Kurt Lewin

Jean Piaget

Gregor J. Mendel

Edward B. Titchener

Ivan P. Pavlov

Max Wertheimer

TOPICS
IN THE
HISTORY
OF
PSYCHOLOGY
Volume 2

TOPICS
IN THE
HISTORY
OF
PSYCHOLOGY
Volume 2

Edited by

Gregory A. Kimble
Duke University

Kurt Schlesinger
University of Colorado

LAWRENCE ERLBAUM ASSOCIATES, PUBLISHERS
1985   Hillsdale, New Jersey   London

Lawrence Erlbaum Associates, Inc., Publishers
365 Broadway
Hillsdale, New Jersey 07642

Library of Congress Cataloging in Publication Data
Main entry under title:

Topics in the history of psychology.   97203

Includes indexes.
1. Psychology—History. I. Kimble, Gregory A.
II. Schlesinger, Kurt.
BF95.T67 1984   150'.9   84-24709
ISBN 0-89859-311-5 (v.1)
ISBN 0-89859-312-3 (v.2)

Printed in the United States of America

Contents

1. OVERVIEW: THE CHRONOLOGY
Gregory A. Kimble   **1**

Contents of Volume 1

Preface

In writing the history of any field of inquiry, there are two important decisions to make: where in time to begin and where to end. At one end of the time scale, speculations about psychological processes go back to classical Greek philosophy and beyond. For centuries thereafter, the treatment of psychological subject matter remained largely in the domain of other disciplines, especially philosophy, where it became inextricably interwoven with epistemology. The chapters of this book tend to glance only briefly at these philosophical antecedents, to review the basic concepts and principles that early investigators were to take for granted. They tend then to move to the end of the last century when the systematic study of psychological processes began.

At the other end of the time scale, every subfield of psychology has been undergoing extremely rapid growth and change, especially during the last two decades. Before that, there had been a fairly gradual evolution of experimental methods, theoretical concepts, and empirical issues. More recently, however, the dominant trends in the field have changed significantly as new approaches gained ascendency. These developments were accompanied by an explosive spurt in new research. Even when the substantive problems remained the same, they were often reformulated, described in a new language, and attacked by new methods. How the old concepts and methods relate to the new is a topic of continuing debate, and sometimes controversy.

A great deal of what has been happening in the most recent years is still too new and controversial to be placed in historical perspective. As Boring wrote, "It is a nice question as to when the past becomes history, as to how old it needs to be before a first stable perspective of it can be limned" (1942, p. iii). The editors invited the contributors to these volumes to end their coverage at a point in time when their respective fields seemed to have been characterized by coherence and closure. For most of them this meant a point in time during the third quarter of this century, which brings us to the threshold of the current era and avoids the controversies of today.

Even within this truncated temporal span, many of the contributors of these volumes describe the work of the earliest years in greater detail than that of the later years. Inevitably, the questions that were asked first and the methods that were developed first set the agenda for a long time to come. Of course, the treatment has been highly selective throughout, with the selection of earlier work guided as much as possible by later developments. To quote Boring again, "Strange as it may seem, the present changes the past" (1950, p. ix).

The volumes of this work consist of nineteen chapters. Seventeen were written by psychologists expert in a particular branch of our field. For this reason, the book as a whole is not organized chronologically, as reflected in our title *Topics in the History of Psychology.* The first chapter in each of the volumes are the editors' attempts to remedy this deficiency. The first volume covers the areas of conditioning and learning, human learning and memory, sensory and perceptual processes, comparative psychology, and physiological psychology. Volume 2 covers the history of behavioral genetics, psychological testing, developmental psychology, drives and motives, sleep and dreaming, psychotherapy, psychopathology, personality theory and social psychology.

In developing this work, the editors had a particular concept in mind which we hoped would make these volumes appropriate as a textbook for a particular course. Psychology is a vast and incoherent field. In spite of this, it is our experience that students and teachers alike yearn for some type of capstone course that will put psychology in perspective. Historical perspective is the obvious candidate. The chapters in this book provide it for most of the important topics in our field.

The problem with a book that mainly provides perspective is that the liberalities of the twentieth-century university curriculum leave students unacquainted with the basic subject matter for which perspective is provided. This leads us, finally, to the description of a course which we believe should be required of all serious senior majors in psychology and would be very appropriate for beginning graduate students. This course would be based on this work supplemented by any of a dozen or so large encyclopedic introductory books that are currently available. These books are of a remarkably high quality; they present the current thinking which our volumes do not, and, most importantly, they change with changes in methods, concepts, data and interpretation. Exposure to the history of a topic, together with a picture of where that history has lead, strikes us as about as useful an integrating experience as we can provide our students.

Gregory A. Kimble
Kurt Schlesinger

Topics
in the
History
of
Psychology
Volume 2

1 Overview: The Chronology

Gregory A. Kimble
Duke University

There is an old fashioned view of learning, which treats the process as a passive and gradual accumulation of the potential for responding, moving steadily toward some physiological limit of effectiveness. Probably most of us think of the history of psychology in similar terms, as the passive record of events as they happened, moving cumulatively forward to the present moment, which represents the highest level of advancement reached so far. This view of history has to be abandoned for much the same reason as the outdated view of learning did. It neglects the constructive behavior of the historian just as the treatment of learning neglected the active involvement of the learner.

This point becomes particularly clear in an effort of the type represented by this chapter, in which I attempt to coordinate the materials developed by a dozen other authors. It takes no more than the first page written by any of them to show that the histories they have written are selective, constructive, and creative. Now, I impose my own perspective on these materials in order to extract common themes and to present a chronology. Surely the result is *a* history of a set of topics in our field, not *the* history of those topics. Now that my work is complete, I wonder if *the* history is even a defensible concept.

THE BEGINNINGS

Fragments of the history covered in this volume go back almost 5000 years, and to the Eastern as well as to the Western World. As early as 2200 B.C., the Chinese, recognizing the importance of individual differences, were using tests to select candidates for office in the imperial government. Even earlier—3000 B.C. or so—speculation had begun about other important topics in the volume.

There was an interest in sleep and dreams, and the notion that dreams might give clues to effective therapy had been developed. The proposed treatments included treatment for mental disorder, indicating that the concept of madness was also achieved early.

Extrapolating backward from later records, there is reason to suspect that a theory of spirit possession may have been a dominant explanation for mental disorder. On similar bases, it seems likely that dreams were given much the same interpretation, that they were messages placed in the sleeping mind by dieties who wanted to communicate with the dreamer. These messages included messages about the future.

Vestiges of such prescientific thinking still exist today but, even before age of the classical Greek philosophers, spiritism had begun to decline and naturalistic accounts of a scattered set of phenomena had been offered. Early in the first millenium B.C., the theory of bodily fluids or humors elaborated later on by Hippocrates had been developed. Anticipating the concept of homeostasis, it had been proposed that disease results from imbalance among these fluids and that cures could be produced by restoring this balance. In separate developments, the brain had been mentioned as a possible locus for disorder. The concepts that psychosis developed from conflict and that catharsis provided by dance, music, and poetry might effect a cure had also been proposed.

The writings of the great Greek philosophers reveal that, even as early as the fifth century B.C., potentially opposing environmental and biological interpretations of psychological phenomena had begun to take recognizable form. Aristotle put forth the conception of the mind as a blank tablet and developed an account of associations, both of which were to become important in environmental interpretations of behavior. At the same time, however, he as well as Plato advocated programs of eugenics, which anticipated a more biological approach to psychology. Hippocrates' theory of humors was in this biological tradition and it was also important in another way. It implied an analysis of behavior that involved the concept of traits of personality, an idea that has persisted to the present time in psychology. For example, Plato's analysis of personality into components devoted to thinking, doing, and feeling presented a way of looking at human experience that reappeared 2000 years later in Sheldon's cerebrotonic-somatotonic-viscerotonic typology. The sophisticated nature of this thinking raises questions as to why progress in psychology was so limited in the next 2000 years. A part of the answer is to be found in the acceptance of these self-same ideas as sacred dogma.

THROUGH THE MIDDLE AGES AND RENAISSANCE

From the point of view of science, the most important influence in the early centuries of the Christian era must have been the discouragement it brought to the development of empirical methods. The emphasis was on the wisdom of established authority and the truths that could be derived from such authority by the method of deductive reason. The scientific teachings of Aristotle became doctrine and Hippocrates' theory of the humors was also accepted. The influence of authority was pervasive; its force was tyrannical; its methods of maintaining adherence to doctrine—the Spanish inquisition, for example—were draconian. The only positive feature of the situation was that the Christian virtue of charity was extended to madness and the treatment of mentally disordered people was more humane than might have been anticipated.

Little record remains of what psychologically relevant ideas were like until the seventeenth century, although scraps of evidence suggest the existence of fairly modern ideas. Procedures for treating mental disorder that sound like behavior modification were occasionally employed. The possible effectiveness of drug therapy had been noted. There were occasional efforts to make formal assessments of personality. And, interestingly, questions about the legal significance of mental condition had been raised.

The printing press was invented late in the fifteenth century. This probably accounts as much as anything for the fact that our history becomes very much richer beginning about 1600 than it had been earlier. By then, three major forces were dominant on the intellectual scene.

The first of these major forces was dualistic thinking, the acceptance of a sharp distinction between mind and body. Christian theology favored this position and Descartes, having invented the concept of reflex, put forth the idea of an extended body interacting with the non-extended soul. The second major force was Newtonian mechanics. Descartes also contributed to developments in this area. He treated the body as an automaton, operated by vital spirits in much the same way as the elaborate statues in some royal gardens were operated by water. The third major force was British empiricism, which resurrected the Aristotelian concept of tabula rasa and accepted the doctrines of elementism and associationism. The primary source of knowledge became sensory experience, a view that made it possible for Francis Bacon to challenge deductivism, to advocate an empirical approach to truth and to recommend inductive reasoning as a basic method. These developments freed science from the shackles of established authority.

EIGHTEENTH CENTURY

The dualistic, mechanistic, elementistic, empirical approach which took definite form in the 1600s was to become the orthodox methodology; it dominates psychology even today. But there is and always has been opposition. In the eighteenth century, the opposition came from the scholars of the Scottish school of psychologists, founded by Thomas Reid. Without being very clear about exactly what he meant by the notion, Reid favored a "common sense" psychology. He had faith in the practical reliability of the senses and was suspicious of the treatments that claimed that bits of experience were fitted together by association. He preferred the term *suggestion* to refer to what others called *association*, possibly because suggestion implied an active power of the mind: One idea actively suggested another; having one idea called up by association implies a more mechanical operation of a passive mind. Reid was opposed to mechanistic interpretations, and indeed to anything that degraded the dignity of man. In that sense, he anticipated later humanistic developments.

Reid also contributed to the development of a faculty psychology by proposing the existence of some twenty fundamental powers of the mind. Toward the end of the century, these faculties were a part of what Gall included in his phrenology. The other part of phrenology was a much increased understanding of the nervous system, which included the concept of localized functions of the brain. The phrenological position was that human faculties are represented in restricted areas of the brain and that a highly developed faculty means a highly developed brain in the appropriate cerebral area. On the further assumption that the increase in brain tissue needs extra volume in the skull to accommodate it, it was suggested that the individual's faculties could be assessed by examining the surface of the head, looking for tell-tale bumps that would reveal the person's strongest faculties. The theory was nonsense, of course, but it was immensely influential. Gall published on the subject in 1790, Spurzheim in 1805. Volumes for the layman continued to appear even in the twentieth century.

The eighteenth century was the century of George III, King of England and one of the most famous cases of mental illness on record. According to most accounts, King George suffered from porphyria, a physiological disturbance, whose symptoms included mental disorder and blood red urine. As was characteristic in those times, the therapy received by George III was probably mostly physical therapy: Blistering, bleeding, purgation, and the like. Already, however, the methods of psychotherapy were becoming available. In 1785, Benjamin Rush (one of the signers of the American Declaration of Independence) published a paper in which he described a treatment for alcoholism that sounds remarkably like twentieth century aversive conditioning therapy. At about the same time, and more importantly for the nearer-term history of psychology, hypnosis, still being called animal magnetism, was becoming popular. It was to remain a topic of controversy well into the nineteenth century.

NINETEENTH CENTURY

It has been said many times that the three most important happenings in the history of ideas were three revolutionary proposals that came as a threat to collective human self-esteem. The first was the Copernican revolution, which overturned our conception of the universe. The earth, rather than being at the center of the universe, had to be accepted as an insignificant little planet whirling through space. Accommodation to this revolutionary idea was not easy, but it seems to have been accomplished. The Copernican conception is no longer controversial.

The same cannot be said for the second revolution—the Darwinian revolution—which robbed man of his status as unique among God's creations. Although the theory of evolution is generally accepted in science, poorly informed people in politics continue their efforts to promote the creationist alternative, and according to a recent poll, as many as 75% of the population of one of our states accept that view as truth. Darwin's own words (1869) can be cited to put the issue in perspective: "I see no good reason why the views given in this volume [Origin of Species] should shock the religious feelings of anyone . . . it is just as noble a conception of the Deity to believe that He created a few original forms capable of self-development into other and needful forms, as to believe that He required a fresh act of creation to supply the voids caused by the action of His laws."

The third suggested revolution was the Freudian revolution, which threatened our claim to special status as the only reasoning organism. In this case, the revolutionary status of the contribution, is now less clear than it once seemed to be. There is no doubt that psychoanalytic theory had a powerful impact on Western culture for something like the first half of this century. Time and research have called many aspects of Freudian theory into question, however. The impact of psychoanalysis on psychology appears to be waning, whatever its residual influence on culture and popular thought.

DARWIN AND EVOLUTION

Evolutionary theory proposed that species develop and disappear as a result of three processes: Heredity, variation, and natural selection.

Heredity means that offspring resemble their parents. Offspring are members of the same species as the parents; they are also like them in physical and psychological characteristics. Large nervous dogs tend to have puppies that grow up to become large and nervous.

Variation means that, although offspring resemble their parents, they are not identical to them; if there are many offspring, they are not identical to one another.

Selection means that some of these varied offspring have a better chance than others of becoming parents of the next generation. Those that have this better chance of becoming parents are, in this sense, more fit than other members of the same species. It is in this way that the "survival of the fittest" occurs.

Darwin's *Origin of Species* was published in 1859. Mendel's work on genetic mechanisms was done only a few years later, but it received little or no attention in the scientific community until the turn of the century. In the meantime, by contrast, evolutionary theory was widely discussed and had its influence on the history of psychology through the work of a heterogeneous collection of individuals. Herbert Spencer put forth the view that evolutionary theory provided an attractive model on which to base a general psychological theory. G. Stanley Hall developed the hypothesis of recapitualation, which held that the evolutionary history of the human species was reproduced in the process of individual human development. In Russia, Ivan M. Sechnov, who was Pavlov's most important intellectual ancestor, picked up the notion of adaptive behavior, calling attention to the fact that most reflexes had this property. (Eyeblinks rid the eyes of irritating substance; reflex coughs do the same for the throat.) Most important of all, several scholars, accepting a biological view of human traits, made the case that traits may be inherited. Dugdale's initial study of the Jukes family is in this category as is Galton's monumental work on hereditary genius.

Galton also participated in another major theme of the 1800s, the development of quantitative thinking in psychology. In the field of intelligence, Esquirol had the general concept of mental age as early as 1838. Only a bit later, tests were being used in America for the selection of people to fill federal positions and there were sporadic unsuccessful attempts to use anthropometric measurement for the assessment of psychological traits.

Fechner published his work on psychophysics in 1860. In addition to having a profound impact in various areas of experimental psychology, this was destined to contribute to the emergence of psychological testing. Ebbinghaus was enormously impressed with Fechner's work and attempted to apply it to the measure of mental fatigue in children. This effort, in turn, was to provide one of the insights used by Binet in the construction of the first successful intelligence tests.

TWENTIETH CENTURY

The three decades from about 1885 to about 1915 were a period in which present-day approaches to psychology were to take definite form. In one way or another, these new approaches were reactions against Structuralism, which was dominant on the psychological scene. A direct descendant from British empiricistic philosophy, the Structuralists, advocated the introspective method and took the position that psychology's major goal was the analysis of human experience into its perceptual elements. Both the method and the goal were too limiting to survive as the only valid way of treating psychological subject matter. By the end of the 30 years just mentioned, Behaviorism, Functionalism, and Gestalt Psychology had all made anti-Structuralist pronouncements; independently of these schools, Psychoanalysis had come forth with ideas that also tended to clash with Structuralist psychology, and interests in animal behavior, child development, and psychopathology had demonstrated the impotence of the introspective method to deal with such subject matters. These developments had all occurred prior to the beginning of World War I.

The two world wars both happened to come at times when psychology was ready for a change. The developments just described came prior to the first world war; they prepared psychology for a period of rapid growth. The war assisted some of these changes and hindered others. The second war came at a time when psychology had taken these earlier themes to a point where many of them had outgrown their usefulness. During this war, as with the previous one, some specialties advanced; others came to a virtual standstill. The positive effects of a war time situation seem, mainly, to accrue to the applied specialties in science. In psychology, mental testing and the clinical/counseling interests were the chief beneficiaries.

The earliest attempts to measure intelligence had been in the Structuralist tradition. For example, prior to Binet, tests had been constructed which included subtests of color naming, two-point threshold, the pressure required to produce pain, and other sensory abilities. Scores on these tests failed to show any correspondence to school grades or teacher's ratings of students' intelligence and were abandoned. Binet substituted tests of vocabulary, memory, reasoning, and other more intellectual processes. This breaking away from the Structuralist tradition marked the beginning of successful mental measurement.

The standardization of psychology tests required the application of statistical tools, which were becoming familiar to psychologists. Galton had invented the concepts of correlation and regression in the nineteenth century. He also understood the statistical phenomenon of regression to the mean, which he called "regression to mediocrity." Early in this century the correlational methods were beginning to be applied to the assessment of test reliability and validity.

During this period, the Binet tests were translated into several languages and they underwent a somewhat informal process of standardization. At the beginning of World War I, such tests were available as instruments for the selection of military personnel. The tests had two main drawbacks, however: (1) They were individual tests, which took too long to administer; (2) they were largely verbal tests, which were useless for testing people who were either illiterate or not speakers of the language in which the tests were written. The heavy influx of immigrants into the United States just before that nation's entry into the war, had already brought home the second of these problems. During the war when hundreds of thousands of personnel had to be tested, these difficulties were dealt with by the construction of the Army Alpha and Beta tests. Both were group tests; the Beta test was a nonverbal test.

While partially solving one set of problems, the Army tests revealed the existence of another set: Factors other than intelligence were related to performance in the military setting. This led to the creation of objective personality inventories, a pioneer effort being that of Woodworth, who constructed a Personal Data Sheet. Rorschach developed his projective ink blot test of personality at about the same time although he did not produce a published report of his work until 1921.

Following World War I, the field of psychometrics exploded. A variety of new intelligence tests appeared. Many were group tests patterned after the Army tests. The Scholastic Aptitude Test (SAT), published by the Educational Testing Service (ETS), is the most important descendant of such tests. Other tests were individual tests. These included the post-war revisions of the Binet tests themselves as well as a series of intelligence tests developed by David Wechsler, of which the current versions are the Wechsler Adult Intelligence Scale (WAIS) and the Wechsler Intelligence Test for Children (WISC).

While these new tests were being developed there were improvements in the scoring systems employed. Terman had introduced the concept of a Mental Quotient (IQ) in 1916, calculated by the well-known formula: IQ = 100 (MA/CA). This measure became standard, and scales with its chief characteristics—a mean of 100 and a standard deviation of about 15—are still employed. The calculations have changed, however. Now, even the Stanford-Binet Test scores are expressed as deviation IQs calculated by the formula:

$$IQ = 100 + S_A \frac{(X - \bar{X})}{S_o}$$

where S_A is an arbitrary standard deviation—usually 15 or 16 to approximate the typical value obtained by the older calculations—X is the raw score on the test for a single individual, $\bar{X}$ is the mean raw score, and S_o is the obtained standard deviation of the population. This measure has the advantage of being calculatable for tests like the WAIS that do not provide scores expressed as Mental Age (MA).

In the field of personality testing, the most important post-war descendants of the Personal Data Sheet are the Minnesota Multiphasic Personality Inventory (MMPI) and the California Psychological Inventory (CPI). The most important projective tests are Rorschach's inkblot test and the more recent Thematic Apperception Test (TAT). The period between the two wars saw the development of objective methods of scoring both of these tests. This set the stage for studies following World War II that evaluated the reliability and validity of these instruments. The results were disappointing and, as a result, the tests have lost favor.

Other applications of the psychometric methods that have developed since the early beginnings are attitude scaling, opinion polling, and testing for vocational and educational interests. These efforts have been remarkably successful, so much so that, soon after World War II, Cronbach (1957) wrote an important paper in which he described two disciplines of scientific psychology. One was the traditional psychology that performed experiments and employed hypothesis-testing statistics. The other was the psychology of individual differences that gave tests and analyzed data with correlational methods.

BIOLOGICAL PSYCHOLOGY

The development of standardized mental tests gave quantitative support to the concept of trait, a way of thinking that dates back several thousand years. With traits like intelligence reduced to numbers, it was much easier than it had been before to ask about the environmental influences that affected them and the extent to which they were inherited. Beginning with the pronouncements of J. B. Watson, the environmental interpretation was to enjoy a few years in the limelight; but before that and again more recently, the biological interpretation has more than held its own in the nature-nuture controversy.

Following Galton's nineteenth century promotion of the notion that genius is inherited and Dugdale's argument that the same is true of individuals at the other end of the intellectual continuum, there were a number of ventures into the field that today we call behavioral genetics. As early as 1906, Woods published on intelligence in royal families; Yerkes' study of the dancing mouse came out in 1907; Goddard published on the Kallikaks in 1912; a year later Yerkes argued for the heritability of wildness; in 1916 Estabrooks presented his genetic interpretation of the family history of the Jukes.

The last of these studies came at a time when we were already well into the Behaviorist Era. Between then and 1940 or so, there were only scattered studies that promoted the argument for a genetic influence on behavior. The investigations with the greatest impact were those which provided evidence for the environmental modifiability of behavioral traits, whether cognitive or affective. The positions taken were extreme. In 1924, Zing Yang Kuo was claiming that even congenital traits (present at birth) are the result of the experience of the unborn, rather than heredity. Somewhat earlier, Knight Dunlap had denied the existence of innate motives or instincts.

By the late 1930s the transition toward a more even-handed position was evident. Twin studies had made a strong case for a genetic factor in the determination of IQ; other family studies had done the same for psychopathology; and in the laboratory, selective breeding studies had begun to demonstrate the heritability of emotionality, aggressiveness and maze brightness.

Developments in quantitative methods helped push the field forward after that. Most importantly, the calculation of coefficients of heritability from the correlations between measured traits of individuals who share varying proportions of genes in common, provided estimates of the strength of genetic influences on human IQ, alcoholism, risk for psychopathology, and various traits of personality. These coefficients of heritability are estimates of the proportion of total variation in a trait that is due to genetic factors. Looked at broadly, this approach leads to an important restatement of the mission of psychology. Rather than a search for the laws of behavior, this mission becomes an attempt to account for the variance in behavior. In this attempt, the laws take on a role of subsidiary significance.

The biological position also had influence on the field of child development, where a biological concept, maturation, was accepted by almost everyone. In 1929, Coghill published his monograph which showed regular sequences in the development of behavior in the salamander, which depended upon neural growth and seemed likely to be independent of experience. Within the next few years, Shirley and Halverson described similar sequences for human motor development and Bridges proposed that emotional development follows one of these maturational courses (mass action-differentiation). Although the neurological data necessary to clinch the case for biological determination were never obtained, studies using the method of cotwin control and other studies that deprived organisms of the experience that might lead to the learning of wide variety of behaviors seemed to minimize the importance of such experience. Gesell's schedules of development often seem to make a similar point.

Independently in the 1920s, Piaget was presenting a position that was also biological in outlook. It incorporated a concept of stages and took the position that these stages are maturational inevitabilities. If experience contributed to development, other data that were available as early as the mid 1930s from the work of the ethologists suggested that the necessary experience was usually available to all members of a species. The essential requirement is for that experience to take place at a time of optimal readiness, a critical period.

This more biological way of thinking, once it took hold, extended in many additional directions. In the area of cognition, Chomsky's theory of generative grammar is strongly biological. Both Erik Erikson in the field of personality development and Kohlberg writing on moral development adopt positions that involve maturational stages.

The biological outlook also began to characterize treatments of emotion and motivation outside the developmental frame of reference. In 1929, the same year as Coghill's monumental publication, Cannon published *Bodily Changes in Pain, Hunger, Fear and Rage* in which he presented his interpretation of these conditions in complex physiological terms. The concept of homeostasis was central to Cannon's treatment. The term homeostasis refers to a set of automatic, self-regulating biological mechanisms utilized by the body to maintain or restore equilibrium whenever the organism is thrown into a state of physiological imbalance. Such imbalance has powerful consequences, some of which we experience in motivational/emotional terms. Scientific attempts to understand the physiology of these effects led to studies of thalamic and hypothalamic influences as well as those of the reticular activating system.

One part of Cannon's theory was a local stimulus theory of drive. According to this theory, motives have associated stimuli that inform the organism of its state of need. Hunger pangs and dryness of the mouth and throat are examples. Psychologists found this mechanism attractive because of a possible relationship to reinforcement. If motives are drive stimuli, then it is conceivable that the mechanism of reinforcement is drive stimulus reduction, the removal of a drive.

This theory did not last long for two reasons: (1) The local stimulus theory could not handle the fact (for example) that animals deprived of the stomach stimuli corresponding to a need for food still became hungry, would eat and even learn a maze to be fed. (2) Some reinforcers seem not to involve drive stimulus reduction: The facts that a baby prefers the stimulus corresponding to a human face and that animals will learn habits that present stimuli, for example, intracranial stimuli, are cases where reinforcers are increases rather than decreases in stimulation. For such reasons, drive stimulus reduction theory and its frail cousin, drive reduction theory, were both abandoned, but not until they had done a great deal to bring harmony to two very different realms of discourse, Psychoanalysis and learning theory.

PSYCHOANALYSIS

Freud's theory of Psychoanalysis was many theories. It was a theory of personality structure, a theory of personality functioning, a theory of personality development, a theory with implications for psychotherapy. It was also a product of its times. Darwinian thinking was reflected in the emphasis Freud gave to the irrational (animal) aspects of human adjustment. More importantly, analytic theory seems to have been modeled after nineteenth-century physics. The central concept in the theory was libido, a generalized energy derived from physiological processes. Just as science had come to understand about other energy, libidinal energy was assumed to be indestructible. It might be kept in check or shunted into indirect expression, but its disappearance from one system meant the eventual appearance of some sort of alternative expression elsewhere.

Freud's theory of psychosexual development was one application of this way of thinking. The normal course of development is one in which libido expresses itself successively in oral, anal, phallic, and finally genital activities. As the individual moves from stage to stage, however, libidinal energy remains at least partly attached to the activities of former stages; the person is fixated at these stages. In periods of stress, behavior may regress to these earlier stages. This general idea also appears in the writings of Lewin and Piaget. Later on, it was to become one of the major conceptions that learning theorists attempted to deal with in their own terms.

In Freudian theory, the structure of personality contains three components, id, ego, and superego, which function at three levels, conscious, preconscious, and unconscious. The id, ego, and superego, however, do not exactly correspond to these three levels of consciousness. Each personality component is represented at all levels, although the id is more unconscious and the ego more conscious than the others. The id represents unacceptable lower instincts of aggression and sexuality. These impulses operate in terms of a pleasure principle; they seek immediate and direct gratification. The tendencies are so offensive to the norms of society that they are usually repressed and remain unconscious, expressing themselves symbolically and indirectly.

The ego is the rational component of mind. It operates in terms of a reality principle, functioning to delay gratification and to confine the individual's behavior to the limits laid down by the culture within which we live. The enforcer in the system is the superego, which corresponds to conscience, guilt, and anxiety; it represents the introjected moral values of society acquired by the individual through identification with the parents.

The elements of this tripartite structure of personality are obviously not in harmony. The tendencies of the id conflict with the inhibitions imposed by the superego. Sometimes the conflict is more than the ego can handle, in part because the impulses of the id are repressed and unavailable to the ego. With some frequency the result is neurosis, to be treated by the methods of analytic therapy. This therapy is aimed at uncovering the repressed conflict and helping the patient accept it. According to Freudian theory, the removal of repression sometimes reveals traumatic childhood experiences that have contributed to the neurotic adjustment. Recalling and reliving these experiences (abreaction) brings relief from the neurotic tensions (catharsis) leaving the individual in a position to develop a new and healthier adjustment.

LEARNING THEORY

At first blush, Psychoanalysis and the psychology of learning, derived from the Behaviorist and Functionalist schools of psychology, seem to have little in common. The Freudian contribution was in the area of human psychopathology; it reflected the insights obtained in Freud's personal treatment of individual clinical cases. The learning theorists, by contrast, remained close to the laboratory; their contributions came from experimental studies, the most influential of which were done with lower animals, studied in groups and analyzed by the impersonal methods of statistics.

What Psychoanalysis and learning theory had most fundamentally in common was the view that behavior now is the result of experience in the past. The recognition of this fact led to several attempts to translate psychoanalytic phenomena into learning mechanisms. The most successful of these efforts grew out of Hullian theory, although Tolman made similar interpretations.

Hull's (1943) treatment of motivation assumed a libido-like concept of generalized drive that was available to supply the energy required for the performance of any and all of an individual's habits. Hull did not employ a concept of the conservation of motivation energy, but assumed that habits were developed because they led to drive reduction. With that difference, however, the parallels between Hullian theory and Psychoanalysis are quite striking. For example, what

Freud treated as stages of personality development, the learning theorists handled quite gracefully in terms of hierarchies of habits. The basic idea was that habits develop to satisfy motives. As the person grows older, the habits of childhood become inappropriate and are superceded by the habits of adulthood. However, the earlier habits remain latent and in times of stress, when the newer habits fail, the individual may return to them. Thus, the Freudian concepts of fixation and regression were interpreted in terms of habit progression and regression.

For the theorist of learning, the activities that the Freudians took to be behavior based on a pleasure principle were consummatory responses tied to drive states. Acts performed in the service of a reality principle were instrumental acts learned because they allow the satisfaction of these drives. This interpretation contains basic elements of the Freudian concept of ego. Superego is perceived as the conditioning of the negative and positive emotions (mostly the former) to response-produced stimulation. (The model for such conditioning was the classical investigation of Watson and Rayner in their study with little Albert, except that the conditioned stimuli for superego development were those produced by unacceptable sexual and aggressive behavior, and the unconditioned stimuli were parental punishment and expressions of approval.) Since much of this conditioning takes place in early childhood, before the individual has developed useful verbal codes for recall, these memories are inaccessible, in other words, repressed.

This interpretation of superego development leads to a behavioristic interpretation of neurotic conflict. It is a special case of approach-avoidance conflict in which the approach component is the expression of id-like urges to sexuality and aggression; the avoidance component is a superego-like conditioned fear of the approach component. Neal Miller's later development of this interpretation added a dimension also suggested by Kurt Lewin. It was assumed that the approach and avoidance tendencies both got stronger as the individual came closer and closer to expressing the prohibited urges, where closeness was symbolic proximity. It was assumed further that sexual anxiety and aggression anxiety increased faster than did the sexual and aggressive tendencies themselves. This meant that at some point short of the direct expression prevented by mounting anxiety, the individual would produce a sexual or aggressive response in some generalized, indirect, substitute or disguised form. The Freudian defense mechanisms were handled in this way.

There were even suggestions that important aspects of analytic therapy could be interpreted in terms of learning principles. The removal of repression would consist in discovering the cues that controlled unhappy habits. Providing these cues would allow the patient to relive the traumatic experience. This in turn would reduce the fearful motives involved, thus removing a part of the basis for the neurosis and putting the individual into a position to acquire new and healthy habits.

HOUSE OF CARDS

The rapproachment between Freudianism and learning theory was one of the high points in the history of psychology. If one had to give a date to the reaching of this pinnacle, one could do no better than to put it exactly at mid-century with the publication of Dollard and Miller's *Personality and Psychotherapy* (1950). But even then the cracks in the foundation of the structure that had been created were visible. When the translations of Freudian ideas were put to laboratory tests, they frequently did not fare well. For example, attempts to create experimental analogues of repression tended to be unsuccessful. The introduction of behavior therapy and drugs was beginning to demonstrate that Psychoanalysis was both inferior and irrelevant to these new therapies. The human behavioral geneticists (e.g., Kallman) were coming forth with strong evidence that at least some forms of psychopathology depended more on inherited biological factors than either the Psychoanalysts or learning theorists would have supposed. And, finally learning theory was having troubles of its own.

Drive And Reinforcement

Hull's theory of generalized drive and Freud's theory of libido both treated drive as an internal state. There is a biological sense in which this must be true, and developments in physiological psychology were helping to make the case. Beach, Morgan, Stellar, and others were providing new evidence for the neuroendocrine bases of motivation, and Lindsley and Magoun added a new dimension to this picture with the report of their classic studies of the reticular activating system. The humanistic psychologists, with their emphasis on internal resources, also treated motives in terms that were compatible (in this respect) with the more traditional views.

But other psychologists were showing that external stimulational factors had motivational properties. The studies of Harlow, Glanzer, and Montgomery indicated the existence of externally triggered motives for exploration and manipulation. Other studies of what was coming to be called incentive motivation showed that rewards had motivating as well as reinforcing properties. The ethologists tied both sexuality and aggression to stimulational factors. Developmental psychologists (e.g., Fantz) showed that the stimulus provided by a human face is attractive to very young babies. All of these developments required a revision of the Hull-Freud conception of drive.

In the meantime, one of the key concepts tying learning theory to personality development was seriously undermined. According to learning theory, such important contributors to personality development as a baby's love for its mother were learned as a result of reinforcement. In this particular case, for example, the mother was treated as a secondary reinforcer who acquired that status because she was the array of stimuli associated with satisfaction and relief from such unpleasantnesses as hunger and wetness. Harlow's work with infant monkeys and surrogate mothers called this interpretation sharply into question by showing that the critical factor is contact comfort, that nourishment has little to do with the development of attachments, and that even the contribution of learning is minimal.

Habit Acquisition

Although the importance of learning turned out to be less than had once been supposed for the development of filial attachments, it continued to be seen as the most important process in personality development when such development is considered more generally. Views of the learning mechanism changed, however.

Traditional learning theory, from Thorndike to Hull, took the position that learning consists of the strengthening of associations that are formed directly between stimuli and other stimuli or (more frequently) responses. Beginning in the late 1940s, Kuenne's study of transposition as well as that of Alberts and Ehrenfreund began to implicate mediating verbal processes. This marked the beginning of a strong cognitive development in the field. In the work of Bandura and others, cognitive, observational learning (modeling) came to be regarded as the most important mechanism by which children acquire the behaviors that identify their different personalities. Others were making a strong case for the acquisition of language in the same way and without much influence of reward and punishment. This newer interpretation is a far cry from the stimulus-response-reinforcement interpretation of Hull and the others, whose theories, up to then, had dominated thinking in the fields of personality development and psychopathology.

Humanism

For some psychologists, observational learning and modeling are too small a step to take, although the step is in the right direction. The reference here is to the humanistic psychologists, Erikson, Maslow, and Rogers. For these psychologists, the missing emphasis in the other accounts is the potential of the individual human being for growth.

For the humanists, the important item on every person's psychological agenda is to develop an acceptable self-concept, to realize one's potential, to achieve self-actualization. For Rogers, the way to achieve this goal is a process of self-discovery and self-acceptance. Rogers' therapeutic procedures were designed to assist in this process. Sometimes, the assistance takes the form of client-centered nondirective therapy; sometimes it is sensitivity training and encounter experiences.

For Maslow, self-actualization requires the satisfaction of lower order physiological needs, and needs for safety, love, and self-esteem. Freed from the necessity of being concerned with these lesser needs, the person can set and attain the goals that represent the best that is possible for the human individual.

Erikson's approach is more developmental. He sees personal growth as taking place from birth to death in a series of stages. Each stage is defined in terms of a conflict to be resolved. In order, these stages of conflict are as follows: To year 1, trust vs. mistrust; years 2–3, autonomy vs. shame and doubt; years 4–5, initiative vs. guilt; ages 6–11, industry vs. inferiority; ages 12–18, identity vs. role confusion; young adulthood, intimacy vs. isolation; middle age, generativity (creative productivity) vs. stagnation; old age, integrity vs. despair. At every stage, the first-mentioned term identifies the adjustment of the individuals who are realizing their greatest potential.

FIELD THEORY

The humanistic psychologists' emphasis on individual worth and dignity picks up a theme that dates back to the eighteenth century and the Scottish philosophers. These philosophers were early opponents of mainstream thinking in psychology because of their criticisms of associationism and elementism and their advocacy of everyday experience and folk wisdom as sources of psychological knowledge. In the 15-year period from about 1910 to 1925, Max Wertheimer, Wolfgang Kohler, and Kurt Koffka reasserted this anti-associationistic, anti-elementistic criticism and founded the school of Gestalt Psychology. Gestalt theory developed as a theory of perceptual phenomena, but it had a profound impact on psychologists with broader interests. Of these, the most influential were Solomon Asch, Fritz Heider, Harry Helson, George Kelly, and especially Kurt Lewin, who developed a more general behavior theory which he called a *field theory*. Lewin took the position that behavior is a function of the person and the environment [B = F(P,E)] and that these two components, person and environment, interacted in ways that made it a mistake to treat them as separate elements. The Lewinians sometimes referred to this interactive way of thinking as the Gallilean as opposed to the Aristotelian mode of thought, which relied more on analysis and classification.

The environment in Lewinian thinking was a perceptual environment, a view that may have been fostered by the close relationship of field theory to Gestalt psychology. The general idea, as George Kelly put it later, was that a person functions in terms of a creative representation of the world rather than in terms of a passive reaction to the physical environment. Helson's concept of adaptation level and Sherif's concepts of social norms and frames of reference were some of the more precise statements of this way of thinking. Lewin used a set of well-known diagrams (see p. 182 for examples) to represent this perceptual environment as well as the position of the individual in it. These diagrams contained quasi-physical representations of the forces (valences and vectors) acting on the individual, the boundaries of the person's life space and the barriers that prevented the achievements of goals. All of these concepts were treated as aspects of a psychological environment that was relatively independent of the physical environment.

The psychology of the 1930s was not yet ready for Lewinian theory. In those days, psychology had finally won its hard-fought battle against subjectivism. The tough-minded philosophy of the logical positivists dominated the scene. Concepts lacking operational definition were unacceptable and Lewin's field theoretical concepts seemed to belong to that category. In actuality, Lewin's concepts could easily have been shown to be operationally sound. The defining operations were to be found in the verbal and other responses of individuals, rather than in physical stimuli. In the words of the most sophisticated philosophers of psychological science, Lewin's concepts are response inferred as are trait concepts like intelligence that are defined in terms of test performance. But the Lewinians never pushed this point and it took another decade or so for field theory to begin to have its influence.

One feature of field theory that contributed to its lack of immediate acceptance was its cross-sectional approach. Although behavior might, as a matter of fact, have historical antecedents, the Lewinians preferred to develop their theories without reference to this history. It is entirely feasible, they argued, to treat the human individual like the golem of Yiddish mythology, created as a fully developed adult without a history, but nevertheless possessing all human psychological characteristics. From what we have already seen of psychoanalytic theory and the views of the learning theorists, who were dominant in psychology at the time, it was clear that field theory struck a strange discordant note. The reactions of these dominant theorists most commonly were to ignore field theory although Tolman incorporated Lewinian concepts in his theorizing, and Hull made an effort to show that field theoretical phenomena could be dealt with by S-R approaches. It was not until a second generation of psychologists influenced by Lewin came on the scene that field theory began to have a significant influence on the field. These were the social psychologists, Festinger, Kelly, and others, who remain active in psychology in the present day.

CONCLUSION

This brief glimpse at more than 4000 years in the history of psychology raises a question: Is it possible to draw significant generalizations about the character of this history. No doubt, different readers will have very different answers to this question. To me, four points came through with greatest force.

The first point is that the history of psychology is mostly a very recent history, beginning toward the end of the nineteenth century. The commonly cited date, 1879, when Wundt established his laboratory, is probably about right for most psychological topics, not just experimental psychology. I see the history as recent in spite of the fact that many of the ideas covered in this volume had been developed by the beginning of the Christian Era. Such concepts as trait, madness, the nature-nurture issue, psychotherapy, psychological tests, unconscious and association had all been developed thousands of years ago, but not much happened to them until recently.

The second point is that our history has been evolutionary rather than revolutionary. There have been no Kuhnian breakthroughs, just a gradual accumulation of knowledge that produces a change in atmosphere, a change in the way in which we think about psychological problems. Freudian theory, our only candidate standing for possible election to the rank of intellectual revolution, no longer seems to have much of a chance of being chosen.

The third point is that progress in psychology appears to come from the application of objective and quantitative methods. The development of mental measurement strikes me as the most important feature of the history described in this volume. In addition to their role in the assessment of individual human traits, tests have contributed a method for clinical diagnosis, a metric for the assessment of behavioral change, and device for measuring public attitudes and opinion and a means of estimating the contributions of heredity and environment to behavior.

The fourth point is that psychology's history has taken it to a point where it seems ready to make important practical contributions. Some of the most promising areas appear to be those of childrearing, social programs, genetic counseling, leadership, legal issues, the prevention of mental illness, and therapy.

Probably there should be a fifth point. It would be the one with which this chapter began: These conclusions and, indeed, the whole chapter, are a filtering of what has already been filtered. They are my interpretation of the interpretations of several authors, whose writings I commend to you.

REFERENCES

Alberts, E., & Ehrenfreund, D. Transposition in children as a function of age. *Journal of Experimental Psychology,* 1951, *41,* 30–35.

Cannon, W. B. *Bodily changes in pain, hunger, fear and rage.* New York: Appleton-Century-Crofts, Inc., 1929.

Coghill, C. E. *Anatomy and the problem of behavior.* New York: Macmillan, 1929.

Cronbach, L. J. The two disciplines of scientific psychology. *American Psychologist,* 1957, *12,* 671–684.

Darwin, C. *On the origin of species by means of natural selection or the preservation of favoured races in the struggle for life.* New York: Appleton, 1869.

Dollard, J., & Miller, N. E. *Personality and psychotherapy.* New York: McGraw-Hill, 1950.

Hull, C. L. *Principles of behavior.* New York: Appleton-Century-Crofts, Inc., 1943.

Kuenne, M. R. Experimental investigation of the relation of language to transposition behavior in young children. *Journal of Experimental Psychology,* 1946, *36,* 471–490.

2 Behavioral Genetics and the Nature-Nurture Question

Kurt Schlesinger
University of Colorado

As with all important issues in psychology, the origins of the nature-nurture question go back to the "ancients," as Descartes called the Greek philosophers, although these philosophers were not really interested in genetic, as opposed to environmental, determinants of behavior. They were trying to understand the nature of knowledge and how it is acquired by the mind. Aristotle believed that experience was all important in shaping the content of the mind. He coined the term *tabula rasa* and, in his formal philosophy, was a strict environmentalist. On other topics, however, Aristotle took positions that were exactly opposite to this one. One of Aristotle's concerns, an interest shared by most Greek philosophers, was how to create "good" societies in the city states of Greece. And here, Aristotle preached a simple **eugenics.** For example, he urged that procreational activities should be restricted to relatively young women and middle-aged men. Specifically, 18-year-old women should conceive children who should be sired by 37-year-old men. He also suggested that procreation should be carried on during the winter months. He argued that is this advice were not followed, a weak and inferior citizenry would result: ". . . as proof of this you may see in those cities where men and women usually marry young, the people are generally small and ill framed . . ."

Plato, the other giant of Greek philosophy, proposed a more ambitious program of eugenics, and he described his ideas in greater detail. Plato also would allow people of only certain ages to have children. For him, the proper ages were between 20 and 40 for women and 35 and 55 for men. Offspring born to parents not within these age brackets were to be exposed to the elements and left to die. Further, only distinguished individuals were to be allowed to have children: "As for those youth who distinguish themselves either in war or other pursuits, they ought to have rewards and prizes given to them, and the most ample liberty of lying with women, so that, under this pretext, the greatest number of children may spring from each parentage.'' In the Greek city of Sparta similar ideas about eugenics were anything but idle speculations. Children born physically defective, or otherwise believed to be ill-bred, were exposed and killed. This was a true selective breeding program, practiced on human population, in a city which, as the crow flies, was only 95 statute miles distant from Athens.

EARLY DOMINATION BY ENVIRONMENTALISM

In spite of these beginnings, what happened in ancient Greece, and what followed until about the turn of the fifteenth century, had little direct bearing on the nature-nurture question as it concerns the inheritance of *behavior*. For this reason, we can skip many centuries and pick up the historical thread with the great Frenchman, René Descartes (1596–1650), whose beliefs were to be of central importance in the history of many of the issues in psychology, including the nature-nurture question. Descartes argued that certain ideas are inherent to the structure of the human mind and cannot be derived from experience. To Descartes it was almost self-evident that our ideas of ''God'' and of ''self'' could not come from experience. These were **innate ideas,** as were the geometrical axioms and our conceptions of time, space, and motion.

Reactions against Cartesian nativism came immediately. Thomas Hobbes (1588–1679), who was Descartes' contemporary, disagreed vigorously and argued that everything we know, all of our ideas, comes from experience which reaches us through our senses. John Locke (1632–1704), who followed Hobbes, also took issue with Descartes' ''innate ideas.'' As mentioned in Chapter 1, he favored the Aristotelian concept of *tabula rasa* and also that all ideas derive from experience. For Locke, ideas were concepts such as ''humankind'' and ''rectangularity'' which were formed as a consequence of sensory experiences or on the basis of ''impressions,'' which were described as kinds of inner sensations. They constituted the basic structural units of the mind. Higher order concepts were ideas assembled into units by **associations,** which were formed because the experiences upon which they were based occurred either successively or simultaneously.

The theory that the structure of the mind was derived from experiences assembled by association was refined by later philosophers in the British tradition. As they relate to psychology, these concepts reached their climax in John Stuart Mill's (1806–1873) laws of association. These laws, which we have met before in discussions of learning, held that two or more ideas were associated on the basis of such attributes as contiguity, similarity, frequency, and inseparability.

These British associationists (or British Empiricists) were to exert a powerful influence upon psychology. The reasons for this effect are not difficult to understand. Psychology emerged from philosophy to establish an independent discipline. The early psychologists were often trained as philosophers, and their approaches to psychological questions reflected these philosophical origins. For the purposes of this chapter, the most important feature of this influence is that, since the British associationists were total empiricists, the early psychologists became strong environmentalists.

Not all of the early psychologists were philosophers. Some of them came to psychology with training in biology, but they were also heavily environmentalistic in their orientation. Why? Although there is undoubtedly more than a single answer to this question, one answer is the immense influence of that giant of late nineteenth-century physiology, Herman von Helmholtz. Helmholtz was not so much a follower of the British tradition as he was a critic of nativism. For Helmholtz, any nativistic view which postulates that the mind has inherent attributes given it by its very structure and a priori intuitions not derived from experience was a naive and nonsensical philosophy. From the point of view of science, it is a view of the world which cannot be tested by empirical methods and must, therefore, be rejected. Because of Helmholtz's stature and reputation, those early psychologists who came into psychology with training in the biological sciences were also heavily environmentalistic in their orientation. But in biology, the seeds of change were already being sown.

THE THEORY OF EVOLUTION

In 1859 Charles Robert Darwin published what he called his "abstract" *On the Origin of Species by Natural Selection*. The ideas Darwin put forth, namely, evolution by means of natural selection, had an immediate impact. (The first edition of the book, a printing of 1500 copies, was sold out the day it was published.) As Cooper (see Chapter 4, Volume 1) points out, the theory of evolution revolutionized the biological sciences to the same extent that Newton's mechanics had altered the face of physics 170 years earlier. The scientific conception of the biological world was changed, and changed forever. Forms of life were now viewed as continuous, the most complex biological forms having evolved from simpler types. The immense chasm between all animals which possessed a more or less mechanical body, and human beings who were endowed with a body and with a unique soul (mind), was at long last closed. Given the facts of anatomical evolution, was there any reason to doubt that human *behavior* had also evolved from simpler types? If the answer to this question was affirmative, and Darwin and many others believed it was, then a comparative psychology was possible. The behavior of animals could now be studied in the hope that what one learned from such observations would tell something about the causes of human behavior. In fact, Darwin did discuss the inheritance of behavior, particularly in his books *The Expression of the Emotions in Man and Animals* and *Animals and Plants under Domestication,* in which he reported his own research on the inheritance of behavior in pigeons.

The history of Darwin's discovery is well known. In barest outline, the history can be sketched as follows: In 1831, when only 22 years of age and fresh out of Cambridge, Darwin obtained employment as a naturalist to sail on a 5-year voyage of discovery aboard H.M.S. Beagle. At that time, Darwin believed in the dogma of creation, that all species had been created simultaneously (probably about 4000 B.C.), and that once created they remained unaltered forever. His studies of living animals, and the fossil record in Argentina and on the Galapagos Islands, convinced him otherwise. By the time he returned to England in 1836, he was certain that animals of all species gradually change over time and that not all species survive. He was certain that animals of all species were modified descendants of previously existing forms.

But how to explain evolution? Darwin was aware of the immense variability that exists in all species. He also knew that animal breeders exploit this variability as they practice artificial selection in order to produce the many and diverse varieties of domesticated plants and animals. What neither the animal breeders nor Darwin understood were the causes which produced such variability or the mechanisms by which such variable traits were inherited.

One theory of inheritance available at that time was Jean Baptiste de Lamarck's theory of the **inheritance of acquired characteristics.** According to Lamarck, bodily changes acquired during an individual's lifetime are passed on to offspring. The usual example for Lamarckian inheritance is that of the giraffe; these animals eat the leaves on the tops of trees, an activity that requires them to stretch their necks. In the process, the neck gets longer, and this trait is passed on to the next generation. Thus, over many generations, giraffes developed into animals with very long necks. Darwin followed Lamarck in believing that bodily changes conditioned by the environment are passed on to the next generation. This idea is incorporated into Darwin's theory of inheritance as *pangenesis,* which is a refinement of the theory proposed by Erasmus Darwin (Charles' grandfather). According to this theory, each organ in the body forms so-called *gemmules,* small particles which are secreted into the blood stream and concentrated in the germ cells. During development, these gemmules regenerate to form organ systems and, ultimately, to produce the next generation of organisms. (We can only speculate what Darwin would have believed had he understood Mendel's paper published some 7 years after *On the Origin of Species.*)

In any case, having now formulated an explanation of biological variation and a theory of inheritance (which was not really necessary to account for selection), Darwin was left with the puzzle of how selection might occur in nature. Darwin found the answer upon reading Thomas Malthus' book *Essay on the Principle of*

Population. Malthus made the point that most species have an almost limitless reproductive potential. Nevertheless, population size tends to remain stable over time. This is because the size of any population is necessarily limited by the resources available to it. In his autobiography, Darwin wrote as follows: "In October 1838 . . . I happened to read for amusement *Malthus on Population* . . . at once it struck me that under these circumstances favorable variations would tend to be preserved and unfavorable ones destroyed. The result of this would be the formation of new species." From this it followed that

> As many more individuals of each species are born than can possibly survive; and as, consequently, there is a frequently recurring struggle for existence, it follows that any being, if it vary however slightly in any manner profitable to itself, under the complex and sometimes varying conditions of life, will have a better chance of surviving, and thus be *naturally selected.* From the strong principle of inheritance, any selected variety will tend to propagate its new and modified form. (p. 13)

This was Darwin's great principle of selection and elimination of the unfit, which Spencer described as **The Survival of the Fittest.** The key to understanding this principle lies in the word *fit.* What does it mean in the context of evolutionary theory? Fitness, of course, includes survival by any means whatsoever, including that of "Nature red in tooth and claw," as Alfred Lord Tennyson described it in his eminently successful poem *In Memoriam* published in 1850 at the very height of the mid-Victorian period of English literature. It is certainly true that organisms must be fit in order to survive. However, in the Darwinian sense, fitness refers strictly to differential reproductive success and not to differential survival. Fitness is defined as the number of offspring that an organism produces, individuals who themselves have reached reproductive maturity. Natural selection will favor any trait that increases the number of progeny produced by an organism. Such traits may be morphological and physiological variables *and* they may be behavioral characteristics. Darwin himself recognized this fact when he wrote that ". . . Besides specialized tastes and habits, general intelligence, courage, bad and good temper, etc., are certainly transmitted . . . and we now know through the admirable labors of Mr. Galton that genius, which implies a wonderfully complex combination of high faculties, tends to be inherited. . ." (Darwin, 1873, Vol. I, pp. 106–107).

The theory of evolution was to have a profound effect on the development of psychology. Darwin set the tone in 1872 in his volume on *The Expression of the Emotions in Man and Animals.* Emotional behaviors, particularly emotional expressions, were analyzed in terms of their fitness value. According to this view, organisms exhibit emotions largely in order to signal their internal states (motives) to conspecifics, and such displays obviously contribute to fitness. As we saw in Chapter 2, Volume 1, this view of behavior as being adaptive contributed to the rise of the functionalist school of psychology. The functionalists held that the proper concern of psychologists should be an investigation of behavior in terms of its functions, the values given behaviors have in the life of animals. Of such values, which could be more important than a contribution to survival? Survival determines the attributes of the coming generations. This observation ties fitness to the science of genetics.

THE BIRTH OF GENETICS

The appearance of the theory of evolution, the emergence of psychology as an independent academic discipline, and the birth of the science of genetics all occurred within a relatively short period of time. Modern genetics was born when Mendel published his *Versuche über Pflanzentybriden* (Experiments on Plant Hybrids) in 1866. As is well known, Mendel's insights into genetics were based on the results of breeding experiments performed on the common garden pea. Mendel studied the inheritance of certain morphological traits—stem size, seed color, seed skin, etc.—in these plants, and he noted that of two alternative traits, say yellow versus green seed color, only one appeared in the first filial (F_1 hybrid) generation when two plants that bred true for the trait in question were crossed. When two such F_1 hybrids were crossed to produce an F_2 generation, the trait that had vanished in the F_1 generation reappeared in one-fourth of the F_2 plants (Mendel's famous 3:1 ratio). When similar experiments were performed in plants that differed with respect to two traits, such as stem size (tall versus dwarf) and seed color, four distinct types were recovered in the F_2 generation—namely, tall-yellow, tall-green, dwarf-yellow, and dwarf-green—and the ratios of these types were 9:3:3:1. The results of these *monohybrid* and *dihybrid* breeding experiments are illustrated diagrammatically in Figure 2.1.

Mendel's genius lay in the great insight with which he interpreted the results of these breeding experiments. He saw that in order to account for the data it was necessary to postulate that each plant carried two factors (today, we call them genes) which mediated the expression of each of the morphological traits that were studied. However, each parent plant passes on only one of these genes to its progeny. In the daughter plant, two of these genes, one derived from the pollen and the other from the ovum, combine to reconstitute a homologous pair of genes. Further, since only one trait expressed itself in the plants of the F_1 hybrid generation, it was necessary to hypothesize that the gene which mediates the expression of that trait was **dominant,** whereas the other gene of the homologous pair was **recessive.** Both recessive genes must be present before the trait which they mediate is expressed. The results of these experiments form the basis of Mendel's first law, the **law of segregation,** so called because the two genes separate (segregate) when *gametes* are formed.

On the basis of the data obtained when two traits were studied simultaneously, Mendel proposed his second law, the **law of independent assortment.** This law

Parent generation = T T Y Y   x   D D G G

$$\downarrow$$

F₁ = T D Y G   x   T D Y G

$$\downarrow$$

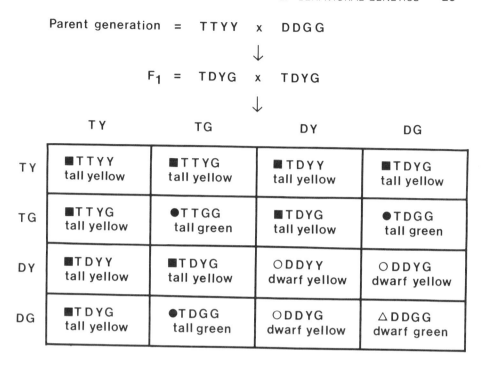

FIG. 2.1   Illustration of Mendel's law of independent assortment. In this case, two true-breeding organisms that differed in two traits were crossed. Four distinct types of organisms were recovered in the F₂ generation, and the ratios of these types were 9:3:3:1. This example Illustrates that the genes that mediate these traits were inherited "independently" of each other.

states that genes which mediate two different traits, say size of the plant and color of the seed, are transmitted independently of each other, an interpretation which explains the 9:3:3:1 ratio observed in F₂ hybrid plants.

The results of these epoch-making experiments were published in 1865—and totally ignored by the scientific community for some 35 years. Even Charles Darwin, Mendel's most illustrious contemporary biologist, was unaware of the birth of modern genetics. Why Mendel's work went unrecognized for so many years is another question that must have a complex answer. However, as Watson (1965) has pointed out, one reason undoubtedly was that the mechanisms underlying Mendel's findings were not known at that time.

In 1900 Hugo de Vries, Carl Correns, and Erich von Tschermak independently rediscovered Mendel's findings. By then, the cytological basis of cell reproduction, mitosis and meiosis, was sufficiently well understood that many geneticists began to see the relations between the behavior of chromosomes during cell division and the results of breeding experiments. In 1903, an American geneticist, Walter S. Sutton, published a paper entitled *The Chromosomes in*

Heredity in which he proposed that Mendel's factors (genes) were located on the chromosomes. It was known that the chromosome number is reduced by one-half during meiosis. Mendel's 9:3:3:1 ratio could be explained if it was assumed that the genes that mediate any two factors are located on separate chromosomes.

Having just attributed Mendel's brilliance to the insight he developed in interpreting his data, it is only fair to mention that good fortune also played a significant role. Mendel was very lucky to have chosen to measure seven morphological characteristics regulated by genes located on different chromosomes. Had any of the characteristics been mediated by genes on the same chromosomes, chances are that the law of independent assortment would have escaped him. Indeed, traits regulated by genes that failed to obey Mendel's second law were soon discovered. The behavior of these genes was explained by the fact that they were located on the same chromosome; that is, that they were **linked.** The degree of linkage, as measured experimentally, always varied between approximately 50% and 100%, and the phenomenon came to be understood on the basis of cytological evidence which revealed that homologous chromosomes come together during meiosis, and an actual exchange of genetic material occurs. This exchange of physical material is called **crossing over**—genes on one chromosome crossing over to the homologue, and vice versa.

Thomas H. Morgan began working with linked genes in the fruit fly, *Drosophila,* exploiting the idea that the farther apart any two genes were on a chromosome, the greater the probability that they would assort independently. Soon, a quantitative relation between the frequency of crossing over and the distance separating two genes on a chromosome was discovered. The choice of *Drosophila* was fortunate, since this animal has only four pairs of chromosomes. Thus, Morgan and his students were able to construct genetic maps of the chromosomes of this insect, each gene occupying a fixed position, or locus. In 1915, Morgan, Sturtevant, Muller, and Bridges published *The Mechanism of Mendelian Heredity,* the definitive work establishing the chromosomal basis of heredity as generally valid.

Gregor Mendel was fortunate in another respect, namely that he had chosen to work with characteristics that were dichotomous. Most traits in nature are not dichotomous, and had Mendel worked with continuously distributed variables he would never have been able to derive the law of segregation or the law of independent assortment. An important case in point is Sir Francis Galton's work on the inheritance of ''genius.'' (See below.) Galton had discovered a relation between genius and familial relatedness which he interpreted as evidence for the heritability of this trait. It was clear, however, that the inheritance of genius did not obey simple Mendelian rules; rather, the genetic effects in successive generations seemed to blend and weaken. From the genius of the parents there was a ''regression to mediocrity'' in later generations. Karl Pearson, the great statistician and student of Galton's, seized upon such evidence to argue that Mendelian inheritance applied only to exceptional cases of little biological significance (McClearn, 1962).

Thus began a great debate between the so-called Mendelians on the one hand and the biometricians on the other. Bateson emerged as the leader of the Mendelians, and Pearson as the leader of the biometricians, and the controversy these two schools of thought generated has had few equals in the history of science in the amount of acrimony it produced. The resolution of the differences between these camps came about when geneticists such as H. Nilsson-Ehle and G. V. Yule proved that a continuous and normal distribution would be produced if a trait is controlled by many genes, each with a small but incremental effect, and if the environment affected these genes in a random way. This resulted in the creation of a field of study known as quantitative genetics, which is of particular significance since almost all behaviors are controlled by **polygenic** (multiple-gene) systems that interact with environmental variables in the most complex fashion.

BEHAVIORAL GENETICS

Behavioral genetics has been defined as that discipline which studies the degree and the nature of the heritable causes of behavior. Intrinsic to such a definition, and it is a very popular one, is the idea that behavioral genetics consists of two inter-related domains of inquiry. On the one hand, such a definition points out that behavioral genetics is statistical in the sense that it tries to estimate the degree to which genetic diversity contributes to the expression of individual differences in behavior. On the other hand, the discipline is biological in that it tries to discover how genes affect the expression of behavioral traits.

It is important to describe at the outset, and hopefully lay to rest, several common misconceptions about behavioral genetics.

1. The first of these misconceptions is that genes determine behavior in a direct sense. Not so. Genes, deoxyribonucleic acid (DNA), have two functions, and two functions only: (a) DNA codes for the synthesis of new DNA, a process referred to as *duplication* or *replication*. (b) DNA codes for the synthesis of another large molecule, another nucleic acid, called ribonucleic acid (RNA), a process referred to as *transcription*. Finally, DNA-like RNA, or messenger RNA as it is more commonly called, controls the synthesis of proteins, a process called *translation*. These are the only known functions of DNA. If genes influence behavior, and we have every reason to believe that they do, then the chain of events which links DNA to behavior must be enormously complex. Suffice it to say that in the entire scientific literature there exists not a single worked-out

example of how this complex chain of events, linking a gene to a behavioral phenotype, might operate. This state of affairs is not unique to behavioral phenotypes. The chains of events linking genes to physiological or morphological traits are also very complex and remain to be discovered in many instances.

It is equally important to point out (directing ourselves still to the same misconception) that, although genetic factors are important in mediating behavior, including complex behavior such as "emotionality," mental disorder, IQ test performance, and (if the sociobiologists are right) even altruism, there are no genes for emotionality, schizophrenia, intelligence, or altruism. When people speak of such genes, they are using a shorthand to describe complex processes. This shorthand is very unfortunate, and it should be avoided.

2. The second common misconception about behavioral genetics concerns the nature-nurture question, and how it is asked. This misconception is largely semantic. It is common to ask whether a given type of behavior is caused by genetic or by experiential factors. When one phrases the nature-nurture question in this fashion, and this is precisely how the question used to be put, one is raising a pseudo-issue; the question has no answer, or at least the answer is always the same. No behavior is determined *either* by genetic *or* by environmental factors; all behaviors are determined by interacting genetic and experiential determinants. The "modern" way of asking the nature-nurture question has to do with variability—a fact of biological life. One can profitably ask how much of the variability in a behavior, measured in a population of organisms, is attributable to genetic factors. This question has an answer which is expressed as a statistic (heritability) that gives the proportion of total phenotypic variability due to genetic diversity in the population in which it is measured. These **heritability coefficients** have values between 1.0 and 0.0. They are the source of the additional misunderstanding to be mentioned here.

3. Coefficients of heritability say nothing about the inheritance of a given trait in an individual; they refer to the fraction of variance in a total population that is the result of genetic factors.

4. A high coefficient of heritability does not mean that the trait to which it applies is immune to the effects of environment. A trait with a coefficient of heritability of 1.0 can be affected substantially by environmental changes. In such a case, all of the individuals in the population would change in exactly the same way to changes in environment, and they would maintain their original ranking on the trait.

5. Coefficients of heritability obtained on one population (i.e., race) cannot be generalized to other populations.

If these last three points had been better understood by the critics of behavioral genetics, psychology could have been spared a great deal of bitter but pointless controversy.

Hereditary Genius

It is usually difficult to date the beginning of an academic discipline with any degree of precision. This is not true for behavioral genetics. In this case, there is no doubt that the founding father was Sir Francis Galton. Behavioral genetics can be said to have been born in 1869 when Sir Francis published an article entitled *Hereditary Genius: An Inquiry Into its Laws and Consequences*. This paper was an expanded version of two pieces that had been published in *Macmillan's Magazine* some 4 years earlier. It is well worthwhile to examine Galton's work on the heritability of genius in some detail for two reasons: first, because the paper is of great historical significance and, second, because the arguments with which Galton had to struggle preoccupy researchers even today.

As most students of psychology know, Galton was interested in studying the heritability of mental abilities, genius in particular. Since he was working at a time that antedated the development of intelligence tests, Galton's first research problem was one of measurement. How does one identify and measure genius? Galton decided to use the "reputation" of individuals as an index. By reputation Galton did not mean the kind of notoriety one gains by any single act, nor did he mean social status. Rather, he defined as genius ". . . the reputation of a leader of opinion, of an originator, or a man to whom the world deliberately acknowledges itself largely indebted." He then set out to identify such individuals, using bibliographical material and direct interviews. The reputations of many eminent scientists, military figures, musicians, poets, religious leaders, etc. were examined, and 1000 individuals were identified who met Galton's criterion of genius. These 1000 eminent men, these geniuses, were found to belong to 300 families. Given that the incidence of genius in the general population was 1 to 4000, the fact that 1000 eminent men came from but 300 families could not be attributed to chance. Therefore, Galton concluded that genius was a familial trait. He did not yet call it heritable.

Galton continued his research by tabulating the degree of eminence of these men as a function of the closeness of their relationship to an index case, the most eminent individual in a given pedigree. The correlations Galton obtained indicated that the degree of eminence of an individual decreased as the biological resemblance to the index case decreased. It was on the basis of this pattern of correlations that Galton concluded that genius was a heritable trait.

It is also possible to explain these data on the basis of an environmentalist argument, the very opposite of Galton's explanation. One could argue that the relatives of famous men are likely to receive important social and educational advantages which could account for their superior achievements. Galton himself recognized that such an interpretation could account for his observations. However, he simply did not believe such an explanation, and he advanced three arguments which he believed made anything except a strictly genetic explanation untenable. First, he pointed out that genius sometimes arose in humble backgrounds. This did not happen frequently, but the very fact that it occurred at all militated against the idea that social status and educational achievement produced individuals of eminence. Second, Galton pointed out that although education in the United States was much more widespread than it was in the United Kingdom, the frequency of genius was approximately equal in these two countries. How could this be, if education was important in producing genius? Third, Galton studied the achievements of adopted kinsmen of Roman Catholic Popes, individuals who are given every social, financial, educational, and political advantage, and he found them to be far less eminent as a group than were the biological relatives of men of eminence.

Sir Francis was very interested in the social applications of his ideas. He wished to improve the human condition by applying genetic principles, notably selective breeding, an enterprise for which he coined the term **eugenics.** He expressed his ideas quite explicitly; for example, he wrote that just as it is possible ". . . to obtain by careful selection a permanent breed of dogs or horses gifted with peculiar powers of running, or of doing anything else, so it would be practicable to produce a highly gifted race of men by judicious marriages during several consecutive generations" (Galton, 1869, p. 1). In order for such a eugenics program to work, Galton thought it necessary to measure the mental abilities of an entire population, which he proposed to do for the population of the British Isles. He established the Anthropometric Laboratory in which 9337 individuals were tested for a wide variety of physical and psychological traits. He failed in his attempts to measure the entire psychological resources of the United Kingdom, but he did obtain a great mass of data which he examined very carefully for hereditary factors in human abilities.

In summary, it is fair to characterize Sir Francis' beliefs as strongly favoring the contributions of heredity in determining mental abilities in general, and genius in particular. No amount of education, he argued, could create genius unless the hereditary predispositions were there in the first place. Conversely, "hereditary genius will out, regardless of adversity" (McClearn, 1962). Finally, it is important to note that Galton did believe in interactions between genotype and environment. For example, he thought that individuals of average talent might be hurt by impoverished environments. However, talent at either end of the distribution was so heavily influenced by heredity that the environment hardly made a difference.

Other Early Family Studies

In the decades following the publication of Galton's work, many other investigators wrote articles on the heritability of behavior in "eminent" and "degenerate" families. Members of the nobility were studied extensively (e.g., Woods, 1906), since genealogical and bibliographical materials were readily available for individuals belonging to the royal houses of Europe. For example, Gun (1930a, 1930b) published two short papers describing the inheritance of behavioral characteristics in the Stuarts and Tudors, respectively. Members of the former dynasty were described as stubborn and unyielding, traits that were said to have been passed on ''down the direct male line.'' The Tudors, on the other hand, were described as studious, a characteristic which was also said to be heritable.

At the other extreme, ''degenerate'' families were studied for the inheritance of criminality and feeble-mindedness. This line of work was begun by Dugdale (1877), who, as a member of the New York State prison commission, had the opportunity to visit and inspect many of the county jails in that state. On one of these visits, he was so impressed by the fact that six inmates in one county jail were related to each other that he traced the lineage of this family back over time. He was able to show that they had all descended from six sisters, and he gave the family the pseudonym ''Jukes.'' He estimated that the descendants of this family had cost New York State in excess of one million dollars for institutional care. Some years later, Estabrook (1916) discovered the real name of this family and was able to trace the descendants of these six sisters over a period of 130 years. In all, he was able to identify 2094 Jukes, of whom 1258 were living in 1915. Half of these individuals were ''feeble-minded.'' In interpreting these data, Estabrook cautiously pointed out that heredity and environment were both important in determining the behavior of members of the Jukes family.

Goddard (1912) published an account of another family to which he assigned the pseudonym ''Kallikak.'' The historical record showed that one Martin Kallikak, a soldier in the American Revolutionary War, had sired two families. One of these families was said to have resulted from a liaison between the soldier and a retarded woman whom he met in a tavern. The other sprang from a marriage between the soldier and a woman he met when he returned home from fighting the War of Independence. Goddard was able to trace many of the descendants of these two different unions. He found 480 progeny that had resulted from the illicit relationship and learned that many of these were judged to have been ''feeble-minded.'' On the other hand, most of the descendants of the legal marriage were judged to have been respectable members of society, and only a few of them had been retarded. In discussing these findings, Goddard concluded that ''feeble-mindedness'' was heritable. Although Goddard discussed his data in terms of classical Mendelian genetics, he stopped short of attributing feeble-mindedness to the action of a single gene.

Although the results of these early family studies are suggestive, it is obvious that they all suffer from a number of serious methodological flaws. One problem has to do with the determination of paternity; for example, the only evidence produced to support the fact that Martin Kallikak had an affair with a retarded woman whom he met in a tavern, and that a child had resulted from this relationship, was a tale Martin used to tell. One can argue about the merits of using such evidence and making such an assumption the basis of a serious scientific argument seems foolhardy, to say the least. A second serious flaw in all of these studies is the fact that the contributions of nature and nurture are hopelessly **confounded:** strong genetic potential and good environmental opportunity tended to occur together as did weak genetic potential and poor environment. What, for example, were the environmental conditions in which the descendants of a retarded tavern maid grew up at the turn of the eighteenth century? One can only guess at the answer to this question, but one's best guess would have to be that these circumstances were less than optimal. A third methodological flaw in many of these early experiments has to do with the way in which the intellectual attainments of the subjects were assessed. In Goddard's stu, for example, one might question the accuracy of the investigator's claim that he used well-trained and competent field workers who could judge an individual's intelligence on the basis of an interview; one might also wonder whether interviewing the acquaintances of deceased subjects yields reliable data.

For all of these reasons, it is fair to say that these early studies provided no hard data on the basis of which one could infer the relative contributions of nature and nurture in determining the intelligence of populations of human subjects. On the other hand, there are modern data suggesting that intelligence is determined, at least in part, by heritable factors, and it is to a consideration of these data that we now turn.

THE INHERITANCE OF INTELLECTUAL SKILL

Research on the inheritance of intellectual abilities began many years ago, and the large number of resulting publications makes it necessary to limit this discussion to a general overview. Inasmuch as nearly all of the work on the inheritance of intellectual skills has used IQ test scores as the dependent variable, a word or two about the **reliability** of these tests seems in order. IQ test scores are remarkably reliable when the tests are given to individuals who are 6 years of age or older. For example, full-scale Stanford-Binet IQ scores have a reliability of 0.91; full-scale scores on the Wechsler Intelligence Scale for Children (WISC) have a reliability of 0.89; the reliabilities of the verbal and performance portions of this test are 0.85 and 0.75, respectively (Cronbach, 1970; p. 222). When these standard intelligence tests are given to younger children, reliability coefficients in the seventies are obtained—lower, but still satisfactory. For example, when the Stanford-Binet was given to 4-year-old children who were then retested either 3, 6, or 12 years later, reliabilities of 0.71, 0.73, and 0.70 were obtained (Cronbach, 1970, p. 231). Thus, IQ tests meet one of the essential requirements necessary for measuring instruments used in any behavioral-genetic analysis; namely, that the measuring instrument be reliable. The arguments about what the tests actually measure and their **validity,** although of crucial importance in other contexts, simply do not apply to studies which propose to assess the relative contribution of genetic factors in determining individual differences in IQ test scores.

Having made the fundamental point, the first question to which we turn in our discussion is whether there is any evidence that the genetic material can affect an individual's performance on IQ tests. We will discuss this evidence under two separate headings: single-gene studies and studies of chromosomal aberrations.

Single Genes and Intelligence

For convenience, we will divide this section into two parts. We will ask first whether there are any single recessive genes that affect performance on IQ tests. Then we will ask if there are any single dominant genes that affect IQ scores.

Recessive Genes.   The best known example of a single recessive gene affecting an individual's performance on IQ tests is **phenylketonuria** (PKU), a heritable disease first described by Følling (1934). Følling discovered that the urine of certain mentally retarded patients contained excessively large quantities of phenylpyruvic acid. Penrose (1935), in a subsequent study, tested the urine of 500 institutionalized mentally retarded patients and found one case in which the urine of the individual contained excessive amounts of phenylpyruvic acid. An investigation of the pedigree of this individual revealed that the patient had a brother who was also mentally retarded, although not institutionalized. When this brother was examined, it was discovered that he suffered from the same biochemical defect. By 1937, it had become clear that PKU was a heritable syndrome caused by a single recessive gene (Jervis, 1937). Numerous studies performed since that time have confirmed this mode of inheritance; one-fourth of the offspring of heterozygous carriers of this disease are affected.

The underlying biochemical defect in PKU is that the affected individuals lack the gene which codes for the liver enzyme *phenylalanine hydroxylase*. Because this is the enzyme that catalyzes the conversion of phenylalanine to tyrosine, affected individuals have high circulating levels of phenylalanine and secrete many abnormal phenylalanine metabolites. What remains unknown about PKU is how the liver pathology produces central nervous system symptoms. The most devastating of the various symptoms is severe mental retardation. It has been estimated that the average IQ of untreated PKU patients is 30, although some patients have IQ scores well within the normal range. Some of the other symptoms shown by PKU patients are a very high incidence of epileptic seizures, accentuated deep and superficial reflexes, microcepahly (small heads), purposeless movements and severe temper tantrums. A number of theories have been advanced to account for these conditions. These include the hypotheses that high levels of circulating phenylalanine, or any of the abnormal phenylalanine metabolites, are toxic to the developing nervous system. In this regard, we should

mention that administration of a diet very low in levels of phenylalanine (Bickel, Gerrard, & Hickman, 1954) leads to improvement in intellectual abilities of PKU patients when dietary treatment is begun very early in life.

In any event, PKU is an example of a disease caused by a single recessive gene that clearly affects performance on IQ tests. There are many other examples of single recessive genes having such effects. Two of the better known are (1) *Lesch-Nyhan* syndrome, characterized by mental retardation, cerebral palsy, and involuntary movements; and (2) *Tay-Sachs* disease, a condition that occurs with high frequency in Ashkenazi Jews. Stafford (1961) and Bock and Kolakowski (1973) have reported on the effects of a single sex-linked gene that influences human spatial visualizing ability.

Dominant Genes.   There are only a few known instances of single dominant genes that affect IQ test scores. This is probably because the dominant genes which result in severe mental retardation usually affect fitness in very deleterious ways, and these individuals do not survive long enough to pass the gene along to their offspring. An exception to this rule is **Huntington's chorea,** a disease caused by a single dominant gene and characterized by involuntary jerky movements of limbs and body and a general mental and physical deterioration that ultimately leads to death. Huntington's chorea produces its effect through a progressive degeneration of the central nervous system, particularly of the basal ganglia. The average age of onset of the disease is 40, although earlier and later ages of onset are not uncommon. In general, however, the symptoms do not develop until the patients are past their reproductive prime. Affected individuals pass the disease on to one-half their offspring. Since it is impossible to diagnose the disease before the onset of the clinical symptoms, genetic counseling is particularly difficult.

When Levitt, Rosenbaum, Willerman, and Levitt (1972) studied the intellectual performance of patients who suffered from retinoblastoma, a malignancy of retinal tissue caused by a single dominant gene, they found that patients with retinoblastoma had significantly *higher* levels of verbal intelligence than did their unaffected siblings.

Chromosomal Aberrations and Intellectual Skill

The human genome consists of 23 pairs of chromosomes. The X and Y chromosomes are referred to as **sex chromosomes.** The other 22 pairs are collectively referred to as **autosomes.** Abnormalities of both types of chromosomes have been found to affect IQ test scores.

Autosomal Abnormalities.   There are, unfortunately, many examples of autosomal abnormalities that produce mental retardation. The best known of these is **Down syndrome** or **trisomy-21.** The condition, first described by Langdon Down in 1866, is characterized by a variety of symptoms. Affected patients are

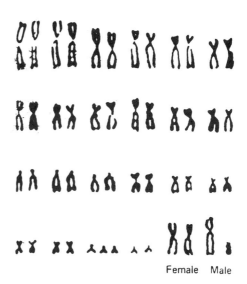

FIG 2.2   This figure illustrates the karyotypes of human males and females with Down syndrome. The pair of X chromosomes and the pair consisting of an X and a Y chromosome characterize females and males, respectively. In addition to these sex chromosomes, the normal human genome includes 22 pairs of autosomes. It can be seen in the illustration that chromosome 21 is present in triplicate in patients with Down syndrome.

Female   Male

mentally retarded; the average IQ of institutionalized patients with trisomy-21 is below 50 (Connolly, 1978). Because patients have upward and outward slants of their eyelids and epicanthal folds, the disease used to be referred to as "Mongolism." Certain peculiarities of the hands and of the finger prints are also characteristic of trisomy-21, and respiratory infections, heart malformations, and leukemia occur at high frequencies among patients with this disease. (There are several types of trisomy-21; the symptoms described above characterize what has been called "standard" trisomy-21.)

It was not until 1959 that Lejeune, Gautier, and Turpin discovered the cause of trisomy-21. By that time, human cytogeneticists had developed techniques which allowed them to visualize the human chromosomes fairly accurately, and Lejeune and his colleagues discovered that patients with trisomy-21 have 47 chromosomes, instead of the normal human complement of 46. Specifically, these investigators discovered that one of the smaller chromosomes, chromosome 21, was present in triplicate in patients with Down syndrome (Fig. 2.2).

The incidence of trisomy-21 is quite high; estimates of the frequency of this disease place it as high as 0.15 percent of all live births. A very high proportion of children with trisomy-21 are born to older women. Penrose and Smith (1966) have provided data indicating that fully 56% of all patients with trisomy-21 are born to women who are 35 years of age or older.

Sex Chromosomal Abnormalities.   Normal human females have two X chromosomes, and the normal human male carries one X and one Y chromosome. Of the many human sex chromosomal abnormalities that have been described, the two most frequently occurring anomalies are XXY (which causes **Klinefelter's syndrome**) and XO (which causes **Turner's syndrome**).

Patients with Klinefelter's syndrome are phenotypically male. However, sexual development is retarded; these patients usually have normal external genitalia, but very small testes. Klinefelter's patients are often mentally retarded. According to Moor (1967), the average IQ of patients with this disease is 84. However, many patients with Klinefelter's syndrome have normal IQ test scores.

Patients with Turner's syndrome are phenotypically female, but they also show a retardation of sexual development. These patients exhibit infantile sexual development, characterized especially by gonadal degeneration. The common belief that Turner's syndrome causes *general* mental retardation was contradicted by Moor's (1967) study in which 60 Turner's syndrome patients were examined and found to have an average IQ of 100. However, Shaffer (1962) has shown that these individuals suffer from a *specific* cognitive defect, characterized by an inability to organize perceptual information. Money (1968) has described Turner's patients as suffering from "visual infantilism" and a deficit in spatial ability.

Many other types of sex chromosomal aberrations have been discovered. Moor (1967) has published a summary of these data as they relate to IQ test scores (see Table 2.1). An examination of these data shows that (1) IQ test scores decrease as the amount of extra chromosomal material increases, and (2) the decrease in IQ test scores is greater for extra X chromosomal material than it is when extra Y material is present. This latter finding can probably be accounted for on the basis of the fact that the X chromosome contains more genetic information than is coded for on the Y chromosome.

The Effects of Heredity on Mid-Range IQ Scores

Although the data summarized above indicate that the genetic material can affect performance on standard IQ tests, the argument has often been made that single-gene studies and studies of chromosomal abnormalities apply only to intellectual abnormality and tell us little about the inheritance of normal intelligence. In order to examine this question, investigators have employed three types of methodologies: (1) twin studies, (2) analyses of resemblance in nonadoptive and adoptive families, and (3) studies of the effect of inbreeding on intellectual skills.

Twin Studies.   To study the nature-nurture question investigators have long used data obtained by examining the behavior of twins. Two types of methodologies are possible: First, data obtained in studies of **monozygotic** (MZ, identical) twins can be compared to data from **dizygotic** (DZ, fraternal) twins, and, second, data obtained in studies of twins who have been reared either together or apart can be compared.

One of the earliest studies using twin data to explore the nature-nurture question with respect to the inheritance of intellectual skills was reported by

TABLE 2.1
Average IQ Test Scores of Individuals Having Various Numbers of
Sex Chromosomes (Numbers in Parentheses)

	O	Y	YY	YYY
O		unlikely to occur		
X	100 (60)	100	76 (6)	80 (1)
XX	100	84 (63)	58 (19)	n.r.
XXX	51 (28)	52 (12)	48 (1)	n.r.
XXXX	50 (3)	35 (22)	n.r.	n.r.
XXXXX	low (2)	n.r.	n.r.	n.r.

n.r. = not reported.
From McClearn and DeFries (1973).
After Moor, 1967.

Thorndike (1905). In this study, a variety of psychological tests, such as simple arithmetic computation, naming the opposite words, etc., were administered to twins and to non-twin siblings. The sample of twins was divided into two, those who were less than 12 years of age and those who were older, and each subject in the study was given a single score. The results were as follows: Twins resembled each other more than did non-twin siblings, and there were no significant differences between the similarities of the scores when the younger and older twins were compared. Thorndike interpreted these results to show that nature influences the development of mental abilities in exactly the same fashion as nature influences the development of physical traits. Thorndike did not distinguish between identical and fraternal twins; indeed, he believed that all twins were genetically the same, differing from each other along a continuum of physical resemblance.

In 1930 Newman reported one of the first studies of the intellectual and personality characteristics of identical twins who had been reared in different homes. The results of this study, based on a comparison of only three pairs of twins, were disappointing from the point of view of a genetic hypothesis. The identical twins reared apart were found to be no more similar in their performance than were fraternal twins reared together. A few years later Newman, Freeman, and Holzinger (1937) reported the results of a study in which the sample of identical twins reared apart had been increased to 19 pairs, and, in addition, data were presented on 50 pairs of identical twins and 50 pairs of fraternal twins reared together. This paper quickly became one of the most influential articles dealing with the inheritance of intellectual skills. The zygosity of the twin pairs was determined by judging their resemblance on 10 physical dimensions. Each subject was given a battery of psychological tests, including the Stanford-Binet intelligence test. The results were that (1) identical twins were significantly more alike in measures of intelligence than were the fraternal twins, the respective correlation coefficients being 0.88 and 0.63; and (2) intelligence

TABLE 2.2
Correlations on Intelligence Test Measures for Monozygotic and
Dizygotic Twins Reared Together and Reared Separately

	Newman et al. (1937)		Shields (1962)	
	Correlation	N	Correlation	N
MZ together	0.88	50	0.76	44
MZ apart	0.77	19	0.77	44
DZ together	0.63	50	0.51	28

After McClearn and DeFries, 1973.

test scores of identical twins reared apart were more different than those of identical twins reared together, the respective correlation coefficients being 0.88 and 0.77. These data plainly imply that nature and nurture are both important in determining an individual's performance on IQ tests.

Several more recent studies have employed essentially the same methodology as that used by Newman et al. (1937). The results of one such experiment (Shields, 1962) are summarized in Table 2.2, which has been adapted from McClearn and DeFries (1973). It can be seen that the IQ test score correlations for identical twins are substantially higher than is the correlation for fraternal twins. Further, the resemblance between identical twins seems to be virtually unaffected by the rearing condition; the correlations between identical twins reared together and identical twins reared apart are essentially the same. In this respect, these data differ from those reported by Newman et al. (1937) in that Shields' study provided little evidence to support the view that experiential factors are at all important in determining an individual's performance on these tests. On this basis, it comes as no surprise to learn that Shields interprets these data to mean that IQ test performance depends upon inheritance.

Kamin (1973, 1974) has severely criticized all of these studies for both political and scientific reasons. On political grounds, Kamin faults the use of intelligence tests in general, and studies which purport to show heritable influences on intelligence test scores in particular, because he believes that the results of such experiments have been used to suppress the advancement of the underprivileged classes in this country. As Loehlin, Lindzey, and Spuhler (1975) have pointed out, it is indeed possible to find ". . . a variety of statements that by today's standards are shockingly bigoted toward ethnic minorities and lower income groups" (p. 293) in the psychological literature of the 1920s. However, and as these authors also note, it is equally easy to find other statements which convey precisely the opposite impression; namely, the results of mental tests have often been used to ". . . circumvent traditional social class barriers by locating and encouraging talented youth from all sectors of society" (p. 293).

One of Kamin's major scientific criticisms is that the degree of separation of twins reared apart is often not very great. The homes in which they grow up are fairly similar. On this basis, Kamin suggests that it is not surprising to find that many of the twin studies have failed to find a lowering of the correlations for identical twins reared apart. This is a sound criticism—up to a point. There is a great deal of evidence to show environmental effects on IQ; it would, in fact, be surprising if the experience of very different environments had no effect (Vandenberg & Johnson, 1968). However, the modern view that functioning intelligence is the product of genetic factors *and* environment can easily accept the predicted effects of such greater differences between the environments of separated twins.

IQ tests measure many different intellectual traits that range from verbal ability to performance skills, from knowledge of vocabulary to the skills of perceptual organization. IQ test scores are thus a composite index representing an individual's performance on all of these varied subtests. Twin studies have also been used to study the inheritance of a number of specific abilities such as verbal ability, verbal fluency, perceptual speed, memory, number ability, etc. Vandenberg (1971) reviewed many of these studies and concluded that heritable factors influence performance on these traits to varying degrees. Verbal and spatial intelligence have higher coefficients of heritability than reasoning and memory: approximately 0.60 as opposed to approximately 0.30. In terms of future twin studies, it seems clear that investigations in which the heritability of specific abilities will be studied constitute an important direction for new research.

Studies of Nonadoptive and Adoptive Families.   Identical twins are a special case of familial resemblance in that they are genetically identical. Fraternal twins have half of their genes in common on the average,[1] as do non-twin siblings and parents and their offspring. First cousins, as well as half-siblings, share 25% of their genes. Given these degrees of genetic relationship, it follows that relatives should resemble each other to varying degrees in terms of their performance on IQ tests, if that performance is influenced by heritable factors. On the other hand, the correlations of IQ test scores for unrelated individuals picked at random from the general population should be zero, and this correlation should become positive when adopted children are compared to their adoptive parents to the extent that environmental factors are important in contributing to performance on IQ tests and to the extent that children are placed into homes without regard to their predicted intelligence. Thus, family correlations and studies of adopted and foster children are important in that they provide data about the relative contributions of nature and nurture with respect to this trait in a population.

A large number of such studies have been performed, many of them more than 40 years ago. Erlenmeyer-Kimling and Jarvik (1963) reviewed the data in

---

[1]The "on the average" clause is very important. Some siblings have many more than half their genes in common; some have fewer.

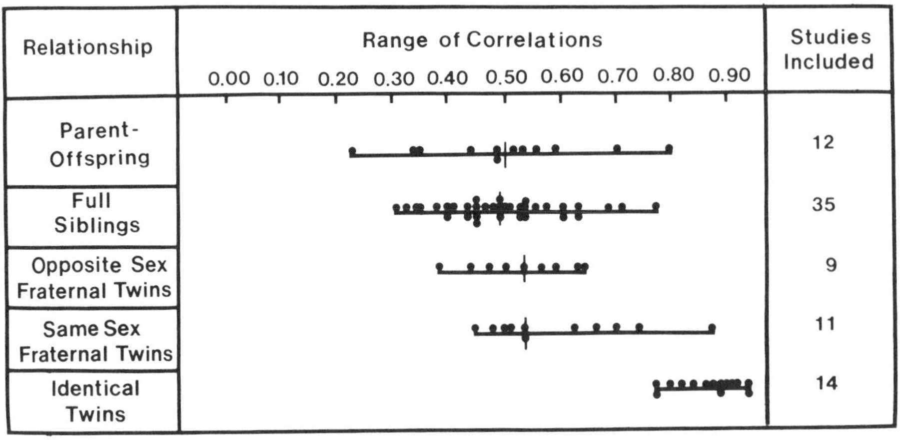

Relationship	Range of Correlations	Studies Included
	0.00 0.10 0.20 0.30 0.40 0.50 0.60 0.70 0.80 0.90	
Parent-Offspring		12
Full Siblings		35
Opposite Sex Fraternal Twins		9
Same Sex Fraternal Twins		11
Identical Twins		14

FIG. 2.3   Correlations for IQ test scores between relatives of varying degrees of genetic relationship. Each point represents an average correlation coefficient; the vertical bars indicate the median correlation for each degree of biological resemblance. (Adapted from "Genetics and Intelligence: A Review" by L. Erlenmeyer-Kimling and L. F. Jarvik, *Science*, 1963, *142*, 1477–1479.)

56 such studies conducted between 1911 and 1962. In this article the authors compared IQ test score correlations between individuals of varying degrees of genetic and environmental relationship. The results of their analysis are reproduced in Figure 2.3. Without discussing the merits of any of these individual experiments, the overwhelming weight of the evidence, when one considers all of these studies, is that both genetic and environmental factors are important in determining an individual's performance on IQ tests.

Inbreeding and Intellectual Skills.   **Inbreeding** is defined as the mating of individuals who are related to each other more closely than would occur by chance. Inbreeding has deleterious effects on traits closely related to fitness, a phenomenon known as **inbreeding depression.** Roberts (1967) has lamented the fact that the effects of inbreeding on behavioral traits have not been studied extensively. Interestingly, one of the few behavioral phenotypes which has been studied from this perspective is performance on intelligence tests.

Cohen, Bloch, Flum, Kadar, and Goldschmidt (1963) studied children of first cousin marriages and compared their performance on the Wechsler intelligence test with that of children of unrelated parents. They reported that the offspring of children of first cousin marriages do less well on subtests of this IQ test than do the offspring of unrelated spouses. Schull and Neel (1965) reported the results of a similar experiment performed in Japan. A Japanese version of the WISC was used, and 486 children of first cousin marriages, 191 children of marriages between first cousins once removed, 188 children of second cousin marriages, and 989 children of marriages between unrelated spouses were studied. Inbreeding also had a deleterious effect on IQ test scores in this study. Finally, Böök (1957) found that the children of first cousin marriages had a 3.5 times greater chance of being mentally retarded than did the children of unrelated parents.

Summary of Studies on the Inheritance of Intellectual Skills

In the preceding parts of this section we have reviewed some of the studies that have investigated the inheritance of intellectual skills, as these are measured by performance on standard intelligence tests. This discussion has been lengthy because the underlying question is intrinsically interesting and because we have chosen this trait to illustrate the methods employed by behavioral geneticists in their attempts to answer such questions when working with human subjects.

The overwhelming weight of this evidence supports the conclusion that differences in IQ test scores are determined in part by heritable factors. We have seen, for example, that single recessive and single dominant genes can affect performance on these tests, as can abnormalities of the sex chromosomes and of the autosomes. Twin research has shown that identical twins tend to be more alike in their performanc on IQ tests than are fraternal twins and that this similarity is not substantially affected when identical twins are reared apart. Family correlation studies and studies of adopted children have also yielded data consistent with the hypothesis that nature is important in influencing an individual's intellectual abilities. Finally, the fact that inbreeding appears to have deleterious effects on measures of IQ suggests that genetic factors affect performance on IQ tests, and that the trait(s) measured by these tests may be related to fitness. In short, all of this research strongly suggests that nature and nurture play an important role in determining the individual differences in IQ test scores that are observed when this trait is measured in populations of human subjects.

A large number of investigators have attempted to estimate the heritable component in the variability of IQ test scores in populations of subjects—**heritability,** in the broad sense, being defined as the proportion of total phenotypic variability which is caused by genetic factors. Estimates of heritability for total IQ test scores vary between 0.40 and 0.80, depending on the particular population being tested, the IQ test that is used, and the statistical procedure employed in any given study. As Loehlin et al. (1975) have suggested, the question of whether heritability for IQ test scores is really 0.40 or 0.80 "might sometimes affect matters of emphasis, but rarely matters of substance." As a general theoretical issue, the question of whether or not genetic factors contribute to the variability in intellectual skills observed in populations of human beings can be answered as follows: Genetic, environmental, and interactive factors all contribute to individual differences in performance on IQ tests.

RACE AND INTELLIGENCE

It is difficult to overestimate the degree to which Western intellectual thought has been preoccupied with racial differences in behavior or the number of atrocities that have been spawned by ideas about racial superiority. Within behavioral genetics, the issue of racial differences in behavior came up in Sir Francis Galton's study of hereditary genius. Galton wanted to determine the proportion of geniuses in different racial groups and made certain estimates based on the historical records available at that time. Each race was then assigned a position on a 16-point rating scale, depending on the relative proportion of genius in the general population. The ancient Greeks were ranked two points ahead of the Anglo-Saxons, who were ranked two points ahead of the "Negro" race. Thus, at least since 1869, some behavioral geneticists have concerned themselves with racial difference in behavior, especially in intellectual abilities.

Before we discuss this question further, it is important to define what biologists mean by the term **race.** Because human populations are to some extent reproductively isolated, they differ from each other in frequency of alleles (alternate forms) for any number of genes. It is this fact that underlies the concept of race. Dobzhansky (1970) has written: "Members of the same species who inhabit different parts of the world are often visibly and genetically different. This, in the simplest terms possible, is what race is as a biological concept" (p. 269). With this definition in mind, it is possible to frame the question concerning race differences in behavior as follows: Given that human populations have existed in relative reproductive isolation and therefore differ from each other with respect to gene frequencies, and given that genes determine the expression of behavior, albeit in very indirect ways, can racial differences in behavior be accounted for on the basis of genotypic differences between the races?

Individual investigators have contributed to an enormous literature on racial differences in behavior, attributing these differences to environmental or genetic causes, depending, or so it seems, more on individual preconceptions than on the weight of scientific evidence. In recent years, discussions of racial differences in behavior have focused on differences in intelligence between Afro-Americans and Caucasians living in the United States. Despite great overlap in the distributions of IQ scores in blacks and whites, the average IQ test score of whites is some 10-20 points higher than that of blacks. The controversy that has arisen does not concern this evidence but whether the difference is to be attributed to genetic or environmental factors.

Much of the early research on black-white differences in IQ test scores has been summarized by Audrey Shuey (1966) in a book entitled *The Testing of Negro Intelligence.* After reviewing all of this evidence, Shuey concluded that the measured differences in IQ test scores between blacks and whites could best be explained on the basis of genotypic differences between the groups. Interestingly, this book caused little debate, probably because the *Zeitgeist* was not yet ripe for the IQ controversy. By 1969, the situation was altogether different, and the modern controversy concerning racial differences and intelligence was launched with the publication of Jensen's long article in the *Harvard Educational Review* (1969). Jensen also reviewed much of the literature on the heritability of intelligence and on racial differences in intelligence and concluded "So all we are left with are various lines of evidence, no one of which is definitive alone, but which, viewed altogether, make it a not unreasonable hypothesis that genetic factors are strongly implicated in the average Negro-white intelligence difference" (1969, p. 82). Any number of investigors have taken Jensen to task for the interpretation he placed on these data. All of these authors point out that environmental diferences are hopelessly confounded with any genetic differences between populations classified as either black or white. Some investigators have gone so far as to suggest that it is impossible to design experiments which will critically distinguish between genetic and environmental explanations of racial differences in IQ test scores. According to Ehrman and Parsons (1975), "If a controversy of this type occurred in laboratory rodents, for example, it would have been resolved long ago because genotypes can be replicated and environments controlled" (p. 298). Given that it is impossible to replicate genotypes in human beings or to control their environments, should we give up all hope of solving this problem on the basis of valid scientific research?

Recent research by Scarr and Weinberg (1976) and by Scarr, Pakstis, Katz, and Barker (1977) suggests that we should not give up hope of solving the race and intelligence question quite yet. Scarr and Weinberg reported on black and mixed-race children who had been adopted by working-class to upper-middle-class white families in Minnesota. The average IQ test scores of these children was 110, well above the performance of black children reared in that part of the country. Further, the evidence obtained from the school districts indicated that these children performed at a higher level than the national average for white children on tests of vocabulary, reading, and mathematics. Scarr et al. (1977) also took advantage of the fact that U.S. blacks, like Caucasians, are a hybrid population. Using a variety of genetic and phenotypic markers, they determined the degree of admixture in a large sample of blacks. Each subject in the experiment was given an admixture score, and all were then given IQ tests. The results showed that there was no significant correlation between the degree of admixture and IQ test scores. Thus, both of these studies failed to provide evidence that the observed differences in IQ scores between blacks and whites are determined by genotypic differences.

THE INHERITANCE OF MENTAL DISORDERS

Modern research on the genetics of mental disorders can be said to have originated with the publication of Kallmann's book, *The Genetics of Schizophrenia,* which was published in 1938. In this book, the author concludes that genetic factors must contribute substantially to the expression of schizophrenic behavior, since this syndrome is much more prevalent in first-degree relatives of diagnosed patients than it is in the population at large. Kallmann's best known work, *The Genetic Theory of Schizophrenia: An Analysis of 691 Schizophrenic Twin Index Families,* was published in 1946. In this study, Kallmann identified 691 schizophrenic **index cases,** of whom 174 had identical and 507 had fraternal twins. Examination of these relatives revealed that 120 of the identical twins of the index cases were schizophrenic (yielding a **concordance rate** of 69%) and 53 of the fraternal twins of index cases were schizophrenic (a concordance rate of 10%).

Between that time and 1977, 12 other twin studies on the inheritance of schizophrenia were reported (see Jarvik & Deckard, 1977). These studies were conducted over a period of some 40 years, in eight countries on three continents. The results were always consistent with a genetic hypothesis; that is, the concordance rates for identical twins were consistently higher than those for fraternal twins. Jarvik and Deckard calculated the concordance rates for all of the reported studies and obtained average rates of 51% for identical twins, whereas that for fraternal twins was only 9%. As with all twin studies, the results of these experiments are difficult to interpret because of the possibility that environmental factors operate differently for these two types of twins. It is possible, for example, that the parents of identical twins create more similar environments for these special children. To the extent that environmental factors contribute to the expression of schizophrenia, this would confound interpretations based on different concordance rates in monozygotic versus dizygotic twins. Another complication arises from the fact that the uterine environments of identical and fraternal twins are different; to the extent that prenatal factors might be important in the etiology of schizophrenia, such differences would complicate interpretations based on comparisons of data from monozygotic and dizygotic twins.

To circumvent some of these difficulties, investigators have compared the concordance rates for schizophrenia in identical twins reared either apart or together. Unfortunately, such studies have been done only on very small samples. In the entire literature there exist very few cases (approximately 24) in which one member of an identical pair had been diagnosed as schizophrenic and the twins had been reared apart. Nevertheless, small as this sample is, the obtained results support a genetic hypothesis. The concordance rate for schizophrenia in identical twins reared apart is not less than that in identical twins reared together; in fact, the opposite is the case. In these studies, the concordance rate for schizophrenia in identical twins reared apart was approximately 70%, whereas that for identical twins reared together was 51%.

A large number of family studies of schizophrenia have been reported. Concordance rates in studies of children, siblings, half-siblings, uncles and aunts, and first cousins of schizophrenic index cases have been calculated. The general finding in these studies is that the relatives of schizophrenics are at much greater risk than are individuals taken at random from the general population. Further,

TABLE 2.3
Morbidity Risk Estimates for
Schizophrenia in the General
Population and for Relatives of
Schizophrenic Index Cases

Population	Percent
General Population	0.9
First Degree Relatives	
Parents of Schizophrenics	4.2
Siblings of Schizophrenics	7.5
Children of Schizophrenics	9.7
Second Degree Relatives	2.1
Third Degree Relatives	1.7

Data from Rosenthal, 1970.
Source: Plomin, DeFries, & McClearn, 1980.

the probability of developing schizophrenia tends to be correlated with the closeness of the relationship to the index case; the closer the relation, the greater the risk. These findings are summarized in Table 2.3.

Studies of adopted children have been used with particular effectiveness in experiments aimed at testing genetic theories of schizophrenia. One such study was reported by Heston (1970). This investigator located a sample of 47 individuals who had been born to schizophrenic mothers and had been given up for adoption before they were 1 month of age. As a control, 50 individuals were located who had been born to normal mothers and who had also been given up for adoption before they were 1 month of age. As adults, these individuals were carefully evaluated; school, police, medical, and Veterans Administration records were checked, and all of the individuals were given detailed psychiatric examinations. All of these data were evaluated by teams of clinicians who did not know whether the records they were examining were those of offspring of normal or schizophrenic mothers. The results indicated that the incidence of schizophrenia was significantly higher in individuals born to schizophrenic mothers. In addition, the incidence of other ''abnormal'' behaviors, such as mental deficiency, antisocial personalities, time spent in penal and/or psychiatric institutions, being discharged from the armed services on psychiatry grounds, etc., was also significantly greater in the children of schizophrenic mothers.

Rosenthal, Wender, Kety, Welner, and Schulsinger (1971) have reported the results of a similar study. These investigators used a less restrictive definition of schizophrenia, classifying individuals along what they called a ''schizophrenic spectrum.'' They studied this trait in offspring of normal and schizophrenic parents, all of whom had been raised in foster homes. The incidence of pathology was found to be 11% in the offspring of normal parents and 21% in the children of schizophrenic parents. In a follow-up study, Kety, Rosenthal, Wender,

Schulsinger, and Jacobson (1975) found that the incidence of schizophrenia in the biological relatives of children born to schizophrenic parents, but raised in foster homes, was much higher than that in the adoptive relatives of children who later became schizophrenic.

All of these results, obtained in studies which have employed very different methodologies, indicate strongly that schizophrenia is influenced by genetic factors. These data have been interpreted to show that the condition is transmitted by a single recessive gene, by a single dominant gene, by a complex polygenic system, or by several single genes each acting independently. As Kidd and Cavalli-Sforza (1973) have pointed out, however, it is premature to interpret these data in this fashion since the results currently available do not allow one to distinguish between these various genetic hypotheses. Nevertheless, it seems quite clear that schizophrenia is a condition which is greatly influenced by heritable factors.

It has been estimated that the incidence of schizophrenia is approximately 1% in the total population. This frequency has remained constant over a considerable period of time, and it is the same over the wide range of populations in which it has been estimated. This high incidence is difficult to explain since schizophrenia is detrimental from the point of view of fitness. Thus, natural selection should operate to decrease the frequency of schizophrenia. The only way to explain such a high incidence, and its relative constancy over time, is to postulate that the heterozygote carrier of the disease, a nonpsychotic individual, is somehow at a selective advantage. Several hypotheses have been advanced to account for the presumed selective advantage of heterozygous carriers of schizophrenia. These include suggestions that carriers have a reduced mortality rate (Erlenmeyer-Kimling, 1968) and that they are more fertile than noncarriers (Huxley, Mayr, Osmond, & Hoffer, 1964). More recently, Jarvik and Deckard (1977) have suggested that heterozygous carriers might have a selective advantage by virtue of their personality structures. These authors suggest that carriers are endowed with a suspicious and seclusive personality that might give them a selective advantage in a hostile environment such as must have existed for long periods of time during the evolution of *Homo sapiens*. They have coined the term "odyssean personality" to describe the schizoid-paranoid traits often observed in carriers.

Although by far the greatest amount of work on the heritability of mental disorders has focused on schizophrenia, the possible role of genetic mechanisms in the etiology of other psychopathologies has also been studied. For example, Luxenburger (1928) and Rosanoff, Handy, Plesset, and Brush (1935) have studied the possible genetic bases of manic-depressive psychoses using twin and family correlation methods. Åmark (1951) has reported data from Sweden indicating that alcoholism is a familial condition, although in this particular study it is difficult to distinguish between the relative importance of environmental and genetic factors. Current research on the heritability of the manic-depressive psychoses and alcoholism suggest that these conditions have a genetic component.

ANIMAL RESEARCH

Since investigators first began to study the possible contributions of genetic factors to animal behaviors, an enormous literature on what loosely might be called "animal behavioral genetics" has accumulated. Much of this research has been performed in the house mouse, *Mus musculus,* and in insects, especially fruit flies of the various species of *Drosophila.* It is possible to classify the research in animal behavioral genetics into three categories depending on the methodologies used in various experiments. These three categories are (1) selective breeding studies, (2) inbred strain comparison studies, and (3) single-gene studies. Although it is clearly impossible to review all of animal behavioral genetics, we will consider several examples of research in each of these categories, focusing our attention on historically important works.

Selective Breeding

Human beings have practiced **selective breeding** for many thousands of years. As a technique for producing desirable varieties of plants and animals, the idea that "like begets like," or selective breeding, can be traced back to approximately 8000 B.C., at which time humans began to domesticate the dog (McClearn & DeFries, 1973). The basic ideas underlying a selective breeding program are quite simple. In such a program, animals with a certain phenotype are selected for reproduction, whereas animals which lack this phenotype are excluded. Several types of selective breeding are possible: In behavioral research the most common type of selective breeding is bi-directional selection. In bi-directional selection, a continuously distributed trait is measured in a genetically heterogeneous population of organisms, this population of organisms being referred to as the base population. Animals at the two extremes of the trait distribution are then chosen for reproduction; those in the middle are discarded. Thus, two selected lines are established which are never allowed to interbreed. Within these two lines, animals at the extreme in the desired direction are bred inter se, and the process is continued for as many generations as is desirable.

Notice that animals are chosen for reproduction on the basis of their **phenotype;** their **genotype** is not known by the investigators. An organism's phenotype is not a perfect indicator of its genotype, nor is the inverse proposition true. However, to the extent that the expression of an organism's phenotype depends on its genotype, selective breeding will succeed in establishing phenotypically distinct lines. Thus, one of the purposes of selective breeding is to show that a phenotype is determined, at least in part, by genetic mechanisms. Or, to put this another way, a successful selective breeding program is prima facie evidence that the trait selected for is determined in part by genetic factors. Further, the results of selective breeding studies allow one to estimate certain genetic parameters such as, for example, heritability. Finally, selective breeding experiments are important because they produce the biological materials that allow one to ask more mechanistic questions about the determinants of the phenotype that was the subject of the selection study.

One of the earliest experiments using this technique with respect to a behavioral trait was performed by Tolman (1924). Tolman tested 82 heterogeneous rats in a maze and assigned each animal a "learning" score based on the number of errors the animals made, the latency to run the maze, and the number of perfect runs through the maze. Nine males and nine females with the "best" learning scores, and nine males and nine females with the "worst" learning scores, were selected for reproduction to establish the so-called "bright" and "dull" lines, respectively. The offspring of these two lines were then tested, and the "brightest" animals in the bright line were mated to each other, as were the "dullest" animals in the dull line. Since the numbers of animals in each of the two lines were quite small, Tolman had to practice inbreeding; in fact, brother-by-sister matings were routinely employed. The results of this early selective breeding experiment were as follows: In the first selected generation, the progeny of the bright line were themselves quite bright, whereas the progeny of the dull line were dull. In the second generation, however, the differences in the learning scores between the animals of the two lines decreased, largely because the animals of the bright line regressed with respect to their performance in learning the maze. Tolman was disappointed with the results of this experiment, and he offered two arguments to explain the behavior of the animals in the second selected generation. First, he pointed out that the measuring instrument—that is, the maze—might not have been very reliable, in which case accurate selection would not have been possible. Second, he argued that inasmuch as the animals had been inbred, inbreeding depression could account for the poor performance of the animals in the bright line. Both of these explanations are potentially correct. Even without these two potential sources of error, however, modern researchers would not be surprised at the outcome of the experiment since two generations of selective breeding are rarely sufficient to produce lines of animals that differ in their performance in a learning situation.

Tolman never returned to research in behavioral genetics. However, he remained one of the few eminent learning theorists who believed that hereditary factors make an important contribution to the individual differences in performance which are ubiquitous whenever animals are studied in learning situations. He coined the acronym "H.A.T.E." to indicate that heredity, age, training, and endocrine factors underlie individual differences in learning. Despite the fact that Tolman turned his attention elsewhere, interest in genetics continued to be high in his laboratory, and two of his students set out to construct a maze of known reliability. The result (Tolman, Tyron, & Jeffress, 1929) was a 17-unit, automated T-maze of great reliability; the odd-even trial reliability of rats running this maze was greater than 0.90. Since the maze was fully automated, the animals did not have to be handled once they had been placed into the maze for any given day. Some additional features of the maze were that the animals ran for food reinforcement and that learning depended on the correct utilization of spatial cues.

Using this maze, Robert Choate Tryon set out to perform what has become the "classic" selective breeding experiment for a behavioral phenotype. This experiment is justly famous, and it has been cited in very nearly every introductory textbook published since that time. Tryon began with a genetically heterogeneous population of some 100 rats, carefully acquired from a wide range of sources to ensure their heterogeneity. All of the animals in this base population were tested in the maze. Predictably, some of the animals learned the maze with ease, making few errors, while others learned the maze slowly and made many errors. The male and female rats which made the fewest errors were mated inter se to establish what Tryon called the "maze bright" line, and the animals which made the largest number of errors were mated to each other to produce the so-called "maze dull" line. In due course these matings produced offspring which were tested in the maze when they reached the appropriate age. The "brightest" rats in the maze bright line were mated to each other, as were the "dullest" rats in the dull line. This procedure was carried out for 21 generations (Tryon, 1940).

The experiment was successful in producing two lines of rats which differed from each other in the number of errors they made in learning the maze (see Figure 2.4). Although the selective breeding was continued for 21 generations, non-overlapping distributions of error scores had occurred by the seventh generation. In other words, by the seventh generation of selective breeding, the "dullest" rat in the bright line made fewer errors than did the "brightest" rat in the dull line.

Although this experiment is a "classic," and although Tryon was successful in selecting for performance in this maze, the experiment is not a good example of how one should perform a selective breeding experiment. A number of weaknesses in experimental design should be noted. First, Tryon systematically inbred while he selected. Since selective breeding depends on genetic variability and variability is decreased by inbreeding, inbreeding should be avoided in a selection experiment. Second, Tryon did not maintain an unselected control line against which the results of selective breeding could be compared. Third, Tryon did not produce replicate selected lines to assure the reliability of the selection procedure. Nevertheless, as we have just pointed out, the experiment was successful. Although Tryon himself did not compute the heritability of the trait which he had selected for, Tyler (1969) performed these calculations and obtained a heritability coefficient of 0.21. This means that the phenotypic variability measured in this experiment depended on both environmental and genetic

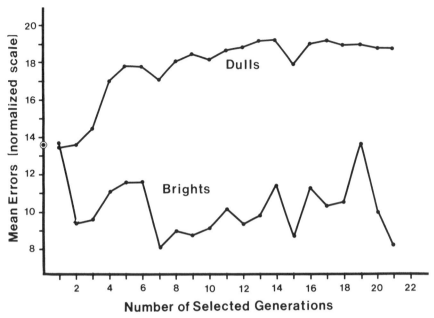

FIG. 2.4   This figure illustrates the results of Tryon's selective breeding experiment. Data are plotted in terms of mean number of errors in learning the maze made by "dull" and "bright" rats as a function of number of selected generations.

factors; 21% of the total phenotypic variability exhibited by these rats in learning this maze can be attributed to genetic factors.

The rats produced in this selective breeding experiment have been used in numerous attempts to discover the underlying factors that contribute to the differences in error scores of maze-bright and maze-dull rats as they learn to run this maze. Here, we will mention only a few such studies as examples of how selectively bred animals can be used in psychological research.

In one such experiment, Tryon was interested in the question of whether or not motivational factors could account for the observed differences in performance. Specifically, could it be that the maze-bright rats were hungrier than the maze-dull rats after 24 hours of food deprivation, and could this be the reason for their superior performance? To answer this question, Tryon tested maze-bright and maze-dull rats under two conditions of food deprivation. Maze-dull rats were run through the maze after either 1 or 2 days of food deprivation, whereas maze-bright rats were tested after having been deprived of food either for half a day or for 1 day. This asymmetry in experimental design was due to the fact that maze-dull rats would not run the maze at all unless they were quite hungry. The results of this experiment were that the maze-dull rats made more errors in learning the maze even when they were hungrier than the maze-bright rats; the error scores were hardly affected by the duration of food deprivation. Using the then popular Hullian conception that drive and habit strength determine performance, Tryon concluded that differences in drive could not explain the superior performance of the maze-bright rats. Accordingly, differences in the potential for developing habit strength must account for the observed differences in performance between these two lines.

Several experiments were performed to discover whether the maze-bright rats were generally better at learning mazes than were the maze-dull rats. Krechevsky (1933) performed an experiment in which he tested maze-bright and maze-dull rats in a maze in which the rats could utilize either spatial or visual cues in their attempts to learn the path through the maze. He found that maze-bright rats tended to use spatial cues, whereas maze-dull rats tended to use visual cues. This result was to be expected since the maze on which these animals had been selected required the utilization of spatial cues. Searle (1949) also performed an experiment in which maze-bright and maze-dull rats were tested in a variety of learning situations. Maze-dull rats were found to be *better* at learning mazes under conditions of escape-from-water motivation, whereas maze-bright rats performed more efficiently under conditions of hunger motivation. The results of these experiments, and others, indicate that maze-bright and maze-dull rats differ from each other in complex ways. They also indicate that the rats had been selected for performance in a rather specific situation. Namely, maze-bright rats are superior to maze-dull rats under conditions of hunger motivation and in mazes in which learning depends on the correct utilization of spatial cues.

Numerous other successful selective breeding programs for behavioral phenotypes have been reported in the literature. These include selective breeding for such diverse behaviors as (1) performance of rats is an automated maze (Heron, 1935); (2) performance of rats in the Hebb-Williams maze, in which animals are required to solve progressively more complex maze patterns (Thompson, 1954); (3) locomotor activity of rats as measured by the number of revolutions animals run in an activity wheel (Rundquist, 1933); (4) locomotor activity of mice as measured by square crossings in an arena (DeFries & Hegmann, 1970); (5) "emotionality" of rats as measured by urination-defecation scores in a novel environment (Hall, 1938); (6) "emotional reactivity" of rats as measured by defecation scores (Broadhurst, 1958); (7) preference for saccharin of rats tested in free-choice situations (Nachman, 1959); (8) susceptibility of mice to audiogenic seizures when the mice are exposed to an intense acoustic stimulus (Frings & Frings, 1953); (9) response to acoustic priming in mice (Deckard, Tepper, & Schlesinger, 1976); (10) sleeping time of mice in response to a single intraperitoneal injection of ethanol (McClearn & Kakihana, 1973, 1981); (11) geotaxis in *Drosophila melanogaster* (Hirsch, 1959); (12) phototaxis in *Drosophila melanogaster* (Hinsch & Boudreau, 1958); and (13) performance of mice on a conditioned avoidance task (Bignami, 1965).

Inbred Strain Comparison Studies

Of all the various techniques available to behavioral geneticists, the use of inbred strains—or, more specifically, **inbred strain comparisons**—is the single most frequently employed procedure. There are several reasons for the popularity of this technique. Before we discuss some of these reasons, a word or two about inbreeding and its effects are in order.

As we have already indicated, inbreeding is defined as the mating together of individuals who are related to each other. Many different systems of inbreeding are possible in sexually reproducing species. For example, brother can be mated to sister, parent to offspring, first cousins to each other, and so forth. Regardless of which system of inbreeding is employed, the results are always the same, and they are twofold: First, inbreeding results in **isogenicity;** that is, it reduces genetic variability until it approaches zero asymptotically. The rate at which variability approaches zero depends on the particular system of inbreeding that is employed—the closer the inbreeding, the faster genetic variability in a population approaches zero. For example, after 20 generations of brother-by-sister mating, isogenicity exceeds 98%. Thus, for all intents and purposes, after 20 generations of brother-by-sister mating, all the animals within an inbred line are genetically identical. Second, inbreeding results in **homozygosity,** which means that the alleles at any given locus are the same. Considering two alleles at any given locus, say A_1 and A_2, individuals possessing two identical alleles, A_1A_1 or A_2A_2, are said to be homozygous, whereas individuals possessing two unlike alleles, A_1A_2, are said to be heterozygous.

By convention, an inbred strain of organisms is defined as a population in which isogenicity is equal to or exceeds that produced by 20 generations of brother-by-sister mating. Inbred strains of many species have been developed, largely for purposes of medical research, although they have also been used extensively in behavioral studies. Inbred strains of mice, rats, guinea pigs, Syrian hamsters, and rabbits are available. The origins and degree of inbreeding of many of these strains have been described (see, for example, Jay, 1963). In addition, so-called "breeds" of many species, including dogs, dairy cattle, etc., are available. Even though such breeds do not satisfy the strict definition of an "inbred strain," the animals within a breed are genetically much more similar than are animals taken from the general population.

The use of inbred animals in psychological research offers many advantages, including the following: First, if an experiment is performed with animals of an inbred strain, it can be replicated with animals of precisely the same genotype, since all inbred animals of a given strain are genetically identical. Second, if an experiment is performed on inbred animals and if variability in the dependent variable is observed, then that variability can be attributed to environmental factors, since genetic variability is effectively zero within an inbred strain. Third, if a trait is measured in animals of more than one strain and if the animals have been reared in identical, or very nearly identical, environments, then the differences in behavior can be attributed to genotypic differences, since such results are prima facie evidence that the trait in question is determined, at least in part, by genetic factors. Fourth, if strain differences in a behavior are observed and if further breeding experiments are performed, the experimenter can estimate certain genetic parameters such as the heritability of that trait in that population. Fifth, if animals of two or more inbred strains differ with respect to a particular behavior, then the experimenter has available the biological material on which further experiments can be conducted in an attempt to discover the underlying variables that mediate such differences.

Strain and/or breed comparison experiments have a long history within psychology. One of the earliest of these studies was carried out by Yerkes (1913), who was interested in traits which he called savageness, wildness, and timidity. To measure these variables, Yerkes observed behaviors such as biting, jumping, cowering, etc., and animals were assigned a score for each of these behaviors based on a 5-point rating scale devised for the purpose. These behaviors were measured in laboratory rats and in wild rats, and similar measurements were made in F_1 and F_2 hybrid generations derived by mating laboratory-reared and wild rats. The animals of the F_1 generation were produced by mating laboratory females with wild males. The results of this experiment indicated that these behaviors are determined in part by genetic factors. Coburn (1922) performed a very similar experiment in which the same behaviors were measured, with the additional refinement that *reciprocal F_1 hybrid crosses* were produced. In other words, F_1 hybrids were produced by mating wild males with laboratory females and, conversely, by mating laboratory males with wild females. The results of this experiment replicated Yerkes' findings (that is, savageness, wildness, and timidity were found to be determined by genetic factors); furthermore, no differences were observed between the reciprocal crosses, indicating that possible maternal effects could be ruled out. Many other experiments of this nature have been reported: For example, Dawson (1932) and Scott (1942), working with inbred strains of mice, measured wildness/tameness and aggression, respectively, and obtained data consistent with the hypothesis that these behaviors are determined in part by genetic factors.

The number of studies in which experimenters have looked for and found strain differences in behavior is truly enormous. Such differences have been obtained in behaviors as diverse as learning, memory storage, hoarding, "emotionality," geotropism, temperature preference, alcohol preference, saccharin preference, locomotor activity, and susceptibility to audiogenic seizures. Further, strain differences in neuroanatomical, neurochemical, and neurophysiological parameters have been found, and these are being studied from the point of view of correlating them with differences in behavior. Observations of large strain differences in the behavioral effects of drugs have led to the recent creation of a new field of study which has been named "psychopharmacogenetics."

All of these data lead one to conclude that most behaviors are determined in part by genetic factors. As we have stated repeatedly throughout this discussion, however, interactions between genotype and environment must also be considered. Unfortunately, few behaviors have been studied from this perspective. We will briefly discuss two lines of inquiry in which such interactions have been investigated.

Ginsburg and Allee (1942) measured aggression in several strains of inbred mice. Aggression was defined as the number of fights initiated and won by an animal when two mice were placed together within a confined space. Large strain differences in these behaviors were observed; mice of some strains initiated and won many more encounters than did the animals of other strains. For example, C57BL mice were far better at winning fights than were C3H animals. These results were taken as evidence that aggression in these animals was determined by genetic variables. Ginsburg and Allee then continued their experiment by manipulating certain experiential factors. Highly aggressive mice of the C57BL strain were given a series of "defeat" experiences; that is, they were placed into situations so contrived that they lost many fights. When the effects of this treatment were studied, these animals from this aggressive strain initiated and won far fewer fights than did animals not given such experiences. Conversely, less aggressive mice of the C3H strains were placed into situations so contrived as to assure that they experienced so-called "victory" experiences. The effects of this treatment were that the animals which had been given these experiences initiated and won more fights than did C3H mice which had not been exposed to victory experiences. Nevertheless, they were less aggressive than were the C57BL animals, and less aggressive even than C57BL mice which had been exposed to a series of defeat experiences. Thus, the results of this study indicate that aggression, at least insofar as this trait was measured in these experiments, is determined by the interaction between an animal's genotype and its experiences.

McClearn (1959) measured locomotor activity in mice of a variety of inbred strains. Activity measurements were made in a brightly lighted arena. The animals were found to differ greatly in their activity, with mice of some strains being much more active than mice of others. In order to determine the generality of these results, McClearn (1961) tested the activity levels of mice of these same strains in four different situations. The results indicated that mice of strains with high levels of activity in the arena tended to be active in all of the other situations, whereas mice from inactive strains tended to be inactive regardless of the apparatus in which they were tested. In examining these data, McClearn noted that animals from albino strains tended to be less active than animals from pigmented strains, an observation that had also been made by other investigators, and he set out to test whether these results might be due to the levels of illumination under which locomotor activity was typically measured. Specifically, Mc-

Clearn (1960) tested the hypothesis that mice of albino strains were "photophobic" and that they would therefore exhibit higher levels of activity if tested under conditions of dim illumination. Accordingly, mice from an albino and from a pigmented strain were tested under two illumination conditions: the standard, bright condition; or dim illumination provided by red light, a wavelength to which mice are very insensitive. The results of this experiment were as follows: Mice of the pigmented strain were more active under bright illumination, whereas the opposite was true for albino animals. However, even when tested in dim light, the albino animals were still less active than were the pigmented mice under that illumination condition. Again, the results of this experiment indicate that behavior, in this case locomotor activity, is determined by the interaction of genetic and environmental factors.

Single Genes and Behavior

The techniques we have just discussed, namely selective breeding and inbred strain comparisons, are most useful for studying behaviors that are polygenically determined. Single-gene studies, on the other hand, are designed principally to test the adequacy of single-locus hypotheses. As we shall see, such studies can also be used to test for the effects of more than one gene.

Single-gene studies of behavioral traits have a long history within behavioral genetics, and such research has been performed both in human beings and in other animals. The two earliest papers on single genes and behavior were published by Yerkes (1907) and by Sturtevant (1915). The former author published an extensive monograph on the so-called *waltzing* behavior observed in some mice, a trait which is passed from generation to generation by a single recessive gene. Sturtevant's experiments dealt with mating behavior in *Drosophila melanogaster*. When this geneticist tested mating behavior in several types of **mutants,** as well as in wild type, normal flies, he found that both normal and mutant male flies tended to mate more frequently with mutant females, probably because these females were less active and therefore less likely to escape from the courting male. Both normal and mutant females tended to mate more frequently with normal males, probably because they were more active and approached the receptive females more rapidly.

Since these early beginnings, many papers on single genes and behavior have appeared in the literature. Lindzey, Loehlin, Manosevitz, and Thiessen (1971) reported that of the 1545 syndromes described by McKusick (1968) in his book entitled *Mendelian Inheritance in Man,* 135 have behavioral consequences in that they cause mental retardation. Of these, 112 are transmitted by single autosomal recessive genes, 7 by single autosomal dominant genes, and 16 by single sex-linked genes. Besides these conditions, many other human behaviors are determined by single genes in accord with the rules of Mendelian inheritance.

These include such diverse behaviors as the ability to taste, particularly a substance known as phenylthiocarbamide (PTC); certain types of color blindness; certain types of epilepsy; and behaviors associated with testicular feminization.

In animals, single-gene studies have been conducted most frequently in mice and in *Drosophila*. In mice, for example, Sidman, Appel, and Fuller (1965) described no fewer than 92 neurological mutations which cause abnormalities in the anatomy, physiology, and neurochemistry of the nervous system. As might be expected, many of these conditions are correlated with behavioral abnormalities. A few examples of such mutations are: (1) *dilute lethal* mice, which suffer from spontaneous convulsions; (2) *Wobbler lethal* mice, which have great difficulty in locomotor activity; (3) *cerebral degeneration*, which causes the cerebral hemispheres and the olfactory bulbs to undergo a progressive degeneration accompanied by an overall degeneration in many types of behavior; and (4) *absent corpus*, in which the animals congenitally lack either all or a part of the corpus callosum and which, unfortunately, has not been studied behaviorally. In addition to these neurological mutants, a number of other single genes that affect behavior have been studied. These include the *albino* locus, which reduces locomotor activity, as we have already mentioned, and which also affects a wide range of other behaviors (including, for example, poor performance on conditioned avoidance tasks); the *brown* locus, which increases grooming activity; and *pintail*, which increases the rates of extinction in conditioned avoidance situations. More recently, Collins (1970) discovered a gene, which he named *asp* (**audiogenic seizure prone**), which increases susceptibility to audiogenic (sound-induced) seizures and is located on the eighth linkage group.

In *Drosophila*, many single genes that affect a wide range of behaviors have been discovered. For example, the *yellow* gene decreases reproductive success in male fruit flies, probably because the animals exhibit abnormal patterns of courtship behavior (Bastock, 1956). More recently, Seymour Benzer and his collaborators have described single genes that affect locomotor activity, visual physiology and behavior, sexual behavior, responses to stress, and several other behaviors (see, for example, Konopka & Benzer, 1971; Benzer, 1973).

Finally, we should also note that effects of single genes upon behavior have been described in animals of many other species. One particularly interesting example is hygienic behavior in honeybees (Rothenbuhler, 1967). The hives of these insects sometimes become infected with a bacterial condition known as "American foulbrood." Under these conditions, the bees engage in hygienic behavior which is regulated by two different genes. When the hive becomes infected, the bees first open the combs in which infected young larvae are located and then remove the dead from the hive. These two distinct behaviors are controlled by two genes; namely, the so-called *u* gene (for uncapping) and the so-called *r* gene (for removal). Rothenbuhler was able to show that the bees which engage in these behaviors are of the *uurr* genotype and that only bees of this genotype engage in both of these hygienic behaviors.

CONCLUSION

The study of learning described by Kimble (Chapter 2, Volume 1) was the expression of a strongly environmentalist commitment which received its most vigorous expression in J. B. Watson's heavy-handed pronouncement, "Give me a dozen healthy infants, and my own specified world to bring them up in, and I'll guarantee to take any one at random and train him to become any type of specialist I might select. . . ." Most American psychologists followed Watson's lead and attempted to write a psychology from which genetic and other biological factors were excluded. Knight Dunlap (1919), for example, published a paper which he titled "Are There Any Instincts?" In this article, instincts were equated with behaviors which were not influenced by experience, and Dunlap's answer to the question posed by his title was decidedly negative. A few years later, Z. Y. Kuo (1924) published a paper in which he discussed the status of psychology, as he saw it at the time, under the title "A Psychology Without Heredity."

During this period in the history of psychology the nature-nurture question was treated in terms that implied that behavior was to be explained either in terms of heredity *or* environment and the theoretical pendulum had swung decidedly in the direction of environmentalism. No one conceived of nature and nurture as interacting, and the behaviorists, at most, yielded slightly in their concession that nature might contribute to the expression of reflexive behaviors, especially as these were observed to emerge during maturation. An example of research that led to this minor theoretical concession was reported by Gesell and Thompson (1929), who introduced the **method of co-twin control** in this paper. In their experiment, one member of a pair of twins was given early and extensive training on a motor task, while the other twin was given less training or none; when performance was assessed later, no differences between the pairs of twins were observed, and the conclusion was that experience does not enhance performance until a requisite level of maturation has been reached. Moreover, experience was seen as all important in shaping those behaviors which were of the greatest interest to psychologists at the time—namely, conditioning and learning.

The behaviorists, and their intellectual heirs, the American learning theorists, reigned supreme for some 40 years, and their views dominated the direction of research. Gradually, however, papers accumulated, published here and there, which threw doubt on the validity of a psychology from which genetics was totally excluded. By 1951, the number of such papers had grown to the extent that Calvin Hall could write a chapter on "The Genetics of Behavior" for inclusion in S. S. Stevens' *Handbook of Experimental Psychology* (1951). Nine years later, the research literature on genetic determinants of behavior had grown to such proportions that Fuller and Thompson (1960) were able to write an entire textbook called *Behavior Genetics*.

It is fair to characterize today's situation by stating that the nature-nurture pendulum has now swung back at least to center and probably a bit to the genetic side of center. For example, a number of universities now offer undergraduate courses in behavioral genetics, and it is possible to obtain advanced degrees in behavioral genetics at four or five American universities. Since Fuller and Thompson's classic textbook, several others have been published (e.g., Thiessen, 1972; McClearn & DeFries, 1973; Ehrman & Parsons, 1976; Plomin, DeFries, & McClearn, 1980). There is an international journal, *Behavior Genetics*, devoted to the publication of research on the inheritance of behavior in animals and human beings. The Behavior Genetics Association was founded in 1970 and now has over 300 members. With only a few exceptions, psychologists today accept the proposition that behavior, *all* behavior, results from interacting genetic and environmental factors. As a result, the nature-nurture question is much less controversial than it once was and has become an empirical issue. The question, "Do genes regulate behavior?", has been translated into . . . "How do genes express themselves in various developmental and environmental circumstances?" (Thiessen, 1972).

REFERENCES

Åmark, C. A study of alcoholism. Clinical, social-psychiatric and genetic investigations. *Acta Psychiatrica et Neurologica Scandinavica*, 1951, Suppl. 70.

Bastock, M. A gene mutation which changes a behavior pattern. *Evolution*, 1956, *10*, 421–439.

Benzer, S. Genetic dissection of behavior. *Scientific American*, 1973, *229*, 24–37.

Bickel, H., Gerrard, J., & Hickman, E. M. The influence of phenylalanine intake on the chemistry and behavior of phenylketonuric child. *Acta Paediatrika*, Upps., 1954, *43*, 64–77.

Bignami, J. Selection for high rates and low rates of conditioning in the rat. *Animal Behaviour*, 1965, *13*, 221–227.

Bock, R. D., & Kolakowski, D. Further evidence of sex-linked major-gene influence on human spatial visualizing ability. *American Journa of Human Genetics*, 1973, *25*, 1–14.

Böök, J. A. Genetical investigation in a north Swedish population: The offspring of first-cousin marriages. *Annals of Human Genetics*. 1957, *21*, 191–221.

Broadhurst, P. L. Studies in psychogenetics: The quantitative inheritance of behavior in rats investigated by selective and cross-breeding. *Bulletin of the British Psychological Society*, 1958, *34*, 2A (Abst.).

Coburn, C. A. Heredity of wildness and savageness in mice. *Behavior Monographs*, 1922, *4*, 1–71.

Collins, R. L. A new genetic locus mapped from behavioral variation in mice: Audiogenic seizure prone (asp). *Behavior Genetics*, 1970, *1*, 99–109.

Cohen, R., Bloch, N., Flum, Y., Kadar, M., & Goldschmidt, E. School attainment in an immigrant village. In E. Goldschmidt (Ed.), *The genetics of migrant and isolated populations*. Baltimore: Williams and Wilkins, 1963.

Connolly, J. A. Intelligence levels of Down's syndrome children. *American Journal of Mental Deficiency*. 1978, *83*, 193–196.

Cronbach, L. J. *Essentials of psychological testing*. New York: Harper and Row, 1970.

Darwin, C. *The variation of animals and plants under domestication*. New York: Orange Judd, 1868.

Darwin, C. *On the origin of species by means of natural selection or the preservation of favoured races in the struggle for life*. New York: Appleton, 1869.

Darwin, C. *The descent of man and selection in relation to sex.* London: Murray, 1871 (New York: Appleton, 1873).

Darwin, C. *The expression of the emotions in man and animals.* London: Murray, 1872.

Deckard, B. S., Tepper, J. M., & Schlesinger, K. Selective breeding for acoustic priming. *Behavior Genetics*, 1976, *6*, 375–383.

DeFries, J. C., & Hegmann, J. P. Genetic analysis of open-field behavior. In G. Lindzey & D. D. Thiessen (Eds.), *Contributions to behavior-genetic analysis: The mouse as a prototype.* New York: Appleton-Century-Crofts, 1970.

Dobzhansky, Th. *The genetics of the evolutionary process.* New York: Columbia University Press, 1970.

Dugdale, R. L. *The Jukes.* New York: G. P. Putnam, 1877.

Dawson, W. M. Inheritance of wildness and tameness in mice. *Genetics*, 1932, *17*, 296–326.

Ehrman, L., & Parsons, P. A. *The genetics of behavior.* Sunderland, Mass.: Sinauer Associates, 1975.

Erlenmeyer-Kimling, L., & Jarvik, L. F. Genetics and intelligence: A review. *Science*, 1963, *142*, 1477–1479.

Erlenmeyer-Kimling, L. Studies on the offspring of two schizophrenic parents. In D. Rosenthal & S. S. Kety (Eds.), *The transmission of schizophrenia.* Oxford: Pergamon, 1968.

Estabrook, A. H. *The Jukes in 1915.* Washington, D. C.: Carnegie Institution, 1916.

Frings, H., & Frings, M. The production of stocks of albino mice with predictable susceptibility to audiogenic seizures. *Behaviour*, 1953, *5*, 305–319.

Følling, A. Über Ausscheidung von Phenylbrenztraubensäure in den Harn asl Stoffwecksekabinakue in Verbindung mit Imbezillität. *Zeitschrift fur physiologische Chemie*, 1934, *227*, 169–176.

Fuller, J. L., & Thompson, W. R. *Behavior genetics.* New York: Wiley, 1960.

Galton, F. *Hereditary genius: An inquiry into its laws and consequences.* London: Macmillan, 1869.

Gesell, A. L., & Thompson, H. Learning and growth in identical infant twins. *Genetic Psychology Monographs*, 1929, *6*, 5–120.

Ginsburg, B. E. & Allee, W. C. Some effects of conditioning on social dominance and subordination in inbred strains of mice. *Physiological Zoology*, 1942, *15*, 485–506.

Goddard, H. H. *The Kallikak family.* New York: The Macmillan Co., 1912.

Gun, W. T. J. The heredity of the Stewarts. *Eugenics Review*, 1930, *22*, 195–201. (a)

Gun, W. T. J. The heredity of the Tudors. *Eugenics Review*, 1930, *22*, 111–116. (b)

Hall, C. S. The inheritance of emotionality. *Sigma Xi Quarterly*, 1938, *26*, 17–27.

Hall, C. S. The genetics of behavior. In S. S. Stevens (Ed.), *Handbook of experimental psychology.* New York: Wiley, 1951.

Heron, W. T. The inheritance of maze learning ability in rats. *Journal of Comparative Psychology*, 1935, *19*, 77–89.

Heston, L. L. The genetics of schizophrenic and schizoid disease. *Science*, 1970, *167*, 249–256.

Hirsch, J. & Boudreau, J. C. Studies in experimental behavior genetics: I. The heritability of phototaxis in a population of *Drosophila melanogaster*. *Journal of Comparative and Physiological Psychology*. 1958, *51*, 647–651.

Hirsch, J. Studies in experimental behavior genetics: II. Individual differences in geotaxis as a function of chromosome variations in synthesized *Drosophila* populations. *Journal of Comparative and Physiological Psychology*, 1959, *52*, 304–308.

Huxley, J., Mayr, E., Osmond, H., & Hoffer, A. Schizophrenia as a genetic morphism. *Nature*, 1964, *204*, 220–221.

Jarvik, L. F. & Deckard, B. S. The odyssean personality: A survival advantage for carriers of genes predisposing to schizophrenia? *Neuropsychobiology*, 1977, *3*, 179–191.

Jay, G. E. Jr. Genetic strains and stocks. In W. J. Burdette (Ed.), *Methodology in mammalian genetics.* San Francisco: Holden-Day, 1963.

Jensen, A. R. How much can we boost IQ and scholastic achievement? *Harvard Education Review*, 1969, *39*(1), 1–123.

Jervis, G. A. Introductory study of fifty cases of mental deficiency associated with excretion of phenylpyruvic acid. *Archives of Neurology and Psychiatry*, 1937, *38*, 944–963.

Kallman, F. J. *The genetic theory of schizophrenia*. New York: J. J. Augustin, 1938.

Kallman, F. J. The genetic theory of schizophrenia: An analysis of 691 schizophrenic twin index families. *American Journal of Psychiatry*, 1946, *103*, 309–322.

Kamin, L. *The science and politics of I.Q.* Hillsdale, N.J.: Lawrence Erlbaum Associates, 1974.

Kamin, L. *Heredity, intelligence, politics and psychology.* Paper presented at the Annual Meeting of the Eastern Psychological Association. Washington, D.C., May 1973.

Kety, S. S., Rosenthal, D., Wender, P. H., & Schulsinger, F. Mental illness in the biological and adoptive families of adopted schizophrenics. *American Journal of Psychiatry*, 1971, *128*, 302–306.

Kety, S. S., Rosenthal, D., Wender, P. H., Schulsinger, F., & Jacobsen, B. Mental illness in the biological and adoptive families of adopted individuals who have become schizophrenic: A preliminary report based on psychiatric interviews. In R. R. Fieve, D. Rosenthal, & H. Brill (Eds.), *Genetic research in psychiatry*. Baltimore: Johns Hopkins University Press, 1975.

Kidd, K. K., & Cavalli-Sforza, L. L. An analysis of the genetics of schizophrenia. *Social Biology*. 1973, *20*, 254–265.

Konopka, R. J., & Benzer, S. Clock mutants of *Drosophila melanogaster*. *Proceedings of the National Academy of Sciences*, 1971, *68*, 2112–2116.

Krechevsky, I. Hereditary nature of "hypotheses." *Journal of Comparative Psychology*, 1933, *16*, 99–116.

Lejeune, J., Gauthier, M., & Turpin, R. Etude des chromosomes somatiques de neuf enfants mongoliens. *Comptes Rendus de l'Academie Des Sciences Paris*, 1959, *248*, 1721–1722.

Levitt, E. A., Rosenbaum, A. L., Willerman, L., & Levitt, M. Intelligence of retinoblastoma patients and their siblings. *Child Development*, 1972, *43*, 939–948.

Lindzey, G., Loehlin, J., Manosevitz, M., & Thiessen, D. Behavioral genetics. *Annual Review of Psychology*, 1971, *22*, 39–94.

Loehlin, J. C., Lindzey, G., & Spuhler, J. N. *Race differences in intelligence*. San Francisco: W. H. Freeman, 1975.

Luxenburger, H. Vorläufiger Bericht Über psychiatrische Serienuntersuchungen an Zwillingen. *Zeitschrift fuer die Gesamte Neurologie und Psychiatrie*, 1928, *116*, 297–326.

McClearn, G. E. The genetics of mouse behavior in novel situations. *Journal of Comparative and Physiological Psychology*, 1959, *52*, 62–67.

McClearn, G. E. Strain differences in activity of mice: Influence of illumination. *Journal of Comparative and Physiological Psychology*, 1960, *53*, 142–143.

McClearn, G. E. Genotype and mouse activity. *Journal of Comparative and Physiological Psychology*. 1961, *54*, 674–676.

McClearn, G. E. The inheritance of behavior. In L. J. Postman (Ed.), *Psychology in the making*. New York: Knopf, 1962.

McClearn, G. E., & DeFries, J. C. *Introduction to behavioral genetics*. San Francisco: W. H. Freeman, 1973.

McClearn, G. E., & Kakihana, R. Selective breeding for ethanol sensitivity in mice. *Behavior Genetics*, 1973, *3*, 409–410.

McKusick, V. A. *Mendelian inheritance in man* (2nd ed.). Baltimore: John Hopkins Press, 1968.

Mendel, G. J. Versuche uber Pflanzen-Hybriden. *Verhandlung des Naturforschuden Vereines in Bruenn*, 1866, *4*, 3–47. (Available in E. W. Sinnott, L. C. Dunn, & Th. Dobzhansky (Eds.), *Principles of genetics*. New York: McGraw-Hill, 1950.)

Money, J. Cognitive deficits in Turner's syndrome. In S. G. Vandenberg (Ed.), *Progress in human behavior genetics*. Baltimore: John Hopkins Press, 1968.

Moor, L. Niveau intellectuel et polygohosomie: Confrontation du caryotype et due niveau mental de 374 malades dont le caryotype comporte un excess de chromosomes X ou Y. *Revue de Neuropsychiatrie Infantile et d'hygiene Mentale de l'Enfrance,* 1967, *15,* 325–348.

Morgan, T. H., Sturtevant, A. H., Muller, H. J., & Bridges, C. B. *The mechanisms of Mendelian heredity.* New York: Holt, 1915.

Nachman, M. The inheritance of saccharin preference. *Journal of Comparative and Physiological Psychology,* 1959, *52,* 451–457.

Newman, H. H. Identical twins. *Eugenics Review,* 1930, *22,* 29–34.

Newman, H. H., Freeman, F. N., & Holzinger, K. J. *Twins: A study of heredity and environment.* Chicago: University of Chicago, 1937.

Penrose, L. S. Inheritance of phenylpyruvic amentia (phenylketonuria). *Lancet,* 1935, *2,* 192–194.

Penrose, L. S., & Smith, G. F. *Down's anomaly.* London: Churchhill, 1966.

Plomin, R., DeFries, J. C., & McClearn, G. E. *Behavioral genetics.* San Francisco: W. H. Freeman, 1980.

Roberts, R. C. Some evolutionary implications of behavior. *Canadian Journal of Genetic Cytology,* 1967, *9,* 419–435.

Rosanoff, A. J., Handy, L. M., Plesset, I. R., & Brush, S. The etiology of manic-depressive syndromes with special reference to their occurrence in twins. *American Journal of Psychiatry,* 1935, *91,* 725–762.

Rosenthal, D. *Genetic theory and abnormal behavior.* New York: McGraw-Hill, 1970.

Rosenthal, D., Wender, P. H., Kety, S. S., Welner, J., & Schulsinger, F. The adopted-away offspring of schizophrenics. *American Journal of Psychiatry,* 1971, *128,* 307–311.

Rothenbuhler, W. C. Genetic and evolutionary considerations of social behavior of honeybees and some related insects. In J. Hirsch (Ed.), *Behavior-genetic analysis.* New York: McGraw-Hill, 1967.

Rundquist, E. A. Inheritance of spontaneous activity in rats. *Journal of Comparative Psychology,* 1933, *16,* 415–438.

Scarr, S., Paktis, A. J., Katz, S. H., & Barker, W. B. The absence of a relationship between degree of white ancestry and intellectual skills within a black population. *Human Genetics,* 1977, *39,* 69–86.

Scarr, S., & Weinberg, R. A. IQ test performance of black children adopted by white families. *American Psychologist,* 1976, 726–739.

Schull, W. J., & Neel, J. V. *The effects of inbreeding on Japanese children.* New York: Harper and Row, 1965.

Scott, J. P. Genetic differences in the social behavior of inbred strains of mice. *Journal of Heredity,* 1942, *33,* 11–15.

Searle, L. V. The organization of hereditar maze-brightness and maze-dullness. *Genetic Psychology Monographs,* 1949, *39,* 279–325.

Shaffer, J. W. A specific cognitive deficit observed in gonadal aplasia (Turner's syndrome). *Journal of Clinical Psychology,* 1962, *18,* 403–406.

Shields, J. *Monozygotic twins.* London: Oxford University Press, 1962.

Shuey, A. M. *The testing of Negro intelligence* (2nd ed.). New York: Social Science Press, 1966. (1st ed., Lynchburg, Va.: J. P. Bell, 1958.)

Sidman, R. L., Appel, S. H., & Fuller, J. L. Neurological mutants of the mouse. *Science,* 1965, *150,* 513–516.

Stafford, R. E. Sex differences in spatial visualization as evidence of sex-linked inheritance. *Perceptual and Motor Skills,* 1981, *13,* 428.

Sturtevant, A. H. Experiments on sex recognition and the problem of sexual selection in *Drosophila. Journal of Animal Behavior,* 1915, *5,* 351–366.

Sutton, W. S. The chromosomes in heredity. *Biological Bulletin,* 1903, *4,* 231–251.

Thiessen, D. D. *Gene organization and behavior.* New York: Random House, 1972.

Thompson, W. R. The inheritance and development of intelligence. *Proceedings of the Association for Research in Nervous and Mental Disease*, 1954, *33*, 209–231.

Thorndike, E. L. Measurements of twins. *Columbia University Contributions to Philosophy and Psychology*, 1905, *13*, 1–64.

Tolman, E. C. The inheritance of maze-learning ability in rats. *Journal of Comparative Psychology*, 1924, *4*, 1–18.

Tolman, E. C., Tryon, R. C., & Jeffress, L. A. A self-recording maze with an automatic delivery table. *University of California Publications in Psychology*, 1929, *4*, 99–112.

Tryon, R. C. Genetic differences in maze-learning ability in rats. *Yearbook of the National Society for the Study of Education*, 1940, *39*(I), 111–119.

Tyler, P. A. *A quantitative analysis of runway learning in mice*. Ph.D. dissertation, University of Colorado, 1969.

Vandenberg, S. G. What do we know today about the inheritance of intelligence and how do we know it? In R. Cancro (Ed.), *Intelligence: Genetic and environmental influences*. New York: Grune and Stratton, 1971.

Vandenberg, S. G., & Johnson, R. C. Further evidence on the relation between age of separation and similarity in IQ among pairs of separated twins. In S. G. Vandenberg (Ed.), *Progress in human behavior genetics*. Baltimore: John Hopkins Press, 1968.

Watson, J. D. *Molecular biology of the gene*. New York: Benjamin, 1965.

Woods, F. A. *Mental and moral heredity in royalty*. New York: Henry Holt and Co., 1906.

Yerkes, R. M. *The dancing mouse*. New York: The Macmillan Co., 1907.

Yerkes, R. M. The heredity of savageness and wildness in rats. *Journal of Animal Behavior*, 1913, *3*, 286–296.

3 The Development of Psychological Testing[1]

W. Grant Dahlstrom
The University of North Carolina at Chapel Hill

As used in psychology, the term *test* denotes a set of stimulus materials, together with both explicit procedures about the circumstances, manner, and sequence in which they are to be presented to a test subject, and detailed instructions that the subject is to be given about what he or she is to do with these materials, in order to draw from the subject a series of actions or reactions by means of which he or she may be typified or characterized in regard to the attribute(s) under consideration. Many tests also include specific ways in which the dependability of the sample of the subject's behavior may be appraised or assessed and hence the comparability of that individual's performance to other subjects examined by means of the same instrument and methods.

Any given test must meet six general requirements which distinguish it from other methods of examination: standardized materials and procedures, optimum motivation, immediate recording, objective scoring, appropriate norms, and established validity. The same requirements hold true for any one administration of a psychological test; a particular test protocol can be faulted by some neglect of or deficiency in any of these requirements. The painful ways in which psychologists have come to appreciate the need for these standards and the reasons for maintaining them in our instruments will become clearer in what follows. The evolution of our test instruments has been marked by heated controversies, blind

[1]Support during the preparation of this chapter was provided by the Kenan Fund of the University of North Carolina at Chapel Hill and the James McKeen Cattell Fund of New York City. My appreciation is deeply felt for their generous support and for the warm hospitality of the Institute of Personality Assessment and Research, University of California at Berkeley, and its director, Dr. Harrison G. Gough, during my leave of absence from UNC-CH.

alleys, false claims, and impressive amounts of hard work, even sheer drudgery. As increasingly important decisions have come to rest upon the results of psychological tests, several basic ethical issues have also emerged for test developers and test users alike (Messick, 1980).

EARLY ORIGINS OF TESTING

Where positions of trust and responsibility (political, economic, military, or judicial) are assigned on the basis of personal favoritism or hereditary privilege, individual differences are of small interest and techniques of appraising such differences in dependable and objective ways get scant attention. In those societies in which such positions are earned by merit, however, the sources, development, and evaluation of ability and competence have received continued study and exploration (Doyle, 1974; DuBois, 1968). Thus, it is quite understandable that school programs and the appraisal of educational outcomes, governmental service and the selection of candidates for official positions, and military organization and the identification of talent for leadership, strategy, or combat have been the sources out of which our testing methods of today have developed. Academic psychology as it has developed in institutions of higher learning in the Western world has played a rather minor role until very recently in either the development of the technology or the formulation of the nature and origins of types of talent, temperament, or personality.

The earliest forms of psychological tests in written history date from the civil service selection procedures of the Chinese emperors. Beginning about 2200 B.C., and developing over the centuries until it was discontinued in 1905 A.D., the formal selection of candidates for various offices in the imperial government came to involve successively more rigorous regional examinations, culminating in Peking with testing sessions which usually lasted 3 days and nights. In addition to the ability to write expertly, create both prose compositions and poetic verse, quote scholarly works of history, law, agriculture, finance, and geography, these procedures obviously sampled the candidates' level of sustained motivation, persistence, and even physical endurance in surviving the experience. These methods of assessment were highly successful and served as a model for systems of personnel selection in the British and German colonial services in the nineteenth century. The United States Civil Service Commission, established in its present form in 1883, also emulated these practices of testing and screening for positions at various levels in the federal government. Although reliance on formal examinations of candidates for positions at the upper levels has been discontinued in favor of credentials of graduation from accredited programs in institutions of higher education, a wide variety of our current trade tests and special aptitude measures date from these early efforts to assure competency and proficiency in governmental service.

Adoption in Western countries of these methods of evaluation and selection that were practiced by the Chinese was obviously very late and quite limited. In Western traditions, such diagnostic efforts were focused instead upon various physical attributes of the individuals under study. Beliefs in the utility of various anatomic, physiognomic, or physiologic indicators to provide insights into a person's ability, disposition, and character date from the earliest Greek writers: Aristotle, Plato, Pythagoras, Hippocrates, and Galen. These authorities gave convincing rationales and explanations for individual differences in intellective insights, wisdom and judgment, emotional control, amiability and tolerance, as well as dispositions to depression, fearfulness, and psychosis.

Upon the rediscovery of these writings and the resurgence of interest in classic theories of human nature after the Middle Ages in Western Europe, features of physique were elaborated into complex systems of characterology. In France, de la Chambre in 1659 developed a schema of personality assessment based upon internal states of the body (cold-hot, dry-moist) which provided explanations of sex differences in temperament and emotionality as well as many important differences among individuals of each sex. An even more elaborate system had been worked out by Huarte in 1575 in Spain. It was based upon hypothesized internal states like those employed by de la Chambre, as well as on body build and physiognomic features, and covered intellective, temperamental, and characterological attributes. Huarte not only provided specific means of character reading but prescribed methods for training and enhancing basic talents and capacities. This work met with great interest and wide acceptance, reflecting less the validity of his methods than the need for some means of dealing with and understanding human differences. His first Spanish edition ran to 1500 copies and went through 26 additional editions in Spanish, 24 more in French, 3 in Latin, 7 in Italian, 5 in English, and 2 in German! Many of the combinations and patterns of personality attributes that Huarte ascribed to various physiologic or physiognomic characteristics recur in the writings over the next 4 centuries, although the specific physical features deemed diagnostic of each pattern continued to change as the systems became more complex.

With the rise in knowledge of the internal workings of the human body, physiological explanations of behavior shifted to a locus in the brain. The result was the discipline of **phrenology,** which maintained that underlying brain structure and, therefore, psychological traits, could be diagnosed from the shape of the skull. Like the beliefs in astrological determiners, these notions had a superficial plausibility and, like zodiacal formulations, they too have been difficult to prove or disprove. Such assumptions, based as they are upon plausible and internally coherent systems, can only be refuted by developing dependable means of measuring both the attributes of physique and the dispositions of behavior and by subjecting these assumptions to explicit test. Although anthropometric techniques were developed early in the nineteenth century, the corresponding psychological instruments were not available until the turn of the twentieth century.

The popularity of the formulations of phrenology led to the development of a number of special anthropometric procedures and instruments. Application of these procedures, employed in the as yet unquestioned phrenological systems, was widespread in the last century. For example, during the American Civil War, a special commission was established in the Union Army to carry out systematic anthropometric studies of recruits. After the war, Gould published a lengthy and detailed report in 1869, focusing on differences in a large number of head and body measurements among various racial groups: whites, blacks, and Indians. Because no dependable measures of intellective ability or personality were available to this Commission, however, no opportunity was provided to refute the assumptions then held about the meaning that these differences implied about the psychological characteristics of these racial groups (Haller, 1971). Only after tests of intellective ability and other psychological characteristics were developed could data be marshalled to refute the stereotyped beliefs in the meaning of a person's body build, head shape, or facial pattern (Paterson, 1930). Like astrological formulations, however, phrenological superstitions persist widely in our folklore even today.

BINET AND GALTON

Toward the end of the nineteenth century, two major attacks on the problem of measuring intelligence were undertaken, one in France, the other in England. In France, Alfred Binet was successful in developing a workable and useful psychometric scale; in England, Francis Galton failed, although making important gains in the related areas of descriptive statistics and psychological scaling. The many similarities between these two men in interest, scholarship, approach, and method are perhaps not so important as the few crucial differences in determining the outcome of their efforts, differences which have also been reflected in the approaches of other test pioneers in efforts to develop dependable and workable devices for the measurement of psychological attributes.

Both Binet and Galton shared the then common view of the structure of the mind. Simple sensations and perceptions, through some form of mental chemistry, are combined and recombined, are transformed and elaborated into complex mental faculties, such as memory, judgment, will power, sympathy, intelligence, honesty, and the like. The newly developed methods of studying mental events in the laboratory dictated that various sensory experiences be generated in a subject and the subject's reactions, reports, and associations be recorded and analyzed. By such elementary processes, it was expected that the laws of combination of such sensations and perceptions would emerge. These laboratory studies required increasingly elaborate instruments for generating stimuli and measuring reactions. Binet and Galton were not only conversant with these instruments and techniques but they had both published research and had even made solid contributions to the development of apparatus for the traditional methods of experimental psychology of the time. Both Binet and Galton were also knowledgeable about and had carried out studies in psychophysics, anthropometry, graphology, and mnemonics.

Although he made some preliminary examinations of subjects of very low ability (Forrest, 1974), Galton's primary interest in carrying out his studies of intelligence lay in the upper levels of ability. With the help of an American student, James McKeen Cattell, he gathered data on samples of undergraduates at Cambridge University by means of the traditional simple sensorimotor and anthropometric measures. Although these data were analyzed statistically, they were not compared to any outside criterion of ability. Cattell himself subsequently applied these methods of study (which he termed ''mental tests'') to students in his class in experimental psychology in 1888 at the University of Pennsylvania (Cattell, 1890; Poffenberger, 1947) and to entering freshmen at Columbia University in 1894. (These measures are essentially those described in Part I of Whipple's *Manual,* 1914.)

In an addendum to Cattell's article in *Mind* in 1890, Galton proposed that data gathered by means of these mental tests be compared to the variations found in the academic performances of these college students, but no such comparisons were carried out by Cattell. Thus, it was not until Wissler (1901) compared Cattell's data on the Columbia University freshmen to the course grades earned by these students that Galton, Cattell, and their colleagues began seriously to doubt their basic assumption that these tasks were sampling essential characteristics of mental ability. By then, Binet had already rejected this approach to the study of intellective abilities and was well launched upon an ambitious program to devise a comprehensive battery of practical measures of complex mental processes in ability and personality (Wolf, 1969, 1973).

However, before the full impact was felt of Wissler's negative findings about the lack of appreciable relationship of the simple sensorimotor tasks to differences in intellective ability among adult subjects, two other important lines of research were initiated on the nature of human intelligence, one in England, the other in the United States, both based at first on the mental tests of Galton and J. McK. Cattell. Charles Spearman, having been called back to England for military duty during the Boer War from his studies in Leipzig with Wilhelm Wundt, took advantage of an opportunity to administer the Galton tasks to all the school children in a small Hampshire village. He also gathered data on the school performance of these pupils and obtained judgments about their abilities from teachers, classmates, and the rector's wife (who presumably knew everyone in the area). In addition, he took pains to readminister his tests to these children in order to establish the stability of their performance on each task. By ingenious analytic procedures, many of his own devising, Spearman (1904a, 1904b) showed that most of these tasks had very little relationship to one another (a fact already documented by Sharp in 1898 in Titchener's laboratory at Cornell) but that their "true" intercorrelations would be higher if proper allowance were made for the attenuating effects of low **reliability** on the basic measurements obtained from these tasks. Moreover, once Spearman had carried out his correction for unreliability, the level of these basic intercorrelations among his simple tasks showed closer correspondence to the correlations which he found between each task and the estimated ability levels of the children. On the basis of his findings on these quite limited tasks, Spearman proposed a theory of the underlying organization of human intelligence. As he saw it, intelligence was not composed of separate faculties, such as memory, judgment, etc., but a single underlying capacity which appeared in varying degrees in each of the various tasks included in the Galton survey. He termed this basic capacity g for **general factor**; each of these tasks also involved its own **specific factor,** s_1, s_2, s_3, etc., a special ability of some kind which was required in dealing with each separate type of problem or task. It was the g factor, however, that was reflected in the ratings of general ability he obtained from those who knew the children and was related in varying degrees to their performances on the component tasks in the survey. This view of the organization of intelligence corresponded well with the general approach of Binet and Simon, to be described below, although it apparently had little immediate influence on their methods of procedure in the next few years. Spearman's formulation met serious objections, however, from Edward L. Thorndike, a student of J. McK. Cattell, who took a diametrically opposite view of the implications of the results of Spearman, Cattell, Wissler, and others in this line of investigation of mental abilities.

Although accepting the basic data that Spearman reported (Thorndike, 1904) and admiring the elegance of the mathematical and statistical analyses that he had carried out, Thorndike strenuously rejected the conclusions that Spearman drew about the existence of a general intellective capacity. Instead, the extremely low intercorrelations among the component measures of the Galton survey and their virtually trivial relationship to school performance led Thorndike to conclude that there was no underlying general capacity serving to limit human intellective development. Rather, he believed that each specific kind of activity was determined by its quite separate learning history in each person's behavioral development. If some degree of correlation does appear among such tasks, the explanation for Thorndike would lie in the obvious overlapping of situational cues or the common kinds of response that these tasks call forth (see Ch. 1, vol. 1 for more on Thorndike's position on such matters). Inferences of common mental capacities to serve as mediating processes were rejected as scientifically indefensible. Since Thorndike's formulation led directly to prescriptions of remedial training and increased stimulation to foster growth in intelligent behavior, his theories proved to be extremely attractive to academic psychologists; his optimistic views quickly gained support in the field of progressive education. The two men, Spearman and Thorndike, although later becoming good friends, remained committed to their opposing views on the nature of human abilities (Thorndike, 1945; Jonçich, 1968).

Early Binet Tests

In marked contrast with Galton's efforts to study the upper levels of intelligence, Alfred Binet placed his primary focus upon children and the lower end of the distribution of ability (Wolf, 1969, 1973). Besides making it easier to formulate tasks that reflect such differences, this age period and ability range provide three kinds of independent criteria of ability that were readily available to Binet and his colleagues: differences in capacity emerging in children at different ages as they normally mature; differences in rate of intellective development of children at any one age (as manifested in schoolroom tasks, as noted by experienced teachers, and as reflected in skipping grades or repeating them in school programs); and differences in levels of mental deficiency among adult residents of institutions for the retarded. By availing himself of these sources of independent evaluation of individual subjects, Binet was able to compare each of a wide array of potential measures of intellective capacity with some independent index of ability and quickly discard most of the methods for studying intelligence then being employed in England, Germany, and the United States (Peterson, 1926). It was not so easy, however, to devise or invent alternative procedures that were equally brief, quantifiable, and practical to sample higher, more complex mental processes. At the first German Congress of Experimental Psychology in 1904, Binet expressed serious discouragement about the feasibility of his program of research. A little over a year later, however, Binet and Simon (1905) published a preliminary version of a scale of general intelligence. It is interesting to examine how Binet went about this task.

In part, Binet borrowed from the work of others; in part, he capitalized on careful studies that he had been making of the psychological development of his own children, Madeleine and Alice; and, in part, he drew upon his own understanding of complex cognitive processes in human behavior. The strongest precedent for this approach came from Herman Ebbinghaus (1897) in his effort to measure the effects of classroom work in producing mental fatigue in pupils of the schools in Breslau. Under a charge by school officials to try to measure the drop in efficiency of a child's mental processes as the school day wore on, Ebbinghaus had administered three kinds of tasks to elementary school children repeatedly over the span of the day: rapid arithmetical calculations, span of memory for a series of digits, and ability to supply correctly various missing letters, syllables, or words to complete simple sentences. Although the tasks were not very useful in assessing mental fatigue, Ebbinghaus took advantage of the fact that the classrooms were not only organized by the usual hierarchy of grades but were further subdivided into fast, average, and slow learners. By separate plots, he showed that each of his ability measures demonstrated the expected progression up the sequence of school grades. Only the sentence completion task, however, showed dependable separations in performance within each grade based on the groupings by the teachers on proficiency in school learning.

From Ebbinghaus's research, Binet borrowed not only the specific tasks of complex mental processes but, more importantly, his means of establishing external (non-test) criteria of intelligence. In 1904 when he accepted the assignment from the Ministerial Commission for the Study of Retarded in the French school system to develop a means of "establishing scientifically the anthropometric and mental differences that separate the normal child from the abnormal; of making these differences exact, of measuring them in some way so that their assessment ceases to be a matter of tact and intuition, but rather becomes something objective and tangible . . ." (Wolf, 1973, p. 165), Binet assembled a variety of short, workable tasks; they were drawn from the psychological studies by Jacobs and Ebbinghaus, the psychiatric research of Kraepelin and Oehrn, and the educational investigations of Münsterburg and Gilbert; from various games and puzzles that he had used to sample the thought processes and methods of approach of his daughters; and from parts of the medical screening procedures developed by Damaye for patients entering institutions for the mentally retarded. By means of the same general approach employed by Ebbinghaus in the Breslau schools, Binet and Simon obtained samples of children from the Paris schools who were judged by their teachers to be normal (i.e., average) at 3, 5, 7, 9, and 11 years of age (about ten at each age level) as well as other children judged to be subnormal. They also sampled residents in the hospital at Salpétrière, patients who were retarded to varying degrees. Each subject was given these various simple tasks in individual sessions. By carefully tabulating the successes and failures on each task of average children at increasing age levels, these investigators were able to determine just how difficult each task was in terms of the age of the youngest children who generally succeeded on it without any trouble. Thirty very brief tasks, selected for inclusion in the first tentative scale, were listed from the easiest to the most difficult. The score for any one child examined on this series was simply recorded as a total number of credits (full- and partial-scores added together). The meaning of any given total score, however, was provided by comparing it to the performances of typical children at each particular chronological age. Thus, a very rough *mental level* was easily established. Binet and Simon tried to make clear, even in this first scaling effort, that older children who obtain scores equivalent to those of very much younger children actually differ in any number of ways, both cognitively and non-cognitively, from the normally developing child. That is, the comparability is in terms of level of comprehension or intellective grasp but not necessarily in special aptitudes or in interest, motivation, sophistication, or other non-intellective characteristics.

Although Binet and Simon were the first to develop and publish a workable scale for school-aged children based upon level of mental development, the concept itself had been introduced earlier by workers in the fields of mental retardation, pediatrics, and jurisprudence. As early as 1838, Esquirol employed such a comparison in depicting the degree of deficiency in some profoundly retarded adults. An alienist (psychiatrist), Dimon, used the same qualitative scaling in his court testimony in 1848 to describe the intellective limitation of a defendant named William Freeman who was accused of killing four people not previously known to him, individuals who seemingly had done nothing to provoke such violent acts against them. Down, the physician who first reported the syndrome of mongolism, proposed in 1887 using a qualitative age scale for various degrees of general mental deficiency. In that same year, in an obscure regional medical journal, an American physician named Chaille published a series of tasks that was organized in order of the age that children normally accomplish them to be used in evaluating infant development up to the age of three years. These early conceptualizations and tentative efforts in medicine, pediatrics, psychiatry, and in the courts document the readiness in these fields for such an instrument as Binet and Simon devised and help to explain the rapidity with which these first mental ability scales were accepted and adopted. With a scale to quantify degrees of difference in mental development, it was then possible to document the continuity of mental growth (Norsworthy, 1906) and to begin the task of measuring the fundamental differences between retarded and normally developing children.

Later Binet Tests

Binet prepared two more versions of his scale of intelligence before his untimely death in 1911; the second was ready in 1908 and the last appeared just before he died. Even his first device, however, exemplified most of the features that Binet considered essential for a scale of this kind. Since he was trying to find out what children could really accomplish if they were trying hard, he sought tasks of high interest that would motivate them optimally. (For example, candy was used in some discrimination tasks.) Since Binet was trying to assess the role of intellective capacity in children who were either not in school or were not making normal school progress, he sought to avoid tasks that required experiences that could only come from advanced school work. (Only a few of the most advanced tasks in the 1905 scale had direct schoolroom content, e.g., telling time and abstract definitions.) Because he wished to sample mental processes that were increasingly complex, he sought to vary the difficulty level by small increments. This requirement was met by employing two sorts of puzzles that inherently involved for their solution the attributes which he believed characterize human intelligence: comprehension, invention, direction, and self-criticism. The two kinds of tasks were *riddles* and *hurdles*. In the former, employing what came to be called the constant-task method, a standard problem is presented to which a variety of responses may be obtained; each response then must be classified and scored by commonly agreed-upon rules (pass-fail or partial credit). Once the solution is obtained, such a task is no longer useful or appropriate to sample that person's intelligence; it may be given again, however, to study memory capacity or to reflect some personality processes. Tasks based upon the method of increasing difficulty (hurdles), on the other hand, can be presented with successively more challenging content until the individual subject fails to solve the task.

(Usually a few additional items at the same level of complexity are given to make certain that the subject's limit has in fact been reliably established.) Scoring agreement is obviously more easily obtained for hurdles than for riddles. Because the procedures were to be used by a variety of different examiners in many diverse contexts (schools, hospitals, or clinics), agreement on scoring had to be another basic requirement for such scales, as Binet saw it.

The 1905 scale had one feature which was not typical of Binet's later versions or of scales developed on his model in the next decade: the series of items were not grouped together in age-levels but were simply ranked in order of increasing difficulty. This format has come to be called **a point scale**; the subject's performance is simply summarized in the total number of credits or points earned without regard to the order of passes or failures, and the psychological interpretation of the score is based on tables of norms from subjects of the same age and background. In the two subsequent scales, Binet organized the tasks by rough age levels so that items too easy or too difficult for the subject need not be administered and items of the same general difficulty level could be changed around in the order of administration to keep the child interested and motivated. Tests organized in this way are called **age scales.** While the 1905 scale was clearly intended for simple screening, the second version (Binet, 1908) was proposed as a means of *measuring* the level of intellective development of each subject in order to guide educational placement and determine level of classroom instruction. Not only was the scaling of the items by mental level elaborated in this scale but different content was also introduced based upon experiences with the 1905 scale by Binet himself and by other investigators. For example, Decroly and Degand, working in a private French-language school in Brussels, tried out the 1905 scale and found that, while it did give roughly comparable separations or placements in scores obtained on their pupils, the scale needed revision. They suggested that less reliance be placed upon memory tasks and more problems requiring ingenuity be included, suggestions consistent with the more advanced levels of ability of the children who were enrolled in their exclusive school. Similarly, Lewis M. Terman, a student working on his doctorate at Clark University, wrote Binet about his own experiences with tasks from the 1905 scale (along with many of his own devising) in examining bright and dull children from the Worcester, Massachusetts school system while studying the characteristics of their mental processes. He indicated that motor tasks were not as discriminating as verbal comprehension items or various logical problems, such as the application of rules of games which require reasoning and deduction.

THE DEVELOPMENT OF MENTAL ABILITY SCALES

The 1908 scale of Binet and Simon proved to be much more acceptable to critics and practitioners alike. Efforts to translate this instrument were soon underway in Italy by Ferrari, in Germany by Bobertag, in England by Johnston and by Burt, and, most notably perhaps, in America by H. H. Goddard. The scale fitted well into Goddard's new research program. Under special funding provided by Samuel Fels, a Philadelphia soap merchant and philanthropist, a research laboratory on the causes of mental retardation had been established in 1906 in conjunction with the Training School at Vineland, New Jersey, and Goddard had been hired as its director. He quickly initiated a study of the background and history of a large family with many members known to the staff at Vineland as retarded, the results of which were published in 1912, using the fictitious name of Kallikak for the family (see p. 31). Goddard became increasingly aware of the need for a dependable method of evaluating and diagnosing mental retardation. From the start, he had begun collecting a variety of tasks (which he called "stunts") that he gave to residents of the Training School in an effort to evaluate the kind and extent of their intellective deficits. One such task was a simple board with various geometric figures cut out of it which Seguin had devised in 1866 for the sensory training of retardates. Goddard posed the task of replacing each cut-out in its proper place in the board as quickly as possible; he counted the number of errors in placement as well as the total time taken. However, Goddard had apparently not made any real headway in organizing his collection of devices into a method of measurement. In fact, the claims by Binet and Simon to have developed a practical intelligence scale in 1905 had not convinced him as being anything particularly different or noteworthy. Goddard had translated and tried out that scale when it appeared but he did not believe it was better than his own set of stunts. He was skeptical that it would be dependable and had decided not to use it; he did, nevertheless, publish his translation (Whipple, 1915). When he saw the 1908 scale, however, his doubts vanished and he took up the task of translation and application with impressive enthusiasm. He published his English-language version in *The Training School* (Goddard, 1910b); it was a direct translation with only a few simple substitutions of sentences made to adapt the procedures to American children. In a short time, he and his assistants surveyed the whole testable population of the Training School (400 children) and published the results (Goddard, 1910a), followed in the next year by a survey of all 2000 pupils in the public schools of Vineland, New Jersey. Although other psychologists were also publishing English-language versions of the 1908 Binet-Simon scale (such as F. Kuhlmann at the Minnesota School for the Feeble-minded, J. E. W. Wallin at the New Jersey State Village for Epileptics, L. M. Terman and H. G. Childs at Stanford University, as well as K. Johnston and C. L. Burt in England), the rather literally translated Goddard version was by far the most widely disseminated in the United States at that time.

Public Response to Early Tests

Through an earlier established program of summer workshops for public school teachers, Goddard developed a means of preparing these teachers to use the Binet-Simon scale. After a brief introduction to the test, these testers went back home to survey their own schools and to identify pupils in need of special help or requiring assignment to ungraded classrooms. Typically, the teachers had little psychological background and no familiarity with measurement or statistical concepts. Through Goddard's missionary zeal, in a very few years hundreds of "mental testers" were launched into American public school systems with great enthusiasm but little psychometric competence. The direct results of Goddard's campaign, however, in the first two or three decades of this century, were strongly negative; to be asked to undergo examination by a mental tester in this country meant that one was already suspected of serious intellective deficiency, or worse. It was not long before strong adverse reactions to his well-intentioned efforts were all too evident. In the hands of a skilled modern clinician, these tasks could give the worker only a very rough estimate of a child's relative standing in intellective development; in the hands of these teachers, the results were often worthless, serving only to upset pupils, their parents, and soon school boards as well. The reaction against these tests (coupled with controversies arising from the interpretation of data from the Army testing program in the next decade) led many liberal writers and politicians to take strong stands against the development and use of psychological tests. This adverse image of tests was partially corrected and later put into proper balance through the efforts of Terman by his complete restandardization of the Binet-Simon scale and his subsequent large-scale testing and follow-up studies of individuals of high intellective ability (Terman, 1925).

First Studies of Validity

It was fortunate that the revisions of their initial scale by Binet and Simon were not uniformly met by so uncritical an acceptance as the reception given them by Goddard. Wallin's and Kuhlmann's versions were closer to restandardizations than mere translations, while the research of Terman and Childs, like that of Burt, involved statistical studies of the items that revealed serious limitations in the scaling of the French instrument. Similarly, in Belgium, Decroly and Degand carried out further examination of the 1908 scale and raised even more complaints about it than the 1905 scale. Binet was sufficiently disturbed about the difficulties that they had encountered that he asked to see their data. In reviewing these protocols, he found problems which have plagued test developers from his day to the present: variations in task instructions and methods of presentation, departures from standard scoring practices, and serious errors in computations. Two other problems were also highlighted in his scrutiny of the Brussels data: namely, the sequence of presentation of material in the curriculum of the Belgian schools differed from the instruction given the Paris children; and consistent differences in test performance between children from different family backgrounds became obvious. To meet the first difficulty, Binet made additional efforts in the 1911 scale to eliminate school-related content from the tasks. (The efforts to extend Binet's work by Terman at Stanford University always involved this issue as well, through several revisions and standardizations.)

Turning to the second problem, Binet had his student, Morlé (Binet, 1911), carry out a special study in Paris of children who were sampled from four levels of socioeconomic status: those living in ease, in mediocrity, in poverty, and in misery. Contrasting the two extreme groups, Morlé found that 16 of the 30 children from the highest class were advanced over their expected level by a year or more, with only four children testing down by a year or more; while in the lowest class, only one child in 30 was similarly advanced and 12 were found to test down by over a year. Binet also obtained data from Katherine Johnston in England that revealed consistent differences there as well in the performance of children from different socioeconomic levels. Johnston had additional data that pointed to possible contributing factors such as the different numbers of pupils in the classes in which children from each social level were being taught. Her data also documented the effects of tasks at the lower end of the 1908 scale being too easy for young children and tasks at the upper end being too hard for the older ones; as a result, the test subjects were not discriminated equally well over the whole range of the instrument.

Binet died before he was able to put such insights into appropriate modifications of his intelligence scale. As it turned out, however, the name of Binet came to be associated with a particular method of scaling of measurements, a format of test organization and administration, as well as a concept of intelligence as a single, pervasive ability to deal adaptively with the world. His concept of age levels anticipated in a crude way the current notion of stages of intellective development as proposed by Piaget, emphasizing the orderliness of mental growth but lacking the precise details of ways in which such progress might be slowed or halted (Pollack, 1971). More importantly, Binet was able to demonstrate in an irrefutable manner the fact that measurement of important human psychological attributes was feasible and worthwhile.

Before turning to the efforts of Terman in carrying forward this fundamental work of devising practical intellective scales, standardizing them on much more dependable samples of normative subjects, and establishing their **validity** against external criteria of "world success" which reflect such ability, note should be taken of a different line of research stemming from Binet as well. Efforts to develop a scale of intelligence modeled on the 1905 version, using a point-scaling format instead of the mental-age organization, were carried out by Robert M. Yerkes at Boston Psychopathic Hospital. The scale appeared a year before Terman's first revision (Yerkes, Bridges, & Hardwick, 1915) and established a clear precedent for an alternative design of American intelligence tests (Goodenough, 1949).

TERMAN AND THE STANFORD-BINET

Early in this century at Stanford University, a number of circumstances combined to provide an unusually favorable place for Lewis M. Terman to work on the development of a definitive version of the Binet-Simon scale of intelligence (Seagoe, 1975). E. P. Cubberley, dean of the School of Education at Stanford, extended to Terman an appointment as assistant professor in 1910 on the recommendation of E. B. Huey, a classmate of Terman's at Clark, who had helped him with the project in his doctoral dissertation. Dean Cubberley was trained at Teachers College of Columbia University with J. McK. Cattell and E. L. Thorndike; he brought to Stanford many of the views and projects which those men had already initiated in New York: measurement and statistical analyses in school administration and classroom practice (Thorndike, 1904); research on the nature and evaluation of human intelligence, centering on the intense and long controversy between Thorndike and Spearman; and objective measurement of school achievement by standardized scales, dating from reactions to Rice's inflammatory attacks on the lack of comparability of achievement among graduates of various school systems around the United States (Rice, 1893). Under Cubberley's leadership, Stanford quickly established excellent relationships with a large number of school systems around the state of California. Terman was able to capitalize on these ties, testing over 700 pupils in his pilot studies of Binet test items with his early collaborator, H. G. Childs. Continuing this project, Terman tested an additional 1000 pupils (more carefully selected to be within 2 months of their birthday at the time of testing) for the final standardization of the new instrument. A number of his young adult subjects were also drawn in part from these schools (senior high school students); the rest of his sample of 400 adults came from contacts in the business and industrial field. Terman was also fortunate in having bright and interested graduate students attending Stanford whom he could attract to help in the numerous chores of test construction: writing test items; administering preliminary versions to research subjects; trying out scoring criteria for the clarity, the precision in application, and the explicitness which generates inter-scorer comparability; making tabulations for discriminability of items to identify the optimal placement in an age scale; and also gathering data on the test subjects (both pupils and adults) to serve as external criteria for the evaluation of the effectiveness of the provisional instrument that Terman was assembling. The efforts of Arthur S. Otis, with his knowledge and skill in data reduction and statistical analyses, were particularly important in this entire venture. He carried out the work on the item analyses and the try-outs of the various early combinations of these items in tentative scales. (At the same time, Otis was collecting and evaluating items that were less suitable to the age-scale format but potentially useful in a point-scale version that could be administered in booklets to whole groups of test subjects.)

Terman was soon able to bring out his completed scale. The published volume (Terman, 1916) covered a number of important aspects of test development and administration over and beyond the specific tasks appearing at each mental age level. Test record forms were also sold by Houghton Mifflin, the test publisher, to professional users. No standard kit of test materials was provided the examiner, however; each user had to collect the items needed to conduct the examination. Terman gave the history, a psychological rationale, and detailed instructions for the administration, recording, and scoring of each task. The items were compared in placement, discrimination, and significance to the location they had in the original scales of Binet and Simon, as well as to their placements by Goddard, Kuhlmann, Wallin, and by others in various European versions. In addition, the general philosophy of such a scale was reviewed and specific criticisms of mental age scaling were taken up in detail and evaluated.

The Intelligence Quotient

Perhaps the most important feature in the 1916 scale was the decision by Terman to incorporate a second summary score, in addition to the mental age, to describe each child's standing on the test, namely, the ratio of the measured performance level to the level expected for a child of that **chronological age.** This index (which he termed the *mental quotient*) was first proposed along with the concept of mental age by W. Stern in 1911 as a better way of describing a child's standing in his own age group than the crude measure of the number of mental levels he or she fell above or below the typical child of that age. That is, if the child "tested down" 2 years when 10 years old, the discrepancy was not as important psychologically as performing 2 years below expected level at the age of five. Because the variability in test performance increases with advancing age, the absolute discrepancy has no uniform or consistent meaning. Stern suggested that the *ratio* of mental age to chronological age would give an index with just such uniformity in describing a child's relative standing; this mental quotient would be constant in its interpretive significance. Terman concurred and introduced this index, which he called the **intelligence quotient, or IQ,** into the 1916 Stanford-Binet scale as a summary score to supplement the mental age. (To avoid using decimals, Terman required that the examiner multiply this ratio by 100 and enter the child's score as a whole number.) The standardization data on the 1916 scale were reported in terms of the IQ; rough interpretive limits were also proposed in relation to general levels of mental retardation, school achievement, grade acceleration, etc. Unfortunately, the narrow meaning of "constancy of the IQ" as understood by Stern and by Terman was soon lost in various storms of controversy over this index that have raged episodically in this country and abroad to the present time. That is, in the next three decades, the issue of the constancy of the IQ took on at least three distinct meanings, each requiring quite

different research data to resolve: (1) the psychometric advantages (noted previously) of this index compared to other competing summarizing scores (mental
age, percentile standing, etc.) as a descriptive measure of an individual's status
in his or her intellective development; (2) the equivalence of an individual's
scores on two different intelligence test batteries (for example, on the Stanford-
Binet vs. the Kuhlmann-Binet) when each test performance is expressed in terms
of an IQ; or (3) the consistency of an individual's performances (earned IQs) in
taking the same test at intervals as he or she grows older. As will be clear in later
sections, problems in test construction, in test administration, in objective scoring, and in standardization on national normative samples, as well as shifts in
rates of mental development over the period of negatively accelerated growth
toward adulthood, all entered into this complex controversy (Jensen, 1980).

The seeds for some of these controversies were present in Terman's standardization data on the 1916 scale. Serious sampling biases had crept into the choice
of the subjects he used to establish the typical adult level of performance on this
instrument: high school students and adults employed in various businesses. An
individual who went on to attend high school in the years before World War I
(and indeed before World War II) was atypical of his age peers; most adults
stopped school at the eighth grade or before. Thus, it was generally the most
academically talented teenagers who were still in school and available for such a
test survey. As a result, the performance level for American adults was set at 16
years of mental age in the 1916 scale. When this scale, in turn, was used as a
standard metric for the large-scale testing program for the military a year later
(see below), too large a proportion of American men were characterized as
mental incompetents and one of the many controversies surrounding mental tests
and the IQ was underway (Block & Dworkin, 1976).

Legal Status of Testing

The same year that the Stanford revision of the Binet scale was published,
Terman served as an expert witness in a murder trial in which the use of the new
mental tests in the courts became a central issue (Terman, 1918). The defendant,
Alberto Flores, was charged with the sex murder of a young girl in Santa
Barbara, California. Although Flores was about 20 years old, the defense consid-
ered him to be so profoundly retarded that he could not know the nature of his act
and they called Terman to testify to this fact. The prosecution contended that
Flores was normal in mental competence and that the only issue in applying the
M'Naghten Rule was the presence or absence of some mental illness. The pros-
ecution employed a psychiatrist to examine Flores and offer medical opinion as
to his freedom from any psychosis and his basic knowledge of right or wrong.
The state also attempted to bar Terman's testimony on these matters on the
grounds that he was not medically trained. A few months before the trial,
Terman had Emily Lamb, a psychologist trained in the use of the new Stanford-

Binet scale, administer the examination to Flores on two different occasions 4 days apart. When Terman saw Flores (after the trial was already underway), he himself again administered the 1916 test and also gave Flores the Yerkes-Bridges Point Scale. Terman was allowed to testify (thereby establishing a precedent for psychologists as expert witnesses in trials of this kind) and was able to document that on repeated examinations Flores had a mental age of $7\frac{1}{2}$ years, not only with Terman's scale but also on the entirely different sample of intellective behavior obtained with the Yerkes-Bridges scale. More important to the issue of the utility of such tests in future applications in the courts, Terman was able to show upon cross-examination that the actual ability levels required to perform the tasks used by the alienist to support his view that the defendant was of normal intellective capacity were all well within the low competence level of 7 years mental age. That is, typical children of early school age were known to be able to do all of the things that the physician had asked Flores to do. Unfortunately for the defense, the State of California had no provision for confining mentally retarded adults indefinitely on the basis of legal incompetence; the jury found Flores guilty but recommended a life sentence rather than the death penalty.

Tests for Special Groups

Prior to World War I, the use of various intelligence tests spread rapidly throughout the country in hospitals, prisons, training schools, and institutions for the retarded, the epileptic, and the mentally ill. Psychologists working with the deaf and blind were also in need of sound intelligence tests, but they realized the inherent limitation of the new scales for children with such sensory handicaps (Pintner & Paterson, 1915). Special adaptations were soon begun. At the School for the Deaf in Ohio, for example, Rudolph Pintner and Donald Paterson, in an effort to circumvent the communication problems of their subjects, gathered together various tasks that could not only be administered by pantomime but required only non-verbal responses. In addition to various formboards, like those adapted by Goddard from Seguin's training materials, Pintner and Paterson profited from the work of several other test pioneers. In their battery, they included tasks from two sources in which examination of abilities had to be made in as non-academic a manner as possible: the juvenile courts and the immigration service. William Healy, a psychiatrist working in the newly established Chicago Juvenile Psychopathic Institute and consulting with the courts of Chicago, had developed a series of pictures, each with some crucial element cut out, which the test subject had to perceive, identify, and locate in an array of plausible alternatives to be able to complete correctly. An individual's performance was summarized by adding up the scoring weights assigned to each of the alternatives selected. Little formal educational content was involved in the discriminations presented in these choices (Healy & Fernald, 1911) and the subjects obviously did not have to speak or write anything. A similar freedom from speech or oral comprehension was characteristic of the tasks developed by the U.S. Immigration Service at Ellis Island in New York to examine subjects from widely different linguistic and cultural backgrounds who were seeking admission to and ultimate citizenship in this country (Knox, 1914). Several of these tasks were also adapted for the performance scale by Pintner and Paterson: a simple digit series to be presented by tapping with one wooden block in increasingly lengthy sequences on other blocks arrayed in a row before the subject (the Knox Cube Test); reassembling a very simple jigsaw picture of a ship (like the one most subjects had just spent a week or more abroad before debarking at Ellis Island) in which total time and errors in putting the pieces into a frame were given differential credit (Glueck Ship Test); assembling the head, arms, and legs to the body of a simple mannikin figure; and constructing the profile of a human head from pieces cut out of the face and ear areas of the puzzle board, also timed to completion. As used at Ellis Island, instructions for the tasks were given in pantomime gestures to circumvent the language barriers that often existed between examiner and test subject. Pintner and Paterson organized these various tasks into a battery and standardized the scoring and scaling against the Goddard-Binet using children who could hear adequately and hence could also be given the more usual Binet tasks. They published their new scale (Pintner & Paterson, 1917) just before the entry of the United States into World War I.

PSYCHOLOGICAL TESTING IN WORLD WAR I

The response of psychologists to the news of the outbreak of war was as immediate, as supportive and patriotic, and as constructive as that of any other professional group. A set of hurried conferences by officers of the American Psychological Association, some meetings with officers of the National Academy of Sciences-National Research Council by psychologists who had recently been elected to the Academy (J. McK. Cattell, G. S. Hall, and E. L. Thorndike), and a special session of the Council of the APA, resulted in the formation within a few months of a set of twelve committees (largely composed of experimental psychologists) who offered their services to the government. Several of these APA committees, under the general direction of Robert M. Yerkes, then APA president, soon joined with the Adjutant General's Office to apply psychological procedures to various military problems. The activities of these psychologists were modeled in part on the role of psychologists in the Canadian Army and the many ways that they had already been contributing to their war effort. Although some of these committees were assigned to such problems as analyses of the psychological processes involved in learning to fly military aircraft, most of the energy was devoted to personnel testing and screening. In some ways these surveys were analogous to the efforts of Gould's Commission in the Civil War using anthropometric procedures; Yerkes and his colleagues developed test instruments and initiated wholesale administration of intellective scales throughout the military establishment. Many of their findings, only partly analyzed and incompletely interpreted, were reported in the *Memoirs of the National Academy of Sciences* after the armistice (Yerkes, 1921).

Army Alpha and Beta Tests

Most influential in shaping the format of the various test instruments that were developed for the Army at this time was the special Statistical Unit in the Division of the Surgeon General, headed by Thorndike and comprised of Arthur Otis from Stanford University, and Louis L. Thurstone, an engineer recently turned psychologist, from the Carnegie Institute of Technology (Yerkes, 1921; Jonçich, 1968). Otis brought with him his pilot work on a group form of a verbal test; it formed the nucleus of the scale developed by the committee on methods, which met in Vineland, New Jersey in May, 1917. Yerkes himself worked with this group, which included Goddard, Terman, Whipple, Wells, Bingham, and Haines. This knowledgeable group of psychologists had a draft form of the verbal scale ready by mid-June for try-outs at various Marine barracks and officers' training camps around the country. After meeting again in early July with these preliminary data before them, the committee on methods then assembled a **verbal scale** (the **Army Alpha Tests**), ready in five different forms; a **non-verbal scale** (the **Army Beta Test**) for illiterate inductees; and an individually administered intelligence scale to be given to men suspected of having emotional problems which presumably would interfere with their taking tests in a group setting. A second try-out of these methods, together with administration of the Yerkes-Bridges scale, the Pintner-Paterson Performance battery, and the Stanford-Binet scale, was completed on 4000 military personnel in July and early August. By the end of August, 1917, routine procedures employing the above instruments, together with a special Army performance scale, were ready for implementation in Army and Navy induction centers around the country. The performance scale was developed to test illiterate or non-English-speaking inductees and others who failed the Beta examination. It incorporated the formboards, puzzles, and cube-tapping tasks from the Pintner-Paterson battery and added a digit-symbol coding task developed by Whipple from the work of Woodworth and Wells (1911); a picture arrangement series (based upon newspaper cartoon strips involving familiar actions but no verbal cues) adapted from work in Belgium by Decroly; a memory for designs task that was elaborated from the ones that Terman developed from Binet; and a series of printed mazes. This last test had been developed in Australia by Stanley D. Porteus. Porteus was at that time director of a school for the retarded in Melbourne; he hit upon pencil-and-paper mazes in his efforts to mirror the abilities needed to get about in a complex urban environment: attention to detail, memory for spatial cues, planfulness and control over impulsive actions, as well as maintenance of an orienting and guiding set of instructions (Porteus, 1915, 1969). He had found that performance on these maze tasks not only reflected the same kind of ability sampled in the Goddard-Binet but that it was also even more independent of classroom training and content than the Binet items. Many of these component tests of the Army performance scale were subsequently incorporated into the performance half of the various point scales of intelligence developed after the war by David Wechsler.

Soon thousands of young men were being screened with these intelligence scales. Those who volunteered the information that they could not read were removed immediately from the test cohort and, together with those few additional subjects who had difficulty with the task of filling out identifying information at the top of the test form, were sent to another room for separate testing. These latter subjects were given the Beta form; all others were given one or another form of the Alpha scale. Very low scorers on either instrument were given additional evaluation on an individual basis by means of the verbal or performance scales. Very high scores on the Alpha were also followed up with an individual examination. Most subjects were simply identified by the particular level or category into which their performance on the Alpha or Beta placed them and sent on through the induction screening procedures. These designations were then used to identify those inductees who were potential candidates for officer training programs, for special assignments in various military units, or for noncombatant duties in labor battalions. In some installations, psychologists were also able to set up procedures to identify special aptitudes or to conduct trade tests to verify claims of the new recruits to special occupational competencies. In some training centers psychologists also served the newly devised function of morale officers.

Research with the Army Tests

In addition to the new psychometric instruments that were constructed for the induction screening and personnel selection, several lines of basic research were carried out in these military settings (Kevles, 1968). The effects of physical exhaustion on test performance were studied by bringing various platoons directly into the testing halls from the road after a fast 20-mile march and retesting them with an equivalent form of the test that they had taken at induction; when compared with units who were fresh on each test occasion, these weary men were found to show no deleterious effects of such physical fatigue on this kind of test performance. Intercorrelations of scores from the various kinds of tasks and instruments, individual and group, verbal and non-verbal, were calculated and studied. Interpretations of these interrelationships varied greatly, depending upon the conceptualizations of the nature of human abilities and aptitudes on the part of the various psychologists and on their methods of data analysis. Many of the alternative explanations made of these data were expanded and defended in long controversies in the period between the two World Wars.

Ratings obtained on men after induction screening, upon completion of various special training programs (e.g., in officers' training camp), in performance in a variety of duty assignments, or in basic training for the infantry or for shipboard duty were gathered and related to the scores on intelligence scales. These non-test data added immeasurably to the empirical bases for the various psychometric instruments and enabled the statistical unit to carry out item analyses, differential comparisons of component tasks in these scales in their discriminatory capabilities, as well as scaling of general ability in the adult male population of the United States.

Problems and Misconceptions

As mentioned earlier, the use of the Stanford-Binet scale to establish the meaning of score levels of the Alpha and Beta resulted in an upward skew in the levels expected for an average adult subject. (Later restandardization of the Stanford-Binet placed the average closer to a mental age of 14 years, rather than 16.) When the general implications were spelled out by the writers of the *Memoirs* after the war, this spurious level prompted a series of wide-ranging articles by the journalist Walter Lippmann in which he attacked the claims and implications of the findings from the use of intelligence tests both in the Army and out (cf. Block & Dworkin, 1976).

In the light of subsequent research on intellective measures of the sort employed in World War I, it is clear that some additional misconceptions and false assumptions were also distorting the interpretation of findings from the Army surveys. Prior to the large-scale application of group tests in these induction centers, the psychologists directly involved in devising and refining test instruments were primarily examining either school-aged subjects who could be counted on to try to do their best when challenged by the examiner, or with adults, as in the Ellis Island setting, who had everything to gain by performing well. Psychologists who themselves were uniformly academically oriented had little experience with or awareness of the way that the motivational level could vary in the population of young men appearing at the Army induction centers. They undoubtedly underestimated the number of men who were seeking to get by with the least burdensome assignments possible. In addition, the earlier work on intelligence tests had been carried out for the most part in settings in which the educational background and curricular patterns of the schools in which the test subjects were enrolled were well known and quite uniform. The findings of the educational crusader J. M. Rice had only hinted at the true range of variation extant in educational quality in schools around the United States; surveys carried out by means of standardized achievement scales in the basic school subjects after World War I revealed the scandalous neglect that many pupils were suffering in impoverished school programs in the more isolated parts of the country. Since the administration of a standardized instrument to a group of subjects presumed that all individuals in that group had comparable opportunities to acquire the component skills required to perform well on the tasks, the examiners in the World War I surveys were often seriously violating this basic tenet of sound psychometric practice. A third general area of concern about the data and conclusions drawn from this testing program is more subtle but probably as important as the motivational and educational variations among the inductees being tested: the differences in home and family backgrounds providing opportunities, incentives, and support for cognitive development and expectations for ultimate success and reward for such endeavor. The data reported in the *Memoirs* included separate tabulations of scores from inductees by state and region, ethnic background, occupation and educational level, as well as the country of origin and length of residence in this country for immigrants. The findings were interpreted by some psychologists and politicians without regard to the distorting factors that were undoubtedly operating and were then used to justify recommendations for various educational, eugenic, and immigrational policies (cf. Kamin, 1974). Although their efforts were not as uniformly conspiratorial nor as successful as it may now seem a half-century later, it is clear that the data from the Army program of intelligence testing provided seemingly scientific underpinning for many stereotypes of ethnic and racial characteristics. It has taken a great deal of careful research to sort out some of the complexities of interacting factors in such test score differences. For example, C. C. Brigham came to quite different conclusions about the World War I data in the *Memoirs* between his first examination of the findings and the later reflections (Brigham, 1923, 1930). Without test instruments, these studies could not have been carried out at all; yet the negative attitudes that some individuals hold about these stereotypes have all too often been carelessly generalized to include the instruments themselves, or even to the application of psychological tests in such research issues. Moreover, without objectively administered and scored intellective measures, the true range of competency appearing in minority groups would not be fully appreciated (Cronbach & Drenth, 1972; Eysenck, 1971; Vernon, 1969; Whitty & Jenkins, 1935).

EARLY PERSONALITY TESTING

During the period of the first World War, two other major developments in psychological testing were also initiated, one stemming from the same wartime group of American psychologists, the other originating in the peaceful atmosphere of neutral Switzerland. As the flow of inductees into the U.S. Army reached floodtide, the efforts of military psychiatrists to identify and screen out emotionally unfit men became totally inadequate. General Pershing, commander of the American Expeditionary Forces in France, became alarmed at the number of psychiatric casualties in his units engaged in trench warfare and called for some more effective methods of screening. R. S. Woodworth was placed in charge of a Committee on Emotional Fitness that undertook the task of develoopng a written form of the questions routinely employed by psychiatrists to appraise emotional stability, and of trying out the resulting questionnaire as a means of reducing the numbers of men who had to be interviewed individually by Army psychiatrists. He gathered a lengthy series of potential items in the form of simple statements describing fears, anxieties, physical complaints, peculiar and bizarre experiences, as well as variations in mood, morale, and self-confidence. These items were administered to diagnosed neurotics and to presumably well-adjusted college students and adults in general, as well as to military personnel and patients in a military hospital. Tallies of the numbers of individuals answering affirmatively to these various emotional symptoms in each of the general groups of respondents enabled Woodworth to eliminate some items which sampled problems that were common to maladjusted and well-adjusted alike (Woodworth, 1919). The set of 116 surviving items was quite homogeneous. The items were printed on two sides of a single page with a place to circle "Yes", "No", or "?" opposite each item; it was given the innocuous title of **Personal Data Sheet** (although the results were referred to as **Psychoneurotic Inventory scores** by the professional personnel). Screening use involved only 10 minutes or so of group testing time; scoring required simply a count of the number of items marked in the significant direction. Split-half reliability was found to be .90. The war ended before this inventory was given very extensive use for screening but it was employed in diagnostic studies of psychiatric casualties in military hospitals in various parts of the United States (Hollingworth, 1920). In slightly altered format this instrument was very widely adopted after the war in business, schools, and clinics before more serious questions were finally raised about the validity of this approach to personality measurement.

The Personal Data Sheet was obviously not the first use of a list of standard questions in psychological research. Numerous opinionnaires and questionnaires had been constructed to obtain information on a wide range of issues. G. S. Hall (1891) employed a large array of such survey instruments to sample the experiences and beliefs of teachers, educators, and pediatricians about the developmental characteristics of subjects at various ages and had written extensively about the implications of his findings from such surveys. J. B. Watson, the radical behaviorist, employed survey questionnaires in assessing wartime morale among Army Air Corps pilots and in efforts to measure the impact upon military troops after viewing propaganda films depicting the ravages of venereal diseases in terms of changes in their attitudes, knowledge, or sexual activities (Cohen, 1979). However, the use of a standard list of items covering emotional symptoms to determine the *degree* of disorder that a given subject may be manifesting did constitute a significant departure from previous applications of questionnaires. The idea that such a set of items could constitute a scale and that scores could be determined comparable in psychometric quality to scores from existing mental ability scales marked an additional advance in the effort to quantify human psychological characteristics.

The Rorschach Test

In retrospect, the step from focusing upon the veridicality of the mental report obtained from an endorsement of a particular item to a concern merely with the total *number* of significant endorsements seems almost trivial; most of the advances in psychological testing involve just such apparently simple shifts from the qualitative to the quantitative. Psychologists have remained interested in the content of such verbal reports in many areas of social and personological research but, as will be described below, they have found that they must be much more circumspect in the conclusions drawn from such content. In an analogous fashion to the development of quantitative methods of verbal reports, the efforts of Hermann Rorschach to devise quantitative indices from the responses of subjects to non-verbal, ambiguous, and amorphous inkblots were equally noteworthy in achieving this all-important shift from qualitative description to quantitative summarization.

Rorschach, a psychiatrist at the Cantonal Asylum in Herisau, Switzerland, worked for several years to develop a large collection of patterns generated by chance from blots of various colored ink. Such random designs had been popular in Europe for over a hundred years as games or pastimes for children to prompt various perceptions and to stimulate their imaginations. Binet had employed such tasks with his own daughters, and a student of Titchener, Stella E. Sharp, included inkblots in her preliminary survey of tasks involving complex mental functions. No general method of summarizing the responses of individuals to the various forms and colors of inkblots had been devised, however, prior to the studies of Rorschach (Ellenberger, 1954). Although trained in the tradition of Kraepelinian psychiatry, Rorschach was deeply interested in the newer formulations of such analytic psychiatrists as Freud, Jung, and their followers. In his preliminary uses of the inkblot materials (which he called his "experiment"), Rorschach noted not only general similarities in response to the task by patients with similar diagnoses but also the systematic differences in responsiveness to various aspects of the blots shown by patients with thought disorders, mood variations, fears and phobias, or intellective defects. These observations led him to conjecture that each different aspect of the ambiguous stimuli—shape, color, location on the card—triggered off particular cognitive and emotional processes in his subjects. These mental processes in turn were centrally involved in the emotional disorders of the patients and even in the temperamental, mood, and thought patterns of the normal subjects he asked to try his experiment. Based upon these insights into the role of these stimulus properties as determinants of the perceptions of his test subjects, Rorschach devised a preliminary scoring format, conducted a number of additional studies on various cognitive and emotional reactions of normals and psychiatric patients on related laboratory tasks to try to confirm his conjectures, and gathered normative data on hospital staff and employees, school children, and adults from various nearby cantons. He reported his various efforts in a monograph after the war (Rorschach, 1921). He was preparing a further report on this method when he died suddenly in 1922 at the age of 37. His approach to personality assessment was uniformly empirical, even opportunistic. For example, his struggles with the printer over the technical problem of faithful reproduction of his final 10-card inkblot series were very trying; the reproductions lacked the uniform saturation of coloring of his own blots. He soon came to see additional potentialities, however, in the shadings and internal details produced by the defective method of reproduction of his cards, making possible such additional determinants as shading, vista, and chiaroscuro in the scoring system. Thus, it is unlikely that Rorschach would have left his "experiment" in just the form in which it now has been preserved by loyal and devoted adherents. For example, he explicitly discussed the pros and cons of developing a parallel series of stimulus cards. His colleagues, E. Oberholzer and W. Morgenthaler, carried on the work that Rorschach had initiated in Switzerland and helped to train numerous students from other countries who eventually spread the technique and lore to all parts of the world.

DEVELOPMENTS IN PSYCHOLOGICAL TESTING BETWEEN THE WARS

In the second decade of the twentieth century American psychology was still a small community; most psychologists knew each other or at least knew each other's work well. Many had studied in Europe and kept in close contact with developments there. With so many caught up in the war effort, working together in the screening centers or training camps, consulting on instruments and data analyses, these psychologists came to know each other even better (Samelson, 1977). Many formed close associations that persisted after the war in new or expanding departments of psychology, in hospitals, clinics, and guidance centers. Their collaborations in research and test development extended over the next decades, leading to many refinements of existing scales and procedures, as well as totally new tests.

Some of the Army tests were published relatively unchanged for use in civilian settings. In the *Memoirs*, Yerkes described these tests and provided full documentation and sample forms of all of the Army measures; Bregman and Wells prepared civilian versions of the Army Alpha; both the Kansas State Teachers College Bureau of Educational Measurement and the University of Nebraska Press published further versions of the Army Alpha for college use. In 1922 Myers published a group non-verbal scale based on the Army Beta. In addition, the key members of the military test development program (Yerkes,

Terman, Whipple, and Thorndike) collaborated in producing the National Intelligence Test for the National Research Council. Each of these men upon returning to his civilian position gave a new impetus to psychological measurement and test development work. It is worth following them in their undertakings in the next decade or two.

Yerkes

Yerkes did not return to the Boston Psychopathic Hospital after the war but took a position on the faculty of the Department of Psychology at Yale. M. A. May joined him there and eventually became head of the Institute of Human Relations. Yerkes, in addition to his editorial work on the report to the National Academy of Sciences for the *Memoirs,* collaborated with Bridges on a revised form of their Point Scale of Intelligence. For many years this scale served as an alternate to the Stanford-Binet. It is likely that the Point Scale would have continued in use and been further revised were it not for the subsequent appearance of parallel forms of the Stanford-Binet in 1937 and the new Wechsler batteries in 1939. Yerkes himself became more involved later in studies of the cognitive behavior of primates but an associate of his at Yale, Arnold Gesell, prepared behavioral measures on infants and pre-school children that served to plot early motor and intellective development. These developmental standards were widely applied in pediatric and child guidance centers in the United States for several decades. (Later performance on the Stanford-Binet by the subjects in Gesell's normative group suggested that the developmental milestones that he established were probably set too high for the general population [Goodenough, 1949]; many of these children came from the academic community of New Haven and, upon entering school, the group was found to have a mean IQ of at least 125.)

Thorndike

As noted above, a significant impetus to the development and application of group tests of intelligence and achievement was provided by Thorndike upon his return to Columbia. He and his colleagues, together with their students, set to work on new intellective and achievement batteries. By 1920, he was able to report to the National Society for the Study of Education that more than one million school children had been administered group intelligence tests during the preceding year (Jonçich, 1968). Thorndike also returned to his earlier interest in the nature and course of development of human intelligence. From the materials used in the military program, he now found new testing formats which would be applicable to the total range of cognitive development from early childhood to the most advanced levels of graduate school. He settled upon four kinds of intellective processes: Completions and Arithmetic reasoning (reflecting well upon Ebbinghaus's original insights), Vocabulary, and the following of Directions (contributions of Binet) (Thorndike, 1926). With this CAVD battery, Thorndike sought to put mental measurement on a par with physical measurements by establishing uniform scaling of intelligence with equal scale intervals and an absolute zero point. Although failing in this attempt, Thorndike clearly documented the distinction between various levels of difficulty of tasks, or the *altitude* of ability needed to succeed on a given level, versus the *range* of competencies at each level. Even today this distinction between altitude and range of intellective capacity is often blurred in evaluating the benefits from well-intentioned efforts to intervene and enhance the intellective development of culturally disadvantaged youngsters.

Cattell

James McKeen Cattell, having been dismissed from his faculty position at Columbia University because of his vigorous anti-war stand (Woodworth, 1944), initiated an effort after the war that had a profound effect for many decades on the quality as well as the quantity of tests of all kinds developed in the United States. While a few long-established firms, such as C. H. Stoelting Company of Chicago, a manufacturer and distributor of medical and physiological equipment since 1886, took on lines of testing materials and produced uniform kits of standard quality, most group tests were produced by textbook publishers with newly established test divisions or by fly-by-night businesses drawn to this first profit-making phase of psychotechnology. These publishers often lacked experience even in the practical requirements of individual and group tests (precise specifications, high quality of materials and production, legibility, ease of marking and scoring), let alone the quality of the basic research supporting these instruments. The numbers of tests that were coming into use increased dramatically, but the quality of research work on them as well as the quality of the printing or manufacture often lagged far behind. Seeing this rapid spread of tests and realizing the difficulties and dangers inherent in such rampant growth, Cattell recognized the need for test standardization, quality control, and professional restrictions in distribution and usage. In 1921, in collaboration with some 200 other psychologists, he established The Psychological Corporation in New York City. This group of psychologists led the way in establishing test guidelines and monitoring test development and distribution. It also extended consultation to potential test users in business, government, schools and colleges in the U.S.

Wechsler

One of the psychologists Cattell asked to serve with him in The Psychological Corporation in getting its consultative services properly launched was David Wechsler, a former student of Cattell's and of Thorndike's, who had also had testing experience in the Army. In addition, Wechsler had spent some time in the laboratories of Spearman and Pearson in England where he was assigned during the war after completing the Army training program. He stayed with The Psychological Corporation only a short time, however; after a period in industrial consultation and in private practice, he assumed the position of chief psychologist in the psychiatric services of Bellevue Hospitals in New York City. Here Wechsler was faced with the examination of emotionally disturbed adults who often balked at being tested with child-oriented tests. Drawing upon his experience with the various scales and measures that had been employed by the mental examiners to test adult subjects in the Army, and guided by Spearman's conceptualization of general intelligence, Wechsler assembled a battery of tests to evaluate adults. It was comprised of 11 sub-tests: 6 verbal (general information, arithmetic, comprehension, similarities, digit span, and vocabulary) and 5 performance scales (block designs, from Kohs's work of 1923; object assembly, adapted from Knox and the Pintner-Paterson batteries; picture completion, similar to the Healy; picture arrangement, from Decroly; and a digit-symbol substitution task, from Whipple). The component scales in this battery were thus not unique to Wechsler but all had a long tradition of development and prior validation. He fashioned them into an organized test by developing standardized scoring procedures and by establishing separate normative values for each component scale, for the two part-scores based upon the verbal and performance sets, as well as for the total composite score. He employed various subject groups from the age of 16 to 60 and determined the relationship of scores on this battery to various other established group and individual intelligence scales. The Psychological Corporation agreed to publish and distribute this scale (Wechsler, 1939); it went through several revisions and extensions, including a parallel form based upon research in the Army psychology program during World War II, and simpler versions for children (the Wechsler Intelligence Scale for Children, and the Wechsler Preschool and Primary Scale of Intelligence [Matarazzo, 1972]). Although the initial standardization of the Wechsler scale was quite parochial, restricted entirely to subjects located in and around New York City, subsequent standardizations sponsored by The Psychological Corporation were carried out on carefully executed representative sampling designs of American adults and children. The format of the Wechsler batteries with equivalent scores obtained from the component sub-tests has enabled psychologists to devise a number of pattern analytic procedures for special diagnostic purposes.

Otis, Terman, and Merrill

Comparable developments in intelligence and achievement testing were soon underway again at Stanford upon Terman's return from the Army. Otis came back with him and soon completed his dissertation which had been interrupted by the war. His research led to the construction of a general group test; it undoubtedly profited from the experience Otis had working with Thorndike and Thurstone in the Statistical Section. Otis published his test (Otis, 1922) and continued to refine and revise it through many editions in the interval between the two World Wars. Terman himself developed group tests and continued work on perfecting the Stanford-Binet. In 1927 Terman enlisted the continuing collaboration of one of his former doctoral students, Maude Merrill (James), who worked closely with him for three decades in preparing the two parallel forms of the 1937 revision (named L and M for Lewis and Maude [Terman & Merrill, 1937]), and later saw the 1960 revision, the combined form L-M, through to completion after Terman's death in 1956 (Terman & Merrill, 1960).

Seashore

As noted above, after the end of the war a number of pre-war efforts were renewed and several new research efforts were launched. Carl E. Seashore at the State University of Iowa continued his program of study of special talent in music, as well as his efforts to devise practical tests for school children and entering college students. Even after he assumed the deanship of the College of Arts and Sciences, Seashore remained active in this area. He was also instrumental in bringing in N. C. Meier with whom he collaborated in developing an art aptitude test, as well as E. F. Lindquist in educational psychology who worked to establish the nation-wide school testing program, the Iowa Every-Pupil batteries, now called (following modifications) the American College Testing Program. R. H. Seashore and H. E. Seashore continued their father's interest in the development of psychometric procedures and scientifically sound applications of testing methods, the former at Columbia University, the latter at The Psychological Corporation.

Strong

A group of applied psychologists that had formed just before the war at Carnegie Institute of Technology was quickly formed again at the end of the hostilities. With W. V. Bingham as head, the department included W. D. Scott, E. K. Strong, C. S. Yoakum, H. D. Fryer, J. B. Miner, and L. L. Thurstone. (D. G. Paterson also spent a couple of years with Scott before going to Minnesota.) This group worked closely with various industries to develop special aptitude measures for employee selection and training. Here Strong also initiated studies on the role of vocational interests as factors in career choice and job satisfaction. In 1923, he moved to Stanford and carried out an extensive, longitudinal research program on the origins, persistence, and significance of vocational interests. He developed a standardized inventory of interests for each sex with empirically derived keys for scores of professions and occupations. Each scale was developed by contrasting the expressed interests of men and women who were successfully established in a given vocation with the endorsement patterns of men in general and women in general (Strong, 1927, 1943). This empirical approach to interest measurement contrasted sharply with the method employed by G. F. Kuder in developing his Vocational Preference Record (Kuder, 1934), the major competing instrument in this field in the ensuing decades. Kuder selected items based upon their content from nine (later ten) broad areas of vocational activity and verified these scale placements by internal consistency studies calculated to develop homogeneous measures of preferences for various kinds of occupations (sales, clerical, computation, personal service, etc.). Subsequent factor analyses of the interrelationships among the numerous specific keys in the Strong Vocational Interest Blank identified some occupational groupings which corresponded reasonably well with the a priori groups envisioned by Kuder.

Upon Strong's retirement, Paterson and his associates were influential in persuading Strong to donate his extensive archival data to the University of Minnesota. A recent revision of this widely used inventory has been developed in a combined form for men and women (Campbell, 1971). The empirical approach to scale construction devised by Strong for inventory responses served as one of the models for the empirical construction of the MMPI, to be described below.

Thurstone

Before Thurstone began his consultation with the Statistical Section, his investigations at Carnegie had focused upon the improvement of trade tests. He helped get that part of the Army psychology testing program well launched and many examiners were trained to administer these procedures as part of the induction screening. He had been increasingly caught up, however, in the correlational analyses among the various intellective scales in the Army batteries and the different ways in which the staff psychologists tended to interpret these results. Back at Carnegie he initiated several investigations of the patterning of abilities, devising several new measures to provide additional scales for his intercorrelational matrices. He continued these studies, in collaboration with his wife, Thelma Gwynn Thurstone, after his move to the University of Chicago in 1924. There they established The Psychometric Laboratory and developed factor analytic methods and concepts with which they hoped to resolve the then raging controversy between Thorndike and Spearman on the organization of human intelligence. The scales they used in these studies were relatively simple, homogeneous **p12point scales** administered to groups of mature subjects (university students or adults) with short time limits. Thurstone (1926) contrasted such measures of ability with the mental **age scales** that were at that time the accepted format for individual testing. His criticisms covered both the heterogeneity of the content included in age scales, at each level and particularly between levels, and the lack of empirical scaling for superior performance once general mental growth has reached a plateau. That is, subjects whose performances as adults fall below the adult mean can be compared directly to the mental age levels established by the typical performances of younger subjects but there are no empirical markers for successively higher levels of ability above the adult mean. (Terman had had to prorate his superior adult levels by scaling deviations proportionately above the general adult norm.) Thurstone's argument was that if deviations upward were scaled by relative frequency then deviations downward should be scaled in the same way to be entirely consistent in the measurement procedure for all subjects. This scaling method as proposed by Thurstone was quickly adopted for group testing formats (Wood, 1962) and many individually administered scales soon followed, most notably the Wechsler batteries. The most recent revision of the Stanford-Binet, form L-M, now includes tables for the **deviation IQ scores** in addition to the traditional mental age scores (Terman & Merrill, 1960). This issue is still not fully resolved, however, since the general age level organization of the Binet-type scales is seen by some investigators as a rough approximation of the stages of cognitive development as proposed by Piaget's theories. There are also continuing efforts to fit the Stanford-Binet into a point-scaled, multidimensional profile format (cf. Terman & Merrill, 1972; Valett, 1965).

Through **factor analytic methods** of his own devising, Thurstone carried out numerous analyses of the interrelationships among the homogeneous scales that he and others were constructing. Similar work was being carried out by T. L. Kelley at Stanford, by G. H. Thomson in Scotland, and by C. Burt in England; all were coming to the same general conclusion: neither Thorndike's atomistic nor Spearman's global conceptualization of human cognitive abilities was defensible. Publications by Kelley (1928), Thurstone (1933), Thomson (1939), and Burt (1940) proposed various groups of factors each less pervasive than those envisioned by Spearman (1927) and less delimited than those conceptualized by Thorndike (1926). This controversy is still a lively one, as witnessed by Jensen (1980). The Thurstones studied younger-aged subjects and developed practical batteries of tests to measure the components of intelligence that they were able to identify over wide ranges of intellective development and capacity. Much of this pioneering work has been extended by J. P. Guilford (1967a, 1967b) and R. B. Cattell (1971) in long series of basic investigations of the components of human cognitive processes. Many of the findings from their studies have yet to be incorporated into practical instruments for educational and clinical use.

College Admission Tests

At the time that the Thurstones moved to Chicago, they began a program of annual revision of a college admission test for the American Council on Education. This arrangement lasted for nearly three decades and the examination, which came to be known as the ACE, rivaled for many years the essay procedures of the College Entrance Examination Board, Miller's Mental Ability

Test, the National Intelligence Test, and other screening measures for college admission (Thurstone, 1925). The ACE was made up of a verbal comprehension and a quantitative reasoning subscale; each was precisely timed. All member institutions in the Council could employ the ACE, and appropriate cutting scores were worked out separately for each college or university. Reliance on subtest time limits in such instruments was justified on the basis of earlier research by the military psychologists that had demonstrated that the rank-ordering of subjects in a group was virtually unaffected even when time restrictions were completely removed; that is, when subjects could have all the time needed to try all items, the absolute numbers of items correct were obviously increased but able subjects did proportionately better and the order among subjects changed very little. (The nice distinction involved in this scaling decision between timed and untimed performances escaped Walter Lippmann in his diatribe against early intelligence tests [Block & Dworkin, 1976]). Therefore, as long as everyone had the same amount of time to work on the component subscales, the more economical and more easily administered timed tests should be as good as the unwieldy untimed procedures. The only notable exception to the use of timed tests in these early group examinations was the Ohio State University Psychological Examination developed by H. A. Toops (1919). He noted that subjects often felt frustrated and self-dissatisfied with the **timed tests** and, even more importantly, that some became so distressed that they could not concentrate on the test content. His examination was a **power test** that allowed subjects time to try to complete every item in an increasingly more difficult series. Since later factor analytic studies documented a special speed factor (i.e., the ability to work various kinds of intellective tasks quickly), Thurstone's own findings would appear to vindicate Toops in his efforts to minimize any potential biases from such special skills in the scores obtained on a test of general intellective ability.

Developments at Minnesota

In this account of the post-war contributions of the psychologists involved in the military program, it should be clear that many of these investigators simply resumed programs of work already underway at the time that the United States entered the war. There were, however, some new undertakings which dated from the Army program that should also be mentioned. One notable example of such a new effort in test construction grew directly out of these wartime associations. In 1919, a department of psychology was established at the University of Minnesota. When R. M. Elliott left the Army, he accepted the position of chairman of the department and persuaded his Army associates, W. S. Foster and D. G. Paterson, to join his faculty. In addition, two other associates from the military program were recruited in closely allied programs at Minnesota: W. S. Miller in educational psychology and J. E. Anderson in the Child Welfare Institute (now the Institute of Child Development). This nucleus of experienced, capable, and hard-headed psychologists quickly initiated a program of research on the abilities needed to succeed in various levels of schooling and in a wide variety of jobs. Although Foster died unexpectedly a few years later, Paterson and his associates, working closely with members of the Employment Stabilization Research Institute and the Industrial Relations Center, carried on with a long series of investigations of the special aptitudes and abilities which are crucial to success in various occupations and vocations. This work culminated in the publication of a series of performance tests for use in guidance clinics, employment services, and industrial centers.

Similarly, under John Anderson's long directorship, the Child Welfare Institute at Minnesota became a center for test development and research on the origins of human abilities. Florence Goodenough, a student of Thorndike's at Columbia who completed her doctoral work with Terman at Stanford, was recruited by Anderson. She explored various non-verbal indices of intellective ability, most notably the development of figure-drawing performance (Goodenough, 1926). Goodenough also carried out work on an instrument to extend the Stanford-Binet scale downward in age level. Her efforts resulted in the publication of the Minnesota Preschool Scale (Goodenough, Maurer, & Van Wagenen, 1932). Goodenough and her associates at the Institute also became involved in a series of studies (and controversies arising from them) on the fundamental question of the modifiability of intellective development over the age range from infancy to adulthood. The scales that had become available for assessing children at different stages in their development provided opportunities to assess the impact of early child-rearing and training, special schooling, foster home placement, and other interventions, on cognitive performance. Many claims for impressive enhancement of intellective capacity were advanced in the literature, particularly by investigators at the Iowa Child Welfare Research Station at the State University of Iowa (e.g., B. Wellman, M. Skodak, H. Skeels, B. McCandless, and others). Investigators at Minnesota, Stanford, and the University of California at Berkeley were highly skeptical of these claims and a vigorous exchange of research reports and commentary developed. Many of these papers were published in two yearbooks of the National Society for the Study of Education (Whipple, 1928, 1940). A more recent publication by the Society (Findley, 1963) covered subsequent research on this problem, and the work of Jensen (1980) discusses the many complex sources of bias that may enter into this kind of research.

In educational psychology at Minnesota, Miller studied the usefulness of group tests at the college and post-graduate level, eventually developing the Miller Analogies Test (Miller, 1944, 1947) which has been very widely employed to supplement the Graduate Record Examinations for selecting applicants to graduate level programs in many different professional fields. Miller's long-time associate, M. J. Van Wagenen, collaborated with Goodenough in her work on the Preschool Scale. He also became a leader in the standardization of achievement tests for a variety of subject-matter areas in the school curriculum. These significant efforts at Minnesota have long rivaled the test development work at such pioneering institutions as Columbia, Stanford, Carnegie Tech, Iowa, and Chicago.

Other Trends

By 1930, hardly more than a decade after the end of World War I, hundreds of new tests were being developed and published, thousands upon thousands of subjects were being examined, here and abroad, and a new profession of clinical psychology was emerging (Reisman, 1966) that was closely identified with the administration and interpretation of psychological tests. Special tests to evaluate deterioration, aphasic disorders, thought disorders, and developmental delay were being devised and special tests for examining handicapped subjects were being improved. The first textbooks in the field of clinical psychology (Louttit, 1936; Porteus, 1941) emphasized the contributions of psychological testing in work with children. Many conceptual problems in the organization and interpretation of multiple measures on a given client, pupil, or patient were worked out pragmatically without guiding theory or concepts (Gough, 1962).

There was a concerted effort on the part of many test developers to improve upon the psychometric and validational characteristics of their scales of ability. Hundreds of concurrent studies were carried out on the relationship of ability or aptitude scales to school and job success (Tuddenham, 1962; Wright, 1968). In addition, a series of longitudinal projects on intellective and personological development was launched in the early 1930s at the University of California at Berkeley by Macfarlane (1938), Jones (1943), and Bayley (1955). The results of these projects continue to appear and document many of the prognostic implications of the early ability and personality scales (Block, 1971). Investigations of age changes of intellective abilities and personality patterns past maturity have also been more recently conducted but with less clearcut findings (Barton, Plemons, Willis, & Baltes, 1975).

REEXAMINATION OF PERSONALITY INVENTORIES

It is important to note, however, that little attention had been paid to the validities of the numerous personality questionnaires that had appeared during the 1920s. After Woodworth had returned to Columbia, he published a slightly altered version of the Personal Data Sheet for adult use and teamed up with V. M. Cady to simplify the items and format for use with elementary school and junior high-school students. A number of similar questionnaires were soon produced; none seem to have been critically examined against outside criteria of personality characteristics or emotional status. Each had no more support than the plausibility of the content of their component items (i.e., **face validity**). Each new device was typically evaluated against existing inventories. Thus, even when Bernreuter gathered several of the various measures of personality and emotional maladjustment into one test (Bernreuter, 1931), his validation studies involved correlating his new versions against scores obtained from the original scale instruments: Thurstone and Thurstone's neuroticism; Laird's introversion-extraversion; Allport and Allport's ascendance-submission; and a self-sufficiency scale of Bernreuter's own devising. It was not long, however, before the same critical reexamination that had already been focused on existing ability and aptitude measures was turned upon personality and adjustment questionnaires.

Validity of Questionnaires

Some of the most systematic and rigorous investigations of the truth-value of the self-descriptions that a subject provides by answering questionnaire statements were carried out by Carney Landis and his associates (J. Zubin, S. E. Katz, J. Page) at the New York State Psychiatric Institute (Landis, Zubin, & Katz, 1935). Using test protocols obtained from carefully selected and matched samples of diagnosed psychiatric patients and non-medical normal adults, these investigators were able to identify a number of sources of invalidity in the content of reports given by both kinds of subjects (lack of understanding of the instructions or the wording of test items, lack of personal insight, unwillingness to disclose sensitive material, emotional confusions and disorientations, foreign language background and other specific linguistic or reading difficulties, inability to decide between response alternatives) as well as lack of actual differences between endorsements by patients and normals in contradiction of the assumptions that underlay what most psychologists were likely to conclude from these various self-reports. Their publications were augmented by further evidence about the ease with which subjects could slant answers to generate particular test outcomes. For example, Terman, in collaboration with Catharine Cox Miles, had constructed a special instrument to assess the personality differences between men and women (Terman & Miles, 1936). This Attitude-Interest Blank was made up of a variety of different subtests which had shown consistent differences between samples of male and female adults (tastes and preferences; emotional reactions such as fears, disgust, etc.; word associations; special information; inkblot interpretations; hobbies; common beliefs; etc.). When applying this scale to study the comparability of male homophilic inverts to women in general, they found that most inverts scored as feminine as, or even more feminine in their self-descriptions than, adult women; but a few feminine men seemed to be giving a distorted, excessively masculine self-report. In a special study of the fakability of this instrument, Terman was able to show that the items on the Attitude-Interest Blank which provided the best separation between men and women were also the most susceptible to change under instructions to deliberately fake the test answers in either a masculine or feminine direction. Other investigators (e.g., Hathaway, 1939) were finding that some data from adjustment inventories like the Bernreuter could actually be interpreted as indicating some forms of psychopathology if the scores indicated *too favorable* an adjustment. Psychologists in the budding field of clinical psychology reacted to these adverse findings about existing personality questionnaires by seeking assessment methods presumably more subtle and less susceptible to such sources of invalidity as deliberate distortion or unconscious slanting. For clinical diagnosis of adult patients at least, **projective tests** like the Rorschach and the Thematic Apperception Test (TAT) seemed to provide a remedy to these glaring deficiencies in verbal reports to questionnaires.

Rorschach Test

As indicated above, the experiment of Rorschach had been preserved by his colleagues in Switzerland. An American psychiatrist, David Levy, spent a year with Oberholzer studying the method and then introduced the instrument and Rorschach's techniques to the United States in 1924 upon his return to New York City. He also encouraged others, such as Samuel Beck and Bruno Klopfer, to obtain training in the Rorschach methods. These psychologists in turn began to encourage the use of the test and to instruct many American clinicians (Reisman, 1966). They offered workshops which drew increasing numbers of psychologists and psychiatrists eager to learn about the complexities of Rorschach scoring and interpretation. Marguerite Hertz, at the Brush Foundation in Cleveland, also began annual training workshops which continue today in her version of Rorschach method. All of these workers prepared basic manuals; the Rorschach test was also included in the Menninger Clinic test battery (Rapoport, Gill, & Schafer, 1946) which helped promote its general adoption. The group of psychologists at the New York State Psychiatric Institute also turned to these procedures but with a somewhat more skeptical regard for the early claims of accuracy and validity (Zubin, Eron, & Schumer, 1965). The Rorschach technique, unfortunately, was found to suffer various inherent difficulties and limitations as well (cf. Cronbach, 1949) and, after a post-World War II explosion of acceptance, its popularity waned to a considerable extent (Reynolds & Sundberg, 1976). A new inkblot instrument designed to offset many of the criticisms advanced against the original Rorschach method (e.g., using two parallel forms, requiring only one association or perception to each blot, more explicit scoring standards, etc.) was published in 1958 by W. H. Holtzman but it has not proven to be an acceptable clinical substitute for the original instrument. In the last few years, however, the traditional Rorschach has had another resurgence in acceptance and popularity (cf. Exner, 1974, 1978).

Thematic Apperception Test (TAT)

The timing in the appearance of the TAT was equally favorable for its acceptance as an alternative to the discredited questionnaires. The background theory and research on this instrument were vastly different from the origins of the Rorschach, however, although it shared a common basis in reliance upon the subject's controlled association processes. The association method has had a long tradition in academic psychology (Woodworth & Wells, 1911) as well as clinical psychiatry (Jung, 1910; Kent & Rosanoff, 1910) and clinical psychology (Payne, 1928). However, the use of story-telling, prompted by a series of ambiguous pictures, as a means of sampling complexly organized associations from a subject's accumulated apperceptive mass, and the method of analyzing these productions to draw personological inferences are unique to the TAT. H. A. Murray, the developer of the test along with his colleague Christiana D. Morgan (Morgan & Murray, 1935; Murray, et al. 1938), entered psychology late, after being trained as a surgeon and a biochemist (Murray, 1967). Upon the invitation of Morton Prince, he joined the staff of the Harvard Clinic at its founding in 1926. He subsequently became competent in psychoanalytic procedures of all three major forms (Freudian, Jungian, and Adlerian) and synthesized his own personality theory. When Murray became its director in 1934, the Harvard Psychological Clinic developed into a center for basic personality research and a model for personality assessment centers that appeared in universities (MacKinnon, 1974), industrial organizations (Cohen, Moses, & Byham, 1974), and the military (Ansbacher, 1941; Murray, MacKinnon, Miller, Fiske, & Hanfmann, 1948) in the next several decades. Murray and the staff of the Clinic carried out intensive studies of normal subjects, supported the studies of an impressive number of future leaders in the area of human personality research (MacKinnon & Dukes, 1962), and generated theoretical and practical advances in personology that have helped to bridge the gap between clinical psychoanalysis and general psychology (Murray, 1967).

The TAT has also had many imitators and derivations and, like the Rorschach, is employed in numerous batteries for clinical assessment (e.g., Rapaport et al., 1946). As originally published, the TAT lacked several of the basic attributes of a standardized test; it was closer in form to a carefully structured interview for sampling a subject's fantasies and momentary preoccupations. The method has been extended in numerous ways, however, many of which provide scoring standards and procedures, normative data, and extensive validational evidence which serve to qualify such versions for full status as a psychological test (Zubin et al., 1965). In its many forms and derivatives, the TAT has rivaled the Rorschach for first place in the area of projective techniques (Reynolds & Sundberg, 1976).

NEW OBJECTIVE TESTS

In spite of the clear swing to projective methods of personality evaluation in the late 1930s and 1940s, a few psychologists continued to employ questionnaire formats with a more sophisticated awareness of the limitations as well as the advantages they possess. For example, G. W. Allport at Harvard collaborated with P. E. Vernon, a British psychologist, in constructing an instrument, called the Study of Values, to measure the basic orientations to the world proposed in Spranger's theory of personality types (Allport & Vernon, 1931; Allport, Vernon, & Lindzey, 1970). (Allport had previously developed an ascendance-submission scale with his brother, F. H. Allport; their A-S measure had served as a criterion in Bernreuter's research on his Psychoneurotic Inventory.) The Study of Values was unusual in at least two ways: it was constructed within a specific theoretical framework rather than as a utilitarian measuring instrument, and it employed a forced-choice format. Although the Study of Values has since been used in research and numerous applications having little bearing upon the theory within which it was developed, the original validational bases for the test imply quite delimited assumptions and conceptualizations about human personality. For example, the appraisal of strength of a particular value is made by this instrument only against the relative strength of other values within a particular test subject. This ipsative scaling from the forced choice does not provide a basis for comparing the amount of a given value commitment of any one person with the strength of that value in other individuals. There is thus a trade-off in the use of such a format that fits well the Spranger type theory but does not permit normative comparisons. The same ipsative scaling has been employed in other inventories, often without full understanding of the limitations it imposes upon the use of general norms.

In addition to the continued use of verbal statements in such theory-based instruments, several psychologists who had previously employed factor analytic methods to study intelligence and to devise new ability scales began to apply the same analytic techniques to data from verbal reports. The Thurstones had constructed the Neurotic Inventory (upon which Bernreuter had relied to develop the neurotic subscale in his test) by factor analytic methods but they did little with this scale except to demonstrate the internal consistency of answers to these statements; that is, real world correlates of this measure were not extensively studied. J. P. Guilford, R. B. Cattell, and H. J. Eysenck each began about this time long series of factor analytic investigations of the domain of personality, both normal and pathological, and each developed numerous instruments and scales based on endorsements to verbal items in self-descriptions. Although many individuals have decried the separate consideration of intellective abilities and personality dimensions and even though R. B. Cattell has explicitly included a measure of general intellective ability in his best known test, the Sixteen Personality Factor Test (Cattell, Eber, & Tatsuoka, 1970), these two general kinds of attributes (abilities and personality characteristics) have not shown much overlapping. Even more importantly, there have been serious questions raised about the suitability of the factor models that had been developed within the ability domain and the geometric representations upon which most of these factor formulations rest for depicting personality variables and interrelationships. That is, the use of such summarization devices as cumulative scales, vector plots (which for abilities invariably fell within the positive manifold), and orthogonal reference planes, often provides only poor approximations to the complexities of human personality. Although this line of research and test development continues unabated (cf. Jackson, 1965), this factor analytic approach to personality inventory construction has been contrasted over the last four decades with a pragmatic, empirical approach employing various external criteria against which to select items and construct scales. This third approach is most clearly demonstrated in the work of S. R. Hathaway and J. C. McKinley (1940, 1942) in the construction of the personality schedule that came to be called the Minnesota Multiphasic Personality Inventory (MMPI).

The Minnesota Multiphasic Personality Inventory

Hathaway, a physiological psychologist turning clinician, and McKinley, a neuropsychiatrist, both at the University of Minnesota, took as their model the radically empirical approach of E. K. Strong in his development of the subscales for his vocational interest inventory. Culling items from many traditional sources (from other tests and texts in abnormal psychology and psychiatry) as well as non-traditional sources (social, political, and religious attitudes; hobbies, interests, and superstitions; personal habits, family relationships, and folk customs), they rewrote them in a uniform format and common vernacular. They also adapted some parts of the Terman-Miles Attitude-Interest Blank related to sex differences in personality. They then began systematic testing of adults in general and of carefully selected groups of psychiatric and medical patients. Hathaway and McKinley constructed item sets from demonstrated differences in the answers of psychiatric criterion groups and comparable adults without known pathology, rather than relying upon psychologists' judgments (Woodworth), conformance with a guiding theory (Allport), or patterns of interitem correlation (Thurstone, Guilford, and others). A series of publications in the early 1940s introduced the component scales; the test was published by the University of Minnesota Press in 1943. The final form of the MMPI profile, or psychograph, was made up of a series of validity indicators and a separate set of clinical scales arrayed in a standard order and employing separate male and female adult norms. This profile, together with scoring keys and record forms, was distributed by The Psychological Corporation beginning in 1947. Since its appearance nearly 40 years ago, it has come to be the most widely used inventory in the United States (Reynolds & Sundberg, 1976) and has been translated into scores of other languages for use in cross-cultural research, differential diagnosis, and computerized test interpretation around the world (Butcher & Pancheri, 1976).

The universally wide acceptance of the MMPI for use in medical, educational, industrial, judicial, as well as basic psychological, research and application (cf. Dahlstrom, Welsh, & Dahlstrom, 1972, 1975) rivals the spread of the Binet scales of intelligence in the first decades of this century. Aside from the demonstrated need for a workable personality instrument in these fields, the success of the instrument is puzzling, even to its inventor (Hathaway, 1978). Part of the explanation undoubtedly lies in the disclaimers of omniscience made by Hathaway and McKinley in acknowledging limitations in their grasp of the subtleties of a person's self-perceptions and in their willingness to use instead empirical data upon which to base item selection for the clinical scales. In addition, the collaboration of Hathaway with his former student P. E. Meehl after McKinley's untimely death led to the elaboration of the preliminary set of validity indicators into an array of sensitive measures that helped to detect many of the major sources of error that Landis and his coworkers had shown affected the acceptability of any given test administration. Few tests even now provide internal checks of this sort on protocol validity. These scales anticipated by 20 years the flurry of concerns in the 1960s over the biasing effects of various response sets on answers to questionnaires and objective inventories. Numerous empirical studies of test slanting carried out at the University of Minnesota and elsewhere had documented the importance of these test-taking orientations and the usefulness of the MMPI validity indicators in measuring their deleterious effects or in offsetting the distortions by various amounts of statistical correction. Important as these attributes of the MMPI format may be, the inherent validities of the instrument for use in general psychiatric and medical settings would not alone have carried it beyond these arenas; the pervasiveness of the emotional conditions that are assessed by the MMPI within widely varying human relationships and interactions have served to assure the relevance of these measures to many diverse human settings.

The MMPI, like many of the other powerful psychological test instruments, has been subject to extensive criticism and debate (cf. Brayfield, 1965; Butcher, 1969). Invasion of privacy, possible racial and ethnic biases, inclusion of item content that may be upsetting or disturbing to some subjects, and many other concerns have been voiced from time to time. Some of the criticisms of the MMPI stem from its original derivational framework of psychiatric diagnosis in a Meyerian psychobiology. Derivatives from the MMPI, like the Minnesota Counseling Inventory (MCI) of Berdie and Layton and the California Psychological Inventory (CPI) of Gough, have used the same empirical construction methods against dependable external criteria and have even included some of the same basic items; they have not, however, designated their component scales by labels which are so pathological or negative, perhaps, as those of the MMPI. (Gough deliberately reversed the scoring of some of the early CPI scales, e.g., the scale for delinquency was scored the other way and called a measure of socialization; on several scales he changed the names to reflect more positive personality attributes and in this way emphasized personality assets rather than liabilities that may be revealed in such scores.) Would the MMPI itself have achieved even wider acceptance if, for example, the authors had inverted the scores on the Depression scale and named it instead Surgent Optimism (with lower scores, then, serving to measure the depths of emotional despair)? The successive compromises that have in fact been made in MMPI terminology (from calling it the Depression scale, to designating it the D scale, and finally to calling it simply scale 2) may have facilitated the introduction of the inventory into areas of general application where it otherwise would not have been welcomed. Strong residual feelings about the content of some items or even the various applications and uses of such devices continue in many quarters today in spite of general liberalization of social attitudes toward mental health problems, greater freedom in public discussion about social and sexual deviations, and growing permissiveness in literary vocabularies and general dictionaries. Efforts to censor, prohibit, expurgate, or purify in the tradition of Thomas Bowdler and Anthony Comstock still persist. In spite of wishful thinking to the contrary, there is reason to believe that many important kinds of psychological appraisal cannot be accomplished without such controversial item content in our personality instruments (Dahlstrom & Dahlstrom, 1980).

PSYCHOLOGICAL TESTING DURING AND AFTER WORLD WAR II

However ill-prepared the United States may have been upon our entry into hostilities in World War II, it should be apparent that American psychology was much better equipped by this time to make substantial contributions to the infinitely greater complexities of modern warfare. The range of problems to which psychotechnology was applied was impressive, but personnel selection and psychological testing undoubtedly still constituted the primary area of application as they did in World War I (Goodenough, 1949). At the end of the war this time, the reports on research and development of these test instruments and the various ways in which they improved upon existing screening and placement in various military training programs ran to dozens of volumes (cf. DuBois, 1947; Stuit, 1947; Vernon & Parry, 1949). As in World War I, experienced psychologists quickly entered the military in all services and brought tests and sophisticated statistical procedures to bear upon the identification of aptitudes and personality characteristics pertinent to various phases of military training, service, and combat. These methods ranged from routine ability and emotional screening in all branches of the military to complex assessment of candidates for the Office of Strategic Services where they would be given dangerous individualized assignments of counter-intelligence (Murray et al., 1948). This time, too, many young men and women were given training and practical experience in testing and psychodiagnosis which attracted them into various fields of psychology upon their discharge from the service. Numerous applied fields of psychology were given new impetus when these service-experienced veterans entered graduate programs in universities throughout the country. This growth was particularly marked in clinical psychology (Reisman, 1966) and the efforts of these new clinicians advanced the application of psychological tests in various batteries along a wide front. Many of these developments have already been anticipated in the previous discussions: the Wechsler batteries which provided new flexibility in testing both normal and physically or emotionally handicapped subjects, thus rendering much less necessary special verbal versions of the Stanford-Binet for the blind (the Hayes-Binet) or new performance scales for the deaf like the one developed by Hiskey; factor-analytic batteries of aptitude and ability measures competing with the older-style single score tests of general scholastic ability; multidimensional instruments based either upon empirical keying or factor-ana-lytic internal consistency scaling to evaluate total personality functioning; as well as an array of projective instruments for which an increasingly rich clinical lore was being developed and published (Klopfer, 1973).

Psychological Tests and Public Policy

As psychological tests have come to play an even greater role in the crucial decisions being made about children and adults, applicants for school admission and for jobs, patients entering or leaving treatment, recipients of special govern-ment benefits, or miscreants in various phases of the criminal justice system, it could be expected that such heavy reliance upon test methods would soon raise fundamental questions about the suitability or appropriateness of their use as shibboleths by our gatekeepers. The criticisms take many forms and the attacks come from several quarters. The basic validity of all ability tests and achieve-ment batteries has been repeatedly questioned (Linden & Linden, 1968), as has the basic concept of a single general intellective ability (Jensen, 1980; Riegel, 1973; Voyat, 1976; Wechsler, 1966). Questions of constitutionality and legality have also been effectively raised in Congress and the courts (Brayfield, 1965) and new regulations introduced in state and federal laws (Ash & Kroeker, 1975). Various ad hominem attacks have also been made (Hearnshaw, 1979; Jensen, 1974, 1978; Kamin, 1974) against individual investigators in fields of study touching upon such emotionally charged questions as racial competence, genetic determinism, and sex differences.

These various attacks have focused on both the test instruments themselves and the professional uses to which they are put; they have become more con-certed and well organized in recent years. As an example of such efforts, Ralph Nader, the militant reformer, has undertaken a vigorous attack on various aspects of the large-scale testing programs now routinely employed by public and private schools and colleges for student guidance and in selection for admission to various programs and training centers. His Public Interest Research Groups have initiated efforts to control such uses of tests by legislation, and Nader has issued a lengthy report on the Educational Testing Service (ETS) at Princeton, New Jersey, one of the largest test publishing and test screening operations in the

United States. The ETS organization was formed shortly after World War II and was an outgrowth of the American Council on Education, the College Entrance Examination Board, and the Carnegie Foundation for the Advancement of Teaching; it combined the admission screening functions that these various organizations had previously carried out separately. The Nader Report on the ETS was prepared by Allan Nairn (1980); it includes criticisms of alleged monopolistic practices, lack of concern for test abuses by subscribers to ETS testing services, lack of predictive validities in the various tests and scales developed and published by ETS, and serious biases from social class, ethnic background, and educational privilege in the test scores earned by subjects being screened for colleges, universities, military programs, and the like. The staff of ETS has initiated efforts to correct errors of reporting and attribution in the Nairn report (ETS Staff, 1980a, 1980b), but a detailed rebuttal has yet to appear.

The Nader PIRG efforts to introduce so-called "truth-in-testing" laws seek to require testing services to report in detail the answers used to score each individual's test performance. Revelation of test content on standardized and copyrighted test instruments constitutes a violation of such copyrights and of professional ethics as well; psychologists are obviously placed in direct conflict with such laws in their professional practice. Contemporary tests cannot be employed in compliance with such statutes and still retain any concurrent or predictive validity. Widespread dissemination of the answers to college admission batteries would reduce such screening efforts to a farce. Ironically, the general impact of the use of such screening measures as the Scholastic Aptitude Test (SAT) over the last several decades of college admissions has been fully in accord with the stated goals of organizations like those of the Nader PIRGs. For example, as noted in the Annual Report of the Educational Testing Service for 1961-62: ". . . In the Ivy League colleges, for instance, the undergraduate body of the 1920s was a homogeneous one with respect to socioeconomic background and a heterogeneous one with respect to intellectual ability. Today the picture is almost reversed—undergraduates in these colleges come from widely varying socioeconomic backgrounds and possess a generally high intellectual ability" (Turnbull, 1968, p. 1424). Many of these reform efforts appear to be particularly short-sighted since the only available alternatives to well-designed and appropriately used psychological tests would appear to be a return to personal recommendations with their associated foibles of limited acquaintanceship, stereotyped perceptions, and nepotisms.

Despite all the polemics, the most telling rebuttals of such criticisms continue to be the ever-growing body of scientific data serving to document the strengths and weaknesses of various test instruments and test procedures. For example, the monumental efforts of the late O. K. Buros and his tireless staff at the Institute of Mental Measurements at Rutgers University enhanced the field of testing for over 40 years by providing critical reviews of tests of all kinds, by pointing out limitations in construction or documentation, and by facilitating choices, purchases, and utilizations through a long series of distinguished yearbooks and other test references (Buros, 1936, 1978). Similarly, the American Psychological Association has provided increasingly explicit and realistic guidelines for psychological tests and manuals (APA, 1954, 1966, 1977). The development of sophisticated formulations about the use of test data in various kinds of applications involving traditional decisions (Cronbach & Gleser, 1965), complex batteries (Gough, 1962), and computerized scoring and interpretation have also increased the precision of test applications and decisions about when tests may most effectively be employed and when and where their usage may be of no advantage or even a distinct disadvantage.

CONCLUSION

Psychology as a science has its beginning with the systematic assignment of numbers to specified attributes of human behavior. The first successful quantifications focused upon simple judgments of sizes, weights, and similar sensory impressions, culminating in the Weber-Fechner laws. Temporal judgments in star transits as well as memory retentions and losses were also quantified and systematized. It was not until the development of various psychological tests, however, that it became possible to measure behavioral attributes of central importance to daily living. With the invention and refinement of tests, the infant science of behavior became relevant and significant to the understanding, prediction, and control of human activities.

The origin of the term test is the Latin word *testum*: the lid or cover of an earthen vessel; also, a crucible or cupel employed in chemical or metallurgical assays. By a form of synecdoche, the crucible itself has come to stand for the process of establishing the genuineness of true worth of the metals rendered molten and separated in the vessel. So, too, a more general definition of *test* gradually emerged in the English language, appearing well before Chaucer's time, as "that by which the existence, quality, or genuineness of anything is or may be determined" (Oxford English Dictionary). For example, the Test Act of 1673 in England established a means by which Catholics and nonconforming Protestants could be excluded from holding office under the crown through various articles of religious faith and practice to which the candidate had to swear and by which he had to abide. In present-day psychology, tests are used, not just to establish the existence of some trait, but to assess its quantitative magnitude as well.

Scientifically based methods to measure human diversity have been available for barely 100 years. Over this relatively short period, however, psychologists have assiduously applied the dictum of E. L. Thorndike: "Whatever exists at all exists in some amount and it can be measured." The impressive array of instruments now available and the huge corpus of scientific findings undergirding their development and application speaks to the energy, determination, and inspiration of several generations of psychologists during the brief history of this research.

Virtually every person in the Western world has by now had some contact with a psychological test; increasingly, citizens in the developing nations are encountering these procedures as well. Entering and leaving school, as well as at choice points along the educational route; entering jobs or retiring; entering or leaving hospitals, prisons, or other institutions: all may be occasions for testing. As active as psychologists now are on a broad array of research topics and problems in psychotechnology, no area of application of our field has had nearly as pervasive nor as extensive an impact upon individual lives as has the development of testing.

During the century of the history of psychological testing, instruments and techniques have been developed largely through pragmatic, cut-and-try methods, guided more by the demands of real-life problems that call for workable solutions than by psychological theory. This trend now appears to be shifting. Results from well-constructed tests of important abilities, motives, and personality characteristics are having a noticeable impact upon scientific theory, and theory in turn is coming to have a role in test revisions and developments. There are still too many areas of psychology in which investigators are satisfied to rig ad hoc scales or measures rather than use more scientifically sound and dependable instruments, thus depriving themselves of the ready communicability of well-established and standardized methods and techniques. The role of psychological tests in scientific research and study is steadily increasing, however, and may soon come to rival the role that these devices play in real-life decisions of our fellow citizens. The result can only be to enhance the dependability of the tests and improve the ways in which they are used.

REFERENCES

Allport, G. W., & Vernon, P. E. *Study of Values: A scale for measuring the dominant interests in personality* (1st ed.). Boston: Houghton Mifflin, 1931. (With G. Lindzey: 2nd ed., 1951; 3rd ed., 1970)

American Psychological Association, Committee on Psychological Tests. Technical recommendations for psychological tests and diagnostic techniques. *Psychological Bulletin Supplement,* 1954, *51,* 1–38. (2nd ed., 1966; 3rd ed., 1977)

Ansbacher, H. L. Murray's and Simoneit's (German military) methods of personality study. *Journal of Abnormal and Social Psychology,* 1941, *36,* 589–592.

Ash, P., & Kroeker, L. P. Personnel selection, classification, and placement. *Annual Review of Psychology,* 1975, *26,* 481–507.

Barton, E. M., Plemons, J. K., Willis, S. L., & Baltes, P. B. Recent findings on adults and gerontological intelligence: Changing stereotypes of decline. *American Behavioral Scientist,* 1975, *19,* 224–236.

Bayley, N. On the growth of intelligence. *American Psychologist,* 1955, *20,* 805–818.

Bernreuter, R. G. *Manual for the personality inventory.* Stanford: Stanford University Press, 1931.

Binet, A. Le dévelopment de l'intelligence chez les enfants. *L'Année Psychologique,* 1908, *14,* 1–94.

Binet, A. Nouvelles recherches sur la mesure du niveau intellectuel chez les enfants d'école. *L'Année Psychologique,* 1911, *17,* 165–210.

Binet, A., & Simon, T. Méthodes nouvelles pour le diagnostic du niveau intellectuel des abnormaux. *L'Année Psychologique,* 1905, *11,* 191–244.

Block, J. *Lives through time.* Berkeley, Ca: Bancroft, 1971.

Block, N. J., & Dworkin, G. (Eds.) *The IQ controversy: Critical readings.* New York: Random House, 1976.

Brayfield, A. H. (Ed.) Special issue: Testing and public policy. *American Psychologist,* 1965, *20,* 857–1005.

Brigham, C. C. *A study in American intelligence.* Princeton, NJ: Princeton University Press, 1923.

Brigham, C. C. Intelligence tests of immigrant groups. *Psychological Review,* 1930, *37,* 158–165.

Buros, O. K. (Ed.) *Educational, psychological and personality tests of 1933, 1934 and 1935.* New Brunswick, N.J.: Rutgers University Press, 1936.

Buros, O. K. (Ed.) *The eighth mental measurement yearbook.* Highland Park, N.J.: The Institute of Mental Measurement, 1978.

Burt, C. *The factors of the mind.* London: University of London Press, 1940.

Butcher, J. N. (Ed.) *MMPI: Research developments and clinical applications.* New York: McGraw-Hill, 1969.

Butcher, J. N., & Pancheri, P. *A handbook of cross-national MMPI research.* Minneapolis: University of Minnesota Press, 1976.

Campbell, D. P. *Handbook for the Strong Vocational Interest Blank.* Stanford: Stanford University Press, 1971.

Cattell, J. McK. Mental tests and measurements. *Mind,* 1890, *15,* 373–381.

Cattell, R. B. *Abilities: their structure, growth and action.* Boston: Houghton Mifflin, 1971.

Cattell, R. B., Eber, H. W., & Tatsuoka, M. N. *Handbook for the 16PF Test.* Champaign, Ill.: Institute for Personality & Ability Testing, 1970.

Cohen, B. M., Moses, J. L., & Byham, W. C. *The validity of assessment centers: A literature review.* Monograph II. Pittsburgh: Development Dimensions, 1974.

Cohen, D. *J. B. Watson, the founder of behaviorism: A biography.* London: Routledge & Kegan Paul, 1979.

Cronbach, L. J. Statistical methods applied to Rorschach scores: A review. *Psychological Bulletin,* 1949, *40,* 393–429.

Cronbach, L. J., & Drenth, P. J. D. (Eds.) *Mental tests and cultural adaptation.* The Hague: Mouton, 1972.

Cronbach, L. J., & Gleser, G. C. *Psychological tests and personnel decisions.* (2nd ed.) Urbana: University of Illinois Press, 1965.

Dahlstrom, W. G., & Dahlstrom, L. E. (Eds.) *Basic readings on the MMPI: A new selection on personality measurement.* Minneapolis: University of Minnesota Press, 1980.

Dahlstrom, W. G., Welsh, G. S., & Dahlstrom, L. E. *An MMPI handbook.* Volumes I & II. Minneapolis: University of Minnesota Press, 1972, 1975.

Doyle, K. O. Theory and practice of ability testing in ancient Greece. *Journal of the History of the Behavioral Sciences,* 1974, *10,* 202–212.

DuBois, P. H. (Ed.) *Army Air Force Aviation Psychology Program. Research Reports: No. 2. The Classification Program.* Washington, D.C.: United States Government Printing Office, 1947.

DuBois, P. H. A test-dominated society: China, 1115 BC—1905 AD. In L. J. Barnette (Ed.), *Readings in psychological tests and measurements.* Homewood, Ill.: Dorsey, 1968.

Ebbinghaus, H. Über eine neue Methode zur Prüfung geistiger Fähigkeiten und ihre Awendung bei Schulkindern. *Zeitschrift für angewandte Psychologie,* 1897, *13,* 401–459. (Reprinted in part in

R. J. Herrnstein, & E. G. Boring (Eds.), *A source book in the history of psychology.* Cambridge: Harvard University Press, 1966.)

Ellenberger, H. F. The life and work of Hermann Rorschach. *Bulletin of the Menninger Clinic,* 1954, *18,* 173–219.

ETS Staff. *Test scores and family income: a response to charges in the Nader/Nairn report on ETS.* Princeton, N.J.: Educational Testing Service, 1980. (a)

ETS Staff. *Test use and validity: a response to charges in the Nader/Nairn report on ETS.* Princeton, N.J.: Educational Testing Service, 1980. (b)

Exner, J. E. *The Rorschach: a comprehensive system.* Volumes I & II. New York: Wiley, 1974, 1978.

Eysenck, H. J. *The IQ argument: race, intelligence, and education.* La Salle, Ill.: Open Court, 1971.

Findley, W. G. (Ed.) *The impact and improvement of school testing programs* (Sixty-second Yearbook of the National Society for the Study of Education). Chicago: University of Chicago Press, 1963.

Forrest, D. W. *Francis Galton: the life and work of a Victorian genius.* London: Elek, 1974.

Goddard, H. H. Four hundred feeble-minded children classified by the Binet method. *Pedagogical Seminary,* 1910, *17,* 387–397. (a)

Goddard, H. H. A measuring scale of intelligence. *The Training School,* 1910, *6,* 146–155. (b)

Goodenough, F. L. *Measurement of intelligence by drawings.* Yonkers, N.Y.: World, 1926.

Goodenough, F. L. *Mental testing: its history, principles, and applications.* New York: Rinehart, 1949.

Goodenough, F. L., Maurer, K. M., & Van Wagenen, M. J. *Minnesota Preschool Scale.* Minneapolis: Educational Test Bureau, 1932.

Gough, H. G. Clinical versus statistical prediction in psychology. In L. Postman (Ed.), *Psychology in the making: histories of selected research problems.* New York: Knopf, 1962.

Guilford, J. P. In E. G. Boring & G. Lindzey (Eds.), *A history of psychology in autobiography.* Volume V. New York: Appleton-Century-Crofts, 1967. (a)

Guilford, J. P. *The nature of human intelligence.* New York: McGraw-Hill, 1967. (b)

Hall, G. S. The contents of children's minds. *Pedagogical Seminary,* 1891, *1,* 139–173.

Haller, J. S. *Outcasts from evolution: scientific attitudes of racial inferiority, 1859–1900.* Urbana: University of Illinois Press, 1971.

Hathaway, S. R. The personality inventory as an aid in the diagnosis of psychopathic inferiors. *Journal of Consulting Psychology,* 1939, *3,* 112–117.

Hathaway, S. R. Through psychology: my way. In T. S. Krawiec (Ed.), *The psychologists,* Volume III. Brandon, Vt.: Clinical Psychology Publishing Co., 1978.

Hathaway, S. R., & McKinley, J. C. A multiphasic personality schedule (Minnesota): I. Construction of the schedule. *Journal of Psychology,* 1940, *10,* 249–254. (Reprinted in W. G. Dahlstrom & L. E. Dahlstrom (Eds.), *Basic readings on the MMPI.* Minneapolis: University of Minnesota Press, 1980)

Hathaway, S. R., & McKinley, J. C. *The Minnesota Multiphasic Personality Schedule.* Minneapolis: University of Minnesota Press, 1942.

Healy, W., & Fernald, G. Tests for practical mental classification. *Psychological Monographs,* 1911, No. 2.

Hearnshaw, L. S. *Cyril Burt, psychologist.* Ithaca, N.Y.: Cornell University Press, 1979.

Hollingworth, H. L. *The psychology of functional neuroses.* New York: Appleton, 1920.

Jackson, D. N. *Personality Research Form manual.* Goshen, N.Y.: Research Psychologists Press, 1965.

Jensen, A. R. What is the question? What is the evidence? In T. S. Krawiec (Ed.), *The psychologists.* Volume II. New York: Oxford University Press, 1974.

Jensen, A. R. Sir Cyril Burt in perspective. *American Psychologist*, 1978, *33*, 499–503.

Jensen, A. R. *Bias in mental testing.* New York: Free Press, 1980.

Jonçich, G. *The sane positivist: a biography of Edward L. Thorndike.* Middletown, Ct.: Wesleyan University Press, 1968.

Jones, H. E. *Development in adolescence: approaches to the study of the individual.* New York: Appleton-Century, 1943.

Jung, C. G. The association method. *American Journal of Psychology*, 1910, *21*, 219–269.

Kamin, L. J. *The science and politics of I.Q.* Hillsdale, N.J.: Lawrence Erlbaum Associates, 1974.

Kelley, T. L. *Crossroads in the mind of man: a study of differential mental abilities.* Stanford: Stanford University Press, 1928.

Kent, G. H., & Rosanoff, A. The study of association in insanity. *American Journal of Insanity*, 1910, *67*, 317–390.

Kevles, D. J. Testing the Army's intelligence: psychologists and the military in World War I. *Journal of American History*, 1968, *55*, 565–581.

Klopfer, W. G. A short history of projective techniques. *Journal of the History of the Behavioral Sciences*, 1973, *9*, 60–65.

Knox, H. A. A scale, based on the work at Ellis Island, for estimating mental defect. *Journal of the American Medical Association*, 1914, *62*, 741–747.

Kuder, G. F. *Kuder preference record.* Chicago: Science Research Associates, 1934.

Landis, C., Zubin, J., & Katz, S. E. Empirical evaluation of three personality adjustment inventories. *Journal of Educational Psychology*, 1935, *26*, 321–330.

Linden, J. D., & Linden, K. W. *Tests on trial.* Boston: Houghton Mifflin, 1968.

Louttit, C. M. *Clinical psychology: a handbook of children's behavior problems.* New York: Harpers, 1936.

Macfarlane, J. W. Studies in child guidance. I. Methodology for data collection and organization. *Monograph of the Society for Research in Child Development*, 1938, *3*, No. 6.

MacKinnon, D. W. *How assessment centers got started in the United States: the OSS assessment program.* Monograph I. Pittsburgh: Development Dimensions, 1974.

MacKinnon, D. W., & Dukes, W. F. Repression. In L. Postman (Ed.), *Psychology in the making: histories of selected research problems.* New York: Knopf, 1962.

Matarazzo, J. D. *Wechsler's measurement and appraisal of adult intelligence.* (5th ed.) Baltimore: Williams & Wilkins, 1972.

Messick, S. Test validity and the ethics of assessment. *American Psychologist*, 1980, *35*, 1012–1027.

Miller, W. S. *Miller Analogies Test.* New York: The Psychological Corporation, 1944. (Form G, 1947)

Morgan, C. C., & Murray, H. A. A method for investigating fantasies: the Thematic Appperception Test. *Archives of Neurology and Psychiatry*, 1935, *34*, 289–306.

Murray, H. A. et al. *Explorations in personality: a clinical and experimental study of fifty men of college age.* New York: Oxford University Press, 1938.

Murray, H. A. In E. G. Boring & G. Lindzey (Eds.), *A history of psychology in autobiography.* Volume V. New York: Appleton-Century-Crofts, 1967.

Murray, H. A., MacKinnon, D. W., Miller, J. G., Fiske, D. W., & Hanfmann, E. *Assessment of men: selection of personnel for the Office of Strategic Services.* New York: Rinehart, 1948.

Nairn, A. *The reign of ETS: the corporation that makes up minds.* Learning Research Project (Ralph Nader Reports), Washington, D.C., 1980.

Norsworthy, N. The psychology of mentally deficient children. *Archives of Psychology*, 1906, No. 1.

Otis, A. S. *Otis Self-Administering Tests of Mental Ability.* Yonkers, N.Y.: World, 1922.

Paterson, D. G. *Physique and intellect.* New York: Century, 1930.

Payne, A. F. *Sentence completions.* New York: New York Guidance Center, 1928.

Peterson, J. *Early conceptions and tests of intelligence.* Yonkers, N.Y.: World, 1926.

Pintner, R., & Paterson, D. G. The Binet scale and the deaf child. *Journal of Educational Psychology,* 1915, *6,* 20–210.

Pintner, R., & Paterson, D. G. *A Scale of Performance Tests.* New York: Appleton, 1917.

Poffenberger, A. T. (Ed.) *James McKeen Cattell: a man of science.* Volume I: *Psychological research.* Lancaster, Pa: Science Press, 1947.

Pollack, R. H. Binet on perceptual-cognitive development, or Piaget-come-lately. *Journal of the History of the Behavioral Sciences,* 1971, *7,* 370–374.

Porteus, S. D. Mental tests for feebleminded: a new series. *Journal of Psycho-asthenics,* 1915, *19,* 200–213.

Porteus, S. D. *The practice of clinical psychology.* New York: American Book Company, 1941.

Porteus, S. D. *A psychologist of sorts: the autobiography and publications of the inventor of the Porteus Maze Tests.* Palo Alto, Ca.: Pacific Books, 1969.

Rapaport, D., Gill, M., & Schafer, R. *Diagnostic psychological testing: the theory, statistical evaluation, and diagnostic application of a battery of tests.* Volumes I & II. Chicago: Yearbook, 1946.

Reisman, J. M. *The development of clinical psychology.* New York: Appleton-Century-Crofts, 1966.

Reynolds, W. M., & Sundberg, N. D. Recent research trends in testing. *Journal of Personality Assessment,* 1976, *40,* 228–233.

Rice, J. M. *The public school system in the United States.* New York: Century, 1893.

Riegel, K. F. (Ed.) *Intelligence: alternative views of a paradigm.* Basel: Karger, 1973.

Rorschach, H. *Psychodiagnostik.* Berne: Birchen, 1921.

Samelson, F. World War I intelligence testing and the development of psychology. *Journal of the History of the Behavioral Sciences,* 1977, *13,* 274–282.

Seagoe, M. V. *Terman and the gifted.* Los Altos, Ca.: William Kaufman, 1975.

Spearman, C. The proof and measurement of association between two things. *American Journal of Psychology,* 1904, *15,* 72–101. (Reprinted in J. J. Jenkins & D. G. Paterson (Eds.), *Studies in individual differences: the search for intelligence.* New York: Appleton-Century-Crofts, 1961.) (a)

Spearman, C. General intelligence objectively determined and measured. *American Journal of Psychology,* 1904, *15,* 201–293. (Reprinted in J. J. Jenkins & D. G. Paterson (Eds.), *Studies in individual differences: the search for intelligence.* New York: Appleton-Century-Crofts, 1961.) (b)

Spearman, C. *The abilities of man.* London: Macmillan, 1927.

Strong, E. K. A vocational interest test. *The Educational Record,* 1927, *8,* 107–121.

Strong, E. K. *Vocational interests of men and women.* Stanford: Stanford University Press, 1943.

Stuit, D. B. (Ed.) *Personnel research and test development in the Bureau of Naval Personnel.* Princeton, N.J.: Princeton University Press, 1947.

Terman, L. M. *The measurement of intelligence: an explanation of and a complete guide for the use of the Stanford revision and extension of the Binet-Simon Intelligence Scale.* Boston: Houghton Mifflin, 1916.

Terman, L. M. Expert testimony in the case of Alberto Flores. *The Journal of Delinquency.* 1918, *3,* 145–164.

Terman, L. M. *Genetic studies of genius.* Volume I. *Mental and physical traits of a thousand gifted children.* Stanford: Stanford University Press, 1925.

Terman, L. M., & Merrill, M. A. *Measuring intelligence.* Boston: Houghton Mifflin, 1937.

Terman, L. M., & Merrill, M. A. *Stanford-Binet Intelligence Scale.* Boston: Houghton Mifflin, 1960.

Terman, L. M., & Merrill, M. A. *Stanford-Binet Intelligence Scale: 1972 norms.* Boston: Houghton Mifflin, 1972.

Terman, L. M., & Miles, C. C. *Sex and personality: studies in masculinity and femininity.* New York: McGraw-Hill, 1936.

Thomson, G. H. *The factorial analysis of human ability.* Boston: Houghton Mifflin, 1939.

Thorndike, E. L. *An introduction to the theory of mental and social measurements.* New York: Science Press, 1904.

Thorndike, E. L. *The measurement of intelligence.* New York: Bureau of Publications, Teachers College, Columbia University, 1926.

Thorndike, E. L. Charles Edward Spearman, 1863–1945. *American Journal of Psychology,* 1945, *58,* 558–560.

Thurstone, L. L. *Psychological Examination for High School Graduates and College Freshmen.* Washington, D.C.: American Council on Education, 1925.

Thurstone, L. L. The mental age concept. *Psychological Review,* 1926, *33,* 268–278.

Thurstone, L. L. *The theory of multiple factors.* Chicago: University of Chicago Press, 1933.

Toops, H. A. *Ohio State University Psychological Test.* Columbus: Ohio State University Press, 1919.

Tuddenham, R. D. The nature and measurement of intelligence. In L. Postman (Ed.), *Psychology in the making: Histories of selected research problems.* New York: Knopf, 1962.

Turnbull, W. W. Relevance in testing. *Science,* 1968, *160,* 1424–1429.

Valett, R. E. *A profile for the Stanford-Binet (L-M).* Palo Alto, Ca: Consulting Psychologists Press, 1965.

Vernon, P. E. *Intelligence and cultural environment.* London: Methuen, 1969.

Vernon, P. E., & Parry, J. B. *Personnel selection in the British forces.* London: University of London Press, 1949.

Voyat, G. The real world of Alfred Binet. In K. F. Riegel & J. A. Meacham (Eds.), *The developing individual in a changing world.* Volume I. *Historical and cultural issues.* Chicago: Aldine, 1976.

Wechsler, D. *The measurement of adult intelligence.* Baltimore: Williams & Wilkins, 1939.

Wechsler, D. The IQ is an intelligent test. *New York Times,* June 26, 1966. (Reprinted in D. Wechsler, *Selected papers of David Wechsler.* New York: Academic Press, 1975.)

Whipple, G. M. *Manual of mental and physical tests.* Part I: *Simpler processes.* Part II. *Complex processes.* Baltimore: Warwick & York, 1914, 1915.

Whipple, G. M. (Ed.) *Nature and nurture:* Part I: *Their influence upon intelligence.* (Twenty-seventh Yearbook of the National Society for the Study of Education.) Bloomington, Ill.: Public School Publishing Co., 1928.

Whipple, G. M. (Ed.) *Intelligence: Its nature and nurture.* Part II: *Original studies and experiments.* (Thirty-ninth Yearbook of the National Society for the Study of Education.) Bloomington, Ill.: Public School Publishing Co., 1940.

Whitty, P. A., & Jenkins, M. D. The case of B—: A gifted Negro child. *Journal of Social Psychology,* 1935, *6,* 117–124.

Wissler, C. The correlation of mental and physical traits. *Psychological Monographs,* 1901, No. 6.

Wolf, T. H. The emergence of Binet's conception and measurement of intelligence: A case history of creative process. *Journal of the History of the Behavioral Sciences,* 1969, *5,* 113–134; 207–237.

Wolf, T. H. *Alfred Binet.* Chicago: University of Chicago Press, 1973.

Wood, D. A. *Louis Leon Thurstone: Creative thinker, dedicated teacher, eminent psychologist.* Princeton, N.J.: Educational Testing Service, 1962.

Woodworth, R. S. Examination of emotional fitness for warfare. *Psychological Bulletin,* 1919, *16,* 59–60.

Woodworth, R. S. James McKeen Cattell: 1860–1944. *Psychological Review,* 1944, *51,* 201–209.

Woodworth, R. S., & Wells, F. L. Association tests. *Psychological Monographs,* 1911, *13,* No. 37.

Wright, L. *Bibliography on human intelligence: An extensive bibliography.* Public Health Service Publication No. 1839. Washington, D.C.: United States Government Printing Office, 1968.

Yerkes, R. M. (Ed.) Psychological examining in the United States Army. *Memoirs of the National Academy of Sciences*, 1921, *15*, 1–890.

Yerkes, R. M., Bridges, J. W., & Hardwick, R. S. *A Point Scale for Measuring Mental Ability*. Baltimore: Warwick & York, 1915.

Zubin, J., Eron, L. D., & Schumer, F. *An experimental approach to projective techniques*. New York: Wiley, 1965.

4

Developmental Psychology

Thomas J. Berndt
Edward F. Zigler
Yale University

The history of developmental psychology goes back nearly a century, to the early 1880s. During this time the field has gone through periods of rapid growth and apparent stagnation, but progress has been made in the specification and solution of the two central theoretical problems of developmental psychology—the description and the explanation of development. Progress has also come through the extension of developmental research to all aspects of psychological functioning, from perception and cognition to personality and social behavior. In their choice of areas of study, developmental psychologists have sometimes been influenced by theoretical viewpoints, but at other times they have been motivated by a concern with pressing social problems of their day. In this chapter we attempt to describe the history of the field from 1880 to 1970. We will consider the theories and the topics of research that were most prominent during different periods, and note those cases when research was focused on important social issues.

During its history developmental psychology has been affected by research in other scientific disciplines, by the major currents in Western intellectual history, and by social trends in the care and treatment of children. These various strands of influence on the field cannot be fully treated in this chapter, but useful information can be found in other sources.

The links between developmental psychology and other social sciences are discussed in Zigler and Child (1973) and Sears (1975). Sears (1975) also comments on the field's relations to the practical professions of education, medicine,

The authors wish to thank William Kessen for his thoughtful and detailed comments on an earlier version of this chapter.

and social work. Senn (1975) provides a brief history of the ties, or lack of them, between developmental psychology, pediatrics, and child psychiatry. There is little information about the history of relations to biology and comparative psychology, perhaps because developmental psychologists have not thought of themselves as separate from those disciplines. The topics of physical and physiological development and genetic influences on behavior have been central to the field since its beginning. This is evident in the fact that the first part of the classic *Manual of Child Psychology* (Mussen, 1970) is titled "Biological Bases of Development." Similarly, in the earliest writings on child psychology (see Kessen, 1965) and in very recent ones, attention has been paid to similarities and differences between the development of the human child and that of the young of other species.

Besides these contemporary influences from other disciplines, the history of child psychology has been affected by the great amount of philosophical writing on the child that preceded the birth of developmental psychology as a scientific field of study. Excellent selections of writings from this tradition and commentaries on them are available (Grinder, 1967; Kessen, 1965). A brief account of the informal and semi-systematic observations of children published in the eighteenth and nineteenth centuries also exists (Dennis, 1949).

The final omission from our history is the wealth of recent writing on the history of childhood itself, which describes historical changes in popular conceptions of the child and in the treatment of children by parents, educators, and government officials (Aries, 1962; Borstelmann, 1977; Bremner, Barnard, Hareven, & Mennel, 1970–1974; deMause, 1974). There is also documentation of changes in the popular advice on childrearing given to parents over the years (e.g., Stendler, 1950; Wolfenstein, 1953).

Examination of the great amount of material just mentioned could allow some future historian to better explain historical changes in the field of developmental psychology, and also document the impact of developmental psychology on other fields and the society at large. Though our goal of describing theory and research in developmental psychology is more limited, it is a necessary part of the larger task.

DEVELOPMENTAL PSYCHOLOGY: DEFINITION AND ISSUES

The field that today is called developmental psychology has gone under other names. At the beginning it was commonly known as "child psychology." This label accurately reflects an early concentration on the child per se, rather than on changes with age from infancy through childhood and adulthood. A shift to the designation of the field as "child development" can be rather arbitrarily set at 1934, the data of the founding of the Society for Research in Child Development.

This name indicates a heightened interest in developmental processes, but a continued emphasis on the child. The change to the label "developmental psychology" can again be rather arbitrarily set at 1954, when Division 7 of the American Psychological Association was renamed the Division of Developmental Psychology. The new label represents an implicit broadening of the field to include human development through the life span as well as the development of other species, but also a narrower focus on exclusively psychological phenomena.

The newer labels, child development and developmental psychology, can occasionally be found in early writings in the field. Moreover, an examination of the titles of major journals in the field will establish that the name "child psychology" has not been entirely abandoned. However, the concept of development is certainly crucial to the present definition, and many different types of evidence show that it has become more important to the field as the years have passed.

But what is development? Many papers and at least one entire book (Harris, 1957) have been devoted to this question. One definition describes a change as developmental "if it can be related to age in an orderly or lawful way" (Kessen, 1960, p. 36). Other writers argue that such a definition is too inclusive. For example, Wohlwill (1970, p. 52) states that age changes should be regarded as developmental only if the changes "are uniform and consistent across a wide range of individuals and environmental conditions." In other words, age changes that are a function of specific experiences, for example growing up in one culture rather than another, would not be considered developmental changes. Such a definition appears overly restrictive, because many age changes are likely to reflect the combined effects of specific experiences and the endogenous factor usually called **maturation.** Wohlwill appears to argue that developmental psychology should be concerned only with phenomena that are primarily a function of maturation.

However, there is an element of truth in Wohlwill's position. Most developmental psychologists would agree that a truly developmental phenomenon involves some influence of maturation (or another biological process—aging). Age changes that solely reflect learning would not be called developmental changes. In other words, developmental psychologists are concerned with age changes that are a function of maturation alone, maturation plus learning, or an interaction of the two (Bijou, 1968). The same factors have been labeled in different ways, as nature versus nurture, or heredity versus environment. The specific phrasing is sometimes important, but it is more significant that this definition of development refers directly to the explanation of age changes. In deriving the definition, we have made the assumption that age changes may be attributed to learning, maturation, or their combined effects.

In other definitions of development the underlying theoretical issue seems to be the description of developmental changes. Several writers (e.g., Kohlberg,

1969; Zigler, 1963) have suggested that developmental changes are those which affect the structure or pattern of a child's responses, rather than changing the strength, frequency, or other quantitative features of the response. These definitions tie the notion of developmental changes to that of developmental stages, for a stage commonly refers to an integrated structure or pattern of responding at a particular age. Stage theories have been questioned, however, by those who argue that age changes are merely quantitative or matters of degree.

In summary, the discussion of definitions has led us to two central issues in developmental psychology. The first is the explanation of age changes, and the possible factors are maturation, learning, or some combination of the two. The second is the description of age changes, and the alternatives are that the changes are only a matter of degree, or that they are transitions to new stages or modes of behavior. While the issues apply to all aspects of psychological development, the answers that are appropriate in different cases are likely to be different. Appreciation of this fact has increased during the history of the field. Nonetheless, vigorous debates have been waged over the description and explanation of development in specific instances.

THE EARLY YEARS OF CHILD PSYCHOLOGY: 1880–1910

The birth of child psychology is often dated at the publication of *The Mind of the Child* by Wilhelm Preyer in 1882. Preyer was a Professor of Physiology at Jena in Germany who turned to the study of the child in order "to arrive at an explanation of the origin of the separate vital processes" (1882/1888, p. ix). The book was what became known as a "baby biography," an account of the author's observations of his own son from birth to age three. Preyer's was not the first baby biography (see Dennis, 1949), but it was distinguished by its comprehensiveness and the systematic character of the observations.

Preyer began his book with a presentation of the sensory capabilities of his son from birth on. He described the development of vision, hearing, feeling, taste, smell, and the emotions of pleasure and discomfort. He compared his observations with those of earlier baby biographies and with information on young animals. He also described the development of will, under which he included the transition from reflex to voluntary movements, the development of imitation, and changes in expressive movements such as smiling and laughing. Finally, he discussed the existence of thinking before language, the development of children's speech as compared with speech disturbances in adults, and the development of the sense of self.

In most of the book, observations were recounted with little attempt to provide a theoretical explanation for them. For example, he referred to the fact that the child at $2\frac{1}{2}$ years confounded "too much" and "too little," saying the former when he meant the latter (1882/1888, p. 173). Preyer did not try to explain the confusion, merely noting that the child also confused different numbers such as "5" and "2." However, in the section on will, Preyer (pp. 241–257) presented a long series of observations on the development of grasping, of which the following are typical:

> In the forty-third week the child without help not only grasps properly with both hands at a nursing-bottle, but carries it correctly to the mouth; the same with a biscuit lying before him. He pulls strongly at the beard of a face that he can reach.
> On the other hand, he grasped at the flame of the lamp in the forty-fifth week; in the forty-seventh, and later, at objects separated from him by a pane of glass, as if they were attainable, and that persistently, with attention and eagerness, as if the pane were not there. (p. 252)

Then Preyer proposed an explanation for these developments, saying that the stimulus that elicits reaching must be repeated often, and the arm movement repeated often, before the ideas of the object and of the movement come to consciousness as representations of the sensations associated with the stimulus and with the movement. When the two representations are aroused in close succession, they are united, "which calls into life the will" (p. 254).

Along with his specific theory of the development of will, Preyer had a general theory of development which included the notions of heredity and learning. Preyer was familiar with Darwin's work and accepted the notion of heredity. He was also well aware of the associationist psychology of his time, and thus sensitive to the impact of learning. However, Preyer tended to attribute all age changes to learning, as if he did not understand or accept a concept of maturation. In other words, he called hereditary what the child possesses at birth, and explained responses that appeared later in terms of learning. It is probably unjustified to make too much of this point, since Preyer did not try to explain all age changes; but it suggests that psychologists only gradually formulated the presently accepted notions of the explanation of development.

While Preyer's book set a standard and a model for many similar works done in succeeding decades, baby biographies fell into disfavor in later years. Researchers worried about the possibilities of biased observation, since the children studied were often the author's own. But other factors were probably more important. The number of children observed was always small and the observations themselves were unstandardized. As a result, making comparisons between different sets of observations was difficult. When inconsistencies were found, they might be due to simple omission by one observer, differences in rate of development of different children, or something else, and there was no way of telling which explanation was correct. Furthermore, methods of standardized testing were developed later, and they seemed to provide more reliable results. Finally, as the field progressed researchers wanted detailed observations of specific aspects of development. Important examples of the new model for naturalistic observation are Piaget's (e.g., 1952) studies of sensorimotor intelligence, Brown's (1973) work on language development, and ethological studies of preschool children's social behavior (Jones, 1972).

In 1883, one year after the publication of Preyer's book, G. Stanley Hall published an article on "The Content of Children's Minds." Hall later founded the *Pedagogical Seminary* (now the *Journal of Genetic Psychology*), which was a major outlet for papers on child psychology. While President of Clark University, he was one of the forces in the development of the child study movement, which attempted to transmit the findings of research on children to parents and educators. For all these reasons, Hall is the recognized founder of child psychology in the United States. And yet his influence on the field was rather weak and short-lived.

Many separate reasons for his quick disappearance from the journals and textbooks can be mentioned, but the overall problem seemed to be Hall's style of working, which was entirely out of keeping with the new scientific psychology. First of all, he did not pick a single topic and pursue it in a series of investigations. He studied any and all topics, from sex to religion to children's dolls, and did a little with each. Second, he did not confine himself to the results of psychological research. He ranged widely through anthropology, history, and biology for ideas, and his papers were filled with comments on these fields. Unfortunately, these comments were often irrelevant to his actual research. Finally, and probably most importantly, the research procedure on which he most heavily relied was the use of questionnaires which were administered by teachers in an entirely unstandardized way to groups of children whose characteristics were unknown. In many cases even the ages of the children who responded were not reported.

A typical example of Hall's work is a paper entitled "The Cat and the Child" (Hall & Browne, 1904). Questionnaires including a set of 12 topics were distributed to large numbers of children. The paper dealt with the answers of 2835 children who had pet cats. The questions themselves were often suggestive, and the answers may reveal more about children's response to suggestion than their actual attitudes toward their pets. For example, Hall asked if the cat "was ever sorry, happy, cross" and "Does it (a) scold, (b) swear, (c) pity, (d) run away, (e) fight" (p. 8). As could be expected, many of the children attempted to provide instances of these things. Hall then concluded that the children were displaying anthropomorphic tendencies.

Hall also quoted extensively from anthropological and historical data to show that the child's response to the cat was that prevalent at earlier periods in the history of the human species. That is, he attempted to provide evidence for the *theory of recapitulation,* which asserts that the development of the individual repeats the stages in the development of the species ("ontogeny recapitulates phylogeny"). For example, he noted that the children were sensitive to very slight movements and actions of their cats and speculated that this power ''was one of the prime survival factors of our anthropoid ancestors'' (p. 13). When faced with the problem that few of the children indicated any of the suspicion and distrust of cats that is frequently noted in folklore, Hall speculated that primitive man must have feared the great cats but also admired ''their lithe forms and graceful motions, the beauty and sleekness of their skins and the fire of their gleaming eyes'' (p. 22).

The carelessness of Hall's methods and the amount of unsupported and far-fetched speculation in his papers were totally unacceptable to later American psychologists, and Hall's reputation quickly declined (McCullers, 1969; Ross, 1972).

A third psychologist of the period, James Mark Baldwin, focused on theoretical explanations of development. Baldwin came to psychology from philosophy, but he retained a greater interest in ideas than empirical research. His major work (Baldwin, 1895) was an attempt to explain the development of thought in terms of the opposing tendencies of *assimilation* and *accommodation*. Assimilation was a new term for habit. The notion of accommodation was novel because it referred to an intrinsic tendency toward adaptive behavior which led to new accomplishments or inventions. Previously, psychologists had attributed inventions to simple trial and error. However, Baldwin's language was difficult, and psychologists of the time had little interest in largely theoretical speculation. Though many of his ideas were accepted and further extended by Piaget (1952), Baldwin did not have much influence on American psychologists.

The overall picture of child psychology from 1880 to 1910 was one of fragmentation and immaturity. In the explanation of developmental changes, Preyer and others stressed the role of learning and gave little consideration to maturation. On the other hand, Hall and his co-workers explained age changes by using a notion of recapitulation. The modern conception of maturation emerged only after the rejection of recapitulation theory (Grinder, 1967). In the description of age changes, the idea of an orderly sequence that was invariant despite variations in rate of development was accepted by Preyer, and the idea of stages which succeeded one another was part of Hall's recapitulation theory. However, in neither case was attention given to the fundamental characteristic of current stage concepts, the notion that the different responses present at a given stage are structurally related.

On the more practical side, child psychology during the period had little to offer the parent or educator. Preyer commented occasionally on the implications of his observations for educational practice and parents' treatment of children, but he usually had no firm basis for his recommendations. Hall believed that his theoretical and empirical writings provided a foundation for advice to parents on disciplinary techniques and advice to educators on the appropriate curriculum for children of different ages. However, his ideas were often out of step with the mood of the times, and psychologists critical of his scientific writings also criticized his pronouncements to parents and educators (Ross, 1972).

MEASUREMENT AND CONFLICTING THEORIES: 1910–1930

During the early decades of the century child psychology remained dominated by a few individuals, but a number of large-scale research studies were also done. Substantial gains were made in the development of theory and the precision of measurement.

The first major achievement during the period was the formulation of the intelligence test by Binet and Simon (1905) in France, and its extension and adaptation to America by Terman (1916). Binet and Simon set themselves the practical problem of distinguishing between normal and subnormal intelligence so that children could be appropriately placed either in regular public schools or in special schools. They deplored the subjective methods for judging intelligence that had been used in the past, citing the lack of comparability among different judges and the possibilities of bias due to factors unrelated to intelligence. To secure a more objective measure, they devised a series of short and simple tests. For example, they asked children for the definition of words or asked them to complete a sentence with an appropriate word (e.g., "The weather is clear, the sky is *blue*."). Binet and Simon first gave each test to a large number of normal children. The age at which roughly 75% of normal children passed a test defined the **mental age** required by the test. Children were considered subnormal if their mental age, as determined from the entire series of tests, was markedly below their chronological age.

Terman (1916) translated the Binet-Simon tests, adpated them for use in America, and added other items. He also suggested that the most meaningful measure of intelligence was the **intelligence quotient** or IQ, the ratio of mental age to chronological age. Since Terman worked at Stanford, his new test was labeled the Stanford-Binet. As Binet and Simon had hoped, the intelligence tests were quick and easy to administer, and they provided a measure that was of reasonable *reliability* and *validity*. Children tested at different times received similar scores, suggesting that a stable feature of their functioning was being measured. Children who did well on the tests also did well in school, suggesting that the tests did measure intellectual ability.

Intelligence tests have been criticized throughout their history. An early criticism was that the tests did not contribute to an understanding of intelligence, for they showed only whether a child was right or wrong, not how he or she had arrived at an answer. Possible biases of the tests against certain cultural groups have also been discussed. These criticisms and others became more forceful as time passed (Cronbach, 1975). In this early period, however, psychologists were pleased to have a measure of intellectual performance that proved to have some reliability and validity, and many of their activities involved the creation of new tests to cover a wider age range and the examination of stability in intelligence test scores as age increased.

The method used in developing the intelligence tests, the determination of the normal or average behavior of children at a given age, was soon employed in the study of other aspects of development. A pioneer in this work was Arnold Gesell. Gesell began his observations of infants' and children's behavior at the Yale Clinic for Child Development in 1911, and he continued with the work until his death in 1961. While he stressed many aspects of the development of the child, he is best known for his summaries of physical and motor development.

Gesell often presented his findings by describing the typical behavior at a given age. For example, he described the 9-month-old in the following way:

> *Motor Development.*   (a) Sits alone; (b) Opposes thumb in seizing cube; (c) Makes a locomotive reaction in prone position.
> *Language.*   (a) Says Da-da or equivalent; (b) Listens with selective interest to familiar words.
> *Adaptive Behavior.*   (a) Brings inset block and form board into exploiting relation; (b) Uses string and pulls ring; (c) Gives definite attention to scribbling demonstration.
> *Personal-Social Behavior.*   (a) Cooperates in rhythmic nursery games; (b) Waves bye-bye or performs similar trick; (c) Plays combiningly with cup and cube. (1928, p. 132)

A 9-month-old whose behavior corresponded exactly with the normal pattern was given a **developmental quotient** of 100, which was analogous to an average IQ score.

Gesell used his normative data not only to indicate a child's level at one point in time, but also to chart the course of development in terms of growth curves which represented a child's status relative to the norm at several different points in time. Through the examination of growth curves, Gesell was able to point out various types of irregularities in development. Some children were consistently below the curve of normal development and others were consistently above it. More unusual patterns were sometimes observed, such as early retardation followed by a later return to the norm. Obtaining these data required repeated observation of the same children, or what became known as *longitudinal study*. Determining different patterns of development in different children remains one of the main reasons for longitudinal investigations (Wohlwill, 1973).

Gesell recognized that development, or growth, the term he more commonly used, could be explained either by learning or by maturation. He clearly presented and convincingly defended the importance of maturation in human growth.

However, he also suggested that the influences of learning and environment on growth were relatively minor. He therefore became a spokesman for the maturationist position in American child psychology (Stoltz, 1958).

Gesell's theoretical viewpoint was soon attacked by John B. Watson, who was a founder of behavioristic psychology. Watson asserted that maturation and heredity were of very little importance for the explanation of development. Rather, he claimed that learning alone could account for any individual differences in psychological functioning that were present during childhood or in adulthood.

Watson sought to demonstrate the truth of his position in a series of experimental studies, which were again a contrast to Gesell's observational method. Watson's (1926) best-known research involved the use of classical conditioning procedures to produce fears of specific stimuli in children. For example, he showed that an 11-month-old infant who initially had no fear of a rabbit would begin to fear the rabbit if its presence was associated with the loud banging of a steel bar. He also demonstrated that such fears generalized to other furry objects.

The experiments of Watson and his students did not go very far toward proving the contention that learning is the major factor in psychological development, for only one type of response was investigated, and only very young children were studied. Nonetheless, a major theoretical controversy over the views of Gesell and Watson soon developed. While one might have concluded that maturation was the most important factor in motor development and the other responses which Gesell studied, and learning was the most important factor in the emotional reactions which Watson studied, it is unlikely that either Gesell or Watson would have been happy with such a resolution (Kessen, 1965; White, 1968). Gesell was led by his medical background as well as his observations to stress biological processes rather than experience. Watson, on the other hand, was committed to the experiment as the method for psychology, and committed to a learning theory as the theory for psychology. The difference in the general viewpoints of the two men prevented any rapprochement on the theoretical level.

The testing movement exemplified by the work on intelligence and Gesell's normative studies had one more offshoot during the 1920s. Hugh Hartshorne and Mark May (1928–1930) collaborated on a comprehensive program of research aimed at the measurement of character. The project was sponsored by the Institute for Social and Religious Research, and it was ultimately intended to contribute to the improvement of religious education and other efforts at character development.

Hartshorne and May assumed that character was made up of several distinct components: knowledge of correct behavior, attitudes or motives toward correct behavior, behavior itself, and self-control. They developed a series of tests to tap each component. For example, in one test of moral knowledge, children were asked to choose what they would say "after they had a stupid time at a party." The alternatives were (a) that they had a delightful time; (b) goodbye and nothing more; (c) that they had a very sad time; or (d) that they hoped the hostess wouldn't invite them again (Hartshorne & May, 1930, p. 610). One test of attitudes consisted of asking how the child would feel if a best friend had done something wrong or something very good. The tests of social behavior included items on cheating, cooperation, and self-denial. Tests of self-control measured children's ability to inhibit the tendency to make a wry face on smelling unpleasant odors and their ability to persist on a dull or very confusing task. Many different samples of children were used, but children often received only some of the entire set of tests. During the 5 years of the research program, thousands of children were tested.

The most commonly cited conclusion of the research was that there is no general trait of honesty, for a child's honesty was not highly consistent across situations. A child who cheated on one test was not especially likely to cheat on another, or in statistical terms, there were few strong correlations between the different measures of cheating (see Table 4.1). However, the correlations were almost always positive, and the average correlation was moderate ($r = .23$). Shortly after Hartshorne and May published their data, other writers argued that the general positive correlations were evidence for a trait of honesty (Allport, 1937). A more recent reanalysis of the data suggested the same conclusion (Burton, 1963), but also suggested that the degree of consistency in children's behavior depends on how consistently parents and others define situations as calling for an honest response and how consistently they reinforce honest behavior.

In making a general assessment of the progress of the field during this period, the clear gains in the description and measurement of intelligence, character, and motor development must be weighed against the consequences of theoretical confrontation between maturation and learning theorists. The debate between Gesell and Watson over the roles of maturation and learning in development may be viewed as fruitless, and as hindering the more balanced study of psychological

TABLE 4.1
Intercorrelations of Tests for Cheating in Different Situations

	Copying	Speed	Peeping	Faking	Home	Athletic	Parties	Stealing	Lying
Copying	—	.45	.40	.40	.17	.29	.12	.14	.35
Speed		—	.37	.42	.19	.34	.17	.17	.25
Peeping			—	.30	.23	.10	.25	.20	.11
Faking				—	*	.30	.12	.35	.26
Home					—	.14	−.02	−.01	.40
Athletic						—	.12	.28	.23
Parties							—	.21	.00
Stealing								—	.13

Adapted from Hartshorne and May (1928, Book II, p. 123). Data were unavailable for asterisked entry.

development. On the other hand, the debate may have focused the attention of psychologists on the concept of maturation for the first time. It may also have forced them to recognize that a full understanding of development could only come through the use of both experimental and observational methods to determine the features of development that are primarily influenced by maturation, other features that are primarily influenced by learning, and still others that involve major influences from both factors. The comments of psychologists active in this early period (see Senn, 1975) suggest that the debate did have a largely positive influence, for serious attention to the explanation of development was part of these psychologists' interest in the following decades.

Finally, to an impressive extent the research of the period was done in response to social needs, or was translated into guidelines for parents and educators. By providing a more accurate basis for classifying children, intelligence tests reduced the errors of assigning children of normal intelligence to schools for the retarded and vice versa. Hartshorne and May's investigations were perhaps most important in correcting the erroneous impression that a single instance of cheating could be used as an accurate measure of a child's character. Gesell aimed his early work toward the medical profession, and toward pediatricians in particular. Though they generally ignored him (Senn, 1975), in later periods his norms for behavior were often consulted by parents. Surprisingly, Watson may have had the greatest influence on childrearing practices, for especially after he left academia he directed his writings at parents (Watson, 1928). Watson emphasized a rigid and unsentimental approach to raising children, but neither his own research nor other research of his time gave him a firm basis for the recommendations. In this respect at least, he continued a tradition established in child psychology by G. Stanley Hall.

A GOLDEN AGE IN CHILD DEVELOPMENT: 1930–1940

Child development began as a self-conscious field of science around 1930 (Sears, 1975). As the concern with development became more prominent, the concern with the psychology of the child per se declined. The tremendous vitality of the field during the decade was not, however, a matter of a change in theoretical emphasis. It can be traced directly to a great increase in the funds devoted to child development research.

During the mid- and late-1920s Lawrence Frank acted on behalf of the Laura Spelman Rockefeller Memorial Fund in negotiating with several universities for the initiation or extension of centers for child development research. The Rockefeller funds were to be spent for the benefit of children, as is indicated by the name, Institute of Child Welfare, given to several of the new centers. Including both new and established centers, the funds enhanced developmental research at Yale, Columbia, Western Reserve, and the Universities of Iowa, Minnesota, and

California. At about the same time, the Fels Research Institute was set up in Ohio, and the Merrill-Palmer School was established in Detroit. A dramatic increase in the number of researchers, the size and scope of research studies, and the number of topics studied soon occurred. Bolstered by this growth, the new group of researchers gathered in 1934 to establish their own professional organization, the Society for Research in Child Development. The organization soon took over the publication of two journals, *Child Development* and *Child Development Abstracts and Bibliography,* and started a new one, the *Monographs of the Society for Research in Child Development.*

Much of the research of the 1930s was an extension of the research topics of previous decades. The heredity-environment or learning-maturation issue received special attention. One of the most famous studies of the period was an investigation of the effects of training on the motor development of twins (McGraw, 1935). In some activities Johnny, the trained twin, was more advanced than Jimmy, the control twin. For example, Johnny learned to roller-skate almost as soon as he could walk, and he learned to swim a distance of 15 feet before he was a year and a half old. However, in the more usual aspects of childhood motor development, such as the waning of reflexes and the ability to walk alone, training had little effect. In other cases, such as riding a tricycle, training was unsuccessful for several months, until Johnny's motor coordination had improved. When Jimmy was introduced to the tricycle, he quickly became as good or even better in riding it than his brother. The conclusion from the research was that learning can have an effect on motor skills, but only if the child is at an appropriate developmental level. Stated more succinctly, the effectiveness of learning is dependent on maturation.

Other research suggested modifications in Watson's ideas about the development of emotions. Bridges (1932) studied emotional expression in the first year of life, in part to test Watson's (1926) claim that the newborn showed three distinct emotions: rage, fear, and love. Bridges concluded that the newborn shows only an undifferentiated excitement in response to stimulation, and that emotional expressions become more differentiated during the infant's first 2 years. The research did not show that emotional reactions to specific stimuli are unlearned, nor did Bridges believe this. However, it suggested the importance of maturation even in the development of emotions. Unfortunately, there are methodological problems in the research which make the conclusions uncertain (Kessen, Haith, & Salapatek, 1970). Information on the development of anger, fear, and other emotions during infancy and childhood was also gathered during the 1930s, especially by Arthur Jersild (1946; Jersild & Holmes, 1935).

In research on intellectual development, the effects of heredity and environment (here these terms are more appropriate than learning and maturation) were investigated during this period. The method of twin study devised by Galton was used with the added comparison of twins reared together and apart (Newman, Freeman, & Holzinger, 1937). In other research, an enriched nursery school environment was provided to some orphanage children, and their IQ gains over the year were compared with those of other orphanage children who were not attending nursery school (Skeels, Updegraff, Wellman, & Williams, 1938). Both sets of researchers concluded that important effects of the environment on learning had been demonstrated, but their methods and the conclusions were criticized by later investigators. The question of genetic and environmental factors in intelligence has always been a heated one, and conclusions asserting the predominance of one factor or the other have always been challenged (cf. Cronbach, 1975).

In addition to research on the explanation of physical and mental development, work continued on the description of age changes. A detailed analysis of the more important achievements in infancy was one goal of the research. Shirley (1931) observed 25 infants at frequent intervals during the first 2 years of life and outlined some of the milestones of motor development, from ability to hold the chin up when in a prone position (1 month) to walking alone (15 months; see Fig. 4.1). Halverson (1931) closely examined developmental changes in a special set of skills, those involving reaching and grasping, during the first year of life. He achieved great precision in his descriptions by the use of motion picture recording of infants' behavior. For examle, he noted that 20-week-old children were likely to use a scooping motion and use both hands to surround a cube placed on a table in front of them. When attempting to surround the cube, the infants often accidentally pushed it out of reach. As the infants grew older they integrated the motions of reaching, opening the hand when near the cube, and clasping the hand over the cube into a single smooth movement.

Results also began to appear from large-scale longitudinal studies of mental and language development (Bayley, 1933, 1935). These studies, at the Institute of Child Welfare in California, the Fels Research Institute in Ohio, and other research centers, were begun in the late 1920s. The studies continued as the children grew older, and expanded to include the measurement of social and personality development. In many cases the subject samples were followed into adulthood, and sometimes the children of the original subjects were studied as well. The great return in descriptive information from the studies and the availability of information that cannot be obtained in any other way have made longitudinal study the most prestigious research design in developmental psychology, though not the most commonly used. However, longitudinal studies have been criticized recently for the lack of comparability of their samples to the general population and for the limitation of their findings to the description of development in one cultural period, that in which the children were growing up. The latter criticism acquires special force in a period of rapid cultural change such as the present, but the extent to which it qualifies the interpretation of results from the longitudinal studies in uncertain (Horn & Donaldson, 1976).

New areas of research were also opened during the 1930s. Great advances were made in techniques for unobtrusive and reliable observation of preschool

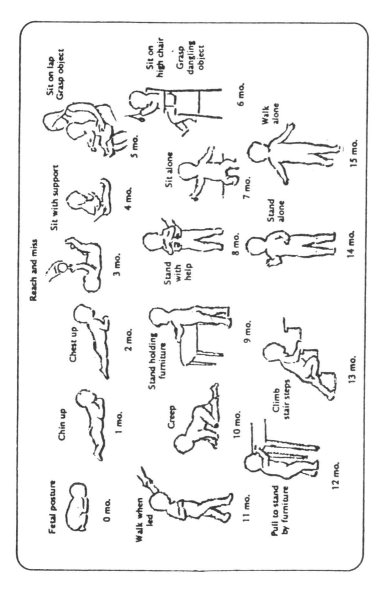

FIG. 4.1. The developmental sequence that leads to walking. (From Shirley, 1931.)

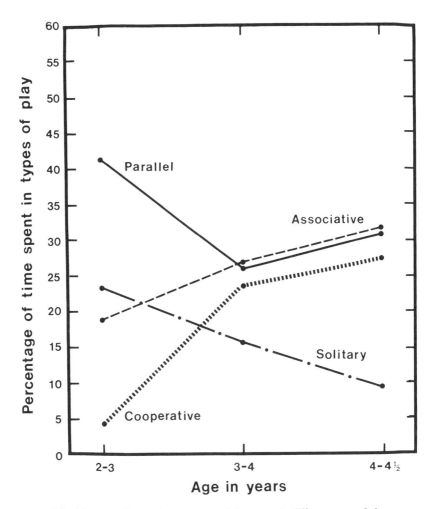

FIG. 4.2.   Age changes in percentage of time spent in different types of play. Percentages do not total 100 because some categories used by Parten are not displayed. (Adapted from Parten, 1932.)

children's social behavior. Normative data on the play behavior of preschool children were obtained by Parten (1932), showing that between the ages of 2 and $4\frac{1}{2}$ parallel play was most common. Children played with the same materials as others near them, but generally ignored the others. Age changes during the preschool years were also identified (see Fig. 4.2). Decreases were found in parallel and solitary play. Increases with age were found for associative play, in which children play with the same materials and converse with one another, and for cooperative play, in which children take different roles in a common activity (e.g., playing house) or work together to achieve a common goal. The results of this early study appear to be valid for preschool children today, although differences between children of different social classes are important (Rubin, Maroni, & Hornung, 1976).

Sympathetic and helpful responses of children at different ages were also studied (Murphy, 1937). These responses were fairly infrequent, but they did increase with age. Results suggested that sympathetic and helpful children were likely also to be more aggressive, but very recent research indicates that the relation is more complex (Yarrow & Waxler, 1976). Child developmentalists also adopted the sociometric technique of Moreno (1934), in which questions about whom children would like to play with and work with are used as measures of popularity, leadership, and the social relations that exist between members of large groups.

At the end of the decade an ingenious combination of experimental and observational methods was used by Lewin and his co-workers (1939) to study the effects of authoritarian, democratic, and laissez-faire leadership styles on school children's behavior. Lewin convincingly demonstrated the negative effects of authoritarian leadership, but he then turned his attention to adult social psychology and the earlier work was not followed up.

Research on children's language and reasoning took new directions with the publication of the early research of Jean Piaget (1926). The greatest interest was aroused by Piaget's claim that young children were *egocentric*. By egocentric Piaget did not mean selfish. Rather, he meant that young children, unlike older children and adults, can only see things from a single point of view—their own—and cannot understand or appreciate the viewpoints of others. As proof of his contention, Piaget showed the nearly complete absence of true communication between children playing together in the same classroom. He described the following observation as typical:

Pie (to Ez who is drawing a tram-car with carriages in tow): *But the trams that are hooked on behind don't have any flags.* (No answer.) (Talking about his tram). *They don't have any carriages hooked on . . .* (He was addressing no one in particular. No one answers him.)

(To Béa), *'T'sa tram that hasn't got no carriages.* (No answer.)

(To Hei), *This tram hasn't got no carriages, Hei, look, it isn't red, d'you see . . .* (No answer.)

(Lev says out loud, 'A funny gentleman' from a certain distance, and without addressing himself to Pie or to anyone else). Pie: *A funny gentleman!* (Goes on drawing his tram.)

I'm leaving the tram white.

(Ez who is drawing next to him says, 'I'm doing it yellow'),

No, you mustn't do it all yellow.

I'm doing the stair-case, look. (Béa answers, 'I can't come this afternoon, I've got a Eurhythmic class.')

What did you say? (Béa repeats the same sentence.) *What did you say?* (Béa does not answer. She has forgotten what she said, and gives Ro a push.) (1928, pp. 6–7)

In the transcript, children receive no answer or receive an irrelevant answer when they talk to others, and they often talk without addressing their comments to anyone in particular. They seem lost in their own world, and usually unaware that they are not being understood by others.

As has often been the case with Piaget, American psychologists were skeptical of his ideas and found difficulty in replicating the findings. Even when procedural differences that could account for the failures to replicate were isolated, American psychologists continued to doubt the assertion that young children's behavior was intrinsically different from that of an adult (McCarthy, 1946). The American position was that the age changes were merely quantitative, or matters of degree. Piaget felt that the data confirmed the existence of truly qualitative changes, or **stages,** during development.

However, in this case the controversy remained fairly localized. Piaget had not yet fully developed his theory of developmental stages, and American psychologists paid little attention to his claim that the egocentricity of the child was not a phenomenon of language alone, but a fundamental feature of the child's reasoning.

Many writers have commented on the lack of strong theoretical positions among child psychologists of this period (e.g., Bronfenbrenner, 1963; White, 1970; Wohlwill, 1973). In particular, Freud's theories of development and the learning theories of Skinner and Hull were virtually ignored. The neglect of Freud is a bit surprising, since he had come to America in 1909 at Hall's invitation, and a chapter by Anna Freud was included in the first *Handbook of Child Psychology* (Murchison, 1931). Freud's notions of the stages of psychosexual development, of the changing relations between children and their parents, and of innate drives were certainly relevant to the field. However, for a long time Freudian ideas were only disparagingly discussed by child psychologists (Jersild, 1933; Sears, 1975). Many different reasons for this reaction could be given. First, Freud's views were based on the psychoanalysis of adults, and especially on the interpretation of dreams. In contrast, psychologists of the period focused on the objective assessment of children's behavior. Freud's speculations might have been difficult to test with such methods. However, Susan Isaacs, working in England, used observations of preschool children as support for Freud's theories (Isaacs, 1933). Perhaps it was that Freud's theories implied that the course of psychological development was toward a more negative psychological state, involving substantial repression and inner conflict, when psychologists wished to assert a more positive view (Zigler, 1963). And finally, perhaps psychologists shared the uneasiness of much of the lay public about open discussions of sexuality, especially in children.

The rejection of the learning theory viewpoint has been attributed to the existence of an implicit genetic point of view among developmental researchers (White, 1970). This seems a bit of an overstatement. The importance of maturation was emphasized in the research on motor development, but the importance of environment was stressed in research on intellectual development. The research on social behavior seems truly atheoretical, focused on method and description rather than explanation.

However, there was a curious gap in the research of the 1930s which might reflect the implicit acceptance of a maturational view of development. Research dealing with the influence of parents or other adults on the child's development was scarce. The role of adults in the various aspects of socialization, such as learning social norms and learning to inhibit socially undesirable behavior, was almost totally ignored. The reason for this state of affairs is not entirely clear. It may be that psychologists felt hesitant about the intrusion into family life that study of socialization might entail, that they preferred to establish methods for measuring social behavior before investigating the antecedents of individual differences in social behavior, or that they felt there was relatively little to be gained from the study of socialization. The last possibility could be rephrased as a rejection of the importance of learning in the development of social behavior. But because of the other possible explanations, it is relatively weak evidence for a biased theoretical viewpoint in child development during the 1930s.

Few of the studies undertaken during this period were of immediate benefit to children, or of immediate applicability to educational reform. In distributing the Spelman Memorial funds, Lawrence Frank was apparently not very interested in immediate benefits (Senn, 1975). His goal was the gradual accumulation of information about all aspects of child development, and he saw the gathering of accurate information as the most important task of his time. While he did not believe that the actual topics of research should be determined by any narrow conception of what was useful, it should be noted that his long-range goal was the eventual dissemination of the information through the education of parents.

LULL AND PREPARATION: 1940–1950

Many child psychologists devoted themselves to war-related research during World War II. Little developmental research was initiated during this time, and the field did not quickly recover after the war. However, reports from the longitudinal studies that had begun in the late 1920s and early 1930s continued to appear. As before, the reports concentrated on physical and mental development, but the interest in this purely descriptive information was waning.

One very important accomplishment during the decade was the acceptance and attempted synthesis of the two theoretical positions that had been ignored by child developmentalists during the 1930s, psychoanalysis and learning theory. The first major results of this fusion were books on aggression and its socialization (Dollard, Doob, Miller, Mowrer, & Sears, 1939) and a social learning theory with emphasis on children's imitation (Miller & Dollard, 1941). The new theory incorporated a notion of motivation, or drives, that was a blend of the ideas of Freud and Clark Hull. The new theory also included hypotheses about the frustration and redirection of drive that owed much to Freud. However, the principles used to explain the acquisition of drives were drawn largely from learning theory. Armed with the new social learning theory, researchers turned to the study of socialization, paying special attention to those phenomena (e.g., aggression, dependency, and guilt) that had been extensively discussed by Freud. Full elaboration of the theoretical approach, and its full application in research, did not come until the following decade, but the crucial beginning steps were made in the 1940s.

A more exclusively psychoanalytic focus was found in studies of the effects of early experience on later psychological development. The major studies examined the effects of institutionalization on infants (Goldfarb, 1943; Ribble, 1943; Spitz, 1945). The findings of retardation or severe disturbances in development, and occasional death from no apparent cause, were generally attributed to lack of maternal contact and nurturance. However, subsequent writers (e.g., Pinneau, 1950, 1955) suggested that lack of physical stimulation or even congenital problems in the infants might have been the major causal factors. The comprehensive examination of the different explanations did not come until later.

REVIVAL AND EXPANSION: 1950-1960

Several reviewers of the state of child psychology in the early 1950s commented on the lack of vigor in the field and the poor quality of the work that was done (e.g., Barker, 1951). But by the end of the decade, the field was clearly booming. The turnaround was due to many factors, but chief among them was the success of the new **social learning theory.** For the first time, developmental psychologists gave serious and sustained attention to the influences of parents and other adults on the development of the child's personality. Fully 50% of the research during the mid-1950s was done on personality development and child-rearing (Radke-Yarrow & Yarrow, 1955; Baldwin, 1956). The best-known of these studies were done by Sears and his co-workers (Sears, Whiting, Nowlis, & Sears, 1953; Sears, Maccoby, & Levin, 1957; Sears, Rau, & Alpert, 1965). In the earliest study, parental behaviors toward the child were rated from mothers' responses in a 3-hour interview. The mother was asked about specific practices during two time periods, the child's infancy and the time of the interview, when the child was 4 or 5 years old. Because of the derivation of some hypotheses from psychoanalytic theory, the questions concerned style of nursing, weaning, and toilet training. The mothers were also asked about their disciplinary techniques, and their "warmth" toward the child was rated from their responses during the entire interview. The mother's behavior was expected to affect the child's dependency and aggression. These were assessed by direct observation of the children in their nursery schools. In the later studies the child was not observed directly. Instead, the mother was asked about the child's behavior in various situations. Then the mother's reports of the child's behavior, and of the parents' behavior toward the child, were related. The results confirmed certain expectations, and included some surprises. For example, children who were more aggressive toward parents, according to the mothers' reports, had mothers who were less warm toward them, more permissive of aggression toward parents, and also more severe in their punishment of aggression (see Table 4.2). The positive correlation between a child's aggression and parents' punishment of aggression has been frequently replicated in later research, suggesting that the parents' punishment serves either as a frustration or as a model of aggression. Although the correlations in Table 4.2 are statistically significant, they are rather small. In the studies, correlations of similar size were found for other aspects of the child's behavior, such as resistance to temptation and the sex-appropriateness of the behavior.

Several other types of investigations were offshoots of the new social learning theory. More indirect assessments of the effects of parents' behavior on children's social and personality development were made by examining social class differences in children's behavior. The assumption underlying this research was that disciplinary techniques and other aspects of childrearing vary with social class. Direct tests of the assumption exposed a great deal of overlap and few significant differences in childrearing between social class groups (Zigler & Child, 1973). The existence of more extreme variations in parental practices between cultures was an instigation for the test of theoretical predictions by cross-cultural study. The first major effort (Whiting & Child, 1953) relied on ethnographer's reports for indices of childrearing practices. Cultural responses to illnesses were also coded from ethnographer's reports, because the responses were assumed to reflect socialization anxiety, guilt, and other consequences of childrearing practices. Some support for the hypotheses was found, but the

TABLE 4.2
Correlations Between Parents'
Childrearing Practices and
Children's Aggression

Reported Childrearing Practices	Reported Aggression toward Parents
Parental warmth	$-.20$
Permissiveness for aggression toward parents	.23
Severity of punishment for aggression toward parents	.16

Adapted from Sears, Maccoby, and Levin (1957).

investigators recognized that more reliable and valid data could be obtained from first-hand observation of behavior in different cultures. Observations were subsequently done in six different cultures, and results of the project have been published gradually over the years (e.g., Whiting & Whiting, 1975). The later reports are not heavily based on the psychoanalytic-learning theory hypotheses, for they reflect the changes in the dominant theoretical orientations of psychology during later years.

The new theory also added impetus to the study of personality, which was conceived as a collection of drive systems. Popular topics were the aggressive drive, the dependency drive, and later in the 1950s, achievement motivation described as a drive. These investigations often used projective techniques, in which the child was asked to interpret an ambiguous picture or complete a story. The child was believed to "project" his own desires and motives into the interpretations or completed stories. For example, to measure achievement motivation children were asked to tell stories starting from very brief verbal cues, such as "A young man is sitting at a desk." The stories children told were coded for achievement imagery, statements that the child was competing with another or seeking to match a standard of excellence. They were also coded for direct comments about the need for achievement, how the person felt if he did or did not attain the goal, and other factors (Winterbottom, 1958). Projective techniques were attractive to researchers because they seemed to provide a clearer measure of motivation than did actual behavior. In a real situation, differences in children's motivation to achieve could be obscured by differences in the rewards or punishments they expected for achievement.

More purely psychoanalytic positions and a variety of other theoretical positions were represented in a second area of research on personality development. The studies of the effects of institutionalization on physical, social, and intellectual development which had begun in the 1940s were continued in the 1950s. One group of researchers continued to assert that the major factor in causing adverse effects was maternal deprivation (Bowlby, 1951). However, severe effects of institutionalization were not found in all of the later studies, and the retardation sometimes disappeared during childhood (Dennis & Najarian, 1957). The new research gave support to the hypothesis that the retardation found in institutionalized infants was due to deprivation in physical or perceptual stimulation and the practice of motor behavior, rather than the absence of the mother. A more recent report (Dennis, 1973) also suggested that intellectual deficits in institutionalized children were due to lack of environmental stimulation, and these deficits were relatively permanent. The stimulation hypothesis has now been tested in a large amount of research on animals, as well as experimental research with human infants (Rheingold, 1956; Thompson & Grusec, 1970).

However, support for the position that maternal contact is especially important to the young infant was obtained from two sorts of research with animals. Ethologists had earlier demonstrated the phenomenon of imprinting, the development of a relatively permanent attachment to an object on the basis of brief experiences with it during a specific, early period in development (Lorenz, 1935). If a satisfactory object was not presented during the "critical period," the young animal was expected never to develop a strong attachment to a member of its species. Equally prolonged effects of separation from the mother early in development were said to occur in humans (Bowlby, 1951). In addition, at the end of the decade reports began to appear from the research of Harlow with rhesus monkeys (Harlow & Zimmerman, 1959). Harlow found that monkeys reared without their mothers vastly preferred to be with a surrogate mother covered with terrycloth rather than one made out of wire, even if the wire mother held the infant's bottle of milk (see Fig. 4.3). The results dramatically indicated the importance of contact comfort in an infant's attachment to adults. Both sets of findings contributed to the later formulation of a more sophisticated defense of the position that contact with a single maternal figure is especially important to the development of the child.

Not all developmental psychologists in the 1950s, concentrated on personality development. During this period learning theory itself acquired a developmental

FIG. 4.3.   Two surrogate mothers and the preference of the infant monkey. Although the wire mother provides food, the infant prefers the contact comfort of the cloth mother surrogate. (Photograph courtesy Dr. H. F. Harlow.)

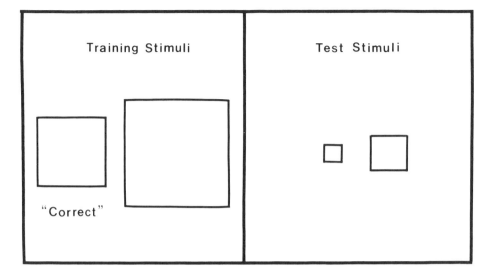

FIG. 4.4.   Training and test stimuli from a transposition experiment. The test stimuli illustrate what is generally known as a "far test" of transposition (Stevenson, 1972), because they are very different in size than the original stimuli.

emphasis. A classic problem in learning is the transfer of a response learned in one situation to a new situation. For example, a child might be trained to choose the smaller of two squares, and then be tested on two different squares, both of which are much smaller than the original squares but one of which is smaller than the other (see Fig. 4.4). Which square will the child choose in the test? If the test squares are much smaller than the original training stimuli, animals pick each of them about equally often. That is, they respond randomly. Kuenne (1946) speculated that young children would respond in the same way as animals. However, she predicted that older children, who have developed a functional language, would conceptualize the correct stimulus in the training series as "the small one" and concistently pick the smaller of the two stimuli during the testing phrases. The expected difference was found between 3- and 6-year-olds, and the result was replicated in a second study (Alberts & Ehrenfreund, 1951). However, later studies were more inconsistent. Attempts to explain the inconsistencies led to further research on the use of language as a mediator of responses. Different types of problems were tried, with different procedures. Most significant about the research was the hypothesis that learning itself is different at different ages. Indeed, it was in learning research that a concern with developmental phenomena was strongest during the 1950s.

    Other areas of developmental research were inactive during this period. The era of longitudinal studies of physical and mental development was over, and little research of this type has since been done. Language research was not strong, and observational studies of children's social behavior, a hallmark of the 1930s, were not common.

In comparison with previous periods, the most striking feature of the decade was the absence of a strong emphasis on age changes. The social learning theory assumed an essentially static model for the relation between children's experiences and later behavior. There was no thought that warmth, for example, might have different effects on 5- and 10-year old children. To take perhaps a more convincing example, there was little concern with possible differences in the factors which lead to resistance to temptation in 5-year-olds and in 10-year olds. A second feature of the decade was the presence of a great amount of research on socialization. The new focus was due to theoretical rather than practical interests. And yet parents were for the first time being provided with scientific evidence on the effects of their behavior toward their children. Not all the information was trustworthy, but it was an advance over the speculation of earlier years.

FROM SOCIALIZATION TO COGNITIVE DEVELOPMENT: 1960–1970

Almost before the findings of the research on personality development were published, disillusionment set in. Although a few relationships were consistently found, the more general picture was one of weak relationships that were not often replicated in different studies, regardless of how comparable the studies were (Yarrow, Campbell, & Burton, 1968). Evidence accumulated that mother interviews were not very reliable sources of data on either the mother's own behavior or her child's behavior. Confidence in the blend of psychoanalytic and learning theories that fostered the research also waned. Finally, the validity of projective tests was questioned because they proved to have complex and often confusing relations to actual behavior. Taken together, these problems led to disenchantment with the entire framework for research on childrearing and personality development that had been used in the 1950s.

Changes came in theory and in method. A newer social learning theory was developed which concentrated almost exclusively on the rewards or punishments which the child expected for a behavior, and the learning of behavior through imitation (Bandura & Walters, 1963). With the new theory came a method of experimental research which focused on the impact of **modeling** on children's behaviors. In one classic experiment, children observed an adult model who made aggressive responses toward a large, inflated "punch-me" doll. As predicted, the children subsequently behaved more aggressively toward the doll than did children not exposed to the model (Bandura, Ross, & Ross, 1961).

The laboratory studies were criticized as very unnatural, and were defended on the grounds that the importance of modeling could be shown in natural settings as well. However, there was also an attempt during the 1960s to study the normal interaction between parents and their children. The earliest of this research focused on the interaction of mothers and infants. The research of the 1940s on maternal deprivation and the ethological studies of imprinting in animals were brought together in a theory of the infant's attachment to the mother (Ainsworth, 1967; Bowlby, 1969), and the research on mother-infant interaction developed out of the new attachment theory. In the theory the infant was described as actively seeking proximity and contact with the mother, rather than being merely a passive recipient of the mother's attention. In addition, the infant was said to be evolutionarily predisposed to comply with the mother's commands, because such behavior was likely to increase the infant's chances of survival (Stayton, Hogan, & Ainsworth, 1971). This stress on such innate tendencies was in sharp contrast with the predominantly environmental view of socialization that had held sway in the field since Watson. Moreover, the stress on the infant's important role in attracting the mother was a contrast to the general view of the infant as simply responding to the actions of others (cf. Bell, 1968). Finally, the belief that the infant was biased toward obedience to the mother was opposite to earlier views that the infant was either neutral or actually resistant to any check on his impulse expression. Such active and positive views of the child did not fit in very well with the social learning theory of the 1960s. The conflict between the differing perspectives is likely to continue, for each reflects a central orientation in socialization research (Zigler & Child, 1973).

The change in socialization research, great though it was, was dwarfed by the tremendous upsurge in research on cognitive development, for the 1960s was the decade for cognitive studies. In the field's two major journals, *Child Development* and *Developmental Psychology*, studies of cognitive development made up more than half of the papers submitted (McCandless, 1970; Siegel, 1967). Most of the work stemmed from the research and theories of Piaget.

Piaget had been writing extensively about the child for 30 years, and he had formulated his general theory of cognitive development during the 1940s and 1950s. Piaget's writings were often difficult to read, and his methods were crude by American standards; but his results were so surprising that attempts to replicate them were soon made (e.g., Elkind, 1961). Most striking was his demonstration that young children do not *conserve* quantity. If 4-year-olds are shown two identical beakers filled with water to the same level, they will say that the beakers have the same amount of water. However, if all the water in one beaker is poured into a thinner and taller beaker, so that it rises to a higher level, the children will say that the new beaker has more water than the other one, "because it comes up higher." The children believe that the simple act of pouring the water into a beaker of a different shape can change the quantity of water, because they define quantity by the height of the water in the beaker. Of course, by 7 or 8 years of age children realize that only adding or removing water can change the quantity of water. They also realize that pouring the water into a new beaker did not change its quantity because the change in height was cancelled out by a change in width. Replication of this experiment and Piaget's other findings took some time, for Piaget had done a great amount of work; but the attempts to replicate were generally successful. American researchers also attempted to understand children's responses on Piagetian tasks by introducing variations in the tasks and examining their effects.

However, developmental psychologists devoted more attention to the test of two hypotheses which seemed critical to the theory. The first was that cognitive development was not a simple function of learning, or of maturation, but rather was a function of the child's attempts to understand the environment with which he came in contact. Piaget's stress on the child's active role was comparable to that in attachment theory. His hypothesis seemed to imply that training children to respond correctly on Piagetian tasks would be impossible. No successful attempts at training were reported in the early 1960s, but success in training conservation of number was reported at the end of the decade (Gelman, 1969). However, writers favorable to Piaget suggested that successful training would be expected with certain groups of children under some conditions (Inhelder & Sinclair, 1969). Thus at the end of the decade the status of the hypothesis was unclear.

The second hypothesis given sustained examination during the 1960s was the claim that the child's various achievements in a single cognitive stage formed a structured whole. Researchers, and sometimes Piaget himself, suggested that evidence for the hypothesis would be the simultaneous acquisition of all the achievements placed at a given stage. Throughout the 1960s evidence accumulated that an entire set of tasks was not mastered at the same time; but once again, other writers (e.g., Flavell, 1971) suggested that the evidence did not amount to a disconfirmation of Piaget's major hypothesis.

Emphases on biologically governed capabilities and functions, on the child's role in his own development, and on stages which describe structures of knowledge and related processes are found to varying degrees in other developmental research during the period. The study of language development received a tremendous boost from Chomsky's (1957) formulation of a structural theory of grammar. For example, it provided a framework for describing changes in grammar that led to changes in question-asking from the use only of a different intonation for questions, to a period when the child fails to invert subject and verb when asking ''wh-'' questions (e.g., ''What you have in your mouth?''), to the final period of correct questions (Brown, Cazden, & Bellugi, 1968). Language development research also became a focus of interest because of Chomsky's (1968) thoretical claims. He argued that his structural account of language was an essential part of a theory of human cognition; and that his linguistic theory provided a fairly precise specification of what innate knowledge the child must have, and what he must add to this innate knowledge, in learning to speak his native language. Chomsky himself did not attempt to directly confirm these hypotheses, but evidence on the biological basis for language acquisition was summarized by Lenneberg (1967).

Notions of stages and structures also appeared in theories of *moral development*. In an extension of Piaget's (1932/1965) original theory of moral development, Kohlberg (1969) described three levels of moral reasoning which could be divided into six stages, the highest of which was not achieved by most people even in adulthood (see Table 4.3). In line with Piagetian ideas of structure, Kohlberg claimed that each of the six stages made up an integrated set of beliefs about morality, and that the highest stages represented a consolidation and integration of separate and contradictory aspects of lower stages. And as in Piaget's cognitive-developmental theory, Kohlberg argued that progress to higher stages was a result of the child's attempts to make sense of his own morality. However, there are methodological problems in Kohlberg's measurement of moral reasoning, and there is substantial disagreement over the validity of his theory (e.g., Kurtines & Greif, 1974; Rest, Davison, & Robbins, 1978; Sullivan, 1977).

The existence of innate capabilities was also a major issue in research on infant visual perception. For example, researchers attempted to determine whether the newborn infant actually perceives the distance of objects from himself, or instead begins life with a two-dimensional view of the world, and only gradually learns to judge the distance of objects on the basis of experience. The two alternative viewpoints had been discussed by Preyer (1882/1888), and their philosophical history goes back much farther. However, experimental investigations of the question only became possible in the 1960s, with the invention of techniques for recording infants' movements and other responses simultaneously (see Kessen et al., 1970). In addition to providing tentative answers to the major theoretical question (Bower, 1974), the techniques allowed more accurate measurement of the visual sensitivity of the newborn and changes in sensitivity with age.

Research on learning remained largely independent of the prevailing shift toward a cognitive view of the child, and was criticized for this reason (Flavell & Hill, 1969). One of the few attempts to make some link between learning studies and cognitive research was White's (1965) paper which listed a large number of learning and cognitive tasks on which there were sharp changes in children's responses between the ages of 5 and 7 years. The shifts in responding could be related to the change, in Piaget's terms, from the preoperational to concrete operational stages of cognitive development. However, learning research was more commonly devoted to the major issue of the previous decade, the use of language as a mediator of responding. The main new development was the proposal that it was attention to various aspects of stimuli, rather than verbal responses, that had the greatest effect on children's learning (Stevenson, 1972).

There are inevitable omissions in the preceding account of developmental psychology during the 1960s, for there was great research activity in many areas

TABLE 4.3
Levels and Stages of Moral Reasoning

Level I—Preconventional

Stage 1—Heteronomous morality (Rules are followed to avoid punishment, to avoid physical damage to persons or property, and because of respect for the power or authority of others.)

Stage 2—Individualism, instrumental purposes, and exchange (Rules are followed if they serve one's own needs and interests. A recognition that others have interests as well leads to acceptance of exchange, reciprocity, or deals between persons.)

Level II—Conventional

Stage 3—Mutual interpersonal expectations and relationships (Rules are followed because of concern with living up to what others expect of you. Concern with "being good" means concern with having good motives, caring for others, and fulfilling stereotypical requirements for mutual relationships [e.g., trust, loyalty, respect, gratitude].)

Stage 4—Social system and conscience (Rules are followed because they are necessary to keep the system going, and because one's conscience demands the fulfillment of the duties to which one has agreed. However, laws may be violated in cases when they conflict with other social duties.)

Level III—Postconventional or Principled

Stage 5—Social contract or utility, and individual rights (Rules are followed because of a sense of obligation that derives from one's social contract. People make and abide by laws for the welfare of all and for the protection of all people's rights. There is the same commitment to family, friendship, and work obligations. Rules may vary in different groups, but they should be based on the idea of utility, "the greatest good for the greatest number." However, life and liberty must be respected in any society, regardless of majority opinion.)

Stage 6—Universal ethical principles (Rules are followed because they reflect self-chosen ethical principles to which one is committed. One's principles are believed to be universally valid principles of justice. They include a stress on the equality of human rights and the dignity of other human beings. When laws conflict with the principles, one acts in accordance with the principles.)

Adapted from Kohlberg (1969, 1976).

and our space permits only brief coverage. The decade is also difficult to summarize because the complexity and sophistication of developmental theories reached new peaks. Descriptions of development often included an attempt to specify the innate, "basic equipment" of the newborn infant. Several theories employed notions of the evolutionary history of the human species (e.g., attachment, language development), and thus were reminiscent of Hall; but the notions were firmly grounded on the advances in biological theory and research during the intervening years. The descriptions of development also concentrated on stages, or interrelationships of different responses at a given age. Though the validity of Piagetian and other stage theories was repeatedly questioned during the decade, the theories increased psychologists' recognition of the need to establish some links between the many different aspects of psychological development.

In explanations of development, many theorists suggested tendencies in the infant and child which promote self-development. The notions varied from Piaget's idea of the child as aiming at increased adaptation to the environment and increased organization of cognitive processes, to the idea of attachment theorists that the child contributes to his own socialization. Attempts to reconcile the existence of these continuously operating processes with the existence of qualitatively distinct stages in development were also made (Kessen, 1962; Piaget, 1970). The active and positive view of the child's role in development came into conflict with older notions of the child as rather passively responding to outside factors, that is, as affected by his environment or as the object rather than the agent of maturation. The new position was often described in terms of an interaction between maturation and learning, but this seems inaccurate. The controversy over the interpretation and significance of the Piagetian training studies suggests that the new and old positions may not be directly comparable. They may instead reflect conflicting paradigms, the relative merits of which cannot be determined by empirical tests (see Kuhn, 1962).

Developmental psychologists were also involved in a major social project during the decade, the implementation of Head Start programs for disadvantaged children. Impetus for the project came from writings which suggested that experience during the first years of life is crucial for optimal development, and in particular, that a person's final level of intelligence is determined more by early environmental influences than by heredity (Bloom, 1964; Hunt, 1961). Many different types of Head Start programs were implemented across the nation. Academic progress was one goal of the programs, but social and physical development were also heavily emphasized. However, in the initial evaluations of Head Start the other goals were largely ignored, and emphasis was placed on the effects of the program on IQ and achievement test scores. Though the initial evaluations suggested that the program had little positive effect in the cognitive realm (Westinghouse Learning Corporation/Ohio University, 1969), methodological problems in the evaluations were subsequently pointed out (Campbell & Erlebacher, 1970; Evans & Schiller, 1970) and later results have often suggested a more positive conclusion (Zigler, 1976).

Probably more important than the Head Start program itself was the central role that developmental psychologists played in the genesis and evaluation of a major social program. The field attained a level of maturity in the 1960s, and this had apparently been recognized in government and society.

CONCLUSION

The history of developmental psychology reveals that great progress was made in the years between the birth of child psychology in the 1880s and the maturity of the field of developmental psychology in 1970. In the description and explanation of developmental changes, a large number of theoretical positions have been developed. Moreover, there is now recognition that the nature of development differs for different phenomena. What is true for the development of reaching behavior in infancy will not necessarily be true for the development of competitiveness in middle childhood.

The topics of concern to developmental psychologists have also increased greatly during the history of the field. Preyer's concern with senses, will, and intellect in the years from birth to three has continued to occupy certain groups of researchers; but concerns with social behavior, with parental influences, and with the age range from three to adolescence and beyond have emerged. Psychologists now view the child not as an entity in itself, but as an individual linked with other individuals in an encompassing physical and social environment.

The extension of psychologists' interests has been due to changes in theoretical emphasis in the field, the availability of new research techniques, and the infusion of theories and research from other disciplines. At certain periods, one factor in the concentration of research interest has been the existence of major problems in the wider society. Recent history suggests that this factor will become more important in the future. In the 1970s psychologists were involved in research sponsored by the Surgeon General on the effects of television on children, in research undertaken by the Office of Child Development on the effects of day care on children, and in research on reading funded by the National Institute of Education.

Research done in an attempt to contribute to the understanding of social problems may be difficult for various political reasons (see Campbell, 1969). In addition, it may be a difficult undertaking for developmental psychologists who have not paid much attention to the generalizability of their findings to natural settings. Methods for doing research that is directly applicable in the real world of children will certainly be more complex, for the influences of various levels of social systems must be considered (Bronfenbrenner, 1977). On the other hand, many psychological processes that have been demonstrated in the laboratory have proven validity in natural settings as well. For example, the predictions of social learning theory regarding the development of aggressive behavior have been confirmed both in the laboratory and in naturalistic studies of television aggression.

The debate should therefore not be between laboratory and field studies, although it may be misinterpreted in this way. Nor should it be a debate between basic research and applied research. It is commonplace in science that the most basic research can often have the most profound applications. The opposite is true as well. Consequently, the major issue, as we see it, is a continuing attempt by developmental psychologists to increase understanding of the child's development, development which is in some respects a function of a particular social and cultural context, and in other respects a function of universal characteristics of the human species. This increased understanding will surely contribute to an increased effectiveness of attempts to solve the problems of children's development in our society and in others.

REFERENCES

Ainsworth, M. D. S. *Infancy in Uganda*. Baltimore: Johns Hopkins, 1967.

Alberts, E., & Ehrenfreund, D. Transposition in children as a fuction of age. *Journal of Experimental Psychology*, 1951, *41*, 30–38.

Allport, G. W. *Personality: A psychological interpretation*. New York: Holt, 1937.

Aries, P. *Centuries of childhood*. New York: Vintage, 1962.

Baldwin, A. L. Child psychology. In P. R. Farnsworth & Q. McNemar (Eds.), *Annual Review of Psychology*. Stanford, CA: Annual Reviews, 1956.

Baldwin, J. M. *Mental development in the child and the race*. London: Macmillan, 1895.

Bandura, A., Ross, D., & Ross, S. A. Transmission of aggression through imitation of aggressive models. *Journal of Abnormal and Social Psychology*, 1961, *63*, 575–582.

Bandura, A., & Walters, R. H. *Social learning and personality development*. New York: Holt, Rinehart, & Winston, 1963.

Barker, R. G. Child psychology. In C. P. Stone & D. W. Taylor (Eds.), *Annual Review of Psychology*. Stanford, CA: Annual Reviews, 1951.

Bayley, N. Mental growth during the first three years. A developmental study of 61 children by repeated tests. *Genetic Psychology Monographs*, 1933, *14*, 1–92.

Bayley, N. The development of motor abilities during the first three years. *Monographs of the Society for Research in Child Development*, 1935, No. 1.

Bell, R. Q. A reinterpretation of the direction of effects in studies of socialization. *Psychological Review*, 1968, *75*, 81–85.

Bijou, S. W. Ages, stages, and the naturalization of human development. *American Psychologist*, 1968, *23*, 419–427.

Binet, A., & Simon, T. Methodes nouvelles pour le diagnostic du niveau intellectuel des anormaux. *L'Année Psychologique*, 1905, *11*, 191–244.

Bloom, B. S. *Stability and change in human characteristics*. New York: Wiley, 1964.

Borstelmann, L. J. American childrearing in historical perspective: 1620–1970. In B. Wolman (Ed.), *International encyclopedia of neurology, psychiatry, psychoanalysis, and psychology*. New York: Van Nostrand, Reinhold, 1977.

Bower, T. G. *Development in infancy*. San Francisco: W. H. Freeman, 1974.

Bowlby, J. *Maternal care and mental health*. Geneva: World Health Organization, 1951.

Bowlby, J. *Attachment and loss, Vol. 1: Attachment*. New York: Basic, 1969.

Bremner, R. H., Barnard, J., Hareven, T. K., & Mennel, R. M. (Eds.). *Children and youth in America: A documentary history* (3 vols.). Cambridge, Mass.: Harvard University Press, 1970–1974.

Bridges, K. M. B. Emotional development in early infancy. *Child Development*, 1932, *3*, 324–341.

Bronfenbrenner, U. Developmental theory in transition. In H. W. Stevenson (Ed.), *Child Psychology*. Sixty-second Yearbook of the National Society for the Study of Education, Part 1. Chicago: University of Chicago Press, 1963.

Bronfenbrenner, U. Toward an experimental ecology of human development. *American Psychologist*, 1977, *32*, 513–531.

Brown, R. *A first language: The early stages*. Cambridge, Mass.: Harvard University Press, 1973.

Brown, R., Cazden, C., & Bellugi, U. The child's grammar from I to III. In J. P. Hill (Ed.), *Minnesota symposium on child psychology*. Minneapolis: University of Minnesota Press, 1968.

Burton, R. V. Generality of honesty reconsidered. *Psychological Review*, 1963, *70*, 481–499.

Campbell, D. T. Reforms as experiments. *American Psychologist,* 1969, *24,* 409–428.

Campbell, D. T., & Erlebacher, A. How regression artifacts in quasi-experimental evaluations can mistakenly make compensatory education look harmful. In J. Hellmuth (Ed.), *Disadvantaged child* (Vol. 3) *Compensatory education: A national debate.* New York: Brunner/Mazel, 1970.

Chomsky, N. A. *Syntactic structures.* The Hague: Mouton, 1957.

Chomsky, N. A. *Language and mind.* New York: Harcourt, Brace, & World, 1968.

Cronbach, L. J. Five decades of public controversy over mental testing. *American Psychologist,* 1975, *30,* 1–14.

de Mause, L. (Ed.). *The history of childhood.* New York: Psychohistory Press, 1974.

Dennis, W. Historical beginnings of child psychology. *Psychological Bulletin,* 1949, *46,* 224–235.

Dennis, W. *Children of the Creche.* New York: Appleton-Century-Crofts, 1973.

Dennis, W., & Najarian, P. Infant development under environmental handicap. *Psychological Monographs,* 1957, *71*(7, Whole No. 436).

Dollard, J., Doob, L. W., Miller, N. E., Mowrer, O. H., & Sears, R. R. *Frustration and aggression.* New Haven, Conn.: Yale University Press, 1939.

Elkind, D. Children's discovery of the conservation of mass, weight, and volume: Piaget replication study II. *Journal of Genetic Psychology,* 1961, *98,* 219–227.

Evans, J. W., & Schiller, J. How preoccupation with possible regression artifacts can lead to a faulty strategy for the evaluation of social action programs: A reply to Campbell and Erlebacher. In J. Hellmuth (Ed.), *Disadvantaged child* (Vol. 3) *Compensatory education: A national debate.* New York: Brunner/Mazel, 1970.

Flavell, J. H. Stage-related properties of cognitive development. *Cognitive Psychology,* 1971, *2,* 421–453.

Flavell, J. H., & Hill, J. P. Developmental psychology. In P. H. Mussen & M. R. Rosenzweig (Eds.), *Annual Review of Psychology.* Palo Alto, CA: Annual Reviews, 1969.

Gelman, R. Conservation acquisition: A problem of learning to attend to relevant attributes. *Journal of Experimental Child Psychology,* 1969, *7,* 167–187.

Gesell, A. *Infancy and human growth.* New York: Macmillan, 1928.

Goldfarb, W. The effects of early institutional care on adolescent personality. *Journal of Experimental Education,* 1943, *12,* 106–129.

Grinder, R. A. *A history of genetic psychology.* New York: Wiley, 1967.

Hall, G. S., & 8rowne, C. E. The cat and the child. *Pedagogical Seminary,* 1904, *11,* 3–29.

Halverson, H. M. An experimental study of prehension in infants by means of systematic cinema records. *Genetic Psychology Monographs,* 1931, *10,* 107–286.

Harlow, H. F., & Zimmerman, R. R. Affectional responses in the infant monkey. *Science,* 1959, *130,* 421–432.

Harris, D. B. (Ed.). *The concept of development.* Minneapolis University of Minnesota Press, 1957.

Hartshorne, H., & May, M. S. *Studies in the nature of character.* (3 vols.) New York: Macmillan, 1928–1930.

Hartshorne, H., & May, M. S. A summary of the work of the character education inquiry. *Religious Education,* 1930, *25,* 607–619.

Horn, J. L., & Donaldson, G. On the myth of intellectual decline in adulthood. *American Psychologist,* 1976, *31,* 701–719.

Hunt, J. McV. *Intelligence and experience.* New York: Ronald, 1961.

Inhelder, B., & Sinclair, H. Learning cognitive structures. In P. H. Mussen, J. Langer, & M. Covington (Eds.), *Trends and issues in developmental psychology.* New York: Holt, Rinehart, & Winston, 1969.

Isaacs, S. *Social development in young children.* London: Routledge & Kegan Paul, 1933.

Jersild, A. T. *Child psychology.* New York: Prentice-Hall, 1933.

Jersild, A. T. Emotional development. In L. Carmichael (Ed.), Manual of child psychology. New York: Wiley, 1946.

Jersild, A. T., & Holmes, F. B. *Children's fears.* Child Development Monographs, No. 20. New York: Teacher's College, Columbia University, 1935.

Jones, N. B. (Ed.). *Ethological studies of child behavior.* London: Cambridge University Press, 1972.

Kessen, W. Research design in the study of developmental problems. In P. H. Mussen (Ed.), *Handbook of research methods in child development.* New York: Wiley, 1960.

Kessen, W. "Stage" and "structure" in the study of children. In W. Kessen & C. Kuhlman (Eds.), Thought in the young child: Report of a conference on intellective development with particular attention to the work of Jean Piaget. *Monographs of the Society for Research in Child Development,* 1962, *27*(2, Serial No. 83), 65–81.

Kessen, W. *The child.* New York: Wiley, 1965.

Kessen, W., Haith, M. M., & Salapatek, P. H. Human infancy: A bibliography and guide. In P. H. Mussen (Ed.), *Carmichael's manual of child psychology.* (3rd ed., Vol. 2). New York: Wiley, 1970.

Kohlberg, L. Stage and sequence: The cognitive-developmental approach to socialization. In D. A. Goslin (Ed.), *Handbook of socialization theory and research.* New York: Rand-McNally, 1969.

Kohlberg, L. Moral stages and moralization: The cognitive-developmental approach. In T. Lickona (Ed.), *Moral development and behavior: Theory, research, and social issues.* New York: Holt, Rinehart, & Winston, 1976.

Kuenne, M. R. Experimental investigation of the relation of language to transposition behavior in young children. *Journal of Experimental Psychology,* 1946, *36,* 471–490.

Kuhn, T. S. *The structure of scientific revolutions.* Chicago: University of Chicago Press, 1962.

Kurtines, W., & Greif, E. B. The development of moral thought: Review and evaluation of Kohlberg's approach. *Psychological Bulletin,* 1974, *81,* 453–470.

Lenneberg, E. H. *Biological foundations of language.* New York: Wiley, 1967.

Lewin, K., Lippitt, R., & White, R. K. Patterns of aggressive behavior in experimentally created social climates. *Journal of Social Psychology,* 1939, *10,* 271–299.

Lorenz, K. Z. Der kumpan in der umwelt des vogels. *Journal fuer ornithologie,* 1935, *83,* 137–413.

McCandless, B. R. Editorial. *Developmental Psychology,* 1970, *2,* 1–4.

McCarthy, D. Language development in children. In L. Carmichael (Ed.), *Manual of child psychology.* New York: Wiley, 1946.

McCullers, J. C., G. Stanley Hall's conception of mental development and some indications of its influence on developmental psychology. *American Psychologist,* 1969, *24,* 1109–1114.

McGraw, M. *Growth, a study of Johnny and Jimmy.* New York: Appleton-Century, 1935.

Miller, N. E., & Dollard, J. *Social learning and imitation.* New Haven: Yale, 1941.

Moreno, J. L. *Who shall survive?* Washington, D.C.: Nervous and Mental Disease Publishing Company, 1934.

Murchison, C. (Ed.), *Handbook of child psychology.* Worcester, MA: Clark University Press, 1931.

Murphy, L. B. *Social behavior and child personality.* New York: Columbia, 1937.

Mussen, P. H. (Ed.). *Carmichael's manual of child psychology* (3rd ed., 2 vols.). New York: Wiley, 1970.

Newman, H. H., Freeman, F. N., & Holzinger, K. J. *Twins: A study of heredity and environment.* Chicago: University of Chicago Press, 1937.

Parten, M. B. Social participation among pre-school children. *Journal of Abnormal and Social Psychology,* 1932, *27,* 243–269.

Piaget, J. *The language and thought of the child.* New York: Harcourt, Brace, 1926.

Piaget, J. *The origins of intelligence in children.* New York: International Universities Press, 1952.

Piaget, J. *The moral judgment of the child.* New York: Free Press, 1965. (Orginally published, 1932.)

Piaget, J. Piaget's theory. In P. H. Mussen (Ed.), *Carmichael's manual of child psychology* (3rd ed., Vol 1). New York: Wiley, 1970.

Pinneau, S. A critique on the articles by Margaret Ribble. *Child Development,* 1950, *21,* 203–228.

Pinneau, S. The infantile disorders of hospitalization and anaclitic depression. *Psychological Bulletin,* 1955, *42,* 429–452.

Preyer, W. *The mind of the child. Part I. The senses and the will* (trans. H. W. Brown). New York: D. Appleton & Company, 1888. (Originally published, 1882).

Radke-Yarrow, M., & Yarrow, L. J. Child psychology. In C. P. Stone, & O. McNemar (Eds.), *Annual Review of Psychology.* Stanford, CA: Annual Reviews, 1955.

Rest, J. R., Davison, M. R., & Robbins, S. Age trends in judging moral issues: A review of cross-sectional, longitudinal, and sequential studies of the Defining Issues Test. *Child Development,* 1978, *49,* 263–279.

Rheingold, H. L. The modification of social responsiveness in institutional babies. *Monographs of the Society for Research in Child Development,* 1956, 21(2, Serial No. 63).

Ribble, M. A. *The rights of infants.* New York: Columbia University Press, 1943.

Ross, D. G. *G. Stanley Hall: The psychologist as prophet.* Chicago: University of Chicago Press, 1972.

Rubin, K. H., Maroni, T. L., & Hornung, M. Free play behaviors in middle- and lower-class preschoolers: Parten and Piaget revisited. *Child Development,* 1976, *47,* 414–419.

Sears, R. R. Your ancients revisited: A history of child development. In E. M. Hetherington (Ed.), *Review of child development research* (Vol. 5). Chicago: University of Chicago Press, 1975.

Sears, R. R., Maccoby, E. E., & Levin, H. *Patterns of child rearing.* Evanston, Ill: Row, Peterson, 1957.

Sears, R. R., Rau, L., & Alpert, R. *Identification and child rearing.* Stanford, Ca: Stanford University Press, 1965.

Sears, R. R., Whiting, J. W. M., Nowlis, V., & Sears, P. S. Some childrearing antecedents of aggression and dependency in young children. *Genetic Psychology Monographs,* 1953, *47,* 135–234.

Senn, M. J. E. Insights on the child development movement in the United States. Commentary by W. Kessen and by L. J. Borstelmann. *Monographs of the Society for Research in Child Development,* 1975, 40(3–4, Serial No. 161).

Shirley, M. M. *The first two years of life: A study of twenty-five babies Vol. 1: Postural and locomotor development.* Institute of Child Welfare Monograph No. 6. Minneapolis: University of Minnesota Press, 1931.

Siegel, A. E. Editorial. *Child Development,* 1967, *38,* 901–908.

Skeels, H. M., Updegraff, R., Wellman, B. L., & Williams, H. M. A study of environmental stimulation: An orphanage preschool project. *University of Iowa Studies in Child Welfare,* 1938, *15,* 1–191.

Spitz, R. A. Hospitalism: An inquiry into the genesis of psychiatric conditions in early childhood. *Psychoanalytic Study of the Child,* 1945, *1,* 53–74.

Stayton, D. J., Hogan, R., & Ainsworth, M. D. S. Infant obedience and maternal behavior: The origins of socialization reconsidered. *Child Development,* 1971, *42,* 1057–1069.

Stendler, C. Sixty years of child training practices. *Journal of Pediatrics,* 1950, *36,* 122–134.

Stevenson, H. W. *Children's learning.* New York: Appleton-Century-Crofts, 1972.

Stoltz, L. M. Youth: The Gesell Institute and its latest study. *Contemporary Psychology,* 1958, *3,* 10–15.

Sullivan, E. V. A study of Kohlberg's structural theory of moral development: A critique of liberal social science ideology. *Human Development,* 1977, *20,* 352–376.

Terman, L. M. *The measurement of intelligence.* New York: Houghton-Mifflin, 1916.

Thompson, W. R., & Grusec, J. E. Studies of early experience. In P. H. Mussen (Ed.), *Carmichael's manual of child psychology* (3rd ed., Vol. 1). New York: Wiley, 1970.

Watson, J. B. Experimental studies of the growth of the emotions. In C. Murchison (Ed.), *Psychologies of 1925.* Worcester, MA: Clark University Press, 1926.

Watson, J. B. *Psychological care of infant and child.* New York: Norton, 1928.

Westinghouse Learning Corporation/Ohio University. *The impact of Heat Start: An evaluation of the effects of Head Start on children's cognitive and affective development.* Clearinghouse for Federal Scientific and Technical Information, Sale Department, U.S. Department of Commerce, Springfield, Virginia, Order No. PB 184329, 1969.

White, S. H. Evidence for a hierarchical arrangement of learning processes. In L. P. Lipsitt & C. C. Spiker (Ed.), *Advances in child development and behavior* (Vol. 2). New York: Academic Press, 1965, 187–220.

White, S. H. The learning-maturation controversy: Hall to Hull. *Merrill-Palmer Quarterly,* 1968, *14,* 187–196.

White, S. H. The learning theory tradition and child psychology. In P. H. Mussen (Ed.), *Carmichael's manual of child psychology* (3rd. ed., Vol. 1). New York: Wiley, 1970.

Whiting, J. W. M., & Child, I. *Child training and personality.* New Haven: Yale, 1953.

Whiting, B. B., & Whiting, J. W. M. *Children of six cultures: A psychocultural analysis.* Cambridge, MA: Harvard, 1975.

Winterbottom, M. The relation of need for achievement to learning experiences in independence and mastery. In J. W. Atkinson (Ed.), *Motives in fantasy, action, and society.* Princeton, N.J.: Van Nostrand, 1958.

Wohlwill, J. F. The age variable in psychological research. *Psychological Review,* 1970, *77,* 49–64.

Wohlwill, J. F. *The study of behavioral development.* New York: Academic Press, 1973.

Wolfenstein, M. Trends in infant care. *American Journal of Orthopsychiatry,* 1953, *23,* 120–130.

Yarrow, M. R., Campbell, J. D., & Burton, R. V. *Childrearing.* San Francisco: Jossey-Bass, 1968.

Yarrow, M. R., & Waxler, C. F. with the collaboration of Barrett, D., Darby, J., King, R., Pickett, M., & Smith, J. Dimensions and correlates of prosocial behavior in young children. *Child Development,* 1976, *47,* 118–125.

Zigler, E. Metatheoretical issues in developmental psychology. In M. Marx (Ed.), *Psychological theory* (2nd ed.). New York: Macmillan, 1963.

Zigler, E. Head Start: Not a program but an evolving concept. In J. D. Andrews (Ed.), *Early childhood education: It's an art! It's a science!* Washington, D.C.: National Association for the Education of Young Children, 1976.

Zigler, E., & Child, I. L. *Socialization and personality development.* Reading, MA: Addison-Wesley, 1973.

5 Drives and Motives[1]

Charles N. Cofer
*University of North Carolina, Chapel Hill,
and Duke University*

In the concept of motivation, psychology comes to grips with a question of great significance: Is human behavior primarily driven by external stimuli or does it arise out of internal forces? Motivational interpretations imply that the second way of putting it is more nearly correct. Even accepting this position, however, there are disagreements as to the precise meaning of such an interpretation. Some think that the internal forces work like external stimuli, impelling an essentially passive organism, i.e., a "patient," into action. Others view these forces as the possession of a voluntary agent who chooses to make responses calculated to serve the individual's purposes.

Until the second half of the nineteenth century, an emphasis on choice and self-determined action marked psychology's use of motivational concepts as they applied to human behavior. At that time, reason was taken to be a uniquely human faculty, one not possessed by lower forms of life. Infrahuman animals were seen as *reacting* passively on the basis of reflex and instinct; homo sapiens *acted* creatively on the basis of reason and will. Darwin was to change all that. With the appearance and widespread acceptance of the theory of evolution, human and lower animal life became continuous, not only in anatomical structure but in behavior as well. From then on it was conceivable that animals could think and reason and, conversely, that human beings were driven by impulse.

---

[1]The field of motivation relates to so many topics in psychology that overlap between this chapter and others—particularly those on learning and those on topics in personality—is inevitable. The emphases, however, are different, and Professor Cofer's treatments of Hullian theory and Freudian theory, for example, add a new dimension to the presentations of Kimble (Chapter 1) and Matarazzo and Garner (Chapter 10). *The Editors.*

The history of how psychology has dealt with this issue—reflex versus reason, instinct versus will, blind impulse versus thoughtful choice, involuntary reaction versus voluntary action, patient versus agent—is the history of the topic of motivation to which we turn now. The history is a history of accommodation and compromise.

MOTIVATIONAL CONCEPTS BEFORE THE TWENTIETH CENTURY

Rationalism

In the great philosophical and theological traditions that have dominated Western thought since the time of the ancient Greeks, there was little or no place for a deterministic concept like motivation. The reason is that action was conceived to be a product of intellect and will, working together. Conduct was a consequence of choice, and choice was thought to be free. If choice is free, of course, it cannot be said to be determined and it cannot be predicted. Such a view removes choice from scientific consideration, as science assumes determination and some degree of predictability for the phenomena with which it is concerned.

It is, of course, the case that wise or right choice was a matter of concern to Greek philosopher and to theologian alike. The Greeks, like Socrates, emphasized the importance of knowledge to the choice of right conduct; knowledge and virtue were conceived as identical. The passions could not be denied, but sufficient knowledge would enable the person to control them.

A somewhat different basis for right conduct appears in the theology of St. Thomas Aquinas (1225-1274) which, as summarized by Gilson (1956), held that the person "has free-will, that is, intelligence and will" (p. 252). An act depends on considerations by the reason or intelligence and by the will. "In every case, it is the understanding alone which apprehends truths, which accepts or rejects them, and which gives orders; but the movement which it receives or transmits always comes from the will. All movement, therefore, remains voluntary, even when it seems to come from the intellect" (pp. 255–256). The will "tends to God directly," whereas in earthly life "our knowledge of God is imperfect and analogical." Hence, in this life the will is nobler than the intellect (Coppleston, 1957, pp. 382-383); following the dictates of the will, then, assures us of right conduct.

An example of the importance of the will to conduct is afforded by its role in the decision as to whether or not a mortal sin has been committed. Mortal sins condemn one to hell, unless repentance and forgiveness occur. However, for an act to be a mortal sin, it must have occurred with intent, with clear knowledge of the act and its consequences, and with full consent of the will. Obviously, we are personally responsible only for the acts, the commission of which meets these criteria.

Determinism

Psychological accounts of behavior and experience are based, more or less, on the assumption that psychological phenomena are determined, not free. Prior to the twentieth century, determinism appears in several philosophical systems. In some, determinism was assumed for all phenomena, but in others it was postulated for only some phenomena. When determinism was assumed, it took the form of a conception like the reflex or it was expressed in terms of the laws of association together with the hedonic principle—that our conduct is governed by the end of obtaining pleasure and avoiding pain.

We review the contributions of Descartes and Hobbes in the seventeenth century. There were, in ancient Greece, many anticipations of the notions that these writers advanced, but we shall begin at the time of the development of modern science, during the sixteenth and seventeenth centuries.

René Descartes (1596–1650).   In Descartes' thinking there was a partial break with rationalism. Like others before him, Descartes considered animal behavior to be machine-like, and he extended this conception to the human species as far as many functions are concerned. However, he left a place for reason to function in the case of the human being, thus preserving free choice for that species in the processes of thinking.

Descartes knew of the views of Andreas Vesalius (1514–1564), who believed that the brain dominates movement through the influence it exerts via the nerves, and he was acquainted with Thomas Harvey's (1578-1667) discovery of the circulation of the blood. He was also impressed by the fact that there were statues in the royal gardens which, activated by water pressure, could perform certain movements like extending an arm or moving into or out of a garden path. He synthesized these various pieces of information into a view of the animal and the human body as machines, as **automata.** In Descartes' account, external stimuli affect a minute thread located in a nerve. Movement of this thread opens certain pores in the brain, these openings allowing animal spirits, a kind of fluid distilled from the blood and stored in the brain, to flow toward the appropriate muscles, causing them to move by inflating them. Thus, muscular action reflected the sensory stimulation in an automatic way. This is the sense of the concept of reflex, a word which means reflected or bent back. Descartes' place in the history of the concept of reflex action is summarized by Fearing (1930). Descartes also regarded the passions essentially in a physiological way. Thus, the passions occur in the soul because of actions taken by the body, as in fear or joy (Mischel, 1969, p. 10). If someone runs away in fear, the "stimulus operates on the animal spirits, nerves, and so on, in such a way that a feeling of fear is produced in the soul while at the same time there are physiological changes" perceived by the soul (p. 10).

The behavior of animals, for Descartes, is explained completely by the mechanisms outlined for external stimulation and the passions. In people, however, there is thinking; this is evidence for a soul. The soul is not a bodily substance but is capable of interaction with the body. The interaction occurs at the pineal body in the brain. Thus, Descartes maintained rationalism, but perhaps his major contribution was to bring together systematically ideas and information that explained the behavior of animals as that of automata and that regarded the human body as a machine also. A logical development of Descartes' views was made by La Méttrie (1709–1751), whose book *L'Homme Machine* appeared in 1748. In this book, he argued that there is no difference between the animal and the human species, the latter being as much a machine as the former, but perhaps more finely constructed (Fearing, 1930, p. 88). Although La Méttrie did not deny thinking, feeling, and consciousness in human beings, he asserted that these activities are due to the brain which has "muscles for thinking as the legs have muscles for walking" (quoted by Fearing, 1930, p. 89).

The history of the study of reflex action is a long and complicated one, and we cannot follow it here. Nevertheless, the reflex, as an automatic unconscious, involuntary, mechanical "reflection" of stimuli, represents a conception that appears through the nineteenth and twentieth centuries. We shall refer to it again in later sections of this chapter. It appears to be central to the idea that behavior must be stimulated in order to occur, and further, that complex behaviors may simply represent combinations of simple reflexes.

Hedonism and Association in British Philosophy.   A strongly deterministic view was taken toward conduct by a number of English writers, starting with Thomas Hobbes (1588–1679), a contemporary of Descartes. Hobbes and the other British philosophers mentioned in this chapter were influenced by the new physics, Hobbes by Gallileo, the others by Newton as well. Hobbes assumed that the human being is a mechanical or material system, the heart being like a spring, the nerves like strings, the joints like wheels. He believed that movement of parts like these underlay all the phenomena of human behavior—not just some of it as Descartes proposed (Mischel, 1969, p. 5). Hobbes was a thoroughly deterministic philosopher.

Hobbes employed two principles, together with the idea of motion, in developing his views. One was **hedonism**, the other **association.** Our actions, Hobbes believed, are motivated by pleasure and by pain. These ends are mediated by "endeavor," an incipient or small movement that is induced by an object. An object known from past experience to be associated with pleasant experiences creates an incipient movement of approach and is accompanied by augmented vital motion—improved circulation of the blood, for example. This state of affairs would lead to locomotion toward the object; on the other hand, the circulation of the blood is impeded by the occurrence of the endeavor aroused by an object with which past experience has been unpleasant. Action toward such an object would be retarded by this change in the blood. Hobbes believed that, whatever we may think, all our actions depend on this hedonic principle.

Like John Locke (see pp. 21–22), Hobbes thought that the human mind, at birth, is devoid of knowledge, that it has no innate ideas. He accounted for the development of knowledge through the effects of experience as governed by the laws of association. The laws, later conceived as principles with the standing of Newton's law of gravitation, added to the deterministic account of human experience and conduct. However they are not motivational laws, and we shall not pursue a discussion of them here. But, in general, both the laws of association and the hedonic principle were applied to the human organism in a way to suggest that that organism is essentially a passive vehicle to be guided in its action and its thought by factors over which it has no control.

There were, of course, other advocates of these doctrines. Among them may be mentioned, in addition to Locke, David Hume (1711–1776), David Hartley (1705–1757), James Mill (1773–1836), and Jeremy Bentham (1748–1832). We cannot enter into a discussion of their particular additions to and variations on the ideas we have attributed to Hobbes. However, their contributions have been summarized elsewhere (Bolles, 1975; Boring, 1950; McReynolds, 1968a,b; Mischel, 1966; 1969; Peters, 1953).

The Person as Agent

The views of Hobbes and his successors were not accepted everywhere. Attacks were made on these views by Thomas Reid (1710–1796) in Scotland and Immanuel Kant (1724–1804) in Germany. Reid's writings were influential in the nineteenth century in France and the United States (Brooks, 1976). Kant's effect on German philosophy was great, and it, more than Reid's, had at least an indirect influence on later English Psychology. We shall discuss Reid and Kant briefly and then go on to other advocates of the person as agent.

Thomas Reid. He proposed a "common-sense" psychology, in which our intuitions about what we perceive and about how we think about our conduct are given credence. Although Reid used the principle of association, he did not accord it the significance given it by the English philosophers, and he rejected the hedonic principle out of hand. He wrote *Essays on the Active Powers of the Human Mind* (1785) in which he treated motivational problems. Reid believed in free will and argued that many of our actions are a consequence of willing. However, he seems to have hedged this belief by suggesting that some actions can be due to instinct, habit, appetite, desire, affections, and passions (strong and turbulent affections). These factors, he said, are present in the natural constitution of the human being, but evidently some of them were subject to control by the will, especially insofar as the will might inhibit the actions which otherwise we might be moved to take. There were also "rational powers," involving will "as well as reason or judgment" and directed toward what is good for us and toward doing our duty (Brooks, 1976, p. 74).

Reid thus countered the proposals of the English philosophers by proposing an active mind and the person as a rational, responsible agent, whose conduct was guided in many aspects by constitutional or innate powers or faculties.

Immanuel Kant.   We do not see the things of the world in themselves, Kant said. Rather, we construct what we perceive. As Russell (1945) has put it, "the outer world causes only the matter of sensation, but our own mental apparatus orders this matter in space and time, and supplies the concepts by means of which we understand experience" (p. 707). Space and time are not based on experience; they are "intuitions" which we know to be true without experience. Similarly, there are categories or concepts which are also part of our constitution and which aid our understanding. These factors seem clearly to suggest an active process in our perception of the world.

Kant rejected hedonism as a principle governing conduct and sought to define the control of action in terms of morality. For Kant, Russell (1945) says, moral concepts "have their seat and origin wholly *a priori* in the reason. Moral worth exists only when a man acts from a sense of duty . . . The essence of morality is to be derived from the concept of law; for, though everything in nature acts according to law, only a rational being has the power of acting according to the idea of law, i.e., by will" (p. 710). Kant spoke of the categorical imperative. One should act only in conformity with this imperative, i.e., that what one does is what one would also will to be a general natural law. For example, the categorical imperative implies that it is wrong to lie, because one would not wish to will that lying be a universal law.

Here, again, we see the person as agent, acting reasonably and responsibly in the light of capacities arising from the constitution.

The Nineteenth Century.   The influence of the British associationists and their hedonic principle continued to be important in the nineteenth century, both in England and in Germany. However, in both places developments after the middle of the century represented a challenge to these doctrines. An important figure was Franz Brentano (1838–1917), who in 1874 published his book, *Psychology from an Empirical Standpoint.* In this work, Brentano made the important point that psychology is concerned with mental acts, not with the contents of those acts. In the experimental methods used in German psychology at the time, there was great interest in measuring the features of conscious experiences, like their intensity. To Brentano, however, "The actual magnitude measured . . . is not the intensity of a color as seen or of a sound as heard, etc., but the intensity of the inner act of seeing or hearing" (Rancurello, 1968, p. 33). There were three classes of acts: representation, i.e., imagining, or thinking; judgment, i.e., accepting something as true or rejecting it as false; and affectivity, i.e., all other psychic acts (Rancurello, 1968, p. 45). Motivational processes would fall into the third class. Brentano divided these processes into " 'lower' or 'sensory' and 'higher' or 'rational' feelings, emotions, desires, and motives" (Rancurello,

1968, p. 60). In the case of these higher states, action stems from the subject rather than from the factors that underlie them. Rancurello thinks this is a causal system, in which the subject is the efficient (or effective) cause and the subject's attitudes are the final cause or purpose. (Efficient and final causes are terms from Aristotle.) In any case, the subject in Brentano's view is an active agent rather than a patient.

Later, Brentano's influence carried over to the school of Gestaltqualität and to the thinking of a number of important German psychologists possibly including Sigmund Freud, who attended his lectures as a student at the University of Vienna. However, for the purposes of this chapter, Brentano's influence on Ward and Stout in England has the greatest significance, because of their impact on William McDougall, a key figure in the history of motivation in the twentieth century.

James Ward (1843–1925) was the first non-associationist to occupy an important place in English psychology, starting with his attack on Alexander Bain's (1818–1903) associationistic views in an article on psychology in the ninth edition of the *Encyclopedia Britannica* in 1886; his revision of this article for the eleventh edition (1911) is often regarded as sealing the doom of the associationistic psychology in England. Ward's student, G. F. Stout (1860–1944), is one of two men (William James is the other) whom McDougall regarded as his mentors (McDougall, 1930, p. 209).

Ward viewed individuals as active, in contrast to the determinists who "regard motives as forces . . ." of which "the man meanwhile seems to play the part of a simply passive spectator" (Ward, 1911, p. 283). Ward compares the two propositions "Hunger makes a man eat" and "Heat makes a glass crack" as follows: ". . . in the one case the active subject changes the situation; in the other the situation changes the passive body" (Ward, 1911, p. 284). Forces, he said, converge on an object, but diverge from a subject. Ward saw activity as an inherent property of the human being, the activity being directed according to that subject's aims and ends. Stout (1896) emphasized striving. "Every emotion, such as fear, anger, indignation, etc., contains in intimate combination both feelings of pleasure and pain and feelings of desire or aversion" (p. 115). Desire or aversion equal striving or conation in Stout's system. He further characterizes these and other words such as activity, endeavor, effort, will, and attention as implying "that the process to which they refer tends by its intrinsic nature in a certain direction or toward a certain end, and that apart from the end to which they are directed they can neither exist nor be conceived" (p. 147).

The Theory of Evolution

In biology, the most important event of the nineteenth century was the publication, in 1859, of *The Origin of Species* by Charles Darwin (1809–1882). Darwin had his predecessors (see Boring, 1950, pp. 468–470; Cofer & Appley, 1964, p. 32), but his formulation of the theory, together with presentation of a mass of supporting evidence, stands as the decisive contribution in the history of the theory. For other discussions of Darwin see pages 21–24.

Prior to the theory of evolution, prevailing opinion had held that the human being was the result of a special act of creation and that, therefore, the human species was discontinuous with other species of animals. Darwin's theory challenged this presupposition. There is continuity among species, the various species having evolved from common ancestors. In the process of evolution some species fail to survive, and among evolutionists there was interest in the reasons for the survival of some and the disappearance of other species. In his voyage on the *Beagle*, Darwin observed that similar animals living in diverse environments had developed characteristics suitable to those environments. He believed that variations in the characteristics of animals of a species could, in the course of time, make some variants more likely to survive in the struggle for existence than others. Hence, new species could emerge whereas old ones could die out. This is the essence of the thesis of natural selection. Certain characteristics promote adaptation to an environment, and animals whose features enable them to adapt, reproduce and survive; their characteristics are passed on to subsequent generations.

Darwin conceived the processes of evolution as deterministic; he saw no purpose or plan in nature. Since species are continuous, this deterministic view applied also to the human species. The result was a shift in thought about humans and non-human animals. The former could be regarded as having properties in common with the latter and conversely. So investigators could study animals with the intent of discovering in them evidences of reason and intelligence, previously denied them. And instincts could be proposed for the human being, to an extent far greater than had been possible before. Peters (1953, p. 66) has epitomized these consequences of Darwin's theory as ''a developing tendency both to humanize animals and to brutalize men.'' We will not follow here the work concerning intellectual capacities in animals but will a little later say something about instinct in the human. The first great exponent in psychology of evolutionary thinking was Herbert Spencer (1820–1903), who had anticipated some of the theory himself. It was also Spencer who was chiefly responsible for introducing Darwinian thinking in America where it contributed to the development of functionalism (Ch. 1, vol. 1). We will mention Spencer briefly in conjunction with the law of effect.

THE TWENTIETH CENTURY

Motivational principles dominated theories of behavior in the first six or seven decades of the twentieth century, as expressed in the assertion (or slogan) that ''all behavior is motivated.'' This domination is an expression of the acceptance of determinism as formulated in Freudian theory and drive theory, both of which rely on ideas of impulsion to get behavior going and to maintain it. Neither point of view is rationalistic, and the behaviorists, together with Freud, reduced the role of consciousness in the control of conduct. Although the behaviorists stressed the importance of learning, their conception of learning was associationistic, the association being modeled on conditioned reflexes in the spirit of reflexology as developed by Pavlov. Motivational notions have had a central role in the theories of learning and in ideas about the occurrence of previously learned behavior after learning is complete. While it seems to be true that Freudian and behavioristic drive theories have dominated most of the century, there have been writers who have objected to these views. Further, as the decades of the 1950s and 1960s came, alternative conceptions have grown in strength, so that by the 1970s cognitive approaches were coming again to the fore.

Evidence of the importance of motivational concepts in this century is afforded by the frequency with which we now use words like motivation and drive. These terms are new in psychology; neither appears in Baldwin's *Dictionary of Philosophy and Psychology* (1911) or in the eleventh edition of the *Encyclopedia Britannica* published in the same year. The term motive, of course, has been in use for a long time, appearing as early as 1412 if not earlier, according to the *Oxford English Dictionary*. Its use, however, was not as an impulse but rather as a feature of conscious experience, as was also often the case for will, volition, and conation or striving. The twentieth century has seemed to be the motivational century, at least until recently.

In the rest of this chapter, we shall review the major motivational ideas of the twentieth century. We begin with Freud and psychoanalysis, go on to William McDougall and instinct theory, review the development of drive theory and its role in learning theories, and indicate the problems that drive theory has encountered. We will consider field and balance theories and the assessment of human motives. Lastly, we will provide some brief comments on the future of motivation theory.

FREUDIAN PSYCHOANALYSIS

Sigmund Freud (1856–1939) has had more influence on Western thought than any other psychologist. His work rivals that of Darwin in its impact on a wide variety of disciplines. He was a determinist and proposed, in contrast to the doctrines of rationalism, that the human being, at base, is governed by unconscious forces that energize or actuate all of the person's behavior, thought, and experience. Freud's view of human nature was not optimistic, although he did think that by achieving knowledge of that human nature one could at least modulate its domination. Thus one's life, despite human nature, could be a productive and comfortable one.

Freud was trained in medicine at the University of Vienna and lived in Vienna most of his life. At the University, as we have learned, he attended Brentano's lectures, although the extent of Brentano's influence on Freud is uncertain. Freud also studied under Ernst Brücke, a physiologist, who, with other physiologists (Helmholtz, Ludwig, and du Bois-Reymond) agreed to fight vitalism. Vitalism holds that there are non-materialistic forces that influence behavior, growth, and development. Brücke, with du Bois-Reymond, pledged to oppose vitalism (Boring, 1950, p. 708) and to argue for the principle that "no other forces than common physical chemical ones are active within the organism" (quoted by Boring, 1950, p. 708). This way of thinking must have influenced Freud profoundly, as his theories seem to be modelled on biophysical principles, even though they came to refer to psychic, rather than physical, energy. Freud, at least in the early stages of his psychoanalytic career, thought in reflexological terms (Bolles, 1975, p. 56). However, with the development of his instinct concept, reflexes themselves were seldom mentioned.

Freud's early career, after his medical degree at Vienna, was spent in research and clinical practice, largely in neurology. In the 1880s he began to work with Josef Breuer, who had been treating hysterical patients by means of hypnosis. Freud studied hypnosis, going to Paris to study with Charcot and to Nancy to study with Liébault and Bernheim. Freud continued to treat hysterics with hypnosis but found the method unsatisfactory. He had discovered that by allowing his patients to talk freely most of the information obtained under hypnosis would appear anyway. Breuer dropped out of the collaboration, leaving Freud to develop his methods and his theories alone.

Early on, Freud discovered the role of unconscious and sexual factors in hysterical disorders and the value of the talking out method (free association) with respect to dreams and other experiences. He formulated his early theories on these bases, but later experiences with patients forced him to alter his position. In the present chapter, we shall ignore Freud's early formulations and review only those that he retained and developed in his later years.

Freud made an important distinction between energy and structure, a contrast that we shall see in other theories. Although motivation is the energy concept in Freud's theories, it will be necessary also to discuss structure in order for us to understand the over-all system.

Energy

Freud postulated a psychic energy, whose source is somehow in bodily processes; he did not pretend to know how the psychic energy arises. Freud also conceived this energy as an irritant, much as we would regard a painful external stimulus, and it was a basic postulate that this energy or excitation must be reduced. He said (1915, p. 63), "The nervous system is an apparatus having the function of abolishing stimuli which reach it, or of reducing excitation to the lowest possible level, an apparatus which would even, if this were feasible, maintain itself in an altogether unstimulated condition." The nervous system "masters stimuli." Freud went on to say that this function is easily executed for external stimuli by reflex movements away from them. With inner or instinctual stimuli, however, the organism cannot move away, and thus such stimuli ''make far higher demands upon the nervous system and compel it to complicated and interdependent activities'' which cause changes in the external world, permitting ''satisfaction to the internal source of stimulation'' (p. 63).

As suggested in this quotation, Freud thought of the psychic energy as instinctual, and ultimately he proposed two classes of instincts: (1) the **life instincts,** which include those that maintain life and serve reproduction, and (2) the destructive or **death instincts.** In the first class, it was the reproductive or sexual instinct which figured in Freud's motivational theory, and he referred to the energy of this instinct as **libido.** The death instinct, **Thanatos,** was not so well formulated in Freud's theory, and its energy source was unspecified. However, it was proposed because of the widespread incidence of aggression, the occurrence of repetition–compulsion (the re-living of traumatic episodes in later life), and the need to have a principle in opposition to the life instincts. The two instincts fused in certain kinds of activities, as in sadistic and masochistic behaviors.

The instincts, Freud said, had four characteristics. First, they have a source, somewhere in the body. Second, they have impetus or force, i.e., degrees of intensity related to the strength of the underlying need. Third, they have an aim, that is to abolish the conditions (the source) from which they spring. Such reduction or abolition of the irritating source is experienced as satisfaction. Fourth, they have an object, i.e., a person or thing, either internal or external, through which the aim of the instinct may be reached.

It should be noted that the objects are not necessarily fixed, so that any of a variety of objects might serve as the instruments of satisfaction for the instincts. Similarly, various aims, short of the ultimate one of achieving reduction of the internal excitation, might be imagined, giving partial relief to the instinctual pressure. However, some discharge of the instinctual energy is necessary; the instinctive urges do not go away with disuse or with suppression. It should be remarked, then, that in Freud's usage the term instinct did not, as it has in some recent uses of the word, mean a fixed action pattern or course of behavior. Instinctive behavior in Freud's sense could be variable as to object and manner of behavioral expression. What was constant were source, impetus, and ultimate aim.

This comment should not obscure the fact that the sexual instinct, to Freud, did undergo systematic or invariant changes in mode of gratification with age. In early infancy the mouth region was said to be the erogenous zone, stimulation of which (e.g., through sucking) gives the greatest instinctual satisfaction. A little later, perhaps by the age of 2 or 3 years, the anal region does so. Finally, the phallic region, at ages of about 4 to 5 years, gives the greatest pleasure. The phallic stage is terminated with the Oedipus complex and is followed by the latency period in which sexual interest is lessened. At adolescence, however, sexuality returns and, if development has been normal, leads to the mature genital stage, the final stage of psychosexual development. This final stage, if reached, does not have the egocentricity or immature object choices of the phallic stage. Freud traced neurosis and psychosis to fixations on an early stage, beyond which some individuals did not progress or to which other persons returned (regressed) after suffering frustrations at a later stage of development. All of us, it can be remarked, retain vestiges of all of the stages, even in maturity, according to the Freudian view.

The Structural Model

Freud conceived of a three-way model of the mental apparatus to deal with instinctual energy (see Fig. 5.1). At its base is the Id, the unconscious reservoir of libidual energy, ". . . a chaos, a cauldron of seething excitement . . ." (Freud, 1933, p. 104). The Id knows no morality, no logic, no reason, obeying only the pleasure principle. It is the basic stuff from which the personality develops. Actually, the personality develops only because the Id is not in contact

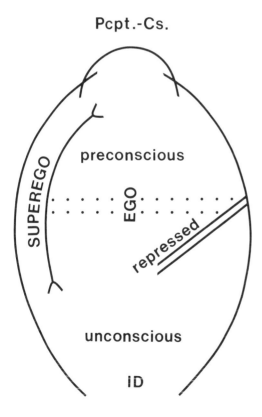

FIG. 5.1. A diagrammatic representations of Freud's structural model. Redrawn from Cofer and Appley, 1964, p. 613, Fig. 12-1b. The figure appeared originally in Freud (1933, p. 111).

with reality and is not able, when discharge of its impulses does not occur, to affect the external world so as to gain its satisfactions. Consequently, another structure, the Ego, appears. Somehow, some of the Id energy is made available to the Ego, which uses this energy to gain satisfactions for the Id, while, at the same time, avoiding the censure and punishment that would accompany the direct and unbridled expression in behavior of Id impulses. The Ego has control of the motor apparatus and functions in accordance with the reality principle. That is, it acts with respect to the real word in attempting to gain satisfactions and to avoid punishments. It is subject to the demands of the Super-Ego, the third component of the personality. This structure develops initially from the prohibitions and punishments emanating from the parents. It serves as one's conscience, and it can cause anxiety and guilt in the Ego. It also contains the Ego-ideal, a standard to the observance of which the Ego aspires. Failure to do so results in loss of self-esteem.

As may be seen from this account, the Ego stands between the demands of the Id and the prohibitions and ideals of the Super-Ego. Freud proposed that the Ego is the seat of the experience of anxiety, and it will go to great lengths to reduce or avoid anxiety. The experience of birth, with its exposure of the infant to stimulation from the environment and to ungratified internal needs, is said to be the model of anxiety. The Ego, getting signals from the Id, reality, or the Super-Ego which foretoken a flood of stimulation like that experience at birth, reacts to prevent the further development of the stimulation. In doing so, it uses defense mechanisms, such as repression, regression, reaction formation, displacement, sublimation, and the like. These mechanisms are not themselves motivational concepts; they are used by the Ego to hold the Id impulses in check or to give them partial relief through activities the true function of which is disguised from reality and the Super-Ego. Thus a person who is motivated to perform seamy sex acts with prostitutes may convert this energy into actions of a highly moral character—condemning prostitution, for example, and attempting to eliminate it. Such a person would be using the defense mechanism of reaction formation.

Reactions to Psychoanalysis

Freud's theories stirred up much controversy, but they have also been applied in numerous areas aside from psychotherapeutic treatment, where they were formulated. Freud's views about the significance of sex, especially in early childhood, aroused much opposition and moral indignation. His theories have been said to be vague and untestable aside from the therapeutic situation in which they arose. His ideas have been said to be culture bound, as they are based on clinical work with a limited sample of Viennese neurotics.

Within the psychoanalytic movement, there have been challenges to Freud's assumptions. Early in the movement, Alfred Adler, Carl Jung, and Otto Rank developed ideas which led to breaks with Freud. More recently, socially and culturally oriented analysts, like Karen Horney, Erich Fromm, and Harry S. Sullivan, have rejected the over-weening importance of the sex instinct, in favor of social and familial conditions evoking anxiety. Further, some analysts like Heinz Hartman, David Rapaport, and their associates have insisted on autonomy for the Ego, indicating that it has an existence independent of conflicts between Id impulses and reality. We register these disagreements but in the present space will not discuss them further.

Freudian ideas have influenced other disciplines, from anthropology to sociology in the social sciences, and art and literature among the humanities. Freud's work has been important in areas of child-rearing and in the views of people toward criminal activity and other aspects of social policy. Psychology marks Freud's influence in such diverse areas as child psychology, personality, social psychology, and abnormal psychology, and in attempts to study psychoanalytic hypotheses in the laboratory.

Freud, as much as or more than anyone, overthrew the rational views of the human being by insisting that human behavior is impelled by intense instinctive forces, operating outside of awareness but affecting us in almost everything we do.

INSTINCT THEORY AND WILLIAM MCDOUGALL

After the theory of evolution, as we have seen, it was conceivable to explain human behavior in instinctive terms to an extent that was greater than had been possible before. However, the concept of **instinct** was seldom well-defined; it had the properties of being inborn, unlearned, and universal in the species but otherwise it varied from rather specific response patterns, as are observed in insects, to purposive actions involving goals, without specific response patterns. To Darwin, instincts were composed of reflexes; to McDougall, instincts could not be reduced to reflexes. There was variation, then, in the way the concept was used.

An extremely mechanistic concept was that of **tropism,** made up of reflexes and in many ways like an instinct. Jacques Loeb (1859–1924) proposed that these "forced movements," for example the orientation of an animal toward a light source, could explain much behavior in lower animals and could be applied to higher animals as well. The light induces movement in the animal, and the animal orientates itself to the light in order to attain equal stimulation on both sides of its bodily axis. Such a conception is clearly that of a Cartesian automaton, and it did not allow for the variability in behavior, even in protozoa, that investigators like H. S. Jennings (1868–1947) observed. Wallace Craig (1918) also reported from his work with doves that internal stimuli lead to instinctive action that is much more variable than Loeb's ideas would permit.

But instincts that were very poorly defined were also postulated. William James (1890) said that the human being has more instincts than any other animal and that the instincts are purposive. He listed about 20 human instincts, varying in kind from locomotion, vocalization and imitation to love, jealousy, and parental love. Numerous other acts and tendencies were called instinctive by other writers, the total listed by one writer or another (Bernard, 1924) being in excess of 5000. The postulation of instincts became so popular that one author (Ayres, 1921) wrote of "the instinct of belief-in-instincts." There were no fixed or certain criteria to determine what acts could be called instinctive, and a powerful movement against instinct explanations developed in the 1920s. This movement was successful, and the word virtually disappeared from the psychological vocabulary until its revival by the ethologists.

An instinct theorist of importance was William McDougall (1871–1938), who, like Freud, made instincts the driving, impelling force of all conduct. His mentors, he said, were Stout and James, but his views were considerably more sweeping than theirs. McDougall's stress on instincts is seen in his comment, "Take away these instinctive dispositions with their powerful impulses, and the organism would become incapable of activity of any kind; it would lie inert and motionless like a wonderful clockwork whose mainspring has been removed or a steam-engine whose fires had been drawn." Further, by the force of some instinct directly or indirectly, "every train of thought, however cold or passionless it may seem, is borne along toward its end, and every bodily activity is initiated and sustained" (1950, p. 38).

McDougall saw the instincts as purposive, i.e., they determine the individual "to perceive, and to pay attention to, objects of a certain class, to experience an emotional excitement of a particular equality upon perceiving such an object, and to act in regard to it in a particular manner, or, at least, to experience an impulse to such action" (p. 30). McDougall postulated a number of instincts, most of them having an associated emotion, and he regarded them as the prime movers of conduct. He said (pp. 15–16) that it is a prime problem to explain how moral and rational conduct could arise in the human species which is, at base, amoral and egoistic, because it is propelled by instincts. This, of course, was also a problem for Freud, one that he handled through the Ego and Super-Ego structures. This problem may be characterized in the question, "Why does the human ever behave morally or rationally?", which contrasts with the question that the rationalist movement would ask: "Why does the human, endowed with reason and moral virtue, ever behave irrationally?"

McDougall saw his question as answered through the controls exercised by society through a system of sentiments into which the instincts and emotions entered. This part of his theory has had little impact. But his instinct theory contained elements that seemed to demand the attention of theorists who were not committed to the doctrine of instincts, i.e., the drive theorists. Peters (1953, pp. 665–666) suggests that the concept of drive "turned out to be the objectively

testable   component   of   McDougall's   more   metaphysical   concept   of
'instinct' . . .''

DRIVE THEORY

The term drive was introduced by Woodworth (1918) to refer to the energy that
makes the structures underlying behavior active. As had Jennings and Craig,
Woodworth pointed to the restless activity an animal may display before being
able to make a consummatory reaction (e.g., eating, drinking). Earlier (1912)
Cannon and Washburn had given an explanation of hunger pangs in terms of
contractions of the empty stomach, and supported their explanation by showing a
correlation between reported pangs and the occurrence of the contractions (see
Fig. 5.2). Drive soon came to be viewed as an effect of tissue needs, or, as
Dunlap (1922) said, desire resides in tissues, and it was regarded on Cannon's
evidence as an irritating stimulus, arising in specific structures. Thus, Cannon
(1934) suggested that thirst arises from dryness in the mouth and throat and that
stimuli in the genital organs and the mammary glands underlie sexual behavior
and the encouragement by a mother of sucking by her offspring. Drives were

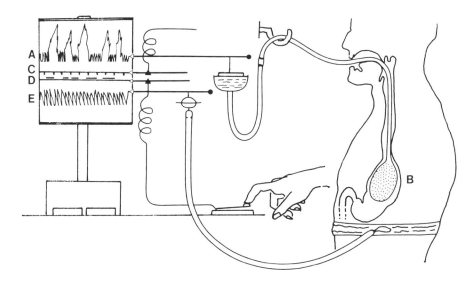

FIG. 5.2.   Diagram of the experimental situation by Cannon and Washburn
(1912). B designates the balloon in the stomach. On the kymograph tracing to the
left, A refers to air pressure changes corresponding to stomach contractions, C to
time in minutes, D to hunger pangs as indicated by the subject, and E to respiration. Redrawn from Cofer (1972, p. 19, Fig. 1). Originally published in Cannon,
W. B., Hunger and Thirst. In C. Murchison (ed.), *Foundations of Experimental
Psychology*, Worcester, Mass.: Clark University Press, 1929.

seen as internal goads to action (Cannon, 1939, p. 76). Cannon's view was a homeostatic one. This is to say that the drive stimuli arise because of deficits or excesses in bodily tissues and they activate behavior which can correct the imbalances by suitable activity leading to consummatory behavior. This is the **local stimulus theory** of drive.

There were other findings that supported drive theory. Richter (1927) summarized evidence that the general or "spontaneous" activity that animals show occurs in cycles; thus after a meal a rat is relatively quiet, but as the next meal time approaches activity increases. Female rats show a 4-day cycle of activity associated with the estrous cycle, the peak of activity corresponding to the stage of sexual receptivity ("heat"). These findings were consistent with the proposition that internal stimuli spur the animal into activity. Richter also observed that the undeprived animal does not eat continuously; rather, Richter thought, the animal eats regularly spaced "meals." The interpretation was that stimuli arising from short periods of deprivation elicit eating.

Another finding from Richter's laboratory (Richter, 1942–43) pointed to the regulatory function of drive states. This function arose from the discovery of specific hungers. If animals are deprived of needed food elements (e.g., salt or thiamine) and are given a choice between the deficient diet and one that contains the needed substance, they often choose the nutritionally desirable one, thus rectifying the imbalance. Although this finding is not congruent with a local stimulus theory of drive, it was consistent with an interpretation of drive as a central state, a physiological condition somehow affecting behavior through the central nervous system (Beach, 1956, Morgan, 1943, Stellar, 1954). Yet another piece of evidence for drive was reported by Warden (1931) and his associates. This evidence came from studies with the Columbia Obstruction Box. In this device, an animal is placed in a starting box with an incentive (food, a mate, young, etc.,) in view on the other side of a grid; the grid can be electrified, and Warden measured the strength of a drive by counting the number of times in a 20-minute interval the animal would cross the electrified grid to reach a given incentive (see Fig. 5.3). Number of crossings increased with length of time since the animal had eaten, drunk, or mated, etc., at least up to 2 days for most of the drives studied. (See Bolles, 1975, pp. 109–124; Cofer, 1972, pp. 17–27; and Cofer & Appley, 1964, Chapters 5, 6, and 10 for more complete discussions of this early literature on drives.)

These studies lent considerable support to the drive concept. However, there are many difficulties with it. Before we turn to these difficulties it will be useful to give a brief presentation of the use of drive as it was employed by Hull (1943) in a major behavior system constructed during the 1930s and 1940s, a system which was widely influential during its development and for a period thereafter (see Ch. 1, vol. 1).

C. L. Hull (1884–1952) began his work as an effort to construct a theory of learning on conditioned response and trial and error principles. In doing so,

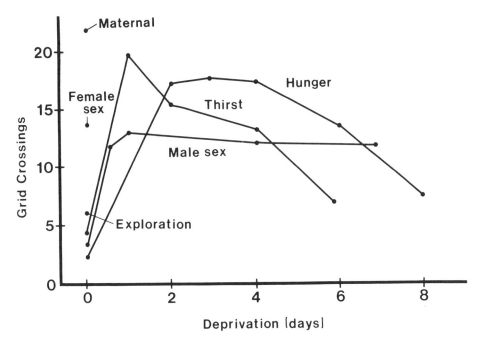

FIG. 5.3. Number of grid crossings in the Columbia obstruction box as a function of deprivation of food, water, and sexual behavior (male rats). Also shown are crossings with no incentive present (exploration), and crossings by females to a male rate (female sex) and to rat pups (maternal). Redrawn from Bolles (1975, p. 121, Fig. 5-1). Originally published in Warden, et al., (1931).

however, he found it necessary to include, as an important component, a motivational theory as well. The learning theory was concerned with the formation of associations or habits that link stimulus conditions (S) with responses (R). In thinking of habits as conditioned reflexes, Hull proposed that **reinforcement** along the lines of Thorndike's (1898) law of effect was necessary. Reinforcement is a concept invented independently by Pavlov and by Herbert Spencer (1880) as pointed out by Bolles (1975, p. 43). Hull defined reinforcement more formally as occurring from the reduction of a drive or of a drive stimulus (1943).

The existence of a habit (H), however, is not sufficient, after the habit has been formed, for the behavior mediated by the habit to occur. Rather, there must be appropriate stimulus conditions and drive energy (D). Hull's formula for the occurrence of a response based on a given habit was $R = f(H) \times f(D)$. Since the combination of habit and drive is multiplicative, the habit could not be displayed in behavior without some level of motivation. Hull thus distinguished between structure (habit) and motivation (drive), in much the way as Freud and especially McDougall seemed to do.

In Hull's theory drive was established by antecedent conditions such as deprivation of needed substances (e.g., food or water) or such as excesses in the body
(e.g., urine, feces, or painful stimulation). These conditions set up states of
need, which are the basis for drives. The needs, he said, ''generate and throw
into the bloodstream more or less characteristic chemical substances, or
else . . . withdraw a characteristic substance.'' These effects ''have a selective
physiological effect on more or less restricted or characteristic parts of the body
(e.g., the so-called 'hunger' contractions of the body)'' which activates receptors
giving rise to the ''drive stimulus'' (Hull, 1943, p. 240).

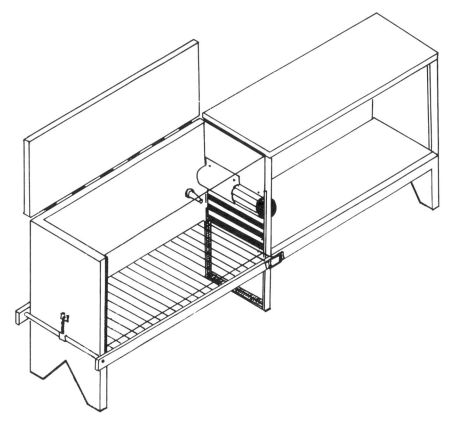

FIG. 5.4.   Apparatus used to study the acquired drive of fear. The left compartment is painted white, the right compartment black. Electric shocks can be given
through the grid floor in the white (left) compartment. The door between the
compartments is painted with black and white stripes. Depending on conditions, it
will drop out of the way when the experimenter presses a button or when the rat
presses the bar or turns the wheel. Redrawn from Cofer and Appley (1964, p. 574,
Fig. 11-8). Originally published in Miller (1951, p. 437, Fig. 1).

For Hull, the drive stimulus was not a motivational factor in behavior; he did not accept the local stimulus theory of drive. Rather, it served as a stimulus to which the reaction was conditioned just as it was conditioned to the acting environmental stimuli. Although drive activated habits, it was not necessary that the same drive as was present during learning also be present to energize a habit. Any source of drive could do so. Hull remarked that this generalized character of drive resembled Freud's libido (Hull, 1943, p. 241).

Hull was aware that the biological drives based on needs were insufficient to account for human behavior, and he proposed in addition learned or **secondary drives.** These drives were acquired through "*situations* associated with drives" (Hull, 1951, p. 21). The paradigm example of the learning of a drive is Miller's (1948, 1951) demonstration that fear can be learned (see Fig. 5.4). Reinforcers other than food, water, and the like were also needed to account for much human learning, and Hull proposed that conditions associated with primary reinforcement could themselves become **secondary reinforcers**. In these ways, Hull extended his basic concepts beyond the animal laboratory in which they were first developed.

Hull's theory had tremendous impact on the study of learning and motivation in experimental psychology, and it was also influential in such fields as social psychology, personality, developmental psychology, and clinical psychology. There was an attempt to integrate it with psychoanalytic theory, with many of whose tenets it seemed compatible. Relevant to these assertions are the books or papers by Dollard, Doob, Miller, Mowrer, and Sears (1939), Dollard and Miller (1950), Miller and Dollard (1941), and Sears (1943, 1944).

PROBLEMS OF DRIVE THEORY

As Hull and others developed the concept of drive during the 1930s and 1940s it was a fairly straightforward example of an **intervening variable. Defining independent variables** were such things as time of deprivation (e.g., in the case of food), stimulus factors (to account for the fact that animals show preferences for particular goal objects such as particular foods or mates) and events in the organism's history (since most drives are modified by experience and some are acquired outright). Attributes of behavior on the **dependent variable** side were such things as level of consummatory activity such as the amount of food or water ingested, level of general activity (e.g., in a running wheel), vigor of performance of a learned response (e.g., running a maze or crossing the barrier in an obstruction apparatus), the particular food selected in a choice situation and performance in the presence of stimuli previously associated with drive or not (in experiments designed to demonstrate acquired motivation).

The intervening variable itself had the energization of behavior $[R = f(H) \times f(D)]$ as its main property. In Hull's theory specifically, however, it had a number of other properties: (1) Drives were additive; combining two or more drives increased the value of **generalized drive.** (2) Drives per se were not directed toward any particular goal or invested in any particular behavior; a habit learned in one drive condition could be energized by a different drive. (3) In order to explain the fact that drives obviously *are* directed, contrary to property (2) just listed, they were hypothesized to have associated **drive stimuli** which acquired directing power as a result of learning. (4) Reinforcement was assumed to be a process of **drive reduction;** demonstrations of learning without drive reduction called into question Hull's concept of drive as well as his concept of reinforcement.

One implication of this view of drive is that it should be possible, experimentally, to manipulate any of the independent variables and, in that way, produce predictable changes in any of the dependent variables one chose to measure. Sometimes such experiments produced the expected outcome. Many experiments obtained orderly relationships between time of deprivation and the vigor, both of consummatory behavior and the performance of a learned response. Too frequently for theoretical comfort, however, the results turned out to give at best weak support for the theory.

General activity (Bolles, 1975, pp. 217–233) turns out to be a complex matter that is responsive to many variables in addition to deprivation. When all these variables are partialled out, there remains a small increase in activity after food deprivation but not from deprivation of other incentives; even in the case of food deprivation, the effect on activity is seen only in the activity wheel. Other devices do not show it. Another problem with activity, as a pure measure of drive, is that animals can learn to anticipate feeding time, when, as in Richter's experiments, feeding occurs at the same time every day. Support for this interpretation was provided by Sheffield and Campbell (1954). They deprived rats of food for 3 days. Then, in one group, the delivery of food was associated with a stimulus change but was not in a second group. Occurrence of the stimulus change in the first group was accompanied by augmented activity but had no effect in the second group. Campbell and Sheffield (1953) also showed that starvation over a 3-day period did not result in an increase in activity.

Studies of **feeding rhythms** or cycles in the rat (Baker, 1953) have indicated that there is an average 2-hour interval between ''meals,'' but that the variability around this average is very large (a standard deviation of 90 minutes). In line with this variability, the sequence of eating and non-eating episodes in individual animals is best described as a random one.

Investigations of stimulus factors began to reveal a pattern of great complexity. Although animals' food preferences usually matched their states of need, there were exceptions. Strong learned preferences for food were found to persist despite the presence of nutritional needs that would dictate other choices (Young, 1959). Thus an animal may choose a sugar solution over one containing a needed protein. Moreover, Rozin and Kalat (1971) found that an animal's choice of diet containing a needed substance like thiamin depends on the alternative diet it is offered. If a new diet is the alternative choice, even one that does not contain the needed substance, it is as likely to be chosen as a new one containing the nutritionally necessary element. Evidently, in the older experiments, in which the animal had to choose between the old, deficient diet and a new, adequate diet, choice of the latter really reflected only an aversion to the old diet which had sickened the animal. The choice made between a new, adequate and a new, inadequate foodstuff does not support the idea of specific hungers.

Studies with the obstruction box were marred by a number of faults. Bolles (1975, pp. 122–123) has pointed out that the data reported by Warden and his associates for the entire 20-minute test intervals differ from those seen early in those intervals. Further, before the tests were run, there were pre-training trials whose effects on learning to cross the grid may have varied with the deprivation conditions. Warden had wished to compare the strengths of drives, but it is impossible to equate the value of different incentives (e.g., food, water, a mate, a litter of pups), so that differences in number of grid-crossings for different "drives" may have been due to incentive differences.

A particular flaw in many of the early drive experiments involving hunger centered on the use of hours of deprivation as an index of motivation. It is now clear (Bolles, 1975) that loss of body weight is a much more important parameter, thus leaving a number of early experiments difficult to evaluate. Bolles' (1975, pp. 270–278) survey of the literature on the stimulus properties of drive shows that the drive stimulus has little functional value, and, similarly, his evaluation of the experiments on generalized drive (pp. 247–257) is that they have not supported Hull's expectations. "There is," he says, "very little support for the idea that different sources of drive are mutually substitutable and mutually additive" (p. 257). There is little basis for the notion that drive sources summate to produce a D, independently of their qualitative differences.

Drive Reduction as Reinforcement.   The aspect of Hull's particular theory that received the greatest and most critical attention was the drive-reduction hypothesis of reinforcement. The notion that animals are motivated to reduce drive stimulation or to reduce tension in general has been attacked in two ways. One is that reinforcement can occur even when there is no decrease of or when there is an actual increase in level of stimulation. The other is that sometimes animals are motivated to seek stimulation, rather than to avoid or reduce it. This second objection is broader than the first and will be considered later in this section.

In the 1950s, a number of studies produced results consistent with the idea that drive reduction is not essential to reinforcement. Thus, it was found that saccharin, a non-nutritive substance, is an effective reward (Sheffield & Roby, 1950) and that it has more reinforcing value than does dextrose, a nutritive sugar not so sweet as saccharin. There is a good deal of evidence that incentive and reward values of substances vary with their palatability, even though nutritive and therefore drive-reduction values do not differ substantially (Young, 1959). There were also reports that increases in stimulation can be reinforcing. Thus, Sheffield, Wulff, and Backer (1951) found that naive male rats will increase their running speed in a runway for the reward of incomplete copulation, an activity that presumably increases stimulation. It has been found that small increases in illumination, the opportunity to explore a complex maze, or to explore novel objects are reinforcing for rats, and monkeys can be reinforced by an opportunity to look through a window at the laboratory environment or to hear laboratory sounds (see Cofer, 1972, pp. 100–101, for a review of these experiments). The fact that animals can be reinforced by and will work for electrical stimulation of parts of their brains was initially interpreted as evidence against drive reduction (Olds, 1955), but this interpretation was largely conjectural.

The kinds of results just summarized led to accounts of reinforcement alternative to drive reduction. Some investigators suggested that consummatory acts are reinforcing, as indicated by the effects of saccharin ingestion and of incomplete copulation (Sheffield, Roby, & Campbell, 1954), without drive reduction. Premack (1965) proposed that an activity will reinforce another one, if its preference value is greater than that of the other one. This view has received some substantiation, but its applicability to the full range of reinforcement phenomena has not been established. Interest in the process of reinforcement seemed to wane in the 1960s, though the use of reinforcement in shaping behavior continues on a wide scale.

Animals and people spend much of their time in activities, and some attention has been paid to the question whether there is a drive for activity, independent of other drives (cf. Cofer, 1972, pp. 74–76). However, it has been difficult to establish that such a drive exists. On the other hand, a number of studies have led to the conclusion that organisms may often be motivated to explore their environments, to manipulate and inspect objects and to escape from situations in which external stimulation has been reduced.

Evidence concerning exploration came from work on rats by Glanzer (1953) and Montgomery (1951). Glanzer used a maze in the shape of a cross (+); he was interested in the question whether the rat after making a turn in this apparatus would, on the next trial, be motivated to enter a new part of the maze or to avoid the turn it had just made. Glanzer was testing an implication of Hull's theory (not developed in this book) that predicted a nonrepetition of the previous turn. In his experiment, Glanzer started the rat in either the upper or the lower arm of the cross, and the animal was forced to turn right or left because access to the arm directly ahead of the starting arm was blocked off. The animal made its turn and was then placed in the starting arm that had been blocked. This time the starting arm on the other side was blocked. Glanzer found that the animal would repeat its prior turn, rather than avoiding it. This means the animal (which was neither hungry nor thirsty nor given any reinforcement for its choice) was avoiding by its second turn the *place* in the maze it had previously visited and was entering the unexplored part of the maze. Montgomery's work, in which elevated mazes of various configurations were employed, also showed that animals would move in the maze to places they had not already visited. These findings were taken as indicating that rats have a tendency to perform locomotory exploration.

Manipulation of objects was explored by Harlow, Harlow, and Meyer (1950). They presented mechanical puzzles that had been assembled to monkeys. The monkeys, which were not rewarded for their behavior by food, water, or other goal objects, manipulated these puzzles and disassembled them. With practice they became more proficient at disassembling the puzzles and showed persistence in working on the puzzles over a number of days. Harlow concluded that this behavior cannot be explained by homeostatic drives and proposed a motive for manipulation.

Inspection of figures was studied by a number of investigators. With infants, for example, Fantz (1958) found that checker-board patterns were more attractive to the infant's inspection than were simpler patterns. Berlyne (1958), with college students, investigated a number of features of figural displays for their effects on inspection time (see Fig. 5.5). He found that complex or incongruous figures were inspected longer than were simple or congruous figures. Complexity was introduced by irregular arrangements of the parts in the figures, by increasing the amount of material in the figures, by making the parts heterogeneous, and by making them irregular. Incongruity is illustrated by pictures in which parts of animals were replaced by parts of other animals or by placing part of an object like an automobile as the rear of a rabbit and conversely.

Reduction of stimulation was provided in experimental situations like the one shown in Fig. 5.6. Volunteer subjects were recruited to participate in an experiment in which they were to lie on a cot, with goggles over their eyes, with cuffs over their hands and arms, and with masking noises from a fan and air-conditioner. They were paid well for participating, and their food, water, and toileting needs were arranged for. The subjects, however, found this situation to be one they could not tolerate for long, most of them terminating their participation before 2 or 3 days had passed. Evidently, the lack of stimulation created a situation the subjects could not endure, and they were motivated to escape from it.

The accumulation of findings on exploration, manipulation, inspection, and sensory deprivation was taken by many writers as contradictory to tension reduction views of human motivation. This evidence (White, 1959) was seen also as contravening Freud's views as well as the drive model.

The demonstrations were given interpretations, of course, as investigators wished to go beyond their simple impact on the concept of tension reduction. Initially, it was proposed that there are non-homeostatic drives, such as those for manipulation, exploration, and for stimuli. However, these ideas seemed hardly to be an advance over tension reduction. Probably the most general view to

EXPERIMENT I

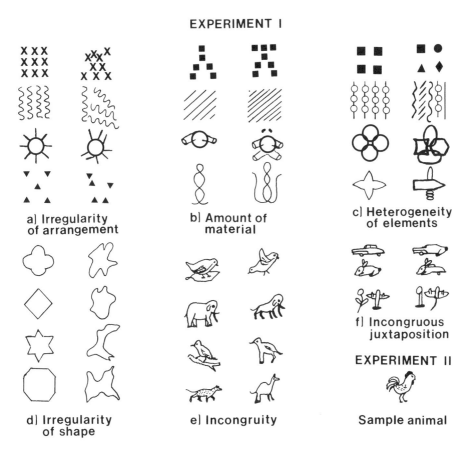

a] Irregularity
of arrangement

b] Amount of
material

c] Heterogeneity
of elements

f] Incongruous
juxtaposition

EXPERIMENT II

d] Irregularity
of shape

e] Incongruity

Sample animal

FIG. 5.5.   Arrangements of visual material designed to produce stimulus complexity. Redrawn from Cofer and Appley (1964, p. 287, Fig. 6-4). First published by Berlyne (1958, Fig. 1).

receive some acceptance combined the concept of arousal with that of adaptation level.

Arousal and Activation Level

Arousal or activation has long been a concept in psychophysiology, but its introduction as a major entry into motivational considerations seems to date from the discovery that impulses from the reticular formation of the brain stem are involved in the degree of activation of the cerebral cortex. This structure is shown in Fig. 5.7. Lesions in this structure at its higher levels produce patterns in the electroencephalogram that resemble those seen in sleep. Alternatively, stimulation of the structure in a sleeping cat produce an EEG characteristic of waking

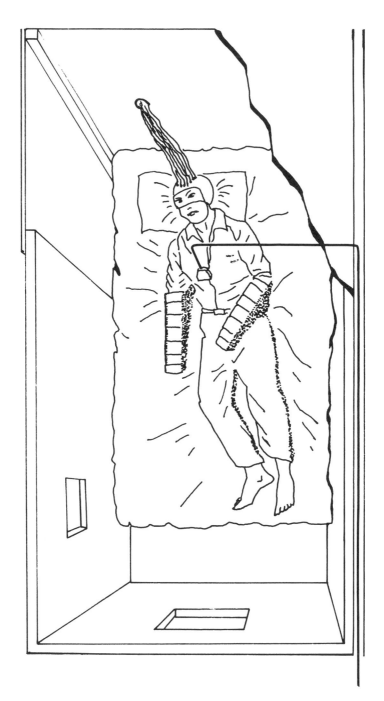

FIG. 5.6.   A diagram of a sensory deprivation chamber showing the subject lying on a cot with cuffs over his forearms and hands and goggles over his eyes. Above the subject's head is an exhaust fan and above the feet an air-conditioner. Redrawn from Cofer & Appley (1964, p. 280, Fig. 6-2). Originally published in P. Solomon et al., (eds.), *Sensory Deprivation: A Symposium at Harvard Medical School.* Cambridge: Harvard University Press, 1961.

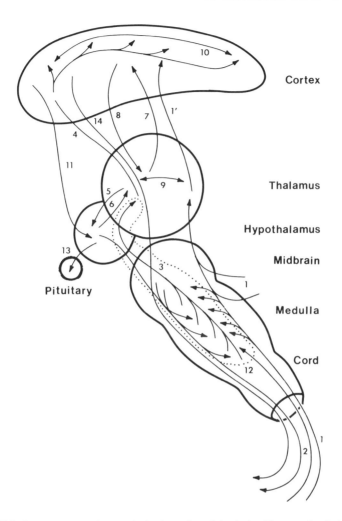

FIG. 5.7. Diagram of the reticular formation of the brain. The cross-hatched portion of the figure shows the formation. Redrawn from Cofer and Appley (1964, p. 400, Fig. 8-4a). Originally published in Lindsley (1957, Fig. 6).

activity (Lindsley, 1957). It was also known (Lindsley, 1957) that activation patterns from deep sleep to excitement are associated with different EEG patterns (see Fig. 5.8). Further, it can reasonably be asserted that behavioral efficiency is low in sleep states and also in excited states. Behavioral efficiency then would be greatest at a level between excitement and relaxed or drowsy states. A theoretical relation between arousal level and behavioral efficiency is shown as an inverted U-shaped curve in Fig. 5.9, as suggested by Hebb (1955). Some evidence was obtained that arousal is related to motivational states (Bartoshuk, 1971) and to behavioral efficiency, though it was never extensive.

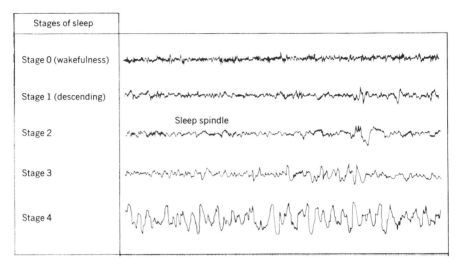

FIG. 5.8. Patterns of EEG, from deep sleep to wakefulness and excitement. Redrawn from Cofer (1972, p. 64, Fig. 9). Originally published in Lindsley (1957, p. 67, Fig. 5).

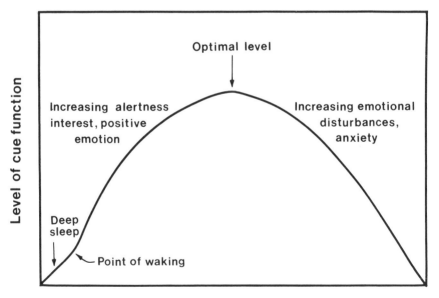

FIG. 5.9. Hypothetical curve showing the relationship between behavioral arousal and behavioral efficiency or level of cue function as an inverted U. Redrawn from Cofer and Appley (1964, p. 393, Fig. 8-3). Originally published by Hebb (1955, Fig. 2).

Adaptation level or AL is a notion stressed by Helson (1964) and developed by him. In essence, Helson's idea is that one adapts to past and current stimuli and takes this level as a frame of reference. One reacts to stimulation in terms of the degree to which they deviate from AL. A number of writers, including Berlyne (1967) and Hunt (1965), have suggested that stimulation is sought because it deviates from the AL; further, it can be argued that increases in stimulation can be rewarding (if they are not too great) because they differ from AL; decreases are also rewarding because they, too, differ from AL.

While these interpretations have generated some interest, they have not gained the attention that was accorded to drive theory. It is almost as if the whole motivation concept was so closely intertwined with drive theory that the fall of the latter cost the concept itself a great deal of its interest.

HUMAN MOTIVATION

Drive theory was developed largely in the context of animal behavior, although it was seen as applicable to human beings. Psychoanalytic theory, of course, was concerned entirely with human motivation, and, except for some studies of incentives (Cofer & Appley, 1964, 769–771), it had little direct competition until the 1930s. Study of human motivation has become prominent since then, and we can divide the work done into the following classes: the assessment of motives, field or balance theories, attribution theory, and humanistic views. This work is much more cognitive than was that carried out under the aegis of drive theory, even when that theory was applied to human behavior. Thus motivation theory is turning again to the active subject, rather than to the patient, who was moved by forces (e.g. drives) with little or no control of them.

Assessment of Motives

Henry A. Murray (1893–   ) was the source of much of the work on human motives, listing a large number of them in his book (1938) which also reported essentially clinical assessments of the motives of a sample of college students. Included in Murray's procedures was a projective test, the **Thematic Appercep-tion Test (TAT),** that Morgan and Murray (1935) had described earlier. Murray saw behavior as dynamically determined through the interactions of **needs** (or motives), which he seemed to regard as impelling forces, and environmental pressures (**press**). Most of the research that his views generated has been concerned mainly with two or three of the needs he proposed: Need for achievement (NAch), need for affiliation, and need for power. Other human motives that have received extensive study are the need for social approval (Crowne & Marlowe, 1964) and anxiety (see Cofer & Appley, 1964, pp. 701–714).

Research on achievement, affiliation, and power has been largely the work of D. C. McClelland (1917–   ) and John W. Atkinson (1925–   ) and their associates. They have typically used a need arousal procedure. The need for achievement, for example, was aroused by involving male college students in a competitive intellectual situation. The TAT was administered under these arousal and (to different subjects) non-arousal conditions. A scoring system for the presence and amount of a need was constructed by looking at the differences in stories written to TAT pictures under aroused and non-aroused conditions. This scoring system then yields a range of scores for stories written without arousal, indicating that people respond differently, in terms of need expression, to identical pictures.

The McClelland-Atkinson group has gone on to explore the relations between the need scores and performance in a variety of situations. A major conclusion from their work is that performance is a function of a complex set of variables; need or motive alone does not determine it, but factors like the subjective probability of success and failure and the incentive value of success and failure are also important. In this conclusion, they agree with some of the observations of Kurt Lewin (see below).

The study of anxiety and social approval has been carried out often with questionnaires, and contrasting groups have been formed based on questionnaire scores. One anxiety questionnaire, the Manifest-Anxiety Scale (Taylor, 1953), was employed to test certain predictions from Hullian theory, and another, the Test Anxiety Questionnaire (Mandler & Sarason, 1952), has been employed to study reactions to success and failure, a factor that enters into the prediction of performance on the basis of NAch. These questionnaires have been employed in a great deal of research, with somewhat mixed results.

Another way of studying anxiety is to use fear-inducing situations. Schachter (1959) employed this procedure and was able to show that social affiliation was greater in certain people who were fearful than in those who were not. Unfortunately, he did not combine his fear-arousing conditions with TAT measures of affiliation.

Field and Balance Theories

A dynamic theory that began about 1912 is Gestalt theory. Its early concerns were primarily with visual perception, and it saw perceptual events as arising from the forces in the visual field. Despite its dynamic character, the founders of Gestalt theory did not discuss motivation, and it remained for Kurt Lewin (1899–1947) to do so.

Lewin (1935) stressed that behavior is a product of a psychological environment, i.e., the way in which the world is perceived by the individual. This perceived world is related to but not identical to the world as a physicist would describe it. Behavior depends on the relations between the needs the individual has and aspects of the environment which function as goals; also there are perceived obstacles and barriers to the securing of the goals and there are intermediate steps (regions of the life space) that must be completed before the goal can be attained. The psychological environment or life space is usually represented as a sausage-shaped diagram, divided up into regions that correspond to these steps or activities (see Fig. 5.10). The person has needs that are states of tension, and goal regions of the life space have attractive or repulsive features (corresponding to approach to or avoidance of the goal region) which endow them with valence. Thus, the person can be represented as functioning within a field of forces, being impelled to those regions with positive valences and repelled by those with negative valence. The person's path through the life space is governed by this force field; automatic as behavior would seem to be according to this account, the field, initially, corresponds to the individual's perceptions and includes mental events and processes that go on in that person's mind.

Lewin did not postulate a list of motives, needs, or drives, but stressed the tension that accompanied intentions. Thus, if one is asked to perform a task and agrees to do so, there is a tension corresponding to the intention to do the task; if work is interrupted before the task is completed, one is likely to remember that task, resume working on it when possible, or carry out a similar substitute task, because the tension remains to be resolved. Lewin and his students set up a great many experiments in which the procedures made it reasonable to infer that goals had been accepted by the participants and that, therefore, tensions existed. In addition, there were studies of goal-setting, as reflected in the level-of-aspiration procedure, studies of frustration, social climates, food habits, and a number of other interesting and socially pertinent problems. Lewin's ideas were applied to group processes, and Lewin can be regarded as the founder of the field of group dynamics, and of a number of other social psychological problems.

One of Lewin's students, Leon Festinger (1919–   ), developed the theory of **cognitive dissonance** (Festinger, 1957). This theory, which has generated much research and controversy, was concerned with conditions conducive to attitude change. The basic postulate of the theory is that we desire to have harmony among our cognitions; if cognitions are not in harmony, they are dissonant, and the resulting dissonance acts like a drive, motivating us to do something that will resolve the dissonance. Thus, if there is disagreement on some issue between two persons, and each person likes the other, there is dissonance, for each, between the cognition of liking the other and the cognition that the other's attitude, opinion, or information on the issue differs. One might be motivated by such dissonance to seek more information, to attempt to persuade the other, to change one's attitude, or to change one's valuation of the other. This theory, which dominated social psychology for a number of years, no longer seems to be as persuasive as it once was, perhaps because its experimental tests involved a great deal of deception, rather contrived situations, and other complex manipulations that were difficult to replicate. Alternative accounts for dissonance phenomena could also be given.

Another person with a Gestalt background is Fritz Heider (1896–   ), who has proposed a **balance theory** in conjunction with inter-personal relations and pro-

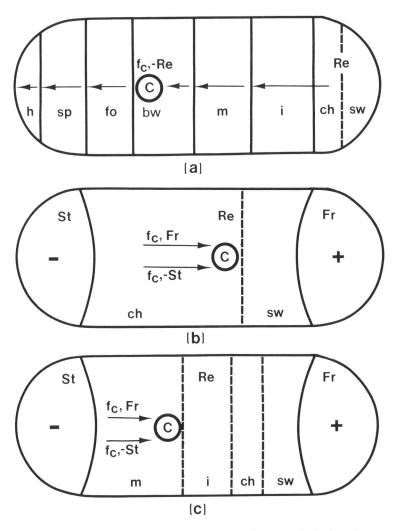

FIG. 5.10. Representations of the life-space according to Lewin. In these diagrams C refers to a child, RE to real eating, H to putting the hand on the table, SP to taking a spoon, FO to putting food on the spoon, BW to bringing the spoon halfway to the mouth, M to bringing the food to the mouth, SW to swallowing, ST to struggle with adults, FR to freedom, FC to force on the child which is negative. Part (a) depicts the situation in the case of a disliked food, (b) the situation as the child starts eating, and (c) the situation at a later stage of learning to eat the disliked food. Redrawn from Cofer and Appley (1964, p. 361, Fig. 7-5), who adapted it from Fig. 37, p. 117, in Lewin, K., *The Conceptual Representation and Measurement of Psychological Forces,* Durham, N.C.: Duke University Press, 1938.

cesses. He has also proposed an **attribution theory,** which some writers (e.g., Weiner, 1972) take as replacing dissonance theory. Heider's basic contention is that we, as average people, attempt to make sense of the world by attributing causes to events, including human behavior. One cannot perceive causes but can infer them. Thus, if we perceive a hostile act on the part of another, we will wish to explain—find a cause for—that act, and will think about the circumstances of the act and will reflect in our explanation our preconceptions about hostility and what causes it.

Attribution theory is a theory of "how a typical observer infers a person's motivation from his action" (Kelley, 1967, p. 193), and, in Heider's writings, has not been developed much as a theory of the observer's motivation. However, one could make attributions as to the causes for one's actions (Heider, 1958, p. 79), and perhaps a self-attributional account of motivation can be developed. Weiner (1972, Chapter 6) has reviewed comparisons of the attributions that have been studied in people who vary in NAch. These are not self-attributions, but it is clear that people with high NAch explain conduct on the part of others rather differently in several respects from the way people with low NAch do.

In field theory, balance and dissonance theories, and in attribution theories, much stress is placed on cognitive processes and evaluations made by the person. Thus the role of the active subject once again receives emphasis, although not perhaps to the extent that someone like Peters (1958) would urge. Peters seems to argue that much of motivation theory is unnecessary, because a great many actions can be understood simply on the basis of the actor's reasons for doing them.

Humanistic Views

Humanistic theories tend to see the person as an active agent, one who has satisfied lower level needs and who is not controlled by anxiety. The response to anxiety is conformity to social pressures, conventions, and standards. These theories have had a prominent role since about 1950, in the writings of Fromm (1941), Syngg and Combs (1949), Horney (1950), Rogers (1951), May (1953), and Maslow (1954). Maslow's formulation is the most systematic from a motivational viewpoint, and we give a brief summary of it here.

Maslow postulated a hierarchy of motives. At the base are physiological needs, like hunger. Next are safety needs, then love and belongingness needs. Needs for deserved esteem follow, and the highest need of the hierarchy is the need for self-actualization.

Maslow argues that if the lower needs are satisfied, the highest level can emerge. When it emerges, Maslow says, motivation is unlike that which the lower needs provide. Among self-actualizing people there is "expression motivation or growth motivation, rather than deficiency motivation . . . our subjects no longer strive in the ordinary sense, but rather develop. They attempt to grow to perfection and to develop more and more fully in their own style . . . For them motivation is just character growth, character expression, maturation, and development; in a word self-actualization (Maslow, 1954, p. 211)."

It is clear that many of the motivational ideas dominant in the twentieth century are taken, by the humanist group, as unrepresentative of what the human being can be. They attribute the failure of most people to achieve the highest level to social and familial sources which inhibit full development. Behavior of people at the highest level would be unpredictable, so that there is a hint in the works of the humanist writers of the rational view of the species which has been under attack since the time of Thomas Hobbes. In this chapter, then, we have come full circle.

CONCLUSION

The theme developed in this chapter is that the concept of motivation was a major factor in introducing determinism into considerations of human beings. The concept was opposed to the idea of free choice or free will that had dominated theological and philosophical thought for many centuries. At the very beginnings of modern science, the principles of hedonism were suggested in English philosophy and the concept of the reflex in French philosophy as replacements for free will. Hedonism and the reflex appeared to treat the organism as a relatively passive participant in the calculus of pleasure and pain and in responding to external stimuli. However, the histories of hedonism and of the reflex were largely independent of each other.

Another significant factor in the emergence of deterministic motivational ideas was the theory of evolution. After the theory was announced, it became possible to consider the human species as continuous with other animal species, rather than being the result of a separate Divine creation. Thus, instincts, which earlier had been reserved for animals, could be postulated for the human species, and intelligence, earlier reserved for the human being, could be considered in species of animals below the human species. Instinct theory, however, encountered many difficulties, and except in psychoanalysis and in ethological studies of animals, the word largely disappeared from psychology's vocabulary in the decades from about 1920 to 1950.

The decline of instinct left learning as a major interest among psychologists in the United States and it left also a void in the explanation of the dynamics of behavior. This void was filled by the concept of drive. Drive was initially believed to be localized in irritating impulses in bodily organs—the stomach in hunger, the mouth and throat in thirst. Drive was considered from the point of view of homeostasis, the idea that when bodily needs arise they initiate behavior that can be instrumental in reducing or eliminating the irritating drive stimuli. A theory of learning held that reduction of such stimuli or of the needs underlying them was essential for learning to occur.

Through much of its history, motivation has been accorded the function of energizing or activating habit or innate structures that in conjunction with external stimuli actually supply the direction and control that behavior displays.

Drive theory shares some important features with psychoanalytic motivation theory, and it was extended to human motivation through the concepts of acquired drive or learned sources of motivation. Human motives that have received attention include anxiety and needs for achievement, affiliation, social approval, and power.

Ultimately, drive theory failed. Most of the evidence that seemed to support the theory could be given alternative interpretations, and findings from experiments on animals and on human beings showed that there are motivations to explore and manipulate the environment, that animals and people are curious, and that they may seek rather than avoid stimulation. The homeostatic character of drive seemed to be disavowed by this kind of evidence, and an arousal concept, closely related to the notion of adaptation level, emerged as a replacement for drive. Meanwhile, however, anatomical and neurochemical studies of such states as hunger, thirst, and sex brought out their very complex character. The theory of acquired motivation was found wanting. The demise of the drive concept has left the field of motivation in disarray, and the arousal concept has not captured the interest that was invested in drive.

The idea that motivation in the human being is a highly cognitive matter has arisen again and is expressed in such views as the theory of cognitive dissonance, other balance theories, and in attribution theory. These theories see the person as an active agent who makes decisions and chooses alternatives on the basis of evaluations of information. Humanistic theories have been developed. They are cognitive as well and stress the idea that social and environmental factors may actually prevent the emergence of a person's human nature, i.e., his or her self-actualization. It is possible that the humanistic theories are rejecting of determinism, though whether this is true is not clear at present.

It is uncertain as to how the field of motivation will proceed in the future. In the writer's view, it seems unlikely that the old models provided by hunger, thirst, and sex and by S-R theory will dominate any longer our conception of the area.

The role of inborn behavior patterns, as described by the ethologists, has had an increasing influence on our understanding of the conditions of learning. They have also stressed stimulus factors that release many unlearned acts, making neither learning nor motivational concepts necessary to account for such acts. Their work has highlighted differences among species in both learning and motivation, and these differences offer problems for those who advocate universal principles of learning and motivation. Universal principles have been the goal of much research on learning and motivation, and it may simply be that they do not exist. Searching for them may no longer be fruitful.

Research with motivation in human beings has, as just indicated, taken a cognitive direction, one which emphasizes choice by an active agent. This approach may lead to stress on the goals of behavior, both in the short and the long term (Irwin, 1971). Goals are related to expectations, and Bolles (1975) sees expectancy as a concept which can explain much in the literature of animal learning and motivation. However, it still remains to be seen what a cognitive theory of motivation based on goals and expectancies would be like. But in some way psychology must deal with the dynamics of action, which is, in sum, the problem of motivation.

REFERENCES

Ayres, C. E. Instinct and capacity: I. The instinct of belief-in-instincts. *Journal of Philosophy,* 1921, *18,* 561–566.

Baker, R. A. Aperiodic feeding in the albino rat. *Journal of Comparative and Physiological Psychology,* 1953, *46,* 422–426.

Bartoshuk, A. K. Motivation. In J. W. Kling & L. A. Riggs (Eds.), *Woodworth and Schlosberg's experimental psychology* (3rd ed.). New York: Holt, Rinehart & Winston, 1971.

Beach, F. A. Characteristics of masculine sex drive. In M. R. Jones (Ed.), *Nebraska Symposium on Motivation.* Lincoln: University of Nebraska Press, 1956. Pp. 1–32.

Berlyne, D. E. Conflict and information-theory variables as determinants of human perceptual curiosity. *Journal of Experimental Psychology,* 1957, *53,* 399–404.

Berlyne, D. E. The influence of complexity and novelty in visual figures on orienting responses. *Journal of Experimental Psychology,* 1958, *55,* 289–296.

Bernard, L. L. *Instinct: A study in social psychology.* New York: Holt, 1924.

Bolles, R. C. *Theory of motivation* (2nd ed.). New York: Harper & Row, 1975.

Boring, E. G. *A history of experimental psychology* (2nd ed.). New York: Appleton-Century-Crofts, 1950.

Brooks, G. P. The faculty psychology of Thomas Reid. *Journal of the History of the Behavioral Sciences,* 1976, *12,* 65–77.

Brown, J. S. *The motivation of behavior.* New York: McGraw-Hill, 1961.

Campbell, B. A. & Sheffield, F. D. Relation of random activity to food deprivation. *Journal of Comparative and Physiological Psychology,* 1953, *46,* 320–322.

Cannon, W. B. Hunger and thirst. In C. Murchison (Ed.), *A handbook of general experimental psychology.* Worcester, Mass.: Clark University Press, 1934.

Cannon, W. B. *The wisdom of the body* (2nd ed.). New York: Norton, 1939.

Cannon, W. B. & Washburn, A. L. An explanation of hunger. *American Journal of Physiology,* 1912, *29,* 441–454.

Cofer, C. N. *Motivation and emotion.* Glenview, Ill.: Scott, Foresman, 1972.

Cofer, C. N. & Appley, M. H. *Motivation: Theory and research.* New York: Wiley, 1964.

Coppleston, F. *A history of philosophy* (Vol. II). *Mediaeval philosophy, Augustine to Scotus.* Westminister, Md.: The Newman Press, 1957.

Craig, W. Appetites and aversions as constituents of instincts. *Biological Bulletin,* 1918, *34,* 91–107.

Crowne, D. P. & Marlow, D. *The approval motive: Studies in evaluative dependence.* New York: Wiley, 1964.

Dollard, J., Doob, L. W., Miller, N. E., Mowrer, O. H., & Sears, R. R. *Frustration and aggression.* New Haven: Yale University Press, 1939.

Dollard, J. & Miller, N. E. *Personality and psychotherapy: An analysis in terms of learning thinking, and culture.* New York: McGraw-Hill, 1950.

Dunlap, K. *Elements of scientific psychology.* St. Louis: Mosby, 1922.

Fantz, R. L. Pattern vision in young infants. *Psychological Record,* 1958, *8,* 43–48.

Fearing, F. *Reflex action: A study in the history of physiological psychology.* Cambridge, Mass.: The MIT Press, 1970. (Originally published, 1930.)

Festinger, L. *A theory of cognitive dissonance.* Evanston, Ill.: Row, Peterson, 1957.

Freud, S. *New introductory lectures on psychoanalysis.* New York: Norton, 1933.

Freud, S. The ego and the id. In J. Strachey (Eds.), *Complete psychological works of Sigmund Freud* (standard ed., Vol. XIX). London: Hogarth Press, 1947. (Originally published, 1923.)

Freud, S. Instincts and their vicissitudes. In *Sigmund Freud, M.D., L.L.D. collected papers* (Vol. IV). (J. Riviere, trans.) London: Hogarth, 1950. (Originally published, 1915.)

Fromm, E. *Escape from freedom.* New York: Farrah & Rinehart, 1941.

Gilson, E. *The Christian philosophy of St. Thomas Aquinas.* (L. K. Shouls, trans.) New York: Random House, 1956.

Glanzer, M. The role of stimulus satiation in spontaneous alternation. *Journal of Experimental Psychology,* 1953, *45,* 387–393.

Harlow, H. F., Harlow, M. K., & Meyer, D. R. Learning motivated by a manipulation drive. *Journal of Experimental Psychology,* 1950, *40,* 228–234.

Hebb, D. O. Drives and the C. N. S. (conceptual nervous system). *Psychological Review,* 1955, *62,* 243–254.

Heider, F. *The psychology of interpersonal relations.* New York: Wiley, 1958.

Helson, H. *Adaptation-level theory.* New York: Harper & Row, 1964.

Horney, K. *Neurosis and human growth.* New York: Norton, 1950.

Hull, C. L. *Principles of behavior.* New York: Appleton-Century-Crofts, 1943.

Hull, C. L. *Essentials of behavior.* New Haven: Yale University Press, 1951.

Hunt, J. McV. Intrinsic motivation and its role in psychological development. In D. Levine (Ed.), *Nebraska Symposium on Motivation.* Lincoln: University of Nebraska Press, 1965.

Irwin, F. W. *Intentional behavior and motivation: A cognitive theory.* Philadelphia: Lippincott, 1971.

James, W. *The principles of psychology* (2 vols.). New York: Holt, 1890.

Kelley, H. H. Attribution theory in social psychology. In D. Levine (Ed.), *Nebraska Symposium on Motivation.* Lincoln: University of Nebraska Press, 1967.

Lewin, K. *A dynamic theory of personality.* New York: McGraw-Hill, 1935.

Lindsley, D. B. Psychophysiology and motivation. In M. R. Jones (Ed.), *Nebraska Symposium on Motivation.* Lincoln: University of Nebraska Press, 1957.

Mandler, G. & Sarason, S. A study of anxiety and learning. *Journal of Abnormal and Social Psychology,* 1952, *47,* 166–173.

Maslow, A. H. *Motivation and personality.* New York: Harper, 1954.

May, R. *Man's search for himself.* New York: Norton, 1953.

McDougall, W. William McDougall. In C. Murchison (Ed.), *A history of psychology in autobiography* (Vol. 1). Worcester, Mass.: Clark University Press, 1930.

McDougall, W. *An introduction to social psychology.* Boston: Luce & Co., 1950. (Originally published, 1908.)

McReynolds, P. The motivational psychology of Jeremy Bentham: I. Background and general approach. *Journal of the History of the Behavioral Sciences,* 1968, *4,* 230–244. (a)

McReynolds, P. The motivational psychology of Jeremy Bentham: II. Efforts toward quantification and classification. *Journal of the History of the Behvaioral Sciences,* 1968, *4,* 349–364. (b)

Miller, N. E. Studies of fear as an acquirable drive: I. Fear as motivation and fear-reduction as reinforcement in the learning of new responses. *Journal of Experimental Psychology,* 1948, *38,* 89–101.

Miller, N. E. Learnable drives and rewards. In S. S. Stevens (Ed.), *Handbook of experimental psychology.* New York: Wiley, 1951.

Miller, N. E. & Dollard, J. *Social learning and imitation.* New Haven: Yale University Press, 1941.

Mischel, T. "Emotion" and "motivation" in the development of English psychology: D. Hartley, James Mill, A. Bain. *Journal of the History of the Behavioral Sciences, 1966, 2,* 123–144.

Mischel, T. (Ed.). *Human actions: Conceptual and empirical issues.* New York: Academic Press, 1969.

Montgomery, K. C. The relation between exploratory behavior and spontaneous alternation in the white rat. *Journal of Comparative and Physiological Psychology,* 1951, *44,* 582–589.

Morgan, C. T. *Physiological psychology.* New York: McGraw-Hill, 1943.

Morgan, C. D. & Murray, H. Method for investigating fantasies—the thematic apperception test. *Archives of Neurology and Psychology,* 1935, *34,* 289–306.

Murray, H. A. *Explorations in personality.* New York: Oxford University Press, 1938.

Olds, J. Physiological mechanisms of reward. In M. R. Jones (Ed.), *Nebraska Symposium on Motivation.* Lincoln: University of Nebraska Press, 1955.

Peters, R. S. (Ed.). *Brett's history of psychology.* London: Allen & Unwin, 1953.

Peters, R. S. *The concept of motivation.* London: Routledge & Kegan Paul, 1958.

Premack, D. Reinforcement theory. In M. R. Jones (Ed.), *Nebraska Symposium on Motivation.* Lincoln: University of Nebraska Press, 1965.

Rancurello, A. C. *A study of Franz Brentano.* New York: Academic Press, 1968.

Richter, C. P. Animal behavior and internal drives. *Quarterly Review of Biology,* 1927, *2,* 307–343.

Richter, C. P. Total self-regulatory functions in animals and human beings. *Harvey Lectures, 1942–43, 38,* 63–103.

Rogers, C. R. *Client-centered therapy: Its current practice, implications, and theory.* Boston: Houghton-Mifflin, 1951.

Rozin, P. & Kalat, J. W. Specific hungers and poison avoidance as adaptive specializations of learning. *Psychological Review,* 1971, *78,* 459–486.

Russell, B. *A history of western philosophy.* New York: Simon & Schuster, 1945.

Schachter, S. *The psychology of affiliation: Experimental studies of the sources of gregariousness.* Stanford, Calif.: Stanford University Press, 1959.

Sears, R. R. *Survey of objective studies of psychoanalytic concepts.* New York: Social Science Research Council, 1943.

Sears, R. R. Experimental analysis of psychoanalytic phenomena. In J. McV. Hunt (Ed.), *Personality and the behavior disorders* (Vol. 1). New York: Ronald, 1944.

Sheffield, F. D. & Campbell, B. A. The role of experience in the "spontaneous" activity of hungry rats. *Journal of Comparative and Physiological Psychology,* 1954, *47,* 97–100.

Sheffield, F. D. & Roby, T. B. Reward value of a non-nutritive sweet taste. *Journal of Comparative and Physiological Psychology,* 1950, *43,* 471–481.

Sheffield, F. D., Roby, T. B., & Campbell, B. A. Drive reduction versus consummatory behavior as determinants of reinforcement. *Journal of Comparative and Physiological Psychology,* 1954, *47,* 349–354.

Sheffield, F. D., Wulff, J. J., & Backer, R. Reward value of copulation without sex drive reduction. *Journal of Comparative and Physiological Psychology,* 1951, *44,* 3–8.

Snygg, D. & Combs, A. W. *Individual behavior.* New York: Harper, 1949.

Stellar, E. The physiology of motivation. *Psychological Review,* 1954, *61,* 5–22.

Stout, G. F. *Analytic psychology* (2 vols.). London: Sonnenschein, 1896.

Taylor, J. A. A personality scale of manifest anxiety. *Journal of Abnormal and Social Psychology,* 1953, *48,* 285–290.

Thorndike, E. L. Animal intelligence: An experimental study of the associative processes in animals. *Psychological Review Monograph Supplements,* 1898, *2*(Whole No. 8).

Tolman, E. C. *Purposive behavior in animals and men.* New York: Appleton-Century, 1932.

Ward, J. *The realism of ends or pluralism and theism. The Gifford Lectures.* Cambridge: Cambridge University Press, 1911.

Warden, C. J. *Animal motivation: Experimental studies on the albino rat.* New York: Columbia University Press, 1931.

Weiner, B. *Theories of motivation: From mechanism to cognition.* Chicago: Markham, 1972.

White, R. W. Motivation reconsidered: The concept of competence. *Psychological Review,* 1959, *66,* 297–333.

Woodworth, R. S. *Dynamic psychology.* New York: Columbia University Press, 1918.

Young, P. T. The role of affective processes in learning and motivation. *Psychological Review,* 1959, *66,* 104–125.

Young, P. T. *Motivation and emotion: A survey of the determinants of human and animal activity.* New York: Wiley, 1961.

6 Sleep and Dreaming

Wilse B. Webb
University of Florida

Sleep and dreams, in their occurrence, are necessarily bound together in time. However, the historical development of the areas was essentially independent. Aristotle treated them independently in chapters of *De Naturalia*. More than 2000 years later, Freud, in *The Interpretation of Dreams* (1900), said, "In such obscure matters [sleep and dreams] it will only be possible to arrive at explanations and agreed results by detailed investigation . . . the literature on sleep is accordingly disregarded" (p. 9).

With such precedents, this chapter first considers the historical views of dreams from the early Greek period through the Freudian "era." The background of sleep research will then be reviewed to the point of the explosive emergence of contemporary sleep and dream research in the 1950s. This resulted in and was partially a result of the convergence of these two areas of concern. The contemporary status of sleep and dream research will then be described and assessed.

HISTORICAL PERSPECTIVES ON DREAMS

For an historical perspective on dreams, I have chosen to emphasize the writings of Aristotle, Cicero, and Freud. I have done so for several reasons. First, they are among the most famous, systematic, and extensive writers of their time. Secondly, of particular historical interest, each presented a conceptualization of dreams which was unique to and beyond his time. They did not simply reflect their historical periods. These three writers, from their unique positions—the naturalism of Aristotle, the socio-philosophical orientation of Cicero, and the psychological stance of Freud—may help us to understand their times by their very differences from those times.

Dreams in the Time of Aristotle and Cicero

While Aristotle and Cicero lived and wrote about dreams some 300 years apart (circa 340 B.C. and 40 A.D.), there was a pervasive concept of dreams across that time span. This concept extended temporally from the fragments of the earliest writings of the Egyptians and Summerians; through the literature exemplified by Homer, the Old Testament, the Grecian plays, and the histories of Herodotus; into the collection of this extended literature by Artemedorus in the later Roman period of the second century A.D. As can be seen from these sources, with minor variations geographically, there was a common theme throughout the known world. The early literature on dreams has been reviewed elsewhere by Webb (1979) and, in detail, by Bonnuzi (1975), Meir (1977) and Oppenheim (1977).

The orientation was a pragmatic one—dreams were messages about the person or the future (primarily the latter) from an extra-ordinary source. Underlying this was a general set of beliefs: The future is fated, and there is a "higher" order involved in that fate. The most common belief about dreams was as follows: A human life is part of a superordinate "plan," the future can most readily be accessed during sleep, and this is typically mediated by a divine intervention.

Examples of the crucial role of dreams in the lives of earlier significant figures are rife: the dreams of the Pharaohs and of the leading characters of the Iliad and the Odyssey; the Old Testatment dreams of Joseph and David; the annals of Cyrus' dreams; Hannibal's responses to dreams; the divination dreams of Sophocles and Socrates; and the dreams of Joseph in the New Testament. Cicero had his brother, Quintus (below), citing a long series of influential dreams in pre-Roman and Roman times. Perhaps the clearest concrete evidence of this concept of the dream can be found in the hundreds of "sleep temples" scattered throughout Greece (Meir, 1977).

Aristotle on Dreams.   In *On Divination by Dreams,* Aristotle wrote of dreams in a strikingly naturalistic manner (Aristotle, 340 B.C.(c)/1931). Dreams are perceptions of sensory-based occurrences. They are, however, residual impressions. "The objects of sense-perceptions corresponding to each sensory organ produce sense-perceptions in us, and the affection due to this operation is present . . . even when they have departed" (p. 459). These residual impressions constitute dreams. The unusual quality of dreams stems from three primary sources: (1) We receive dreams but do not exercise reason or opinion during sleep; (2) residual impressions may have particular impressiveness since they are not "extended or obscured" by "the intellect and the senses working together"; and (3) uncontrolled, they are like "little eddies being formed in rivers . . . often running what they were like when first started out but often, too, broken into other forms'' (p. 460).

Given this position, it is not surprising to find Aristotle rejecting the dominant theme of divine dreams: "It may be concluded that dreams are not sent by God. . . . Nor are they designed [to reveal the future]. . . . They have a divine aspect, however, for Nature [their cause] is divinely planned" (p. 463).

Aristotle's examination of the issue of divination is, again, naturalistic. Dreams may be related to the future as tokens, causes, or coincidences. Physicians may attend to dreams as tokens: "Movements which occur in the day time are, unless very great and violent, lost sight of. . . . In sleep the opposite takes place, for then even trifling movements seem considerable . . . the beginnings of all events are small, so, it is clear, are those also of diseases and other affectations" (p. 463). Indeed, some dreams may be "causes" of the future: "For as when we are about to act, or engage in any course of action, or have already performed certain actions, we often find ourselves concerned with these actions, or performing them in a vivid dream; the cause whereof is that the dream-movement has had a way paved for it from the original movements . . . conversely . . . movements set up first in sleep (may) prove to be starting points of actions to be performed in the daytime" (p. 463). Aristotle, however, discussed "most dreams" as coincidences relative to the future, especially "all such as are extravagant, and those in which the dreams have no initiative such as the case of a sea fight, or of things taking place far away. . . . The probability is that many such things should happen. As, then, one's mentioning a particular person is neither token or cause of this person's presenting himself, so, . . . to him the dream is . . . neither token nor cause of its fulfillment, but a mere coincidence of its (so-called) fulfillment" (p. 463).

He leaves us with wise words about interpretation: "The most skillful interpreter of dreams is he who has the faculty of observing resemblances—dream presentations are analogous to forms reflected in water . . . if the motion in the water be great, the reflection has no resemblance to its original . . . in a similar way, some such thing is a troubled dream . . . for the internal movement effaces the clearness of the dream" (p. 464).

Cicero on Dreams.   Cicero considered dreams in his treatise, *De Senectute, de Amicitia, de Divinatione* (translated by W. A. Falconer, 1923). He included two kinds of divination: artificial, which "depends partly on conjecture and partly on long continued observation," e.g., astrology, augury, portents; and natural, which were "dreams and prophecies."

Cicero presents his arguments in a classical rhetorical form. He, first through his brother Quintus, presents the arguments in favor of divination. These follow primarily the arguments of the Stoics. After first citing the prevalence of belief in divination from earliest times, he gives three arguments: (1) The human soul is an emanation of the Divine Soul and hence they are in contact. (2) The contact is enhanced when the soul is unencumbered by the senses and flesh. (3) Fate is an orderly succession of causes and thus is predictable.

Cicero's response to the issue of the prediction of Fate centers mostly on "artificial" divination. Elements of the core of his arguments are: (1) the "unnatural connections" between portents and predicted events (the connection between "cleft in a kidney" and a naval victory makes no sense); (2) while the observations of our senses do yield predictions, e.g., the physician and the pilot, this is not divination but skilled performance; and (3) things do occur by "chance" and these are not predictable.

Cicero argues that whatever theory one holds for dreams, they are "phantoms and apparitions." But we place little faith in our waking delusions and hallucinations and certainly not in those of the insane or drunk. Why then value dreams? He adds that if he wishes to solve a problem in geometry, physics, or logic, to learn to play a lute, or to be cured, he would consult the "peculiar knowledge of those arts and science . . . if I want to sail a boat I would not pilot it as I might have dreamed I should."

Clearly, argues Cicero, this is not the work of God: (1) Most dreams are ignored, thus God is either ignorant or he does a vain thing. (2) If God was "consulting for our own good," he would send us clear visions while we were waking rather than unintelligible ones while asleep. (3) Since at least some dreams are not true, why would he send false dreams with no distinguishing marks? He summarizes: "Do the immortal gods, who are of surprising excellence in all things, constantly flit about, not only the beds, but even the lowly pallets of mortals . . . and when they find him snoring, throw at him dark and twisted visions . . . or does nature bring it to pass that the ever active soul sees in sleep phantoms of what it saw when the body was awake?" (p. 517).

Cicero does not find the time of sleep propitious for wisdom or divination. "When the soul is supported by the bodily members and by the five senses, its powers of perception, thought, and apprehension are more trustworthy. . . . When the soul itself weakened in sleep . . . many sights and sounds . . . are seen and heard in all manner of confusion and diversity" (p. 527).

Tellingly, he refutes the argument that by "long continuing observations . . . and recording of the results an art has been evolved." After first arguing that he can see no possible connection between a "phantom" dream and a future physical event, he further denies the possibility of establishing such connections. "For they (dreams) are of infinite variety and there is no imaginable thing too absurd, too involved, or too abnormal for us to dream about. How then is it possible for us either to remember the countless and ever-changing mass of visions or to observe and record the subsequent results? . . . As a rule we do not believe a liar even when he tells the truth . . . (yet) if one's dream turns out true . . . they (the Stoics) establish the character of the countless others that are false" (p. 533–535).

Between Cicero and Emerging Science

The naturalism of Aristotle and the witty and scathing rhetoric of Cicero did not stem the prophetic interpretation of dreams. The popularity of this approach was crowned by five volumes of Artemedorus of Daldis in the second century. These were an exhaustive review of the dream interpretations in the classical world in combination with Artemedorus' own interpretation of more than 3000 dreams. While giving prototypical indexings of particular dreams and their meaning, Artemedorus emphasized the individual dreamer and the context of the time of the dream. These volumes were republished in 1518 under the title *Oneicritica* and published in English translation in 1606. The continued popularity of this approach to dreams is attested to by a volume by Thomas Hall imprinted in London in 1576. It is titled: *The most Pleasaunte Arte of the Interpretacion of Dreams, Whereunto is Annexed Sundry Problems with Apte Aunsweares Neare Agreeing to the Matter, and Very Rare Examples, not the Like Extant in the English Tongue.*

There is, however, a landmark in the history of dreams which dramatically entered the course of philosophy in the seventeenth century and today continues to reverberate within it. In his *First Meditation*, Descartes cites his dream experiences as a central point of his skepticism of the senses. He reports, "For example, there is the fact that I am here, seated by the fire, attired in a dressing gown, having the paper in my hands, and other similar matters. . . . At the same time I must remember that I am a man and consequently in the habit of sleeping, and in my dreams representing to myself the same things."

The epistemological puzzle of the status of dreams as sensory data clearly contributed to Descartes' central theme of "doubt." Moreover, the puzzle raised continued as a lively issue throughout subsequent philosophical inquiries, and its contemporary status is reviewed in *Philosophical Essays on Dreaming* (Dunlop, 1977). It is also to be noted, however, that Descartes attributed the development of his philosophy and his life to three "revelatory dreams" (Maritain, 1944).

In a book relating dreams and theology, Kelsey (1968), after a lengthy review of the role of the dreams in the Bible, cites the extensive writings of the early Church fathers and the culmination of theological concern through the period of Enlightenment. He notes that the present absence of theological considerations is a relatively recent development.

Dreams in Freud's Time

A major review of the status of the dream between 1860 and 1910 has recently appeared (Vande Kemp, 1981). This review notes that "theologians no longer regarded dreams as bona fide revelations . . . Philosophers were concerned primarily with their metaphysical implications, and literary critics emphasized only their frequently inaccurate portrayal in literature" (p. 88). In short, the dream

TABLE 6.1
Time Distribution of
Publications Cited in Freud's
Interpretation of Dreams

Period of Time[a]	Number of Publications
Pre–1800	16
1800–1849	23
1850–1859	16
1860–1869	10
1870–1879	17
1880–1889	38
1890–1899	94

[a]Note differences in yearly groupings.

had lost its potency as a popular force. There is little evidence that the leaders of society—statesmen or men of power—were guided by their dreams. In poetry, the dream was more typically a literary device, as in Wordsworth's *Dream of a Slave* (dreaming of his preslave times) or in Poe's elaborate fantasies of a dream world. The "dream books" were still sold, but they were ragtags of Artemedorus' rigid dream "meanings."

Contrary to opinion, however, Freud did not create the "scientific" interest in dreams. Freud himself provides the background in *The Interpretation of Dreams* (1900/1965), and Vande Kemp (1981) extends it. Freud's book (Third Revised English Edition) cites 214 publications prior to 1900. Table 6.1 presents the time distribution of these references. Eight major books are cited by Freud: Burdach (1838), Scherner (1861), Hildebrandt (1875), Strumpell (1877), Maury (1878), Radestock (1879), Spitta (1882) and Delboeuf (1885).

Substantial figures in the developing science of psychology are also cited: Fechner (1860), Wundt (1892), Calkins (1893), Titchener (1895) and Woodworth (1897).

However, Mary Calkins (1893) described the status of the literature of the 1890s as follows:

The phenomenon of dreaming has rarely been discussed or investigated in a thorough and in an experimental manner: of description, of theory, of discussion, of poetical analogy and illustration there has been no end; of accurate observation almost nothing . . . The most scientific books—those of Maury and of Tissie— have been wholly and chiefly the results of the observations of abnormal subjects and in the interest more or less distinctly of pathology. . . . The fullest discussion of the subject—the work of Radestock and Spitta—are largely compilations of the recorded dreams of other people. (p. 312)

Freud's own evaluation of the literature he reviewed was succinctly stated: "Many stimulating observations are to be found and a quantity of interesting materials bearing upon our theme, but little or nothing that touches upon the essential nature of dreams or that offers a final solution of any of their enigmas'' (1900/1965, p. 36).

Space does not permit a summary of this literature or even a summary of Freud's 120-page review. However, a few samples should be given to indicate the character of the developing literature.

In the first of eight questions which Freud examined, ''the relationship of dreams to waking life,'' the literature reveals two positions: Dreams are independent of our waking life, or ''the preponderant view'' that dreams are consequences of our waking life. Freud, of course, holds the latter position. In considering ''memory of dreams,'' Freud reviews the efforts to account for the less than apparent relationship between dreams and waking life. He cites a series of authors' reports of dreams in which the source was an event that was not accessible to immediate memory but was discovered to have actually occurred many years previously. Freud (1900/1965) describes these as ''hypermnesic'' dreams. He devotes several pages to dreams derived from childhood as a particular form of hypermnesic dreams. While many dreams are clearly related to the immediate present, he finds evidence that this is not linearly related to salience: ''For what is found worth remembering is not, as in waking life, only what is most important, but on the contrary what is most indifferent and insignificant as well'' (p. 42). Freud notes Hildebrandt's belief that dreams derive ''from incidental details, from worthless fragments . . . of what has been recently experienced or of the remoter past'' (p. 52). Although Hildebrandt believed we could explain the genesis of every dream, that would require ''dragging to light once again every kind of indifferent moment of the past from the oblivion in which it was buried'' (p. 53). Freud remarks that if the author had but followed that path, ''it would have led him to the very heart of the explanation of dreams'' (p. 54).

In discussing the forgetting of dreams, Freud (1900/1965) cites Strumpell heavily. Besides appealing to ''intensity'' and ''repetition,'' Strumpell anticipates ''meaningfulness'' as a variable in recall: ''If words are properly arranged and put into the relevant order, one word will help another, and the whole, being charged with meaning, will be easily taken up in memory and retained for a long time. . . . It is in general as difficult and unusual to retain what is nonsensical as it is to retain what is confused and 'disordered' '' (p. 78). He finds in Strumpell a clear statement of secondary elaboration: ''Thus it may easily happen that waking consciousness unwittingly makes interpretations in the memory of a dream: we persuade ourselves that we have dreamt all kinds of things that were not contained in the actual dream'' (p. 79).

Freud on Dreams.   In writing *The Interpretation of Dreams*, Freud's purposes, as he stated in the first paragraph of the preface, were two fold: ''to give an account of the interpretations of dreams,'' and to establish ''their theoretical value as a paradigm.'' He specifically delineates his theoretical intent in the first paragraph of the book: "Every dream reveals itself as a psychical structure which has meaning and which can be inserted at an assignable point in the mental activities of waking life. . . . I shall endeavor to elaborate the processes to which the strangeness and obscurity of dreams are due and to deduce from the processes the nature of the psychical forces by which concurrent or mutually opposing forces are generated" (p. 35).

Combining his observations of dreams and the "contradictory" literature, Freud accomplished his purpose by the introduction of an organized set of hypotheses: "There is, at the present time, no established psychological knowledge under which we could subsume what the psychological examination of dreams enables us to infer as a basis for their explanation. . . . On the contrary, we shall be obliged to set up a number of fresh hypotheses which touch tentatively upon the structure of apparatus of the mind and upon the play of forces operating in it" (p. 549).

The basic elements of the "fresh hypotheses" are well known. Briefly: (1) The meaning of the manifest content (the dream itself) was comprehended in terms of the latent content; (2) the latent content was expressing unresolved wish fulfillment; (3) these utilized the "day residues" and, to a lesser degree, sensory stimuli for expression; (4) "dream work" comprised of symbolism, condensation, and displacement, and "loosened" association occurred to make the impulses expressed acceptable; and (5) dreams must (and do) use "concrete imagery" for expression.

There is little doubt that Freud believed he had made new and substantial contributions to the psychology of the dream: "My presumption that dreams can be interpreted at once puts me in opposition . . . to every theory of dreams with a single exception . . . [Scherner]. . . . As we have seen scientific theories of dreams have not room for any problem of interpreting them, since in their view a dream is not a mental act at all, but a somatic process signalizing its occurrence by indications registered on the mental apparatus" (p. 128). Later he says, "If I proceed to put forth the assertion that the meaning of *every* dream is the fulfillment of a wish, . . . I feel certain in advance that I shall meet with the most categorical contradictions" (p. 167). Elsewhere he states: "Every attempt that has hitherto been made to solve the problem of dreams has dealt directly with their *manifest* content as it is presented in our memory. . . . We are alone in taking something else into account. . . . We have introduced a new class of psychical material between the manifest content of dreams and the conclusions of our enquiry; namely, their *latent* content, or [as we say] the 'dream-thoughts,' arrived at by means of our procedure. . . . It is from these dream-thoughts and not from a dream's manifest content that we disentangle its meaning" (p. 311).

Freud's perceptions of his contribution to an understanding of dreams are readily traced. They are explicitly stated in the preface to later editions of *The Interpretation of Dreams*. In the first 6 years after publication only 351 copies were sold. Freud's disappointment was expressed in the preface of the Second Edition (1909):

If within ten years of the publication of this book (which is very far from being an easy one to read) a second edition is called for, this is not due to the interest taken in it by the professional circles to whom my original preface was addressed. My psychiatric colleagues seem to have taken no trouble to overcome the initial bewilderment created by my new approach to dreams. The professional philosophers have become acustomed to polishing off the problem of dream-life (which they treat as a mere appendix to conscious states) in a few sentences—and usually in the same ones; and they have evidently failed to notice that we have something here from which a number of inferences can be drawn that are bound to transform our psychological theories. The attitude adopted by reviewers in the scientific periodicals could only lead one to suppose that my work was doomed to be sunk into complete silence. (p. xxv)

In the preface to the Third Edition, which followed shortly (1917), Freud wrote: "This new turn of events may please me; but just as formerly I was unwilling to regard the neglect of my book by readers as evidence of its worthlessness, so I cannot claim that the interest which is now being taken in it is proof of its excellence" (p. xxvi).

In the 1932 English Edition (the last to contain a preface by Freud), satisfaction was at last expressed: "This book, with the new contribution to psychology which surprised the world when it was published (1900), remains essentially unaltered. . . . It contains even according to present-day judgments, the most valuable of all the discoveries it has been my good fortune to make. Insight such as this falls to one's lot but once in a life time" (p. xxii).

Freud's attitude toward the content of his contributions is also clear in these prefaces. In the Second Edition, he wrote: "I am glad to say that I have found little to change in it . . . the essence of what I have written about dreams and their interpretations, as well as about the psychological theorems to be deduced from them—all this remains unaltered: subjectively at all events, it has stood the test of time" (p. xxv).

However, in the Sixth Edition (1921), Freud's perspective had become a defensive one in response to the increasing number of critics and modifiers of his position. In this preface he wrote: "Thus my assumption that after an existence of nearly twenty years this book has accomplished its task has not been confirmed. . . . On the contrary, I might say that it has a new task to perform. . . . If its earlier function was to offer some information on the nature of dreams, now it has the no less important duty of dealing with the obstinate misunderstandings to which that information is subject" (p. xxx).

In his 1932 *New Introductory Lectures on Psychoanalysis,* Freud stoutly maintains his position: "I feel sure you are impatient to have what changes have been made in our fundamental views on the nature and significance of dreams. . . . I have already warned you of this. . . . There is little to report to you" (p. 27).

Variations on Freud.   This, of course, was Freud's own perception. Stekel, who wrote extensively on dreams and was an early follower of Freud, stated that

Freud complained about the failure of dream interpretation to advance. He found this, however, to be "one of the distressing instances in which this overwhelmingly great man has shown himself as petty".

Freud's theory of dreams has been subject to continuous criticism and alternative statements. Among the earliest critics were Freud's nearest disciples: Adler, Jung, and Stekel. Procedurally, they tended to the view of free association as leading away from the dream. At a conceptual level, the manifest content was reemphasized. Wish fulfillment was questioned. Childhood sources were replaced by immediate conflicts. The core force of sexuality was denied, and rigid symbolism was repudiated.

Space and intent does not permit a detailing of the "variations" and critiques on the Freudian theme. They have been extensive. The major positions—those of Adler, Jung, Silberer, Lowy, Hall, French, Ullman, Erickson, and Boss—are accurately reviewed by Jones in *The New Psychology of Dreaming* (1970). The plethora of variations is emphasized by Jones in his review chapter:

> The reader may question why it is that such well-regarded writings as those of Maeder, Stekel, Horney, Sullivan, Fromm, Binswanger, and Bonime were not included . . . from the point of view of the psychology of dreaming it may, I think, be safely said that no significant heuristic leads have been overlooked . . . in this writer's judgment French has incorporated Maeder; Lowy has included Stekel; Ullman has improved on Horney and Sullivan; Hall has incorporated Fromm; Boss has covered Binswanger; and Bonime has brought to a high classical polish the roughly presented suppositions of Lowy. (p. 42)

We shall return to the dream as the stream of inquiry merges into the area of contemporary research.

THE BACKGROUND OF SLEEP RESEARCH

The enigma of the dream is wrapped in the mystery of sleep. However, unlike the fulsome speculations about dreams, the ancient literature on sleep is sparse. As with dreams, we shall trace the course of developments of sleep research by focusing on individual landmark writers.

Aristotle and the Classical Period

The religious or literary works of the early Greek period contain few references to sleep. Characters simply slept or they did not. Within sleep they were freed to dream marvelous dreams.

However, there were rudimentary theories of sleep among some of the natural philosophers, particularly the early physicians. Alecemon, the physician of Crotone, a contemporary of Pythagorus in the sixth century B.C., suggested that sleep was due to a retreat of the blood in the veins and awakening to an engorgement of the veins. Empedocles, an early materialistic philosopher writing in the fifth century B.C., attributed sleep to a cooling of the blood; death ensued when the cooling was complete.

The Hippocratic collection of some 70 works compiled about 200 years after the death of Hippocrates (circa 370 B.C.) contained a number of references to sleep. Sleep in this system was also a cooling of the blood. Since the Hippocratic system was based upon a balance among four humors—blood, phlegm, and black and yellow bile, the changes in the blood associated with excessive sleep and insomnia were of diagnostic importance.

Aristotle (circa 330 B.C.) wrote a chapter on sleep in *Parva Naturalia*. While dead wrong in its details, it is remarkable in its naturalistic orientation and its observational data base. Aristotle conceived of the heart as the seat of the sensitive soul (sensation). It also controlled the blood system. On the basis of these assumptions, as well as observations of the sleep of animals and infants, sleep after meals and wine, and differences between swooning and coma, Aristotle reasoned sleep to be a natural physiological event resulting from the nature of the surround and the condition of the person. When the blood evaporates from the heart, it rises to the head and, becoming cooled, it descends and cools the heart. Sleep ensues and the sensitivity of the special senses (seeing and hearing) is lost. However, unlike a coma, the general capacity to sense remains, thus permitting dreams. This, then, was an active inhibitory theory. Aristotle further conceived of sleep as a "conservative" period: to the cessation of motion was added a period in which "nutrition and growth" was "especially presented."

With the exception of Galen's second-century omnivorous inclusion of sleep in his extensive writings, sleep commentary after Aristotle drifts almost exclusively in the realm of poetry until the eighteenth and nineteenth centuries.

The Quickening Pace

The full history of the development of sleep research would require describing the development of the life sciences. The pattern of sleep "research" up to recent times is primarily one of the rapidly emerging findings about human physiology which would occasionally "spill over" and be applied to the problem of sleep. These developments across the 1800s are reviewed in detail by Manaceine (1899) and Pieron (1913). Kleitman (1963), drawing heavily on Pieron, also reviews the earlier "theories" of sleep. However, he notes that, "Since newly discovered facts render previously accepted alleged facts obsolete, the theories based on the latter are mentioned here only for their historical interests or for their amusing aspects" (p. 341).

With a similar intent, two nineteenth century books written for the general public which combine anecdotes and "science" are mentioned here. In 1842,

Edward Binns, M.D., published *The Anatomy of Sleep*. Chapter I had the following subheadings: Questions Posed, Definition of Sleep, Sound Sleep, Narcotic Sleep, Animals Sleep More Than Man, Monkeys—Do They Reason?, Absence of Sleep Cannot Be Long Sustained, Damien, Luke, Ann Moore, Means of Inducing Sleep, Luxurious Indulgence of the Harem, The Art of Procurring Sleep No Longer a Desideratum, How Discovered, and The Late Mr. Gardner; His Severe Suffering. The definition of sleep was "the art of escaping reflection." His "art of procurring sleep," given 391 pages later, was as follows:

> Let him turn on his right side, place his head comfortably on the pillow, so that it exactly occupies the angle [of] a line drawn from the head to the shoulder . . . the respiration is neither to be accelerated or retarded . . . the attention must now be fixed on [breathing] . . . the very instant that he brings his mind to conceive this apart from all other ideas, consciousness and memory depart; imagination slumbers, fancy becomes dormant, thought subdued; the sentient faculties lose their susceptibility; the vital or ganglionic system assumes the sovereignty . . . he no longer wakes, but sleeps. (p. 391)

The reference to the vital or ganglionic system refers to a conclusion drawn from three chapters on comparative anatomy that give examples of periods of sleeplessness. Binns concludes that the organ of sleep "will be found between the cervical and lumbar vertebrae in the Ganglia formed from the nerves given off by this portion of the nervous system" (p. 350).

A second "how to" book of the period was *Sleep: or the Hygiene of the Night*, by W. W. Hall, M.D. (1870). Hall's premise was that the cause of insomnia is "impure air" in the sleep chamber. If "sound and regular sleep is prevented, the mind sooner or later fails of its elasticity, its vigor, and its life, to be followed by nervousness, weakness of intellect, softening of the brain, insanity and death" (p. ii). After excursions into the evils of masturbation and the virtues of marriage, and an intensive examination of the Black Hole of Calcutta incident, Hall recommends that bed chambers be 12 feet square (per person) and well ventilated. This is complicated, however, by the fact that,

> such a room is often crowded by furniture and other items: . . . besides the soap for washing, which is constantly sending off out its emanations, there are damp towels and beddings and combs and brushes, and the clothing worn during the day, which, as to some persons, is alone sufficient to taint the air of a whole room in five minutes after it is laid off. Besides these, if inner doors are left open during the night, emanations from cellars and warm kitchens, and slops of various kinds, are constantly ascending . . . it is an almost unknown thing that any sleeper . . . gets one single breath of real pure air in the whole night. (p. 55–56)

Hall recommends warm feet, a cool body, a hard mattress, a large ventilated chamber, and sleep alone. When these things fail, "there remains but one of two safe alternatives, either marriage or the consultation of a physician of known ability and of high character'' (p. 195).

There was a clear pattern, however, in the development of sleep research. The rapidly advancing life sciences were bringing forth new and exciting findings about vascular circulation, respiration, digestion, secretion, temperature, the chemical constituencies, and the neurology of the human body. Most of these showed substantial changes during sleep, and the observed changes added to the description of these processes. The changes often were taken as ''causes'' of sleep; for example, congestive or anemic theories of sleep were based upon the circulatory findings. We have elsewhere described the early scientific background as follows: ''During the early period there was an overwhelming impression of sleep research as an orphan of uncertain parentage living within a larger family of powerful aunts and uncles who, occasionally, gave sustenance and attention to the waif'' (Webb, 1975).

The Emerging Field

The emerging field of sleep research is summarized by the American edition of Marie de Manaceine's *Sleep: Its Physiology, Pathology, Hygiene and Psychology* published in 1899. This was a translation and enlargement of an early publication in Russian and French. The book was edited by Havelock Ellis. Manaceine was one of the earliest systematic experimenters specifically concerned with sleep per se. She had reported extensive studies of sleep deprivation in puppies in 1884.

The book is divided into four chapters concerned with physiology, pathology, hygiene, and psychology (dreams). Each part reviews the extant literature. The chapters, with substantial overlap, contain 128, 167, 107, and 171 references, respectively. The list of references are a Hall of Fame of the life sciences in general: Haller, Purkinje, Cajal, Pfluger, Tarchanoff, J. Miller, and Helmholtz. In the more direct psychology lineage we find references to Wundt, Lotze, Fechner, Bain, Titchener, Calkins, and Jastrow.

The chapter on physiology reviews the studies of change in respiratory vasomotor, hemotologic, digestive, and skeletal muscular system during sleep. Manaceine also reviews the early studies of the ''curve of sleep'' obtained from threshold measures by Kohlshulter in 1867. These are considered to be the earliest experimental studies of sleep. The theories of sleep are reviewed: ''localized'' theories, e.g., the thyroid or arachnoid plexus, vasomotor theories of anemia or congestion; ''chemical'' theories, e.g., carbonic acid or oxygen change; or ''historical'' theories, e.g., Cajal's theories of neuroganglia ''amoeboid activity.'' Manaceine concludes with a ''psychophysiology theory'' which hypothesizes (1) a ''fatigue'' of the cortical area, (2) voluntary withdrawal from sensory and mental stimulation, and (3) a diminished blood supply.

The chapter on pathology includes a discussion of insomnia, narcolepsy (which mixes with hypersomnia), somnambulism, and hibernation. The chapter concludes with a startlingly modern "split brain" hypothesis. The hygiene chapter includes discussions of the changes with aging and effects of varied illnesses and considers a wide range of influences such as light, temperature, body position, and ventilation. The chapter on psychology discusses dreams, and reviews almost exactly the same material reviewed by Freud (see above). Manaceine writes that in sleep the consciousness is freed from determination by circumstances of the present moment and thus "may think, feel and judge" as it did "at some earlier stage of development." Manaceine directly anticipates Jung's concept of the "collective unconscious": "It is even possible to hold that consciousness is still further extended, and that the consciousness of the species, and even its predecessors, may be represented in sleep . . . the world of our once-forgotten past . . . it may be also the forgotten past of the race" (p. 317–318).

The next major landmark was Henri Pieron's *Le Probleme Physiologique de Somniel* (1913). The acceleration of sleep research in the nineteenth and into the twentieth century can be seen in Table 6.2, which displays a temporal analysis of the books and articles cited by Pieron.

Pieron, however, found this plethora of work more challenging than satisfying. In his preface he described the earlier work as "abundant" in amount but "poor" in results.

In regard to the causes of sleep, Pieron wrote that one is submerged by the number of hypotheses. "It would be difficult to find an idea, on sleep genesis, even absurd, for which there was uncontestable priority" (p. 320). Unfortunately, the facts for such hypotheses are nonexistent; "they are analogies, coincidences or the observations of some hypnotic effect or comatose state" (p. 320). In fact, Pieron notes that some authors boldly commit themselves to hypotheses "because there are no facts." He sadly suggests that "it would be an excellent thing [if] theoreticians would turn to experimental control" (p. 321).

The book is divided into four parts. The first part (105 pages) describes what was known about the physiological concomitants of sleep: changes in circulation, respiration, digestion, secretion (sweat, tears, and urine output), temperature, and sensory-motor processes. The second section (108 pages) examines "analogous" states: comatose states, marcolepsy, lethargies and somnambulances, "provoked" states (anesthesias, drugs, electric sleep, and hypnosis), and hibernation. The third section (105 pages) presents Pieron's experimental work in his development of a hypnotoxin theory. The fourth part reviews the extant theories of sleep. These are divided into "partial" theories (those directed at the mechanisms of change in sleep and waking) and "complete" theories concerned with the more general question of the "why" of sleep and waking. The partial theories include "vasomotor" theories of cerebral anemia and congestion, nervous system theories of decreased stimulation, and inhibition of "sleep center" theories. The complete theories examined are humoral theories;

TABLE 6.2
Time and Language Distributions of
Publications Cited by Pieron (1913)

	Average Number of Publications per Year	Total Number of Publications
Period of time		
1500–1700		4
1700–1800		12
1801–1820	.3	
1821–1840	1.1	
1841–1860	3.5	
1861–1880	8.5	
1881–1890	13.9	
1891–1900	29.4	
1901–1905	33.6	
1906–1910	36.4	
Language		
French		627
German		289
English		150
Italian		91

hydration and dehydration theories; biochemical change theories; and "toxic" theories such as lactic acid, carbonic acid and urotoxins. The last part (27 pages) is a summary of the "facts," an outline of Pieron's hypnotoxin theory and a critique and answer to the critique.

The primary thrust of research from the second decade of the 1900s into the "modern" era of the 1950s was essentially determined by developments in neurophysiology. As this research technology advanced in stimulation and surgical procedures, it simultaneously expanded its conceptualization of nervous system functions. For sleep research in particular, the era of the 1920s, 30s, and 40s was predominantly a search for a sleep "center."

The stage for this search was set by Mauthner's clinical observations of encephalitica lethargica in 1890. However, the specific central nervous system focal center was posited by Von Economo, from similar observations of an epidemic of encephalitis in Austria in 1916 and 1917. In 1925, he explicated the notion of a central regulator of sleep consisting of two parts: a center of vigilance, and a center of sleep.

Primary contributors in these developments were Hess in the 1920s using electrical stimulation of various brain areas, Ranson in the 1930s using lesion procedures, and the development and application by Bremer of the techniques of "cervea isole" and "encephale isole" in the late 1930s. These developments are reviewed intensively by Lemain, Clemencon, Gomis, Pollin, and Salvo (1975, pp. 57–69) and more generally by Kleitman (1963, pp. 202–206, 359–382). A particularly critical development was the work of Morruzi and Magoun in 1949 relative to the reticular "activating" system. Basically, it appeared that the "waking" center might have been located, since stimulation of this area in the sleeping cat resulted in an activated electroencephalogram (EEG). In the same year, Lindsley, Bowden, and Magoun reported that a deactivation of the area yielded a synchronized EEG, a sign of sleep.

Systematic relationships between the presence of sleep and changes in the EEG were noted by the Davis-Harvey-Loomis group during the 2-year period between 1935 and 1937. These were codified in a paper in the *Journal of Experimental Psychology* (Loomis, Harvey, & Hobart, 1937). The changes in sleep were classified into five "stages" labeled A through E. Blake and Gerrard (1937) also published an article on brain potential changes and sleep.

Surprisingly, this measure was not extensively exploited as an index of the all-night sleep process. The early studies basically used EEG sleep characteristics as a test condition to increase understanding of the waking EEG. Others examined the relationship of a particular EEG state to such independent variables as threshold measures or evoked potentials. Not until 1946 do we find a study comparing all-night characteristics (stage totals, number of stage changes) for normal and depressed individuals. As late as the 1950s, Russian research almost exclusively utilized the motility measures of sleep. Indeed, in 1964, when we published a detailed analysis of all-night sleep patterns in young adults (Williams, Agnew, & Webb, 1964), the introduction stated that "there is an absence of data relative to the normal EEG sleep pattern of the human" (p. 376).

The Merging of Sleep and Dreams

The crucial finding that presaged the contemporary era of sleep and dream research merged the more general investigations of sleep, the increasingly focused central nervous system studies, and the persistent exploration of the dream. In a *Science* paper in 1953, Aserinsky and Kleitman noted the systematic presence of "rapid, jerky and binocularly symmetrical" eye movements (REM) associated with low voltage and irregular high frequency EEG. To confirm the conjecture that this particular eye activity was associated with dreaming, they awakened 10 subjects during 27 eye movement conditions and 23 non-eye movement occasions. Twenty of the eye movement awakenings resulted in reports of "detailed dreams," whereas 19 of the noneye movement awakenings "disclosed complete failure of recall." They concluded that: "The fact that these eye movements, EEG patterns, and autonomic nervous system activity are significantly related and do not occur randomly suggests that these physiological phenomena, and probably dreaming, are very likely a manifestation of a particular level of critical activity when it is encountered normally in sleep" (p. 274).

The response was quick and vigorous. In 1955, Dement published a comparison of normal and schizophrenic REM sleep. In 1957, Dement and Kleitman published two extensive normative papers on REM sleep and its relation to dream recall and added this stage of sleep to the description of ongoing sleep. In 1958, REM sleep was tied with neurophysiology when Dement reported on the REM state analogue in cats (Dement, 1958). Jouvet in Lyon, after working with Magoun, also began his extensive explorations of "active" sleep in the cat (Jouvet & Michel, 1959).

The early work in this area has been well reviewed by Snyder (1967). He cites 18 studies from 1955 through 1965 which focused on differentiation of recall from REM and non-REM awakenings. These involved 271 subjects, 2464 REM awakenings and 1604 non-REM awakenings. Many experimental studies examined the effects of presleep stimuli, incorporation of stimuli presented during sleep, factors affecting recall, etc.

But the discovery of REM sleep did far more than enhance the exploration of cognitive state during dreaming and the experimental approach to dreams. Investigations of the REM periods became the dominant research theme. During the decade of the 1960s and into the 1970s, sleep research predominantly was concerned with the neurophysiology of the REM period, the ontogeny of REM, the phylogeny of REM, and the physiological and psychophysiological concomitants of REM. A particular example of this is seen in deprivation experiments. In 1960, Dement published his classical paper on REM deprivation in human subjects (Dement, 1960). The Brain Information Service (BIS) annual bibliographies of 1970 and 1971 list 76 experimental studies of sleep deprivation, 40 of which were REM deprivation studies.

CONTEMPORARY SLEEP AND DREAM RESEARCH

We have dated contemporary sleep research from the time that sleep and dream research merged as described above. The growing sophistication of neurophysiological research, the conjunction of an electrophysiological measure and the presence of the dream, and the discovery of the analogue of the REM state in animals and infants fell on the fertile soil of available research funds of the 1950s and 1960s. Three books appeared in quick succession: *The Nature of Sleep*, a CIBA symposium report (1961); *Sleeping and Waking* (Oswald, 1962); and Kleitman's 1963 revision of his 1939 *Sleep and Wakefulness*. A particular stimulation to the research grew from a gathering at the University of Chicago in 1960 of the active researchers in sleep. About 25 people attended, and the Association for the Psychophysiological Study of Sleep was begun in the following year.

The dynamics of the field and a sense of its growth can be inferred from the sleep literature. Kleitman's 1963 book has an exhaustive bibliography of 4637 articles to that date. Rechtschaffen and Eakins (1967) extended this bibliography from 1964 through 1967. In 1968, the Brain Information Service (BIS) began publishing annual bibliographies of the world-wide literature of sleep and dream research (Chase, 1968–1982). Using categories listed in the BIS bibliography, Table 6.3 presents the percentage distribution of the research articles for five selected 5-year periods and the 2 most recent years available. The two earliest periods are from Kleitman's bibliography, the 1963–1967 period is from the Rechtschaffen-Eakins bibliography, and the later three periods are from the BIS listings.

Across these periods about 40% of the research has been focused on the internal determinants and concomitants of sleep (neurophysiology, physiology, biochemistry, pharmacology, and endocrinology). Within this grouping there have been significant trends. Neurophysiological research rose sharply to a peak in the middle 1960s and has since declined. Physiological research declined with this rise and has remained at a low steady state into the present. The "wet physiology" (biochemistry, pharmacology, and endocrinology) peaked later, and pharmacology continues to be a primary focus of research. Pharmacological studies of hypnotics are now a central feature of the field. The area labeled "Sleep Disturbances" includes research on the relationships between pathological conditions and sleep. It also includes a small amount of research relating personality to sleep. The area clearly declined as research turned to the laboratory in the 1960s, but recently it has become the central focus. Ontogenetic and phylogenetic studies have held a steady interest across time. The increasing trend in recent years is primarily the result of clinical concerns about sleep of infants and the elderly. The sleep deprivation area, which includes total, partial, and selective stage deprivation, rose sharply in the 1960s. The rise can be almost

TABLE 6.3
Percentage of All Articles Related to Sleep Published During
Selected 5-Year Periods and During 1979–80

	1926–1930	1946–1950	1963–1967	1968–1972	1973–1977	1979–1980
Neurophysiology	10	14	24	16	12	10
Physiology	15	13	5	4	5	7
Biochemistry[a]	13	15	13	20	6	4
Pharmacology[a]	—	—	—	—	12	14
Endocrinology[a]	—	—	—	—	4	4
Sleep disturbances	26	19	14	16	20	25
Ontogeny/phylogeny	10	7	7	8	9	11
Sleep deprivation	3	1	13	6	4	3
Dreams	4	6	6	5	5	4
Biorhythms[b]	—	—	—	4	5	5
Others	19	25	18	21	18	13
N/Yr	50	100	450	650	1500	1950

[a]Separate coding introduced in 1973.
[b]Not assessed prior to 1968.

exclusively attributed to the emergence of REM deprivation studies. Dream research refers here to cognitive studies involving dream recall. The figures, of course, by reference to research publications do not reflect clinical usages or interest in dreams. The coding "biorhythms" was introduced in 1969 and signifies the strength of this conception of sleep. Much of this research is directly applied to problems generated by shiftwork and jet lag. The "other" category reflects a wide range of subject matter and articles: general reviews and books, electrosleep, hypnosis and sleep, sleep therapy, the influence of external stimuli on sleep and dreams, behavior relationships, altered states of consciousness and biofeedback, and instrumentation and methodological developments.

The interdisciplinary nature of this effort is apparent. It moves across the biochemical substrata, the action of single nerve cells, the neurophysiological network, the interactions of sleep with endocrine systems and physiology, the ontogeny of sleep, the phylogeny of sleep, pathological conditions and psychopathology relations, the interactions with performance and learning, the effects of external stimuli and schedules, the relations to drugs, and the entire panorama of these variables in relation to dreams. Scientists from many disciplines are involved in sleep research. We find biochemists, neurologists, physiologists, pediatricians, pharmacologists, psychiatrists, psychoanalysts, and zoologists—and, of course, psychologists. The latter group has tended to focus on the interrelations between sleep and behavioral manifestations and on the cognitive aspects of dreams.

Within the disciplines involved, sleep, as an area, remains of marginal interest; it is a peripheral concern of many, but central to none. This is typified by the relationship to psychology. A survey of the major introductory textbooks of 1960 (Webb, 1961) revealed that four made no reference to sleep, one had two paragraphs, and the most extensive treatment was two pages. A survey of 10 recent introductory tests (Webb, 1981) found that all include sleep and the number of pages ranges from 3 to 17. In most cases sleep is treated as an "altered state of consciousness," along with hypnosis and drug-induced states.

Clearly, as seen in the bottom row of Table 6.3, the field has grown rapidly since the 1950s. That this essentially exponential increase in publications exceeds the general explosion of research publications can be judged by comparison with research publications in psychology. The numbers of *Psychological Abstracts* for the years 1950, 1967, 1972, 1977, and 1980 were 6563, 17202, 24326, 27009, 26831, respectively. Thus, the increase in papers was 4-fold, while sleep research papers increased 20-fold.

CURRENT PERSPECTIVES

Difficulties of achieving "current perspective" are pointed to by the two nuances of the word "perspective": "capacity to view things in their true relations or relative importance," and "a visible scene, especially one giving a distinctive impression of distance'' (Webster's Collegiate Dictionary). Sleep research sprawls across a wide range of particularized concerns, and each plunges into complexities of techniques. Each effort holds an importance, and its complete comprehension demands particular expertise. Understanding of its ''true relations'' may lie in the future. The problem that an active participant in a field faces in achieving Olympian ''distance'' is as great as that of a foot soldier midst a battle in a great war. This final section is written within these limits of ''perspective.''

Sleep research in our modern era has ridden the broad and convenient shoulders of electroencephalograms of human and animal sleep. Currently, however, there are recognized needs and efforts to move beyond this familiar terrain. Computers are permitting an almost overwhelming extraction of indices and analyses. For example, recent evidence indicates that Stage 4 (slow waves of high amplitude) does not disappear or diminish with aging, but that the waves merely diminish in amplitude while maintaining their frequency-defined presence. An increasing interest in sleep in the context of diurnal (24-hour) variations in behavior has emphasized the limits of this descriptor in relation to subjective evaluations and sleeping/waking patterns. This has led also to an increasing concern beyond the structure of sleep toward pattern descriptors of sleep within 24-hour periods—delays in sleep onset, awakenings, number of sleep episodes, and the like.

Sleep, however measured, may be considered as a dependent variable, i.e., responsive to one or more independent variables. In this paradigm we may group these independent variables as central nervous system, phylogeny, ontogeny, time schedule, and precursor and pharmaceutical variables.

The relations between sleep and waking and the central nervous system have been intensively explored. Stimulation and lesion exploratory techniques have failed to reveal *a* sleep center, but have emphasized that this is a complex and interactive system. Current efforts have moved toward an emphasis on neurochemical and neuronal unit activity. The most recent search for the sleep ''humor'' centers has focused on the peptides. The neuroanatomy and neurophysiology of desynchronized, or REM, sleep are better understood and clearly are centered in the pontine reticular formation.

The phylogenetic studies of sleep continue to extend the measurement of sleep characteristics across species. However, because ''good'' measures tend to carry incompatible requirements, the accumulation of data, while steady, is slow. For example, a good measure requires 24-hour observations (because of diurnal variations) in a ''natural'' setting with an accurate designation of sleep and waking patterns, as well as of sleep structure. Unfortunately, natural settings restrict measurement accuracy, and often even observation (e.g., of burrowing or far-ranging animals), whereas accurate laboratory measurements drastically impose restriction on the natural sleep response. These data, however, furnish the prime source of ''theories'' about the function of sleep, e.g., energy conservation, instinctual, or behavioral adaptation conceptualizations.

The ontogeny of sleep has been extensively explored in the neonate through approximately 6 months of age, particularly in regard to electrophysiological development. Developmental change in sleep during early childhood is almost completely unexplored, and the latter years of the human lifespan have only recently received the attention of sleep researchers.

Time schedules of sleep refer to essentially four variables: prior wakefulness, sleep length, sleep displacement (onset and termination times), and time-free environments. The sleep structure and patterns of human sleep have been shown to be systematically related to changes in these variables. For example, sleep onset latency and amount of Stage 4 sleep are functions of prior wakefulness; sleep length seems chronically irreducible below about 4 hours; sleep displacement such as shift work schedules or "jet lag" disrupt the temporal organization of the sleep structure; and the biological "day" in time-free environments extends to an average "day-length" of about $25\frac{1}{2}$ hours. All of these research efforts find close relations to the results of biological rhythm research.

Perhaps because of the difficulties of defining and controlling the independent variables, the influence of daily activities has had limited exploration. However, the effects of exercise, an easily definable and measurable activity with considerable face validity as a determinant variable, have been experimentally evaluated. In general, amounts of exercise across a wide range from bed rest to substantial levels have little effect on sleep structure after onset. Similarly, within a healthy population, such variables as moods and set or personality traits show limited effects on the sleep process. Perhaps the most convincing evidence of the limited effects of antecedent factors on the sleep process is the lack of differences between the sleep of healthy young males and females.

Investigations of sleep-surround variables have focused on auditory stimuli. While the threshold studies of Kohlschutter were previously cited as the earliest experimental studies of sleep, the problems have provided ample room for further explorations and future discoveries. Clearly, thresholds are related to the intensity and relevance of the signal; to subject variables such as age, expectancy, preconditioning and sleep stage; and to response variables varying from evoked potentials to complex information processing. This area extends into the complexities of habituation to signal input and learning during sleep.

Under the goad of commercial enterprise and consumer and FDA regulations, the effectiveness of sleep control by the pharmaceutical "sleeping potions" of today has been extensively explored. So far the "magic bullet" has not been found. The general approach has been pragmatic testing of new compounds, and the dangers of chronic usage are well established.

Sleep may also be viewed as an independent variable, i.e., variations in sleep may be related to various dependent variables. The general approaches have been to study the effects of total sleep deprivation, partial sleep deprivation, selective deprivation of particular sleep stages, and schedule variations. The effects of these sleep variations on waking behavior have been elusive and disappointing. While increasing sleepiness is the apparent result of total deprivation, physiological effects are ephemeral and the effects on performance are heavily task dependent. The effects of chronic partial deprivation within the tolerable range of a minimum of about 4 hours of sleep are seen primarily in mood changes and sleepiness. Although literally hundreds of REM deprivation studies on both human and animals have been conducted, no certain consequences have yet emerged. As with total deprivation, it appears that whatever the consequences, they are likely to center on affective responses rather than physiological or performance changes. The most impressive effects of schedule variations are revealed in response decrements that appear in the time from which sleep was displaced. Recent interest in sleep disorders has accelerated studies of the change in general physiological systems such as pulmonary and vascular functions. A highly active area of research is the study of sleep apneas, or breathing difficulties, as contributory to sleep disturbances.

These approaches to sleep as a dependent or independent variable have been generally nomothetic in emphasis. The presence of individual differences, however, is apparent and has been given emphasis by the recent trends which have focused on sleep disorders. The impressive range of individual differences can be emphasized by noting that while the average length of sleep ranges between 7 and 8 hours across most populations measured, the standard deviation is approximately 1 hour. The area of sleep disorders has emphasized deviations from normative sleep such as insomnia, sleep walking, night terrors, nightmares, enuresis, sleep talking, and intrusions of sleep involving hypersomnia and narcolepsy.

Fortunately, the data and the field are maturing to the point that summary statements are increasingly forthcoming. Detailed treatments of most of the areas I have mentioned are available in the literature. Three major symposia have been published: *The Sleeping Brain* (Chase, 1972), *Aspects of Human Efficiency: Diurnal Rhythms and Sleep Loss* (Colquhoun, 1972), and *The Experimental Study of Sleep: Methodological Problems* (Lairy & Salzarulo, 1975). The ontogeny of sleep is intensively covered in *Sleep and The Maturing Nervous System* (Clemente, Purpura, & Mayer, 1972). An atlas of human EEG from 2 years through 70 years and its relation to clinical disorders is available (Williams, Karacan, & Hursch, 1974). Two recent volumes review the pharmacology of sleep (Williams & Karacan, 1976) and sleep disorders (Williams & Karacan, 1978). Four less technical volumes are available (Dement, 1974; Hartmann, 1973; Meddis, 1977; Webb, 1975). Cross-sectional views of the field can be found in the published papers of the European Sleep Congress (Koella & Levin, 1973, 1974, 1976) and in yearly volumes of the BIS bibliography of sleep (Chase, 1968–1982). Finally, there have been two *Annual Review of Psychology* articles: "Physiological Psychology: Sleep" (Williams, Holloway, & Griffiths, 1973), and "Sleep and Dreams" (Webb & Cartwright, 1978).

Contemporary dream research has been shaped by the established connection between the neurophysiological state of activation signaled in the EEG and the presence of the cognitive state of dreams. A substantial number of studies have explored the concomitance of cognitive quality and quantity of recall on awakening and EEG states. In general, REM awakenings can be accurately differentiated from non-REM awakenings; the former are more dream-like, while the latter are more thought-like. The quality of cognition varies across the night (becoming more intense) and shows interconnections both across REM periods and between REM and non-REM periods. A number of studies using the laboratory-evoked dream have continued the efforts to describe the quality of dream cognition in terms of content and dynamics. This extends the efforts to code or index the dream. A recent book (Winget & Kramer, 1978) summarizes attempts to classify dreams. The most extensive research in this area has been that of Hall and Van de Castle (1966), who studied "home" dreams.

Webb and Cartwright (1978) describe and summarize three essential experimental approaches to the dream: their relations to trait-like characteristics (e.g., differences between sexes, cultures, and psychopathological conditions); their relations to specific states (e.g., presleep films, the laboratory surround, and signals presented during sleep); and dreams as an independent variable (i.e., the effect of dreaming on waking behavior). They summarize the evidence supporting the conclusion that dreams reflect waking emotional concerns and styles and that the relationship between the "target" (a specific state stimulus) and the dream is ephemeral. The approach to the latter area (dream function) has been primarily through the experimental suppression of REM with an inferred "excision" of the dream. The authors conclude that REM deprivation produces a wider variance in waking performance than does non-REM deprivation and that the behaviors most affected are in the domains of emotion and activity level.

Table 6.3 shows that studies concerned with dream content per se have continued at a steady but low level in terms of percentage of sleep research. This conceals the fact that the absolute amount of research on dreams has risen across the years. One may infer from this that the indexing of the dream by the EEG has permitted increased effectiveness of experimental work, although this has not yet yielded a dramatic insight in unlocking the enigma of the dream.

The extent of the binding of sleep and dreams that resulted from the discovered interrelationship between the electrophysiologically defined REM data and the cognitive characteristics of dreams is to be seen in a new conceptual schema about dreams and their formation developed by McCarley and Hobson (Hobson & McCarley, 1977; McCarley & Hobson, 1977).

These investigators have attempted to integrate the extensive findings about the role of the central nervous system during the REM period with cognitive data on dreams. It is called an "activation-synthesis" hypothesis. Simply summarized, it recognizes periods of activation of the central nervous system, at roughly 90-minute intervals, arising from the pontine reticular formation. These are motivationally "neutral" sensory and muscular command signals which engender the dream experience. They are synthesized by the forebrain as it attempts to interpret these signals. The "impulse" of the dream is a neurophysiological event, not unconscious needs, wishes, or motivational states. The "dream work" is not that of disguising (Freud) or "expressing" (Neo-Freudian) needs, lifestyles, or motive states; rather, it is more that of "signal processing."

The proposal is a theoretically sophisticated one. McCarley and Hobson (1977) recognize that their concept is in the midst of the mind-body paradigm and dilemma. Thier choice is the "isomorphic" path. As stated by the authors:

> We suggest that the most useful strategy . . . is to regard the mind and brain concepts as coming from different linguistic and conceptual systems . . . we do not seek to reduce physiological to psychological events or psychological to physiological events. . . . Nor do we view psychological events as causing physiological events or vice versa. Instead we view the proper strategy . . . as seeking areas of contact between the conceptualization of physiology and psychological theory. Mind-body isomorphism is our name for this strategy. (p. 1338)

The form of presentation is interesting. It is clearly in confrontation with the Freudian schema. The inadequacy of the neurological base of Freud's thinking (drawn primarily from his Project for Scientific Psychology) is reviewed. Current knowledge of the physiology of the somatic period of dreaming is detailed, and the possible "psychological" or mental state of dreams is then superimposed on this model. The resultant discrepancies from the Freudian construct are noted.

This theory marks yet another point in the constant struggle to bridge the mind-body issues sharpened by the advancing discoveries about the central nervous system. Freud (1900/1965) had found it necessary in his approach to take a different position: "Scientific theories of dreams have no room for any problem of interpreting them, since in their view a dream is not a mental act at all, but a somatic process signalling the occurrence by indications registered on the mental appratus" (p. 128).

It can be reasonably guessed that the relationships between neurophysiological correlates of sleep and the mental states associated with sleep as precursors, concomitants, and consequences will remain as fundamental challenges.

CONCLUSION

From this review of sleep and dreams, it is clear that these areas have not been of central concern in the development of contemporary psychology. They remain of peripheral interest. Of the *13,800* articles appearing in the *Psychological Abstracts* from January through June, 1981, 218 were indexed under "sleep" and 45 under "dreams."

The apparent lack of interest in these topics is puzzling. As a behavioral event, sleep constitutes roughly a third of the daily behavior of a human adult and two-thirds of that of a neonate. Furthermore, it is a condition before which all other behaviors bow down when it is present and which modifies behavior when it is wanting. As a state of mind, sleep is clearly psychologically challenging; it is a reversible and differentially responsive period of "non-mind," as well as a breeding ground for a "third" state of unconsciousness, the dream.

There are a few obvious contributors to this neglect. Much of the development of contemporary psychology, certainly from the 1920s, has been ordained by behaviorism (of both a small "b" and a large "B" type). From this perspective, sleep has limitations. Is this non-behaving really a behavior? Even if considered a "behavior," it is sharply restricted in its variability. More critically, at the core of behaviorism's concern is the mutability or modifiability of the behavior. Sleep is not a response controlled by learning or desire. In this context, sleep is likely to be viewed as a biological system such as digestion or the circulation of the blood—a homeostatic system with limited responsivity to learning, reinforcement, or motivation. Those interested in the sensory or information input side of psychology see their interests disappear with the onset of sleep. In short, sleep can be viewed as a variable which fits neither our theoretical conceptions nor our methods of study.

Psychological interest in dreams has also probably been stunted by our behavioral orientation. When mental events were of central concern to psychology, our psychological forefathers (Wundt, Titchener, Woodworth, Jastrow) and a foremother (Calkins) wrote on dreams. However, with few exceptions, e.g., Calvin Hall, the area was abandoned to the psychoanalysts and clinicians by the developing science of psychology. A part of the reason undoubtedly was, and continues to be, the intractible experimental problems of measurement and the philosophical status of dreams as behavior. Simply, the stimulus event must remain forever inaccessible and the "behavior" dependent upon a verbal report for which no "confirmation" is available.

With the return of "consciousness" to psychology, the topic of sleep has shyly returned to the introductory texts. There is a small "boomlet" in studies concerning behavioral control of sleep onset. These are welcomed since a full comprehension of the realm of human behavior will necessarily require an understanding of the dark domain.

REFERENCES

Aristotle. *The works of Aristotle* (Vol. III). W. D. Ross (Ed.). Oxford: Clarendon Press, 1931.

Aserinsky, E., & Kleitman, N. Regularly occurring periods of eye mobility and concomitant phenomena during sleep. *Science*, 1953, *118*, 273–274.

Binns, E. *The anatomy of sleep.* London: John Churchill, 1842.

Blake, H., & Gerrard, R. W. Brain potential during sleep. *American Journal of Physiology*, 1937, *119*, 692–703.

Bonnuzi, L. About the origins of the scientific study of sleep and dreaming. In G. Lairy & P. Salzarulo (Eds.), *Study of human sleep: Methodological problems.* Amsterdam: Elsevier, 1975.

Calkins, M. W. Statistics of dreams. *American Journal of Psychology,* 1893, *5,* 311–324.

Chase, M. (Ed.). *Annual sleep bibliography and sleep research.* University of California, Los Angeles: Brain Information Service: Brain Research Institute, 1968–present.

Chase, M. *The sleeping brain.* University of California, Los Angeles: Brain Information Service: Brain Research Institute, 1972.

CIBA Foundation Symposium. *The nature of sleep.* G. E. W. Wolstenholms & M. O'Connor (Eds.). London: Churchill, 1961.

Cicero. *De senectute, de amicitia, de divinatione.* W. A. Falconer (Trans.). Cambridge, Mass.: Harvard Press, 1923.

Clemente, C., Purpura, D., & Mayer, F. *Sleep in the maturing nervous system.* New York: Academic Press, 1972.

Colquhoun, W. P. *Aspects of human efficiency: Diurnal rhythm and loss of sleep.* London: The English Universities Press, Ltd., 1972.

Dement, W. C. The occurrence of low voltage, fast electroencephalogram patterns during behavioral sleep in the cat. *Electroencephalography and Clinical Neurophysiology,* 1958, *10,* 291–296.

Dement, W. C. The effect of dream deprivation. *Science,* 1960, *131,* 1705.

Dement, W. C. *Some must watch while some must sleep.* San Francisco: Freeman, 1974.

Dunlop, C. E. M. *Philosophical essays on dreaming.* Ithaca: Cornell University Press, 1977.

Freud, S. *The interpretation of dreams.* J. Strachey (Trans.). New York: Avon, 1965.

Hall, C. S., & Van de Castle, R. L. *The content analysis of dreams.* New York: Appleton-Century-Crofts, 1966.

Hall, W. *Sleep: or the hygiene of the night.* New York: Hurd & Houghton, 1870.

Hartmann, E. *The functions of sleep.* New Haven: Yale Press, 1973.

Hobson, J. A., & McCarley, R. The brain as a dream generator: an activation-synthesis hypothesis of the dream process. *American Journal of Psychiatry,* 1977, *134,* 1335–1348.

Jones, R. M. *The new psychology of dreaming.* New York: Grune & Stratton, 1970.

Jouvet, M., & Michel, F. Corrélations électromyographique due sommeil chex le chat décortiqué et mésencéphalique chronique. *C. R. Soc. Biol.* (Paris), 1959, *159,* 422–425.

Kelsey, M. T. *God, dreams and revelation.* Minneapolis: Augsburg, 1968.

Kleitman, N. *Sleep and wakefulness.* Chicago: University of Chicago, 1963.

Koella, W., & Levin, P. (Eds.). *Sleep, Sleep 1973, Sleep 1974.* Basel: Karger, 1973, 1974, 1976.

Lairy, G. C., & Salzarulo, P. (Eds.). *The experimental study of human sleep: methodological problems.* Amsterdam: Elsevier, 1975.

Lemain, G., Clemencon, M., Gomis, A., Pollin, B., & Salvo, B. *Strategies et choix dans la recherche: a propos des travaux sur le sommeil.* Paris: Groupe d'Etudes et de Recherches sur la Science, 1975.

Loomis, A. L., Harvey, E. N., & Hobart, G. A. Electrical potentials of the human brain. *Journal of Experimental Psychology,* 1937, *21,* 127–144.

Manaceine, Marie de. *Sleep: its physiology, hygiene, and psychology.* New York: Charles Scribner's Sons, 1899.

Maritain, J. *The dreams of Descartes.* New York: Philosophical Library, 1944.

McCarley, R., & Hobson, J. A. The neurobiological origins of psychoanalytical dream theory. *American Journal of Psychiatry,* 1977, *134,* 1211–1221.

Meddis, R. *The sleep instinct.* London: Routledge & Kegan, 1977.

Meir, C. The dream in Ancient Greece and its use in temple cures. In G. Von Gruenbaum & R. Callois (Eds.), *The dream in human society.* Berkeley: University of California, 1977.

Oppenheim, A. Mantic dreams in the Near East. In G. Von Gruenbaum & R. Callois (Eds.), *The dream in human society.* Berkeley: University of California, 1977.

Oswald, I. *Sleeping and waking: physiology and psychology.* Amsterdam: Elsevier, 1962.

Pieron, H. *Le probleme physiologique du sommeil.* Paris: Masson & Cie, 1913.

Rechtschaffen, A., & Eakins, D. *Sleep and dream research, a bibliography.* (Q701). University of California, Los Angeles: Brain Information Service: Brain Research Institute, 1967.

Snyder, F. In quest of dreaming. In H. A. Witkin & H. B. Lewis (Eds.), *Experimental studies of dreaming.* New York: Random House, 1967.

Vande Kemp, H. The dream in periodical literature: 1860–1910. *Journal of the History of the Behavioral Sciences,* 1981, *17,* 88–113.

Webb, W. B. An overview of sleep as an experimental variable (1940–1959). *Science,* 1961, *134,* 1421–1423.

Webb, W. B. *Sleep: the gentle tyrant.* Engelwood Cliffs, N.J.: Prentice-Hall, 1975.

Webb, W. B. A historical perspective of dreams. In B. Wolman (Ed.), *Handbook of dreams.* New York: Van Nostrand Reinhold, 1979.

Webb, W. B. The return of consciousness. In L. T. Benjamin, Jr. (Ed.), *The G. Stanley Hall lecture series.* Washington, D.C.: American Psychological Association, 1981.

Webb, W. B., & Cartwright, R. D. Sleep and dreams. *Annual Review of Psychology,* 1978, *29,* 223–252.

Williams, H., Holloway, F., & Griffiths, W. Physiological psychology: sleep. *Annual Review of Psychology,* 1973, *24,* 279–316.

Williams, R. L., Agnew, H. W., & Webb, W. B. Sleep patterns in young adults: and EEG study. *Electroencephalography and Clinical Neurophysiology,* 1964 *17,* 376–381.

Williams, R., & Karacan, I. *Pharmacology of sleep.* New York: Wiley & Sons, 1976.

Williams, R., & Karacan, I. *Sleep disorders: diagnosis and treatment.* New York: Wiley & Sons, 1978.

Williams, R., Karacan, I., & Hursch, C. *EEG and human sleep.* New York: Wiley & Sons, 1974.

Winget, C., & Kramer, M. *Dimensions of dreams.* Gainesville: University of Florida Press, 1978.

7 Psychotherapy*

Joseph D. Matarazzo
Oregon Health Sciences University

No matter what its form, cost or setting, all that is meant by psychotherapy is the service that one human being, a helper, renders another, a sufferer, toward the end of promoting the latter's well being. The common elements in both ancient and modern forms of psychotherapy are a sufferer, a helper, and a systematized ritual through which help is proffered. Although the specific purposes in consulting a psychotherapist are as numerous and unique as the individuals who seek such help, the basic reasons have always been to obtain assistance in (1) removing, modifying or controlling anxiety, depression, alienation, and other distressing psychological states, (2) changing undesirable patterns of behavior such as timidity, over-aggressiveness, alcoholism, disturbed sexual relationships, and the like, or (3) promoting more positive personal growth and the development of greater meaning in one's life through more effective personal functioning, or through the pursuit of new educational, occupational, recreational, or other goals which will better allow expression of the individual's potential.

Psychotherapy without fee is as old as history, and the healing effects of an intimate human relationship have always been recognized. Psychotherapy for a fee had its historical roots in early fiscal exchanges between ancient high priest or priestess and supplicant, naturopathic physician and patient, philosopher-teacher-advisor and student, clergyman and sinner, and attorney and client. Psychotherapy practiced by that name for a fee began about a century ago with Freud who saw the process as a means of earning a living and, equally important, as a

---

*The reader interested in pursuing the ideas presented in this chapter in considerable greater detail will find them in Durant (1939), Ehrenwald (1976), Ellenberger (1970), Frank (1973), Jones (1953), Masserman (1965), Schofield (1964), Shapiro (1971) and Zilboorg (1941).

means of providing a more scientific basis for the study of personality. We shall return to Freud's contributions after a brief description of some earlier history. We pick up the story with Mesmer, an eighteenth and early nineteenth century precursor of Freud.

MESMER AND HYPNOTISM

Franz Anton Mesmer (1734–1815), Austrian physician, dabbler in physics, and huckster par excellence, took Paris by storm in 1778 with his demonstrations before scientific and lay audiences of a "new" physical phenomenon which he called **animal magnetism.** Actually the phenomenon was not new. Accounts of trance-like states induced by having the individual fixate on a luminous object were recorded on an Egyptian scroll dating back to the third century A.D.

Mesmer preached that every illness was a manifestation of disturbances in a mysterious ethereal fluid which, operating like magnetism, made animate and inanimate entities subject to influence and disruption by the stars. By applying magnets to the body of a subject Mesmer was able to produce peculiar trance-like states and even convulsions. Occasionally these alleged magnetic influences also produced spectacular cures in conditions such as blindness, paralysis, and convulsive disorders.

Despite these accomplishments Mesmer was vilified at first by the medical-scientific community. It was clear that the eighteenth century was not yet ready to discard either the soul or the devil in the interpretation of mental disorder and the practice of psychotherapy. **Mesmerism,** as it universally was called, had attracted such notoriety in England that in 1837 the Council of University College in London decreed that its practice be forbidden within the hospital.

At about this same time, on the other hand, Professor John Elliotson was so impressed with animal magnetism that he resigned his chair in medicine and devoted himself completely to its study and therapeutic use. In 1842 a British surgeon, Dr. Ward, reported to the unbelieving and unimpressed Royal Medical and Chirurgical Society that he had successfully amputated a leg without anesthesia while using only Mesmer's technique. But ether had been discovered between 1800–1818 and surgery (and medicine) did not follow his (or Dr. Elliotson's) lead except for unsystematic and sporadic episodes of revived interest which have continued to the present. In contrast to medicine and surgery, psychiatry and abnormal psychology seemed more generally ready to accept the potential therapeutic value of mesmerism.

Through most of the nineteenth century psychiatry continued to treat severe mental illness (**psychosis**) with bleeding, blistering, purgation, restraining, dunking, and a few nonspecific drugs. Persuasion, exhortation, and other forms of moral treatment were tried occasionally but were repeatedly discarded as ineffective treatments for such mentally ill persons. The **neuroses** received little attention at all. After resigning his chair in medicine, Elliotson turned to the treatment of patients with **hysteria** (physical conditions such as blindness and paralysis without demonstrable physiological bases) and in the 1840s he began to assert that, in contrast to drugs, mesmerism was the treatment of choice for hysteria and the other functional nervous disorders. Elliotson thus was among the first practitioners to draw attention to the neuroses in contrast to the insanities as a legitimate area of psychological and medical therapeutic interest.

It is an important historical fact that neither Elliotson nor others offered any plausible explanation of the etiology of hysteria. Another Englishman, James Braid (1795–1860), soon began to provide an explanation, however. The explanation came in two parts. The first part of the explanation called attention to the hysterical patient's unusual degree of susceptibility to hypnotic influence. In his contribution Braid introduced the modern words *hypnotism, hypnotize,* and *hypnotic* and discarded Mesmer's theory of an internal magnetic fluid which moved around the body under the control of the hypnotizer's magnetic stimulus. Braid offered, instead, the opinion that the influence of the hypnotizer was due primarily, if not solely, to the deep unconscious reactions of the patient under hypnosis. At the time (1842) Braid was writing the concept of the unconscious as a factor in psychological illness was not widely accepted. Braid's speculation, that hypnosis could tap these unconscious attitudes and states, constituted the second critical insight in the eventual unraveling of the puzzle of hysteria as a vehicle in the development of psychotherapy. Unfortunately, this second insight was a premature idea in 1842 and it would lie dormant until picked up by Freud a half century later. Although Braid's views were well known in England throughout the nineteenth century, even as late as 1891 the British Medical Association showed its ambivalence about hypnosis when it would neither approve nor reject a report on hypnotism from one of its committees. Rather, it merely "received" the report without comment or action.

There was no such ambivalence about hypnotism in France during the last half of the nineteenth century. There, two schools of hypnosis were flourishing. The first was in Nancy where a French country general practitioner, A. A. Liébault (1823–1904) was using hypnosis extensively in his practice, treating patients with hysteria as well as those with a wide variety of other medical and psychopathological conditions. One of his associates in Nancy was Hippolyte Bernheim (1840–1919), an early internist who had left Strasbourg in 1871 where he was a university professor renowned for his work on typhoid fever and pulmonary and cardiac disease. Bernheim learned hypnosis from Liébault and, although using it less indiscriminately than the latter, he also became very proficient in its study and use and soon helped make Nancy a leading center for the study of hypnosis. As he gained his reputation Bernheim came to believe, as had Elliotson decades earlier in London, that hypnosis was the result of suggestion, and that hypnotic suggestion was an appropriate therapy for a wide variety of diseases of the nervous system as well as for a number of other medical conditions.

This latter view was opposed by Jean-Martin Charcot (1825–1893) who founded a rival school of hypnosis at the Saltpetriere in Paris. Charcot believed that hypnosis was suitable only for the treatment of hysteria. In 1882 he presented a paper to the French Academy of Sciences in which he described a variety of states which he could produce at will under hypnosis, but only in patients with hysteria. This so impressed the members of the Academy that they reversed their century-old condemnation of mesmerism, perceiving Charcot's use of hypnosis as a more respectable technique than Mesmer's. Soon physicians throughout Europe were traveling to Paris to study the phenomena of hypnosis under Charcot. Although Charcot recognized the importance of autosuggestion and imagination in the treatment of hysteria, and also confirmed Braid's observation of the hypnotizer's influence on the manifestations of the hysterical patient's symptoms, he saw hysteria through the eyes of a neurologist and not those of a psychologist or psychiatrist. To him the symptoms of hysteria, despite their psychic components, were the by-products of some type of physical shock to the nervous system. Admitting that the etiology of hysterial symptoms was different from that of the true neurological symptoms, Charcot was not quite able to totally forsake neurology for psychology in his attempt to understand hypnosis or hysteria.

Bernheim disputed Charcot's restriction of hypnosis to hysteria. In a well-received 1886 textbook coauthored with Henri Beaunis, he put forth the more general view promulgated earlier by Elliotson that hypnosis was a universal psychological reaction based on suggestion and was applicable to everyone. The Nancy school thus was pitted against the Parisian school.

At length, in a showdown between the two schools, Bernheim's more psychological and general views prevailed over Charcot's more physiological and restricted explanations. Also to prevail was Bernheim's just mentioned broader view that the importance of suggestibility extended beyond the psychopathological condition of hysteria to a wide variety of abnormal and normal mental and physical conditions. Bernheim believed these latter mental and physical conditions could be brought about by various types of personal-subjective or interpersonal stimuli, including many which are not readily evident to the conscious mind. (This concept of humans experiencing multiple mental states, some of which were unconscious, was not new. St. Augustine in his *Confessions* remarked that his old pagan personality, of which nothing seemed to remain in his waking state, still must exist inasmuch as it was revived at night in his dreams.) As for the role of suggestion in neurosis, Bernheim repeatedly demonstrated that he could suggest a previously nonexistent symptom to a patient under hypnosis and that such a symptom later would remain in the waking state. In 1891 he published his famous *Hypnotism, Suggestion and Psychotherapy* which elaborated and further developed his view.

Bernheim gave the study and treatment of neurosis respectability and, through the role assigned to suggestibility, he attempted to gain insight into behavior in general. He differed from the earlier legions of philosophers who had written about personality because he based his observations on some 10,000 cases that he and his colleague Beaunis had studied and not on armchair philosophizing. Although Bernheim did not take the next step, that of evolving a system of psychotherapy based on his keen psychological insights, his tentative conceptions were the first important effort to produce a general understanding of human behavior and its motivation from the perspective of the study of psychopathology rather than on the basis of philosophic systems.

FREUD AND PSYCHOANALYSIS

Sigmund Freud (1856–1939) was born in Austria-Hungary (Moravia) during this period of ferment over hypnosis in England and in France. During the years when he was a student of biology, physiology, and medicine, and then a specialist in neurology, Freud also developed an avid interest in early Egyptian, Greek, and Roman literature and culture, British philosophy, and French neuropathology. He translated the works of John Stuart Mill and Charcot into German. Freud thus combined in one mind a monumental store of the literary, philosophical and scientific knowledge of his day. His lifelong study of these varied disciplines added considerable breadth to the products of his formal studies. Not that Freud was uninfluenced by these latter sources of knowledge. From his physiology teacher Brücke, Freud accepted the proposition, first implied 2200 years earlier by Hippocrates, that all human functioning, including the workings of the mind, could be reduced to a physical-chemical basis. Recourse to vitalism, an élan vital, or other religio-philosophic explanations of the workings of the body or mind were utter nonsense to Freud who showed great promise as a research experimental physiologist in Brücke's laboratory both before and shortly after he graduated from medical school in 1881.

After his medical degree and an internship, a travel grant in 1884 took Freud to Paris, where he studied with Charcot and also learned about the exciting ideas of Liébault and Bernheim. While there he learned first hand that some forms of muscular paralysis, blindness, and deafness, although crudely mimicking conditions brought on by physical trauma and neurological disease, could be brought on by severe psychological stress. Furthermore, and equally surprising, these conditions could be made to disappear temporarily under hypnosis, thereby revealing the presence of unconscious psychological forces not typically recognized in the person's waking awareness.

In Paris Freud also came into contact with the work of Pierre Janet (1859–1947), another leading French neuropathologist who was establishing his reputation studying a variety of unusual mental states (somnambulism, fugues, hypnotic states, hysteria). One of the very most unusual of these states was that of **multiple personality,** the phenomenon made popular in this generation through books and movies such as *Three Faces of Eve* and *Sybil*. Janet became an expert on these patients who could switch from one personality to another in a single conversation, appearing totally oblivious when in one mental state of the existence of these other co-existing personalities. Janet correctly surmised that every human mind had the capacity for different states, some of which were conscious and others not. Although unconscious, the latter states were capable of considerable influence on conscious experience. Freud would later make this observation central to his theory of personality development and psychotherapy.

Leaving Paris and Charcot, Freud returned to Vienna to begin his practice of neurology. He quickly resumed there an old friendship with Joseph Breuer, a scientifically-oriented physician and Freud's earlier financial benefactor, who for several years had been experimenting with the use of hypnosis in patients similar to those Freud had just seen being treated in Paris. However, unlike Charcot who enjoyed demonstrating such patients for his disciples' edification and speculating about early traumatic events which left a residue in the patient's unconscious mind, Breuer the practicing physician was spending his days in Vienna treating them.

Shortly before Freud had left to study with Charcot, Breuer had discovered that one such young patient, Anna O, showed considerable relief from her hysterical symptoms when he merely asked her to describe the life events she thought about immediately preceding the onset of such symptoms, life events which he had come to conclude were the psychic trigger for the symptoms. Breuer termed this new type of treatment of hysteria **catharsis,** or the **talking cure.** All of this had made a strong impression on Freud and he attempted to discuss the case of Anna O with Charcot during his Paris fellowship, but the great master showed little interest.

Upon his return to Vienna and his reassociation with Breuer, Freud began experimenting both with Charcot's hypnosis and with Breuer's talking cure with his own patients. Gradually between 1884 and 1895, Freud developed his own method (a hybrid treatment combining features of hypnosis and the cathartic method) which he soon came to call the **free association** method. Some writers believe that Freud's devising of this method was one of his two greatest accomplishments. The second, soon thereafter, was the development of his insights into *psychosexual development*. These latter revelations came about through his own self-analysis in which he discovered his early sex life including the famous *Oedipus complex*.

It is important to point out that at the time Freud introduced the method of free association as a therapeutic tactic it was also widely practiced as a method of research. The first recorded scientific study of the association process was published in 1879 in the journal *Brain* by Francis Galton, at the time when Freud was in medical school. Galton's work was an introspective study of his own associations. This report may have provided the German psychologist Wundt with the framework for the first true experiment on free association in 1880. Quite likely it also helped Wundt launch the formal method of **introspection** which would serve as the foundation for the school of structural psychology, developed by Wundt, and brought to America by E. B. Titchener who studied under Wundt. Soon after Wundt's 1880 publication another American psychologist, James McKeen Cattell, who had also studied in Wundt's laboratory, published an article (1889) in *Mind* which described a study of the individual associations given by subjects including the most popular responses to each word presented. In 1892 Kraepelin would apply Cattell's method in an attempt to diagnose schizophrenia and to understand its etiology. Thus it is clear that free association as the mirror of unconscious processes was an idea that was ready for acceptance when Freud began using it as the foundation of his method of psychotherapy.

Freud's Free Association Technique

Freud's development of the technique of free association as a method of treating troubled individuals was important because the glimpses into the human personality that such verbalizations afforded soon led to a theory of personality development, a particular view of the bases of psychopathology, and important insights into the forms that psychotherapy should ideally take.

Freud records that the discovery of his unique brand of free association was accidental. He had been treating a patient with hysteria, Frl. Elizabeth von R, who could not be hypnotized. Frustrated, Freud remembered a remark of Bernheim's to the effect that one's experiences under hypnosis were only apparently forgotten afterwards; they could be brought into consciousness if the therapist forcibly insisted that the hypnotized person *did* remember the experiences. Putting this recollection together with the knowledge that suggestibility, hypnosis, and hysteria tapped a common mechanism, Freud guessed that Bernheim's observation might also hold for the memories "forgotten" by patients with hysteria. He therefore insisted that this first patient "concentrate" on and report everything which came to her mind, totally without censorship. Freud gave the following description of this first therapeutic use of free association with Frl. Elizabeth von R in an 1893 article and reprinted the case in *Studies on Hysteria* which he published in book form with Breuer in 1895:

> In this extremity (over my inability to put her under hypnosis) the idea occurred to me of resorting to the idea of applying pressure to the head . . . [and] instructing the patient to report to me faithfully whatever appeared before her inner eye or passed through her memory at the moment of pressure. She remained silent for a long time and then, on my insistence, admitted [as others would do spontaneously while under hypnosis that on my pressure] she had thought of an evening on which a young man had seen her home from a party, of the conversation that had taken place between them and of the feelings with which she had returned home to her father's sick bed.

This first mention of the young man opened up a new view of ideas the contents of which I now gradually extracted. It was a question here of a secret, for she had initiated no one, apart from a common friend, into her relations with the young man and the hopes attached to them. (p. 145)

Freud then goes on and describes in this article the insights she and he derived from Frl. Elizabeth von R's further free associations, the analysis of them and their guessed meanings in her psychic life, and the temporary relief from the hysterical symptoms she received from this first form of psychoanalysis (the psychodynamic interpretation of her free associations). Freud also acknowledges that subsequently, still not being familiar with this new technique, he occasionally returned to urging, pressing, and questioning Frl. Elizabeth von R. Whereupon, at one point, she reproved him for interrupting her free flow of thought and associations by his questions. He quickly sensed the importance of this point for his technique of analyzing troubled psyches and thereby added a refinement to his newly evolving method of psychotherapy; namely, never interrupting the patient's free flow of associations.

Soon thereafter, in his treatment of Elizabeth von R and other patients, Freud came to understand the importance of three powerful by-products which would manifest themselves during free association and become the critical elements of his psychoanalytic method: (1) The patient's emotional **abreaction** and reliving of earlier painful experiences in the consultation room; (2) **resistances** to revealing some of these experiences; and (3) the highly charged **transference** relationship or bond between sufferer and helper which verbalization of such hidden memories would invariably induce and whose analysis would be the heart of the treatment. The existence of strong bonds between physician and patient or priest and supplicant had been recognized for centuries; but never before had it deliberately been fostered, and used as the essential basis of treatment. What also was new was that Freud's free association method, and its therapeutic by-products were being described in the scientific periodicals and thus being made subject to independent scrutiny, criticism, and attempts at verification. This placed Freud's method in a scientific context and removed psychotherapy from the magical-religious framework of earlier healers.

It is interesting for our historical discussion to recall, as mentioned above, that Freud's opinion was that he accidentally stumbled upon the powers of free association. However this may be, it also is the case (also mentioned earlier) that Freud was an avid student of Greek drama and one cannot help but speculate that he was familiar with the early writings of the playwright-philosopher, Aristophanes (448–380 B.C.), a friend, rival, and critic of Socrates. The drama *The Clouds* written by Aristophanes contains a scene in which a troubled individual, Strepsiades, consults Socrates for help. Socrates invites Strepsiades to lie on a couch (*Klinikos*), to think completely freely and thereby to reach an understanding of his problem by this indirect Socratic technique. But Strepsiades intones that he does not know exactly what his troubles are, except that he has difficulty falling asleep at night and is tense and anxious by day. Socrates again requests that he lie on the couch and then simply to say *anything that comes into his mind.* At which point Strepsiades lies on the couch, begins to talk and immediately is talking about the moon. Socrates encourages his now embarrassed supplicant with, "That is all right, go ahead and talk about the moon if you want to." Strepsiades does and his free associations reveal the fantasy that if only he could capture the moon and put it in his pocket it no longer would wax and wane, there would no longer be a first of the month, Strepsiades therefore would have no more debts to pay, and his sleepless nights and anxiety and tension would disappear.

This play, written about 390 B.C., contains insights into the human personality, its workings and its conscious and unconscious motivations, which are remarkably current, and antedated by 2400 years the works of Janet and Freud. However, neither Aristophanes nor Socrates nor any of the succeeding generations of philosophers took three important additional steps; steps Freud did take as a scientist-practitioner of the helping arts. *First,* working simultaneously as therapist and scientist, Freud checked his insights about human nature and tested their generality, first in one human being, then another, and another. *Second,* he made refinements in these insights as inconsistencies and new material required. *Third,* he checked the validity of any emerging generalizations against one additional criterion: the potential of such an insight to help a sufferer reconstruct his or her personality and thereby find relief from suffering. This Freud would do in a burst of his most creative insights and intellectual accomplishments from about 1895 to 1920.

Freud's Theory of Personality

The use and refinement of the free association method permitted Freud, in just two decades, to develop his revolutionary conceptions of the working of the human psyche. His brilliant new conceptions included *libido theory,* the theory of *instincts,* the concepts of *repression, infant sexuality,* and the triparte structure of the psychic apparatus (*id, ego,* and *superego*). Freud's earlier work with hypnosis and patients with hysteria had prepared him for the discovery of the importance of *unconscious life.* These insights were followed by the development of a psychoanalytic perspective on slips of speech and lapses of memory which had formerly seemed trivial. These and other forms of "psychopathology of everyday life" were what Freud called paths on the royal road to the unconscious. Freud's concept was that unconscious life stemmed from the id and was acquired in the development and later functioning of personality. In such a conception, free association, the interpretation of dreams (including Freud's own), and the process of analysis itself (again including Freud's own) all provided rich sources of information on the functioning of the unconscious. Soon

Freud was to recognize *fear,* and its derivative *anxiety,* as basic components of all neurotic disorders. From there the next step was the insight that the neuroses are faulty versions of the individually learned attitudes and habits by which all of us attempt to cope with psychic distress. The learning of neurotic adjustments is no different from the acquisition of the more efficient attitudes and habits acquired by the normally functioning human being. These epoch making contributions to personality theory, promulgated between 1895 and 1915, served as the framework for Freud's psychoanalytic form of psychotherapy.

Before leaving Freud's personality theory it will be interesting to point out some of the early historical antecedent of Freud's works. These include an historical antecedent of the tripartite theory of id, ego, and superego. Freud's theory holds that the id, reflecting base, primary instinctual needs demanding instant gratification is governed by the **pleasure principle.** By contrast, the ego in its attempt to repress or otherwise keep the id in check is governed by the **reality principle** of social rewards and punishments. The superego, a product of rewards and punishment growing out of situations involving ethical and moral issues is the negotiator and arbitrator between the other two. Freud adopted the terms id and ego in 1923 from the writings of Nietzsche and a German writer (1920s) by the name of Groddeck. However, as will be shown below, the basic idea of an id and ego battling within a single psyche was clearly of much earlier and ancient origin. Examine first the following quotation from Freud's 1923 book *The Ego and the Id:*

> The ego . . . which is that part of the id which has been modified by direct influence of the external world . . . represents what we call reason and sanity, in contrast to the id which contains the passions . . . Thus in its relation to the id it is like a man on horseback, who has to hold in check the superior strength of the horse; with this difference, that the rider seeks to do so with his own strength while the ego uses borrowed forces. The illustration may be carried further. Often a rider, if he is not to be parted from his horse, is obliged to guide it where it wants to go; so in the same way the ego constantly carries into action the wishes of the id as if they were its own. (p. 30).

Now compare the above quotation with the following metaphor from Plato, writing in the fourth century B.C.:

> Of the nature of the [human] soul . . . let me speak briefly, and in a figure. Let the figure be a composite—a pair of winged horses and a charioteer . . . one of the [horses] is noble . . . and the other is ignoble . . . and the driving of them gives a great deal of trouble . . . The right-hand horse is upright and cleanly made; . . . he is a lover of honour and modesty and temperance . . . he is guided by word and admonition only. The other is a crooked and lumbering animal . . . hardly yielding to whip and spur. Now when the charioteer (beholds his beloved maiden), and has his whole soul warmed through sense, and is full of the prickings and tinglings of

desire, the obedient steed, then as always under the government of shame, refrains from leaping upon the beloved; but the other, heedless of the pricks and of the blows of the whip, . . . forces (the other two) to approach the beloved and to remember the joys of love . . . the charioteer . . . with a . . . violent wrench drags the bit . . . of the wild steed . . . and forces his legs and haunches to the ground and punishes him sorely. And when this has happened several times and the villain has ceased from his wanton way, he is tamed and humbled, and follows the will of the charioteer . . . (Quoted in Ehrenwald, 1976, pp. 158–159.)

The similarity between the two passages is striking.

There were also early anticipations of Freud's theory of **dream interpretation.** As stated earlier, one of the most important contributions made by Freud was his discovery that dreams were a powerful source of information about the existence and the workings of the unconscious, including information about the battles of id, ego, and superego in the development of neurosis. This idea that dreams were a mirror of one's inner life occurs in the writings of the Babylonians, Egyptians, Greeks, Romans, and all the subsequent cultures. One author whose works were well known to Freud was the early writer Artemidorous who stated in his *Interpretation of Dreams* that, ''Dreams and Visions are infused into men for their advantage and instruction . . . Hippocrates is of opinion, that whilst the body sleeps, the spirit is awake . . .''Artemidorous then describes five types of dreams and reiterates the view prevalent from the time of Plato on that the deeper, symbolic meaning of dreams is not accessible to the dreamer himself and must be interpreted by a priest or other similarly annointed person.

As the above quotation indicates, Hippocrates (circa 469–399 B.C.) also wrote about the nature of dreams. In one passage he claimed that:

He who forms a correct judgment of those signs which occur in sleep, will find that they have great efficacy in all respects; for the mind . . . imports a certain portion of its influence to every part of the body, namely to the senses, to the hearing, seeing, touch, walking, action, and to the whole management of the body, and therefore its cognitions are not then in its power . . . Whosoever, then knows how to judge of these correctly, will find a great part of wisdom.

As we shall see next, Freud's discovery of the power of unconscious processes, their role in personality, and their revelation in dreams, and in the free associations on his couch, were an important landmark in this historical evolution of ideas.

Psychoanalysis: The First Scientific Psychotherapy

Inasmuch as Freud was developing his theory of personality and his method of psychotherapy in parallel, it is not surprising that the key elements of the psychoanalytic method of therapy follow cogently from the theoretical propositions which he offered about personality. The earlier theories about the human condition and the corresponding psychotherapists of each era—the shaman, priest, philosopher, naturopathic physician, and teacher—were doomed to failure from the scientific perspective. Their premises were literary, religious, and existential and, thus, not subject to verification by others. As a result each generation that produced great philosophers or theologians found itself with dozens upon dozens of interesting treatises on the nature of man, including proposals on how to help his troubled being, but no two of these treatments showed any similarity.

As was pointed out above, by contrast with these other writers, Freud published his views in the scientific journals, most of which had their beginnings in the nineteenth century. He was thus the first writer to explicitly tie psychotherapy to the broad sweep of empirical science which had profoundly affected the Western countries. As he had in his description of the case of Frl. Elizabeth, Freud continued in each subsequent published case to describe how insights from the patient's free associations, each slip of the tongue, every dream fragment, every neurotic symptom, could be traced to an identifiable antecedent in the patient's life history and thus understood against the patient's conscious and unconscious personality dynamics. There was, of course, a potentially perilous difference between Freud's science and that of most other sciences. Although all scientific observation contains an element of the subjective, Freud's role was more than that of mere observer. He served as a highly trained sounding board who elicited information and catologued and interpreted it. Freud's aim was to undo the damage done by harmful life experiences. Success meant the disappearance of the object of Freud's scientific observation.

In Freud's psychoanalytic therapy, the therapist helped the patient to relive his or her past, in five daily 1-hour sessions per week on the psychoanalytic couch. By judicious use of the **transference relationship** and interpretations of verbal content relating to it, the therapist could help the patient readjust the faulty attitudes, and reaction patterns established toward significant persons in early life. The method of free association induces a flow of highly personal, emotionally charged expressions of unconscious thoughts, feelings and wishes, many of them shocking and embarrassing. These expressions fostered the complex dependency—love-hate interaction—with the analyst which Freud termed the transference relationship. As this transference develops in each psychoanalysis, the patient relives, and describes for the therapist to interpret, the important elements of the damaging early attitudes, feelings, and patterns of relationship which he or she had gradually developed toward parent and sibling in childhood. As these are analyzed and understood by the patient, insight occurs with an attendant emotional release as the bonds of these earlier, inefficient thoughts, feelings, and habit patterns are left behind on the couch.

The above in overview are the essentials of Freud's contribution to the establishment of scientifically-based psychotherapy. The psychoanalytic method (including *abreaction, transference, resistance, interpretation,* and *insight*) attempted to explain personality maldevelopment and its psychotherapeutic reconstruction by recourse to more general principles. These principles offered an understanding of normal development in the same terms that they explained the neurotic sufferer's symptoms of distress, inefficient personality, and faulty interactions with others. A summary of the main features of Freud's psychoanalysis, and their comparison with the two other major classes of psychotherapy we will review, are shown in Table 7.1.

It was not long before Freud was vilified by many of his Viennese colleagues as a medical heretic whose interest was fixated on the sexual fantasies of his frustrated female patients. Almost at the same time, however, Freud's work was widely acclaimed by American psychologists such as William James and Putnam who invited him, along with Carl Jung, to America in 1909 to deliver a lecture at Clark University. Within another 2 decades or so (1910–1939) the sheer magnitude of Freud's published works brought him acclaim in England, France, other Western countries, and finally in his own Vienna.

Following 1923, Freud's writings were chiefly refinements of his earlier creative insights. No further comparable contributions, either to personality theory or therapeutic method were to appear. Driven out of Vienna by Hitler, Freud moved to London in 1938 where he died a year later at the age of 83.

Freud's greatest impact was in America. His work found ready acceptance on many university and college campuses. Of particular importance was a wedding of psychoanalytic theory and empirical psychology. Thomas French at Chicago and John Dollard and Neal Miller at Yale made important translations of portions of the theory into behavioristic terms. It seemed to many psychologists and psychiatrists in those days that the joint interest of learning theory and psychoanalysis in the effects of early experience would provide the means of bringing the two together in a single comprehensive theory. Simultaneously, however, other voices were beginning to be heard.

Helpers other than psychoanalysts were giving help to the needy. These practitioners came from a ''softer,'' nonscientific background. Members of the clergy were providing help for their troubled flocks; social workers were doing case work and counseling with troubled families and individuals. These helpers were soon to be joined by the first influx of clinical psychologists. Trained in the universities, they were grounded in the empirical methods of psychology but, in addition to work in experimental and physiological psychology, they had had courses in clinical and social psychology and the psychology of personality. One of the men who would rank among the most influential of this group was Carl Rogers.

CARL ROGERS AND NONDIRECTIVE THERAPY

Carl Rogers (1902–   ) would add an important chapter to the history of psychotherapy. A product of American academic psychology with its devotion to objective study, he was the first empirical scientist (in 1942) to make the details of a

TABLE 7.1

Main Features of Psychoanalytic, Humanistic-Existential and Behavioral Approaches to Psychotherapy[1]

Issue	Psychoanalysis	Humanistic-Existential Therapy	Behavior Therapy
Basic human nature	Innate, biological, libidinal (id) instincts, primarily sexual and aggressive, press for immediate release, bringing man into conflict with social reality.	Man has free will, choice, and purpose; he has the capacity for self-determination and self-actualization.	Like other animals, man is born with basic needs and the capacity for learning, which develops in terms of the same basic principles in all species.
Normal human development	Growth occurs through resolution of conflicts during successive developmental crises and psychosexual stages. Through identification and internalization, more mature ego controls and super ego character structures emerge.	A unique self-system and self concept develops from birth on. The individual develops his personally characteristic modes of perceiving, feeling, etc.	Adaptive behaviors are learned through reinforcement and imitation.
Nature of psychopathology	Pathology reflects inadequate conflict resolutions and fixations in earlier development, which leave overly strong impulses and/or weak controls. Symptoms are partial adaptations or substitute gratifications, or defensive responses to anxiety.	Incongruence exists between the depreciated self and the potential, desired self. The person is overly dependent on others for gratification and self-esteem. There is a sense of purposelessness and meaninglessness.	Symptomatic behavior derives from faulty learning of maladaptive behaviors. The symptom is the problem, there is no "underlying disease."
Goal of therapy	Through insight, attainment of psychosexual maturity, strengthened ego functions, reduced control by unconscious and repressed impulses.	Fostering self-determination, authenticity, and integration by releasing human potential and expanding awareness.	Relieving symptomatic behavior by extinguishing or replacing maladaptive behaviors through the use of relaxation and other behavioral modalities.
Role of therapist	An investigator, searching out by use of dreams, slips of speech and	An authentic person in true encounter with patient, sharing experi-	A trainer, helping patient unlearn old behaviors and/or learn new

	lapses into long silences and interpreting root conflicts and resistances; detached, neutral, and nondirective, to facilitate transference reactions	ence. Facilitates patient's growth potential. Transference discounted or minimized.	ones. Control of reinforcement is important; interpersonal relation is of minor concern.
Necessary qualifications and skills	Highly trained in theory and supervised practice; much technical and professional knowledge. Must have firm self-knowledge, to avert dangers of countertransference.	Personal genuineness, coupled with empathy for and unconditional positive regard for the client valued over professional training and formal knowledge.	Knowledge of learning principles primary; understanding of personality theory and psychopathology secondary; no concern with self-knowledge. Actual interventions can be done by nonprofessional assistant.
Time orientation	Oriented to discovering and interpreting past conflicts and repressed feelings, to examine them in light of present situation.	Focus on present phenomenal experience; the here-and-now.	Little or no concern with past history or etiology. Present behavior is examined and treated.
Role of unconscious material	Primary in classical psychoanalysis, less emphasized by neo-Freudians and ego psychologists. To all, of great conceptual importance.	Though recognized by some, emphasis is on conscious experience.	No concern with unconscious processes or, indeed, with subjective experience even in conscious realm. Subjective experience shunned as unscientific.
Psychological realm emphasized	Innate as well as learned motives and feelings, fantasies and cognitions; minimum concern with motor behavior and action outside of therapy.	Perceptions, meanings, values. For some, sensory and motor processes.	Behavior and observable feelings and actions. Emphasis on extra-therapeutic behavior in the every-day world.
Role of insight	Central, though conceived not just as intellectual understanding but as it emerges in "corrective emotional experiences."	More emphasis on awareness, the "how" and "what" questions rather than the "why."	Irrelevant and/or unnecessary

[1] Adapted from Korchin (1976, pp. 375–376).

therapeutic interaction available for study by others. Freud was the first to publish examples of these clinical interactions but when he wrote in 1890, sound recording instruments had not yet been invented, let alone used in psychotherapy. As a result Freud's descriptions rarely contain any of the actual free associations of his patients. Rather, Freud summarized and editorialized such verbalizations in his accounts in order to make a particular clinical or theoretical point. It reamined for Rogers (1942) to publish a verbatim transcript of a complete psychotherapy, the psychotherapy of "Herbert Bryan."

The therapy Rogers used was his own brand, his newly introduced **nondirective psychotherapy.** It comprised only eight interviews. The interested reader will find in Rogers' book a detailed discussion of how to actually carry out nondirective psychotherapy. The description will not be summarized here, however, because within one decade, Rogers would disavow the method as too sterile and subject to too much abuse.

This first example of a scientist-professional submitting his own helping technique and the responses of his client, in print, to verification or refutation by others would be followed by the eclipsing of Freud and psychoanalysis as the most powerful force in modern psychotherapy. For this reason if no other, it came as a surprise to many who followed Rogers' writings when in the middle 1960s, following the publication of a coauthored book on research on psychotherapy with schizophrenic and other severely disturbed patients, Rogers turned away from the original version that he had sparked, and upon which he had embarked in 1942, for the more personal, existential perspective. This new perspective of Rogers was one based on premises dramatically different from the empirical-scientific perspective of Freud, most of today's psychology, psychiatry, and medicine, and even Rogers himself during his first three decades as a psychotherapist.

A Return to Earlier Existential Leanings

Interestingly, 2 decades of empirical research, from about 1945 to 1965, played a major role in Rogers' switch from *empiricism* to *existentialism* as his guiding philosophy. Conducting highly creative empirical research with several successive groups of younger co-workers on psychotherapy sessions revealed to Rogers the operation of powerful human forces in therapy. These forces were quite different from the therapeutic forces of *resistance, insight, emotional abreaction, transference,* and the like which Freud described. Rogers' wellsprings of positive change grew out of forces unleashed within the sufferer when a sustained facilitative climate for personal exploration and change was created by the helper. It would take Rogers some 15 years to complete his own understanding of this climate and the personal power or vitalism which it would help release.

In the years prior to writing his 1942 book on nondirective counseling, with its emphasis on such therapeutic techniques as *accepting* the client and *reflecting back* his or her feelings, Rogers had been a student at Union Theological Seminary in New York City and next a budding future psychologist at Teachers College of Columbia University. He acknowledges that during his formative years he was influenced by the writings of such humanist-oriented nonpsychologists as Frederick Allen, Otto Rank, and a social worker-psychologist, Jesse Taft. It thus is not surprising that Rogers' 1942 psychotherapy would be flavored more by these "softer" sides of the human enterprise than by academic psychology, or that the role assigned the therapist was that of being nondirective and a good listener.

Despite the success of the 1942 book and the legions of beginning psychotherapists it helped educate, Rogers found himself increasingly dissatisfied with the directions his nondirective psychotherapy was taking. Specifically he was displeased with the mechanical, often phoney-sounding attempts of many young psychotherapists to mimick his compassionate nondirective style of reflecting back to the client what the latter was saying, expressing, or groping with. They seemed to forget entirely that the purpose of this tactic was merely to create the conditions to help the client discover his or her own true personal self. To combat this unfortunate development Rogers (1951) published another book, *Client-Centered Therapy: Its Current Practice,* the title of which was intended to underscore the point that the essence of psychotherapy was not the therapist's technique but a client-centered process and that only through self-exploration could a troubled client discover and harness his or her potentialities. Those who overemphasized his nondirective method had missed the whole point, that it was merely a facilitative technique to encourage the client to do the real work of self-exploration, to discover his or her untapped psychological healing forces and to accomplish *self-actualization.*

In the following years, Rogers and his colleagues continued their research, seeking to identify the critical effective ingredients (summarized in Table 7.1) which a humanistic psychotherapist brings to or creates in the psychotherapy. In 1957 Rogers suggested that there were three of these essential ingredients. *First,* the therapist communicates a *genuineness* in his or her person as helper; communicates that he or she is an authentic, real, living, behaving person in contrast to one who merely is manifesting a phoney professional facade. *Second,* the therapist shows acceptance and *unconditional positive regard* and caring for the client and his or her human potential no matter how ill-developed, unattractive, inept, inarticulate, defensive, disturbed, or immature that person currently is. *Finally,* in the moment-to-moment conduct of psychotherapy, the therapist so sensitively understands the client's underlying feelings and the fumbling quality of the client's search for a personal inner self that this understanding is sensed, and experienced by the client as an accurate, *empathic understanding.* That is, through creating these three facilitative conditions the psychotherapist gives signals that he or she as helper is "being with," and is totally understanding of what the sufferer is experiencing, feeling, and trying to bring forth, reconcile, and understand. Rogers repeatedly wrote that for a client to be understood in this deep, thoroughgoing, and accepting sense by a genuine person who communicates prizing and caring, is a very profound experience which helps unleash in the client deeply rooted powers, inherent in all of us, for self-actualization and further growth as a unique human being.

In Rogers' account of the essential ingredients of psychotherapy, a recurrent theme is that these conditions create an equality between client and therapist. This is a major difference between Rogers' view and Freud's concept of deliberately encouraging a transference which would foster an infantile dependency in the patient. For Rogers, Freudian psychoanalysis was carried out between two very unequal humans; doctor and patient, superior and subordinate, with the former directing the process of reconstructing an ill-formed person with base, libidinal drives, insisting that the patient proceed through therapist-preconceived stages of psychosocial development required for maturity. By contrast, Rogers sees the helper and sufferer working together in a relationship between equals, with the sufferer determining his or her own goals as he or she works toward becoming a more fully functioning, self-actualized person.

On this last point Rogers parted company, not only with Freud but also with all but a few of the other psychotherapists who had been trained in psychology, medicine, and other disciplines between 1920 and 1960. By this time in his own career, Rogers had decided that the empirical behavioristic psychology, so widely accepted by his contemporaries, was poorly suited to his purposes. As Rogers saw it, the basic fault lay in the orientation toward technology that was inherent in the approach, something that had come about through the adoption of a philosophy of science that was not appropriate to handle the human drama he witnessed as a practicing therapist.

Psychology's acceptance of what Rogers now saw as the wrong set of orienting commitments is not difficult to understand. By 1960 the scientific method as it was used in physics, chemistry, mathematics, and the space sciences had achieved unimagined heights in technology. The ambition of Freud and almost all twentieth-century psychotherapists had been to emulate these accomplishments. To this end, they had accepted an inappropriate methodology, or so at least it seemed to Rogers. Reflecting on this overemphasis on and awe of technology, Rogers concluded that he and other psychotherapy practitioners and researchers had followed the wrong god, had espoused the wrong philosophy of science. And, in a series of steps, beginning in 1960, Rogers turned away from empirical science and returned to the philosophic-religio-humanistic view of man first clearly articulated in ancient Greece. When the present writer asked Rogers to comment on the above description of his attitudes toward science he wrote back,

> I have given up doing empirical research myself, and have doubts about its value in such a subtle field. I believe a phenomenological type of research holds more

promise—and some of our most useful research was phenomenological in nature. My three years of consulting experience at California Institute of Technology, where I became well acquainted with theoretical physicists of Nobel prize calibre, made me realize how narrow is the vision of most of us psychological scientists. These men were far-out dreamers, not simply experts in tools like statistics. (Rogers, personal communication, August 4, 1977)

Self: Experiencing and "Being With" One's Uniqueness

In common with writers of ancient Far Eastern philosophy, and Aristotle, who believed that the soul (psyche) has "powers of self-nourishment, self growth" and that "plants share with animals and men the nutritive soul—the capacity for self-nourishment and internal growth," Rogers took the position that man has an inherent tendency to develop all his capacities in ways that serve to maintain or enhance the organism. That is, a reliable and persistent tendency in all animate beings, when free to operate, moves the individual toward what can be called growth, maturity, and life enrichment. Rogers used the human infant in a normal environment as a simple example to clarify his meaning. The maturing infant first learns to walk. In spite of bumps, failure, and frustrations, it moves toward a more enhancing, enriching mode of locomotion which better serves the developing self. So too in psychological growth and self-actualization: As human beings develop, interpersonal and environmental circumstances can impede them from moving in actualizing directions. Environmental elements can slow or stop the inherent actualizing tendency so that it manifests itself in inept, immature, and even in self- or socially destructive ways. This comes about in part because the individual has too little understanding of his or her unique and personal self.

As the infant slowly develops a concept of physical self as differentiated from surrounding objects and persons and things, it develops a partial psychological concept of self, of "me as a person." This latter concept is available to awareness beginning early in life but it is not necessarily in awareness. It can be called up at will, as a constant referent of "I" or "me," and helps guide the individual's feelings, thoughts, and behavior. In ordinary experience, however, people have little practice at communicating with this inner self. A major accomplishment of successful Rogerian psychotherapy is helping the individual to make this contact.

Rogers' Role in the Human Potential Movement

The human potential movement occurred during the period of alienation and disillusionment which swept much of the civilized countries of the world between the end of World War II in 1945 and the present time. One of the most highly visible aspects of this movement was the emergence of **encounter groups** as ways of helping people deal with the distresses that are so common in the modern world. Some of these groups were sponsored by the psychotherapeutic establishment, but many of them arose in other contexts. Executives began to take 2-week courses in encounter groups designed to help them recognize their impact on other human beings and from such recognition become more effective in their day-to-day interpersonal interactions. College students and their professors formed comparable groups on many campuses for the purposes of similar **sensitivity training.** Adult self-help groups formed in some churches. Soon suites in large city hotels were being used for weekend encounter groups set up for people with a variety of objectives.

Rogers left academia at age 61 when he resigned from the University of Wisconsin in 1963 and moved to the Western Behavioral Sciences Institute in La Jolla, California. This was a year when the United States was in the earliest stages of its involvement in what would be a very unpopular war. The country's college youth and shortly individuals of all ages began to participate in disruptive activities of passive and then not so passive resistance that challenged the very fabric of the country's social, cultural, economic, and governmental structures. It is interesting to compare Rogers' reaction with that of Freud's in a comparable period of social upheaval. After World War I, when in semi-retirement, then in his sixties, Freud was deeply moved by the carnage the world has just lived through. He developed the theory that man must have a basic instinct for self-destruction which he called *Thanatos*. Also in his sixties in 1963, Rogers, finding that he could not commit his time on a regular basis to individuals, used the energies he previously had employed in individual psychotherapy for the direction and guidance of encounter groups made up of the alienated young, disillusioned adults, and groups of the hard drug users. Rogers was called upon to use his encounter methods in ugly biracial and intercultural confrontations. He attempted his approach with segments of the leadership of the parties at war in Northern Ireland's militant Catholics, militant Protestants and the English caught between. He helped organize the first of what would be human *potential-enhancing group experiences* for some 900 leaders in academic medicine. Each year these people came in small groups to La Jolla for experiences designed to help them contribute to humanizing the practice of medicine.

Since 1960, Rogers has written books designed to foster growth-enhancing educational climates (*Freedom to Learn*), marriages (*Becoming Partners*), personal growth (*On Becoming a Person*, and also *Carl Rogers on Encounter Groups*) and the personal power inside each of us (*Carl Rogers On Personal Power: Inner Strength and Its Revolutionary Impact*). The latter (Rogers, 1977) was published during his 75th year and includes a collection of papers he published during the 1960s and early 1970s. It also contains some recently written and still unpublished essays in which he continues to describe, through the present, his own continuing personality change. Each of these recent books and essays represents a progressive refinement of the single theme stated above: that every organism, including human, has a natural tendency toward growth, self-actualization, and a striving toward reaching one's full potential.

Other Existential and Humanistic Therapists

The views of Rogers and of Freud, described so far in this chapter, leave no doubt that opinions of what psychotherapy is or should be are colored by the personal, professional, and cultural experiences of the theorist-practitioner. Therefore, because people differ, there are many versions of humanistic, existential therapy that exist today. The interested reader will find summaries of the views of these existentialist writers in most textbooks on psychotherapy, personality theory, and clinical psychology. Notable among these recent leaders are the Americans Abraham Maslow, Rollo May, Sidney Jourard, and Fritz Perls. Equally well-known leaders in European and Middle Eastern psychotherapy are or were Kierkegaard in Denmark, Sartre in France, Heidegger and Jaspers in Germany, Buber in Israel, Frankl in Austria, and Jung, Binswanger, and Boss in Switzerland.

It is important for the student of psychotherapy to understand that Rogers and the other modern existentialists write little about the actual technique of existential psychotherapy. Their main emphasis is on the idea that existential analysis is an alternative view of understanding human existence, one that is a backlash against the overemphasis on technique, technology, and the conversion of twentieth-century man into a robot. In common with Rogers they feel that modern society has a tendency to view the human being as an object to be calculated, managed and, following Freud, even "analyzed." These modern existentialists charge that Freud and others, especially the behavior therapists whom we shall introduce next, believe that self-understanding follows from use of the appropriate therapeutic technique. They believe just the opposite; namely, that technique should follow understanding. The primary task of the therapist is first to seek to understand, to "be with" or "get with" the client in that client's private, personal world. If that can happen, technique and method will take care of themselves.

BEHAVIOR THERAPY

The views of the existentialists are diametrically opposed to those of a new breed of scientifically oriented psychotherapists, the behavior therapists. **Behavior therapy** has its roots in the scientific tradition of Hippocrates and later Freud, but it developed during the same period as humanistic therapy. The most immediate antecedents of behavior therapy are a series of the breakthroughs in empirical knowledge in the tradition of Pavlov, Bekhterev, Guthrie, Hull, Jacobson, Skinner, Mowrer, and Miller. Before we consider these modern contributions a look at some of the early precursors of behavior therapy is in order.

Historical Anticipations

One of the great philosophers of the Middle Ages was the Jewish philosopher-physician Moses Maimonides (1135–1204) whose writings reveal a beginning insight into the role of the passions in the diseases of the body and the psyche. At a time when theology and superstitition ruled men's minds, Maimonides was advocating the use of a type of therapy for patients suffering from moral vice as well as psychic distress that is remarkably similar to that found in today's textbooks on behavior therapy and behavior modification. Ehrenwald (1976) provides these surprisingly modern-sounding examples taken from the writing of Maimonides.

> Let us take, for example, the case of a man in whose soul there has developed a disposition [of great avarice] on account of which he deprives himself [of every comfort of life], and which, by the way, is one of the most detestable of defects, and an immoral act as we have shown in this chapter. If we wish to cure this sick man, we must not command him merely [to practice] deeds of generosity, for that would be as ineffective as a physician trying to cure a patient consumed by a burning fever by administering mild medicines, which treatment would be inefficacious. We must, however, induce him to squander so often, and to repeat his acts of profusion so continuously until that propensity which was the cause of his avarice has totally disappeared. Then, when he reaches that point where he is about to become a squanderer, we must teach him to moderate his profusion, and tell him to continue with deeds of generosity, and to watch out with due care lest he relapse either into lavishness or niggardliness.
>
> If, on the other hand, a man is a squanderer, he must be directed to practice strict economy and to repeat acts of niggardliness. It is not necessary, however, for him to perform acts of avarice as many times as the mean man should those of profusion. This subtle point, which is a canon and secret of the science of medicine, tells us that it is easier for a man of profuse habits to moderate them to generosity, than it is for a miser to become generous. Likewise, it is easier for one who is apathetic (and eschews sin) to be excited to moderate enjoyment, than it is for one burning with passion, to curb his desires. Consequently, the licentious man must be made to practice restraint more than the apathetic man should be induced to indulge his passions; and similarly, the coward requires exposure to danger more frequently than the reckless man should be forced to cowardice. The mean man needs to practice lavishness to a greater degree than should be required of the lavish to practice meanness. This is a fundamental principle of the science of curing moral ills, and is worthy of remembrance. (pp. 190–191)

Advice and prescription such as the above was not new with Maimonides; similar forms of behavior therapy are found in the writings of the ancient Babylonians, Greeks, and Romans, and also the philosophers of the Far Eastern Worlds. Writing 400 years ago, Shakespeare knew about the effectiveness of behavior modification principles when he had Hamlet chastise his mother for her adultery by urging her to mend her ways as follows:

> Assume the virtue even if you
>   have it not
> For use almost can change the
>   stamp of Nature
> Or overcome the Devil or
> Throw him out
> With wondrous potency

Act III, Scene 4, 168.

One of the most successful modern treatments of alcoholism by the methods of conditioned aversion leads to another point of historical perspective. This form of therapy takes place in a treatment room resembling a cocktail lounge, complete with bar and expected accouterments. It consists of using as an unconditioned stimulus a powerful emetic (a drug that induces vomiting) which is injected by a nurse or physician while the patient is seated on a stool in the "bar." The patient receives a favorite drink which remains on the bar while he or she drinks several glasses of warm water. The therapist studies the patient's neck and mouth muscles, breathing, and flushing of the face for signs of imminent wretching. Seconds before this occurs, the patient is asked to take a big gulp of the favorite alcoholic drink. If the therapist's timing is correct, a bout of wretching into a large basin attached to the stool immediately follows the ingestion of the alcoholic drink. The patient is then offered another drink, and then another, and finally returned to bed where more wretching will follow. A day of rest in bed is allowed the next day. In five such sessions, repeated every other day, the patient is offered a full range of other beverages—wines, beer, liqueurs—as well as the first requested favorite drink. By the third treatment, patients are nauseous at the sight or smell of the alcohol in any form, and thus are showing a beginning conditioned response. By the fifth treatment, usually given on the tenth to fourteenth day after hospital admission, most patients show successful conditioning and return home, usually committed to a life of sobriety. Research shows that some 60% still have not taken their first drink 12 months later. These patients do, however, return to the hospital for "booster" reconditioning sessions over the next 12 months, and as often as they feel they need to from that point on. In conditioning terms, the obvious *conditioned stimulus* in this treatment is the sight, smell, and taste of alcohol, although the room set up as a bar may also serve a similar function. The *unconditioned stimulus* is the nausea-producing emetic. The *conditioned* and *unconditioned responses* both are wretching.

An interesting historical fact is that a description of this form of conditioning therapy for an alcoholic person was provided by Benjamin Rush 2 centuries ago. Rush was an early American physician, signer of this country's Declaration of Independence, and a pioneer of what a century later would become the field of psychiatry. His paper, published in 1785 and reprinted in the 1943 *Quarterly Journal of Studies on Alcohol* contains this as one of the prescriptions for treating the alcoholic person during the era of George Washington and our revolutionary forebearers:

> I once tempted a . . . man, who was habitually fond of ardent spirits, to drink some rum [which I placed in his way] and in which I had put a few grains of tartar emetic. The tartar sickened and puked him to such a degree, that he supposed himself to be poisoned. I was much gratified by observing he could not bear the sight nor smell of spirits for two years afterwards . . .
>
> This appeal to that operation of the human mind, which obliges it to associate ideas, accidentally or otherwise combined, for the cure of vice, is very ancient. It was resorted to by Moses, when he compelled the children of Israel, to drink the solution of the golden calf [which they had idolized] in water. This solution, if made as it probably was, by means of what is called hepar sulphuris, was extremely bitter, and nauseous, and could never be recollected afterwards, without bringing into equal detestation, the sin which subjected them to the necessity of drinking it. Our knowledge of this principle of association upon the minds and conduct of men, should lead us to destroy, by means of other impressions, the influence of all those circumstances, with which the recollection and desire of spirits are combined. (pp. 339–340)

Almost 2 hundred years later, Wolpe, one of the modern leaders in behavior therapy, would develop a form of therapy which utilized what Wolpe calls the principle of **reciprocal inhibition, or counterconditioning.** In this process a strong, pleasurable or positive response, which is incompatible with the patient's neurotic (usually **phobic**) response, is conditioned to the same stimulus which habitually elicits this negative response, thereby weakening and extinguishing the latter. Benjamin Rush also proposed such a procedure utilizing reciprocal inhibition in the treatment of alcoholism in the following passage:

> The love of ardent spirits has sometimes been subdued, by exciting a counter passion in the mind. A citizen of Philadelphia, had made many unsuccessful attempts to cure his wife of drunkenness. At length, despairing of her reformation, he purchased a [barrel] of rum, and after tapping it, left the key in the door of the room in which it was placed, as if he had forgotten it. His design was to give his wife an opportunity of drinking herself to death. She suspected this to be his motive, in what he had done, and suddenly left off drinking. Resentment here became the antidote to intemperance. (p. 340)

There are numerous additional examples from ancient and more modern times which could be provided. Suffice it to state that despite all the excited pronouncements that psychology has embarked on a new behavioral age of psychotherapy coming from the converts to the practice of behavior therapy, its roots are clearly obvious in the quotations from Maimonides almost a 1000 years ago and the procedures are explicit in the writings of Rush 2 centuries ago.

Modern Behavior Therapy

The beginning reader of the literature in this area should be forewarned that, just as there currently are dozens of existential psychotherapies, there is a similar profusion of varieties of behavior therapy. These therapies go by such names as *behavior therapy, conditioning therapy, behavior modification, modeling,* and *biofeedback.* Specific forms of therapy within one or another of these broad categories are *counterconditioning, systematic desensitization, flooding, aversive conditioning, assertive training, sexual dysfunction therapy, token economy therapy* (for whole wards of patients), *relaxation training,* and many others. Their main features are summarized in Table 7.1.

These modern behavior therapies each have their roots in current scientific developments, just as earlier therapies in the same tradition did. Freud, for example, developed his brand of psychotherapy out of that era's great advances in neurology, especially the discovery of the role of co-existing mental states in psychopathology and their neuromuscular manifestations. Modern behavior therapy was spawned by the great discoveries in learning and conditioning which occurred during the twentieth century. The behavior therapists' guiding theme is that neuroses and other behavioral dysfunctions are maladaptive habits that have been unintentionally learned; their correction, therefore, will also be a matter of relearning.

Systematic Desensitization.   As has been mentioned elsewhere in this book (Ch. 1, vol. 1), Watson and Rayner conditioned a fear of a white rate in an 11-month old child, Albert, by sounding a loud, frightening noise behind him each time the previously unfeared rat appeared. The learned fear then generalized to other small animals and even to other inanimate furry objects. Watson and Rayner suggested that it might be possible to remove (extinguish) such a fear by similar conditioning techniques and, in fact, in 1924 Mary Cover Jones did just this in a 3-year old boy, Peter. She succeeded by pairing the pleasant experience of eating with presentations of a rabbit toward which he had previously shown fear. This was accomplished in a series of sessions during which the rabbit was brought gradually nearer to the child.

Wolpe utilized this method as the basis of a whole new approach to therapy some 35 years later. The chief difference was that deconditioning was more often accomplished in the presence of imagined fearful objects than it was in an actual fearful setting. Treatment of a fear of riding in an elevator or an enclosed car will serve as an example. Starting first with pleasant or at least innocuous imaginary scenes, and teaching the patient how to produce in its presence a pleasant state of relaxation (through the use of Jacobson's autosuggestion method) the behavior therapist takes the patient through a carefully constructed individualized graded **hierarchy** of increasingly unpleasant imagined scenes. For example, a man afraid of riding in an elevator might first imagine writing the word elevator, next looking at a picture of one, then standing in front of one, walking in and quickly out of an elevator, riding up one floor, and so on. By stopping at each scene and practicing relaxation as a pleasant state that is incompatible with the anxiety, the patient during a behavior therapy session soon is able to talk about and otherwise confront in imagery situations which heretofore were severely anxiety-producing and disabling. Jacobson's method of **progressive relaxation** which is used whenever tension occurs in the treatment room (or later in the real world) involves tensing and relaxing particular muscle groups on the suggestion of the therapist. With practice the patient learns to distinguish the sensations of tension and relaxation and soon can produce relaxation at will. In time, although again in slow steps, the patient finally goes out into the world and practices relaxation there. In the process the patient learns to deal with the elevator, closed car, presence of a snake, feared parent or employer, or other fear-producing situation which brought the need for therapy.

Operant Methods.   Even as Wolpe was conceiving his new therapeutic approach, a student of Skinner at Harvard, Ogden Lindsley, forsook the pigeons and white rats of the experimental laboratory and set up shop in the nearby Metropolitan State Hospital just outside of Boston. In this clinical setting Lindsley treated regressed patients on the back wards with a modified Skinnerian **operant conditioning** technique which involved delivery of a reward such as food whenever the patient produced nonpsychotic behavior and withheld reward whenever psychotic behavior occurred.

The success achieved by Lindsley was so great that soon whole wards of state hospitals across the country were being turned into behavioral treatment laboratories, with Ayllon and Azrin and many others pioneering a whole new psychotherapeutic technology during the 1950s and 1960s. Nurses and psychiatric technicians were trained to give tokens for any sign of normal behavior to very sick patients. In turn these tokens could be exchanged by such patients for entrance to the cafeteria, better sleeping quarters, hospital beauty salon, etc. Along with the introduction of the powerful newly perfected tranquilizing drugs and the new concept of removing the locks on the state hospital doors to provide free access to the hospital grounds, this new behavioral technology would help to cut the populations of this country's hospitals by 67% in the next 25 years (1955–1980).

Their population had risen over the years from the first patient admitted by Benjamin Rush to a Connecticut state hospital in 1772 to a national census of almost 600,000 patients in 1955. Today there are only 200,000 patients receiving treatment in this country's network of state hospitals.

Modeling Therapy. Wolpe's systematic desensitization procedure was inspired by the work of Hull; the operant methods just described were direct applications of Skinnerian procedures. Both Hull and Skinner were stimulus-response theorists. They believed that learning occurred as a result of doing and specifically rejected the idea of learning through observation. Other learning theorists, of whom Tolman was the most important, accepted the concept of observational learning. This conception also found expression in the work of another group of behavior therapists.

One of these therapists, Albert Bandura, took the position based on **observational learning** that most human behavior, including neurotic and normal behavior, is learned by **identification** with and **modeling** of significant others. This led him to a prescription for the treatment of behavior dysfunction based on the premise that guided participation of watching a therapist serving as a model will lead to imitation and the learning of such skills by the patient. Bandura correctly reminded psychology that the fears of learning to drive an automobile and to speak in public are neither acquired nor extinguished by reading a book written by existentialists. Nor are they quickly left behind on the psychoanalyst's couch. Yet, these same two fears are easily overcome by most individuals through observing and emulating a confident driver-teacher or an inspiring high-school or college teacher of rhetoric. Millions of Americans have learned, for example, to overcome the fear of public speaking from the rapid learning and emulation that takes place at Toastmasters Clubs throughout our land.

Sexual Disorders. In the area of sexual disorders, the behavior therapies have offered a new and seemingly very effective treatment. Frigid and impotent patients and those suffering the anguish associated with premature ejaculation were believed by Freud to be suffering from neurasthenia and hysteria, and were treated by him and his followers by the laborious process of free association and its hoped for resulting personality reconstruction; all with little apparent success. Masters and Johnson, a physician-psychologist, husband-wife team, revolutionized the treatment of such sexual dysfunctions beginning around 1960. Their approach was strictly a behavioral one; namely rewarded, guided practice of small steps with a spouse who has been instructed and thus made a surrogate-therapist. The successes achieved by these two behavior therapists led to a substantial increase in the number of sexual therapists operating in private practice, and in medical school and university outpatient clinics. In a few years behavior therapists were using behavioral methods to treat people diagnosed as inorgasmics, homosexuals, pedophilacs, and transvestites, as well as individuals totally lacking in sexual desire. Success in some of these areas today is reported to be substantial.

Biofeedback and Behavioral Medicine as NeoBehavior Therapies

Mowrer had discovered some 40 years ago that a bedwetting child could be successfully treated if a buzzer went off to wake the child as soon as the first drops of urine made contact with a normal appearing but specially rigged bedsheet. After a few nights of such conditioning, the child would awaken and go to the bathroom before releasing the urine. Following this behavioral treatment of what had hitherto been seen as a medical problem, other psychologists, psychiatrists, and physicians began to report comparable successes with the treatment of a number of such problems. By the 1960s the list had come to include uncontrollable vomiting, facial tics, anorexia nervosa (a condition in which young women, in the main, stop eating until they drop to 50 or 60 pounds in weight and die), and related medical, neurological, and psychiatric disorders.

In 1969 Neal Miller, in an article in *Science,* summarized a series of studies in which, by the use of Skinnerian reinforcement strategies, he and his associates had trained animals to bring a number of internal bodily functions seemingly under self-control. The bodily functions thus trained included blood pressure, urine formation, heart rate, body temperature, and bowel distensions. Together with other demonstrations of a similar kind, often with human subjects, this work led to a new form of therapy called **biofeedback.** Using sophisticated equipment for monitoring and displaying to the patient the moment to moment fluctuations in blood pressure, skin temperature, heart rate, muscle tension, blood volume, or brain waves, a host of investigations began to report the success in treatment by biofeedback and other self-conditioning methods of headache, muscle tension, high blood pressure, nervousness, Raynaud's disease (in which one's finger tips and toes become so cold that they lose all blood circulation and bring on excruciating pain), tics, bedwetting, and a host of comparable disorders. A new subspecialty in medical psychology and medicine was being born. The name given to it was **behavioral medicine.** As this field has developed its scope has expanded. It now includes the helping of patients who want to quit smoking, give up drugs, lose weight, take their insulin or follow the prescribed treatments for other conditions where therapy fails for lack of compliance to a regimen that is known to be effective. It also includes individuals who are healthy and want to remain so by jogging, eating low cholesterol and other more healthful foods, abstain from alcohol, and so on. A brief historical review of the developments in medicine and in psychology which led to the emergence of *behavioral medicine* and *behavioral health* as viable, interdisciplinary specialties is available elsewhere (Matarazzo, 1980, 1982).

CONCLUSION

Despite a dearth of textbooks on how it is practiced, and whether the experience be with a modern fee-for-service Freudian, existential, or behavior therapist, or with the earlier shaman, priest, naturopathic physician or philosopher-teacher-helper, men and women from the dawn of time have reported feeling better after talking with a caring, trusted other person. It is the sufferer's faith in and expectancy of help from such a ritual that for countless millions has provided relief from anxiety, despair, alienation and a wide variety of lesser or greater problems and miseries. Discussion of a serious personal problem with a friend, shaman, priest, teacher, psychotherapist, or family member, or a headache or other disturbing symptom with a physician or psychologist, often is all that is necessary for relief. In all of these interactions, the same elements—sufferer, helper, and ritual—have been the core ingredients of psychotherapy from its first appearance at the time of primitive man to its modern forms and practices.

One of Freud's contributions to this history was his passionate commitment to putting the practice of psychotherapy on a scientific foundation. With matching affect, Rogers has argued that the philosophy of modern science is unsuited to the understanding of either the forces for wellness residing within a person or how these forces are released in the presence of a caring, prizing psycho-therapist. The modern behavior therapists, although aligning themselves with Freud in a belief in the utility of modern science, are *personae non gratae* in both these camps. They are accused of being mere symptom-removing technicians by both the Freudian and the Existentialist therapists.

It would be as foolish to attempt to compare the relative merits of these three forms of psychotherapy as it would be to attempt to compare the differential values of the diets of persons living in India, the USSR, and the United States. These national food preferences evolved as workable solutions to unique sets of ecological and cultural conditions. So it was and is with the history of psycho-therapy. In the Victorian atmosphere of nineteenth-century Paris and Vienna, personal psychological stress and its repression demanded by prudish mores frequently led to hysteria and a variety of other disorders related to unconscious anxiety (neurasthenia and obsessive compulsive neurosis). Not surprisingly, the psychotherapy developed by Charcot, Bernheim, Janet, Breuer, and Freud was specifically suited to both the symptoms of these disorders and to the basic defects in the sufferer's early life history associated with their etiology. Thou-sands upon thousands of such sufferers, in Europe, England and the United States' who were treated by psychoanalysts between 1895–1950, reported relief from the misery associated with psychoneurological or psychological afflictions.

But the America of 1930–1965 which spawned Carl Rogers and the other existentialists was different from Freud's Vienna. The patients and clients who sought help from Rogers in his University of Chicago counseling center offices and at La Jolla, and the legion of psychotherapists he helped to train to treat them, were not suffering from hysterical blindness, impotence, and so on. Rather, they were college educated young and middle aged adults who in the 1940s and 1950s were trying to find out who they were, where they had been, and where they each might better go in search of self-actualization. In the 1960s and 1970s they were individuals who did not like America's involvement in an unpopular war, or who felt shy, inhibited and alienated in college or in the work force, each of which seemed to them to be a highly impersonal, mechanical unit of society. Two to five years (with as many as 400–600 visits) on a Freudian psychoanalyst's couch simply was not the appropriate help for such individuals, and Rogers, sensing this, developed a psychotherapy and encounter group discussion approach that was considerably shorter (averaging closer to 20–30 visits). It was aimed more at releasing the individual's own unique potential as an adult than at exploring for a year or two or more the individual's childhood relations with mother, father, siblings, and related significant others.

But Rogers' approach did not seem to help legions of other sufferers; those, for example, who were afraid to leave their home or drive an automobile lest they have an anxiety attack so severe they could not catch their breath. For persons with these and related conditions psychoanalytic therapy was appropriate but, as just mentioned, a time-consuming process. At mid-twentieth century Wolpe, building on the knowledge base provided by Pavlov, Hull, Jacobson, and the other behaviorists, showed that a therapy built on the concepts of reciprocal inhibition and counter conditioning could improve such conditions, also in 20–30 visits. Concurrently Masters and Johnson, as well as Bandura and other social psychology-oriented psychotherapists, used learning theory knowledge, often liberalized to include an acceptance of observational learning and modeling, to treat the phobias and sexual dysfunctions. These specific conditions do not respond as effectively to existential psychotherapy.

Other behavior problems are more effectively treated by the methods of behavioral medicine than they are by any of the therapies mentioned so far. Bedwetting, smoking, overeating, cold hands, and other highly specific biomecial dysfunctions are poorly suited to the methods employed by existentialist, psychodynamic, and psychoanalytic practioners or, for that matter, by the methods used by Wolpe and others who have developed behavior therapies similar to his. But techniques of behavioral medicine aimed exclusively at such symptoms have been demonstrated to be very effective.

Additionally, a whole family of more severe psychological dysfunctions (psychoses), once treated by psychotherapy, are now being treated successfully by psychopharmacological therapy. These disorders include not only depression and schizophrenia, in which the treatment of choice usually *is* drugs but, also, existential anxiety and certain more purely psychodynamic conditions, for example, the obsessive compulsive disorders.

What may one reasonably conclude from all of this? Quite simply that psychology and the related behavioral sciences have achieved considerable success during the past 50 years in establishing a knowledge base that ties type of disorder to appropriate treatment. This evolving knowledge base and the millions of hours of clinical experience actually doing psychotherapy accumulated by practitioners during the past century have provided the psychotherapists with the ingredients with which to develop the various forms of psychotherapy described in this chapter. Neither this vast clinical experience, nor the scientific knowledge which serves as its foundation, nor their combination, is sufficient, however, to allow anyone to claim that one form of psychotherapy is superior to the others. Instead, we realize today that we must address a more sophisticated set of questions such as (a) which form of psychotherapy practiced by (b) a helper with which types of personal characteristics is (c) most effective with patients with which type(s) of problem(s)? Reviews of the literature (Bergin & Garfield, 1971; Bergin & Strupp, 1972; Garfield, 1981; Garfield & Bergin, 1978; Kiesler, 1966, 1971; Matarazzo, 1971; 1980) suggest that we are actually beginning to ask these more sophisticated questions and to get some beginning answers. From the activities which are currently underway in the science and practice of the psychotherapies it probably is not too optimistic to predict that by the end of this century many different types of human suffering will be treated successfully as we learn more and more about the nature of the sufferer-helper-ritual interaction.

REFERENCES

Bergin, A. E., & Garfield, S. L. (Eds.). *Handbook of psychotherapy and behavior change: An empirical analysis.* New York: Wiley and Sons, 1971.

Bergin, A. E., & Strupp, H. H. *Changing frontiers in the science of psychotherapy.* Chicago: Aldine, 1972.

Durant, W. *The story of civilization: The life of Greece* (Vol. 2). New York: Simon and Schuster, 1939.

Ehrenwald, J. *The history of psychotherapy: From healing magic to encounter.* New York: Jason Aronson, 1976.

Ellenberger, H. E. *The discovery of the unconscious: The history and evolution of dynamic psychiatry.* New York: Basic Books, 1970.

Frank, J. D. *Persuasion and healing: A comparative study of psychotherapy.* Baltimore: The Johns Hopkins University Press, 1973.

Garfield, S. L. Psychotherapy: A 40-year appraisal. *American Psychologist, 1981, 36,* 174–183.

Garfield, S. L., & Bergin, A. E. (Eds.). *Handbook of psychotherapy and behavior change* (Rev. ed.). New York: Wiley and Sons, 1978.

Jones, E. *The life and work of Sigmund Freud* (3 vols.). New York: Basic Books, 1953.

Kiesler, D. J. Some myths of psychotherapy research and the search for a paradigm. *Psychological Bulletin, 1966, 65,* 110–136.

Kiesler, D. J. Experimental designs in psychotherapy research. In A. E. Bergin & S. L. Garfield (Eds.), *Handbook of psychotherapy and behavior change: An empirical analysis.* New York: Wiley and Sons, 1971, pp. 36–74.

Korchin, S. J. *Modern clinical psychology: Principles of intervention in the clinic and community.* New York: Basic Books, 1976.

Masserman, J. H. Historical-comparative and experimental roots of short-term therapy. In L. R. Wolberg (Ed.), *Short-term psychotherapy.* New York: Grune & Stratton, 1965, pp. 23–50.

Matarazzo, J. D. The practice of psychotherapy is art and not science. In A. R. Mahrer & L. Pearson (Eds.), *Creative developments in psychotherapy.* Cleveland: Case Western Reserve Press, 1971, pp. 364–392.

Matarazzo, J. D. Behavioral health and behavioral medicine: Frontiers for a new health psychology. *American Psychologist,* 1980, *35,* 807–817.

Matarazzo, J. D. Behavioral health's challenge to academic, scientific and professional psychology. *American Psychologist,* 1982, *37,* 1–14.

Rogers, C. R. *Counseling and psychotherapy.* Boston: Houghton Mifflin, 1942.

Rogers, C. R. *Client-centered therapy.* Boston: Houghton Mifflin, 1951.

Rogers, C. R. *Carl Rogers on personal power.* New York: Delacorte Press, 1977.

Rogers, C. R. *A way of being.* Boston: Houghton Mifflin, 1980.

Rush, B. An inquiry into the effects of ardent spirits on the human body and mind. Published circa 1785 and reprinted in *Quarterly Journal of Studies on Alcohol,* 1943, *4,* 321–341.

Schofield, W. *Psychotherapy: The purchase of friendship.* Englewood Cliffs, N.J.: Prentice-Hall, 1964.

Shapiro, A. K. Placebo effects in medicine, psychotherapy, and psychoanalysis. In A. E. Bergin & S. L. Garfield (Eds.), *Handbook of psychotherapy and behavior change: An empirical analysis.* New York: Wiley and Sons, 1971, pp. 439–473.

Zilboorg, G. A history of medical psychology. New York: W. W. Norton & Co., 1941.

8

Psychopathology: I. From Ancient Times to the Eighteenth Century

Winifred B. Maher
Brendan A. Maher
Harvard University

This chapter and the one following present an overview of the salient features of the history of psychopathology—the history of the *suffering* (pathology) of the *mind* (psyche) as reflected in theories about, attitudes toward, and treatment of this condition through the centuries.

The terms used will be both modern (e.g. "psychopathology", "abnormal behavior", "mental illness") and archaic—those contemporary to the period under discussion. As mental illness has so often been associated with shame, contempt, and fear, the earlier terms gradually acquired a pejorative flavor and new ones were substituted which initially were considered to be neutral or more objective and scientific. However, the old terms meant pretty much the same thing as the new terms replacing them. "Mad," for example, was an old English word meaning emotionally deranged and came in turn from an ancient root word meaning crippled, hurt; "insanity" comes from the root word "sanus" or free from hurt or disease, and thus "insane" means hurt or unhealthy; "lunacy" refers to the periodic nature of many psychopathological conditions and perhaps was originally intended to differentiate periodic madnesses from those in which the state was chronic and unremitting; "mania" refers to excess of passion or behavior out of control of the reason. We may note that "neurotic" was originally coined to refer to diseases due to malfunctioning of the nervous system; as some psychopathologies seemed to have no organic basis, the word "psychosis" was introduced to refer to these functional or non-biological disorders of the mind.

THE BASES OF HISTORICAL ANALYSIS

Problems of Interpretation

We shall begin by considering a simple fact. European archaeologists have unearthed Stone Age skulls in which there are holes generally symmetrical in shape. These appear to have been purposively cut and they vary in size, shape, and location from skull to skull. As the edges of the holes in many of the skulls show healing, it appears likely that these were the result of surgery and that many persons survived the procedure. Stone Age man left no record to tell us why this operation was done, hence our explanations are entirely a matter of conjecture. It is instructive to consider some of the conjectures that have been advanced.

Cutting away pieces of bone of the skull is a surgical procedure known as *trepanning* or *trephining*. Two centuries ago the editors of the first edition of the Encyclopaedia Britannica (1768) had this to say: "The operation of the trepan is the making of one or more orifices through the skull, to admit an instrument for raising any pieces of bone that by violence are beaten inwards upon the brain, or to give issue to blood or matter lodged in any part of the cranium" (p. 684, Vol. III). This description was written as part of a discussion of contemporary surgical methods. We might conjecture that a similar, though cruder, approximation of the procedure had been practiced by Stone Age man, and to the same end. Examination of stone axes suggests that one of the first conditions which early man might attempt to treat in his fellows would be traumatic focal damage to the skull. This conjecture is supported by Wilkinson (1975) who says "Many of the prehistoric trephined skulls from Peru and Europe, especially the latter, indicate trauma, usually skull fracture. Not surprisingly, there is a fairly high correlation between frequency of trephination and evidence of weapons of the smashing variety, as opposed to cutting and slashing implements. Trephination in such cases was directly therapeutic—to remove bone splinters and relieve pressure. Similarly, reports of recent primitive skull surgery . . . indicate that skull fracture and headache precipitated by trauma are common events leading to skull surgery" (p. 100).

Amongst psychologists, we find a different hypothesis. In one elementary text-book of abnormal psychology, Page (1971) tells us that trephining might be explained by "the intriguing speculation that Paleolithic man not only accepted the notion of spirit possession [to explain abnormal behavior] but worked out an ingenious cure: chipping a hole in the head of the 'possessed' persons to facilitate the departure of the evil spirits" (p. 75). The speculation mentioned by Page becomes a "fact" when cited by other writers. A subsequent text asserts flatly "Archaeological evidence indicates that Stone Age people had a rather direct way of dealing with spirits through a crude surgical technique called trephining" (CRM Books, 1977, p. 5). Thus, by looking at an antique skull with a hole in it, modern psychologists divine (1) that the owner of the skull with a hole in it, alas poor Yorick, was mad, (2) that his contemporaries believed his madness to be caused by evil spirits lodged in his head, and (3) that the hole had been bored in his skull to cure his madness by releasing the evil spirits.

To complicate matters further, the Danish archaeologist, Rasmussen (1956) remarks that "by most primitive people sickness was considered to be caused by supernatural forces—witchcraft, soul theft or obsession with evil spirits which were treated by magic rites. But conjointly with these there are *rational curing methods* built on the practical experience of countless generations. *Most astonishing of these operations is trephining* which was successfully performed in Europe already in the Stone Age" (pp. 20-21; italics added).

Trephining provides us with an example of the problems and prejudices that plague historical analysis in the field of abnormal behavior. On the one hand we have the undisputed fact that trephining is a crude but reasonable technique for removing bone splinters, blood clots, and the like from an injured skull. We also have some archaeological opinion that it was used in this way as a rational treatment by Stone Age man and was probably independent of his belief, if any, in spirit possession. In addition, Wilkinson, (1975) after examining skulls dating from 500 B.C. in Mexico, speculates that the trephined individuals may have been used as guinea pigs for the experimental development of surgical and drilling techniques and tools. On the other hand we have unsupported speculation that trephination was employed to let evil spirits out of the head—a speculation which has been rapidly elevated to the status of a firm conclusion. With these contradictory explanations in mind, let us consider some basic propositions about the method of historical analysis.[1]

Historical Evidence

The history of abnormal psychology is inferred from a wide but often incomplete assortment of documents. Such sources of information include medical treatises; philosophical, theological, and psychological discussion; legal documents in-

---

[1]At present, mental illness afflicts men and women in roughly equal proportions and across a wide range of ages, from childhood to old age. If we assume that was true of the incidence of mental illness in prehistoric man, and if trephining had been done in order to release demonic spirits believed to be trapped inside the head of the mentally ill, then the trephined skulls should belong to both sexes and all ages. On the other hand, if trephining were done to treat focal head injury received in battle or in accidents, including hunting injuries, the skulls should predominantly be those of males in the prime of life.

Since trephining to release evil spirits would be a ritual operation, we could expect that the particular placement of the hole would be similar in skulls found in a given locale and dated for a given time period. However, if the skull had been trephined to relieve injury, the size and location of the hole would vary with the site of injury and should occur most often on those parts of the skull most vulnerable to damage from blows. The photographs pulbished to support the "spirit" hypothesis seem more consistent with the head injury explanation.

cluding laws pertaining to the management of the mentally ill and records of court cases; autobiographies, biographies, diaries, letters, general histories, drama, and creative literature in which mental disorder is described. There are also many descriptions of feigned madness in these sources. Although the symptoms fabricated by individuals might be discrepant with the informed views of professional observers of actual psychopathology, these enactments do indicate what behaviors were popularly considered to be insane.

For much of the history with which this chapter is concerned there is insufficient documentary evidence to permit us to be confident in the conclusions we draw. It is difficult to verify the facts available and particularly difficult to evaluate their significance. Many significant events simply were not documented in the first place and when they were the documentation was often biased or falsified in order to give a slanted picture of those events. Documentation is often lost or destroyed, accidentally or deliberately (either because of its importance or because of its apparent lack of importance). Thus, even when there are documentations of some event, it is not always clear that these may be taken at face value. Without a complete record it is difficult to know what significance, if any, to assign to isolated data. We err, for example, to assume that any finding is necessarily typical of an age: some items have been kept down through the ages simply because they are atypical. For example, the fact that charlatans throughout history preyed, for profit, on the ignorant, the gullible, and the desperate with bizarre quack methods of treatment for bodily and mental disorders tells us nothing about beliefs and theories and practices amongst the educated, the sensible or wary, and those with alternative therapies available to them. Without a complete record, all we can say about some practices or beliefs is that they existed: not whether they did or did not represent a dominant trend for the period in which they existed.

We can imagine a future historian trying to piece together an understanding of our own time. From journals and text-books he might deduce that people viewed the world in terms of relativity theory; from the daily papers, that this was an age of widespread belief in astrology. From publisher's records he would learn that the best-selling book was the Bible: from church attendance records he would conclude that only a minority of people believed in the religions that were founded on the Bible. He would find records to show that more and more people completed high school and went to college, and simultaneous reports that fewer people knew how to read because so many had been watching television instead. Would this historian decide that this was an age of science, of superstition, of religious faith, or literate culture, or of illiterate spectatorism? He could point to material consistent with any of these conclusions. In this case the very wealth of documents would tell him that ours is an age where contradictions flourish. If, however, the surviving documents were few and scattered he might well be misled into deciding that one of these themes was truly dominant.

Historical reconstruction, even of periods within the last two centuries, is greatly dependent upon partial evidence. The further back we go, the more fragmentary become the data. An instructive exhibit in the British Museum in London shows the reconstruction of a metal helmet found in the sixth century Sutton Hoo burial trove. Only a few shards of metal survived but from these archaeologists built a replica of the helmet as they thought it would have been when new. Some time later it became possible to examine the metal more closely with improved techniques. These revealed hinges previously unsuspected: a new model was built, substantially different from the first but accomodating more closely to the new data. Both models are hypotheses and both are based upon limited material. Only one or the other may be correct. Both may be wrong. So it is with our history—based upon limited materials it too is limited and provisional—and may be wrong.

Historical Analysis

History is hypothesis. Using such materials as are available, the historian constructs a description of events, ideas, and trends that might characterize a particular period of time. Their hypotheses color the way in which historians search for and evaluate further evidence. Before the first hypothesis is even constructed, the historian makes, implicitly or explicitly, certain assumptions. We cannot understand history intelligently unless we examine these assumptions.

A popular view of the history of Western man is that over the centuries there has been a progression, often faltering but nonetheless continuous, from ignorance, superstition, brutality, and a kind of functional stupidity towards knowledge, rationality, humanity, and general intellectual superiority. This view tends to be accompanied by the belief that this progression moves in time through a series of steps or periods in which old practices are replaced by new and better practices, and faulty conceptions replaced by less faulty. This has been particularly true of the popular histories of psychiatry, abnormal psychology, and medicine which, to quote Peter Sedgwick (1982) ". . . treat the social past as a slope tending towards the medical present, which becomes the apex of all previous endeavors; an incomplete and provisional peak, to be sure, but one whose incompleteness does not mar the grand conception of the long ascent itself. This liberal, evolutionist history of psychiatry is distinguished by a special emphasis on the barbarism of past ages . . ." (p. 129).

An alternative view is that mankind has always faced certain kinds of problems and has attempted various solutions to them. Each solution appears satisfactory for a while but is found to bring new problems in train. For example, the problem of exploitation and misery of the indigent madman is solved by providing asylums. Asylums create new problems relating to individual liberty and bureaucracy and these lead to a demand to close the asylums and return the patients to the community. Thus we can look at human affairs as proceeding not linearly but in cycles. Actual improvements may come not so much from more intelligent and humane ways of looking at problems but from the accretion of improved practical technologies and new materials or even from the rediscovery of old techniques long forgotten. Competing and even conflicting conceptions may exist side by side, not only in the same time period but in the same individual.

Many people who subscribe to the belief that history is the course of increasing human intellectual sophistication also cherish the view that this has been accompanied by increasing social concern for the sufferings of others. To begin to doubt this view we need only remember that the massacre of Jews, gypsies, and others during World War II was the work of a scientifically sophisticated nation, that it occurred in the twentieth century, and that it involved numbers of victims far beyond any recorded previous excesses. Human capacity for savagery has not diminished over the centuries and technological developments can serve to make it more "efficient" and terrible.

Putting aside such cataclysms we may observe that care and concern for those who cannot care for themselves is made easier by available economic resources. This truism has two implications. One is that the rich get better medical care than the poor. When we seek to describe the way in which patients were treated at any given time in the past we must recognize that the picture we obtain will depend upon the social class that we study. The second implication is that the industrial and agricultural technologies that produce a higher standard of living for the normal competent invididual also provide the basis for better standards of care for those troubled or incompetent members who turn to the community for help. The fact that the material quality of the care now given to psychiatric patients is generally better than that given 200 or more years ago is a tribute not necessarily to improved social sensitivity to their needs but to availability of greater wealth with which to meet them.

In this chapter the present writers try to approach the history of psychopathology from a position of description and understanding rather than interpretation and judgment. This has involved us in certain assumptions. First we assume that the people of previous centuries were as intelligent, perceptive, and energetic as their present-day descendants. Second, we assume that the application of these qualities was limited then, as it is now, by material resources and available technology. Third, we assume that the value placed upon human life and freedom from suffering was then, as now, relative to conditions of peace and war; plague and famine; life expectancy; racial, class and religious prejudice. We assume that ignorance, superstition and hatreds were neither necessarily worse nor less then than now and must be understood in the context of their own times if we are to make sense out of the facts that are available to us. We ought to regard simplifications and broad generalizations with healthy scepticism. Always we must ask: What is the evidence?

THE PROBLEM OF PSYCHOPATHOLOGY

There seems to be little doubt that man has regarded some kinds of behavior as abnormal, pathological, or mad from the beginning of recorded time. Ulysses, we are told, did not wish to join King Agamemnon in his expedition to Troy. When summoned to fulfill his oath of military service to the king, he pretended to be mad and went ploughing the sea sand with oxen, sowing salt. The king's messenger, suspecting fraud, took Ulysses's baby son and laid him in the furrow where the ploughshare would strike and kill him. Ulysses swerved to avoid the child and thereby was judged to be sane and required to take part in the Trojan war. Feigning madness to avoid army service has a long history!

In Snorri Sturluson's history, *Heimskringla: Sagas of the Norse Kings*, written early in the thirteenth century (Laing, trans. 1961), we can read an account of the madness of King Sigurd:

> Latterly it happened that he could with difficulty govern his own mind and reason . . . It is told that King Sigurd, one holiday in Easter, sat at table with many people . . . and when he came to his high seat, people saw that his countenance was very wild, and as if he had been weeping, so that people were afraid of what might follow. The king rolled his eyes, and looked at those who were seated on the benches . . . Then he seized the holy book which he had brought with him from abroad, and which was written all over with gilded letters: so that never has such a costly book come to Norway. His queen sat by his side. Then said King Sigurd . . . "I had two things which were dear to me above all when I came from abroad, and these were this book and the queen; and now I think the one is only worse and more loathsome than the other, and nothing I have belonging to me that I more detest. The queen does not know herself how hideous she is; for a goat's horn is standing out on her head, and the better I liked her before the worse I like her now; and as to this book, it is good for nothing." Thereupon he cast the book on the fire which was burning on the hall floor, and gave the queen a blow with his fist between the eyes. The queen wept; but more at the king's illness than at the blow, or the affront she had suffered. (p. 305).

A minor house-servant alleviated the king's madness by rescuing the book and expressing the sadness of the company at the king's "melancholy and ill-health."

There is a direct allusion to madness in the Bible, 1 Samuel. David, afraid of being recognized by the king of Gath ". . . changed his behavior before them, and feigned himself mad in their hands, and scrabbled on the doors of the gate, and let his spittle fall down upon his beard" (21:13). David was allowed to depart unmolested because the king decided he was mad and deemed him therefore to be harmless.

Criteria By Which Psychopathology is Defined

To most people these examples probably appear to be intuitively obvious instances of abnormal behavior. However, intuition is not enough to define psychopathology. We must provide systematic criteria by which this judgment is made. When we examine the range of human actions that have over the centuries been defined as psychopathological, certain characteristics emerge.

I. Behavior which is Injurious to Self or Others

A. *Self-Injurious Behavior.* Self-injurious behavior, from suicide and self-mutilation to the destruction of personal property, raises questions as to the psychological state of the individual. Such behavior may include the failure to keep oneself clean and groomed (note the previous example of David allowing his spittle to dribble down his beard), to eat properly when an adequate diet is available, or to take rest when fatigued. We assume that there is a normal human motive to survive and prosper and when somebody behaves in ways that do not correspond to this motive we suspect psychological disorder.

For King Sigurd to assault a loving wife and to destroy a costly book which he heretofore had valued highly was maladaptive, for these acts did not seem to serve the king's self-interest. A man wastes his time to sow salt in the sea sand and Ulysses knew that this maladaptive act would create the suggestion of madness. In the case of Ulysses, however, the agents of the king knew that mad behavior might be feigned in order to avoid military service and they therefore contrived a situation to reveal that Ulysses was, in fact, sane.

In order to determine whether self-injurious behavior is evidence of psychological disturbance we need to know the cultural context in which it occurs. Thus, for a long period of time in Japan, the practice of hara-kiri was considered the only possible way for a dishonored individual to restore personal and family honor; under such circumstances, suicide would not be seen as an insane act. Self-mutilation is taken to be evidence of psychopathology unless it results in some significant gain for the individual. Soldiers have been known to shoot themselves in the foot in order to achieve discharge from the army. In some societies for a beggar with no alternative means for livelihood to mutilate himself to enhance his credibility as a beggar and therefore to increase the likelihood of receiving charity from others would not be regarded as mad. Injuries inflicted on the self as a form of religious penance or purification are not regarded as evidence of mental illness if the practice is accepted in the culture in which it occurs.

B. *Behavior Injurious to Others.* Violent and destructive behavior directed against the life, physical welfare, and property of others is also taken as evidence of insanity when it does not serve the self-interest of the individual perpetrating the act. For a parent to mutilate a child ordinarily would be taken as *prima facie* evidence of insanity—castration of one's own child would be an insane act, but if a parent acquiesced in this mutilation during a particular period in Italian history because the child possessed musical talent and was destined for an operatic role as a castrato, the act would have been regarded as a reasonable one and in the child's best interest. To kill a loved one who, because of illness or injury, is suffering intolerably has been viewed as immoral or as criminal, but not as mad. If a person murders another without motive of gain, vengeance, military defense or aggression, or self defense or defense of a valued other, the murderer might be regarded as insane; however, if the murderer profited through inheritance by the murder, or was satisfying a recognizable motive for revenge or patrotism or defense, the individual would be regarded not as insane but as either criminal or heroic.

II. Poor Reality Contact (Disorders of Thought and Perception)

We often impute psychopathology to those whose perceptions of their environment or whose beliefs and thought processes seem to be seriously at odds with those of other people.

A. Disorders of Thought and Delusions. The expression of beliefs that seem incredible to others is often taken to be a sign of poor reality contact and therefore symptomatic of psychopathology; such include unfounded suspicions of others, lack of judgment or poor judgment of one's capacities, inability to foresee likely outcomes of particular actions so that behavior appears to be inconsistent with intent, and so on. Cervantes' Don Quixote may have become mad because according to his literary creator over-perusal of books on knight errantry overheated his imagination and dried up his brain, but the symptoms of his aberration were the delusional beliefs, engendered by the content of the books, upon which he acted.

Because the judgment that a particular belief is plausible is so heavily dependent upon majority opinion, this often constitutes a shaky basis for establishing psychopathology. There was a prolonged period in Western history when many people believed in the existence of witches capable of controlling the weather, of turning themselves and others into animals, of generating disease in people, domestic animals and crops, and the like. In those days, a person with these beliefs was considered normal. Today, a person expressing such beliefs might be regarded as deluded and in need of treatment. As the Victorian psychiatrist, Bucknill (1854) commented ''. . . a few hundreds or even a few scores of persons entertaining the same belief as that of a deluded patient, his ideas on the subject would have been of infinitely less value as a symptom of insanity'' (pp. 74-77).

B. Hallucinations. Another component of poor reality contact is to be seen in disorders of perception. A person may hallucinate voices in a room in which he or she is alone, may claim that one side of his or her body has shrunk to a much smaller size, may report visions, or describe other perceptions that appear to be directly contrary to or unsupported by the sensory evidence available. Such reported experiences, unshared by others, would be regarded as symptoms of psychological disturbance.

III. Disorders of Affect

Emotional reactions inappropriate in nature or degree to the individual's personal situation are regarded as symptomatic of psychopathology.

Sometimes people express feelings of distress or anxiety that appear disproportionate to any actual problems they face. Individuals themselves may complain that they feel inordinately sad, with no compelling reason, and may seek help to alleviate their distress, or they may believe that their depression is understandable but the reasons they give for their feelings may sound exaggerated or even absurd to others. When this happens, we tend to define their behavior as pathological. Excessive expressions of elation or joy when circumstances do not seem to warrant such pleasure may also indicate pathology. The age of the individual is taken into consideration—children are expected to show greater distress and pleasure over trivial events than are adults. When circumstances would normally engender strong emotional reactions in others, failure to respond appropriately with either distress or pleasure can be pathological.

IV. Erratic Behavior

Even when the actual behavior is considered to be within normal limits, dramatic or unpredictable shifts in attitudes, beliefs, moods, or behaviors may be taken to signify pathology. An ordinarily religious person who suddenly announces complete loss of faith or an individual without prior religious conviction who abruptly becomes fervently devout; a parsimonious individual who suddenly begins to speculate in extravagant money making schemes or gives away large sums of money, or a previously generous person who begins to hoard income; a suspicious person who unaccountably becomes unusually trusting or the trusting soul who begins to harbor dark suspicions of others; a person who is cheerful and optimistic one day, despondent and pessimistic the next without obvious changes in circumstance, and so on, all might suggest psychic abnormality.

Madness tends to be differentiated from temporary states induced by brief intense emotional experiences, crowd contagion, drug or alcohol ingestion, or those states of religious or mystical ecstasy and inspiration alluded to above.

Modern psychopathologists have just begun to establish objective criteria by which the presence and the variety of mental illnesses can be diagnosed. Valid and objective diagnosis that commands agreement between two specialists who can observe the patient at first hand is hard to come by. When the patient is long dead and has left only fragmentary records of his or her behavior, any diagnosis that is offered now must be regarded as fraught with the probability of error. Even more unreliable is a present day judgment that such persons would have been judged mad by their contemporaries, whether specialists or members of the general public.

Bearing the above criteria in mind, we note that definitions of good mental health have always tended to accept the psychological processes of the average person as establishing the standard against which pathology is judged. Most people experience some personal distress from time to time; most people have acted in ways that were maladaptive on occasion; most people have probably experienced unusual beliefs and perceptions. Definitions of psychopathology have always tended to compare behaviors with the norm rather than with an ideal of perfect freedom from any signs of psychological malfunction. As this norm varies from one place to another and from one historical period to another, even from one age group or gender, race or ethnic group or class to another, the specific behavior, including thoughts and emotions expressed by the person, that provokes a diagnosis of psychopathology varies accordingly within rather wide limits. What has been constant throughout history is the application of deviations from contemporary norms of reasonable behavior as the criteria for regarding behaviors as indicative of mental illness. This normative aspect of judgments of psychopathology is treated humorously in Act V, scene 1 of Shakespeare's *Hamlet*:

Hamlet:	"Ay, marry! Why was he sent into England?"
Clown:	"Why, because 'a was mad. 'A shall recover his wits there; or if 'a do not, 'tis no great matter there."
Hamlet:	"Why?"
Clown:	" 'Twill not be seen in him there. There the men are as mad as he."

(which has provoked appreciative laughter in audiences from Shakespeare's time to our own).

If the individual's behavior deviates from the norm in ways which do not compromise that individual's essential welfare or that of the group or society in which he or she lives, the behavior may be regarded as merely eccentric— perhaps even highly desirable, as in the case of divine inspiration occurring in a religious or religio-political setting. If, however, the behavior is such that it interferes markedly with normal social functioning, it might be interpreted as pathological and efforts made to understand, treat, or isolate it. Further, a distinction may not always be made, nor even always possible, between people who create two sorts of social problems, the madman and the social revolutionary. Let us consider the instructive case of one Arise Evans, born in 1607, and described by Hill (1976):

Evans often exhibited deranged behavior, was subject to visions and given to prophesizing, and forced himself and his politically inflammatory ideas on the powerful. To quote Hill: "In the cruel and brutal world of mid-seventeenth century England men were hanged, drawn and quartered for having the wrong ideas. . . But Arise could hang about Charles I's court for days on end, and deliver a message from God to the King that he and his kingdom were to be destroyed'' (p. 75), and it was reported he claimed to be Christ. Nothing much happened—Evans lobbied bishops and learned doctors who ''took refuge in flight and barricaded their doors against him.'' He was, at the instigation of his family, for a short time confined as mad and dangerous, but he was released, married, raised a family and continued his political provocation. He was imprisoned for a time for seditious activities but was released because he was certified mad, and continued his sometimes demented, sometimes inspired political agitation, preaching, prophesizing, writing books, issuing pamphlets, and haranguing people in positions of power. As a madman, Arise was treated with tolerance; as a political agitator, with surprising tolerance. Because he was known to be mad his political harangues were not taken seriously. People, mad or sane, may be neglected, mocked, and rejected when they are judged to be unsightly, unseemly in conduct, embarrassing, annoying or even merely boring or tiresome. When this behavior constitutes a recurring source of nuisance to the community they may be physically abused or confined. When their behavior appears to constitute an actual public threat, either by violence to others or by disruption of the social fabric, then the community response may escalate to include severe physical punishment, perhaps to the point of torture or even execution. From the point of view of the social order the fact that somebody is creating a problem may be more important than diagnosing the cause of the problem; the vigor of the reaction to the problem is more likely to be determined by the perceived magnitude of the threat that it presents than by its origins. The lone revolutionary is less of a problem than the charismatic madman. Whether the individual is punished for treason or treated for sickness may depend upon the impact that he has in society. Hill, for example, concludes that ''Arise Evans had the good fortune to have few followers.'' Had it been otherwise he might have perished on the scaffold. It is better to be thought a madman than a heretic or a traitor.

Theories of Causation of Psychopathology

The general criteria by which psychopathology has been defined down through the ages have perhaps differed less from place to place and time to time than have the various theories of pathogenesis current at different periods of history. But even these share certain aspects. Behind differences in terminology we may discern familiar theories surviving over the centuries, and changing often in detail but not in general conception (e.g., such terms as ''humoral balance'' can be viewed as a crude approximation to ''biochemical balance'').

The conditions, agents, events, etc. which have been suggested throughout history as possible causes of psychopathology can be classed into two major categories: *Biological* and/or *Psychological-Experiential*. These two categories are not mutually exclusive; indeed, many theorists believe that the psychological causes in the final analysis can be translated into the biological. Psychopathologists have differed and do differ in the relative importance they attach to one or the other, and these differences are paralleled by differences in viewpoint about the psychological structure of the human being. If "mind" is viewed as a function of the brain with its nervous connections throughout the body, then behavior is assumed to result from a complicated interplay of biological activity, influenced not only by direct biological states but indirectly by environmental stimuli which although "psychological" in nature are understood to translate into physiological states and activity. It is however, possible to hold this "monistic" view about the "mind-body" relationship and yet emphasize psychological-experiential causes as being sufficient to an understanding of behavior. From this viewpoint, only psychological causes would be considered to be important in understanding psychopathology as any behavior obviously affected by primarily biological causes would be assigned to problems of general medicine and physical health. For example, although it would of course be recognized that brain tumors may result in serious psychological malfunctioning, persons so afflicted would be considered problems for neurologists and not for psychopathologists, who would confine their attention to problems of behavior originating in "psychic conflicts," "emotional traumas," and the like.

Some psychologists hold, implicitly or explicitly, to a more or less examined theory of "dualism"—i.e., that the "mind" and the "body" are two separate, although interacting or paralleling, entities. This venerable philosophical position is much less explicitly common in the twentieth than in earlier centuries, although in effect it is often implied. If somehow causative agents act upon the immaterial "mind" (or "psyche" or "soul"), then it is necessary to postulate ways in which the body, composed of matter, can influence the immaterial mind which in turn is taken to be capable of governing the actions of the material body. The dualistic position on the mind-body relationship maintains that the key role of mind (psyche, soul) is independent of purely bodily control. Although not an inevitable corollary, this position does allow for the possibility that other nonmaterial agents might influence the mind directly. One such set of agents includes benign or malignant—or even indifferent—spirits, apparitions, divinities, or demons and divine retributions, another set includes archetypes, cosmic consciousness, racial memories, premonitions, occult "magnetic" and "astral" forces, suggestions, and various paranormal phenomena. Thus a third category of causes, the supernatural, has been postulated. Although the psychological-experiential may be translated into physical or biological terms (a learned behavior, although "psychological," might be described in terms of neural and therefore physical and biological connections), the supernatural is held to work either directly upon "mind" or indirectly through manipulation of physical agents but at no juncture is it assumed to be susceptible of translation into physiology.

I. Biological Causes

A. *Constitutional causes (diathesis).*   Over the centuries it generally has been recognized that some behavior deviations are present from birth onwards. By and large, today these behavior anomalies tend to be classified as *mental retardation;* in previous centuries individuals with such afflictions were known as "natural fools" (i.e. fools by birth or nature, rather than by accident or otherwise). It is usually assumed that a constitutional disposition, inherited or congenitally acquired, is responsible. This chapter is not concerned with this category of psychopathology as such conditions are more properly part of the history of developmental or child psychology. Constitutional explanations of psychopathology which becomes clinically evident in later life (usually puberty or thereafter) tend to fall into either one of two frameworks:

1. The constitutional disposition is considered to be *necessary and sufficient* for the development of the psychopathology; the basic cause usually is assumed to be genetic and the condition believed to be irreversible and therefore incurable.

2. The constitutional disposition is a *pre*disposition; it is *necessary* but *not sufficient* for development of the condition. It is assumed that the individual is born with a constitutional vulnerability (a "weak" constitution) which, unless certain stresses occur (and the stresses might be almost inevitable in the course of living) might escape manifestation of the psychopathology. This theory is currently known as the *diathesis-stress* model. The nature of the precipitating stress or stresses which have been hypothesized have been either biological or psychological-experiential and have included any of the various events or agents listed below.

Other theories do not assume a constitutional disposition or predisposition for psychopathology, holding that the introduction of a sufficiently stressful or pathogenic agent or event into the biological or psychological space of the normally functioning and constituted individual may be sufficient to generate psychopathology.

Each of the following physical agents or events have been suggested, by one name or another, as having the potential of causing psychopathology through damage to the structure or interference with the proper functioning of the nervous system, either directly or indirectly. In the latter case, conditions leading to malfunction of other parts of the biological system are believed in turn to impede the normal function of the nervous system (e.g. circulatory malfunction resulting in cerebral hemorrage which damages the brain).

B. Physical stressors

1. traumas and injuries
2. tumors and obstructions
3. toxins, including drugs, alcohol, poisons, pollutions of air, water and food, and toxins hypothesized to result as bodily by-products from fatigue, unhealthy food, disease, etc.

4. infections or invasion by disease pathogens
5. excessive physiological stress or "over-use" of the body (particularly of the nervous system) by over-work and physical exertion, excessive study, excessive sexual activity or abstinence, fervour of emotional excesses, fasting, over-indulgences, etc.
6. physiological imbalances occasioned by various dietary deficiencies or excesses.

II. Psychological-Experiential Causes

The following are, or have been, assumed (1) capable of creating stress for an already consitutionally predisposed individual or (2) sufficiently pathogenic to cause psychopathological malfunctioning in a normally constituted person.

A. *Psychological Traumas or Stresses*   (to which the psychopathology is a reaction): e.g. grief, prolonged fears, severe disappointments (jilting by a lover, loss of a job, etc.) social consequences of injury or illness (e.g. despondency or withdrawal from social interactions, because of blinding, crippling) and so on.

B. *Intense motivations and/or emotions; conscious or unconscious conflict of motives*   (which disrupt psychological functioning).

C. *"Loss" of some psychological faculty*   (e.g. loss of will or diminution of capacity to govern appetites, emotions, course of conduct; loss of reason or diminution of capacity to direct behavior in accordance with probable consequences.) We note here that such hypothesized losses have served at times to explain the psychopathology and at other times to define it. Shakespeare mocks this glib etiology in Hamlet, V:1:

Hamlet: "How came he [Hamlet] mad?
Clown: "Very strangely, they say."
Hamlet: "How, strangely?"
Clown: "Faith, e'en with losing his wits.
Hamlet: "Upon what ground?"
Clown: "Why, here in Denmark. . ."

D. *Learning of the maladaptive behavior*   (learning of incapacitating or inconvenient emotional reactions to certain recurring situations; learning of inappropriate or inadequate problem solving or social behaviors).

E. *Motivations which are served by the psychopathological behavior;*   (in which the abnormal behavior, far from being intrinsically maladaptive is in fact satisfying a particular motive or cluster of motives which may be unconscious or inaccessible to the person's awareness).

F. The environment—general, social, cultural, economic, political stresses and forces (which prevent the individual from attaining or maintaining psychological well-being).

G. Guilt (in which the psychopathology results as an inevitable moral consequence of indulging in various vices; or in which the psychopathology is a punishment meted out by the self because of internalized feelings of guilt and sin.)

Treatment of Psychopathology

Throughout the course of history there is a constantly recurring list of therapies for mental illness, each related in one way or another to the symptoms of and/or the supposed causes of the pathology. Although ideally therapies are devised to effect cures, they are often merely palliative, intended to relieve symptoms whilst the disease process does or does not run its course. And although therapies have often been derived from theories of causation, at times the theories of causation have been contrived to rationalize the treatments used. Therapies have been developed by physicians, priests, psychiatric and psychological specialists, interested laymen, charlatans, and quacks; the therapies vary accordingly. Treatments in general have been undertaken to meet the patient's need, to meet the needs of the patient's family or friends or community to do something for or about the patient, to solve social problems presented by the patient's condition. Treatment therefore may not be primarily intended to be therapeutic. The patient may be placed under custodial care in order to protect the patient from his or her own self neglect or abuse or the consequences of poor judgment; to allow time for rest, freedom from responsibility, proper diet to effect improvement; to protect others from the violence, problems, embarrassment, or inconvenience caused by the patient—or all of the above.

Therapies which have been used throughout the centuries include those intended to be:

cathartic (i.e., to abruptly rid the patient of the noxious agent causing the symptoms, which includes the use of emetic and purgative medicines to rid the body of toxins; dramatic performances or reenactments of traumatic experiences to rid the mind of disturbing emotions; exorcisms to drive out demons).

shocking (intended to surprise the patient out of the mad state or to jolt the nervous system back to normal, as by unexpectedly plunging the patient into cold water, submitting him/her to convulsive electric shock, and so on).

soothing (quieting the agitations by music, rocking motions, sedative drugs, massage).

supportive and reassuring (pep talks, unconditional acceptance).
restorative of normal balance (diet, blood letting, emetics, and purgatives designed to restore a normal physiological balance; counseling to restore a balanced and rational view).

Other therapies have attempted to:

promote understanding (through rational analysis of motives, dreams, circumstances).
establish improved adjustment through re-learning (by encouraging the patient to industriously apply him/herself to the mastery of crafts in order to systematically organize behavior which is socially useful and personally rewarding; by techniques designed to teach the patient new emotional reactions, or new patterns of behavior which will better satisfy the patient's needs or lead to less conflict with others. This has been attempted through rewards and positive reinforcements and through punishments and aversive conditioning.).

HISTORY OF PSYCHOPATHOLOGY

The Earliest Times

The very early history of psychopathology is scant in the extreme and we must be extremely hesitant to draw inferences from the few available data. There are a few records of psychological therapy dating from 3000 B.C. in Egypt and Mesopotamia. The Egyptian I-em-hotep is said to be the first physician recorded in history (c. 2680 B.C.). After his death he was revered as a deity and patron of medicine. Temples were erected in his honor in which patients with psychological problems were encouraged to sleep. The healer-priest suggested to them that their dreams would reveal the treatment appropriate for their disorder. Illness was believed to be of divine origin and it followed that treatment consisted largely of magical-religious practices. Dream interpretations, incantations, religious rituals, and suggestion were employed. We see here two themes which recur throughout history. One is the belief that psychological and bodily ailments can be matters for divine intervention and that shrines have curative powers. The other is that sleep has psychotherapeutic properties and that dreams provide clues to the patient's problems.

Early views about madness have been inferred from Biblical references. For example, Miller (1975) says "Deuteronomy 28:23,34 views madness as punishment for disobeying the commandments" (p. 528). This selection describes the terrible punishments to be meted out to the people of Israel should they forswear their god. These include inflammation, blasting and mildew, marital infidelity, general perishing and destruction, "a sore botch that cannot be healed, from the sole of thy foot unto the top of thy head," infertile vineyards, locusts, and "madness, and blindness and astonishment of heart." The reference to madness is obviously incidental; madness, like anything nasty, could be visited on mankind as an expression of the awesome power of an enraged god. As such, this Biblical reference gives us no information about early views specific to psychopathology (or of dermatology, marital infidelity, or crop failure!)—but rather more than we might like to know about possible consequences of incurring divine wrath.

In ancient Israel, as in other communities and other times, it was accepted that occasionally a particular person might serve as a vehicle for divine revelations to the people from their god, and that in a state of trance this prophet might utter oracular messages to be interpreted by the community or by priests. Rosen (1968) points out that such a prophet might be considered mad by some, but in the main was allowed to act as he wished providing that what he said and did was not too threatening to the prevailing views of the political-religious groups in power. A discrimination was made between prophets and the actually mentally ill and between both and those persons feigning either divine inspiration or madness—the political manipulator and the malingerer. The prophet, the manipulator, and the malingerer exhibit their behavior only under certain (and for the prophet, socially sanctioned) conditions.

As for the mentally ill, according to Rosen, their psychopathology was regarded by the Israelites (as indeed by most people of that time and later) to be a private matter, to be dealt with by the family or immediate community as long as the abnormal behavior did not present a problem of public safety and convenience or create legal problems (e.g. as those relating to property). Often allowed to wander freely about their home community or countryside, the mentally deranged were not officially mistreated as public policy, although they were often mocked and teased by bystanders. If their behavior was violent or otherwise socially disruptive and if they came from wealthy families, an attendant might be hired to supervise them; otherwise, they might be kept confined in their own homes—sometimes locked up or chained if they were inclined to violence.

References in the Talmud make it clear that a supposition of insanity brought legal consequences. Those considered to be mentally deranged could not be held legally responsible for their actions. They could not therefore be held responsible for causing bodily harm, but restraint could be ordered or imposed to prevent the mad person from doing more harm. Exempt from legal responsibility, the insane person could not, as a consequence, be allowed to enter into contractual arrangements no more than could a child. For example, a madman could not testify in a court of law, dispose of property, enter into or terminate a marriage agreement. A mentally ill man could not legally divorce his wife—however, since only the husband could terminate the marriage contract, there was no way for the sane wife of a mentally ill man to obtain a divorce. If the mental illness were periodic, actions taken during the periods of lucidity were considered legal. These general provisions were to apply throughout much of Western Europe for centuries, and the legal problems presented by those considered mentally ill are with us still.

Greece and Rome: The Classical Ages

The first substantial documentation of an early history of psychopathology begins with the period of Greek and Roman influence, between about 700 B.C. and 600 A.D.

Madness is depicted in early Greek literature and drama. Ducey and Simon (1975) summarize concepts that they have inferred from these sources. The more serious forms of madness, akin to present day concepts of psychosis, were dramatized as arising from severe conflicts within the individual. Conscience (an inner sense of right and wrong) played a major role in these conflicts but the madness itself comprised a divine retribution meted out to the guilty person. Madness was thus presented as a form of punishment for wrongdoing, something administered by supernatural beings, the Furies, who pursued the miscreant. Therapeutic consequences were believed to result from talking about the conflict—the process of *catharsis*. Attendance at dramatic performances, with their accompaniments of music, dancing and poetic language was also seen as cathartic.

Five hundred years before the birth of Christ, the Greeks had begun to develop a practical and empirical profession of medicine, a body of theory and practice based on observations of the symptoms of disease as seen by the examining physician. Symptomatic of many diseases are the quantitative and qualitative changes in bodily excretions—e.g., alterations in amount and in color, consistency and odor of urine, blood, phlegm, bile, feces, which return to normal when the patient regains health. Classical Greek medicine evolved from the observation of these changes—observation limited of course by the lack of microscopes, biochemical assays, or even eyeglasses. From these observations it was concluded that illness results from an imbalance of bodily fluids and that cure logically entails restoring the balance. The need for scientific verification of hypotheses was not recognized; explanations were accepted as sufficient if they were logical and plausible.

Our knowledge of these developments in Greek medicine is based on the assemblage of medical papers preserved from 450-350 B.C. and known collectively as the Hippocratic Corpus. Sometimes attributed in whole to the physician Hippocrates, these are of various authorship. Diverse in subject matter and style, the papers tend to reject magical-religious explanations of disease in favor of empirically ascertained natural causes. The most interesting of these, from the viewpoint of the psychopathologist, is the paper dealing with epilepsy, or the "sacred disease." The author says:

I do not believe that the "Sacred Disease" is any more divine or sacred than any other disease but, on the contrary, has specific characteristics and a definite cause . . . It is my opinion that those who first called this disease "sacred" were the sort of people we now call witch-doctors, faith-healers, quacks and charlatans . . . By invoking a divine element they were able to screen their own failure to give suitable treatment and so called this a "sacred" malady to conceal their ignorance of its nature. By picking their phrases carefully, prescribing purifications and incantations along with abstinence from baths and from many foods unsuitable for the sick, they ensured that their therapeutic measures were safe for themselves. (Lloyd [ed.] 1978: pp. 237-238)

The paper speculates that epilepsy is hereditary and that the brain is the seat of the disease due to blockage of the passage of phlegm from the brain. The author goes on to say that:

It ought to be generally known that the source of our pleasure, merriment, laughter and amusement, as of our grief, pain, anxiety and tears is none other than the brain . . . it is the brain too which is the seat of madness and delirium, of the fears and frights which assail us, often by night, but sometimes even by day; it is there where lies the cause of insomnia and sleep-walking, of thoughts that will not come, forgotten duties and eccentricities. (pp. 248-249)

From these teachings emerged a school of medical thought, to be developed further by the Roman, Galen (129-198 A.D.). The Hippocratic-Galenic writings were later translated and elaborated by Arabic scholars and served as a major source for Avicenna (980-1036 A.D.) whose vast compendium of medical knowledge served as the chief textbook for physicians well into the Renaissance. The general tenets of this school were to be a major influence in Western conceptions of disease, both bodily and psychological, well into the eighteenth century. The basic postulate held that a balance of four humors was ordinarily maintained in the body and was essential for both physical and mental health. It was assumed that nutriments were converted into the humors through a process of "pepsis" or "coction" and that each humor was elaborated by a different organ—blood by the heart, choler or yellow bile by the liver, melancholer or black bile from the spleen, and phlegm by the brain. It was held that the humors partook of the qualities (cold and hot, moist and dry) of the basic elements (earth, fire, water, and air) of which the world was believed to be composed; the relative proportions of these qualities determined the temperament of the individual. Although the humors fluctuated with diet and climate and the balance changed with age, an individual tended to have a predominance of one or another of the humors which determined his or her character. This supposition gave rise to a four-fold classification of temperament: sanguine (blood dominant), phlegmatic, choleric, melancholic—all terms still in use to describe temperament. It was believed that disease arose from serious disturbance of the balance of the humors;

the origin of these imbalances (or "dyscrasias") could be congenital and con-stitutional, or they could arise from environmental and experiential sources (changes in climate, unhealthy diet, overwork, grief, fever, etc.). From the symptoms of the disease, the physician could diagnose the particular type of imbalance and determine the appropriate course of treatment which logically consisted of techniques designed to restore a healthy balance. Thus the use of special diets and of bleeding, purgation, and emetics can be understood as attempts to restore a healthy humoral balance by providing proper nutrition to restore deficiencies or by draining away superfluous humors.

Psychological aberrations were considered to be due to abnormal states of the brain resulting from humoral imbalance. Torpor and apathy, for example, were thought to result from corruption of the brain by excess phlegm; insomnia and delirium were believed to be due to overheating of the brain by blood. Depres-sion was believed to result from a suffusion of the brain by melancholer, or black bile, and we still refer to the depressed patient as "melancholic." Observations of psychopathological behaviors can be read in the Hippocratic Corpus and in the case histories complied by Galen. In the latter there are good clinical accounts of "delirious" disorders, with detailed enumeration of symptoms, including in-coherence of speech, amnesias, mutisms, anorexia, and elaborate delusions.

The therapies rationalized by humoral theories were to continue in use by medical practioners for centuries. Thus as late as 1795, Benjamin Rush of the Pennsylvania Hospital recommended bleeding lunatics of a maximum of 40 ounces of blood in order to restore peace of mind by ridding the head of excess blood (quoted in Hunter & McAlpine, 1963).

The humoral theories were biological and materialistic; mental disorder was understood as resulting from malfunction of the brain due to generalized biological imbalances. In contrast to these there were psychological theories which attributed psychopathology to failure to exercise reason to control emotion and impulse or to regulate conduct. These ideas originated in concepts of psychophysical dualism developed by Greek philosophers, most notably Plato (429-347). These ideas not only shaped Greek speculation about abnormal behavior but were to profoundly influence later Western thought about psychopathology.

Plato taught that the body, composed of matter (and subject to change, decay, and death) was created to house the separate, self-moving, immaterial, and (in part) immortal psyche (or soul). It is the psyche that imparts life to the body and, through its attribute of "eros," movement. "Eros" is manifested at the lowest, most basic level as sexual desire, the seeking to mate and reproduce; at the next higher level as a general striving for satisfaction; and at the highest level as a searching for truth and beauty. (Freud's concept of Libido in its instinctual and sublimated aspects is very similar and possibly derivative). In his creation myth *Timaeus,* Plato describes the psyche as two-fold consisting of (1) the rational, immortal aspect with its capacity for deliberation and reason and (2) the irra-tional, and mortal, aspects which have the capacity to sense and feel. The latter are characterized by (a) passions and bodily hungers, particularly those associated with nutrition and sex and by (b) spirit (courage, impulses) which provides impetus for action either in the interest of sensual gratification or, if properly subordinated and regulated, in the interests of the rational psyche with its concern for perfection and knowledge. The two aspects of the irrational psyche are located in the lower parts of the body, the sensual and passionate being located in the "belly and the members" and the spirited in the chest, whereas the rational aspect has its seat in the head. To function properly, the lower sensual and spirited aspects of the psyche, the passions, impulses, and emotions, ought to be subordinated to and regulated by the rational aspect, the three aspects thus being integrated to achieve the goals of reason. Reason is in abeyance when the person is asleep or drunk or disturbed by strong passion. Under such circumstances, the unleashed appetites strive for sensual pleasures and the psychic processes resemble those of the beasts, which lack reason, or of madmen. Sexual desire is one of the strongest sensual passions; in the Republic, Plato describes the passion of sexual love as a "frantic and savage monster" which puts considerable strain on the reason's attempts at control until age brings "profound repose and freedom from this and other passions."

Plato developed a psychology of conduct in which he attempted to demonstrate how human beings might live a virtuous life guided by ideal principles elucidated by the exercise of reason. Divergence from ideal human conduct results from failure to use reason to moderate passions and emotions, and to direct conduct. This could occur because (1) of a disease of the imagination (that is, of the capacity to unite sensory images into new ideas) hence depriving the reason of material to act upon; (2) of ignorance, the reason itself being enfeebled or insufficiently developed due to faulty education and experience; (3) the individual allows impulse and passion to dominate reason. Without the exercise of self control and the conscious application of the principles of virtuous conduct (knowledge of social regulations, ideas of law and justice, etc). the person behaves like a savage or a madman. Whatever the cause, madness arises from the dominance of impulse, passion, and appetite over reason; madness could be cured therefore by a restoration of, or the development of, the rational process, to be achieved through dialectical discussion. Unlike catharsis which is intended to achieve emotional *release,* dialectical discussion is intended to achieve emotional *control;* it is a purely rational process and is aimed at valid self knowledge through logical and philosophical analyses. Catharsis, on the other hand, is anti-rational and encourages madness. Madness for Plato was not so much a disease as it was a moral disorder, a failure of the psyche to properly control and integrate behavior and, as such, it follows that the treatment of madness should be psychological and re-educative rather than biological.

The later Christian belief that the soul is immortal and strives for goodness owes a great deal to the Platonic philosophy. The idea that irrational and self-indulgent conduct is sinful—and therefore that madness is a form of divine retribution—is related to Plato's ideals of conduct. The belief that madness comprises loss of reason, to be restored by adherence to divine directives of conduct, is also related to Platonic philosophy.

Succeeding centuries show the influence of Plato's ideas in various ways. The view that the restoration of mental health depends upon reestablishing the dominance of reason over the passions is clearly set forth in the nineteenth-century philosophy of moral treatment (p. 314). Freud was to reformulate many Platonic concepts—notably that conflict between passion (especially sexual) and social regulation lies at the root of psychological disturbance.

Evidence of popular notions about psychopathology in ancient Greece is available in historical accounts. Herodotus, the Greek historian whose work was probably published before 425 B.C., presented the history of Cambyses II. Cambyses, son of Cyrus the Great, reigned over Persia between 530 and 522 B.C. Herodotus suggests that Cambyses was probably mad because of the reports of his alleged atrocities in Egypt which included religious sacrileges and gratuitous violence—e.g., the murder of his brother, his pregnant wife, and others. Herodotus mentions some possible motives for Cambyses' behavior but decides these are insufficient to explain it as he killed his brother, wife, various soldiers, and priests on slight pretexts and, further, since he committed religious sacrileges Herodotus concludes, "I hold it then in every way proved that Cambyses was very mad; else he would never have set himself to deride religion and custom" (p. 51). As for why Cambyses became mad, Herodotus is not sure; he suggests Cambyses may have become so as a result of divine retribution (Cambyses had killed a ritual calf supposed to have been a reincarnation of Apis, an Egyptian god), but goes on to suggest that perhaps the madness "grew from some of the many troubles that are wont to beset men; for indeed he is said to have been afflicted from his birth with that grievous disease which some call 'sacred.' It is no unlikely thing then that when his body was grievously afflicted his mind too should be diseased" (pp. 43-45).

We may conjecture that the philosophy of Plato and others had little impact on the quality of life of the common people, either in Greece or later, during the period of the Roman Empire. Application of medical theory was undoubtedly intermingled with existing practices of the peoples that were absorbed into the Roman Empire. The practice of medicine continued at two levels; the wealthy relied on the service of physicians trained in the Hippocratic-Galenic traditions, the poor continued the use of herbs, charms, and other traditional or religiously based procedures to alleviate disease. The impact of sophisticated thought about psychopathology may have been slight for the majority of people.

From early times, mankind has grappled with the problem of whether or not the mentally ill should be held responsible for their actions. As in ancient Israel, the Romans established a legal status for the mentally ill as early as the fifth century B.C. The mentally ill were declared to be legally incompetent, a position that has been elaborated and modified ever since. Judges were empowered to determine the legal competence of the mentally ill to contract marriage, to obtain a divorce, to enter into contracts, to make a will, or to testify before a court. Since they were not considered responsible for themselves, courts were charged with allocating responsibility for the mentally ill to others (e.g., relatives, the community, etc.) Some centuries later, we find in the code of Welsh laws promulgated by the Celtic king, Hywel Dda (909-950), references to the incapacity of the insane to act as judges or to be held responsible for obligations.

The Middle Ages

Division of the past into chronological periods is arbitrary; the periods rarely correspond closely to distinct shifts in patterns of belief. However, it is convenient to consider the history of psychopathology, as it is history in general, in terms of conventional epochs. One of these is the "Middle Ages," conventionally dated from the fifth or sixth century into the fifteenth. The beginning of the Middle Ages may be defined as that time in the history of Europe at which Roman hegemony had disappeared, territories had reverted to control by indigenous peoples, and the spread and consolidation of the Christian church had begun. The resulting culture was largely compounded of classical, Christian and pagan traditions, and varied from place to place and time to time. Knowledge of the physical world consisted of commonsense observations, inspired intuitive guesses, irrational and rational superstitions, and religious speculation. Amongst the educated, a miniscule class, it included fragments of lore derived from Arabic, Roman, and Greek sources. This knowledge was preserved, and often distorted by transcription, in Latin translations; it was virtually unavailable, except insofar as it percolated by word of mouth, to the overwhelming majority of people. Nascent science was suspect; procedures which established control over natural events could be used for malevolent or selfish purposes, overlapping in intent with the practice of magic.

Correlated with the disintegration of Roman control and hastening the process were barbarian invasions, military uprisings, civil disorders, and migration of peoples. The social consequences of these conditions were exacerbated by sporadic famine and by cycles of epidemic disease with extremely heavy mortality rates. In those times of social and economic change, when all too often the population was coping with or recovering from the effects of famine, plague, and warfare, a mental disorder would have had to be disruptive indeed to call attention to itself or to divert the efforts of others to control or cure it.

Psychopathology and Witchcraft: Rumors and Realities

Many recent histories of abnormal psychology have accepted almost without question the view that the Middle Ages were characterized by the definition of many mentally ill people as witches. An archetypical example of this view is put forth in the influential book, the *History of Medical Psychology* (Zilboorg &

Henry, 1941). Scientific psychiatry, the authors claim, had surrendered to a primitive demonology which led to persecution of the insane as witches. "Hundreds of thousands of mentally sick fell victim to this violent reaction [witch hunting]. Not all accused of being witches and sorcerers were mentally sick, but almost all mentally sick were considered witches, or sorcerers, or bewitched" (p. 153). Elsewhere, Zilboorg (1935) asserts, "No doubt is left in our minds that the millions of witches, sorcerers, possessed and obsessed were an enormous mass of severe neurotics, psychotics and considerably deteriorated organic deleria . . . for many years the world looked like a veritable insane asylum without a proper mental hospital" (p. 73).

Zilboorg's history provided the basis for routine repetition by later psychopathologists. Ullman and Krasner (1975) say that the fifteenth-century treatise on witchcraft, the *Malleus Maleficarum*, can be regarded as a contemporary manual for the treatment of mental disorders. Other authors develop this theme: "With it [*Malleus Maleficarum*] as a guide, literally hundreds of thousands of women and children were condemned as witches and . . . burned at the stake . . . in this climate all naturalistic thinking about mental aberration was swept away" (Zax & Cowen, 1976; p. 41). "Before the nineteenth century, people in Western Civilization, except for profound observers and thinkers like the Greek physicians Hippocrates . . . and Galen [sic] . . . thought that 'madness', or extremely abnormal behavior, indicated possession by evil spirits . . . well into the sixteenth century people who were thought to have consorted with or to be possessed by the devil were often burned as witches" (Altrocchi, 1980; p. 17 & 19). "During the early years of the medieval era the mentally ill were considered misdirected souls and were treated by the clergy . . . later . . . witchcraft became the accepted explanation . . . if confessions were not forthcoming at the stake, asphyxiation, strangulation, beheading, or for the lucky ones, brain surgery followed" (Kleinmuntz, 1980; p. 539-540). "The Dark Ages: The return of Demonology. With the death of Galen in 200 A.D., medical advances ceased and the dark era of medical ignorance and fearful superstition returned to blanket the civilized world. The teachings of the Greco-Romans were banned as pagan, mental illness was again seen as a form of possession . . . Medical psychology ceased to exist, and the struggling roots of psychiatry were supplanted by demonology . . . 'It is contrary to true faith' became the authoritative decree that dispensed with any heretic who would believe that there were natural explanations for mental illness" (Suinn, 1975; p. 7 & 9).

These writers suggest that no view other than that of supernatural and demonological causation of mental illness had significant currency much before the eighteenth century; further, that this had expression in the witchcraze which in turn can be understood as masking the goal of persecuting and exterminating the mentally ill. Suinn, we note, alleged that the heretic of the Middle Ages was martyred for holding naturalistic hypotheses about human psychopathology. This view has become so much a standard feature of textbooks of abnormal psychology that it deserves careful scrutiny—the more so because unthinking acceptance of it has served as a substitute for the serious study of the state of psychopathology in those times. We will therefore consider the "facts":

Dates. Witch hunting was not characteristic of the Middle Ages: the witch-craze occurred during the Renaissance and Reformation, from the end of the fifteenth through the seventeenth century. One of the last spasms of the witch-craze took place in Salem, Mass. in 1692 and the last legal execution of a condemned witch, according to Trevor-Roper (1967), was in Glarus, Switzerland in 1782. Although the correct chronology of the witchcraze is recognized by many authors, they continue to interpret the witchcraze as a manifestation of persecution of the mentally ill.

Numbers. It is claimed that an enormous number of people were executed as witches during the witchcraze (estimates range from "hundreds of thousands" to "nine million or more".) This may be true; however, accurate figures for the number of victims are impossible to obtain. Such estimates are speculative and hearsay. It is commonly, and regretfully, conceded by historians that figures given in early documents are notoriously unreliable. There were no methods for arriving at accurate statistics. Ziegler (1969) points out that "A large figure . . . might be expressed as though exactly calculated but this was merely so as to heighten the dramatic effect. When the Pope was assured by his advisers that the Black Death had cost the lives of 42, 836, 486 throughout the world . . . what was meant was that an awful lot of people had died" (p. 52). G. G. Coulton (1961) cautions: "We must note the wild extravagance of medieval writers and even statesmen, wherever large numbers are concerned. The Commons, in 1371, voted a tax on the supposition that there were 50,000 parishes in England. In fact there were less than 9000" (p. 396). Without seeking to minimize the horror, Coulton asserts of the Inquisition and heresy trials that "fewer were actually burned than is often supposed. Bernard Gui, one of the most active inquisitors, convicted altogether 930 heretics; he committed only 42 to the stake, 307 to prison" (p. 106). Trevor-Roper (1967) claims "The figures commonly given for the execution of witches in England are grotesquely exaggerated . . . Lea . . . estimated the number of victims in Britain as 90,000 . . . but Mr. C. L. Ewen's careful study . . . has discredited all such wild guesses. He concluded that between 1542 and 1736 'less than one thousand' persons were executed for witchcraft in England" (p. 89). If figures for witchcraft executions are exaggerated by a factor of 90 in Britain it is likely the figures for Europe are inflated also. This is particularly so when a careful distinction is not drawn between witchcraft trials, criminal trials in which witchcraft was secondary, and heresy trials proper.

Demographics. The concensus amongst historians seems to be that the number of female exceeded the number of male victims, but given that there are no reliable figures anyway there are certainly none available for the distribution of condemned witches by sex and by age. When extracts from witch trials are examined, it is by no means clear that the accused were typically the deluded and melancholic old women of popular psychiatric discussion. Characteristics of the continental witchtrials were strikingly different in several important respects from witchtrials in England. Currie (1968) points out that the continental witch-trials combined a system of unlimited legal power with a compelling motive for persecution as the court was empowered to confiscate the property of the accused; as a result "a significant proportion of continental witches were men, and an even more significant proportion of men and women were people of wealth" (p. 22). In contrast, "English courts did not have the power or the motive to systematically stigmatize the wealthy and propertied . . . the accusations . . . were directed against socially marginal and undesirable individuals who were powerless to defend themselves" (p. 27)—often women and usually from the lower classes.

Diagnosis.   As for the mental status of accused witches, it is at best a dubious enterprise to attempt diagnosis of mental illness at a remove of three to fifteen hundred years. Further, if the behavior in question was not considered to be psychopathological when it occurred, the reactions to it at the time reveal little about attitudes towards psychopathology then current.

Psychoanalysts are particularly enthusiastic about their skill in discerning psychopathology and its causes from minimal cues. Solomon Meyer (1915) claimed that "by a most thorough and far-reaching analysis of a single dream, we can . . . root up the entire life history of the dreamer" (p. 19)! Creativity as a substitute for historical accuracy has a venerable past. The ninth century historian, Agnellus, explained how he contrived to write a complete series of lives of his predecessors: "Where I have not found any history of any of these bishops and have not been able by conversation with aged men, or inspection of the monuments, or from any other authentic source, to obtain information concerning them, in such a case, in order that there might not be a break in the series, I have composed the life myself, with the help of God and the prayers of the brethren" (Coulton, 1961; pp. 66-67). The conclusion that the persons accused as witches were actually mentally ill also may be based on imaginative inference. We paraphrase Agnellus: "Where we have not found any history of these witches and have not been able by conversation with aged men or from any other authentic source to obtain information concerning them, in such a case, we have composed the history of their psychopathology ourselves, with the help of our theory and the support of our professional colleagues."

Discussion.   We of the twentieth century are skeptical of magic and mysticism. This skepticism invites the conclusion that persons must be mentally deranged if they confess themselves to be witches. If, however, belief in the potency of witches is sufficient evidence for a post-hoc psychiatric diagnosis of mental illness, we would be forced to the conclusion that the accusers of witches were also insane. Documentary evidence suggests that the accusers were convinced that the persons they accused were in fact witches; they believed themselves justified, indeed morally obligated, to compel their victims to confess and they used, if necessary, the threat or the actuality of appalling torture from which final release of death was denied until the accused did confess. Nonetheless, it has not been concluded that sane people were persecuted by the insane during the witchcraze. Belief in witchcraft per se does not define mental illness. Such belief has been held until recent times and in fact has never been wholly abandoned.

The Christian Church and Heresy, Witchcraft, and Psychopathology.   It is instructive to leaf through the indexes of general histories of Western Europe for the centuries spanning the beginning of the Middle Ages to the 1700s. Witchcraft trials typically are discussed in the space of a paragraph to a page or two of text. Witchcraft trials are treated by historians as a final excrescence of the trials for religious heresy for which the Inquisition was developed.

The early Church condemned belief in demons as superstitious fancy and discouraged the practice of magic. Punishment for dabbling in magic consisted mainly of penances of fasting and prayer. If magic were involved in the commission of a crime, the crime itself was punished in accordance with the law. In contrast to this mild censure of witchcraft beliefs and practices, the Church began as early as the eleventh century to assemble the machinery of the Inquisition in order to identify, punish, and if deemed necessary to destroy heretics whose thinking, teaching, and behavior might pose a threat to the totalitarian fabric of the Christian Church. Heresy was believed to menace salvation of the soul. A wrong committed in thought, opinion and belief, heresy was not necessarily revealed in overt behavior; the problem of establishing legal proof of heresy was therefore difficult and attempts to establish a procedure to do so finally led to a total subversion of justice. Heresy trials served to stem temporarily the rising tide of criticism against and pressure for reform of the religious absolutism of the Christian Church; inevitably the trials themselves began to generate mounting criticism of Church tyranny. It became difficult to mobilize popular support for the punishment of persons whose only demonstrated crime might be disagreement with Papal authority on matters of religious doctrine. It became expedient to particularize charges against suspected heretics in a way that could polarize popular sentiment in favor of the Inquisition at the expense of the accused heretic. Increasingly, charges were made of pacts with the Devil. "Witch" came to define a fully participating and voluntarily consenting partner with forces of evil, embodied in the Devil, opposed to God, and conspiring to overthrow Christianity. The danger "witches" posed to the community was not the nuisance of individual psychopathology but the religious-political threat of heresy. Witchcraft trials on the continent of Europe appear to have been an expression of a desperate attempt to force compliance with official Church doctrine. It has not been claimed that heretics as such were mentally ill; witches were a special case of heretic. In addition, church theologians had had a difficult time explaining why disease, crop failure, and other misfortunes happened in a world governed by an omniscient, omnipotent, and absolutely benevolent deity and so they had recourse to the supposition of an opposed principle of evil with which certain members of the community were freely co-operating to bring about such calamities. Accusations of witchcraft generally served to demonstrate to an anxious populace that the established Church was vigorously combatting the forces causing the all too frequent disasters of daily life.

Once the legal machinery to prosecute witchcraft was established, it could serve a variety of social, legal, political, and economic purposes, including that of maintaining its own bureaucracy; e.g., to persecute others considered undesirable within and without the community, as a vehicle for political and economic intrigue, to implement personal hatreds, etc. The mentally disturbed may well have been peculiarly vulnerable to involvement in the witchcraze and some, perhaps many, may have been caught up in it. But the mentally ill can not be considered to have been the focus of the witchcraze or a cause of it. Trevor-Roper (1967) summarized the witchcraze as the "social consequence of renewed ideological war with the accompanying climate of fear" (p. 67). Boyer and Nissenbaum (1974) conclude that "whatever else they may have been, the Salem witch trials cannot be written off as a communal effort to purge the poor, the deviant or the outcast" (p. 33). Cohn (1975) states: "Financial greed and conscious sadism, though by no means lacking in all cases, did not supply the main driving force: That was supplied by religious zeal . . . The great witchhunt can in fact be taken as a supreme example of a massive killing of innocent people by a bureaucracy acting in accordance with belief, which unknown or rejected in earlier centuries, had come to be taken for granted as self-evident truths" (pp. 254-255). In his survey of literature dealing with the question of the psychiatric status of accused witches, Spanos (1978) has concluded that there is little evidence of psychopathology in these people. Schoeneman (1977) points out alternative psychological explanations for the behavior of the accused during the witchcraze.

The Christian Influence

Christianity brought into the furthest reaches of Europe two ideas that directly affected the perception and treatment of the mentally ill. The first of these was the emphasis upon the Christian duty of charity towards the poor or sick of any description. The other was the central conception of man as engaged in a struggle with the powers of evil, the prize being the salvation of his soul and everlasting life. Charity, according to the teaching of the Church, was an essential ingredient in the attainment of salvation; without it, man was "a sounding brass and a tinkling cymbal." The phenomenal spread of Christianity might be attributed to these two ideas. Christianity offered solace to people who experienced hardship as daily routine on a scale that can hardly be imagined today. In the face of pestilence, Christians gave help to the stricken; in the face of death, Christianity offered the consolation of salvation.

For tribal peoples of diverse and barbaric culture, inhabiting forest and swamp, without general law or language, the spread of Christianity represented a remarkable advance in general enlightenment, including the care and treatment of disease. The provision of care for the distressed appeared on the scene almost as soon as the Christian missionaries had succeeded in securing a stable foothold in new lands, and the provision of such care tended to secure their success in converting the local peoples. The Church was responsible for extending and developing hospitals well beyond anything known in classical times.

Almshouses and charitable hospitals were established for the aged, the sick, and the poor. In Great Britain, hospitals attached to monasteries had been founded at St. Albans by 794 A.D. and in York in 937 A.D. In Prague, a monastic hospital was opened in 929 A.D. In Norway there is mention, in 1170, of a hospital attached to Trondheim cathedral. Allderidge's research (1979) led her to conclude that although documentary evidence for the early medieval period is scant, it is "sufficient to suggest that in many instances the insane were regarded as, and treated alongside, the sick of other categories"; Allderidge adds "though it is worth bearing in mind that one reason we hear so little about it during this period may be that insanity did not present a very large problem" (p. 322). However, it is likely that some of the mentally ill who were not cared for by their families were extended help and protection in such institutions. Later, in 1326, the Georges Hospital of Elbing, under the auspices of the Teutonic Knights, built a few cells for the mentally ill, as was done in 1375 in the Municipal Hopsital of Hamburg and in 1385 in the hospital of Erfurt, amongst others. The first asylum specifically for the mentally ill was built in Valencia in 1409. The Hospital of St. Mary of Bethlehem ("Bedlam"), founded in London in 1247, sheltered, among others, the indigent too deranged to care for themselves or considered dangerous to the community. It does not appear that large numbers were so confined; Bethlehem held only about 15 or 20 persons until 1630 when it was enlarged to accomodate 50 or 60—and in the period prior to 1547 it did not house exclusively lunatics.

It has been claimed by a number of authors, notably Foucault (1967), that in the Middle Ages, large numbers of the insane were placed aboard boats, to be sailed from port to port segregated in this manner from society. The present authors, in a recent investigation, have been unable to find any actual evidence in support of this assertion (Maher & Maher, 1982).

In addition to those persons cared for in almshouses and hospitals and those under the supervision of their families, many more whom we might today regard as mentally disturbed, existed marginally in town and country. Some of these begged for a living. The unfortunates housed in "Bedlam" were released to beg when they were considered no longer likely to harm themselves or others. John Aubrey, writing of the life of Sir Thomas More (1478-1535) describes an encounter More had with an assaultive "Tom O Bedlam". Aubrey explains:

Till the breaking-out of the Civil-warre [1644], Tom O Bedlams did travell about the Countrey: they had been poore distracted men that had been putt into Bedlam, where recovering to some sobernesse they were truncated to goe a begging, e.g. they had on their left arme an Armilla or Tinne printed in some workes: about 4 inches long: they could not gett it off. They wore about their necks a great Horne of an Oxe, in a string or Bawdrie, which, when they came to an house for Almes, they did sound; and they did putt the drink given them into this Horne, whereto they did putt a stopple. Since the Warres I doe not remember to have seen anyone of them" (Aubrey, in Dick, 1972; p. 375)

Thomas More wrote, himself, in 1533 of an encounter he had with a lunatic who:

had fallen into these frantick heresies, fell soon after into plaine open franzye beside. And all beit that he had therefore bene put up in Bedelem, and afterward by beating and correccion gathered his remembraunce to him and beganne to come again to himselfe being thereupon set at liberty, and walkinge aboute abrode, his old fransies beganne to fall againe in his heade . . . he used in his wandering about to come into the churche, and there make many mad toies and trifles, to the trouble of good people in the divine service, and especially woulde he be most busye in the time of most silence, while the priest was at the secrets of the masse aboute the levacion . . . [More arranged that this man be apprehended and] "bounden to a tree in the streets before the whole towne, and ther they stripped him with roddes therefore till he waxed weary and somewhat lenger. And it appeared well that hys remembraunce was goode ineoughe save that it went about in grazing til it was beaten home. For he coulde then verye wel reherse his fautes himselfe, and speake and treate very well, and promise to doe afterward as well. (quoted in Rosen (1968); pp. 152-153)

We do not know if the lunatic described by Aubrey as assaulting More was the same as the one More is writing about in the quote above, and if so whether or not the assault on More occurred before or after the date of the beating. Be that as it may, it is evident that beating a deranged individual who was disruptive of public order was an acceptable treatment (a treatment, not a punishment per se as it was used in the same spirt as is aversive conditioning today, to bring about a change in behavior). Allderidge (1979) mentions that by 1348, the Common Law of England sanctioned the beating of one's mad relatives with a rod (we do not know how many people availed themselves of this right, or under what conditions of provocation if any); by 1482 it was also lawful in England to imprison someone who appeared likely to cause serious property damage (e.g. burning down a house).

Psychopathology and Demon Possession

When the cause of an event is not obvious, supernatural concepts provide the handiest explanation. The concept of demonic possession was popular during the Middle Ages and after. Demonic possession refers to the supposed occupation of the body of a victim by malevolent spirits responsible for certain bizarre symptoms. This notion was not confined to explanations of psychopathological symptoms. Demons were supposed to be one of the causes of physical disorder and sicknesses in general. The concept of invading demons may be a primitive approximation to germ theory, a point which is illustrated prettily in Kipling's story "Eye of Allah" in which monks are dismayed to discover that a crystal lens reveals a world of swarming devils habiting a drop of stagnant water.

Many people in medieval Europe elected for natural explanations if such were available. Demonic causes tended to be invoked under certain circumstances. Allderidge (1979) points out that "it is usually forgotten by the demoniac theorists that if you opted for crying in the wilderness rather than during a church service you would have a better chance of ending up as a saint." (And we note that More's lunatic who disturbed church services ended up being tied to a tree and beaten.)

The Old Testament taught that an authoritarian and sometimes vindictive God punished individuals or groups who transgressed his edicts; the punishments ran the gamut of the serious misfortunes common to the experience of mankind. Later, Christian theologians transform this God into an understanding, forgiving, loving, and absolutely benevolent deity. Such a God could not visit catastrophe on the people he had created. Therefore, over time, the concept of Satan and his minions, the minor demons, was elaborated. God had endowed mankind with reason, the capacity to deliberate, and as a result mankind was enabled to make a free choice between the goodness of God (and eternal salvation) and the wickedness of Satan (and a life of worldly rewards and sensual pleasures, to be followed by eternal damnation). Punishment and retribution were not meted out by God, but incurred by mankind's own choices and visited on it by Satan—who always rewarded his adherents with torment. Since a beneficent creator would not create evil in humans made in his own image, the temptations to ignore Christian doctrine, to break the holy commandments, and so on were held to come not from internal human and natural impulses but from without—from the devil; struggles of conscience and psychological conflict were objectified as struggles with demons. Abbot Guibert of Nogent writes of his childhood in the late eleventh century: "Even in the tender years of childhood, I was aware that the desire for a good endeavor which burned in my heart enraged the Devil in no small measure to stir up wickedness in me" (Benton, ed. 1970; p. 80). Often the devil was introduced into discussion not primarily to explain an actual situation but to serve in a morality tale. As for the mad—ordinarily, they were assumed to lack reason and thus they could not be held responsible for their choices of action. They were more to be pitied than condemned. However, it was possible to think of deranged persons as being tormented by demons, perhaps as a result of their own behavior or at the behest of another individual acting as intermediary between the Devil and the victim. This view was most likely to be entertained when the disturbed person displayed episodic bizarre behavior. However, if a person—by our contemporary standards sane or otherwise—blasphemed against God, or the sacraments, terrible consequences might be expected to follow. Guibert of Nogent describes such a case:

> At that monastery, I saw a woman who in her outrageous anger with her little son, among other abuses which that foulmouthed person hurled against the innocent child, even cursed his baptism. Instantly seized by a devil, she began to rave madly and to do and say horrible things. After she had been brought to the church and shown to the brothers, and had been restored to her senses by prayers and exorcism she learned from her torment not to curse the Lord's sacraments [and we hope, not to abuse her child]. (Benton, ed. 1970; p. 80)

Psychopathology and Medieval Eclectism

Although notions of demonology flourished in medieval religious, lay, and even medical speculation, rational and naturalistic theories and observations continued to be influential. This is evident in the historical, biographical, medical, legal, and creative literature of the times. Explanations of psychopathological behavior were not confined to demon possession; they embraced a diversity of ideas derived from common sense, classical medicine and philosophy, folklore and religion. In medieval descriptions of mental illness there is most typically an interweaving of statements variously implying natural (biological and psychological) and supernatural causation. It is difficult to assess which was considered most important; it is also difficult to discern what was intended to be taken literally and what metaphorically. This is illustrated in the following extracts. The first has been abbreviated from a letter from Marsilia, Abbess of St. Anne at Rouen, to Bono, Abbot of St. Amand in Flanders:

> In the year 1107, in the village of Lissy, a woman was *so hard beset by the Devil that she was first distressed by various fantastic and malignant cogitations, and then, losing her natural senses,* set all her wits to work to make an end of herself by hanging or drowning or in some other fashion, in the absence of her attendants. This she would have done but that her husband had oftentimes come in suddenly and hindered her. *For she had been deluded by a silly woman, restless and garrulous, who had beset her with her lying stories at home, in the fields, and in the streets, persuading her that her husband hated her and loved another woman with whom he sinned in secret. She, believing these lies even as our mother Eve believed the serpent, fell into a deadly melancholy;* and forgetting God and the Christian faith, she set all her purpose on ending her wretched life by some diabolical artifice. (quoted in Coulton, 1910: p. 128; italics added)

Margery Kempe, in the fourteenth century, described her behavior as a crying mystic—a woman who fell into "crying and roaring" whenever she thought on the sufferings of Christ, something which she did very frequently:

> . . . and as soon as she perceived that she would cry, she would keep it in as much as she might that the people should not hear it, to their annoyance. *For some said that a wicked spirit vexed her; some said it was a sickness; some said she had drunk too much wine;* some wished she was in the harbour; some wished she was on the sea in a bottomless boat; and thus each man as he thought. (quoted in Ross and McLaughlin, 1977; pp. 681-682; italics added)

Rosen (1968) provides a description by Gaspar Ofhuys (1456-1523) of the mental illness of Hugo van der Goes, a Flemish painter of note who had joined the Roode Clooster, near Brussels. "Hugo was struck by a strange disorder of his imagination. He cried out incessantly that he was doomed and condemned to eternal damnation. He would even have injured himself had he not been forcibly prevented . . . " Ofhuys goes on to discuss possible causes for the illness: "Certain people talked of a peculiar case of *frenesis magna,* the great frenzy of the brain. Others, however, believed him to be possessed of an evil spirit . . . In truth, what it really was that ailed him only God can tell." He then suggests it might be a "natural disease" (due to melancholic foods or the consumption of strong wines which heat the body juices) or to have been caused by certain sufferings of the soul like restlessness, sadness, excessive study and anxiety and "Finally, frenzy may be caused by the virulence of noxious juices, if such abound in the body of a man who inclines to that malady." In addition, Ofhuys suggests that the malady had been ordained by God in order to punish and humble van der Goes who had developed too high an opinion of himself because of the esteem in which his art was held. The Prior, Father Thomas, recalling that King Saul's depression had been alleviated when David played his harp for him, ordered music to be played frequently in Hugo's presence, and arranged other entertainments and recreations to divert Hugo from his melancholic obsessions.

Each of the above derives from descriptions written by members of the Christian Church. Although each mentions the possibility of demons disturbing the sufferer's mind, each also details other possible etiologies for the disorder. Punitive exorcisms are not visited upon the mentally disturbed person. The suggestions put forward to explain the disorders are as varied and as insightful, if not more so, as those suggested by Herodotus in the case of Cambyses. The extracts do not support the popular assertion that all naturalistic explanations of mental illness had been swept away during the Middle Ages. Progress had not been made, perhaps, but the Middle Ages did not represent a retrogression to demonology and exorcism as the major explanation and treatment for mental illness.

Physicians continued to ply their trade during the Middle Ages, and treatment continued to be based on the venerable Hippocratic-Galenic concepts. The mentally ill often received no treatment, being cared for or not by their families. Some, if they or their family could afford the fees, sought medical treatment. Others were treated by priests; they came voluntarily to the priest for counsel and help; or they were brought to the priest by their relatives, friends or neighbors; or they were referred to the priest by physicians despairing of effecting a cure by "natural" or medical means. We note that if one takes one's malfunctioning automobile to a body-shop, it is likely to be returned with the dents pounded out and a paint job. Medical men treated their patients with drugs and diet and bloodletting. Priests treated their clients with counseling and if necessary, prayers and incantations. According to Rosen (1968), priests on occasion arranged to subsidize pilgrimage to a religious shrine for the mental sufferer, as did the secular authorities at times. In extreme cases, priests resorted to exorcism. The latter was used primarily it would appear in those cases where all else had failed and the presenting symptoms were a bewildering array of convulsions, local paralyses, garbled incoherent speech, and so on. And perhaps exorcism worked, at least occasionally. It is reported that similar symptoms responded dramatically to the equally bizarre ministrations of Mesmer some centuries later.

Legal Measures

During the Middle Ages, as throughout recorded history, laws were devised to minimize the social impact of mental disturbance. In Norway, in the thirteenth century, there was compulsory boarding out for the poor and mentally ill. Swedish county laws stipulated that the insane be supervised by their sane relatives; the relatives were liable to fines if their charges eluded supervision. These laws also provided for the imprisonment of insane persons likely to injure themselves or others. Legislation in Sweden in the thirteenth century assigned guardians to protect and conserve the property of persons deemed mentally irresponsible. Indeed, mental disorders were called "surveillance diseases" in old Icelandic laws.

R. Neugebauer (1978) draws attention to the extensive legislation enacted in medieval England to protect the property and civil rights of the mentally ill and to provide care for them. The *Prerogative Regis* dating from the thirteenth century, decreed that the king should be custodian of the lands belonging to "natural fools," ultimately rendering the profits therefrom to the rightful heirs; the lands of persons considered "non compos mentis" were to be conserved and returned if the property owners should recover. It is clear here that a distinction was made between persons suffering from congenital subnormality—i.e., natural fools, and those who developed a psychological disturbance after birth—non compos mentis; the former were assumed to be incurable, whereas recovery was considered possible for the latter. Persons thought to be mentally deranged were examined before a jury of 12 or more individuals, who used in their inquiry common sense measures not dissimilar to many used still. Orientation, memory, and ability to perform simple intellectual tasks were assessed. Neugebauer cites from such trials examples of psychiatric disturbance being assigned to organic and to psychological causes; e.g., to a blow on the head (in 1291), to fear of the father (in 1366), to a fever (in 1490).

The Renaissance Through the Seventeenth Century

Scientific progress had already begun to falter before the disintegration of the Roman Empire and it had stagnated by the time the Christian Church began to establish cultural and religious control over Western Europe. During the middle ages, educational institutions were evolved by the Church to meet the needs of religion and the Church controlled the administration and regulated the teaching in the universities as these were founded. The Church viewed earthly life as a preparation for the life beyond; intellectual fervor was focused overwhelmingly on the health of the soul. Interest in the welfare of the body and the improvement of earthly life was distinctly secondary. The emphasis was on revelation, not observation. Scientific analysis and synthesis was incompatible with the authoritarian and conservative attitudes of the Church. New general constructs about the nature of life almost inevitably would conflict with Church dogma. In such an atmosphere there could be little of the vigorous interchange of differences of opinion essential to the growth of science. Furthermore, books were very limited in number and availability until sometime after printing was developed in the fifteenth century. It is easy to underestimate the implications of the fact that until the latter part of the fourteenth century, paper was little known in Europe and although the copying of books had begun as a branch of trade in the fourteenth century they were laboriously copied by hand. Students attended universities not to read books but to hear them; early teaching consisted in large measure of lecturers reading copies of ancient books aloud to students.

All this was to change, gradually at first, but accelerating in the fifteenth and sixteenth centuries. Increasingly, dissent with the established Church was to lead on one hand to alternative religious establishments; on the other, it contributed to the increasing secularization and individualization of thought and action which came to characterize the Renaissance and after. Technological improvements and innovations made possible dramatic advances in all manner of human endeavor. The technology of printing created opportunities for authorship and the cross-fertilization of ideas and discoveries on a scale never before realizable. The increasing use of the vernacular hastened this process. The revival of interest in Classical learning led to the rendering of fresh and accurate translations of Greek and Roman books and stimulated new evaluation of their contents. There was a burgeoning of interest in exploration and speculation of all kinds and medicine, like other fields of inquiry, profited.

Patterns of treatment accorded the insane, as in previous centuries, varied with time, place, economic resources, and custom, and ranged from fear and hostility to indifference to compassion. The poor, helpless, and sick including the mentally ill were often exposed to hardship occasioned by cruelty, abuse, and neglect, but there were also attempts to understand the problems and to deal with these constructively and humanely. With the rise of local governments, civil authorities took increasing responsibility for the welfare of the populace. Hospitals gradually passed from ecclesiastical to municipal control. For example, Henry VIII handed the Hospital of St. Mary of Bethlehem over to the city of London in 1547 to be used exclusively to house lunatics. The Act of 1601 in England stipulated that County Justices should nominate a small number (two to four) of householders in each parish, who in cooperation with the local Churchwarden would serve as Overseers of the Poor, putting the unemployed to work and raising money by taxation for the relief of those who could not work. This act consolidated a number of separate measures which had been enacted over previous years in attempts to solve the problems created by increasing numbers of unemployed and indigent people. Begging and vagrancy had posed increasing problems for communities—the numbers had become oppressive and many of the beggars, it was complained, were aggressive and threatening. Legislation was passed to control vagrancy and begging. The insane were no longer to be "truncated to goe abegging." Instead, all unemployable paupers, including the insane, were to be given relief through municipal and county authorities, and these included the Idiots, Lunaticks, Blind, Lame, etc. as well as orphans too young to work and the aged and decrepit. Because local parishes were responsible for the care of their own indigent members, the insane who were strangers to a community were often returned to the town from which they had come, at public expense. In practice authorities avoided action except when the paupers had no relatives to turn to or when the safety of the community was threatened by violent behavior. Many early institutions which housed the insane included the sick, crippled, blind, incurables of various sorts, "debauched girls" and prostitutes, the aged. With minimal provision for special needs, these institutions perpetuated rather than solved social problems.

When individuals judged to be insane had property but appeared unable to manage it effectively, guardians were appointed. As in the past, attempts were made to improve on the solutions to the legal problems posed by the mentally ill; Neaman (1975) has summarized the legal enactments dealing with insanity as characteristically balancing protection, privilege, and deprivation.

A recently published book by MacDonald (1981) presents an analysis of a series of case histories written between 1597 and 1634 by the Reverend Richard Napier, an astrologer, alchemist, Anglican divine, and parson of a parish in rural Buckinghamshire, England. Although he did not hold a medical degree, he was a medical practitioner—not unusual in England at the time. The casebooks detail 60,000 consultations. Napier's clients came from all but the poorest quarter of the population living near him. MacDonald concluded from his analysis of these records that only 5% of Napier's patients presented mental as distinct from bodily symptoms—which suggests that the criteria for seeking help for psychological suffering was much more stringent then than now. The patients with mental problems fall into two groups; those who presented a danger to others or who were so incoherent and disordered as to be unable to care for themselves, and those suffering from melancholia. Only a very few were defined by Napier as "mad"—as lacking all capacity to reason; only 20 of 2039 patients with mental symptoms who were seen by Napier had ever been chained or beaten—which puts the allegation that the mentally ill were routinely abused and mistreated into some doubt. Napier's treatments, as we would expect, were eclectic; he used medicines based on Galenic theory, prayers, magical amulets—and doubtlessly a good deal of pastoral counseling. He assigned the causes of the mental disturbances to marital problems, frustrated love, jealously, fear, bereavement, economic problems, and the like. Many of his patients thought themselves bewitched, indicating that the general population seriously considered the supernatural as a cause of their afflictions.

Inquiry into the genesis of psychopathology continued to be limited to occasional theological and philosophical speculation, and to empirical observation—events that occurred in some kind of conjunction with the pathology were taken to be causal. Explanations were often a colorful blend of plausible conjecture and fancy.

Unfettered by requirements of concensus and verification, Renaissance writers indiscriminately ascribed the genesis of mental illness to a virtually encyclopedic list of antecedents. The pages of Robert Burton's *Anatomy of Melancholy*, first published in 1621, present a breathtaking compendium of precursors of melancholy. Burton, quoting Greek, Roman, Arabic, and contemporary authors, in addition to his own observations, says:

> General causes are either supernatural or natural. Supernatural are from God and His angels, or by God's permission from the devil and his ministers (p. 178) . . . Natural causes are either primary and universal, or secondary and more particular. Primary causes are the heavens, planets, stars, etc. by their influence (p. 206) . . . Secondary peculiar causes . . . are either . . . inward, innate, inbred; or else outward and adventitious, which happen to us after we are born (p. 210) . . . Amongst these passions and irksome accidents, unfortunate marriage may be ranked . . . Parents many times disquiet their children, and they their parents (pp. 368-9) . . . others are as much tortured to see themselves rejected, contemned, scorned, disabled, diffamed, detracted, undervalued, or "left behind their fellows" . . . loss of liberty which made Brutus venture his life, Cato kill himself, and Tully complain (p. 370) . . . Many men catch this malady by eating certain meats, herbs, roots, at unawares (p. 372) . . . But the most immediate symptoms proceed from the temperature itself and the organical parts, as head, liver, spleen, meseraic veins, heart, womb, stomach, etc. and most especially from distemperature of spirits . . . or from the four humours in those seats, whether they be hot or cold, natural, unnatural, innate or adventitious, intended or remitted, simple, or mixed. (p. 398)

Theophrastus Bombast von Hohenheim (1493-1541) typified the iconoclasm and spirit of free inquiry of the Renaissance. He took the name Paracelsus to signify his superiority to Celsus, the noted first-century medical writer whose *De medicina*, one of the first medical books printed (1478), had become the most popular medical textbook of the Renaissance. Paracelsus fulminated against traditional Galenic concepts and dramatized his antipathy to orthodox medical practices by publicly burning the *Canon* of Avicenna in the public square of Basel. His own theories combined alchemical, astrological, and biological speculation. He viewed disease as a process of deviation from health resulting in metabolic disturbance and treatable through drugs and chemical compounds. He wrote on the topic of insanity and described causes as various as the malign influence of the moon, spiritual separation from God, sin, intestinal worms, retained feces, poor diet, excessive drink. He is credited with originating concepts seminal to the development of modern biochemistry, but his speculations on insanity cannot be regarded as having materially advanced the understanding of psychopathology. Nor can they be considered an improvement on those of Celsus, who, although he advocated resorting to punishment on occasion, recommended such reasonable treatments for the insane as rest, occupational therapies, distraction, emotional support and encouragement, music, diet, and drug therapies.

Medical thought continued to be dominated by the theory that human ailments were caused by imbalances of the four humors. Thomas Nashe, writing in the late 1500s, gives us a picturesquely compelling description of this supposed etiology of madness:

> So this slimy melancholy humor, still thickening as it stands still, engendreth many misshapen objects in our imaginations . . . so from the fuming melancholy of our spleen mounteth that hot matter into the higher region of the brain, whereof many fearful visions are framed . . . Herein specially consisteth our senses defect and abuses, that those organical parts, which to the mind are ordained ambassadors, do not their message as they ought, but by some misdiet or misgovernment being distempered, fail in their report and deliver up nothing but lies and fables. (Nashe, in Wells [ed.], 1964)

The general understanding of the public that psychopathology could have many different kinds of causes, including that of dynamic response to stress and conflict, is illustrated in Shakespeare's plays. Shakespeare's audiences had no difficulty understanding that Lear had been driven mad by the rejection of his daughters once he had divided his kingdom amongst them; when he says "I am a very foolish, fond old man, fourscore and upward, not an hour more or less; and, to deal plainly, I fear I am not in my perfect mind" (IV, vii, 60) lack of official psychiatry did not prevent comprehension of his plight. Lady Macbeth's deranged state is clearly presented as eventuating from guilt over the murder she had done: "Canst thou not minister to a mind diseased, Pluck from the memory a rooted sorrow, Raze out the written troubles of the brain, And with some sweet oblivious antidote Cleanse the stuffed bosom of that perilous stuff Which weighs upon the heart?'' (V, iii, 40) is written with as much insight and perhaps more compassion than many commentaries on case histories today. Hamlet still stands as a case history exemplar for illustration of psychogenic causation of madness.

Conceptions of psychological disturbance change slowly. The seventeenth century was to see the growth of ideas that would, in due course, lead to scientific formulations of mental illness. These changing conceptions came into being in a climate of criticism of the old ideas.

Changing Conceptions of Mental Illness

Physicians, by and large, continued the application of Galenic principles to the diagnosis and treatment of mental illness. Supernatural explanations of disordered behavior were advanced mainly when the behavior in question seemed not to be amenable to understanding with more conventional medical concepts.

The Belgian physician, Weyer (1515-1588), argued in his major work, *De Praestigiis Demonum* (1563), that possession by the devil was the source of many disorders, but that the devil was particularly able to work his will on the old, the melancholic, the demented, the physically ill, and children. Here we see the blend of theological supposition and empirical observation that was to move towards emphasis upon empirics in the century to follow.

This mixture persisted long after in popular thought but by the 1600s medical dissertations began to issue from the universities of Europe attaching demonological and irrational residues in medical thinking. Diethelm (1971) provides an extensive review of this period in medical history, from which we can examine selected examples.

Rhenanus submitted a dissertation to the University of Marburg, on the topic of lycanthropy. Lycanthropy is a disorder wherein the patient is believed to change into a wolf during the hours of darkness—a tendency recently exploited by the makers of cinematic ''horror'' productions. Wolves and wild dogs were realistically feared by those who dwelt near forests in medieval times and it is not surprising that the European folklore of the time evolved the superstition that some of these wolves were human beings transformed into werewolves by the power of evil magic. ''Schizophrenic and paranoid patients'' (according to Diethelm's post-hoc diagnosis) ''believing that they had been changed into dogs or wolves, imitated the behavior of these animals, leaving their homes at night and going about the city, walking on all fours and howling like a wolf until dawn. They were said to visit cemeteries, breaking into graves and stealing bodies, which they carried around on their shoulders. These patients were described as having a pallid complexion, dry and hollow eyes, showed an extraordinary thirst and had sores on their shins caused by their frequent falls. Some of them bit people, like a dog . . .'' (Diethelm, 1971; pp. 132-133)

Rhenanus considered these persons to be delusional and rejected the notion that there was any possibility that such transformations could occur, magically or otherwise. He did, however, comment that if the person appeared as a wolf to others this happened through the agency of the devil, who distorted the perceptions of men.

A similar mixture of scientific skepticism with residual acceptance of some demonology, is to be found in the work of Buching at Halle, Germany. He conceded the power of the devil to influence men's bodies and minds through the elements, particularly via the air. This influence, however, was regarded as moderated by more mundane factors such as food and drink. "It is possible for a person's diet to predispose him to vulnerability to diabolical influence, especially if it creates melancholy. Southern Europeans drink wine and cultivate lively interests which keep melancholy away, and among them one rarely hears of a concern with witches, while Northern Europeans drink beer and eat coarse food. Among them tales of ghosts and demons abound" (quoted by Diethelm, 1971; p. 134). Buching distinguished between those diseases in which the devil played a part and those in which a purely natural explanation was appropriate. Demonic etiology was assumed when the patient spoke in languages of which he had no prior knowledge, displayed unnatural strength, vomited foreign objects such as keys, or had convulsions with no prior symptoms.

Medical writings of the seventeenth century examined many of the popular folk medicine practices of the day, including the use of amulets, love potions, and the like. Some writers now began to suggest that these potions or "philtres" might work their results either because of actual chemical components, often dangerous, or through the imagination of the user—i.e. the "placebo effect."

The Evolution of Medical Empiricism

Medicine of the seventeenth century was to be increasingly influenced by "empiricism." In the twentieth century, the term *empirical* has a generally positive connotation, while the term *theoretical* may conjure up associations of impractical activities of a purely academic nature. During the seventeenth and eighteenth centuries, the situation was almost exactly the opposite. Medical practitioners were of two kinds. One group consisted of people who possessed the degree Doctor of Medicine, largely trained in Galenic traditions; the other consisted of barber-surgeons, apothecaries, and other semi-trained or untrained individuals with an everyday working knowledge of medical practice. To become a Doctor of Medicine in Great Britain required only that the aspirant be a graduate of Oxford or Cambridge University and have delivered either three written or six spoken lectures on one of the books of Galen. No evidence was demanded that the newly qualified physician could amputate a limb, deliver a baby, or stitch up a wound. These latter activities were undertaken by barbers, midwives, and others who had learned their "trade" as apprentices or had simply set up in business for themselves.

Medical practitioners who did not know Galen but did know practical techniques were often referred to contemptuously as "mere empiricks." The barber who knew how to bleed a patient but did not know the theoretical propositions upon which this practice was based was regarded as much inferior to the university graduate who knew the significance of blood in the four-humor scheme, but had never bled a patient.

It was against this prejudice that empirical curiosity had to develop. Galenic treatments were based upon traditional principles which included the regulation of air, food, drink, rest and exercise, sleep and waking, excretion and retention, and mental affections. This was sought through such devices as keeping air moist with vases of water, pleasant through the scent of flowers, providing chicken broth and a diet low in salt, massage and warm baths, the use of syrup of poppies or opium for the induction of sleep, and the avoidance of matter that could provoke unpleasant emotions. Particular importance was attached to the use of bleeding, it being felt that this served to draw off unhealthy humors from the brain and heart. Also highly regarded were other methods designed to "evacuate" undesirable humors. The famed Hellebore of the ancient Greeks is a powerful purgative. Burton's 1621 *Anatomy of Melancholy* recommended tobacco as suitable to produce a healthy vomit. . . "Divine, rare, super-excellent tobacco . . . a sovereign remedy to all diseases. A good vomit, I confess, if it be well qualified, opportunely taken, and medicinally used." Other substances employed to the same effect included senna, aloes, and (somewhat plausibly) half-boiled cabbage.

Empirical medicine was to become increasingly important. Much of the reason for this lay in the discoveries made in anatomy and physiology, discoveries revealing the inadequacy of the humoral theory of bodily function. Harvey's discovery of the circulation of the blood in 1628, Galvani's demonstration of the electrical properties of the nervous system, Willis's atlas of the anatomy of the nervous system, all formed a part of the general invigoration of natural science that was evident in the seventeenth century and thereafter.

We can make at least one generalization about theories of psychopathology throughout the centuries reviewed here: they were eclectic. Possibly no one believed in any one single theory of the cause of psychopathology. This hectic eclecticism was to be replaced, in the coming years, with the belief that scientific investigation would reveal *the* cause of the disorder and thus the nostrum or panacea that could cure or prevent it.

In his book *Principia* published in 1687, Sir Isaac Newton unified disparate terrestrial and heavenly phenomena and reduced the complexity of the intricate patterns of motion of the celestial bodies to the operation of his universal law of attraction, a law simple enough in prinicple to be understood by most educated people (if they didn't bother with the mathematics!). Alexander Pope put it this way: "Nature and nature's laws lay hid in night: God said, Let Newton Be! and all was light." After Newton, philosophers and scientists in the emerging specialities were to look for unifying explanatory concepts. Newton's success engendered the hope amongst physicians and psychologists that the scientific approach would finally reveal a fundamental law of psychology that would explain all the diverse phenomena of human behavior, normal or otherwise.

REFERENCES

Allderidge, P. Hospitals, madhouses and asylums: cycles in the care of the insane. *British Journal of Psychiatry*, 1979, 134, 321–334.

Altrocchi, J. *Abnormal Behavior*. New York: Harcourt Brace Jovanovich, Inc., 1980.

Aubrey, J. *Aubrey's Brief Lives*. Reprint, Harmondsworth: Penguin, 1972.

Benton, J. F. (Ed) *Self and Society in Medieval France—The Memoirs of Abbot Guibert of Nogent (1064?–c. 1125)*. New York: Harper & Row, 1970.

Boyer, P., & Nissenbaum, S. *Salem Possessed. The Social Origins of Witchcraft*. Cambridge, Ma.: Harvard U. Press, 1974.

Bucknill, J. C. *Unsoundness of Mind in Relation to Criminal Insanity*. London: Longmans Green, 1854.

Burton, R. *Anatomy of Melancholy*. (Reprint edition) New York: Random House, 1977.

Celsus *De Medicina I Books I-IV* (Trans. W. G. Spencer) Cambridge, Ma.: Harvard U. Press, 1971.

Cohn, N. *Europe's Inner Demons*. New York: Basic Books, Inc., 1975.

Coulton, G. G. *Life in the Middle Ages*. New York: MacMillan, 1910.

Coulton, G. G. *Medieval Panorama, Vol. II. The Horizon of Thought*. London: Collins, 1961.

Currie, E. P. Crimes without criminals—Witchcraft and its control in renaissance Europe. *Law and Society Review*, 1968, 3, 1–26.

Diethelm, O. *Medical Dissertations of Psychiatric Interest Printed before 1750*. Basel: Karger, 1971.

Ducey, C., & Simon, B. Ancient Greece and Rome. In J. G. Howells (Ed.), *World History of Psychiatry*. London: Balliére Tindall, 1975.

Encyclopaedia Britannica, Vol. III. Edinburgh: A. Bell & McFarquhar, 1768.

Foucault, M. *Madness and Civilization*. New York: American Library, 1967.

Hill, C. *Change and Continuity in 17th Century England*. Cambridge, Ma.: Harvard University Press, 1976.

Hunter, R. & Macalpine, I. *Three Hundred Years of Psychiatry 1535-1860*. London: Oxford University Press, 1963.

Herodotus *The Histories Book III*. (Reprint edition) A. D. Godley (Ed.). New York: Putnam, 1921.

Kleinmuntz, B. *Essentials of Abnormal Psychology, 2nd Ed*. San Francisco: Harper & Row, 1980.

Lloyd, G. E. R. (Ed.) *Hippocratic Writings*. Harmondsworth: Penguin, 1978.

Page, J. D. *Psychopathology*. Chicago: Aldine, 1971.

Plato *Timaeus and Critias*. (Reprint edition). Harmondsworth: Penguin, 1979.

MacDonald, M. *Mystical Bedlam—Madness, Anxiety and Healing in Seventeenth-Century England*. Cambridge University Press, 1981.

Maher, W. B. & Maher, B. A. The ship of fools—stultifera navis or ignis fatuus? *American Psychologist*, 1982, 37, 756–761.

Meyer, S. Analysis of a single dream as a means of unearthing the genesis of psychopathic affections. *Journal of Abnormal Psychology* 1915-1916, (10), 19–31.

Miller, L. Israel and the Jews. In J. G. Howells (Ed.), *World History of Psychiatry*. London: Bailliére Tindall, 1975.

Neaman, J. S. *Suggestion of the Devil*. Garden City, N.Y.: Anchor Books, 1975.

Neugebauer, R. Treatment of the mentally ill in medieval and early modern England: A reappraisal. *Journal of the History of the Behavioral Sciences*, 1978, 14, 158–169.

Rasmussen, H. (Ed.) *Prehistoric Dane*. Copenhagen: Fabrik Automatic, 1956.

Rosen, G. *Madness in Society*. London: Routledge & Kegan Paul, 1968.

Ross, J. B. & McLaughlin, M. M. (Eds.) *The Portable Medieval Reader*. Harmondsworth: Penguin, 1978.

Schoeneman, T. J. The role of mental illness in the European witchhunts of the sixteenth and seventeenth centuries: An assessment. *Journal of the History of the Behavioral Sciences*, 1977, 13, 337–351.

Sedgwick, P. *Psychopolitics*. New York: Harper & Row, 1982.

Spanos, N. P. Witchcraft in histories of psychiatry: A critical analysis and an alternative conceptualization. *Psychological Bulletin*, 1978, 85, 417–439.

Sturlnson, S. *Heimskringla: Saga of the Norse Kings* (Trans. S. Laing). London: Dent, 1961.

Suinn, R. M. *Fundamentals of Behavior Pathology, 2nd Ed.* New York: Wiley & Sons, Inc., 1975.

Trevor-Roper, H. R. *The European Witch-Craze of the 16th and 17th Centuries*. Harmondsworth: Penguin, 1967.

Ullman, L., & Krasner, L. *A Psychological Approach to Abnormal Behavior, 2nd ed.* Englewood, N. J.: Prentice-Hall, Inc., 1975.

Zax, M. & Cowen, E. L. *Abnormal Psychology (2nd ed.)* New York: Holt, Rinehart & Winston, 1976.

Ziegler, P. *The Black Death*. London: Collins, 1969.

Zilboorg, G. & Henry, G. W. *A History of Medical Psychology*. New York: Norton, 1941.

Zilboorg, G. *The Medical Man and the Witch during the Renaissance*. Baltimore: John Hopkins University Press, 1935.

Wells, S. (Ed.) *Thomas Nashe—Selected Works*. Cambridge, Ma.: Harvard University Press, 1964.

Wilkinson, R. G. Techniques of ancient skull surgery. *Natural History*, 1975, 84, No. 8, 94–101.

9 Psychopathology: II. From the Eighteenth Century to Modern Times

Brendan A. Maher
Winifred B. Maher
Harvard University

In this chapter we take up the developments that affected conceptions and treatment of the mentally ill beginning with the eighteenth century. Needless to say patterns of historical change do not accommodate themselves neatly to the turn of the centuries, and thus our boundaries can be only approximate. However, the eighteenth century does encompass the beginning of major changes in the history of Western civilization, changes that affected views of man and set the groundwork for philosophies and practices that are still with us. Two of the most important themes are those generally known as the Age of Enlightenment, and the Industrial Revoluation.

THE AGE OF ENLIGHTENMENT

By the middle of the eighteenth century there had become evident in European thought a rising enthusiasm for reason, empirical knowledge, and the critical examination of society on these bases. Many who took this approach saw themselves in opposition to the doctrines and influence of the Christian churches. While it is true that vigorous debates ensued between those who supported the ecclesiastical definitions of truth and those who saw truth as residing in the empirical method, the confrontation was much more complex than that. Astronomical observation, for example, was much advanced by Jesuit scientists and some of those who promoted the new enlightenment hoped to find in it the basis of a natural religion.

The leaders of this new movement were to be found everywhere in Europe, but particular importance attached to a group of French writers known as the "philosophes." Their thinking led them—and much of Europe with them—to adopt an intellectual cultural style that possessed many threads. One was the critical examination of Christian belief and practice, an examination that was to lead to a thorough rejection of much of it, and an accompanying admiration for the achievements of classical antiquity that Christianity had replaced. Another and related theme was the critical examination of those social and political institutions under which Europeans lived and which also took their roots from previous religious justifications. This trend was given great impetus by the reports of travelers to distant lands and their observations about the vast differences between one culture and another with regard to their institutions, customs, and beliefs. Comparisons are the basis of scientific curiosity and it was from these that the beginnings of a genuine social science arose to replace the authority of divine revelation.

Prominent contributors to this movement were such French philosophes as Voltaire, Montesquieu, Diderot, Rousseau, while from Britain came the philosophers Hume and Locke, the writer and lexicographer Samuel Johnson, and others. As it is the work of the British group that had the most immediate impact upon psychology we must make more than a passing mention of their contributions.

John Locke belongs chronologically to the seventeenth century, his life extending from 1632 to 1704, but the impact of his ideas becomes most evident in the century following his death. The key work was his *Essay on Human Understanding* which appeared in 1690. A detailed account of this work is beyond the scope of the present chapter but we may examine the main thrust of Locke's ideas. Locke proposed that human knowledge—the content of the mind—consisted only of material that had already been experienced by the individual. Two processes were important in the development of knowledge: One was the process of direct sensation, such as seeing, hearing, etc.; the other was an inner process of reflection that organized and examined the received sensations. Reflection could only operate with what had been received. There were no innate ideas and, at the beginning of life, the mind was as a blank slate, or *tabula rasa*. His position was known as *empiricism* and his psychology was *associationism*, which is to say that ideas became formed by the association of experiences.

Locke's work rejects the notion that truths can come from authority, or that certain ideas are an inborn and inevitable part of human nature. As such his influence was clearly antithetical to revealed religious truths; it also implied that the environment ultimately determined the nature of a man's mind. Ideas were formed by experience and, hence, could be reformed by different kinds of experience. Psychological disturbances could thus be ascribed, in at least some cases, to the influence of prior experience creating harmful ideas, which, in turn, affected behavior.

Half a century later the British philosopher David Hume was to dedicate to Locke, amongst others, his work *A Treatise on Human Nature*. Hume was a complete empiricist, repeating many of Locke's views about the nature of ideas, but adding the further assertion that man was constituted in such a fashion as to pursue his own interests. Society thus arose from the composition of the individual interests of its members, and this formed the basis of moral principles. The separation of moral and ethical principles from their previous religious foundation as absolute, and their replacement upon a basis of empirical social science provided the grounds upon which the solution of real social problems such as poverty, crime, and madness could be achieved through scientific social arrangements. As we shall shortly see, these social problems were reaching proportions that defied management by traditional means. Empirical social science was not only intellectually attractive, it appeared to offer a practical solution to new and intractable problems of a society moving towards an industrial age. The empiricism of the philosophers and new social scientists was paralleled by an increasingly triumphant empiricism in the natural sciences, and in medicine. Here the discoveries of the seventeenth century, including Harvey's demonstrations of the circulation of the blood, Galvani's discoveries of the electrical properties of the nervous system, Willis's atlas of the anatomy of the nervous system, gave impetus to a more empirical approach. Techniques of surgery and medical care increased also. The British Lying-In Hospital, for example, reported a newborn mortality rate of 1 baby in 15 in 1759 but a rate of 1 in 118 in 1799. Epidemics of typhoid and small pox had largely disappeared and the value of empirical practices was more and more obvious.

THE INDUSTRIAL REVOLUTION

In the Western world the eighteenth century saw the beginnings of the great changes in society to be known later as the *Industrial Revolution*. For many historians, this epoch began in Lancashire, England in 1764 when James Hargreaves invented the spinning jenny—a crude early machine which enabled one worker to spin as much yarn as 16 had done before. This invention, and the myriad others that followed, wrought profound changes in the economic and social basis of Western society. These changes are still going on.

Social Effects of the Industrial Revolution

Among these changes were the creation of great individual wealth in the industrialized nations, increasing optimism about the power of applied science to solve the problems of human material want, the destruction of feudal social arrangements, and the growth of the great cities. In these cities arose a mass of urban poor, living in conditions of degradation and misery and lacking a familiar social fabric within which to solve their difficulties. Problems that had been handled at the local or parish level needed a new approach which led to the growth of a central bureaucracy and large institutions. Poverty amongst the employed as well as the indigent led to popular reform movements aimed at a more equitable distribution of political and economic power and bringing in their train a re-awakened awareness of the plight of all those who stood in want of simple sustenance and elementary protection.

Contributing to this panorama of wealth and misery were the many major wars waged by powers bent on extending their territorial possessions and upon acquiring a monopoly of world trade. The demands of warfare accelerated the progress of technology, and increased the pace of the industrial revolution. They culminated, as the century came to a close, in the French Revolution and the Napoleonic wars. In their wake came changes in the Western world and European empires that included all facets of social life.

During this century we find that ideas about the causes of mental illness were affected by several influences. These were the development of medical eclecticism, the rise of philosophical conceptions of natural law, the growth of movements to reform the lot of the individual, and the increasing pressure for the government to solve social problems through institutional means.

Medical Eclecticism

As we have already seen, eighteenth-century medicine was much influenced by the classic Hippocratic-Galenic teachings. Some of the treatments could even be found in occasional use by rural physicians up to the middle of the nineteenth century. An edition of Burton's *Anatomy of Melancholy* was published for medical use as late as 1821.

There was, however, a growing trend towards a re-evaluation of the causes of illness generally, including mental illness. Although handicapped by the lack of an adequate base of sciences relevant to medicine, this trend was characterized by a search for causes of psychological disturbance in factors in the environment and from bodily malfunctions more specific than the humoral theory provided.

A good example is to be found in the work of the British physician, George Cheyne who, in 1753, published his classic *The English Malady: or a Treatise of Nervous Diseases of All Kinds*. In this he dealt extensively with depression. Depression, or melancholia as it was termed, was regarded as a disorder peculiarly common to Britain. Observers noted an unusually high suicide rate amongst the English. One satirical advertisement appeared in *Gentleman's Magazine* of 1755 advising ". . . noblemen, gentlemen and others who . . . have incurred such reflections as render life intolerable" to try a new preparation called Stygian Spirit, "only one guinea a phial and free to deserving cases" which would enable them to commit suicide even while in company without distressing or inconveniencing those around them!

Cheyne attributed illness to bad air, climate, and the difficulties of living in overgrown and overpopulated cities. Of London, he wrote

> The infinite number of fires, sulphurous and bituminous, the vast expanse of tallow and foetid oil in candles and lamps . . . the clouds of stinking breaths and perspira-

tions, not to mention the ordure of so many diseased, both intelligent and unintelligent animals, the crowded churches, churchyards and burying-places, with putrified bodies, the stinking butcherhouses, stables, dunghills, etc. and the necessary stagnation, fermentation, and mixture of such variety of all kinds of atoms are more than sufficient to putrefy, poison and infect the air twenty miles around . . . which in time, must alter, weaken, destroy the healthiest constitutions of men. (quoted in Harms, 1967; p. 59–60)

In the year that Hargreaves invented the spinning jenny, Robert Whytt, President of the Royal College of Physicians in Edinburgh, published his *Observations on the Nature, Causes, and Cure of those Diseases which have been commonly called Nervous, Hypochondriac or Hysteric.* In this work he comments about those disorders that ". . . have lately been treated under the names flatulent, spasmodic, hypochondriac, or hysteric. Of late, they have also got the name of nervous; which application having been commonly given to many symptoms seemingly different, and very obscure in their nature, has often made it to be said, that physicians have bestowed the character of nervous on all those disorders whose nature and cause they were ignorant of" (quoted in Harms, 1967; p. 62). He suggested that a "diminution of the moving power of the nerves" caused some disorders, producing a debility of the whole body. A complete loss of this power would lead, he felt, to partial or complete palsy.

Another departure from prior tradition is to be seen in the work of F. C. G. Scheidemantel. His book, *The Passions as a Means of Cure,* is the first known attempt to provide a systematic text in the field of psychosomatic medicine. In it, Scheidemantel traces the effects of emotions on bodily functions including skin temperature, the vascular system, and the nervous system generally. He wrote: "The moment a person becomes scared his arms and legs tend to become rigid. Like lightning a sensation strikes the pit of the heart, one has a feeling that the thorax is too tight. One gets pale and cold; a chill runs through the body. The skin of the entire body contracts and gooseflesh develops. The eyes seem paralyzed and unable to move. The scared person . . . is unable to make a decision and therefore unable to escape . . . has a rapid, short and irregular pulse" (quoted in Harms, 1967; p. 48). As a description of bodily changes in emotion this is still valid. While we now have devices to measure skin temperature and pulse rate, the underlying pattern that they reflect is much as Scheidemantel presented it. He also emphasized the role of childhood experiences of insecurity and guilt in generating later vulnerability to psychosomatic disease, particularly when combined with a melancholic temperament.

Electrical Treatment

A new trend was developing in the latter part of the eighteenth century that, from primtive beginnings, was to persist in one form or another to the present day. This was the application of electricity to the treatment of bodily and mental ills of all kinds. To understand the origins of this we must consider briefly the enormous expansion of popular interest in all kinds of science during that period. Newton had propounded the principles of gravity—the attraction of one physical body to another; gravity had been overcome with the gas-filled balloons of the Frenchmen, the Charlières and Montgolfières; the experiments of Franklin had inspired an interest in such devices as lightning rods, and man was becoming fascinated by this wonderful and invisible force that seemed to fill the universe and affect everything. Galvani had demonstrated the role of electrical impulses in the activation of muscles and hence, by implication, in all behavior. From all of this two propositions seemed to emerge. One was that invisible electrical forces were all around us and had great power to affect material bodies; the other was that human health and behavior were particularly controlled by these electrical forces.

From these propositions it was not surprising that attempts were made to apply electrical current directly to diseased limbs or organs in the hope of curing them. Darnton (1968) describes the situation as follows: "Some scientists reported that electric charges made plants grow faster and that electric eels cured gout. (After being thrown daily into a tub of water containing a large electric eel, a boy recovered from an irregularity in the use of his limbs. The experimenters did not record whatever shocks his psyche received.)" In 1750, Benjamin Franklin had applied electric current to the treatment of what appears to have been an hysterical disorder in a young woman and, in France, enthusiastic amateurs of the electrical treatment applied current to chains of people in the belief that electricity acted as a kind of miraculous potion that would cure disease.

In the *Encyclopaedia Britannica,* Volume II, of 1771, we find that Medical Electricity has already found a place as a part of the discussion of electricity: "The first application of electricity to the cure of disease was made by M. Jallabert, professor of philosophy at Geneva, on a locksmith whose right arm had been paralytic for fifteen years. He was brought to M. Jallabert on the 26th of December 1747, and was compleatly cured by the 28th of February 1748. In this interval he was frequently electrified, sparks being taken from the arm, and sometimes the electrical shock sent through it" (p. 484). The success of this case appears to have encouraged others to try electrical treatment for paralyses for the passage goes on to summarize successes with these problems, tetanus, palsy, St. Vitus's dance, deafness (of 17 years' standing), even toothache, headache, and "obstinate obstructions in two young women."

The use of the direct application of electrical current to patients with motor and sensory disorders was to continue for a century and a half from its inception. In the 1890s we find Freud employing electrical treatments and massage to the cure of patients diagnosed as suffering from hysterial disorders, a procedure that he later abandoned as he developed the techniques of psychoanalysis. Electrical treatments retained an appeal to the popular imagination for a long time. In the years between 1900 and 1905, for example, patents were granted for such inventions as "Gessmann's Improved Electric Dry Battery to be used in connection with Hat or Head Bands"—a flexible strip of metal with two insulated electrodes requiring only water to activate it and thus provide the wearer with an electrical "tonic." The patent specifications added that "people who perspire very much need not do this" (Dale & Gray, 1979, p. 88); or, Romain and Anidjah's Improved Electropathic Socks, which had strips of copper and zinc interwoven into the sole, the object being "to provide a means for generating a slight electric current which may be passed through the body," presumably for purposes of general health. (Dale & Gray, 1979, p. 144).

Within hospital settings, the use of quite substantial generating machines for the electrical treatment of patients became evident in the nineteenth century, and will be discussed later in this chapter. At this point it may suffice to note that the magical powers of electricity, the "subtile, invisible fluid" of the early physicists had seized the interest of both scientists and the general public, providing a framework for later applications, and, more dramatically perhaps, the rise of Mesmerism and hypnosis.

Mesmerism

In eighteenth century France, the years that saw the rise of interest in electrical treatment saw the appearance of the technique and movement originated by Anton Mesmer. Mesmer, a Viennese, studied medicine in his native city, writing a dissertation in 1766 entitled "The Influences of the Planets on the Human Body," a work which reflected the influence of a Jesuit professor of astronomy at Vienna, Father Hehl, who had tried out the curative effects of magnets on the bodily illnesses of patients. Theories relating magnets, magic and the supposed influence of the stars had been common in folklore long before Mesmer began writing on the topic. His own theories were rejected and ridiculed by orthodox Viennese medicine, and he left for Paris in 1777. Here, for a while at least, he was an outstanding success. Arriving in Paris in 1778 he announced that he had discovered an extremely fine fluid that existed everywhere, surrounding and entering into all bodies. Mesmer did not claim to have actually seen this fluid but argued that it must exist to account for the manner in which celestial bodies exerted gravitational influence on each other—an influence that could not occur, so he supposed, in a vacuum. The powers of this fluid could be brought to earth through the use of suitable conductors and could be made to enter the bodies of patients with beneficial results for their health. The body was analogous to a magnet, and sickness was due to the presence of some obstacle to the free flow of the magnetic fluid in the patient's body. These obstacles could be overcome by massaging the "poles" of the patient's body. This would restore the free flow of fluid by inducing a convulsion that reflected a magnetic crisis—to be followed by the restoration of a harmonious balance to the person's fluid state—and, incidentally, bringing him into harmony with the total magnetic balance of nature.

Mesmer performed this massaging through a series of passes and manipulations upon the body of the patient. However, the most dramatic procedures that he created included the use of tubs, filled with iron filings, known as *baquets*. Each tub was filled with the filings and with bottled or "mesmerized water," arranged in the form of the spokes of a wheel. From the lid of the tub protruded iron rods which the patients could apply to the sick area of the body. Joined together around the baquet, patients held hands and transmitted the magnetic fluid to each other. All of this took place in clinics designed to increase the likelihood of a crisis.

> Heavy carpets, weird astrological wall decorations and drawn curtains shut him (the patient) off from the outside world and muffled the occasional words, screams and hysterical laughter that broke the habitual heavy silence. Shafts of fluid struck him constantly in the sombre light reflected by strategically placed mirrors. Soft music played on wind instruments, the pianoforte or the glass "harmonica" . . . sent reinforced waves of fluid deep into his soul. Every so often fellow patients collapsed writhing on the floor, and were carried . . . into the crisis room. (Darnton, 1968, p. 8)

There is little doubt that some of his patients were cured of their ailments by these procedures. However, most judges of the matter conclude that the disorders themselves were essentially hysterical, i.e., without organic basis, and that the cures were similar to those achieved by faith-healing and other suggestion techniques both before and since Mesmer's time. However, his activities came to the attention of the authorities and provoked the opposition of French medical circles, as they had in Vienna. A Royal Commission was appointed to inquire into the validity of mesmerism. Its membership was distinguished: four physicians (including a Dr. Guillotin, later to become famous for his lethal invention, and to perish by it himself during the French Revolution) and five members of the Academie of Sciences. These included Lavoisier and Benjamin Franklin. The commission conducted a series of experiments to test the mesmerists' claims and found them to be unsupported. They found that when a woman was informed, falsely, that she was being mesmerized by a mesmerist behind a door she went into a crisis even though there was nobody there. A patient was given five cups of water, one of which had been mesmerized, but she went into convulsions after drinking from one of the other four. These observations and others led the committee to report that Mesmer's fluid did not exist and that the effects of mesmerizing were due entirely to the imaginations of the mesmerized patients. While the committee was observing mesmeric "cures" conducted by one of Mesmer's associates, D'Eslon, Mesmer himself had left for Switzerland and was not present in Paris when the damning report of the committee was published.

The report was not accepted passively by the mesmerists. Deluges of pamphlets, speeches, and other media of attack on the report were issued. The burden of these retorts was that the report was designed to maintain the privileges of the conventional physicians and to prevent the benefits of mesmeric treatment from reaching their patients. Opinion differed widely. Lafayette, for example, was favorably inclined toward mesmerism, and continued to be interested in it even after the report of 1784.

However, in succeeding years the followers of Mesmer tended to drop some of the more flamboyant accouterments of the mesmeric treatment and to emphasize, instead, the altered state of consciousness, or "mesmeric somnambulism" into which their patients fell. Chief amonst the demonstrators of this effect was the Marquis de Puységur. With his brother, he found that upon mesmerizing a shepherd boy on their estate, the latter fell into a seeming sleep and then stood up, walked and talked according to their instructions. In this way the emphasis shifted away from assumptions about animal magnetism to interest in the somnambulistic state and its role in bringing about cures of illness. The modern techniques of hypnosis began to arise and the mesmeric phase gave way to the beginnings of hypnotism. Hypnotism, as a term, did not appear until 1842 when it was introduced by the Scottish physician, James Braid. Until then, terms such as "nervous sleep" or "mesmeric anesthesia" were common.

The full impact of the mesmeric movement upon ideas about madness was not to appear until the nineteenth century, and then in the areas of hysterical and hypochondriacal disorders. Public ideas about the more serious forms of mental illness continued to be influenced by factors somewhat removed from either medicine or the new development in natural science.

Natural Law and the Consequences of Behavior

Philosophical ideas about human society were, in the eighteenth century, affected by the concept of "natural law." According to this view there were certain natural consequences to behavior such that actions long regarded as sinful, such as drinking, gambling, or whoring, naturally led to madness, disease, and poverty. The alcoholic with delirium tremens or the patient in the terminal stages of syphilis-induced paresis could thus be seen as suffering an inevitable and natural outcome of their own behavior. On the other hand, wealth, health, and prosperity came from habits of industry, sobriety, and the like; the rewards were not to be seen as "prizes" given for good behavior, but as natural effects of this behavior.

Nowhere, perhaps, does one see these principles more clearly depicted than in the work of the English engraver-painter, William Hogarth. The same year that saw the appearance of Cheyne's treatise also saw the publication of the first plate of a famous series of engravings by Hogarth, *The Rake's Progress*. Eight scenes portray the degeneration of young Tom Rakewell from his beginnings as a fashionable dandy through his escapades in tavern, gambling house, and brothel until, in the final plate, he ends incarcerated in the Bedlam Hospital in a state of hopeless lunacy. Many psychopathologists have used this plate (see Fig. 9.1) as though it were Hogarth's intention to depict the inhumane conditions in which Bedlam patients lived. This is a debatable conclusion. The main intent seems to be to point up the degraded state to which Rakewell's behavior had brought him.

FIG. 9.1. In this engraving by the British artist William Hogarth, we see a popular representation of madness as the inevitable consequence of the vices engendered by wealth and self-indulgence. The new patient, Tom Rakewell, has just entered the Bethlehem Hospital, London ("Bedlam"), ruined in mind and body by drink, gambling and prostitutes. Attendants are apparently removing the chains used to restrain him on the way to hospital. The purpose of the artist was to present the folly of corruption rather than to criticize the hospital. (National Library of Medicine. Negative 59-236. Artist William Hogarth. Original engraved circa 1735. Plate 8 from an eight-plate series entitled "The Rake's Progress".)

The verses captioned to the picture state: "The headstrong Course of Youth thus run, what Comfort from this darling Son? His rattling Chains with Terror hear, behold Death grappling with Despair. See Him by Thee to Ruin sold, and curse thyself and curse thy Gold." The other inmates shown in the scene represent various forms of lunatic folly. We see a "bishop" with paper mitre and cross, a "king," a left-handed violinist with the sheet music on his head, a blind man looking through a telescope and, perhaps most allegorical of all, a patient trying to cast the compass of the earth and finding it overshadowed by a large British coin.

Hogarth's works reflect an ambivalence about the origins of social problems. On one hand they arise from individual weakness of character and are therefore in the form of natural deserts for folly. Yet, they also arise from the corrupting effects of wealth and position upon society generally. These provide the pitfalls and temptations; it requires strength of will and wise choice to reject the temptations and live the good life. We may regard Hogarth's work as less of a reliable documentary account of the treatment of the mentally ill than as an index of the popular anxieties that were accompanying the drastic reshaping of English life towards an urban mass form.

There is little doubt that conditions in Bedlam were grim. They were grim in medical hospitals, in the military and naval services, in the factories, mines and mills, in the poor-houses and prisons, and in the tenements and alleys of the great cities.

The Social Care of the Mentally Ill

By the eighteenth century, in Great Britain and elsewhere, there were a number of hospitals dedicated to the care and treatment of psychological disorders. Bedlam, one of the earliest, was joined in 1751 by the newly opened St. Luke's Hospital in London, which was established by public charity because lunatics were ". . . incapable of providing for themselves and their Families, are not admitted into other Hospitals" and "the Expences necessarily attending the Confinement and other means of Cure, are such as People even in midling Circumstances cannot bear, it generally requiring several Months, and often a whole Year before a Cure is complete" (Allderidge, 1979, p. 329).

Accomodation for mental patients was also built as additions to general medical hospitals. An annex of this kind was built to the Manchester Infirmary in 1766, likewise in Liverpool. The decision to treat the mentally ill in a general medical hospital has been hailed as a conceptual advance in the latter part of the twentieth century. Whether or not it results in better treatment for patients remains to be seen, but it is clear that the idea is more than two centuries old.

Some of the hospitals built at this time exclusively for the care of the mentally ill were placed in rural areas. Some modern behavioral scientists have regarded this as part of a tacit conspiracy to handle the mentally ill as scapegoats, isolating them from society somewhat in the manner of criminals. However, at least some of these hospitals were located away from the cities because of the belief that pure air, exercise, and healthy occupation such as gardening would be beneficial to the inmates. It is possible that an additional reason might have been the more mundane but no more malevolent consideration that land in the country costs less than in the towns.

Many patients were cared for in the various private madhouses that flourished at this time. These originated in the practice of boarding mentally ill individuals in homes where the proprietor was willing, for a fee, to take care of them. British private madhouses were as likely as not to be owned and operated by non-medical persons—frequently clergymen. From contemporary descriptions it is clear that private madhouses ran the gamut from curative to catastrophic. The poet William Cowper was a resident of a private madhouse known as the Collegium Insanorum during the period of a suicidal depression in 1763. Allderidge (1979) reports that Cowper was sufficiently pleased with conditions there that he stayed for a year after he had recovered. When he left he took with him as a servant the attendant who had looked after him during his illness. At the other end of the spectrum was the madhouse of a Mr. Spencer in Wiltshire, England. The conditions of his establishment were described to Parliament in 1815. Part of the accomodation was comprised of six compartments, each 9 feet by 5 feet, opening onto a passage that looked into a dunghill and pigpen. Three of these cells had floors of bare earth, all had bare unplastered walls, there was neither light nor ventilation except when the doors were opened, and the patients were chained to beds consisting of boxes filled with straw.

Dreadful though these conditions were their prevalence does not necessarily indicate a peculiar viciousness in the treatment of the mentally ill. Braudel (1974) tells of the living conditions of the Irish immigrants coming into London about the same time: "They . . . lived ten or twelve to one windowless room and accepted wages well below the general rate as dockers, milkcarriers, labourers at the brick-yards or even lodging house keepers" (p. 436). Peasants living in the countryside of Burgundy he describes as "sleeping on straw . . . with no bed or furniture and separated from the pigsty by a screen" (p. 204–205). Patients housed in windowless cells hard by the pigsty were, unfortunately, sharing the general misery and squalor in which large segments of the poor population of Europe lived. Injustice was distributed impartially to the sane and insane alike.

Many suffering from psychiatric disorders were to be found in the gaols and workhouses of the period, or confined in their homes. We cannot estimate with confidence the relative proportions of those inside institutions and those outside. As in the Middle Ages, a number of the mentally ill wandered as vagrants from place to place. That this was a problem in Great Britain can be seen from the Vagrancy Act passed in 1714 that empowered Justices of the Peace to confine "Persons of little or no Estates, who, by Lunacy, or otherwise, are furiously Mad, and dangerous to be permitted to go abroad." A later act of 1744 also required the parish responsible for the "Lunatic" to bear the expense of curing as well as maintaining the patient during the attack of madness—a recognition of the necessity to provide treatment as well as confinement that has recently been rediscovered in contemporary judicial decisions.

The Beginnings of Reform

Although there were hospitals in which humane care was given to patients as medical thought of the time defined it, the lot of those incarcerated in many of them was desperate in the extreme. The situation has been well put by Jones (1972) writing of the management of the Bedlam Hospital: "They provided care and treatment of a kind when this was otherwise unknown and had no precedents against which to test their methods. An institution for the reception of violent patients can never be wholly a pleasant place, and, however enlightened the policy of the authorities, there will always be patients who suffer extremely through delusions of persecution, depression or squalid habits that defy the most patient and sustained attempts at cleanliness'' (p. 17). She goes on to point out that the policy of these particular authorities was not enlightened, even by eighteenth-century standards. Dr. Thomas Monro, the Superintendent of Bedlam, described the treatment of patients: "Patients are ordered to be bled about the latter end of May, or the beginning of June, according to the weather, and after they have been bled they take vomits once a week for a certain number of weeks; after that we purge the patients. That has been the practice invariably for years; it was handed down to me by my father, and I do not know any better practice'' (Jones, 1972, p. 16).

Conditions and practices such as these were to generate a widespread movement for the reform of the care of the mentally ill throughout Europe generally. A government inquiry in England in 1763 (the year that Hogarth's Tom Rakewell entered Bedlam) had led to an Act of Parliament in 1774 whereby private madhouses were to be regulated and supervised by independent inspectors. It included provision that nobody should be confined to them who was not mentally ill—a provision arising from the not uncommon and notorious practice of incarcerating inconvenient family members, wives, parents, and the like under the pretext of their madness. Medical direction of these establishments was also mandated. Many private citizens took an active part in the campaign for reform of the care of the mentally ill. Daniel Defoe, author of *Robinson Crusoe* was an active participant in these efforts. Dean Swift, best known for his work *Gulliver's Travels*, became one of the Governors of Bedlam. At his death he left most of his wealth to found a "House for Fools and Mad" in Dublin—St. Patrick's Hospital—in 1746.

The Great Reformers: Chiarugi, Pinel, and Tuke

The growing movement towards reform reached dramatic proportions in the second half of the century. Particular importance attaches to the work of the Italian physician, Vincenzo Chiarugi (1759–1820), appointed in 1788 as superintendent of the newly opened *Ospidale di Bonifazio*, a hospital for the mentally ill in Florence. One year later he published regulations for the conduct of the hospital, stressing the need for humane care, the reduction of restraint to an absolute minimum, and the provision of work and recreational activities for patients. Chiarugi also published works on psychiatry, emphasized the need for detailed case histories, and for the design of hospital quarters that would be both safe and comfortable for the patients.

Chiarugi's historical precedence has been sometimes forgotten due to the greater publicity attached, somewhat erroneously, to the work of the French physician Pinel (1745–1826). In 1793, a few years after Chiarugi had published his regulations, Pinel was appointed physician at the Bicêtre—a dungeon-like hospital for the sick, including the insane, in Paris. At the time of his appointment the French Revolution was in full course. Upon taking up his position Pinel met Jean-Baptiste Pussin, a former tanner who was then superintendent of the seventh ward of the hospital, a ward designated for the care of incurable mental patients. Pussin, a former patient in the hospital had found employment there after having recovered from the scrofula for which he had been treated. Pussin had instituted humane and firm policies for the care of patients on Ward 7 and these were in effect when Pinel arrived. Two years later Pinel was promoted to Director of the Salpêtrière, a woman's hospital in Paris. He quickly sought the transfer of Pussin to the Salpêtrière because "He combines a rare intelligence and years experience with human feelings and unshakeable firmness" (Weiner, 1979, p. 1129). The transfer was approved but did not take place immediately. While Pinel was settling into his new position at the Salpêtrière, Pussin, at the Bicêtre, took the daring step of removing the chains from patients presumed to be dangerous, using only the straightjacket when actual violence threatened. The results were successful in bringing about improvement in the behavior of these patients and demonstrated the possibility of controlling violence by less oppressive means. When Pussin finally joined Pinel at the Salpêtrière in 1798, these policies were instituted there.

The myth of Pinel as the liberator has been symbolized by two well-known paintings, both products of artistic imagination. Figure 8.2 reproduces one of these, "Pinel frees the madwomen at the Salpêtrière", painted in 1878 by Tony Robert-Fleury. We may surmise that the author of this liberation, Pussin, is the figure depicted wearing an apron, standing near Pinel. Pinel's own reputation stands firmly on his great contributions to psychiatry, three works entitled *Philosophic Nosography, Treatise on Insanity,* and *Clinical Medicine.* There is no doubt that Pinel was himself a humane and liberal physician, but as Weiner (1979) points out, the reforms so often attributed to Pinel can perhaps be understood as arising from a new spirit of enlightenment in social and political thought of the time rather than to the ideas of one or two medical leaders.

A third reformer of importance was the Englishman, William Tuke. In 1792 he founded the York Retreat, an institution for the mentally ill, based upon humanitarian principles. Tuke was not a physician. He was a wholesale tea and coffee merchant, a Quaker dedicated to philanthropy on the basis of his religious convictions. The York Retreat was directed by the Tuke family for several generations. Tuke's son Henry, and his grandson Samuel, neither of whom had medical training, continued the program of treatment. This approach became known as "moral treatment" or "moral management." A great grandson of William Tuke, Daniel Hack Tuke, was medically educated and became a leading figure in psychiatry of the Victorian period.

Pinel, Chiarugi, and Tuke all independently sponsored the movement towards humane treatment of the mentally ill. Each came from a different context. Pinel

FIG. 9.2. In this scene, painted eighty years after the event, Pinel is shown ordering the removal of chains from patients at the Salpetriere Hospital in Paris, 1798. The scene is symbolic and fictional as the actual author of the liberation was an attendant, Pussin, here shown wearing an apron, standing near Pinel. (National Library of Medicine. Negative No. 60-93. Artist: Tony Robert-Fleury, 1876. Engraving by Goupil.)

worked in the context of democratic reform with its emphasis upon the liberty and rights of the humblest individual. Chiarugi, a Florentine, came to his views through the intellectual influence of the Enlightenment. Religious motives inspired Tuke. However, by the turn of the century the groundwork for the reform of treatment of the mentally ill had been laid and was to develop steadily as the Victorian age approached.

The Case of George III

One of the most famous mental patients of the eighteenth century was King George the Third of the United Kingdom. The exact nature of his illness is still unknown although it has been suggested that he suffered from porphyria—a metabolic disorder with accompanying psychological disturbances (Macalpine & Hunter, 1969). As in so many important historical cases there is some confusion about the circumstances surrounding the care of the King. It is instructive to compare three different versions of the same events, two by modern writers, the other by a contemporary eye-witness. Thus Howells and Osborn (1975) comment: "The treatment of the royal patient was entrusted to a number of physicians until Dr. Francis Willis and his son, John Darling Willis, took charge of him. Nothing was spared: the suffering and indignities meted out to the King of England included bleeding, blistering, scarifying, purging, emetics, and solitary confinement away from his family" (p. 192).

Jones (1972) tells us that Dr. Francis Willis was a former clergyman turned physician who ran a private madhouse in Lincolnshire. He was called in, reports Jones, because the Government of the day wanted somebody who would give an optimistic prognosis, thereby forestalling the possibility that the Prince of Wales would be declared Regent during his father's disability. The Prince was in favor of a different political faction and, it was supposed, might replace the Government of the time with his preferred candidates. Willis's first step, according to Jones, "was to acquire ascendancy over the mind of his patient by intimidatory means . . . the King was immediately separated from his wife and family and kept in constant fear of the strait jacket" (p. 35).

Fanny Burney, an authoress and diarist of the period, lived for some years as a lady-in-waiting to the Queen and witnessed many of the happenings surrounding the King's illness. These she recorded in her diary. Her account of the first episodes of illness emphasizes the anxiety felt by everybody concerned lest they inadvertently provoke the royal patient. The Queen was much terrified by the behavior of the King. Early in the development of the King's disorder he ". . . at dinner, had broken forth into positive delirium, which long had been menacing all who saw him most closely; and the Queen was so overpowered as to fall into violent hysterics" (Burney, edited by Gibbs, 1940; p. 221). From this time the Queen herself avoided personal contact with the King, although she continued to reside under the same roof and was compassionately concerned about his welfare. Whether she separated herself from the King because of medical advice or because she was afraid of him is unclear, but the separation occurred well before Dr. Willis was appointed. On December 4th, 1788, Miss Burney wrote: ". . . told this evening that Dr. Willis, a physician of Lincoln, of peculiar skill and practice in intellectual maladies, had been sent for by express. The poor Queen had most painfully concurred in a measure which seemed to fix the nature of the King's attack in the face of the world" (p. 240–241). Dr. Willis, a footnote adds, was selected because "His methods differed from those of the other doctors in the important articles of common sense and kindness" (p. 240).

Clearly, from this account, the decision to call Dr. Willis was a public admission that the King was mad. By calling him to the case the Government of the day hastened the movement to appoint the Prince to be Regent. It was in fact discussed a mere 12 days later in Parliament. However, on the day that the discussion was held news came that the King's condition had improved and hence the question of his replacement by the Prince of Wales was dropped for the time being.

Thus, one set of accounts suggests that Willis was called in mainly to serve the political purposes of the Government and, upon arrival, began to treat the King with callous inhumanity. This version is attractive to those who believe that an enlightened attitude towards the mentally ill is a relatively recent achievement. An alternative explanation is that the authorities responsible for the King's welfare did what they perceived to be reasonable, calling in a physician with some reputation in the treatment of mental illness. The treatment applied to the King was in line with the prevailing medical opinion of the day; that it involved suffering and indignities does not mean that the physicians were singularly insensitive. Rather it meant that the King then, as with Heads of State now, received the best attention currently available. Indeed, Fanny Burney reports that Sir Lucas Pepys, physician to the King and responsible for many of the medical decisions that were made, expressed to her the fear that his life and those of the other doctors involved would be in danger should the King not recover. "All the physicians received threatening letters daily, to answer for the safety of the monarch with their lives" (p. 231). Such, she remarked, was the "high tide of affection and loyalty that the King had inspired in the people of the country." The royal physicians had every incentive to do the best that could be done. That they did what they did tells us much about the state of medical knowledge at the time; it gives us no basis for imputing inhumane motives to their actions.

Whatever the truth of the case, it appears that the mental illness of King George the Third created a precedent for more open discussion of mental illness and this, in turn, contributed to the climate of reform that was already in being.

Phrenology

For centuries man speculated upon the possible connection between bodily characteristics and behavioral tendencies. In the sixteenth century, for example, the Italian Giambattista Porta published a book, *On Human Physiognomy*, in which he tried to demonstrate that men's heads bear resemblances to those of particular animals and that this resemblance, in turn, provided a basis for concluding that the psychological characteristics of the man would resemble those of the animal in question. As the study of anatomy developed, it was accompanied by an increasing focus upon the size and shape of the brain inferred from the contours of the skull as correlates of character. In the last decades of the eighteenth century this approach was to be given full expression in the work of Franz Josef Gall (1758–1828), a physician trained in Vienna.

Gall believed that the brain consisted of 27 different "organs" each of which controlled a different psychological tendency; the larger the segment of skull covering a specific organ, the larger the organ and therefore the more marked the psychological propensity that it governed. By examining a person's head, the relative propensities of the individual could be estimated. Gall's system, known as phrenology, caught the popular imagination. Interest in it persisted well into the latter part of the nineteenth century. Ceramic models of the human head, mapped according to phrenological definitions of organ location, could be found in many households.

Not all Victorians shared this enthusiasm, however. Dickens, in his *Sketches by Boz* presents an account of phrenology in one of the meetings of the "Mudfog Association for the Advancement of Everything." At this fictitious meeting a Professor John Ketch exhibits the skull of a notorious murderer, Mr. Greenacre. (The public executioner of some fame at that time was known as Jack Ketch— and presumably situated to acquire skulls!) Dickens writes: "A most animated discussion upon this interesting relic ensued; and, some difference of opinion arising respecting the real character of the deceased gentleman, Mr. Blubb delivered a lecture upon the cranium before him, clearly showing that Mr. Greenacre possessed the organ of destructiveness to a most unusual extent, with a most remarkable development of the organ of carve-ativeness." The proceedings are interrupted by Professor Ketch who realizes that he has mistakenly presented a carved coconut shell. He produces another skull but this provokes dispute as to whether or not it is really Mr. Greenacre's or a hospital patient's, a pauper's, or perhaps even a monkey's.

Phrenology did not long survive in scientific medicine. We should note however that the basic strategy of seeking to locate different psychological functions in specific brain areas or neurological networks became the core of later neuropsychology.

THE NINETEENTH CENTURY

The First Decades

War and revolution dominated the European scene as the eighteenth century drew to a close. The political consequences of these events were to color reactions to deviant behavior in various ways. In Great Britain, as in the rest of Europe, the excesses of the French Revolutionary Terror, coming hard on the heels of the American War of Independence, greatly alarmed the middle and upper classes. Fears that similar uprisings might occur in other parts of the world became intense. Repressive measures were undertaken to control "seditious thinkers" among the laboring classes and the indigent. Radicals were tried for treason. Protest meetings were broken up and their leaders executed or transported to forced labor in the colonies. These policies were rationalized by the claim that the masses of people were morally inferior and incapable of taking a responsible role in their own government.

If fear of political revolution spurred actions repressive of the dissident poor, they were sustained by forces inherent in the developing Industrial Revolution.

With the rise of the mechanized mill, foundry, machineshop, and mine there came into being a large class of wage-earning laborers viewed by the employer as "units" in a complex industrial machine. These units were profitable or not depending upon the willingness of the employee to work hard for low pay. Inefficient units could and should be scrapped. Mechanical efficiency had produced such spectacular economic consequences for nineteenth-century society that efficiency came to be regarded as an end in itself—a "good" that required no further proof.

Many of the masters of industry had risen from the ranks. They perceived their own success to be a tribute to their virtues—hard work, thrift, and temperance. Any failure of others to rise in similar fashion could be assigned to the lack of these virtues. Sentiments of this kind were systemized and exemplified in the philosophy of the Utilitarians. Following the teaching of Jeremy Bentham, they stressed the value of simplicity, frugality, efficiency, and social planning. Untrammeled laissez-faire economics would necessarily result in the development of this kind of efficiency.

For the mentally ill, this state of affairs had certain consequences. The wealthy patient might gain access, if lucky, to private institutions such as the York Retreat. For the poor or "pauper lunatics" it was necessary to establish public institutions along scientific lines. An essential assumption of those who built these institutions was that the taxpayer should be called upon to contribute as little as possible to the support of unproductive people. This meant that space, food, care, and other components of institution life were to be at a bare minimum—and certainly not such as to make the institution more attractive than the world of work. In Great Britain the provision of public asylums was made possible by an Act of Parliament in 1808 but was not compulsory until a later Act of 1845. Commissions of inquiry into the conditions prevailing in public institutions and the many private "madhouses" were conducted in 1815 and revealed many abuses along with some humane practices. By the middle of the nineteenth century the establishment and inspection of asylums had been placed on firm footing in the United Kingdom. The preceding half-century had been one of humane care and terrible abuse existing side by side, biological and psychological explanations intermingled in unsystematic fashion, but with an emerging trend towards organized public responsibility for the mentally ill and towards the development of the study of psychopathology along scientific grounds.

The United States

Developments in the United States during this period followed a broadly similar course, although the social conditions differed somewhat from those in England. Class attitudes were less encrusted, and the country was proportionately less urbanized and industrialized. By the beginning of the nineteenth century several asylums had been established by private philanthropy. The Hartford Retreat, the Bloomingdale Hospital, and the Friends' Asylum of Frankfort were early foundations of this kind. Public asylums were also built, and in 1833 the Association of Medical Superintendents of American Institutions for the Insane was established. The 13 charter members included such leading figures as Isaac Ray and Pliny Earle.

Moral Management

Behind the conduct of these new and reformed institutions in France, Britain, and the United States there lay a philosophy often referred to as *moral management* or *moral treatment*. Moral, in the sense used here, means what we would now call "psychological," and not specifically what would be ethical. The well-balanced person was one in whom the feelings or passions were under the control of the reason and will; the psychologically disturbed patient was one in whom this balance had been lost and must needs be restored. For the essential principles we can turn to the writing of Samuel Tuke, grandson of William Tuke and, like his father and grandfather before him, the guiding force in the operation of the York Retreat. In his *Description of the Retreat, an Institution near York for Insane Persons of the Society of Friends* (1813) Tuke wrote of the three basic tasks of the moral management approach. These were (1) to find the means by which the patient could be strengthened in his control over his own disorder, (2) to discover what means of coercion might be permissible when restraint is absolutely necessary, and (3) how the general comfort of the insane might be promoted.

Self control was clearly the central goal of moral management, and this could not be promoted by the induction of fear and coercion. Perhaps one of the most complete expressions of the principles of moral management came from the pen of John Connolly; superintendent of the Hanwell Asylum in England:

> Wherever they go they meet kind people, and hear kind words; they are never passed without some recognition, and the face of every officer is the face of a friend. In the evening, the domestic meal of tea refreshes them. Their supper and their bed are not negligently prepared. Day after day these influences operate, and day by day mental irritation subsides, and suspicions die, and gloomy thoughts gradually disperse, and confidence grows and strengthens, and natural affections re-awake, and reason returns. (Connolly, 1856, p. 13)

John Bucknill gave an account of the desirable state of normal mental health as follows: "It is that condition of the mind in which the emotions and the instincts are in such a state of subordination to the will, that the latter can direct and control their manifestations; in which moreover the intellectual faculties are capable of submitting to the will sound reason for its actions. Such coordinate action of the faculties is termed sanity" (Bucknill, 1854, p. 27–28). Supporting themes of the moral management philosophy were the therapeutic value of work and of the opportunity for physical tranquility and seclusion when the patient felt the need of it.

Treatment in these institutions included not only moral management, but also some more traditional techniques. Confinement and restraint of patients had not been abandoned in quite the dramatic way that is implied by Pussin's unshackling of the inmates of the Bicêtre. Some patients, unfortunately, were violent and likely to assault others or injure themselves. Not all psychotic violence could be ascribed to the physical conditions of the hospitals of the time. The Friends' Asylum, for example, never employed the chains that were a feature of earlier times, but did use leather restraints and solitary confinement to control violent patients.

Pliny Earle, the Superintendent of Bloomingdale Hospital, published in 1848 an account of the principles of moral treatment. "The primary object," he wrote, "is to treat the patients, so far as their condition will possibly admit, as if they were still in the enjoyment of the healthy exercise of their mental faculties." The actual components of this approach included (1) manual labor "requiring a degree of exercise of the body sufficient to preserve and increase the activity and vigor of all its organs, as well as to promote sound and healthful sleep . . ."; (2) religious worship, for all who wished to attend—although Earle comments that for "such as are very melancholy, disposed to excessive contemplation upon religious subjects, and hopeless of salvation for themselves, the tendency is thought to be injurious and they are not permitted to attend"; (3) recreational exercise, including walking and carriage riding; (4) instruction. With respect to the latter, Earle inaugurated a lecture series at Bloomingdale which included talks on subjects as diverse as Chemistry, "Physical, Intellectual and Moral Beauty," "History and Description of Malta," and "Greece as it was in 1838." These lectures were attended, he reported, by an average number of 70 patients whose "attention and deportment would compare favorably with that of the audiences ordinarily attendant upon lectures" (Earle, 1848; pp. 26–35).

Restraint, at Bloomingdale, had been substantially curtailed, but Earle concluded that the current "philanthropic" view that the only restraint that should be applied was by the attendants holding patients was mistaken. There was, he felt, "greater irritation produced in a patient by being held by the hands of attendants, than by having his limbs confined by mechanical appliances. In the former mind struggles with mind, in the latter, with matter alone." Restraining devices used at Bloomingdale included the camisole, long sleeves and leathern muffs for the hands, and an apparatus for confining patients to bed.

The Decline of Moral Management

Unfortunately the very successes of moral management led to circumstances that produced its downfall. An unspoken ingredient in the effective use of moral management was the relatively small size of the asylums concerned, the favorable staff-to-patient ratios, and the homogeneity of the patient groups likely to be admitted. When the Hanwell Institution was opened in Middlesex it provided 300 patient beds. Connolly joined it in 1839, 8 years after its opening and then began the moral management regimen. By 1846 it had an inpatient census of 900, and the local authorities wished to double this. Connolly urged that this would render the policy of individual attention to patients impossible to maintain; with 900 it was already stretched to the limit. To house the excess patients from London workhouses and the private madhouses another enormous asylum, of 1000 beds, was built at Colney Hatch. By 1897 it housed over 2500 patients. Reports in Massachusetts and in London urged that 250 patients was the maximum that could be dealt with along moral management lines in any one institution, but the pressures to house the large numbers of urban and pauper patients increasingly to be found in the cities overrode this and led to the growth of the very large state or county hospitals which came to dominate the latter part of the nineteenth-century care of the mentally ill.

Large numbers of patients led to an abandonment of moral treatment for the more mundane but pressing task of custodial care. As these barrack-like institutions became crowded with the poor and destitute the early optimism about cure that typified the moral management period eroded, to be replaced by pessimism associated with the growing bulk of chronic inmates and the low rates of discharge. This, in turn, gave fuel to that view of mental illness that regarded it, along with crime, disease of all kinds, and the condition of "pauperism" as evidence of individual degeneracy. From this point of view the care of the mentally ill was an act of reluctant charity performed by a society which would be better off without such members in its midst. As their degeneracy rendered them incapable of ever being fully functioning citizens, it was a waste of time and money to try to make them so. Custodial care was the minimal humane provision to be made, at the least cost; there were those among the Social Darwinists who regarded this care as a frustration of the processes of natural selection that would have eliminated the degenerate and hence, by this criterion, such care was immoral.

Medical Hypotheses

While humanitarians were concerned with conditions of inmates, and the social planners with the control and cost of social deviants, the psychopathologists were becoming increasingly empirical in their search for the causes of mental illness. Medical treatises of the day argued that the brain was the seat of insanity, but that the brain could be affected by both physical causes and by "moral" causes. Moral causes were what we would now tend to class as either psychological or environmental causes. Thus in a work entitled *Eleven Chapters on Nervous and Mental Complaints*, Moseley (1838) listed the main agents affecting normal brain function. These included: (1) heredity, (2) child rearing practices, (3) damage arising during pregnancies, e.g., the "brutal conduct of (poor) husbands toward their wives while pregnant,'' (4) lack of emotional control due to parental indulgence of childhood wishes and tantrums, and (5) lack of exercise of the brain. In this latter connection, Mosely commented, ''For demonstrative evidence of this position, we have only to look at the numerous victims to be found among females of the middle and higher ranks who have no strong motives to exertion, or any cause to exert themselves for honour or gain: no interests that call forth their mental energies, or to prevent, by their employment, these energies sinking into feebleness by disuse'' (p. 124–125).

Many writers speculated that substances in the blood might be responsible for triggering psychopathology through its effects on the brain. Thus Noble (1853) pointed to the probable role of chemical substances in mental illness by observing that the general principle was already established from the well-known effects of opium, alcohol, *cannabis indica,* and chloroform. Possible sources of trouble were constipation, or ''loaded colon'' but Noble generally conceded that there was no very exact knowledge of the kinds of chemical agents in the blood that might cause brain malfunction.

Burrows (1828) remarked that the nervous disorders of the upper classes could be traced to their ''habitual luxury and the vices of refinement,'' but that in the lower classes, these disorders were due to intemperance and excess.

The early part of the nineteenth century was thus characterized by several themes. Social distresses were generally attributed to the deficient characters of the victims. Lunacy, crime, and poverty were social problems that could not be solved by changing the conditions that gave rise to them as the ''fault'' lay with the individual and not with his environment. Improvement could only be expected if the individual cultivated desirable habits by an exercise of the will; where he failed to do so, the resulting social problem that his behavior created should be managed in the most efficient and least expensive way. The processes by which bad habits led to insanity depended upon impairment of brain functioning.

THE LATE NINETEENTH CENTURY: THE ROOTS OF MODERN PSYCHOPATHOLOGY

Superficially, the second half of the century did not appear appreciably different from the first half. However, it revealed signs of movements that were to lead to striking changes in conceptions and treatment of mental illness.

Development of Medical Science: The Infectious Disease Model

For centuries there had been a powerful school of medical thought that argued that disease was caused by miasma, gaseous emanations coming from rotting earth, dead bodies, swamps, or the like. However, as early as 1546 this view had been opposed by the germ theory, which argued that the source of many diseases was the spread of germs by contact. In the case of insect-borne diseases such as malaria, contemporary observations were not inconsistent with the miasma theory. A French military expedition in 1805, sent to suppress a rebellion in Santo Domingo, was destroyed by yellow fever. This disaster prompted the French authorities to make a thorough study of the spread of the disease. This they did with great care and concluded that person-to-person contagion could not explain the mode of infection. So severe was the blow that this dealt to the germ theory that there were many attempts to eliminate the quarantine regulations that had prevailed in many Mediterranean ports on the ground that they were surviving remnants of superstition. British liberals, for example, pressed for the removal of quarantine procedures as unwarranted infringements on individual liberty. By the 1880s, this state of affairs had been dramatically reversed.

Claude Bernard, in 1865, published a book *Introduction to Experimental Medicine* in which he demonstrated clearly the value of the experimental method in discovering the mechanisms responsible for disease. In the same year Pasteur had shown the role of bacteria in diseases of silk worms; within a few more years, scientists were to discover the bacilli responsible for leprosy, anthrax, tuberculosis, and cholera. As each disease surrendered its secrets to the search for pathogens, there developed the techniques of immunization and the possibility, at last, of control and cure. The scientific triumphs of the infectious disease model profoundly influenced medicine and led to its enthusiastic extension to other diseases.

For practical purposes, the essential components of the infectious disease model were as follows: (1) For each disease there is a specific causative agent or pathogen—a bacillus or bacterium. (2) To identify this pathogen it is first necessary to have comprehensive and scrupulous observation and description of the disease syndrome. (3) Wherever the disease is found, there the pathogen will be found; wherever the pathogen is introduced, there the disease will develop. (4) Any treatment that prevents the pathogen from entering the body will prevent the disease. Any treatment that eliminates the pathogen from the body will cure the disease. (5) As a rule, prevention can be achieved by creating a mild infection with the pathogen, this conferring an immunity to subsequent infections.

This approach, sometimes loosely termed the "medical model," came to be predominant in thinking about psychopathology. It has remained important to the present day, not the least because it proved successful in understanding paresis (due to syphilitic infection), the toxic psychoses, and others.

Along with these developments there was occurring a rapid expansion of knowledge of the central nervous system and its relation to behavior. Broca reported his finds about the "speech" areas of the brain in 1861. The Russian physiologist Sechenov published his classic work *Reflexes of the Brain* in 1863, followed in 1873 by his paper *How and By whom Shall Psychology be Studied* in which he explicitly rejected the concept that the study of consciousness could form the foundation of a scientific psychology. In 1870 the German military physicians Fritsch and Hitzig established the location of the motor centers of the brain. These achievements, together with the work of Hermann Munk in Germany, J. Hughlings Jackson and David Ferrier in Britain, and others, had profound implications for psychopathology. Disturbed behavior could be understood as the result of damage to particular parts of the central nervous system, regardless of the source of the injury.

Evolutionary Theory

The year 1859 saw the publication of Charles Darwin's epochal work, *The Origin of Species*. It had an immediate impact on many areas in the range of human thought, upon biology, religion, geology, archaelogy, and upon psychology. Its effects upon abnormal psychology can be seen in two different themes. One of these emphasized the view that differences between individuals and classes might be traceable to genetic factors. Francis Galton, a British investigator of individual differences applied this strategy to an investigation of the hereditary transmission of superior ability in families, publishing his book, *Hereditary Genius: An Inquiry into its Laws and Consequences* in 1869. Hereditary factors seemed not only to be logical candidates to explain the origin of mental illness, and personality differences, but also to place mental illness into the category of general biological unfitness which in the ordinary course of natural selection would militate against survival. In its most extreme form this view was to be taken up by those who promoted eugenic doctrines, namely that it was in the general interest of society to assist in the elimination of the unfit, thereby giving nature a helping hand, so to speak. Mild versions of the eugenic philosophy suggested the discouragement or prevention of reproduction by those showing signs of "degeneracy." The twentieth century was to see a more brutal application of eugenic ideas in the hands of Nazi Germany, where many of the mentally ill were murdered as a matter of policy.

For some writers the mentally ill patient exemplified a kind of general hereditary weakness which might equally well express itself through physical illnesses, "hereditary pauperism", crime, and the like. We can see this view not only as a derivative of some aspects of Darwin's work, but perhaps also as a reflection of a growing pessimism about the tractability of social problems. The sciences, natural and social, and the enormous achievements in technology generally seemed not to have accomplished much in the removal of the old problems of human society. For reasons that we have already examined, the early optimism of the moral management movement had given way to the custodial pessimism of the large hospitals—a pessimism that readily allied itself to convictions of the hereditary, and therefore incurable, nature of human miseries. This view was particularly associated with the writings of the French physician, Morel. His "degeneration hypothesis," advanced in 1857, has been described by Rosen (1968) as follows: "He [Morel] defined degenerations as pathological deviations from the normal type, which are transmitted through heredity and which develop progressively to death. Degeneration was due to intoxication, social milieu, pathological temperament, heredity, and acquired congenital insults of various kinds. Once acquired the various generations of the family went inexorably to their doom."

At the time of writing this hypothesis has disappeared, as has much of the force of the eugenics movement that was associated with it. In its place the careful identification of the role of genetic and environmental factors in specific disease categories has been developed with the aid of more sophisticated methods of quantitative analysis and more caution in the interpretation of findings.

A second theme arising from the work of Darwin was to be found in the importance attached to the concept of instinct as a basis for human behavior. If it were true that man had evolved from animal ancestors, and that animal behavior could best be understood in terms of instinctual control of acts, then perhaps man could be understood in the same way. Anthropology, a newly developing area of investigation, drew attention to the common features of human behavior across widely divergent cultures, reinforcing the idea that permanent and powerful instincts influenced human behavior in ways that could be, at most, only partially modified by civilization. This theme was to reach full fruition in the work of Freud, and in his conclusion that in the struggle between primitive instinctual forces and the pressures of the demands of civilized society lay the genesis of much psychological disturbance. Thus, we find the ideas of Darwin being a basis for offering conclusions that all men ran the risk of psychological disturbance by virtue of their social arrangements, and that some were doomed to disaster by virtue of hereditary taint that owed nothing to conflict of motives at all.

The Rise of Experimental Psychology

The latter part of the nineteenth century saw the beginnings of experimental psychology. Psychopathology was to feel the impact of this in many ways, but perhaps first through the work of the psychiatrist Emil Kraepelin (1856–1926). Kraepelin worked in Wundt's Leipzig Laboratory in the 1880s, moving to Heidelberg in 1890 and later to Munich. At Heidelberg he opened a laboratory for the experimental study of psychopathology where he embarked upon a series of studies of psychological functioning in patients and normal subjects. These encompassed problems of fatigue, alcohol and drug intoxication, motor activity, memory, and learning. A particularly important series of investigations of associations was conducted by Kraepelin's colleague Aschaffenburg.

Kraepelin influenced investigators from other countries who worked with him at Heidelberg, notably the American Hoch and the Briton W. H. Rivers. Hoch was appointed in 1893 as the first director of the clinical laboratories at the McLean Hospital in Belmont, Massachusetts. Studies of a neurological and psychological nature were conducted in these laboratories as both were regarded as aspects of a single science. By 1904, however, a separate psychological laboratory was opened under the direction of Shepherd Franz and later directed by Frederick Wells. Other laboratories were opened in the United States, notably at the New York Psychiatric Institute in 1896 and at the Worcester State Hospital in Massachusetts in the 1920s (Maher & Maher, 1979).

The Origins of Dynamic Psychology

The attempt to apply experimental psychology to problems of psychopathology had scarcely started when there began to develop a movement which was to dominate twentieth century thinking about these problems for many decades. This movement was psychoanalysis.

It is not possible here to do more than touch the major elements of the history of psychoanalysis. One of the most important of these was the apparent relationship between hysteria and hypnosis, noted by Mesmer and others.

The director of the psychiatric department of the Salpêtrière Hospital, J. M. Charcot (1825–1893), was deeply interested in the syndrome of disorder known as hysteria. This diagnostic term was applied to a wide range of bodily symptoms where no evidence of underlying bodily malfunction could be found to account for them. Seizures similar to epilepsy were often reported, as well as memory losses, anaesthesias, paralyses, and the like. The catalog of malfunctions that could be removed or created by hynosis was very similar to those that were classified as hysteric. The young Viennese physician, Sigmund Freud, spent the year 1885 working with Charcot at the Salpêtrière; on his return to Vienna he used hypnosis as a therapeutic technique with hysterical patients. However, the cures that he wrought with hypnosis seemed, in some cases, not to be permanent; the symptom that had been removed by suggestion was replaced by a new symptom. While dealing with this difficulty Freud learned from a colleague, Joseph Breuer, of a young woman, ''Anna O,'' who Breuer claimed had been cured of hysterical paralysis (and other symptoms) by the experience of remembering the situation in which the symptom had first appeared and by expression of the emotion that had been associated with it.

From these components Freud began to develop his first theory of neurosis dated by the appearance of his book *On the Psychological Mechanisms of Hysterical Phenomena* (1893) which he co-authored with Breuer. This emphasized the role of childhood trauma of a sexual nature as the origin of adult neurosis. The traumatic incident was assumed to have been repressed beyond conscious recall but the accompanying emotional element continued to influence behavior, finally eventuating in actual symptoms. Recall of the traumatic event and re-experiencing the emotion served to drain off the emotional charge and permit reconstruction of the personality along more mature lines. Quite early in these formulations Freud ran into a serious problem. This was that the traumatic sexual incidents that his patients "recalled" frequently turned out to be fictitious. They could not be the cause of neurosis because there was no evidence that they had ever happened! This led to a reformulation of the theory in which emphasis was now placed upon "unconscious sexual wishes"; the conflict between unconscious sexual fantasies and fear of punishment was deemed sufficient to provide the basis for later neurosis even though the fantasy had never been acted out or experienced in reality.

The details of an enormously complex and frequently changing theory of neurosis and personality development are beyond the limits of this chapter. From the point of view of our history the main interest lies in the effect of the rise of psychoanalysis upon contemporary developments in scientific psychopathology. They were many and they were profound.

Psychoanalysis in the United States

In 1909, Freud delivered a series of invited lectures at Clark University in which he set forth the main tenets of his theory and reported with enthusiasm his belief in the effectiveness of psychoanalytic techniques in the treatment of neurotic patients. These lectures had a substantial impact upon the thinking of psychiatrists in the United States. They marked the beginning of a period in which psychoanalysis was to come to dominate the practice and training of psychiatry for nearly half a century.

Psychoanalysis was, by and large, unsympathetic to experimental investigations into problems of psychopathology. The preferred method was the interpretation of observations made upon individual patients during the course of psychotherapy. A significant footnote to the history of the period cites the response of Freud to the enthusiastic report of the American psychologist, Saul Rosenzweig, that he had demonstrated repression in the laboratory. "I cannot put much value on these confirmations," replied Freud, "because the wealth of reliable observations on which these assertions rest makes them independent of experimental verification" (Shakow & Rapaport, 1964; p. 129).

Experimental work in psychopathology did continue in a few laboratories, notably those of David Shakow at the Worcester State Hospital and Joseph Zubin at the New York State Psychiatric Institute. Psychoanalytic hegemony was such, however, that the main expansion of experimental work in abnormal behavior was not seen until the middle of the twentieth century.

Psychoanalysis in Europe

In no country in Europe did psychoanalysis achieve the influence and status that it reached in the United States. Psychoanalytic publications were founded in nearly all parts of Europe and psychiatrists turned to the practice of psychoanalysis in some numbers. Nonetheless, the predominant themes of European psychiatry continued to be drawn from the traditions of biomedicine and social management that had begun to come to strength in the Victorian period.

THE TWENTIETH CENTURY: THE MODERN PERIOD

As the nineteenth century drew to a close the Western world presented a picture of seeming tranquility and rational optimism. Science and technology were advancing with increasing rapidity in almost all fields. Medicine was at last well into stride as a discipline based upon modern science. Movements for social reform were gathering strength—even though the actual conditions of life for millions of people in Europe and the United States were those of great hardship and little hope. Contemporary writers describe the period 1900–1914 as one of unusual calm and prosperity, a golden time recalled with nostalgia after it had passed. There were, it is true, portents that were scattered but disquieting. Military preparations in Europe were being carried out at a rate incompatible with the expectation of a long period of peace. A revolution in Russia had shaken the throne of the Tsar and produced a short-lived popular constitution. Bombings and assassinations by self-styled anarchists caused alarm and indignation. Nevertheless there were few who came to adulthood in the first decade of the century with the prescience to foresee the storm that was about to burst upon the world with such fury in the war of 1914–1918.

It is difficult, perhaps impossible, for those of us born since that time to comprehend the magnitude of the changes brewed in the trenches of Flanders. By 1918, millions of people were dead, a new political ideology had taken a firm grip on Russia and the fabric of Western culture had sustained damage that could not easily be knit up. The reverberations of these events were to be seen in World War II, and are with us at the present time.

One of the immediate effects of World War I was the rise of cynicism and disillusionment about the rationality of human beings. Man had proved to be savage and self-destructive. The optimism of the opening decade of the century had succumbed to the evidence of international folly on a massive scale. Bitter disenchantment with the post-war state of affairs provided an ideal ground for the acceptance of psychoanalysis with its emphasis upon the irrational and darker side of human nature; this acceptance was to come sooner, more widely, and last longer in the popular culture of the West than it did within the mental health professions. One American writer (Sullivan, 1932) commented, "The medium through which Freud's ideas were impressed upon the country and altered its standards, consisted mainly of the novelists, dramatists, poets, critics, college teachers . . . Chatter of all that stirred the air wherever intellectuals met; by the 1920's there were more than 200 books dealing with Freudianism" (pp. 165–174).

A second effect was that the combat itself had produced brain and nervous system injuries in unprecedented numbers. Henry Head in the United Kingdom and Kurt Goldstein in Germany were both deeply involved in the treatment of such injuries. From their work they developed theories of brain functioning that led us into the period of modern neurology.

Yet a further consequence of the war was the major economic depression that began in 1929 and improved only slowly up to the opening of the Second World War in 1939. Public services were curtailed or abandoned, including the funding of mental hospitals and the support of scientific and medical research. The hospitals that had been built by the Victorians as part of the humane reform of the care of the mentally ill now stagnated for lack of resources, evolving gradually into the drab custodial institutions of recent memory. While the spread of psychoanalysis was leading to a growth of individual psychotherapy, it had little impact upon the treatment of the in-patients of the mental hospitals of the time.

Finally, we should note that a by-product of the war was the impetus that it gave to the study of individual differences. This arose mainly from the military need to identify the intelligence of army conscripts for purposes of assignment or rejection from the service. Clinical psychology, in the form of psychological testing, was given a substantial boost by this development and was to keep psychologists firmly within the field of psychopathology even though their experimental activities languished.

Somatic Therapies—Convulsive Techniques

Insofar as psychiatric practice was not controlled by psychoanalysis, it tended to reflect a continuation of the view that biological and genetic factors were of major importance in the more serious forms of psychopathology. Lacking a solid science of neuropsychology upon which to base the treatment of these disorders, therapies developed mainly on the basis of empirical observation.

The first of these was the discovery that malaria had a therapeutic effect upon general paresis—a finding for which the German, Julius Wagner von Jauregg received the Nobel prize in 1927. The effects of infections and their accompanying fevers upon mental illness had been known for some time, but von Jauregg was the first to establish this relationship scientifically using malaria to induce fevers. In the decades that followed there came the convulsion treatments, using insulin, metrazol, and electric current. Howells and Osborn (1975) have described this period as one in which "Each form of treatment was adopted with the same lack of discrimination with which it was abandoned. But while discrimination was lacking enthusiasm was not . . . The most therapeutic element in this therapeutic programme was enthusiasm harnessed to the belief in the possibility of change" (p. 201).

It is instructive to examine the development of electroconvulsive therapy. Like most "modern" forms of treatment it has a long history. Even before Galen, the Mediterranean electric torpedo-fish or crampfish had been applied to affected parts of the body and appears to have been considered particularly effective in the treatment of headache. By the eighteenth century the use of electricity in the treatment of bodily and mental ills had come into use in several places. John Birch, a surgeon at St. Thomas's Hospital in London applied electric current to the head of a depressed patient. Six small shocks were passed through the brain on each of three successive days. The patient improved and returned to work, remaining well for seven years (Clare, 1976). William Battie, the first superintendent of St. Luke's Hospital in London, noted in his *A Treatise on Madness* (1758) that one species of spasm, however caused, would put an end to whatever other spasm had been troubling a patient. W. Oliver, in 1785, reported his use of camphor in inducing a seizure in a melancholic patient. Camphor is extracted from a particular type of laurel tree and has been in medical use in one way or another for centuries. Dr. Oliver's patient became dizzy after taking the camphor and soon after this, ". . . his senses returned to him, and something like a flash of lightning, he said, preceded their return. He now quitted his confinement and trials were made of his behavior in various companies, at different houses. Parties were formed for him, at his own house; he became natural, easy, polite, and in every respect like himself and played his game at whist with great accuracy'' (Oliver, 1785; quoted in Clare, 1976, pp. 224–225).

Camphor-induced seizures were used irregularly in the following centuries. In the early 1930s, Laslo Meduna discovered that convulsions could more reliably be induced by using an extract of synthetic camphor, known as metrazol. While this technique was being improved, an Italian psychiatrist, Ugo Cerletti, was investigating the changes in brain tissue brought about by the application of electrically induced convulsions in animals. Reading of Meduna's use of metrazol convulsions for therapeutic purposes, Cerletti decided that it would be appropriate to try out his electrical techniques on human patients to see if a similar benefit might be obtained.

Cerletti first examined the possible dangers of such a procedure by investigating the differences in the current necessary to produce a convulsion in pigs and the current levels that were lethal to the animal. Noting that the difference was large he concluded that it would be safe to apply convulsive-level shocks to human patients without danger of injuring them. Cerletti then needed an appropriate patient. A man found wandering and incoherent at the Rome railroad station had been brought to the hospital by the police. He could give no explanation of himself and exhibited severe disorder of thought. Cerletti gave the patient a brief shock of low voltage, which failed to produce a convulsion; the patient, in fact, burst into song. Cerletti ordered another shock of somewhat higher voltage to be given. Over the expressed concern of the staff, this was done and a full convulsion resulted. This treatment, first administered in this way in 1938, became widely popular throughout the Western world. At the time of writing it is in substantial use in the treatment of certain kinds of depression, with which it appears to have highly useful effects. The development of electroconvulsive shock therapy has been completely "empirick"; the mechanism by which it produces therapeutic effects is still unknown.

Somatic Therapies—Psychopharmacology

Drugs have been used for therapeutic purposes in psychiatry from time immemorial. Opiates—the "syrup of poppies"—served for centuries to quiet the agitated patient. By the mid-nineteenth century a spectrum of sedatives was in use for the same purpose. In the 1950s modern psychoactive drugs were introduced. *Chlorpromazine* and *Reserpine* were the first of these. Reserpine, in its herbal form *rauwolfia* had long been known as a therapeutic agent. The Arab physician, Avicenna, had used it in the treatment of mental disorders, a fact that provides us with another of the many examples of cyclical "rediscovery" of old knowledge in the field of psychopathology.

In the years that followed the introduction of these major tranquilizers there was a rapid expansion of interest in the development of new compounds—a development that led directly to the possibility of dispensing with physical restraints in hospitals and the maintenance of individuals on an out-patient basis who would formerly have had to be kept in the hospital. Psychopharmacology provided a practical therapy, widely available, that could be administered inexpensively by any therapist with appropriate medical training. Although there were, and are, some criticisms of the use of pharmacological treatment it is clear that it has to all intents and purposes, replaced both psychotherapy and the other somatic therapies in the treatment of most forms of serious psychopathology.

Biopsychology

One natural consequence of the new psychopharmacology was a revival of enthusiasm for biological approaches to psychopathology. The new drugs clearly achieved their effects by biochemical means; it was logical to hope that biochemistry would hold the key to understanding the etiology of psychological pathologies. Additional impetus was given to this approach by contemporary discoveries in the neuropsychology of consciousness. These were to take the study of disorders of consciousness out of the realm of the purely "mental" and to reinforce the conviction that wherever such disorders were found they might be understood in biopsychological terms rather than as outcomes of a metaphorical struggle between one kind of consciousness and another.

The Return of Experimental Psychopathology

The work of Hull and the Yale group, the reviving interest in biopsychology, and the appearance in the 1950s of the first of the new type of clinical psychologist trained in the techniques and concepts of experimental psychology provided the ground for the full growth of an experimental psychology of abnormal behavior—the experimental psychopathology first envisaged by Kraepelin three-quarters of a century before. At the time of this writing, the role of experimental psychopathology has been secured—with a concomitant emphasis upon limited, controlled studies of specific pathological processes rather than upon the formation of grand total theories of abnormality.

CONCLUSION

As we look back over the centuries covered so briefly in this chapter the durability of certain themes strikes the eye. The phenomena of abnormal psychology elicit explanations drawn from biology and from environmental stress. From time to time and from place to place, one or other of these explanations may tend to dominate the thinking of psychopathologists. This dominance is often uncertain, almost always temporary. Biological treatments often continue in various forms over long periods of time. Thus, camphor becomes metrazol, rauwolfia becomes reserpine, the electric torpedo-fish becomes ECT and so forth. The same is true of psychological treatments. Music, rest, removal of excitement, fresh air, and exercise persist as methods of management regardless of the theory that underlies their employment. Behind these continuities and behind the swings of emphasis from biology to environment there can be detected some steady progress. The newer medications—the tranquilizers—appear to be markedly better than the opiates that they replaced. Disorders once mysterious are known to have a biological origin; the biological and genetic nature of some others is becoming increasingly obvious.

When we turn to the problems of the social care of the mentally ill progress seems less clear. The situation has been well put by Allderidge (1979):

The received version of the history of the care of the insane consists largely of myth and folklore, tempered by a strong dash of wilful ignorance . . . It runs roughly as follows, give or take a century or two here or there (which is about the accepted level of precision): from the dawn of history, or just before, or just after, until about the middle of the nineteenth century, nothing happened at all: or (depending upon *where* you received your version) the mentally disordered were indiscriminately exorcised, or burnt, or left to wander at will, or chained up and beaten, or all four. From the middle of the nineteenth century they were all rounded up and driven into enormous asylums (where, according to a subtle sociological variation, mental illness was invented) and were left to vegetate until the 1950's. Around 1960 dawned the enlightenment, and it was suddenly revealed that everything that had ever happened before—whatever it was—was completely wrong, and probably intentionally malicious too: and over the years following there were gradually also revealed a number of brand-new ways of putting it right, all different and mutually incompatible (not to mention expensive) . . . I propose to you . . . that we have been going round in circles for at least the last 750 years; that there are very few, if any, ideas on the public and institutional care of the mentally disordered which have not been round at least once before; and that on the evidence of past experience the likelihood that we are yet at the millenium, if only we had the money, seems remote. (p. 321)

The problem of the civil rights of the patient versus the need to protect him or her from exploitation becomes the choice between the patient wandering the street versus the patient incarcerated in an institution. The problem of institutionalization becomes a question of expensive, small units incorporated in the community versus larger, cheaper units built at some distance from the center of population which they serve. Each option brings some human distress in its train. Human distress prompts society to move to the opposite tack, adopting the solution that was abandoned by the previous generation because of the problems that it had caused. We may hope that a different distribution of social resources may lead to more effective applications of methods that have failed in the past. But we should not assume so without careful study of the work of our predecessors. It has been properly remarked that whoever ignores history is doomed to repeat it.

REFERENCES

Allderidge, P. Hospitals, madhouses and asylums: cycles in the care of the insane. *British Journal of Psychiatry*, 1979, 134, 321–334.

Braudel, F. *Capitalism and material life 1400–1800*. London: Fontana Collins, 1974.

Bucknill, J. C. *Unsoundness of mind in relation to criminal insanity*. London: Longmans Green, 1854.

Burney, F. *The diary of Fanny Burney*. London: Dent, 1940.

Burrows, G. M. *Commentaries on insanity*. London: Underwood, 1828.

Burton, R. *Anatomy of melancholy*. (Reprint edition) New York: Random House, 1977.

Cheyne, G. *The English malady or a treatise on nervous diseases of all kinds*. London: Strahan & Leake, 1734.

Clare, A. *Psychiatry in dissent*. London: Tavistock, 1978.

Connolly, J. *The treatment of the insane without mechanical restraints*. London: Smith, Elder & Co., 1856.

Dale, R., & Gray, J. *Edwardian inventions*. London: Allen, 1979.

Darnton, R. *Mesmerism and the end of the Enlightenment in France*. Cambridge: Harvard University Press, 1968.

Dickens, C. *Sketches by Boz*. Oxford: Oxford University Press, 1957.

Earle, P. *History, description and statistics of the Bloomingdale Asylum*. New York: Egbert, Hovey & King, 1848.

Encyclopaedia Britannica, Vol. II. Edinburgh: Bell & McFarquhar, 1768.

Harms, E. *Origins of modern psychiatry*. Springfield, Illinois: Charles Thomas, 1967.

Howells, J. G., & Osborn, M. L. Great Britain. In J. G. Howells (Ed.), *World history of psychiatry*. London: Balliere Tindall, 1975.

Jones, K. *A history of the mental health services*. London: Routledge & Kegan Paul, 1972.

Macalpine, I., & Hunter, R. Porphyria and King George III. *Scientific American.* 1969, 221, 38–46.

Maher, B. A., & Maher, W. B. Psychopathology. In E. Hearst (Ed.), *The first century of experimental psychology.* Hillsdale, New Jersey: Lawrence Erlbaum, 1979.

Moseley, W. E. *Eleven chapters on nervous and mental complaints.* London: Simpkin Marshall & Co., 1838.

Noble, D. *Elements of psychological medicine.* London: John Churchill, 1853.

Rosen, G. *Madness in society.* London: Routledge & Kegan Paul, 1968.

Shakow, D., & Rapaport, D. *The influence of Freud on American psychiatry.* New York: International Universities Press, 1964.

Sullivan, M. *Our times: The United States 1900–1925, Vol. 4.* New York: Scribner, 1932.

Weiner, D. B. The apprenticeship of Philippe Pinel: a new document, "Observations of Citizen Pussin on the insane". *American Journal of Psychiatry,* 1979, 136, 1128–1134.

10 Approaches to Personality Theory

Ruth G. Matarazzo
Ann M. Garner
University of Oregon Health Sciences Center

Few branches of psychology are more complex, controversial, and wide-ranging than those dealing with human personality. Our attempts, over the centuries, to comprehend others, to satisfy our need to interact with them, and to predict what they will do has led to an unending variety of descriptions and explanations of personality. These efforts at understanding may or may not deserve the title of "theory," depending upon how stringently one applies the term. They do illustrate, however, the wide range of assumptions, methods, and conclusions that continues to characterize the broad field of personality study.

There are at least three factors which contribute to this diversity. For one thing, there is no single, generally accepted definition of "personality." Personality may be seen as a property of a person or as a field of study; it may take on connotations of value, so that one is said to have a "good" or "bad" personality; it may refer to biological or to social aspects of behavior; it may be considered the product of the environment or its determinant; flexible or unchanging; the central core of the person or a collection of characteristics. Seldom do two theorists in the field begin with, or generate, the same basic definition of the phenomenon.

Secondly, the source of data from which personality theories are fashioned varies widely. Some of the earliest and most elaborate theories derive from clinical observation of persons who show some form of pathology. Others stem from responses of large populations of subjects to items on scales of personality assessment. Some are based on behavior in narrowly defined laboratory situations as, for example, the animal studies of Miller and his associates at Yale. Others employ field or naturalistic situations as their testing ground, as we shall see in the discussion of Maslow and other phenomenological theorists.

Finally, and most significantly, there have been differences over time in preferred types of theory and explanation. Partly this was the consequence of the state of psychological science, and of related sciences, at different times. Precise genetic theories, depending upon chromosomal variations, for example, could be constructed only after the development of sophisticated laboratory techniques for staining and microscopy. Modern trait interpretations became possible with the development of factor analysis. But styles of explanation also depend upon the Zeitgeist: Darwinian evolutionary theory made possible Freud's biological explanations of personality development. Decades later, an emphasis on societal forces and concern with social change supported field and environmental explanations of behavior. Theoretical styles are also personal: a Hullian psychologist is more likely to pursue hypothetico-deductive forms of explanation; a psychologist trained in the Koffka-Kohler-Lewin tradition will look at personality through the eyes of a field theorist.

With all this variation—with different definitions of personality, different styles of explanation, and different sources of data—it is difficult to identify systematic historical trends that are specific to personality theory. The field of personality is so broad that its history becomes the history of psychology. Within this general history, however, a sub-history that seems most important today may be roughly defined. It begins just before the turn of the twentieth century, with the motivational concerns of the psychoanalytic schools, which depended heavily upon the hypothesis of tension-reduction and upon the biological characteristics of the human organism. It proceeds to the incorporation of the philosophy of the German schools of Gestalt and personological psychology within field and self-theories of personality. Trends toward the mathematical analysis of traits and toward an increasing attention to cognitive variables—both influenced by the English tradition—begin to emerge. A growing concern with learning processes and the importance of the environment then leads to stimulus-response and finally to social learning explanations of personality.

Within each broad historical influence there have also been trends in time. Thus, early Freudian concepts have evolved into quite different patterns at the hands of contemporary psychoanalytic writers such as Erikson, Murray, and White. The social factors emphasized by Adler and Horney—who differed from each other—are represented in quite different ways in the contemporary writings of Rotter and Bandura. It is this macro/micro development over time, encompassing both the broad sweep of change in general psychology and the more restricted development within separate theoretical frameworks, that has guided the organization of the present chapter. We begin with early approaches to personality theory, and proceed in rough historical sequence to comtemporary notions of learning and behavior. Within each general approach, however, we endeavor to discern and describe developments from early expressions of the theory to contemporary points of view.

It must be emphasized again that the trends are by no means clear. It is the nature of personality theory that it proliferates and becomes more fragmented with time, rather than focusing more sharply. There are many constructs, many definitions, but few complete theories.

EARLY APPROACHES

Personality theory resembles its parent psychology in one significant way: as Ebbinghaus remarked a long time ago, it has a "long past but only a short history" (Boring, 1950, p. vii). Although this volume is concerned primarily with the short history of psychology, still some orientation to the long past may be useful. We shall see that at least three ancient schools of thought continue to survive, in varying forms, within contemporary explanations of personality. Two other more recent schools, representing nineteenth-century physiology and philosophy, also continue to affect the field. Almost all of the theories reviewed in this chapter owe some debt to one or more of these schools.

The three approaches stemming from ancient times are (1) the doctrine of the humors; (2) physiognomy; and (3) literary characterology. The humoral doctrine is probably the oldest personality theory on record; it grew from the notion of cosmic elements (air, earth, fire, water) advanced by Empedocles around 450 B. C. and taught that humanity reflects nature. People express within their own bodies all the properties of the cosmos. Hippocrates, around 400 B. C., specified four basic humors, or bodily fluids, corresponding to the four cosmic elements. For example, the humor corresponding to the cosmic element *air* was thought to be *blood;* that corresponding to *water* was believed to be *phlegm.* From these assumptions it is a short step to the specification of temperaments related to the humors. If blood predominated in the body, a *sanguine* temperament would develop; if phlegm was the predominant humor, a *phlegmatic* temperament would result. Although the particular elements were abandoned long ago, the presumed relationship between bodily state and emotion is still part of our thinking about individual differences in temperament. We shall meet it again in both constitutional and type theories.

Physiognomy, the notion that personality can be inferred from bodily—especially facial—appearance, is commonly thought to have originated in an ancient Aristotelian treatise. Although the authority for such a view is doubtful, contemporary theories of constitution and type continue to assume that people depend upon facial expression and appearance in making judgments of others. The logic of this notion may be what has permitted its survival: if personality has a physiological basis, then physical aspects of the individual may indeed reveal idiosyncrasies of temperament.

Two thousand years ago, Aristotle's pupil Theophrastus perfected a literary form called "character writing," which exemplifies the approach to personality known as literary characterology. A "character" is a brief, written description of a common "type" of human, being so simplified and delineated that it is easily and universally recognized. Theophrastus wrote at least thirty such "characters,'' each defining and illustrating a type of person. An example of a character written by Theophrastus is ''The Distrustful Man.''

Distrustfulness is a disposition to suspect all men of dishonesty. The Distrustful Man is this sort of man. When he has sent one of his slaves to buy provisions he sends another one after the first to find out exactly what they cost. In travelling he carries his own money and sits down every few hundred yards to count it. In bed he asks his wife if she had locked the money chest, if the cupboard is sealed and if the bolt on the outer door is shut; although she says ''yes,'' up he jumps naked out of bed, lights the lamp and goes the rounds without his shoes to see they are all right; and then has great difficulty in getting to sleep. He has witnesses at hand when asking interest from his debtors to prevent their repudiating the debt. He sends his cloak to be cleaned, not to the best fuller, but to the man who gives best security. When he is asked to lend drinking cups he generally refuses, unless it is a relative or an intimate friend, and would almost test each cup with fire and weigh it; he would like to ask security for them. He tells the slave who accompanies him to walk in front and not behind, so that he can watch him and prevent him escaping on the way. If a buyer asks: ''When can I pay you, I haven't time at present''; he answers: ''Never mind, I will stay with you until you have time!''

Analysis of successful ''character'' writing reveals that it is the internal consistency of the samples of conduct described that makes the character credible. This is a foreshadowing of the notion of a dominant or central trait which we shall see in contemporary type and trait theories. Later literary characterologists altered the approach, and wrote their descriptions without naming a dominant trait but, rather, describing a style which entered into every activity. Such writings anticipate the concept of personal style, to be found particularly in our later discussion of cognitive theory.

Two nineteenth-century schools which evolved from these earliest approaches continue to exert influence upon contemporary personality theory. The major figures in these schools were Francis Gall and John Stuart Mill. Gall's (1822–1825) system of phrenology called attention again to the importance of traits, or faculties. Indeed, Gall's theory has been said to provide the first systematic conceptualization of traits. Gall was attempting, in arguing for distinct faculties of the mind and corresponding ''organs'' of the brain, to specify a mind-body relationship—a matter of less concern to psychologists today than in the early nineteenth century. In more contemporary terms, however, modern workers in the field of personality assume that there is a correspondence between personality patterns and somatic responses. In a sense, modern constitutional psychology, trait psychology, even the methematical factorial approaches, may be seen as related to Gall's early views.

The philosopher John Stuart Mill's *science of character* was to provide an ''exact science of human nature'' (Mill, 1843). Here the underlying argument was that collections of proverbial wisdom, derived from adages, maxims, popular literature of all ages, could be referred to psychological laws and thus be tested. Although this system made little advance, due largely to the fact that associationism was the major, if not the sole, explanatory principle available at the time, still some of Mill's followers maintained a line of inquiry which is to be seen in contemporary personality theory. The theory of sentiments, as expounded by Shand (1915) and elaborated by McDougall (1926), for example, placed emphasis upon emotional dispositions as the elements of personality. McDougall's notion of hierarchies of sentiments, with self-regard at the top, seems to foreshadow the hierarchies of needs and motives developed by the phenomenological personologists of the twentieth century.

A related, because opposing, line of influence is to be found flowing from the writings of Bain, who chose to counter Mill's theory with a tripartite system of faculties. He developed the concept of "psychic energy," and argued that the faculties functioned as channels for the flow of this energy. The similarity to early classical psychoanalysts—Freud and Jung in particular—seems obvious; both systems deal with a finite amount of energy, with the flow into one area or another shaping the personality structure. To these nineteenth-century psychodynamic personality theories, we now turn.

PSYCHOANALYTIC APPROACHES

One of the earliest, and certainly one of the most comprehensive, efforts at systematizing our information concerning human personality was that of Sigmund Freud (1856–1939). From his clinical observations of patients Freud developed, over a span of many years, an elaborate description of the structure and functioning of personality (1932). The description changed markedly over Freud's long and productive professional life as a result both of his own continuing clinical experience, and discussion and controversy with his students. Starting from a hypothetical system of energy (libido) exchange within areas and levels of the individual personality, and leaning heavily upon analogies from nineteenth-century physics and biology, psychoanalytic theory evolved in two major directions: (1) toward greater emphasis upon the independent functioning of that part of the personality called the ego, and thus toward cognitive activity; and (2) toward increasing recognition of the importance of social factors in personality development.

Within psychology, both classical psychoanalytic theory and its more recent variations have met with acceptance, skepticism, indifference, or downright hostility. But the basic psychodynamic orientation has remained an important influence upon personality study, often guiding the choice of problems for investigation; even though direct tests of the theory elude the researcher. The theory is controversial, but aspects of it persist. As one writer in the field puts it, "Why for so many psychologists is the major theory one which was formulated more than a half century ago?" (Sechrest, 1976).

Freudian Psychoanalytic Theory

For purposes of this chapter we must focus upon Freud's theory of personality, ignoring the very considerable contributions of the psychoanalytic movement as a whole to twentieth-century culture; and to techniques of therapy (for further discussion of psychoanalytic theory see chapters 5, 6, and 7). The movement itself grew out of nineteenth-century Darwinism and, to some extent, from German metaphysical and literary trends which are refelcted in the writings of Schopenhauer and Nietzsche. The theory reflects these influences, insofar as it deals with basic biological drives as sources of energy, with the effectiveness of habitual behavior in achieving tension reduction, and with life-and-death instincts. Of the many life instincts, the one which Freud emphasized most strongly was sex; among the many expressions of the death instincts, one considered highly important by Freud was aggression. The theor also reflects the state of psychiatric knowledge at the time of Charcot and Bernheim, two of Freud's teachers. Indeed, it was in the course of treating hysterical patients that Freud began his study of the neurotic process, which was to eventuate in the concepts of the unconscious, of repression, of symptom formation, and of symbolization.

As its name implies, psychodynamic personality theory deals, in large part, with conceptualized energy and its deployment. In Freudian theory, the main energy or motivational forces of the personality are seen as constitutional, internal, deriving from that part of the personality structure called the id. These forces are chiefly sexual ("life" instincts) and aggressive ("death" instincts); increases in their intensity may become intolerable and require immediate tension reduction. The direct discharge of tension by the id can be accomplished only by means of images. Actual tension reduction in the environment is the province of a second part of the personality structure, called the ego. This conceptualized structure has as its function the testing of reality, the delaying of immediate biological gratifications, thinking, planning, and decision-making. In contrast to the id, the ego uses cognitive processes to aid in its functioning. A third part of the personality structure, the superego, represents the standards of parents and of society which, according to the theory, have been internalized in the course of personality development.

Freud postulates a constant conflict among the ego, id, and superego. Id impulses seek immediate gratification; the restraining and judgmental functions of the superego and of reality inhibit gratification; and the ego is characterized as the locus of the interplay—often termed a "battleground." The id says, "Go ahead, do it now." The ego says, "Wait, think it over." The superego says, "Don't do it at all or you'll hate yourself later." Subsequent writings by Freud's daughter, Anna Freud (1946), outlined the defenses developed by the ego in dealing with this intrapsychic conflict. The conceptualization of the ego as an embattled, energy-less, relatively weak part of the personality structure led to much controversy, and to the development of a trend which seeks to strengthen the position of the ego in personality theory.

Two other aspects of Freudian theory deserve mention, although a complete exposition of the system is impossible here. In keeping with nineteenth-century thought, Freud conceptualized the mind as functioning on different levels of consciousness. Much of the conflictual, tension-reducing, or adaptive functioning of the various parts of the personality were considered to go on outside the subject's awareness. The concept of the unconscious, foreshadowed long before in the writings of Leibnitz, Herbart, and others, became an explicit part of Freudian personality theory. In addition, as part of his system of energy transformation, Freud postulated certain stages of personality development organized around the focus of sexual energy. Individual differences in personality structure at adulthood were seen to represent different "vicissitudes" met by the sexual impulses at various developmental stages. For instance, the individual whose development is fixated at the early oral stage may show such personality traits as dependency, love of food and eating, optimism, and gullibility.

The reception which Freudian theory received in Victorian Europe is too well-known to require repetition here. Freud himself described his theory as a "psychological blow" to humanity's egocentrism, comparable to the "cosmological blow" administered by Copernicus, and to the "biological blow" administered by Darwin. Certainly the forces contributing to the stormy reception of the theory were many and complex. For present purposes, however, only the immediate effects upon the development of personality theory need be considered.

Freud's Students

A number of Freud's students and associates contributed to the extension and alteration of his theory in ways that stimulated new approaches to the study of personality. Alfred Adler (1870–1937), for example, with his emphasis upon social interest and interpersonal interaction (Adler, 1927; Mosack, 1973), may be considered a forerunner of the social learning theories of personality to be considered later in this chapter. Adler (1870–1937) was a contemporary and associate of Freud who broke away from the psychoanalytic group in Vienna and established his own school of Individual Psychology which stressed ego and social forces, and placed less emphasis upon sex. He saw the person as a social being who relates to others, cooperates with the group, and places the welfare of the group above individual concerns. The basic striving is for security. Everyone strives for superiority, often involving unrealistic goals, necessitating failure which is a great source of unhappiness. A child is aware of inferior status and must strive to compete. He must bow to powerful authorities who control those things he wants and needs. The mature, well-adjusted adult strives for self-perfection and social contribution.

Carl Jung (1875–1961), another early associate of Freud, expanded the psychoanalytic theory of personality in at least two directions (1928, 1933). He elaborated the theory of the unconscious by developing the concept of the collective unconscious, as compared with the personal unconscious. This concept encompasses the ideas and images which have accumulated over many generations, and which are shared by all human beings. It is conceived to be the evolved and evolving foundation of human personality structure. Jung also greatly widened the empirical base upon which psychoanalytic personality theory stands, by using examples from anthropological and cultural observations—from myths, visions, fairy tales, dreams, alchemy, primitive literature, and art, as well as more contemporary clinical and laboratory material.

It is Jung's conceptualization of psychological attitudes or orientations, however, which we consider to foreshadow certain of the trait and type theories summarized below. In Jung's system, the attitude of extraversion points the individual toward the outer world, while the attitude of introversion points him toward the subjective world. Although both orientations are present in the individual, one usually is dominant, lending the distinctive quality of extraversion or introversion to the personality.

Otto Rank (1884–1937), with his emphasis upon the self and upon the very earliest experiences of the human organism (1929, 1936), has influenced some of today's phenomenologically oriented theorists, as well as contemporary workers with children. Each of these men represents a separate branch of psychodynamic theory. From each a discernibly different trend has developed.

The "Neo-Freudians"

As was suggested earlier, the relatively weak position of the ego in classical Freudian theory became a point of controversy as time went on. Freud himself gradually strengthened the position of the ego as he saw it, but it remained for several writers of the late thirties to deal both with the autonomous nature of the ego and with the role of social interactions in personality development. One of these neo-Freudians, Karen Horney, emphasized social learning to the extent that her writings seem more easily comprehended when discussed with social theorists or humanists. Thus her ideas are presented later in this chapter despite the fact that her roots were in psychoanalysis.

Hartmann (1952; Hartmann, Kris, & Lowenstein, 1946), postulated a "conflict-free sphere" of the ego: the ego develops not from the id but from independent roots which later become the processes of perception, memory, and thinking. Such a conceptualization leaves the way clear for the gradually increasing emphasis on cognitive functioning which, as we shall see, characterizes one contemporary trend in personality study.

The writings of Erikson best exemplify the neo-Freudian psychosocial theory of personality (1950, 1959). Erikson's epigenetic view of ego development assumes a sequence of phases, in each of which a developmental task must be solved. Each phase is defined by extremes (basic trust vs. mistrust; intimacy vs. isolation). A satisfactory solution finds a balance between the extremes. In this lifelong course of development, however, there is constant coordination between the individual and social environment; and the relationship between individual and society is one of mutuality. A great many contemporary efforts at explaining human personality deal with the same matter of the interaction between individual and society, as will be seen in the later section on social learning theories.

Still other students of psychoanalytic theory are not concerned with altering the theory as much as they are influenced by it in the development of their own point of view. An outstanding example of such a theorist is Harvard psychologist Henry Murray, who owed much to Jung, but whose painstaking development of a system of motivation closely linked to physiological processes is uniquely his own (Murray, 1938). In Murray's system, the concepts of need, press, and thema, represent respectively the personal, environmental, and interactional determinants of behavior, and permit the inclusion of an unusually wide range of variables to account for the complexity of human personality. Some of these concepts have been used as the basis of diagnostic tools whose application in the clinic and in the field has kept Murray's "personology," as he chooses to call it, alive over many decades. One such well known clinical instrument is the Thematic Apperception Test, in which the subject makes up stories in response to a series of pictures. It is then possible to derive from the stories the particular patterns of need, press, thema, and conflict which characterize the subject's personality.

In the long run, however, Murray's influence on the later development of psychoanalytic theory made itself felt through the contributions of the students he gathered about him at the Harvard Clinic. Nevitt Sanford, Silvan Tomkins, and Robert White, to mention only a few, carried forward the investigation of psychoanalytic theory and eventually developed their own influential approaches to personality.

Even this brief and admittedly incomplete account of the rise and development of the psychoanalytic theory of personality points up two characteristics mentioned earlier. The theory has continued to stimulate new theorizing and also to guide many experimental and clinical investigators in their choice of variables for research (Sears, 1943; Kline, 1972). At the same time, the findings from such studies are often contradictory, of uncertain validity, or trivial. The theory does not lend itself easily to objective test; concepts are often inadequately defined; laws and principles are stated so generally as to defy precise predictions; and the distance between observable behavior and "intrapsychic" variables is a gap too wide to span. This theory was influential during the first half of the twentieth century. Its effect could be seen in many aspects of our culture—in literature, the arts, and philosophy, as well as personality theory, research, and clinical practice. At present, the psychoanalytic orientation is still part of western culture, although its influence is gradually waning as other theories and positions develop. Indeed, the skepticism aroused by the theory has served to stimulate the search for more acceptable alternative explanations of human personality.

CONSTITUTIONAL APPROACHES

Another early and persistent approach to the study of personality attempts to link behavioral tendencies to biological constitution. This approach was anticipated in the writings of Hippocrates, mentioned earlier. Some present-day hypotheses of a relationship between endocrine or autonomic functioning and personality characteristics seem to echo the ancients' emphasis upon bodily fluids. And modern theories of personality type, discussed below, owe much to earlier typologies based upon biological characteristics.

Two fundamental questions underlie the constitutional approach to personality: (1) Are there basic differences in response which are present at birth, which persist as consistent parts of the individual's personality? (2) If so, what determines these differences? Are there identifiable genetic or constitutional factors determining individual differences in physical structure and psychobiological function? Or are these differences reflections of variations in the environment within which the individual develops? It is the age-old question of hereditary and environmental determinants which we confront here, as complex in the area of personality as in disease susceptibility, delinquency, or intelligence test performance.

Enough evidence has accumulated over the years to permit some tentative answers to these questions. Although they lead to a constitutional point of view, these answers do not define a ''theory'' of personality. Rather, the constitutional psychologists maintain a particular orientation toward the phenomena of personality: that congenital differences in structure and function largely determine individual differences. They say little or nothing about the structure of personality systems, about the units of behavior which make up personality, or about the character of energy which arouses the individual.

Concern with constitutional factors, of course, is to be found, in greater or less degree, in most of the more comprehensive theories discussed in this chapter. The classical psychodynamic view, presented earlier, assumes that the basic motivational forces or instincts are constitutional. Trait and type theories, to be presented later, likewise assume some effect of biological functioning upon individual personality. It is their major, if not exclusive, emphasis upon constitution as a personality determinant that distinguishes constitutional psychologists from other students of personality.

Congenital Difference in Response

A long line of studies, over the past several decades, suggests that animals of many species share a few major dimensions of temperament. Early in their lives, rats and mice, dogs, and primates show measurable individual differences in such behaviors as aggression, fearfulness, and dominance. There is evidence that these differences are inherited, and longitudinal studies of some species indicate that the idiosyncratic patterning of these behaviors persists throughout life, imparting an individual character to the animal.

Students of human infant and early child development have also succeeded in identifying individual differences in basic physiological functioning shortly after birth. Some human infants are more reactive than others in sympathetic, parasympathetic, or motor functioning (Richmond, Lipton, & Steinschneider, 1961). Some are active and noisy, others quieter (Escalona, 1968; Friedman, 1967). An increasing number of investigations indicate that such early identified behaviors persist at least throughout the childhood of the individuals (Murphy, 1962; Neilon, 1948), and some studies have found them persisting into the adult years (Bayley, 1968).

There seems little doubt, therefore, that basic differences in responsiveness are present at birth, and that they may persist for many years in the lives of individuals. It is from the second question, that of the factors which determine these differences, that constitutional points of view toward personality emerge.

Constitutional Determinants

It is possible to continue the line of reasoning begun with Hippocrates, and to explain personality in terms of constitution, without analyzing in detail the possible genetic and intrauterine factors contributing to a particular physique or temperament. In recent years, such reasoning has been employed more in explanations of pathological behavior than of more normal reactions. Thus the German psychiatrist Kretschmer (1925) observed relationships between physique and the behavior typical of two major forms of behavior disorder: manic-depressive psychosis and schizophrenia. Using a detailed and systematic method of measurement, Kretschmer identified three main types of physique: the asthenic (frail, lean, narrowly-built); the athletic (muscular, broad-shouldered, tapering); and the pyknic (rounded, plump). Kretschmer's studies of psychiatric patients yielded evidence for increased frequency of schizophrenia among asthenic physical types, and higher frequency of manic-depressive psychosis among pyknic types.

Although certain assumptions implicit in Kretschmer's work suggested a similar relationship between physique and behavior in normal persons, studies which might have shed light upon this point were not carried out. It remained for an American psychologist and physician, William Sheldon, to pursue the study of physical structure as it relates to normal behavior. His writings sought to identify the major structrual elements of the human body and the major varieties of human temperament (Sheldon, 1940, 1942). Later he applied his findings to the study of delinquency (Sheldon, 1949).

By means of a specialized photographic technique, Sheldon obtained approximately 4000 pictures of male college students. From these, a team of judges identified three primary components of physical structure. Endomorphy is characterized by softness and roundness; mesomorphy is typified by strength and toughness; and ectomorphy is shown by fragility and delicacy. The similarity to Kretschmer's system is obvious, although Sheldon's method of deriving components is superior to that of the earlier investigator. In the Sheldon system, for any individual there can be identified a ''somatotype,'' which represents the patterning of the three primary components described above.

The specification of dimensions of temperament proceeded, in Sheldon's work, with similar painstaking care. Beginning with lengthy lists of trait names, paring them down, and then studying a group of male subjects for one year, Sheldon and his associates were able to identify three clusters of traits which eventually emerged as three components of temperament. Viscerotonia is characterized by the seeking of comfort, sociability, need for people, and affection. Somatotonia involves desire for physical adventure, risk-taking, and need for vigorous physical activity. Cerebrotonia is typified by inhibition, need for privacy and concealment, and restraint. Sheldon's studies of the degree of association between components of physique and dimensions of temperament reveal significant correlations between temperament and physique.

Later applications of Sheldon's methods to psychiatric groups and to delinquents led to a certain amount of support for the generality of his approach, although the question of environmental influence upon later behavior always arises. For example, the ectomorphic boy, who is fragile and less muscular, is unlikely to undertake physical feats which would bring him to the favorable attention of his peers. He is not the boy who is chosen first for the football team or praised for his toughness. He is therefore more likely to remain on the periphery of peer groups, and to seek and eventually to find satisfaction in solitary pursuits. Social stereotyping of various body types further compounds the situation. The non-athletic, ectomorphic boy, for example, may be seen by others as non-participating, unsure of himself, and inhibited. Subsequently, others' responses and expectations may well serve to evoke and reinforce these characteristics.

Perhaps because of the complexity of the research designs involved, or because American psychologists have not systematically pursued constitutional problems, relatively few studies have grown out of Sheldon's system. Current emphasis is rather upon certain isolated genetic phenomena—which Sheldon would consider important but not central items for investigation.

Genetic Determinants

Recent statistical and laboratory advances in research on human genetics, described elsewhere in this book, have made contemporary studies of the genetic aspects of personality immensely productive but enormously complex. As in the case of constitutional psychology, early studies focused upon abnormal behavior. Kallman's lengthy series of investigations on the familial incidence of psychiatric disorder, for instance, (Kallman, 1953) were classical groundbreaking efforts in this regard. So also were family studies of giftedness and mental retardation.

Genetic studies directed exclusively toward normal personality, however, are not so numerous. Although the genes are assuredly implicated in congenital response differences (discussed above), in constitutional determinants, and indeed in all the human behavior which the theories seek to explain, large-scale efforts focused on the genetics of personality are rare. One research method which has proved useful is that of comparing monozygotic ("identical") with like-sexed dizygotic ("fraternal") twin pairs. Monozygotic twins, who develop from the same ovum, have identical genetic structure while dizygotic twins, who develop from two ova, differ in genetic makeup. Studies of the relative similarities and differences between members of the two types of twin pairs can yield some information on the relative contributions of heredity and environment and to the characteristic under investigation. This method has yielded information concerning possible genetic contributions to infant behavior (Wilson, Brown, & Matheny, 1971), to performance on paper-and-pencil personality tests (Gottesman, 1963; Dworkin, Burke, Maher, & Gottesman, 1976, 1977), and to other ingredients of personality. In general, indices of concordance in these studies suggest greater similarity between monozygotic than dizygotic twins, which would argue for some genetic determination. It should be noted, however, that the indices for personality traits are in general lower than those for many other aspects of the individual's behavior. At present, only the trait of introversion-extraversion has been found to have a respectably high coefficient of heritability.

Chromosomal Aberrations

Perhaps the most fruitful contemporary investigations of the genetics of personality have emerged since the development of new staining techniques which make possible the direct identification of chromosomes in human subjects. Two examples of identified chromosomal abnormalities will serve to indicate the complex interweaving of constitutional and environmental determinants in these cases.

1. Down's Syndrome   is now considered to be the result of an extra chromosome at locus 21. The predominant symptoms of this syndrome are intellectual impairment and a wide variety of physical defects. However, *Down's syndrome* children have often been thought to show a particular personality pattern: they are presumably more sociable, more compliant, and happier than other children with comparable handicaps. Although there is some evidence supporting this stereotype (Domino, Goldschmid, & Kaplan, 1964; Silverstein, 1964), the desirable personality traits depend to a significant extent upon the child's environment.

2. *Anomalies in Sex Chromosomes.*   Recently, the discovery of additional male sex chromatin in certain men has led to speculation concerning behavioral manifestations which could be related to this chromosome abnormality. The identification of a small number of males with a 47, XYY karyotype in populations of prisons and psychiatric hospitals raised the question of a relationship between extra male chromosomes and aggressive behavior (Casey, Segall, Street, & Blank, 1966). Evidence to date suggests that the relationship, if any, is far from simple. Attempts to assess aggressive behavior with objective measures do not support such a relationship (Owen, 1972; Witkin, et. al. 1976). Moreover, other factors also presumably characteristic of the XYY pattern, such as tallness and borderline intelligence test scores, may predispose an individual to unusually aggressive behavior, given the appropriate environmental stimulation (Jarvik, Klodin, & Matsuyama, 1973). Thus, even if aggressive behavior were found to be associated with this chromosomal pattern, it may well be accounted for by the combination of limited intellectual capacity and unusual height, as these characteristics affect and are affected by the behavior of others in the environment.

Inborn Errors of Metabolism

Certain abnormal conditions resulting from defective genes also shed light upon the contribution of constitutional factors to personality. For example, abnormal genes may prevent the proper development of enzymes which are necessary for normal metabolism (Stanbury, Wyngaarden, & Frederickson, 1972). Again, the primary consequences for the individual are in the areas of intellectual and neurological development. In certain of the syndromes, however, personality factors are thought to be involved as well. In *phenylketonuria* (PKU), for example, early dietary treatment often goes along with improvement in attention, self-control, and socially appropriate behavior. The *Lesch-Nyhan* syndrome (Fernald, 1976), on the other hand, is characterized by persistent aggressive behavior, which is exceedingly difficult to control, and is directed both toward the self and other persons. Here again, however, the contribution of environmental factors to the development and persistence of the personality patterns must not be overlooked.

APPROACHES EMPHASIZING TRAITS AND TYPES

As we have just seen, attempts to describe people by traits or types was probably the earliest approach to personality theory and goes back at least to the ancient Greeks. The belief that physique and temperament or personality are related led to further attempts to define personality types and establish traits associated with body build. As stated previously, Kretschmer (1888–1964) hypothesized a relationship between body build and the tendency to develop one or another type of mental illness. Kraepelin (1856–1926) earlier had many of the same ideas. Further explication and later refinements of such constitutional typologies have been discussed in the section on constitutional and genetic theories.

These constitutional "type" theories were forerunners of more complex theories which included both constitutional tendency and psychogenic factors. For example, Jung (1933) categorized invidivuals as introverted or extraverted according to whether they tend to be withdrawn and absorbed with their inner thoughts and feelings, or outgoing, friendly, and responsive primarily to events going on about them. Jung saw this as one's basic orientation to life, and a natural expression of constitutional tendencies. The ways of experiencing (sensing, interacting, feeling, and thinking) would be modified to some degree by this orientation.

The concept of introversion-extraversion as providing a basic dichotomy among individuals has persisted to the present time, with introversion often having the connotation of neuroticism but also creativity. This personality dimension was one which Hermann Rorschach attempted to measure through the individual's perception of ink blots (Rorschach, 1942); it is one of the clinical scales on the Minnesota Multiphasic Personality Inventory (Hathaway & McKinley, 1943); and it continues in the theoretical writings of such individuals as Hans Eysenck (who, however, uses the concept differently, and postulates a relationship to Pavlovian conditionability). At the present time, introversion-extraversion is thought of as a continuum and a matter of degree rather than as an either-or categorization. Thus an adolescent girl termed introverted may be very warm and outgoing with familiar people, with people who extend themselves to be friendly, or among individuals who share common interests. Conversely, another girl termed "extraverted" by her classmates may withdraw to her room at home and avoid responding to her family. Some of the problems created when one attempts to assign an individual to a type may be avoided by describing the individual in terms of a constellation of traits.

Gordon Allport (1897–1967) was a Harvard Ph.D. who later taught at Harvard for almost 40 years. His method of studying personality was by means of the individual case, and via this method he discovered "traits" which provide some predictability or consistency to the individual's behavior. Allport (1937) differentiated between secondary traits which tell little about the total life style of an individual, central traits or generalized tendencies, and cardinal traits, which describe the orienting focus of a person's life. Traits are equated with the adjectives which we typically use in describing people's behavior and by means of which we say that they are similar. Secondary traits are numerous and apply to many people; however, central traits become relatively more unique to the individual, and there are perhaps only 5-10 which apply to him or her. Cardinal traits are even more unique, and reflect the individual's tendencies to strive toward future, life-unifying goals. When we understand the unifying themes of the individual's life, we become aware that some surface behaviors which appear inconsistent are really not (e.g., obtaining excellent science grades and mediocre grades in the arts when the student is focused upon a career in science).

Traits, of course, always occur in conjunction with other traits, and may be manifest under certain circumstances and not others. The more central the trait, the more different circumstances under which it is manifest. Thus many situations may become functionally equivalent in eliciting behavior described by the trait. For example, for an individual with the trait of competitiveness, a card game, a school examination, and a debate are all likely to evoke competitive behavior. One problem with the concept of traits is that we often think of them as both *describing* behavior and as *causal* agents of that behavior. In actual fact, we are only labeling behavior and cannot then attribute causation to the trait label. Trait theorists do, however, see them as underlying tendencies which help to account for the relative consistency of human behavior.

Raymond Cattell (1905–), born and educated in England, spent most of his research career at the University of Illinois. His work reflects the English tradition of interest in the measurement of traits and individual differences (Cattell, 1946), as well as the intercorrelation of these measurements, as initiated by an English mathematician, Carl Spearman. For Cattell, "personality is that which permits a prediction of what a person will do in a given situation." In line with this definition, he developed and administered multitudes of tests, obtained life history data, questionnaire data, and then performed elaborate statistical analyses upon them, seeking "common traits." By further intercorrelating and factor analyzing all the observed traits, Cattell empirically has found clusters or "source traits" which he believes to be the underlying cause of the surface behaviors, and allow us to predict behavior (see Table 10.1).

Some of Cattell's hypothetical "traits" are primarily determined by constitution and some by the environment. Twenty major traits seem to have emerged from this research, some with familiar names such as emotional stability, intelligence, dominance, and anxiety. Others have names which do not immediately convey their meaning. For example, *parmia* is an acronym derived from "parasympathetic" and "immunity to threat." It is hypothesized to underlie the behavior of boldness, spontaneity, and non-susceptibility to inhibition. *Comention* is conformity or cultural amenability through good parent-self identification, while *abcultion* is abhorrence or rejection of cultural identification.

Although Cattell has written a great deal, and developed several measures of personality variables; (Cattell, 1957), his work to date remains relatively unrelated to that of other theorists.

Hans Eysenck (1916–) was born in Germany, completed his education in England, and has been at the University of London Institute of Psychiatry since 1955. He, like Cattell, is an empiricist who uses factor analysis and other statistical procedures to isolate the dimensions of personality (Eysenck, 1947, 1952). His three primary dimensions are introversion-extraversion; neuroticism-

TABLE 10.1
Overt Manifestations of Personality and Their
Relevant Dimensions

A Surface Trait

Sociability, sentimentalism, warmth	*vs.*	*Independence, hostility, aloofness*
Responsive	vs.	Aloof
Affectionate	vs.	Cold
Sentimental	vs.	Unsentimental
Social interests	vs.	Lacking social interests
Home and family interests	vs.	Lacking home and family interests
Dependent	vs.	Independent
Friendly	vs.	Hostile
Frank	vs.	Secretive
Genial	vs.	Cold-hearted
Even-tempered	vs.	Sensitive

A Source Trait

Dominance	*vs.*	*Submission*
Self-assertive, confident	vs.	Submissive, unsure
Boastful, conceited	vs.	Modest, retiring
Aggressive, pugnacious	vs.	Complaisant
Extra-punitive	vs.	Impunitive, intropunitive
Vigorous, forceful	vs.	Meek, quiet
Willful, egotistic	vs.	Obedient

Questionnaire items	*Dominance Indicators*
Do you tend to keep in the background on social occasions?	No
If you saw the following headlines of equal size in your newspaper, which would you read?	(a)
a) Threat to constitutional government in foreign country by dictator	
b) Physicists make important discovery concerning the electron	

From Cattell, 1950, 1965.

stability; and psychoticism-nonpsychoticism. Eysenck has a strong constitutional-genetic bias, believing that much of human behavior is determined by inherited characteristics of the autonomic nervous system. This has led him to the study of identical and fraternal twins. His theory resembles those of Cattell and Allport insofar as he finds single, surface behaviors which cluster and are related to deeper habitual responses, traits and types, the latter consisting of clusters of

FIG. 10.1.   The results of modern factor analytic studies of the intercorrelations among traits. To illustrate the long-term nature of such views, Eysenck provided an inner circle that shows the classical four temperaments assumed by theorists in ancient Greece who believed that personality was determined by body fluids. (Eysenck, 1964.)

traits. Figure 10.1 presents a summary of the structure of personality proposed by Eysenck.

Eysenck has done considerable research on his own theory, and has measured multiple behavioral and physiological variables which he has attempted to correlate with his dimensions of personality. In general, there are both positive and negative studies regarding his theoretical ideas. For example, in a study of identical versus fraternal twins he found a significantly higher correlation between the former on neuroticism scores, giving some support to his constitutional-genetic leaning. There are differences of opinion about Eysenck's methods of factor analysis and the significance of his dimensions of neuroticism, psychoticism, and introversion-extraversion. His theory, like that of Cattell, tends to be relatively apart from the writings of other theorists.

HUMANISTIC APPROACHES

The theories just discussed emphasize constitutional and environmental determinants of personality. A different view has been provided by the humanistic theorists. This movement stems from European humanistic-existential philosophy which emphasizes human purpose, values, ability to symbolize, capacity for self-determination (Kierkegaard, Sartre, Heidegger), and ability to rise above animal needs. The humanists view humankind as having the potential for growth throughout life under conditions which make this possible. They are interested in the individual's unique, immediate, conscious experience, rather than stimulus-response connections, constitutional characteristics, or universal basic drives. Humanistic psychologists believe that only under adverse conditions are higher qualities submerged by instinctual needs or perverted to become destructive. Humanistic theories tend to be less systematic and precise than those which are more behaviorally oriented, and their concepts less easily measured. Two recent influential humanistic theorists are Abraham Maslow and Carl Rogers (1902–). Both are modern descendents of William James who was concerned with the concept of the self in his *Principles of Psychology* (1890).

Abraham Maslow

Maslow (1908–1970), a Ph.D. From the University of Wisconsin who taught at Brandeis, called the basic, physiological and self-oriented drives—hunger, sex, security, selfishly-oriented love—deficit needs and distinguished them from the uniquely human, higher needs which he called meta-needs or the need for growth (Maslow, 1943). Meta-needs include unselfish love, artistic achievement, the thirst for knowledge, and altruism. Development and expression of the weaker meta-needs depends upon at least partial satisfaction of basic needs. Deficit needs, themselves, are organized hierarchically, the organism semi-instinctually giving precedence to the more basic ones. The most basic are the physiological needs which, when fulfilled, cease to be active so that other needs become predominant. Safety needs are next in the hierarchy—the need for security and some control over one's environment. When safety needs are unfulfilled, the individual experiences fear, insecurity, and anxiety.

Love needs are next in the hierarchy, the exact form of the need changing through the course of life. For example, the infant requires love and nurturance for survival and growth. Later, immature love is based on "deficit needs" or the desire to fill one's own requirements for attention and affection. More mature love, however, involves seeking friendships and a heterosexual partner, becoming a parent, and giving of oneself to others. The next ascending hierarchical needs are first for respect from others and, then, for self-esteem. Self-esteem is initially derived from status achieved relative to others, and is strongest in early adulthood. With added maturity, it lessens, while the need for internally-derived self-esteem becomes more dominant and the individual becomes able to move in the direction of self-actualization (Maslow, 1954).

Self-actualization is, for Maslow, the highest form of human endeavor—a disciplined self-expression which motivates diverse cultural and intellectual achievements. The need to develop one's potential, however, is found among relatively few individuals. The major characteristics of self-actualizing people, as defined by Maslow, are summarized in Table 10.2. While the self-actualizing, cognitive need leads to cultural, intellectual, and other achievements, its frustration has the negative consequence of engendering egocentricity, lack of task-orientation or involvement with people, and anhedonia, the inability to experience happiness.

Maslow's work has had an important influence on psychology, but most particularly on the recent existential group movement which is concerned with the free expression of "self" and a hedonistic experience of "joy." Maslow did not specify his theory in sufficient detail to make possible experimental verification, and the experimentation which has been stimulated by his theory has not produced clear-cut results. His concern with self-actualization led him to analyze the lives of 49 people whom he considered to be self-actualizers. Among these were Lincoln, Jefferson, Eleanor Roosevelt, and Einstein, as well as some of his personal friends.

Carl Rogers

The importance of inner experience, and the concept of a universal drive toward growth and increased perfection are found also in the theory of Carl Rogers, who is probably most noted for his development of the "client-centered" or "non-directive" approach to psychotherapy (1942). Rogers earned a Ph.D. from Columbia University, worked at a Child Guidance Clinic for 10 years, and then remained at the University of Chicago until retirement. He continues to be professionally active in California at the Center for Studies of the Person. Rogers' personality theory has had its greatest effect upon clinical application—individual psychotherapy, group psychotherapy, and the human potential movement—and upon notions of the important or therapeutically sufficient ingredients in therapist behavior. This is not surprising inasmuch as the theory essentially grew out of Rogers' experiences as a therapist.

Like Maslow's, Rogers' theory is positive and humanistic in its view that a basic striving for self-actualization is universal in the human species (Rogers, 1951, 1961). The cornerstone of Rogers' theory is the self-system, which in-

TABLE 10.2
The Attributes of Self-Actualizing College Students

1. An efficient perception of reality	The ability to make accurate judgments of self and others which are undistorted by personal needs, fears, anxieties, beliefs.
2. Acceptance of self and others	Freedom from shame, guilt, and anxiety; a lack of defensiveness or pose.
3. Spontaneity; simplicity and naturalness	This implies a flexibility of behavior but not necessarily unconventionality.
4. Problem-centered	A sense of mission and purpose in life which leads one to tasks one feels it is a duty to perform; a concern with philosophical–ethical issues.
5. Quality of detachment; need for privacy	A preference for solitude; dignity under stress; high concentration; a responsible self-decision-maker.
6. Autonomy; independence from culture and environment; will; an active agent	The assumption of responsibility for one's own development; a person independent of the opinions of others.
7. Continued freshness of appreciation for nature, art, children, etc.	A sense of recurrent pleasure in one's environment.
8. Mystic experience: the Peak Experience	The capacity to feel ecstasy, wonder, awe; a sense of valued happenings; the intensification of experience.
9. Feeling for mankind	A capacity (or identification) for sympathy and affection toward others.
10. Good interpersonal relations	A capacity for love and identification; the attainment of deep ties with a few individuals or a small circle of friends; a person attractive to others.
11. Democratic character structure	A non-authoritarian in attitude and behavior; the ability to be friendly with many people of different backgrounds and to learn from others.
12. Discrimination between good and bad means and ends	A sustained and coherent sense of ethics and values with a focus on ends and not on means.
13. Philosophical and unhostile sense of humor	Humor that is not hostile, superior, or authoritarian; the ability to poke fun at oneself and at other humans in general.
14. Creativeness	Originality and inventiveness; a freshness of perception toward the environment.
15. Resistant to enculturation	A reasonable degree of conventionality in how one does things without being either a rebel against authority or lacking the courage to challenge authority when necessary, particularly in the face of injustice.

Adapted from Maslow, 1970.

cludes the self-concept. People are well adjusted to the extent that their ideas of self are congruent with both what they want to be and what, in fact, they are. Discrepancies between ideal and actuality lead to negative emotions and suffering because of the frustration that results from trying to be something that one is not.

Lack of congruence between the real and perceived self may lead the person to deny or block out of experience certain facts and perceptions. Thus a man who has an inaccurate estimate of his own artistic ability may be angry or suspicious of those who seem unappreciative of his talent; and anxious about allowing others to see his work, or he may block out of awareness or memory the critiques which are given. Client-centered therapy, which emphasizes the therapist's unconditional positive regard and empathic understanding, intends to free the client from threat or anxiety and the rigidity which it engenders, thus bringing the individual's self-concept more closely into line with reality. One first develops positive self-regard by experiencing it from another. Increasing self-regard enables the individual to increase self-understanding and self-acceptance, thus becoming freer to realize one's innate potential for growth. The freedom to be oneself, to like oneself, and grow into what one most naturally *is*, produces a feeling of joy and satisfaction.

The fully functioning human being must be self-aware, "open" to experience, and authentic, must like oneself, live in the present, and trust one's own feelings in deciding on personal directions to take in life. When people are free to love themselves and to develop in their own ways, humankind's basically good nature emerges. Destructive tendencies result from psychopathology and thwarting of the self-actualizing tendency. One must, of course, conform to some cultural expectations, but the person should not conform to the extent of playing prescribed roles which do violence to the real self. Acceptance of others and self-acceptance are the way to happy, productive living and self-actualization.

Rogers has been an extraordinarily important figure in personality theory and psychotherapy over the past 30 years. His theory is, to some degree, capable of experimental validation. Considerable research has been done on Rogers' theory as it applies to psychotherapy (Rogers & Dymond, 1954). Rogers was one of the foremost early challengers to the predominance of psychoanalytic theory and its form of psychotherapy. His theory of therapy seemed most appropriate to the college counseling population on which it was developed. He emphasized the *present* and *strengths* of the individual in contradistinction to psychoanalytic emphasis on the *past* and on *pathology*. Research on Rogers' theory is still actively pursued, with considerable controversy over the means of measuring such variables as accurate empathy, unconditional positive regard, and genuineness. Rogers has been criticized as being naively optimistic regarding human nature, and impractical in underemphasizing the specific skills, self-discipline, emotional control, and task-orientation required in our culture for optimum development.

FIELD-THEORY APPROACHES

Kurt Lewin (1890-1947) was born and educated in Germany, came to the United States in 1932, and held positions at Stanford, Cornell, the University of Iowa, and finally at MIT, where he was director of the Research Center for Group

Dynamics. Lewin had a widespread effect upon many areas of psychology including learning theory, social psychology, group theory, child psychology, and personality theory. In fact, his research and theorizing cut across many traditional divisions of psychology as he attempted to schematize the individual in his/her environment and predict behavior. Lewin's field theory (1936) was an outgrowth of late nineteenth-century physics which developed the ideas of configuration, motion, and force. Lewin asserted that human behavior is a function of all the positive and negative forces or vectors operating upon the individual at a given time, as well as the person's perception of those forces. His theory emphasized the importance of the individual's psychological environment or life space in determining behavior at a particular time. This life space is always changing as external factors are continually entering and leaving it.

Lewin used quasi-mathematical formulae to describe his ideas (e.g., $B=f(P,E)$ where B is behavior, P is the person in his current state, and E is the environment as he experiences it) and a kind of topology to present them. As in Figure 10.2, the person, P, is represented by a circle, the perimeter of which symbolizes the boundary which separates the person from the environment. The psychological environment is represented by the surrounding area, indicating that P is acted upon by the environment. The world outside the life space impinges on it to a greater or less degree inasmuch as the boundary of the life space may be at times more or less permeable, and may be more easily permeated by certain events than others. The needs of the individual are represented by differentiating regions within the person space, while the valences (negative and positive values) within the environment are represented by differentiating regions within the life space. Thus a need, thirst, would be represented as part of the person space, while water would be pictured as a valence in the environment. The need generates tension which exerts pressure toward motoric behavior until a state of equilibrium is reached. Lewin both explains and predicts behavior by means of his system. Major concepts are those of "tension-systems" or needs; "fluidity" or the extent to which one need may affect another; "valence" or the positive-negative pull of an aspect of the environment, and "goals." An alteration in any of the above can change the prediction of behavior. (For a closely related discussion of Lewinian theory, including a presentation of these topological diagrams, see pages 180–183.)

Lewin was interested in motivational conflicts and is well known for his diagrams of approach-approach, avoidance-avoidance, and approach-avoidance tensions, as well as his predictions of behavior under these conditions. His and his colleagues' experimental work, both with animals and human beings, tended to corroborate his hypotheses. He is also noted for his work on finished versus unfinished tasks. He hypothesized that, when people are stopped from completing a task, a tension-system or need to complete the task remains. Ovsiankina (1928) predicted and verified that, shortly after being interrupted, people given a choice of activities will tend to choose to return to complete unfinished tasks.

The events of World War II moved Lewin to study social conflict and to become involved in action research designed to improve understanding of soci-

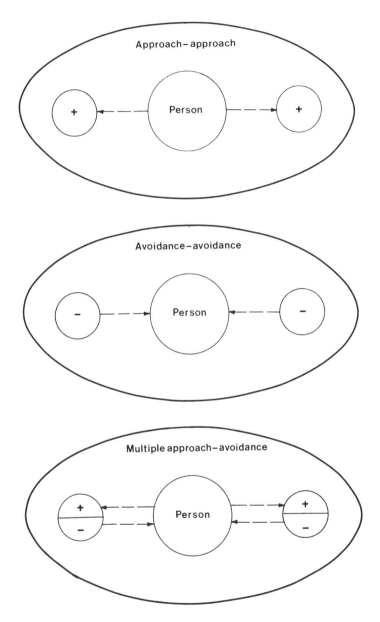

FIG. 10.2.   Simplified diagrams for the other three forms of conflict. The arrows in this case represent direction of locomotion (approach and avoidant tendencies) rather than Lewinian vectors.

etal problems and hopefully to find the means of ameliorating them. Thus he became interested in leadership, group productivity, cohesion, inter-group conflict, and societal influence (Lewin, 1939, 1948), and ingeniously applied his concepts to the study of these phenomena. He and his students were influential in establishing the area of small group research which has mushroomed over the past 30 to 40 years, and he could well be considered a father of industrial psychology.

STIMULUS-RESPONSE APPROACHES

Personality theory began in armchair theorizing, and was extended by Freud to the clinical analysis of individual patients while, simultaneously, S-R theories were emerging from the animal laboratory and human learning experiments. The latter two important influences on psychology—Freud's psychoanalytic theory and Pavlov's "conditioning" and learning theory—(see Chapter 2, Volume 1) were brought together at the Yale Institute of Human Relations. The Institute was established in 1933 for the purpose of engendering collaboration among psychology, psychiatry, sociology, and anthropology, and attracted an outstanding group of social scientists. Two of the early, primary writers were John Dollard, who obtained a Ph.D. in Sociology in 1931 from the University of Chicago, and Neal Miller, who earned a Ph.D. in Psychology from Yale in 1935. The psychologists associated with the Institute in those early years were strongly influenced by the learning theorist, Clark Hull, who developed a sophisticated and detailed S-R theory. Some of Hull's students and young collaborators had received psychoanalytic training, and some of them were well versed in anthropology and sociology. Five of them (Dollard, Doob, Miller, Mowrer, & Sears, 1939) brought out a book called *Frustration and Aggression,* which was an initial attempt to relate Freudian and Hullian concepts. They elaborated Freud's theory that frustration of instinctual drive leads to aggression and translated it into learning-theory concepts.[1]

Mowrer (Ph.D. in Psychology from Johns Hopkins in 1932) conducted a considerable number of laboratory studies in which he combined psychoanalytic and learning theories. Many of these are included in his volume, *Learning Theory and Personality Dynamics,* (Mowrer, 1950). One of his best-known contributions is his elaboration of an earlier-suggested dual theory of learning. In it he postulated that, while instrumental or drive-reducing behaviors require learning through reward or reinforcement, emotional responses may be learned simply through contiguity or association (see Chapter 2, Volume 1). Thus an autonomic or visceral response such as fear or anger may be learned as a cogni-

---

[1]Other attempts at integrating psychoanalytic theory and the Pavlovian theory of conditioning had originated in psychiatry. See Kimble (1967).

tion or set associated with other instrumental behaviors, or with the situation which instigated the instrumental behaviors. While the fate of the latter learning (e.g., fighting in response to anger) may depend upon reinforcement, the emotional concomitant may be independent of it. For example, a boy may continue to feel hostile and unable to behave effectively when he is called a "sissy," although he has learned to ignore it. Mowrer hypothesized that such strong emotions may engender neurotic problem behaviors such as tending to isolate oneself in order to avoid anxiety or hostility. Thus, strong, non-useful emotions may prevent a person from using good judgment or acquiring effective instrumental behavior.

Dollard and Miller (1950) went on to translate additional aspects of Freudian theory into researchable, Hullian concepts (see pp. 11–15). Freud's "libido" or pleasure principle was equated with the primary, physiological drives (sex, hunger, thirst), which for Hull were basic to the learning process. The organism learns to behave in ways which have been followed by drive-reduction or reward. The appropriate behavioral responses are set off by cues. Thus, for the infant, the sight of its bottle is a cue which leads to generalized motor activity and reaching, which are then rewarded by the mother's giving a bottle, the ingestion of milk, and the cessation of stomach contractions. Secondary, mainly psychological drives are learned through association with the primary drives. Thus, suppose that a hungry infant cries to no avail and suffers this strong drive while alone in its crib, not knowing when or whether those cries will be answered. The infant may develop anxiety associated with the cues and drive state of hunger, the cues associated with being in its crib or, by generalization, anxiety regarding the state of being alone in other locations. Anxiety then becomes a learned drive in response to the formerly neutral cues of being in the crib or just being alone. If the mother consistently fails to respond to the infant's cries, the latter response will gradually decrease to near zero probability of occurrence, or will become "extinguished." Enough experiences of non-reinforcement could lead to a more generalized attitude or expectancy, manifested in passivity or perhaps even infantile depression (hopelessness).

Dollard and Miller hypothesize that the most important drive conflicts may occur in infancy because the infant is relatively powerless to satisfy its own needs and does not have the discriminative power to separate, e.g., a genuinely fearful situation from one which may be relatively benign. For adults in our culture, primary drives are usually fairly easily satisfied, but the learned drives (to achieve love, friendship, fame, or reduce anxiety, anger, etc.) may be subjected to considerable frustration. That is, it is not immediately apparent how to satisfy them so that trial and error responses must be tried. This kind of learning dilemma is experienced whenever the individual has no habitual, drive-reducing response to a given situation. When new responses are attempted, their fate depends upon whether they are reinforced. They may be causally, accidentally, or only intermittently reinforced, giving rise to either adaptive or maladaptive learning which persists. The effects of reward or drive-reduction are not necessarily conscious, however.

One of Dollard and Miller's greatest contributions is their formulation of the role of conflict in generating neurotic anxiety, explaining why it is persistent in the absence of further frightening experiences, and how it may be elicited by previously neutral cues. Miller's demonstration was with white rats, who were shocked each time they were placed in a white box, and allowed to escape to a "safe" black box. After they were no longer shocked in the white box, the animals continued to show fear of it. They were motivated to continue to learn new escape responses in the absence of shock, with very little diminution of fear. After partial extinction of fear, they showed spontaneous recovery of the anxiety over time. Dollard and Miller (1950) compare this to the anxiety of the individual who, for example, is afraid of German Police dogs after having once been bitten. The individual thereafter avoids these dogs so that the fear is never extinguished by learning that most German Police dogs will not bite. Furthermore, the anxiety may generalize to all large dogs, those which bear the greatest resemblance to a German Police dog generating the most fear. On the basis of their theory, the best way to "undo" the fear would be to enable the individual to be near dogs in many non-threatening situations, and learn positive responses to the animals—responses incompatible with fear. This paradigm, in fact, turns out to be good therapy—in both the laboratory and the consultation room.

Dollard and Miller made the occurrence of anxiety understandable and predictable, defining it in terms of learning variables which are presumed to have acted during acquisition of the fear. They translated Freud's concept of repression into avoidance of thoughts which arouse fear and are thus painful. It is an anticipatory response of "stopping thinking," which is reinforcing because it avoids pain. Their theoretical analysis makes the individual's fearful behavior predictable. Working from Hull's concept of goal gradient (see Chapter 2, Volume 1), they extended the concept to deal with approach-avoidance conflict. They hypothesized that the closer one comes to an object which has a positive or negative valence, the stronger the associated tendency to approach or avoid the object. The child who fears a dog will tend more and more strongly to run away as the dog comes closer. Similarly, the closer a child gets to the ice cream shop, the stronger the tendency to run toward it. They hypothesized that, when the propelling drives are very strong and fear is very great, as may happen in the case of sexual drive and sexual anxiety, simultaneous approach-avoidance conflicts can be incapacitating, destructive, and the basis for neurotic maladjustment.

Dollard and Miller hypothesize that the child whose early years are marked by reinforcing experiences will become optimistic, self-confident, and resourceful. Similarly, the child whose early years were full of experiences of frustration, punishment, and fear will become passive, anxious, despondent, show "neurotic stupidity" caused by repression, and lack confidence and resourcefulness. The implications for child-rearing are apparent, and much the same as those principles promulgated by Freud. That is, they would recommend relative permissiveness, relative freedom from frustration, the use of positive reinforcement, and minimization of fears.

Another of Dollard and Miller's theoretical contributions was the promotion of Hull's idea that drives such as fear lead to responses which can, themselves, be cue-producing and lead to further responses which are mediated by that cue. Language and thoughts fall into this category, and may intensify, reduce, or direct the action initially associated with the drive. For example, fear of public speaking may produce quivering which further intensifies anxiety as the speaker fears that others will notice this physiological sympton of anxiety. In a positive vein, the dieter who is hungry and reaches for a cookie may think of the calories involved and redirect action with the decision to drink a glass of water, instead. The individual who typically responds with explosive anger when frustrated can generate the self-instruction to "count to ten," relax the muscles and react more effectively as a result. The idea of controlling responses through self-mediated verbal cues is one which has been emphasized, more recently, by social learning theorists and cognitive behavior therapists.

Sears (a Ph.D. in Psychology from Yale in 1932), is another author of the original *Frustration and Aggression* book who has devoted attention to experimental and empirical evaluation of psychoanalytic theory, especially as applied to child development (1943; Sears, Maccoby, & Levin, 1957). He has emphasized the significance of the interactions between parents and children, and has done important work in elucidating the influence of child-rearing practices upon personality. For example, punitive mothers were found to have children who were rated by their teachers as behaving non-aggressively in school, but had high fantasied aggression, while the children of non-punitive mothers showed more overt than fantasied aggression.

Wolpe, a psychiatrist who earned his M.D. in South Africa in 1948, has spent most of his professional life at Temple University Medical School. Like Dollard and Miller, he sees anxiety as a classically conditioned response which produces neurotic, maladaptive behavior designed to avoid anxiety-producing cues. This formulation led him to develop a system of systematic desensitization designed to eliminate anxiety associated with specific stimuli (Wolpe, 1958). With this method of therapy, the anxious individual is first taught how to relax. Then the patient practices relaxing while imagining situations that are mildly anxiety-producing. Having accomplished that, the individual gradually learns to relax to all of the situations, in an individualized hierarchy of their degree of anxiety arousal, until it is possible to relax to all of them. Inasmuch as relaxation is incompatible with anxiety, the individual becomes able to tolerate more and more of those situations which had previously evoked fearful reactions.

B. F. Skinner earned a doctorate in psychology from Harvard in 1931, and spent approximately the last 25 years of his professional career there. Skinner may well go down in history as the most influential psychologist of our times, his only competition for this distinction being Sigmund Freud. Skinner has contributed most directly to the psychology of learning (Ch. 1, vol. 1), but his influence on personality theory and psychotherapy has been considerable (Skinner, 1953, 1954). While not a personality theorist himself, he has stimulated an important extension of contemporary learning theory to the area of personality theory and to its application in the clinical arena. Wolpe has also extended learning theory to clinical practice, an important difference between Wolpe and Skinner being that Wolpe uses a classical, autonomic conditioning paradigm, while Skinner sees maladaptive behavior as operant behavior maintained by reinforcement. He would alter undesirable behavior by non-reinforcement, and promote more desirable behavior by positive reinforcement. A variety of techniques based upon his formulations have, in fact, become important both in research and in applied settings.

Cognitive Theory

We have said that theoretical approaches to personality, considered historically, seem to have proceeded from a strong emphasis upon biological drives, instincts, or needs, then to systems involving the self as central, and finally to a more situational position where environmental variables and learning are crucial. We have seen also that the early theories are concerned with the internal feeling or emotional aspects of human experience; and we might expect that this concern would diminish with the emphasis upon the directly observable which characterizes behaviorally oriented views. Such a description might seem to imply that personality theory, with the exception of the humanistic view, derives from the more or less mechanistic views of biological impulse on the one hand and of environmental determination on the other—a sort of push-pull conceptualization which excludes reference to personal choice or personal styles of perceiving, remembering, and thinking. Although such a description may be accurate for some approaches, nothing could be further from the truth in the case of the cognitive approaches to personality.

There are hints of the importance of cognitive variables in the very earliest theories of personality. From Plato onward, systems describing the major faculties of man have included *thinking,* along with *doing* and *feeling.* "Understanding," as an element, was considered too general for the phrenologist Gall; but his system still included such cognitive terms as constructiveness, comparison, causality, and language. Both English and German philosophers, seeking to explain "mental" phenomena, included ideas and perceptions as units.

In the modern period, every position described thus far in this chapter has dealt in some way with cognition. One example may be found in the neo-Freudian theories where the ego is lifted from its weak position in early psychoanalysis to an independent, conflict-free sphere with intellectual functions. The inclusion, in most constitutional typologies, of a bodily structure related to thinking or introspecting (as in Sheldon's *cerebrotonia*) is another. In the humanistic self-theories, where the person becomes central, the motivational systems contain "cognitive" needs. Indeed, where such systems are hierarchical, the cognitive needs occupy a lofty position, reminiscent of the "higher mental processes" dealt with by nineteenth-century psychologists. As we have seen, stimulus-response and social learning approaches to personality have also included learned cognitive processes.

A small group of theorists, especially active in the fifties but still influential, made cognitive activities the focus of their approaches to personality. Of them all, George Kelly (1905–1966) exemplified best the unique quality of cognitive personality theory (1955, 1969). In one way, Kelly's theory was an attempt to explain personality without a separate motivational construct. In another, it was a theory which makes the person central, an active creator of hypotheses and categorizer of experience. Although emotional responses are not eliminated from this system, Kelly's view lays greater stress on the cognitive processes of thought and perception.

Briefly, the Kelly theory, termed constructive alternativism, holds that people, like scientists, form hypotheses by which they attempt to predict and control their experiences. Human beings thus have the creative capacity to represent the environment, not merely to respond to it. They "construe" their own environments by means of personal interpretations. Their personal processes are channelized by the ways in which they anticipate events. Persons may differ from one another in the construing of events, so that each individual has an idiosyncratic construct system. Individuals differ also in their cognitive complexity, and in their cognitive styles. The person's system is made up of dichotomous constructs, for example, "good-bad." In order to develop a Kellian construct, one must specify a similarity between two events, and a difference between these and a third. "Chromatic-achromatic," "pleasant-unpleasant," "young-old," "lively-dull" are other examples of constructs. It is hypothesized that persons choose from their supply of dichotomous constructs the alternatives that they anticipate will provide the greatest opportunity for the extension and definition of their systems for interpreting the environment.

Kelly's theory was derived in part from his experience with troubled college students whom he saw in psychotherapy over many years. Perhaps for that reason, the theory is considered by many to be over-intellectualized and unduly narrow. However, it has stimulated considerable research, and has generated a useful diagnostic tool, the Role Construct Repertory Test. This test is a means of identifying the constructs with which people give meaning to events around them, thus interpreting the world and rationalizing behavior. In taking the test, the individual names significant persons (e.g., parents, siblings, friends), and then judges all possible combinations of three of these persons in a dichotomous manner. Two of the three persons must be judged as the same in a specified way, and must differ from the third along that same dimension. From such responses, it is possible to specify the content of the constructs which make up the individual's personality system or the important dimensions along which the social environment is interpreted.

Leon Festinger earned a Ph.D. at the University of Iowa in 1951 and has spent many years at Stanford. In his theory, the relevant units for study are *cognitions*, defined as opinions, beliefs and knowledges. The basic concept is that of cognitive dissonance, which refers to a relationship which exists between pairs of cognitions. For example, if a person feels fearful in an environment in which there are only friendly persons, there is a dissonant relationship between the two knowledges. The consequence of dissonance is discomfort and tension, so that when cognitive dissonance exists, the person will employ means of reducing it. Festinger's writings describe the variety of ways in which such reduction may occur, such as changing either the behavior or the environment. Festinger's theory is more related to attitude change, or to motivation, than to personality (see pp. 387–388) but concepts very much like those of the theory of cognitive dissonance appear in a number of personality theories, most clearly, perhaps, in that of David McClelland.

McClelland earned a Ph.D. in psychology from Yale in 1941, and has been at Harvard for many years. His theory is concerned with discrepancies between expectations and occurrences (McClelland, 1953). In attending to such discrepancies McClelland is close to both Kelly and Festinger. He is also close to them in the units of personality he postulated: motives (affective dynamisms), traits (habits of doing) and schemata (cognitions)—a trio which, it will be recalled, is traceable back to ancient times. Among the important cognitions is *expectancy*, a unit which refers to events in the future and is comparable to Kelly's ''construct'' and Festinger's ''cognition.''

In one important respect, however, McClelland differs from the other two theorists: he makes the degree of inconsistency between expectancy and occurrence crucial. Unpleasant feelings and avoidance of the situation occur only when the degree of dissonance is large; small discrepancies, he argues, are pleasant. Thus, the tendency is to minimize large discrepancies between expectation and occurrence, while maximizing small ones.

At present, two trends seem to be developing from the early cognitive positions. In the first trend, the cognitive theories are becoming increasingly social in orientation; a convergence of cognitive personality theory and social learning psychological theory seems inevitable. To be sure, the cognitive approaches to personality have always concerned themselves to some extent with social phenomena. But, particularly when the concepts of dissonance and disequilibrium are employed, increasing attention is given to such social variables as attitude and person perception. Indeed, one contemporary theorist, Walter Mischel, has already brought together some of these notions into what he calls a "cognitive social learning" conceptualization of personality (Mischel, 1973).

Mischel (Ph.D. in Psychology, Ohio State, 1956), has been at Stanford University for the past 20 years. He begins with a general skepticism of trait theory, and his system is soon revealed as one in which personal constructions, social interactions, and individual differences in values are significant. His basic units, called cognitive social learning person variables, focus upon both the individual's cognitive activities and upon his behavior patterns. Five basic units are identified: (1) competencies to construct diverse behaviors: the person constructs reality in much the same manner as Kelly's subjects construe it; (2) encoding strategies: the grouping of informational inputs from situations; (3) outcome expectancies, concerning the consequences of different behavioral possibilities in the situation; (4) subjective stimulus values, or individual differences in the value of response-contingent outcomes; and (5) self-regulatory systems and plans. Echoes of Kelly are to be heard in this system, although it is more broadly social and more heavily dependent upon contemporary research in social learning than are the others.

In the second trend, there is growing emphasis on a dimension of individual differences which might be called cognitive styles. There are many ways in which individuals construe their environments; dissonance depends upon personal knowledges, which vary widely among people; degrees of discrepancy between expectancy and occurrence are perceived differently by different subjects. In the presence of such diversity, the challenge is great to classify, type, or diagnose. Contemporary systems of cognitive style represent attempts to meet that challenge.

Among the many styles which have been identified and then studied extensively are the analytic vs. the global (or field-dependent vs. field-independent [Witkin, 1964]); reflective vs impulsive (Kagan, 1966) and internal vs. external locus of control (see below). These styles all seek to identify individual differences in approaches to problems, and all focus upon cognitive behavior. It should be noted that in this situation Mischel has guided his own research in a different direction. Rather than attempting to classify or diagnose, he has obtained experimental evidence for "cognitive transformations" by which individuals can guide and control their own behavior. Such transformations make for highly idiosyncratic organizations of behavior, rather than types.

SOCIAL APPROACHES

Another important trend in the conceptualization of personality is one that emphasizes the importance of the social environment in shaping emotions, cognitions, and behavior. Some neo-Freudians can be so classified, as well as some psychologists who are closer to the learning theory model. While environmental factors are considered in all personality theories, it is the particular emphasis on the importance of human interactions that has led to the grouping of a few representative writers under the above heading.

Psychoanalytically Oriented Social Theories

Karen Horney (1885–1952) was born in Germany and trained there as a psychoanalyst, but spent the last 20 years of her life in the United States. She did not agree that personality is largely determined by instincts, but emphasized the influence of the social environment and the role of faulty training in the development of intrapsychic conflict and neurosis (Horney, 1937, 1939). As with Freud, anxiety was a central concept as were the individual's learned mechanisms for reducing it. For her, anxiety-reducing strategies involve moving toward, against, or away from people. She called these the individual's social orientation. She identified (1) a self-effacing solution (striving for love); (2) an expansive solution (striving for mastery); and (3) resignation (striving for freedom). Any of the three orientations can become fixed and thereby limiting to the individual—e.g., being overly compliant to achieve acceptance; being overly aggressive and demanding; or avoiding others, being self-sufficient and apart from society. These neurotic needs are made into "virtues" by the maladjusted individual (e.g., compliance, consideration for others, submission). The normal individual integrates the three orientations, and is capable of using them flexibly. As can be seen, Horney has much in common with the humanistic or self theorists.

Horney hypothesizes 10 neurotic needs which, if abnormally strong, can lead one to pursue an idealized version of the self and avoid recognition of the *real* self. In a manner similar to Rogers', Horney posits an *ideal* self or the image we would like to pursue, and the *real* self, or what one's capabilities and achievements actually are. A healthy person has an accurate idea of the real self although pursuing higher achievements, whereas the neurotic has an inaccurate self-picture and may engage in a self-defeating "search for glory." False pride results from faulty self-evaluation, and may engender self-condemnation and feelings of inferiority when the unrealistic goals are not met. Failure often only intensifies the need, resulting in a vicious circle of anxiety and striving. Also, neurotic pride may necessitate avoidance of situations where true performance could be evaluated. Caution and oversensitivity thus may be apparent, along with hatred of the real self and false pride in the idealized self. A partial solution may be sought in daydreams.

Horney was one of the first to emphasize the importance of family attitudes and practices, which interact with broader circumstances and cultural factors to produce the particular characteristics of an individual, and to point out the need for constructive family and societal conditions. She sees self-knowledge and a warm, encouraging, but also guiding environment as the keys to favorable growth through acceptance of the real self and avoidance of anxiety.

Horney made important insightful contributions to the understanding of neurosis and maladaptive behaviors, although they are not readily accessible to laboratory measurement and verification. While her own writing, in the psychoanalytic tradition, did not involve empirical validation outside the clinical consultation room, her ideas are related to others which later were subjected to some experimental validation (Rogers' self vs ideal self; Sears' investigations of family climate). Her writing is, in any case, influential in its application to psychotherapy and has been a source of help and self-understanding to troubled intellectuals who have engaged in self-analysis (Horney, 1942). She stressed the importance of realistic self-appraisal in the light of an individual's experiences with success and failure. She shares the emphasis of Maslow and Rogers on accepting the real self, working to improve it, but working with one's innate potential rather than establishing an unrealistic ideal which is unattainable. Her ideas are positive, optimistic, and emphasize self-actualization. She sees culture as making us neurotic when we are subjected to its forces in a destructive fashion.

Social Learning Theories

Traditional learning theorists have emphasized the need for immediate reinforcement during the acquisition of new instrumental behaviors.[2] That is, it has been hypothesized that there must occur, shortly after the behavior, a reward, either primary (e.g., food, water, sex) or secondary (something which has previously been associated with a primary reinforcement). More recent social learning theorists have hypothesized that complex human behavior cannot all be learned in this way—asserting that S-R theorists unrealistically atomize behavior, not explaining how it emerges in full-blown complexity. They do not deny that consequences are essential in eliciting behavior, but state that reinforcement is not necessary for *cognitive* learning to take place.

Albert Bandura obtained his doctorate in psychology from the University of Iowa in 1952, and has taught at Stanford for approximately 30 years. He and Richard Walters (1918–1967) emphasized the importance of observational learning (Bandura & Walters, 1963). Children learn what to do and how it is done through observing adult models, and later they learn new behaviors or modify

---

[2]The version of learning theory challenged by the social learning theorists is now dated (see Ch. 1, vol. 1). The possibility of learning with long delays of reinforcement has been accepted for some time; a reinterpretation of reinforcement in terms of information, rather than satisfaction, is compatible with observational learning. It is now commonly recognized that "habit" and "expectancy" are similar concepts. Some of this profound shift in perspective represents an effect of social learning theory upon more basic learning theory. *Editors*

old ones through imitation of friends and associates (modeling). Bandura and Walters hypothesize that we can, in this way, learn new behavior without necessarily experiencing reinforcement. If this be the case, it is particularly important in the formative years to have good, competent, pro-social models. These may be real-life models or symbolic models encountered in books or on television. Bandura, Walters, and others have conducted numerous studies showing that children imitate the behavior and attitudes of parents and of models who are presented in real-life or on a television screen. The effect is more potent when the models appear to be similar to the observer, prestigious, or successful. The ''successful'' model is one who is observed to be earning reinforcement for the behavior (vicarious reinforcement).

Julian Rotter earned his Ph.D. in psychology from the University of Indiana in 1941, and has spent a large part of his career at the University of Connecticut. He is a clinical psychologist with an orientation which leans toward learning theory of the Tolman variety (Rotter, 1954; Rotter, Chance, & Phares, 1972). He hypothesizes that, on the basis of past experience, we develop expectancies that specific behaviors will be followed by a certain outcome. An expectancy may be so strong that we perceive the outcome we expect, even if it is not fully justified. Our future behavior is determined and restricted by our expectancies (often of failure, so that we avoid situations in which we have felt inadequate previously) as we attempt to fulfill our needs.

Expectancies are based both on the number and quality of previous reinforcements. We may value some reinforcements considerably more than others, and consequently seek them avidly even though the probability of achieving them may be small. For example, the pursuit of recognition may lead one to many sacrifices, hard work and the abandonment of other psychologically less important reinforcements such as sleep, social contacts, etc. As with Horney and Adler, it is important to have realistic goals, and neurosis often involves having minimum goal levels which are too high. If minimum goals are too high, the individual does not feel satisfied or reinforced by partial achievement—e.g., the fellow who could date a girl he likes for the prom but cannot be satisfied because he was refused by the most popular girl in his class. Rejection may only lead to intensified attempts to date her, leading to frustration and self-depreciation.

Happiness and good adjustment depend upon having realistic expectations— neither too high nor too low. Unreasonably low expectations deny satisfaction and engender boredom and depression. It is important for an individual to be able to delay immediate, less important gratification in the interest of long term, more significant gratification (e.g., forego favorite foods in order to lose weight; lose sleep in order to pass an exam). It is also important for an individual to feel in *control* of obtaining reinforcement (e.g., to feel that working hard enough will earn a grade that is deservedly high, and that the instructor will not examine or grade capriciously).

CONCLUSION

By this time it is clear that there are many historical trends represented in personality theories, most of them reflecting the sweep of the history of modern psychology as a science. These theories have sought to deal with the recurring questions which arise when attempts are made to account for the complexity, diversity, and consistency of human personality:

1. What are the sources of human *motivation?* Here the answers have ranged across a spectrum from the conceptualized energy of psychoanalytic theory to notions of constitutional predisposition, thence to hierarchically ordered needs, to cognitive disequilibria and dissonances, and to biologically defined drives.
2. What are the structural *units* of which personality is fashioned? Again, many answers have been proposed, from the psychoanalytic concepts of id, ego, and superego, to traits, types, habits, cognitions, responses, and interactions.
3. What *orientation* should the theorist maintain? Here the inner-outer, self-situation dichotomies pose the dilemma which the personality theorist faces.

Thus the elements or components of a general theory of personality seem to be available. Despite this obvious fact, however, no general theory has been recently advanced, nor does one seem to be forthcoming. Rather, a series of "mini-theories" have emerged, each derived from or related to a particular focus of research. For example, theories of conflict resolution, based upon animal investigation, appear. Theories of locus of control, of attribution, of dissonance, of social modeling are promulgated. But the integration of these part-components into a total explanatory system continues to elude us. Perhaps these current concepts have led us as far as they can, and a general theory awaits a new and different point of view.

In this situation, it is presumptuous to make predictions as to the direction which future theory-construction might take. It may be reasonable, however, to identify the next steps which could follow from the trends we have identified in this chapter. It would appear that a general personality theory of the future must continue to represent the social-behavioral position at which we have now arrived. Whether this means that personality as a field of study is to be encompassed by a wider field called social psychology remains to be seen. It would appear also that a truly general theory of personality must be oriented in three directions: toward biological predispositions and events, toward cultural forces, and toward the inner self. It is the simultaneous operation of these three variables which accounts in large part for the complexity of human personality. And perhaps most importantly, it would appear that only a theory which is susceptible of objective test—whether in the laboratory or in the field—will be sufficiently in harmony with modern psychology to prevail.

REFERENCES

Adler, A. *The practice and theory of individual psychology.* New York: Harcourt, 1927.

Adler, A. *Problems of neurosis.* London: Kegan Paul, Trench, Trubner, 1929.

Allport, G. W. *Personality: A psychological interpretation.* New York: Holt, 1937.

Bandura, A., & Walters, R. *Social learning and personality development.* New York: Holt, Rinehart & Winston, 1963.

Bayley, N. Behavioral correlates of mental growth: Birth to 36 years. *American Psychologist,* 1968, *23,* 1–17.

Boring, E. G. *A history of experimental psychology* (2nd ed.). New York: Appleton-Century-Crofts, 1950.

Casey, M. D., Segall, L. J., Street, D. R. K., & Blank, C. E. Sex chromosome abnormalities in two state hospitals for patients requiring special security. *Nature,* 1966, *209,* 641–642.

Cattell, R. B. *The description and measurement of personality.* Cleveland: World Book, 1946.

Cattell, R. B. *Personality and motivation structure and measurement.* New York: Harcourt, Brace & World, 1957.

Dollard, J., Doob, L. W., Miller, N. E., Mowrer, O. H., & Sears, R. R. *Frustration and aggression.* New Haven: Yale University Press, 1939.

Dollard, J. & Miller, N. E. *Personality and psychotherapy.* New York: McGraw-Hill, 1950.

Domino, G., Goldschmid, M., & Kaplan, M. Personality traits of institutionalized mongoloid girls. *American Journal of Mental Deficiency,* 1964, *68,* 498–502.

Dworkin, R. H., Burke, B. W., Maher, B. A., & Gottesman, I. I. A longitudinal study of the genetics of personality. *Journal of Personality and Social Psychology,* 1976, *34,* 510–518.

Dworkin, R. H., Burke, B. W., Maher, B. A., & Gottesman, I. I. Genetic influences on the organization and development of personality. *Developmental Psychology,* 1977, *13,* 164–165.

Erikson, E. *Childhood and society.* New York: Norton, 1950.

Erikson, E. Identity and the life cycle. *Psychological Issues,* 1959,*I,* 1, Monograph 1, 18–172.

Escalona, S. K. *The roots of individuality.* Chicago: Aldine, 1968.

Eysenck, H. J. *Dimensions of personality.* London: Routledge & Kegan Paul, 1947.

Eysenck, H. J. *The scientific study of personality.* London: Routledge & Kegan Paul, 1952.

Fernald, C. D. The Lesch-Nyhan syndrome: Cerebral palsy, mental retardation & self mutilation. *Journal of Pediatric Psychology.* 1976, *1,* 51–55.

Festinger, L. *A theory of cognitive dissonance.* Stanford, California: Stanford University Press, 1957.

Friedman, D. G. Personality development in infancy: A biological approach. In Y. Brackbill (Ed.), *Infancy and childhood.* New York: The Free Press, 1967.

Freud, A. *The ego and the mechanisms of defense.* New York: International Universities Press, 1946.

Freud, S. *New introductory lectures on psychoanalysis.* New York: Norton, 1933.

Fuller, J. L., & Thompson, W. R. *Behavior genetics.* New York: Wiley, 1960.

Gall, F. J. *Sur les fonctions du cerveau.* Paris: 1822-25.

Gottesman, I. J. Heritability of personality. *Psychological Monographs,* 1963, *77,* 1–21.

Hartmann, H. The mutual influences in the development of the ego and id. *The Psychoanalytic Study of the Child,* 1952, *7,* 9–30.

Hartmann, H., Kris, E., & Loewenstein, R. M. Comments on the formation of psychic structure. *The Psychoanalytic Study of the Child,* 1946, *2,* 11–38.

Hathaway, S. R., & McKinley, J. C. *The Minnesota Multiphasic Personality Inventory* (Rev. ed.). Minneapolis: Univeristy of Minnesota, 1943.

Horney, K. *The neurotic personality of our time.* New York: Norton, 1937.

Horney, K. *New ways in psychoanalysis.* New York: Norton, 1939.

James, W. *Principles of psychology.* New York: Dover, 1950.

Jarvik, L. F., Klodin, V., & Matsuyama, S. S. Human aggression and the extra Y chromosome: Fact or fantasy? *American Psychologist,* 1973, *28,* 674–682.

Jung, C. G. *Contributions to analytical psychology.* New York: Harcourt, 1928.

Jung, C. G. *Psychological types.* New York: Harcourt, 1933.

Kagan, J. Developmental studies in reflection and analysis. In A. H. Kidd & J. L. Riviore (Eds.), *Perceptual development in children.* New York: International Universities Press, 1966.

Kallman, F. J. *Heredity in health and mental disorder.* New York: Norton, 1953.

Kelly, G. A. *The psychology of personal constructs* (2 vols.). New York: Norton, 1955.

Kelly, G. A. Man's construction of his alternatives. In B. Maher (Ed.), *Clinical psychology and personality: The selected papers of George Kelly.* New York: Wiley, 1969, 66–93.

Kimble, G., Garmezy, N., & Zigler, E. *Principles of general psychology* 4th ed.). New York: Ronald, 1974.

Kline, P. *Fact and fantasy in Freudian theory.* London: Methuen, 1972.

Kretschmer, E. *Physique and character.* New York: Harcourt, 1925.

Lewin, K. *Principles of topological psychology.* New York: McGraw-Hill, 1936.

Lewin, K. *Resolving social conflicts.* New York: Harper, 1948.

Lewin, K., Lippitt, R., & White, R. K. Patterns of aggressive behavior in experimentally created "social climates." *Journal of Social Psychology,* 1939, *10,* 271–279.

Maslow, A. H. Higher and lower needs. *Journal of Psychology,* 1943, *25,* 433–436.

Maslow, A. H. *Motivation and personality.* New York: Harper & Bros., 1954.

McClelland, D. C., Atkinson, J. W., Clark, R. A., & Lowell, E. L. *The achievement motive.* New York: Appleton-Century-Crofts, 1953.

McDougall, W. *Physiological psychology,* London: Dent, 1905.

McDougall, W. *Outline of abnormal Psychology,* New York: Scribner's, 1926.

Mill, J. S. *System of Logic.* New York: Harper, 1846.

Mischel, W. Toward a cognitive social learning reconceptualization of personality. *Psychological Review,* 1973, *80,* 252–283.

Mosack, H. (Ed.). *Alfred Adler, his influence on psychology today.* Park Ridge, N.H.: Noyes, 1973.

Mowrer, O. H. *Learning theory and personality dynamics.* New York: Ronald, 1950.

Murphy, L. B. *The widening world of childhood.* New York: Basic Books, 1962.

Murray, H. *Explorations in personality.* New York: Oxford University Press, 1938.

Neilon, P. Shirley's babies after 15 years: A personality study. *Journal of Genetic Pschology,* 1948, *73,* 175–186.

Owen, D. R. The 47, XYY male: A review. *Psychological Bulletin,* 1972, *78,* 209–233.

Rank, O. *Trauma of birth.* New York: Harcourt, Brace & World, Inc., 1929.

Rank, O. *Will therapy.* New York: Alfred A. Knopf, Inc., 1936.

Richmond, J. B., Lipton, E. L., & Steinschneider, A. Observations on differences in autonomic nervous system function between and within individuals during early infancy. *Journal of Child Psychiatry,* 1961, *1,* 83–91.

Rogers, C. R. *Counseling and psychotherapy.* Boston: Houghton-Mifflin, 1942.

Rogers, C. R. *Client-centered therapy: Its current practice, implications and theory.* Boston: Houghton-Mifflin, 1951.

Rogers, C. R. *Becoming a person.* Boston: Houghton-Mifflin, 1961.

Rogers, C. R., & Dymond, R. *Psychotherapy and personality change.* Chicago: University of Chicago Press, 1954.

Rorschach, H. *Psychodiagnostics.* Berne: Hans Huber, 1942.

Rotter, J., *Social learning and clinical psychology*. New York: Prentice-Hall, 1954.

Rotter, J., Chance, J., & Phares, E. *Application of a social learning theory of personality*. New York: Holt, Rinehart & Winston, 1972.

Sears, R. R. Survey of objective studies of psychoanalytic concepts. *Social Science Research Council Bulletin*, 1943, No. 51.

Sears, R. R., Maccoby, E. E., & Levin, H. *Patterns of child rearing*. Chicago: Row, Peterson, 1957.

Sechrest, L. Personality. *Annual Review of Psychology*, 1976, *27*, 1–27.

Shand, A. *Foundations of Character*. London: McMillan, 1926.

Sheldon, W. H. (with E. M. Hartl & E. McDermott). *Varieties of delinquent youth: An introduction to consititutional psychiatry*. New York: Harper, 1949.

Sheldon, W. H. (with S. S. Stevens). *The varieties of temperament: A psychology of constitutional differences*. New York: Harper, 1942.

Sheldon, W. H. (with S. S. Stevens & W. B. Tucker). *The varieties of human physique: An introduction to constitutional psychology*. New York: Harper, 1940.

Silverstein, A. B. An empirical test of the mongoloid stereotype. *American Journal of Mental Deficiency*, 1964, *68*, 493–497.

Skinner, B. F. *Science and human behavior*. New York: Macmillan, 1953.

Skinner, B. F. *Contingencies of reinforcement*. New York: Appleton-Century-Crofts, 1954.

Stanbury, J. B., Wyngaarden, J. B., & Fredrickson, D. S. (Eds.), *The metabolic basis of inherited disease*. New York: McGraw-Hill, 1972.

Wilson, R. S., Brown, A. M., & Matheny, A. P., Jr. Emergence and persistence of behavioral differences in twins. *Child Development*, 1971, *42*, 1381-1398.

Witkin, H. A. Origins of cognitive style. In C. Scheerer (Ed.), *Cognition: Theory, research, promise*. New York: Harper & Row, 1964.

Witkin, H. A., Mednick, S. A., Schulsinger, F., Bakkeström, E., Christiansen, K. O., Goodenough, D. R., Hirschhorn, K., Lundsteen, C., Owen, D. R., Phillip, J., Rubin, D. B., & Stocking, M. Criminality in XYY and XXY men. *Science*, 1976 *193*, 547–555.

Wolpe, J. *Psychotherapy by reciprocal inhibition*. Stanford, Ca.: Stanford University, 1958.

11 History of Social Psychology

Edward E. Jones
Princeton University

The task of covering the history of a major psychological subdiscipline in a single book chapter is, in fact, an impossible challenge if one is to do justice to the range of topics and guiding ideas that have molded its current shape. This review cannot pretend, therefore, to be comprehensive; it will selectively emphasize the experimental approach to problems of social influence and social cognition. This selective emphasis helps both in restricting the time period to be reviewed and in permitting me to ignore the many contributions of sociological and anthropological analysts to the casting of social psychological problems.

The field of social psychology grew out of the recognition of human diversity within cultural uniformity. It is a truism that people are alike in some respects and differ in others. Some of these differences may be characterized in terms of cultural uniformities and the uniformities of social class or position. However, there is a residue of uniqueness that can only be captured by focusing on the specific intersection of the biological and the social. Some (e.g., Cottrell & Gallagher, 1941) have expressed the hope that social psychology would become ''the biochemistry of the social sciences.'' This will be true to the extent that social psychology is able to capture the underlying processes wherein individuals are responsive to the social stimuli provided by others.

From the point of view of understanding social influence, the central problem of social psychology is how to conceptualize the sources and modifiers of influence so as to make a coherent predictive science, one that transcends the particularities of given instances where one person is affected by the presence or behavior of another. At the same time, we must conceptualize the receiving organism in such a way as to account for the influence process (as well as the influencing process) in terms of relevant cognitive and motivational constructs.

In line with this definition of our subject matter, we find social psychology flanked by the study of social structures and processes on the one hand (sociology, anthropology, political science, and economics) and of personal structures and processes on the other (personality, developmental, and differential psychology). Social psychology becomes a distinctive subject matter when it is realized that the archetype of man intersecting with society is the interpersonal moment; the most fruitful place to study influence processes is in the family, in the small group, in persuasion episodes involving salesmen, educators, or politicians, and in structured interactions known collectively as "games," often featuring negotiation and bargaining. The key (though certainly not the sole) target of social psychology is to understand the processes that mediate direct interpersonal influence in the contexts where it most naturally occurs.

OVERVIEW AND CURRENT STATUS

As it currently exists the field of social psychology is solidly established as a part of psychology in all major American academic departments. (This is not to ignore those approaches to social psychological questions that are pursued in sociology departments.) The core literature supporting the field is undoubtedly the experimental report, though important research efforts of a more applied sort often involve multiple regression, path analysis, and other correlational techniques based on questionnaire or interview data. The field has just passed through an upheaval of self-criticism and soul searching. The criticism has centered around how to make social psychology more relevant to contemporary problems, a set of pressures augmented by student protests and demands during the sixties. In fact, the field has always been characterized by a tension between investigations that are directly relevant to contemporary social issues and those that are primarily relevant to the development of underlying theory. A similar tension exists between investigations embedded in the natural environment and laboratory studies characterized by the purity of variable manipulation. To some extent these tensions are reflected in a discrepancy between the kind of social psychology presented in textbooks (where social relevance and naturalism are typically stressed) and the kind of social psychology one finds in the prime research journals (where connection with theory is more clearly valued). The field has also had a long preoccupation with appropriate methodology and there has been a persistent conflict between those who see the importance of experimental manipulation and unobtrusive measurement on the one hand and those who champion the dignity and inherent privacy of each potential subject on the other hand. There is little prospect that this conflict will soon be resolved, but it is clear that there will always be necessary ethical constraints limiting the procedures available to the social psychological investigator.

In spite of these inherent tensions with regard to methodology, point of attack, and ideological consistency, the contemporary mood of the field has settled into a period of relative calm in which investigators have returned to their primary task of generating new empirical data. There is much to be done, new techniques of analysis are available, new theoretical distinctions assert themselves. So, as an early English physicist said in another context, "the dogs bark and the caravan moves on."

The present route of the caravan is not that easy to map, however. There is unquestionably an emphasis on cognitive processes in relation to behavior—especially how impressions of other persons are formed, how decisions about the self-concept are made, and more generally how we understand and make sense out of the social environment around us. One wing of cognitive social psychology has turned toward algebra in developing models for the processing of information. Those in other wings have resisted this trend as artificializing. Research and theory building continue in the area of dyadic interaction where there is a particular interest in the varieties of interdependence and their modification through social interaction.

But not surprisingly, much of the research in contemporary social psychology is an attack on social problems: aggression and violence, helping behavior, the effects of crowding and other environmental conditions, conservation and the social dilemmas that grow out of the energy crisis, and so on. There is a rapidly accumulating body of research on social psychology and the law, concerned with testimony, jury decision making, and procedural underpinnings. Many social psychologists are concerned with sex role stereotypes, their prevalence and the ways to mute their effects. Minority group prejudice has always been a topic of great importance in social psychology and it remains so.

With this sketchy description of contemporary social psychology in mind, let us turn to the historical highlights to gain a better understanding of how the study of social influence emerged as an experimental field.

PRE-TWENTIETH CENTURY FORERUNNERS

Allport (1954, 1968) has contributed a very useful summary of the historical antecedents of modern social psychology. He finds an impressive continuity in the problem focus of nineteenth-century social theorists and contemporary investigators, although it is possible to question this conclusion. True, one could relate the current interest in helping behavior to Herbert Spencer's (1870) interest in sympathy; conformity research was preceded by the preoccupation of Gabriel Tarde (1903) with the laws of imitation; and group dynamics owe something to the earlier debates over collective representations (Durkheim, 1898) or the group mind (McDougall, 1920). And yet the recent research on such topics yields such differentiated and cumulative insights that the continuity of topic labels is actually misleading. It is as if we were to compare modern reinforcement theory or the work on operant conditioning schedules to earlier assertions about the importance of hedonism. The undoubted difference in both cases is the contribution to theoretical development of a cumulative methodology and a refined body of data. Because of the availability of experimentation as a research paradigm, pronouncements about social influence need not pass each other unnoticed in the misty night or resolve into quibbles about definition and taxonomy. Empirical research involves mutual implication and the continuing re-examination of the ability of current theory to support incoming data generated under carefully specified experimental conditions.

The advent of appropriate methodology may actually have been delayed by certain assumptions made by our most famous forerunners. Wilhelm Wundt, often described as the father of experimental psychology, was impressed with the distinctiveness of individual and social psychology. He argued that the study of man's higher mental processes required a methodology separate from the study of images and sensations. And Wundt was therefore pulled in the direction of the natural history (*Geschichte*) analysis of language, custom, and myth and away from any kind of experimentation or laboratory data collection from individual subjects. Thus we have what Boring (1950) calls the first true psychologist emphasizing the importance of the experimental approach, but excluding social psychology from its province.

But sometimes people don't get the word, labels are ignored, and new paths are opened as if by accident. In 1898 Triplett discovered that children will wind fish reels faster in the presence of others than when alone. While he spoke in terms of "dynamogenesis" and the liberation of "latent energy not ordinarily available"—concepts that are more descriptive than explanatory—his study is often cited as the first experiment in social psychology (a claim that is disputed in a recent article by Haines & Vaughan, 1979). And it is interesting that what we would now call **social facilitation effects** is one of the few areas of experimental research that has persisted through the decades of this century. More broadly speaking, the comparison of performance under individual versus group conditions was social psychology's first foot in the experimental door. The question of whether we do better when others are present, and whether it makes a difference if we are competing or cooperating, arises so naturally from informal observations of children in school rooms or workers on farms and factories that no special theoretical soil was necessary as a precondition for this persistent line of research inquiry.

THE 1908 FULCRUM: ALTERNATIVE PATHS TO THE UNDERSTANDING OF SOCIAL BEHAVIOR

For the historian it is a happy coincidence that the first two texts with social psychology in their title were both published in 1908. (Earlier "social psychology" treatises were considerably less comprehensive in scope; e.g., Tarde, 1898; Orano, 1902; and Tokutani, 1906). It should be noted that this was before the behaviorist revolution and before the writings of Freud had made their impact on psychology. The first to appear was Ross's text, a treatise that owed much to the French proponent of the laws of imitation, Gabriel Tarde. Later that year, McDougall offered a bold formulation of an instinct doctrine. What is interesting is that these two such different approaches can be seen as the prototypes of two radically different perspectives that remain distinct throughout the subsequent history of social psychology. Ross was interested in the interaction process, "the psychic planes and currents that come into existence among men in consequence of their association." His was a *sociological* social psychology and much of his text concerned examples of cultural diffusion. McDougall's approach, on the other hand, was strongly *biopsychological*, showing the heavy influence of evolutionary themes. In fact, he saw his task as that of developing a general psychological approach to man's innate tendencies upon which a social psychology could build. The inclusion of "An Introduction to . . ." in his title was intended literally to mean "that which comes before." Although the instinct doctrine was the major legacy of his text, McDougall devoted considerable effort to an explanation of "moralization," or how the instincts were transformed into sentiments through experience.

AUTONOMOUS EMPIRICISM AND THE IMPACT OF BEHAVIORISM: F. H. ALLPORT

If Ross and McDougall were prototypes, neither really founded a school or generated a loyal following. Their books were read with interest and, especially McDougall's (which went through 23 editions), stimulated controversy and discussion. Quite independently of either text, the experimental research that had begun with Triplett continued with work by Moede (done in 1913, though not published until 1920) and Allport (1920) on attention, learning, and forgetting in co-acting groups.

Discussion of this research found its way into F. H. Allport's influential 1924 text, *Social Psychology*. Allport was something of an imperialist in that he included in his social psychology text practically everything that was not strictly at the physiological level. Whereas today we would expect separate texts on child development, personality, language, and emotion, these topics were all covered at some length in Allport's text. Allport saw social psychology as comprising "the stimulations and reactions arising between an individual and the *social* portions of his environment" (p. 3) but he emphasized that it was a social psychology of the individual and should not be extended to encompass such factors as "crowd consciousness" or the "group mind."

The impact of behaviorism, of a stimulus-response approach, on Allport is clear. He did not completely throw out consciousness, as Watson (1919) wanted to, but he treated consciousness as an accompaniment of reactions to stimulation and not part of the cause–effect linkage between stimulus and response. Behavior was explanatory, consciousness descriptive. A characteristic exercise was to cast imitation within a learning framework. He was not completely able to avoid circular reasoning—he viewed imitation as a conditioned response to the conditioned stimulus of another's similar response—but much of his analysis was a common sense attack on the prevalent view that imitation was instinctive (as it was in McDougall's concept of "primitive passive sympathy") or intrinsically motivated. His emphasis on the instrumental function of imitation in achieving other goals was very similar to Miller and Dollard's later (1941) treatment of matched-dependent behavior.

Allport's text helped to define the boundaries of social psychology and establish the field on an objective, experimental basis. His was the first text to present and organize the experimental data on social facilitation effects, one of the first to talk at length about the measurement of personality traits and individual attitudes, and distinctive in its emphasis on language and communication. There is an extensive treatment of nonverbal, gestural behavior, a topic of considerable contemporary interest. In fact, the entire text has a ring of surprising modernity.

But Allport certainly did not define the field once and for all. During the twenties there was endless controversy about terminology and units of analysis. McDougall's treatment of human proclivities and group processes had been penetrating, but his rhetoric was flamboyant and provocative. His **instinct doctrine** was a flung gauntlet to the behaviorists (including F. H. Allport) who attacked him mercilessly. By 1932 he had changed his terminology to the more palatable label *propensities*. Similarly, McDougall's 1920 treatment of group processes was dramatically titled *group mind*, implying a group consciousness that he later vigorously denied. (Second edition, 1928). Even in the first edition, in fact, we find him quoting from Barker with approval, "the group-mind exists only in the minds of its members. But nevertheless it exists" (p. 25). In any event, objective experimentation did not immediately dominate the post-Allport scene. There was still room for the kind of dispute that could never be empirically resolved.

THE ASCENDANCE OF MEASUREMENT AND METHOD

By the end of the twenties, a handful of psychologists were conducting experiments on a highly selected sample of problems—particularly, problems involving the comparison of group versus individual performance. This issue was, perhaps, chosen as much for its convenience or its accessibility to common sense experimental methods as it was for its practical or theoretical importance. Social psychology had become an area capable of textbook demarcation, but it was an area lacking in relevant theory. As Cottrell and Gallagher (1941) have argued, "social psychologists conducted a kind of clearing house for the theoretical output of other social scientists. They battened on the research efforts in other fields, but offered little in the way of research return from their own field'' (p. 48).

Social psychology at the onset of the thirties was also very much handicapped by the lack of appropriate methods for its subject matter. On the stimulus or situational side, investigators were limited to such concrete comparisons as presence versus absence of others, the use of particular incentives (e.g. praise versus reproof), or whether or not the subjects were competing with others for a reward. On the response side, investigators were constrained to use quantitative measures of performance or other measures of attention, learning, or forgetting that had been developed in the field of educational testing or in the laboratory work of experimental psychology.

It will be claimed later that the determination of independent situational variables awaited the development of a fundamental methodological position that supported theory construction in social psychology. This development was successfully sponsored by Kurt Lewin toward the end of the thirties. But the measurement of relevant social responses (particularly attitudes) was tackled first, within the programs of Louis Thurstone and Rensis Likert. In 1929 Thurstone and Chave published a classic monograph on "the measurement of attitude." In it they espoused the application of psychophysical methods to the measurement of a person's position along an attitudinal dimension such as pro- anti- religion. Their adaptation of the *law of comparative judgment* was ingenious. The eventual purpose of their method was to develop a collection of statements falling at different points along a particular pro-con dimension. The problem was how to determine with any degree of precision what the "scale value" or location of a given statement should be. This was done by applying the logic that the distance between two statements was a function of the number of people who agreed that they were different. If 90% of a group of judges rated statement A as more pro-religion than statement B, whereas 65% rated A as more pro than C, C could not only be placed between A and B but the distance between these statements could be stated as a conversion of the percentage of judged difference figures. By variants of this basic method (the most popular being the *method of equal-appearing-intervals*), a group of statements could be developed by judges to form a scale. This scale could in turn be administered to subjects whose own position on the dimension could be scored as the median scale value of endorsed items, or a similar measure of central tendency. An example of an early Thurstone scale measuring attitudes toward the Chinese is presented in Table 11.1.

Thurstone's scaling procedures were essentially rational and required a separation of judges from eventual subjects. It was assumed that a judge's own opinion would not bias his relative placement of items, and the method required that the items be straightforward and clearly related to the belief or issue in question. In 1932, however, Likert employed a very different and more clearly empirical approach to the measurement of attitudes. His method was to generate

TABLE 11.1
An Early Thurstone Scale for Measuring Attitudes Toward the
Chinese[1]

This is a study of attitudes toward the Chinese. On the other side of this page you will find a number of statements expressing different attitudes toward the Chinese.

    √ Put a check mark if you agree with the statement.
    X Put a cross if you disagree with the statement.

Try to indicate either agreement or disagreement for each statement. If you simply cannot decide about a statement you may mark it with a question mark.

This is not an examination. There are no right or wrong answers to these statements. This is simply a study of people's attitudes toward the Chinese. Please indicate your own convictions by a check mark when you agree and by a cross when you disagree.

    √ Put a check mark if you agree with the statement.
    X Put a cross if you disagree with the statement.

Scale
value

Scale value		
6.5	1.	I have no particular love nor hate for the Chinese.
10.1	2.	I dislike the Chinese more every time I see one.
4.7	3.	The Chinese are pretty decent.
7.2	4.	Some Chinese traits are admirable but on the whole I don't like them.
.5	5.	The Chinese are superior to all other races.
8.7	6.	The Chinese as part of the yellow race are inferior to the white race.
3.5	7.	I like the Chinese.
2.8	8.	The more I know about the Chinese the better I like them.
11.0	9.	The Chinese are aptly described by the term "yellow devils."
1.8	10.	The high class Chinese are superior to us.
5.2	11.	The Chinese are different but not inferior.
11.5	12.	I hate the Chinese.
4.1	13.	Chinese parents are unusually devoted to their children.
7.7	14.	Although I respect some of their qualities, I could never consider a Chinese as my friend.
1.2	15.	I would rather live in China than any other place in the world.
9.7	16.	There are no refined nor cultured Chinese.
6.0	17.	The Chinese are no better and no worse than any other people.
3.4	18.	I think Chinese should be kept out of the United States.
2.2	19.	I consider it a privilege to associate with Chinese people.
10.6	20.	The Chinese are inferior in every way.
9.4	21.	I don't see how anyone could ever like the Chinese.
3.0	22.	Chinese have a very high sense of honor.
3.6	23.	I have no desire to know any Chinese.
1.4	24.	Chinese people have a refinement and depth of feeling that you don't find anywhere else.
9.8	25.	There is nothing about the Chinese that I like or admire.
3.9	26.	I'd like to know more Chinese people.

[1]From Thurstone (1931) pp. 234–235. Scale values were not printed on the blanks given to subjects.

statements about the target issue without any necessary restriction that the statements were on their face related to the issue. The items could then be administered to groups of pre-test subjects with instructions to indicate the degree of agreement or disagreement with each one. Total scores for each subject could be gained by scoring each item in terms of degree of agreement (reversing those phrased in the negative) and summing these item scores. Each item could then be evaluated for each pretest subject sample in terms of its contribution to the total score. If the items were concerned generally with political liberalism, for example, endorsement of some items would correlate more highly with the total score than others. The diagnostic (high correlating) items could then be retained for further use. This procedure could be repeated over several pretest samples until a relatively robust and purified scale resulted. It may be noted that the **Likert scale** essentially is built by the subjects themselves, acting as subjects and not rational judges. It may also be noted that the Likert approach might be more suitable for detecting unpopular or prejudiced attitudes because the items need not have an obvious surface-relationship to the issue involved. The *authoritarian personality* scales developed in the late 1940s (Adorno, Frenkel-Brunswik, Levinson, & Sanford, 1950) were constructed by the Likert method for this reason. For example, it was predicted theoretically, and determined empirically, that subjects who endorse the item "people are born with an urge to jump from high places" are high in authoritarianism and in antisemitism. This could not have been discovered or determined with the Thurstone method.

During the thirties there was both the beginnings of a concern with the structure and functioning of **attitudes** and an accounting of their distribution in different classes or groups. The former emphasis is reflected in Gordon Allport's chapter on attitudes in Murchison's 1935 *Handbook of Social Psychology*. Allport analyzes the history of usage of the term and considers, for example, whether attitudes have their own motive power (concluding that at least some do) and whether attitudes can be either individual, defying nomothetic measurement, or common and measurable (yes they can, he concludes).

A more descriptive approach is reflected in many of the chapters of Murphy, Murphy, & Newcomb's *Experimental Social Psychology*, published in 1937. Much of the research described therein amounted to a mapping of the terrain, a series of headcounts to determine the distribution of attitudes in a particular population. Such efforts said little about the functional significance of attitudes and had little if any relevance for social psychological theories dealing with the central concerns of interaction, influence and interpersonal understanding. They represented an (understandable) flexing of methodological muscles.

A related development was the refinement of *sampling techniques* which permitted the growth of **public opinion polls.** George Gallup, Elmo Roper, and Archibald Crosley each used the sample survey method to forecast correctly the outcome of the 1936 presidential election. Use of this method rapidly became widespread, not only in the political prediction arena, but in the commercial sphere where opinions about consumer products and advertising campaigns were systematically gathered. Governmental bodies such as the U.S. Department of Agriculture also made extensive use of sample surveys. It might be noted, however, that the development of appropriate sampling and questioning techniques had a much greater impact on the growth of empirical sociology than on social psychology itself. This was particularly true when, in the fifties, the sample survey was wedded to computer analysis.

Of somewhat greater relevance for psychology was the introduction of **sociometric measurement** by J. L. Moreno in 1934. This technique involved the simple questioning of group members regarding those fellow members with whom they would choose to associate in some activity. More generally, the sociometric method has come to include any procedure that involves choice, preference, or liking among group members. It can readily be seen that from such statements of preference certain aspects of group structure can be derived. For example, cliques of friends within the group can be discerned and groups can be characterized in terms of the presence of such clique cleavages, the mutuality of choice, and the concentration of attraction toward a few members. In addition, individuals can be readily identified as sociometric "stars" (heavily chosen by others) or isolates. The addition of dislike dimensions provides many further possibilities of group characterization.

Sociometric measures have become ubiquitous in social psychological research, and have been used in applied research on morale and leadership as well as basic experimental research on such topics as the rejection of opinion deviates (Schachter, 1951) or the measurement of in-group cohesion (Sherif, Harvey, White, Hood, & Sherif, 1961). Sociometric indices were also effectively used in the fascinating study of *hysterical contagion* by Kerckhoff and Back (1968) and in many other field studies in both psychology and sociology.

Jenkins (1947) provides an interesting example of the use of sociometric analysis for detecting good and poor morale states in groups having the same formal structure. Figure 11.1 presents the sociograms of two naval air squadrons. The 17 men in each squadron were asked to consider the men they knew (inside the squadron or out of it) and to state anonymously their personal preferences regarding whom they would like to have fly beside them. They were also asked to name men they would *not* like to have beside them. A solid line in Figure 11.1 represents a choice; a dotted line represents a rejection. Circles within the boxes indicate members of the particular squadron. We would expect to find much higher morale and more effective leadership in Squadron A than in B. In Squadron A the Commanding Officer (CO) and the Executive Officer (XO) are both well liked, there are no cliques, and there are no choices (only rejections) of those outside the squadron. In Squadron B, on the other hand, we find two mutual admiration cliques, several out-group choices, a Commanding Officer toward whom the men are indifferent, and an Executive Officer who is thoroughly disliked.

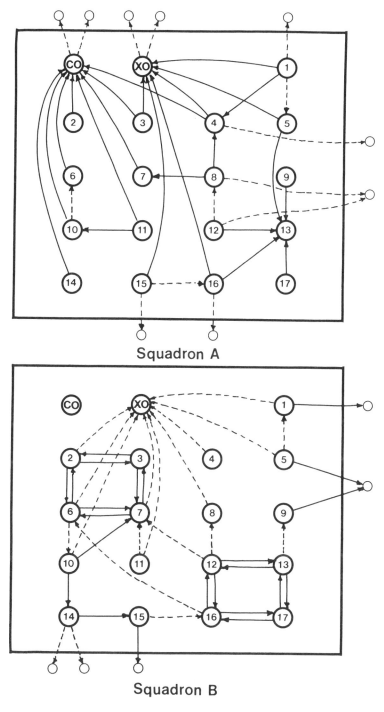

Squadron A

Squadron B

FIG. 11.1 Sociograms of two naval air squadrons. (Jenkins, 1947; reported in Krech and Crutchfield, 1948).

FIELD THEORY

To some extent, the development of theory in social psychology awaited the generation of reliable data that needed to be explained and integrated. But the reverse was even more true. Social psychology was very slow to develop indigenous theory and this unquestionably handicapped its emergence as an experimental science. Without some kind of bridging theory of interpersonal processes, would-be experimenters were thwarted by what might be called the generalization question. That is, how could an experimenter claim that his findings on 30 male college sophomores were in any important sense generalizable to a broader population of human beings or even of American college males? Sociology essentially confronted the generalization question by abjuring the laboratory experiment and attempting to construct or test theories through survey methods (see above) in which sample representativeness was an important consideration. Psychologists, on the other hand, developed and refined experimental techniques that would test the plausibility of general process theories in restricted concrete contexts. In the late twenties and thirties this became increasingly true in studies of animal behavior in which psychologists like Hull and Tolman attempted to theorize about general learning processes from data produced by rats in mazes. Thus there was developing a broad context in American psychology nurturing the importance of theory as a bridge between concrete experimental findings. It is not too surprising to find that as the experimental tradition developed in social psychology, researchers became more preoccupied with the conceptual generality of their findings than with the representativeness of their samples. Theories were useful to the extent that they predicted superficially different but conceptually similar relations in a variety of contexts. It was Kurt Lewin who, more than anyone else, stimulated and provided the philosophical rationale for this approach.

Lewin was a refugee from the Nazis who arrived in this country to stay in 1933, making the rather remarkable shift from Berlin's Psychological Institute to Cornell's department of home economics. He moved shortly thereafter to the Iowa Child Welfare Research Station where he began to apply his basic theoretical predilections to the study of **group dynamics** and to train a number of students who were to play an important role in social psychology. In 1945 he moved to MIT and organized the *Research Center for Group Dynamics*. He died prematurely in 1947. Lewin was to an extent influenced by the Gestalt psychology triumvirate Wertheimer, Kohler, and Koffka, but he was by no means a classic Gestaltist. Whereas Gestalt psychology traditionally emphasized perceptual and cognitive structures, Lewin was much more intrigued with questions of motivation and the dynamics of feeling and action. If a Gestaltist, he was a "hot" Gestaltist.

At least as important as his contact with the leading Gestalt psychologists was Lewin's assimilation of Cassirer's philosophical teachings. These he wove into his own **field theory** which is described in a variety of publications appearing from

1939–47. This theory was not the usual set of assumptions and propositions from which empirical hypotheses were deduced by formal logic. It was more like a language or point of view. Lewin himself described the theory as "a method: namely a method of analyzing causal relations and building scientific constructs" (1944, in Cartwright, 1951, p. 45). Lewin did use a terminology borrowed from force-field physics. Instead of behaving or responding, organisms "locomoted" through a field of bounded "regions" impelled by "forces" or drawn by "valences" along power "vectors." Much more important than the specific terminology was Lewin's movement away from conceiving man as a bundle of propensities confronting a structured social system. For certain purposes he conceived of the person as a point in psychological space, constrained to move in certain valent directions by the characteristics of that space. A typical conceptualization is presented in Figure 11.2 depicting a child caught in a field of forces whose relative strengths will determine whether or not he will finish his homework. One may note in such imagery an invitation to experimentation, or at least an invitation to the kind of theorizing that in turn could lead to experimentation. If one views man as the product of a long developmental history, one emphasizes the uniqueness and the distinctiveness of his responses to a common environment. If, on the other hand, one views man as a point at the intersection of environmental forces, the emphasis is on the contemporaneous perceptions and related actions he shares with others in that same position. Through experimentation, one hopes that such common action patterns can be determined.

Lewin had glimmerings of an ultimate theory that was highly abstract and expressible in the new mathematics of **topology.** Of much greater historical importance, however, was his recognition that one must initially proceed with crude approximations; with what he called "quasi-concepts" like hope, expectancy, frustration, and level of aspiration. Lewin openly and persistently advocated the experimental method, but at least as important were the experimental examples provided by Lewin and his students. Two of these students, Lippitt and White, conducted a series of studies on "leadership atmosphere" in the late thirties (reported first in Lewin, Lippitt, & White, 1939) that were path-breaking in their procedural audacity. Children's groups (five in each) were formed to carry out such extracurricular activities as making masks. Children were assigned to groups in such a way as to make them as comparable as possible in the range of personality types and level of popularity involved. Each group was led by an adult who played, initially, one of two carefully constructed roles: he was either consistently **autocratic** or **democratic.** In subsequent experiments a third role, **laissez-faire,** was added to the design. Unlike the democratic leader who solicited agreement and helped guide the group along its chosen course of action, the laissez-faire leader was no more than a passive resource person available for consultation.

Five observers took continuous notes on the behavior of the leader and the children in each group. Categories of observation were devised so that quantitative indices of such actions as "hostile criticism," "friendly cooperation,"

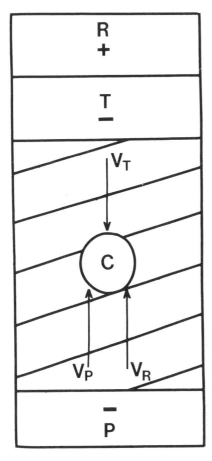

FIG. 11.2. A child (C) who confronts the unpleasantness of his homework task (T), the punishment (P) of a bad grade if he does not do his homework, and the reward (R) of a good grade if he does. Resolution will depend on the relative strengths of the task valuence (V_T) and the reward and punishment valences (V_R and V_P). (Adapted from Lewin, 1935, p. 157.)

"giving instructions," could be used to compare the different leadership atmospheres. Different experimental events were arranged to explore the reactions of the children in the different experimental groups. At times the leader was deliberately late, at other times the leader left the group and a janitor entered to make standard hostile comments. It was also arranged that clubs would simultaneously meet in adjacent areas, so that out-group scapegoating could be studied.

It was found that two kinds of reactions developed to autocratic leadership, aggressive and apathetic. Democratic leadership was uniformly preferred to both autocratic and laissez-faire atmospheres. Scapegoating and blowing off steam in the absence of the leader was minimal in the democratic groups, but very apparent in the others. Productivity was approximately the same in the democratic and autocratic groups, but considerably lower in the laissez-faire.

From the perspective of current experimental designs, the Lewin-Lippitt-White experiments were rather crude and confounded. A number of compromises were made in an attempt to get more information from fewer groups than a fully counter-balanced design would require. But the experiment had a number of features later to be more generally associated with the Lewinian approach:

1. A complex situational **independent variable,** in this case leadership atmosphere, was manipulated, and systematic observations provided a quantitative check on the success of that manipulation. (See Fig. 11.3).
2. Every effort was made to keep the setting as natural as possible and to inhibit self-consciousness in the subjects. One can speculate about the impact of observers, unobtrusive though they tried to be, but the boys did not know that they were experimental subjects and presumably they acted in a relatively natural way, as in any extracurricular club.
3. Theoretical considerations led to the initial choice of independent variables, but changes and additions were made in follow-up experiments as a function of initial observations.
4. The detailed observation of social behavior as a **dependent variable** reflected an interest in interpersonal processes rather than merely the products or outcomes of interaction (e.g., ratings of satisfaction, number of masks made).
5. Follow up interviews were conducted to assess each child's phenomenal perceptions of the experience. An attempt was made, in other words, to capture the **psychological environment** or **life space** of each subject.

The actual effects of such an experimental demonstration on subsequent developments are difficult to assess, but at the very least the study represented a clean break from the kind of experiment varying such objectifiable parameters as the presence or absence of a co-actor, the balance of praise versus reproof, or the age or sex of the subject in a suggestibility experiment. In summary, Lewin's contribution was basically atmospheric: while only a few of his own experiments exemplified his message, the message was nevertheless persistent and it was propounded in a great variety of ways. He provided a rationale for theory-based experimentation and for the idea of *conceptual generality* of a relationship across contexts rather than simple *empirical generality* across samples. As early as 1926 he said, "the quantitative level most propitious for experimental analysis varies from case to case and laws shift little as a function of this level." And 14 years later he made more specific the way to implement conceptual generality: "to prove or disprove the theory of tension systems, it seems much more important to find a variety of derivations from this theory which should be as different as possible from each other, and to test as many as possible of these derivations, even if this test should be rather crude quantitatively at the beginning" (1940; in Cartwright, 1951, p. 9).

I have singled out one salient facet of Lewin's contribution to an experimental social psychology. In addition, Lewin made numerous contributions to applied

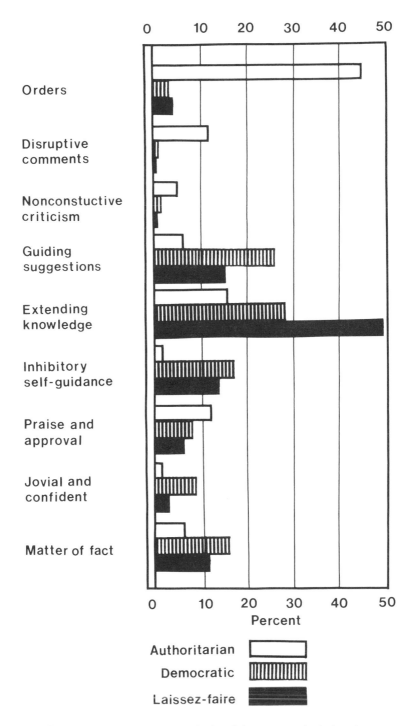

FIG. 11.3. A comparison of the behavior of the average authoritarian, democratic, and laissez faire leader. (From Lewin, Lippitt, and White, 1939.)

social psychology and was himself a consultant to industry, government, and social service organizations. He was the founder of group dynamics, an approach to interactions in groups that laid the ground work for such subsequent movements as T-groups and certain kinds of encounter groups. In addition to his writing, he attracted and trained a distinguished group of students who went on to the center stage in social psychology. Perhaps the most influential of these was Leon Festinger.

Social Comparison

Festinger's first highly influential achievement was the publication of a theory of **social comparison processes** in 1954. Festinger presented his theory in the form of postulates and corollaries, reminiscent of Hull's earlier theoretical hypothetico deductive efforts (see Ch. 1, vol. 1), and probably intended to emphasize that social psychology had "come of age." In addition to the most formal theorizing yet to appear in social psychology, Festinger reported the results of a number of experiments specifically designed to test hypotheses about our sensitivity to others' opinions and abilities in coming to terms with our own. Festinger proposed that there are large areas of judgment in which "reality" cannot be measured by centimeters, grams, or seconds. In these areas reality depends on consensus; it is socially defined. When a person finds himself in disagreement with others about the nature of this reality, he will be motivated to handle the discrepancy in some way. He may either change his own opinion, try to persuade others to change theirs, or decide for one or another reason that the other is irrelevant as a comparison person. Festinger spelled out in some detail the independent variables that should affect the resolution of opinion and ability discrepancies. A number of his students conducted experiments manipulating group cohesiveness (the attraction of the group to its members), issue relevance, degree of discrepancy, and other sources of pressure toward uniformity in a group. The theory was a tour de force in tieing together conformity, rejection of deviates, and instrumental communication.

Some sample findings from research spawned by social comparison theory included:

1. Pairs of subjects induced to believe that they would be attracted to each other showed greater movement toward ultimate agreement in composing a story to fit a picture (Back, 1951).
2. Subjects in groups led to believe in their homogeneity of interests and abilities showed a greater and more persistent tendency to communicate to opinion deviates than subjects previously informed of their heterogeneity of interests and abilities (Festinger & Thibaut, 1951).
3. Subjects whose opinions on a topic were previously anchored in a congenial, cohesive group, showed greater resistance to change when subse-

quently confronted by a paid participant trying to argue them out of their position (Gerard, 1954).

4. Groups participated in a discussion that was either what they had volunteered for or unrelated to their expectations. In the former case (the high cohesive, high relevant condition) a paid participant playing the role of a persistent opinion deviate in the discussion received a greater volume of influence attempts and then was more emphatically rejected than in the latter case (Schachter, (1951).

Social comparison theory was even more ambitious in attempting to show the comparability in certain respects of opinions and abilities. The opinion deviate in a highly cohesive group either tries to exert influence on others or moves toward the group's modal opinion. Similarly, the performance deviate in a cohesive group either tries to bring the performance of others closer to his own (if he has any actual or psychological control over them) or he tries to bring his own performance up (or down) to their levels. In a rather remarkable study, Radloff (1966) showed that subjects were more accurate in estimating their true scores on a pursuit rotor task[1] if they believed that they had performed comparably to many others who had preceded them in the experiment. This is consistent with Festinger's claim that people wish to know their abilities and learn about them from comparisons with others, but the specific mechanisms at work in the Radloff study have never been determined.

An extremely important offshoot from the theory of social comparison was Schachter's (1959) work on the *need for self-appraisal* as a determinant of *affiliation.* In a series of realistic experiments, subjects were threatened with shock and given the choice of waiting alone or with others in a similar predicament. Schachter's major finding was that highly anxious subjects preferred to affiliate before being shocked (they in fact never were) in order to calibrate through social comparison their own level of fear. Schachter's student Wrightsman found, in addition, that experienced anxiety became more homogeneous in groups of subjects waiting together before an expected drug injection. Thus the effects of social comparison on emotional experience were similar to those predicted for opinions and abilities.

Schachter followed the implications of the Wrightsman finding into a broader theory of emotional experience. He proposed (1964) that **emotional states** are a

---

[1]The pursuit rotor is an apparatus used to study and measure the acquisition of a motor skill. Think of a phonograph turntable rotating at 60 RPM. Toward the outer edge of the rotating disc there is a target about the size of a dime set flush with the surface. The subject is given a hinged pointer or "stylus," about eight inches long, with a right-angle bend about an inch from one end and a wooden handle about an inch from the other. The subject grasps the stylus by the handle and attempts to keep the bent point in contact with the rotating target. The subject's score is the amount of time the stylus makes such contact, often measured over a series of trials, each of about one minute's duration.

combination of physiological arousal and cognitive labeling, and showed that vastly different emotional states could result from the same physiological arousal in different social contexts. Schachter's subsequent research into obesity and nicotine addiction has moved him out of social psychology proper, but his approach to emotional experience, as we shall see, played a vital role in the emergence of attributional approaches to social explanation.

The Lab-Field Approach

Festinger, Schachter, and their students also made important contributions to the development of methodology in social psychology. Inherent in the Lewinian message was the importance of going back and forth between the laboratory and the "field." Festinger and his students embraced the lab-field approach with enthusiasm. In addition to numerous experiments with college student subjects in arbitrary group settings, Festinger, Schachter, and Back (1950) conducted a field study in a campus housing project in which they attempted to define relations between friendship structure, communication, and opinion homogeneity on a crucial issue of concern to all residents. While it is difficult to specify the causal direction, these authors found that highly cohesive residential courts (those with a high proportion of in-court to out-of-court friendship choices) tended to show greater opinion agreement.

As we shall see, the lab-field approach also characterized Festinger's subsequent research on cognitive dissonance. But before we consider that important contribution, let us return to the late thirties and pick up the social influence story in its relative infancy.

Frames of Reference and Biased Perceptions.

In 1932 Sir F. C. Bartlett summarized a series of studies in *Remembering* that showed how social factors determined the fate of recall. When asked to reproduce a 300 word folk story that contained a number of unfamiliar notions and obscure connections, his English subjects assimilated the story to their own system of culturally determined cognitive categories, or, as Bartlett called them, *schemata*. Bartletts' subjects condensed, highlighted, and rationalized the story to enhance its apparent coherence and consistency. His systematic observations were similar to those that had often been made by students of the psychology of courtroom testimony. As far back as the turn of the century, psychologists had been interested in showing how witnesses assimilate recalled experiences to their expectations, and distort them in line with their motives. But Bartlett brought such considerations into the mainstream of psychological research.

It surely comes as no surprise to us now to learn that our recollections and interpretations of events are biased by our cultural history and our current motives, but such a point of view came rather late to a psychology concerned with "pure memory" and therefore concentrating on the remembering of nonsense syllables—supposedly uncontaminated by "meaning."

Our cultural background thus provides a **frame of reference** within which we interpret events. In an important series of experiments done shortly after Bartlett's book, Sherif (1936) dramatically showed how such frames of reference can be bred in the laboratory. Subjects, either alone or in groups of two or three, were exposed to a stationary light in an otherwise dark room. They were asked to indicate when the light started moving and to estimate how far it moved. It is a common and compelling illusion (**autokinetic effect**) that such a light will indeed be seen to move, but the stimulus context is obviously very ambiguous. When the individual faces the light alone, he rather quickly develops a personally characteristic range within which his judgments fall. Sherif referred to this as the individual's *norm*. If the subject is exposed to the judgments of others, either prior to or after making his own estimates, his judgments will converge toward a group norm. If the individual is then reexposed to the light in isolation, he will carry over the group-established norm and his judgments will continue to be influenced.

Sherif (1947) ventured to propose that "the psychological basis of the established **social norms,** such as stereotypes, conventions, customs and values, is the formation of common frames of reference as a product of the contact of individuals" (p. 85). Whether one wishes to generalize that widely or not, his experiments beautifully dramatize the cognitive interdependence of persons confronting an ambiguous situation and set the stage for hundreds of conformity experiments in the following decade.

Before following up the implications of Sherif's pioneering work for conformity research, however, we should note that he sustained the line of argument originating with Bartlett and continuing into the 1940s with an explosion of experimental research concerning the effects of past experience and motivation on the perception of relevant stimulus materials. By the mid forties, many investigators had shown that inferences and interpretations are affected by the state of the organism, whether the state was established by food deprivation, prior reinforcement, or fear arousal. This development was undoubtedly fostered by the increasing impact of Freudian theory on academic psychology. J. S. Bruner and his colleague Postman picked up the concern with motivational factors and carried the battle directly into the heartland of perception psychology. From 1946 until roughly the mid fifties, Bruner, Postman, and their students showed how motives, values, and prior experiences affected such standard perceptual measures as magnitude estimation, threshold (speed of identification), illumination judgment, and color matching. While such manipulations as thirst and such correlates as parental income produced unstable perceptual effects on size judgments of motive-relevant materials, effects that were difficult to replicate, expectancies based on prior cultural or laboratory experiences clearly affected relevant perceptual responses. Such controversial notions as *perceptual defense* (not seeing threatening symbols or words except after lengthy exposure) emerged in this era and questions of motivational control of cognitive activity remain a central area in social psychology.

Asch's Classic Conformity Experiments

Sherif showed that people's judgments will be interdependent in a highly ambiguous situation, but it was almost 20 years before the limits of ambiguity were tested in a series of **conformity** experiments by S. E. Asch (1956). It is interesting to note the origins of Asch's interest in the problem of social influence on cognitive judgment. Asch had been very much influenced by his senior colleague Max Wertheimer, the eldest of the Gestalt triumvirate. Asch himself was (and remains) a ''cold'' Gestaltist and very much impressed with our needs to make rational sense out of experience. He surmised that if subjects were exposed to unambiguous perceptual comparisons *after* confronting several other subjects making unanimously erroneous judgments, they would reject any inherent pressures toward uniformity and report the correct, the independently derived, answer. Subjects were to make a simple judgment of which of three comparison lines were the same length as a standard. There was literally no ambiguity about the correct answer, as shown by control subjects who were essentially errorless when reporting their judgment in isolation. Asch was surprised when so many of his college student subjects denied the visual evidence in favor of the underlying consensus. On the average, subjects made between 4 and 5 errors out of a possible 12. Three quarters of the subjects made at least one pro-majority error, and this turned out to be true in a variety of different samples of subjects. The distribution of errors in three separate experiments is presented in Table 11.2. Though Asch's faith in the rationality and good sense of his subjects was somewhat shaken, his painstaking analysis of the subjective strain induced by the conformity conflict in many of his subjects inspired a number of investigators to pursue the determinants of conformity and independence.

Essentially, this research established that people conformed either because they thought the majority was correct, or because they were so reward- and punishment-oriented that they did not particularly care about accuracy. In fact, the underlying conditions of conformity in perceptual judgment situations, such as those studied by Asch, were essentially the same as those proposed by Festinger in a paper (1950) antedating his social comparison theory: social reality (accuracy oriented) and group locomotion (social reward oriented). Under a variety of different labels (cf. Jones & Gerard, 1967) a number of other theorists have emphasized this distinction between the individual's dependence on the group for information and his dependence on the group for rewards and acceptance.

TABLE 11.2
Distribution of Errors in Experimental and Control Groups

Number of Errors	Control group[a] (N = 37)	Experimental groups			All Experimental Groups (N = 123)
		Group I (N = 70)	Group II (N = 25)	Group III (N = 28)	
0	35	17	5	7	29
1	1	4	2	2	8
2	1	7	1	2	10
3		12	1	4	17
4		3	1	2	6
5		5	2	0	7
6		2	4	1	7
7		3	0	1	4
8		7	4	2	13
9		3	2	1	6
10		4	1	1	6
11		2	0	2	4
12		1	2	3	6
Mean	0.08	4.01	5.16	4.71	4.41
Median	0.00	3.00	5.50	3.00	3.00
Mean per cent	0.7	33.4	43.0	39.3	36.8

[a]Subjects in the control group were not exposed to the judgments of others before expressing their own. (From Asch, 1956, p. 10).

Communication and Persuasion: Attitude Change

If one really wished to emphasize the antiquity of social psychology, he would do well to know Aristotle's discussion of persuasive speech in *Rhetoric* (1941 edition, originally fourth century BC.). Aristotle saw persuasive speech as divorced from the particular content involved and distinguished three modes of persuasion: that depending on the positive character attributes of the speaker, that depending on putting the audience in a receptive frame of mind, and that dependent on the apparent proof contained in the speech itself.

The study of attitude or opinion change was remarkably slow in capturing the attention of experimental social psychologists. Though the study of attitudes had been almost equated with social psychology by Watson (1925) and even earlier by Thomas and Znaniecki (1918), one finds, in fact, only a small handful of studies dealing with the processes of **attitude change** until the Second World War. Instead, as McGuire (1969) points out, from 1920 to 1945 attitude theorizing had "become top heavy with conceptual elaboration including contentious questions of definition, analysis into components, and distinctions between attitudes and related concepts" (p. 137).

The Second World War shifted many of the priorities within social psychology, as it did within the other social sciences. In particular, the Information and Education branch of the U.S. Army conducted a number of surveys and experimental studies to assess the impact of morale films and internal army "propaganda" (e.g., concerning the likelihood of a long war with Japan after VE day). A psychologist heavily involved in many of these studies was Carl I. Hovland, who returned to Yale after the war and established a very influential attitude change project. This project attracted young scholars from a variety of universities and generated a stream of collaborative research under Hovland's general direction. The classic *Communication and Persuasion* (Hovland, Janis, & Kelley, 1953) clearly established the value of an experimental paradigm that Lasswell had earlier anticipated by his didactic phrase: "Who says what to whom with what effect." Hovland and his colleagues explored a number of *source variables* (such as prestige, expertise, and credibility), *message variables* (such as whether or not a conclusion is drawn in the communication), and *context variables* (whether a particular reference group is made salient) and the effects of these variables on changes in opinion. A series of more specialized volumes followed dealing with order effects (Hovland, 1957), personality and persuasibility (Hovland & Janis, 1959), cognitive consistency factors (Hovland & Rosenberg, 1960) and the role of assimilation and contrast (Sherif & Hovland, 1961). Research on attitude change through these and many other contributions moved from a strangely neglected area to the center stage of social psychology. By the end of the sixties, attitude change took more space in social psychology text books than any other topic (McGuire, 1969, p. 138, estimates 25%). Shortly thereafter, however, the attitude change output receded in volume to a steady but not torrential stream. For the most part, the attention of social psychologists shifted to the themes of a strongly cognitive social psychology: consistency, dissonance, and eventually attribution theory became the dominant research focus of the seventies. But before turning to these developments, let us drop back to discover the impact of the forties and fifties on investigations and theories dealing with group processes.

Conceptions of Interdependence: The Psychology of Small Groups

We have emphasized in our earlier discussion the relative continuity of experimental research on group problem solving. Kelley and Thibaut could build on Dashiell's 1935 handbook chapter in writing their own for Lindzey's 1954 *Handbook of Social Psychology*. However, Kelley and Thibaut correctly noted that a great proportion of the research on group functioning was quite innocent of penetrating theory. The research, though continuous during the twenties, thirties, and forties, was quite empirical and rarely grappled with the crucial processes in a group's "locomotions" toward a goal. The subtleties of social influence were not laid bare and little was known or discovered about power strategies and the conditions affecting their successful employment. Conceptions of leadership were basically noninteractive, and tended to avoid group dynamics considerations. Investigations in the thirties and forties often involved a search for the personal characteristics of the effective leader. This search was not tied into a broader theory of influence processes.

Part of the problem was remedied by the success of the Lewinian group dynamics movement. At least, Lewin presented a language that facilitated treating the group as a system of interrelated parts and personally advocated a concern with micro-processes rather than global descriptions or quantifications of group products. Many of Lewin's students in the Research Center for Group Dynamics at MIT developed interesting theories about such different aspects of group process as identification with the group goal, communication as a substitute for mobility, and the dynamics of cooperative interdependence.

Influential theoretical accounts of group functioning with a definite psychological flavor were also advanced by sociologists Homans (1950) and Bales (1950). In a tradition established by Barnard in 1938, both of these authors emphasized the distinction between task oriented (external system) functions and social-emotional (internal system) functions in groups. Theoretical analysis was further advanced by Kelley and Thibaut's (1954) lucid identification of group problem-solving variables, and their attempt to distinguish between group influences on individual solution attempts on the one hand and factors influencing the combination or pooling of these attempts on the other. Their contribution provided a rational framework for organizing those portions of the social interaction literature concerned with group problem solving.

The same authors (Thibaut & Kelley, 1959) made a more basic and general contribution five years later in a book that introduced a **social exchange** framework into social psychology. Essentially, the framework dealt with the outcomes for the interacting parties that are consequences of their actual or potential responses to each other. By the ingenious use of *payoff matrixes* conceptualizing the response repertoires of two or more individuals, Thibaut and Kelley could consider the response combinations that would provide the greatest satisfaction to each party and thus locate the most likely drift of their social behavior. In this way, Thibaut and Kelley developed a taxonomy of interpersonal power relations and provided the prototype of a social exchange theory. "You scratch my back and I'll scratch yours" is the underlying exchange axiom.

In their analysis of power and dependence, the notions of social comparison were crucially applied. Thus a person's power in a given relationship depended on the attractiveness of alternative relationships into which he could conveniently enter. This feature of social comparison was missing in Homans' otherwise similar formulation that appeared two years later (Homans, 1961). Nevertheless, it is interesting that Homans and Thibaut and Kelley independently reached almost the same place from rather different origins. Thibaut and Kelley were influenced by Homans' earlier *The Human Group* (1950) and by developments in economics of game and decision theory (Luce & Raiffa, 1957). Homans, on the other hand, was more explicitly influenced by the operant conditioning paradigm of B. F. Skinner. In any case, both formulations emphasized the exchange of reward and punishment in social interaction, and through this vehicle we are better able to understand norms, power, social dependence, and more generally, group formation and maintenance. It is interesting, incidentally, that in the 1974 revision of his 1961 book, Homans explicitly incorporates many features of Thibaut and Kelley's analysis—including the exchange or payoff matrix.

Game theory entered social psychology through a number of pathways in the late fifties and sixties. The most prominent path was the *mixed motive game* and especially the sub-type known as the **prisoner's dilemma.** Important features of the prisoner's dilemma game are brought out in Luce and Raiffa's (1957) description:

> Two suspects are taken into custody and separated. The District Attorney is certain that they are guilty of a specific crime, but he does not have adequate evidence to convict them at a trial. He points out to each prisoner that he has two alternatives: to confess to the crime the police are sure they have done, or not to confess. If they both do not confess, then the District Attorney states he will book them on some very minor trumped up charge such as petty larceny and illegal possession of a weapon and they would both receive minor punishment; if they both confess they will be prosecuted, but he will recommend less than the most severe sentence; but if one confesses and the other does not, then the confessor will receive lenient treatment for turning state's evidence, whereas the latter will get "the book" slapped at him. (p. 95)

The prisoner, thus, may cooperate with his fellow suspect (not confess) or he may compete with him (confess). Figure 11.4 portrays the structure of a typical prisoner's dilemma game in matrix form. Morton Deutsch appears to be the first social psychologist who recognized the implications of this game for studying cooperative behavior and its reliance on mutual attributions of trust. In 1960 he conducted an experiment exploring the effects of different motivational orientations on the frequency of cooperative choices in a dyad.

Quite rapidly, many other variations appeared of experimental games involving the mixture of incentives for both competition and cooperation (thus the generic term "mixed motive game"). By now there is a substantial game literature extending from the elementary question asked by Deutsch through the most complex questions involved in bargaining and negotiations for real payoffs. The massive international experiment conducted by Kelley and his colleagues (Kelley, Shure et al., 1970) illustrates how sophisticated and complex the designs in this area have become: At eight laboratories, three in Europe and five in the

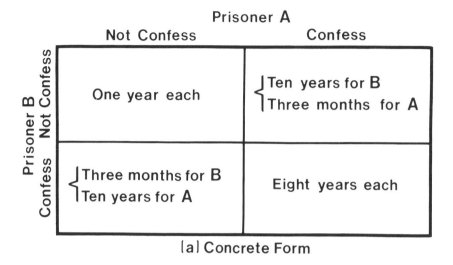

(a) Concrete Form

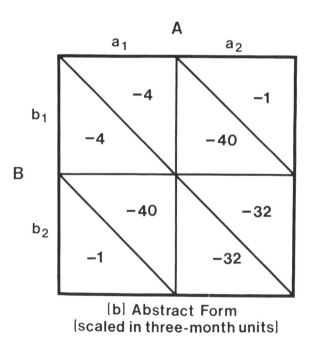

(b) Abstract Form
(scaled in three-month units)

FIG. 11.4. Two ways of representing a typical prisoner's dilemma game. In the abstract matrix, values above the diagonals accrue to prisoner A, those below the diagonals to B. (From Jones and Gerard, 1967, p. 563.)

United States, different investigators conducted essentially the same experiment featuring a complex negotiation involving the choice of interdependent versus independent action. The negotiation "game" was either played for points or money, the difficulty level of the problems was varied, and in some conditions one subject was made systematically more dependent on reaching agreement than his partner. The major finding that held across the different experimental sites was that increasing the value of the stakes had a beneficial effect on negotiation when cooperation yields clear mutual gain and exploitation is difficult. (There were also intriguing differences attributed to the meaning of cooperation in the different cultural contexts.)

The Dissonance—Consistency Era: Cognition on Center Stage

While the study of interactive behavior in group process was being stimulated by these applications of economics and reinforcement theory, an influential assortment of social psychologists were becoming preoccupied with the cognitive processes underlying social behavior. This preoccupation grew out of a long-standing empirical interest in **interpersonal perception** (or **impression formation**) on the one hand, and the theoretical concerns of Fritz Heider on the other.

Prior to his experimental research on conformity, discussed in an earlier section, S. E. Asch (1946) contributed a path-breaking article on impression formation. Whereas earlier research on the perception and evaluation of other persons had emphasized the determinants of judgmental (or diagnostic) accuracy, Asch shifted the concern to an investigation of the *processes* of impression formation. Employing an ingeniously simple paradigm, Asch presented subjects with adjective strings purported to describe a person. One such string, for example, was "the person is intelligent, skillful, industrious, warm, determined, practical, cautious." Subjects were asked to write a brief sketch of the person thus described and to check those traits among a list of further adjectives that were judged as applicable to the person. Other subjects were confronted with an adjective string identical to the above example except that the word "cold" was substituted for "warm." The resulting impressions were dramatically different as a function of the switch of these particular attributes. The "warm" person was described as much more generous, good-natured, popular, and sociable. The "cold" person was generally described more negatively but was nevertheless judged to be slightly more reliable and restrained. Asch used these and other similar experimental results to argue for the dynamic interaction among trait qualities in the impression formation process. The meaning of each trait is modified by the context provided by the other traits, giving rise to an organized Gestalt of the entire person. This classic experiment spawned a crucial shift in the person perception area from a concern with judgmental outcome to a concern with perceptual process.

Fritz Heider's work introduced a different set of considerations that were nevertheless quite compatible with Asch's viewpoint. Heider published two seminal articles in the same period of the middle forties (1944, 1946), each of which led to a rather separate line of theory construction and related research. In 1946, Heider attempted to conceptualize the relations between affective attitudes and cognitive organization. In particular, he argued that we tend to have the same positive or negative feelings about objects or persons who are cognitively associated with each other, who belong together. From such considerations derived a burgeoning interest in cognitive consistency which was elaborated further in Heider's 1958 book, in Newcomb's theorizing about communicative acts (1953), in Osgood and Tannenbaum's concern with the congruity of message source and content (1955), in Cartwright and Harary's elaboration of Heider's earlier notions (1956), and in Festinger's introduction of **cognitive dissonance** theory (1957). Since Festinger's theory became such a pivotal paradigm in social psychology, I shall deal with this at some length. Subsequently, I shall return to consider Heider's second seminal paper and its influence on attribution theory.

The Theory of Cognitive Dissonance

The notion that man is more comfortable with consistent than with inconsistent cognitions has been proclaimed by many psychologists and philosophers. Man is not only rational most of the time, he is (as Freud especially noted) a rationalizer. He wants his attitudes and beliefs to support rather than contradict his behavior, and he wants his cognitions tied together in a coherent, mutually reinforcing system. Such basic assumptions characterize a variety of consistency theories that appeared in the late fifties and early sixties. What Festinger did was to consider the motivational implication of those inconsistencies that are from time to time thrust upon us, and the result of his work was to establish indelibly the power of the experimental method in weeding out theoretical alternatives in social psychology.

Festinger's theory can be very simply stated. Two cognitions can be either relevant or irrelevant. If they are relevant, then they must be either consonant or dissonant. To say that two cognitions are dissonant is to say that one does not follow from the other, or that one follows from the converse of the other. Dissonant cognitions produce an aversive state which the individual will try to reduce by a change in one or both of the cognitions. If a heavy smoker is exposed to statistics showing that smoking leads to lung cancer, he can change the cognition about how much he smokes ("I'm really only a light smoker") or perceive the statistical data as hysterical environmentalist propaganda and attempt to discount it. Where Festinger went beyond the other consistency formulations was in recognizing, and exploiting the recognition, that some cognitions are more resistant to change than others. Cognitions about behavior, in particular, are resistant to change. It is hard to convince ourselves that we did not just knock over the punch bowl if we in fact did, that we did not endorse a particular opinion when we just espoused it, and so on.

In following up the implications of this combined notion of inconsistency reduction and differential resistance, Festinger and his students were led into a series of studies of what was later dubbed "forced compliance." This paradigm involved a crucial experimental condition in which subjects were induced to engage in some action that would normally be dishonest, embarrassing, or at least counter to their own prior attitudes. However, the induction was subtle enough to leave the subject with a feeling that he had a choice and was behaving voluntarily. The experimenters were able to show convincingly that such subtle behavioral inductions lead to accommodating changes in belief, attitude, or values. For example, if a subject was cajoled into writing an essay in favor of the neutron bomb, when previously he was much opposed to it, a subsequent measure would typically show a moderation of the anti-bomb stand. If, however, he was merely assigned such an essay (with no choice) there would be no such attitude change. In theoretical terms, the "fully chosen" behavior was dissonant with the existing attitude; perception of behavior was resistant to change, so therefore there was a resultant attitude change.

Later experimenters were to refine the general prediction of attitude change under the illusion of choice and to highlight the importance of (a) felt responsibility and (b) the perception of potentially harmful consequences. Many other issues were illuminated by the investigators of dissonant cognitions. It was well established that people devalue the non-chosen alternative after making a very close and important decision (e.g., Brehm, 1956). (It would be dissonant to continue to place a high value on a voluntarily foregone option.) Moral inhibitions are internalized in children induced to reduce temptation with "insufficient justification" (Aronson & Carlsmith, 1963). It was shown in a variety of contexts that "people learn to love that for which they suffer" (Festinger, 1961). This principle was even extended to animal maze running behavior (Lawrence & Festinger, 1962). Preference for the goal box is greater the more difficult the maze. (The pain or suffering of such effortful learning must be justified to reduce dissonance.) Some investigators found evidence that standard dissonance producing conditions create a state of generalized arousal that functions like other drive states in energizing well-learned responses and interfering with new learning (e.g., Cottrell & Wack, 1967). Others found that the usual consequences of dissonance reduction, such as attitude change, did not occur if the dissonance could be attributed to a reasonable source of tension symptoms such as a just-ingested pill (Zanna & Cooper, 1974).

It might be sensibly proposed that cognitive dissonance research marked the clear emergence of social psychology as a cumulative experimental discipline. From Festinger's extremely simple and rather vague initial theoretical statement, the theory evolved through experimental refinement to include a set of well articulated systematic relationships (cf. Wicklund & Brehm, 1976). Inherent in this development were many of the features encouraged by Lewin in the construction of a theory of behavior causation: here was a middle-range theory being used to generate testable positions. These findings were conceptually replicable in a variety of superficially different domains, and yet the findings were not self evident without the theory to house them. Many of these experiments involved the kind of stage management first noted in the Lewin, Lippitt, and White studies discussed earlier. While most of the research was laboratory based, there were also many excursions into field settings to check on the empirical utility of the developing theory.

But the wave of dissonance research also aroused considerable controversy. Initially, this controversy centered around methodological shortcomings, and the validity of the results themselves were questioned (e.g., Chapanis & Chapanis, 1964). And since the research typically involved rather elaborate deceptive scenarios, dissonance studies sharply raised ethical issues that remain very much alive today. Eventually, as the methodological shortcomings were reduced by increasingly elegant designs, and the main body of **forced compliance** findings were no longer in serious dispute, alternative theoretical notions were offered to account for them. Bem (1967) proposed that many of the findings attributed to cognitive dissonance reduction could more parsimoniously be explained in terms of self perception. The individual who was induced to "choose" to behave counter attitudinally, interpreted the data of his own behavior-in-context to imply the presence of an attitude congruent with the observed behavior. Subjects were conceptualized as if they were their own observers, trying to make sense out of their own actions against the perceived situational backdrop.

Although Bem derived his argument initially from the "radical behaviorism" of Skinner, his contribution fit nicely into a broader development of attribution theory that was accelerating at the end of the sixties. This in turn grew out of Heider's second assumptive framework, to which we now turn.

The Emergence of Attribution Theory as a Framework for Research

In 1944, Heider published a classic paper on phenomenal causality in which he dealt with causation and action as linked perceptual units or Gestalten. In his 1958 book he delved more deeply and broadly into the conditions and consequences of attributing a particular cause to explain a particular action. This was a book rich in examples from the perception of self and others in drama, fiction, and everyday life, and dedicated to the importance of understanding the naive psychology of the man on the street. If we can understand the terms in which Everyman constructs social causation, we can understand what animates his actions and decisions.

Heider's writings did not have an immediate impact on a field suspicious of phenomenal "introspection" and speculations about cognition, but as social psychologists became more impatient with the shallowness of behavioristic theorizing, Heider's attributional scaffold became a more and more attractive building site. In 1965, Jones and Davis presented a theory of **correspondent inferences,** designed to specify the conditions under which behavior is taken at face value as an indicator of underlying dispositions. They proposed that when we observe another in action, information about his identifying characteristics is gained to the extent that (a) the effects of his action differ from the effects of other actions available to him, and (b) the effects are not those that everyone would seek.

This paper tied together a literature on the role of contextual factors in person perception and it spawned a group of experiments on the attribution of attitudes, abilities, and emotions. But Kelley's seminal paper 2 years later finally began to generate the momentum that carried **attribution theory** into the focal position it now holds. Kelley (1967) was able to integrate Heider's ideas with Festinger's emphasis on social comparison. He showed how Schachter and Singer's (1962) theory of emotion was basically an attributional account, and he publicized Bem's work as an attributional alternative to dissonance theory. Kelley discussed the conditions under which we confidently attribute our perceptions and judgments to environmental states and objects. Our perception of such states and objects must be consistent, distinctive, and in agreement with the perceptions of others. If not, the perception will be judged as personally biased or idiosyncratic.

Subsequent developments in attribution research and theory are difficult to summarize because they touch on such diverse concerns as ability evaluation, emotion perception, psychotherapy, language usage, actor-observer differences, interpersonal conflicts, and ingratiation. Attribution theory itself is difficult to characterize because it is comprised of several sub-theories which in turn involve more of the provision of a taxonomy and a perspective than a set of predictive hypotheses. Much of the research on attribution has treated these sub-theories as normative models of rational inference that are often honored by real subjects in the breech.

More recently, social psychologists have entered the broader domain of general inference processes and judgmental heuristics. Buildling on the data of attributional biases, as well as the work of Tversky and Kahneman (1974), Nisbett and Ross (1980) have identified a variety of human shortcomings in reaching conclusions from available evidence about the self, other persons, and events. Their approach suggests that many processing short-cuts that have survived because of their general usefulness can lead to serious errors of understanding when misapplied. This provocative review constructs a wide and inviting bridge between the domains of social and cognitive psychology.

Attribution theory and derivative approaches to human inference and intuition have definitely stamped the seventies as the era of cognitive emphasis in social psychology. One might venture a guess that the present decade will mark an increased concern with the role of affect and arousal. An important paper by

Zajonc (1980) pleads for a turn in this direction. Though we normally think of affect as following from cognition (believing that one must identify or discriminate before evaluating or preferring), Zajonc argues persuasively for the temporal primacy of affective response systems and their relative independence from cognitive recognition response systems. Affect may be generated by the most primitive or minimal discriminations, and the subsequently elaborated cognitions typically incorporate the affective response and are to an extent determined by it.

The works of Zajonc, and of Nisbett and Ross, converge to raise considerable doubt about the validity of our phenomenal awareness of what determines our actions, our beliefs, and our feelings. Although interest in attribution was originally premised on the causal role that attributions play as determinants of behavior, there are increasing signs that in many important respects we are often out of touch with the true determinants of our behavior and are readily seduced into offering salient cultural stereotypes and rationalizations in answer to "why?" questions. In any event, the precise relations between cognition, affect, and behavior remain very much a mystery. But the mystery is a provocative one that will undoubtedly continue to generate research in the decades to come.

Other Recent Developments

As noted at the outset, a sizable body of contemporary research in social psycholog is focused less on cognitive or affective theory than on the application of empirical findings to the solution of social problems. Many have contributed their time and training to the evaluation of ongoing social programs, and under the impetus of gifted methodologists like Donald Campbell (1969) such evaluation research may be an exceedingly important arena for testing and suggesting hypotheses. A complementary strategy has been to address social problems in laboratory microcosm. Thus, considerable research effort has been expended on the antecedents of aggression, of helping behavior, of attraction, of obedience to authority, and on the effects of inequity of outcomes, of crowding, and other "environmental" conditions. There will undoubtedly continue to be important clusters of research addressed to the understanding of identifiable social problems like violence, ethnic prejudice, drug and alcohol abuse, sex role stereotypes, depression, marital conflict, and so on. There is every reason to expect, furthermore, that attempts to explain such phenomena will comprise theoretical suggestions that may be of basic importance in understanding the socially relevant dimensions of human nature.

CONCLUSION

The history of social psychology is difficult to segregate from historical accounts of research on learning, memory, information processing, motivation, or personality. It is hard to conceive of a human function that is not affected by the implied or actual presence of others. Nevertheless, the field can be roughly identified with those who clearly stress the role of social contexts in attempting to understand feeling, thought, and action. Social psychologists—especially those who favor the experimental approach—have tended to focus on common or modal responses to definable social settings and the interpretations that underly these responses. While not denying the obvious importance of individual differences when attempting to predict responses to complex life events, social psychologists have genreally sought to arrange unambiguous inputs for their subjects so as to tap a common level of meaning. The general assumption is that our knowledge of human nature will advance more rapidly through observing the consequences of controlled variations in situational input than by measuring the complex end-products of individual social histories.

This way of looking at things, as I have stressed, reflects the impact of a Lewinian revolution on social psychology. E. G. Boring might caution us about the *zeitgeist* and suggest that the developments I have described were an inevitable product of converging forces in the evolution of social science. Perhaps, but Lewin's admonitions and prescriptions provide an illuminating script, at least, for describing the transformation of a discipline from about 1935 to 1960. The transformation involved a movement away from personality taxonomies and the measurement of attitudes to a concern with functional relationships between shared human characteristics and specifiable social settings.

As a consequence of this transformation we now have certain kinds of cumulative knowledge about the determinants of conformity and independence. We understand more clearly some of the subtleties of social comparison: when, and with whom, and for what reason we turn to others for information about the validity of our opinions and the level of our abilities. More than two decades of intensive research informs us about how people handle cognitive inconsistencies—especially when these inconsistencies were foreseeable or avoidable and dissonance is aroused.

The Lewinian transformation stressed the interplay between experimentation and theory. When we looked at the history of small group research we noted an increasing emphasis on the theoretical underpinnings of basic interaction processes. The earlier concern with product and performance gave way to a concern with communication flow, the vicissitudes of group cohesiveness, and the pooling and weighing of individual member insights in reaching a group decision. No longer were the secrets of leadership sought in personality profiles; the secrets are buried in the intricacies of group process. Models of interdependence and related research on exchange, negotiations, and bargaining have brought laboratory study in touch with important human concerns.

Social psychologists have never strayed far from a concern with the phenomenal experience of the man-in-the-street, and Heider amplified this concern with his penetrating analyses of naive psychology. His work gave rise to an attributional approach which grew to dominate the social psychology of the seventies. The outlines of what is attributional and what is more generally cognitive have become increasingly blurred in the most recent past as the discipline has moved steadily toward rapprochement with more general studies of thinking and information processing.

This review has selectively highlighted the experimental approach to social psychological problems. There is an articulate minority of social psychologists who may view my remarks as the dying gasp of a maladaptive breed and who question the very possibility of effective and illuminating experimentation on social psychological processes. Some have criticized the artificiality of the controlled laboratory situation and the culture-, time-, and place-boundedness of experimental findings (cf. Gergen, 1973; Schlenker, 1974). Others have objected to the manipulative and deceptive aspect of experimentation and the misapplications of scientific models from the physical sciences (Harré & Secord, 1973). In my opinion, however, the alternatives have not been clearly enough stated to cause abandonment of Lewin's dream of an experimental social psychology. There are good reasons to resist the transmutation of social psychologists into historians, journalists, or humanists. Each approach has its own contributions to make to our understanding of the human condition, but let us not ignore the special advantages of control, quantification, and comparison. I hope that the present chapter provides some justification for the conviction that a cumulative, objective, science of social behavior is not just a future possibility; it is happening under our very eyes.

REFERENCES

Adorno, T. W., Frenkel-Brunswik, E., Levinson, D. J., & Sanford, N. *The authoritarian personality*. New York: Harper and Row, 1950.

Allport, F. H. The influence of the group upon association and thought. *Journal of Experimental Psychology*, 1920, *3*, 159–182.

Allport, F. H. *Social psychology*. Boston: Houghton Mifflin, 1924.

Allport, G. W. Attitudes. In C. Murchison (Ed.), *A handbook of social psychology*. Worcester, Mass.: Clark University, 1935. Pp. 798–844.

Allport, G. W. The historical background of modern social psychology. In G. Lindzey (Ed.), *Handbook of social psychology*. Cambridge: Addison-Wesley, 1954. Pp. 3–56.

Allport, G. W. The historical background of modern social psychology. In G. Lindzey & E. Aronson (Eds.), *Handbook of social psychology* (2nd ed.). Reading, Mass.: Addison-Wesley, 1968.

Aristotle. *The basic works of Aristotle* (R. McKeon, Ed.). New York: Random House, 1941. (Original date unknown.)

Aronson, E., & Carlsmith, J. M. Effect of the severity of threat on the devaluation of forbidden behavior. *Journal of Abnormal and Social Psychology*, 1963, *66*, 584–588.

Asch, S. E. Forming impressions of personality. *Journal of Abnormal and Social Psychology*, 1946, *41*, 258–290.

Asch, S. E. Studies of independence and conformity: A minority of one against a unanimous majority. *Psychological Monographs*, 1956, *70* (9, Whole No. 416).

Back, K. W. Influence through social communication. *Journal of Abnormal and Social Psychology*, 1951, *46*, 9–23.

Bales, R. F. *Interaction process analysis*. Cambridge: Addison-Wesley, 1950.

Barnard, C. I. *The functions of the executive.* Cambridge: Harvard University Press, 1938.

Bartlett, F. C. *Remembering.* Cambridge, England: Cambridge University, 1932.

Bem, D. J. Self-perception: An alternative interpretation of cognitive dissonance phenomena. *Psychological Review,* 1967, *74,* 183–200.

Boring, E. G. *A history of experimental psychology* (2nd ed.). New York: Appleton-Century-Crofts, 1950.

Brehm, J. W. Postdecision changes in the desirability of alternatives. *Journal of Abnormal and Social Psychology,* 1956, *52,* 384–389.

Campbell, D. T. Reforms as experiments. *American Psychologist,* 1969, *24,* 409–429.

Cartwright, D. (Ed.). *Field theory in social science.* New York: Harper, 1951.

Cartwright, D., & Harary, F. Structural balance: A generalization of Heider's theory. *Psychological Review,* 1956, *63,* 277–293.

Cottrell, N. B., & Wack, D. L. Energizing effects of cognitive dissonance upon dominant and subordinate responses. *Journal of Personality and Social Psychology,* 1967, *6,* 132–138.

Cottrell, L. S., & Gallagher, R. *Developments in social psychology 1930–1940 (Sociometry Monograph No. 1).* New York: Beacon House, 1941.

Chapanis, N. P., & Chapanis, A. C. Cognitive dissonance: Five years later. *Psychological Bulletin,* 1964, *61,* 1–22.

Dashiell, J. F. Experimental studies of the influence of social situations on the behavior of individual human adults. In C. Murchison (Ed.), *Handbook of social psychology.* Worcester, Mass.: Clark University, 1935. Pp. 1097–1158.

Deutsch, M. The effect of motivational orientation upon trust and suspicion. *Human Relations,* 1960, *13,* 122–139.

Durkheim, E. Représentations individuelles et représentations collectives. *Revuede métaphysique,* 1898, *6,* 274–302. (Transl. D. F. Pocock, *Sociology and philosophy.* New York: Free Press, 1953.)

Festinger, L. Informal social communication. *Psychological Review,* 1950, *57,* 271–282.

Festinger, L. A theory of social comparison processes. *Human Relations,* 1954, *7,* 117–140.

Festinger, L. *A theory of cognitive dissonance.* Evanston, Ill.: Row, Peterson, 1957.

Festinger, L. The psychological effects of insufficient reward. *American Psychologist,* 1961, *16,* 1–12.

Festinger, L., Schachter, S., & Back, K. *Social pressures in informal groups: A study of human factors in housing.* New York: Harper, 1950.

Festinger, L., & Thibaut, J. Interpersonal communication in small groups. *Journal of Abnormal and Social Psychology,* 1951, *46,* 92–99.

Gerard, H. B. The anchorage of opinions in face-to-face groups. *Human Relations,* 1954, *7,* 313–326.

Gergen, K. J. Social psychology as history. *Journal of Personality and Social Psychology,* 1973, *26,* 309–320.

Haines, H., & Vaughan, G. M. Was 1898 a "great date" in the history of experimental social psychology? *Journal of the History of the Behavioral Sciences,* 1979, *15,* 323–332.

Harré, R., & Secord, P. F. *The explanation of social behavior.* Totowa, N.J.: Littlefield, Adams and Co., 1973.

Heider, F. Social perception and phenomenal causality. *Psychological Review,* 1944, *51,* 358–374.

Heider, F. Attitudes and cognitive organization. *Journal of Psychology,* 1946, *21,* 107–112.

Heider, F. *The psychology of interpersonal relations.* New York: Wiley, 1958.

Homans, G. C. *The human group.* New York: Harcourt, Brace, 1950.

Homans, G. C. *Social behavior: Its elementary forms.* New York: Harcourt, Brace, 1961. (Rev. ed., 1974.)

Hovland, C. I. (Ed.). *Order of presentation in persuasion.* New Haven: Yale University, 1957.

Hovland, C. I., & Janis, I. L. (Eds.). *Personality and persuasibility.* New Haven: Yale University, 1959.

Hovland, C. I., Janis, I. L., & Kelley, H. H. *Communication and persuasion.* New Haven: Yale University, 1953.

Hovland, C. I., & Rosenberg, M. J. (Eds.). *Attitude organization and change.* New Haven: Yale University, 1960.

Jenkins, J. G. *The nominating technique, its uses and limitations.* Paper delivered at Eastern Psychological Association Annual Meeting, Atlantic City, 1947. (Cited in Krech & Crutchfield's *Theory and problems of social psychology.* New York: McGraw-Hill, 1948.)

Jones, E. E., & Davis, K. E. From acts to dispositions: The attribution process in person perception. In L. Berkowitz (Ed.), *Advances in experimental social psychology* (Vol. 2). New York: Academic, 1965. Pp. 219–266.

Jones, E. E., & Gerard, H. B. *Foundations of social psychology.* New York: Wiley, 1967.

Kelley, H. H. Attribution theory in social psychology. *Nebraska Symposium on Motivation,* 1967, *14,* 192–241.

Kelley, H. H., Shure, G. H., Deutsch, M., Faucheux, C., Lanzetta, J. T., Moscovici, S., Nuttin, J. M. Jr., Rabbie, J. M., & Thibaut, J. W. A comparative experimental study of negotiation behavior. *Journal of Personality and Social Psychology,* 1970, *16,* 411–438.

Kelley, H. H., & Thibaut, J. W. Experimental studies of group problem solving and process. In G. Lindzey (Ed.), *Handbook of social psychology.* Cambridge: Addison-Wesley, 1954. Pp. 735–785.

Kelley, H. H., & Thibaut, J. W. Group problem solving. In G. Lindzey & E. Aronson (Eds.), *Handbook of social psychology* (Vol. IV). Reading, Mass.: Addison-Wesley, 1968. Pp. 1–101.

Kerckhoff, A. C., & Back, K. W. *The june bug.* New York: Appleton-Century-Crofts, 1968.

Krech, D., & Crutchfield, R. S. *Theory and problems of social psychology.* New York: McGraw-Hill, 1948.

Lawrence, D. H., & Festinger, L. *Deterrents and reinforcement: The psychology of insufficient reward.* Stanford: Stanford University, 1962.

Lewin, K. Formalization and progress in psychology. *University of Iowa Studies in Child Welfare,* 1940, *16*(3), 9–42.

Lewin, K. Constructs in psychology and psychological ecology. *University of Iowa Studies in Child Welfare,* 1944, *20,* 1–29.

Lewin, K. Comments concerning psychological forces and energies, and the structure of the psyche. In D. Rapaport (Ed.), *Organization and pathology of thought.* New York: Columbia University, 1951. Pp. 76–94. (Originally published, 1926.)

Lewin, K., Lippitt, R., & White, R. K. Patterns of aggressive behavior in experimentally created "social climates." *Journal of Social Psychology,* 1939, *10,* 271–299.

Likert, R. A technique for the measurement of attitudes. *Archives of Psychology,* 1932, No. 140.

Lindzey, G. *Handbook of social psychology.* Cambridge: Addison-Wesley, 1954.

Luce, R. D., & Raiffa, H. *Games and decisions: Introduction and critical survey.* New York: Wiley, 1957.

McDougall, W. *Introduction to social psychology.* London: Methuen, 1908.

McDougall, W. *The group mind.* New York: G. P. Putnam's Sons, 1920. (2nd ed., 1928.)

McDougall, W. *The energies of men: A study of the fundamentals of dynamic psychology.* London: Methuen, 1932.

McGuire, W. The nature of attitudes and attitude change. In G. Lindzey & E. Aronson (Eds.), *Handbook of social psychology* (2nd ed.). Reading, Mass.: Addison-Wesley, 1969. Pp. 136–314.

Miller, N. E., & Dollard, J. *Social learning and imitation.* New Haven: Yale University Press, 1941.

Moede, W. *Experimentelle Massenpsychologie.* Leipzig: S. Hirzel, 1920.

Moreno, J. L. *Who shall survive?* Washington. D.C.: Nervous and Mental Disease Publishing Co., 1934.

Murchison, C. (Ed.). *Handbook of social psychology.* Worcester, Mass.: Clark University, 1935.

Murphy, G., Murphy, L. B., & Newcomb, T. M. *Experimental social psychology* (Rev. ed.). New York: Harper, 1937.

Newcomb, T. M. An approach to the study of communicative acts. *Psychological Review,* 1953, *60,* 393–404.

Nisbett, R. E., & Ross, L. *Human inference: Strategies and shortcomings of social judgment.* Englewood Cliffs, N.J.: Prentice-Hall, 1980.

Orano, P. *Psicologia sociale.* Bari: Laterza, 1902.

Osgood, C. E., & Tannenbaum, P. H. The principle of congruity in the prediction of attitude change. *Psychological Review,* 1955, *62,* 42–55.

Radloff, R. Social comparison and ability evaluation. *Journal of Experimental Social Psychology Supplement 1,* 1966, 6–26.

Ross, E. A. *Social psychology.* New York: Macmillan, 1908.

Schachter, S. Deviation, rejection, and communication. *Journal of Abnormal and Social Psychology,* 1951, *46,* 190–207.

Schachter, S. *The psychology of affiliation.* Stanford: Stanford University, 1959.

Schachter, S. The interaction of cognitive and physiological determinants of emotional state. In L. Berkowitz (Ed.), *Advances in experimental social psychology.* New York: Academic Press, 1964.

Schachter, S., & Singer, J. E. Cognitive, social, and physiological determinants of emotional states. *Psychological Review,* 1962, *69,* 379–399.

Schlenker, B. R. Social psychology and science. *Journal of Personality and Social Psychology,* 1974, *29,* 1–15.

Sherif, M. *The psychology of social norms.* New York: Harper Bros., 1936.

Sherif, M. Group influences upon the formation of norms and attitudes. In T. M. Newcomb & E. L. Hartley (Eds.), *Readings in social psychology.* New York: Holt, 1947. Pp. 77–90.

Sherif, M., Harvey, O. J., White, B., Hood, W., & Sherif, C. *Intergroup conflict and cooperation: The Robbers' Cave experiment.* Norman: Institute of Group Relations, University of Oklahoma, 1961.

Sherif, M., & Hovland, C. I. *Social judgment.* New Haven: Yale University, 1961.

Spencer, H. *The principles of psychology* (2nd ed., Vol. 1). London: Williams and Norgate, 1870.

Tarde, G. *Etudes de psychologie sociale.* Paris: Giard & Briere, 1898.

Tarde, G. *The laws of imitation* (transl.). New York: Henry Holt, 1903.

Thibaut, J. W., & Kelley, H. H. *The social psychology of groups.* New York: Wiley, 1959.

Thomas, W. I., & Znaniecki, F. *The Polish peasant in Europe and America* (5 vols.). Boston: Badger, 1918–1920.

Thurstone, L. L., & Chave, E. J. *The measurement of attitude.* Chicago: University of Chicago Press, 1929.

Tokutani, T. *Shiyakai shinrigaku.* Tokyo: Sheinodou shiyoten, 1906.

Triplett, N. The dynamogenic factors in pacemaking and competition. *American Journal of Psychology,* 1898, *9,* 507–533.

Tversky, A., & Kahneman, D. Judgment under uncertainty: Heuristics and biases. *Science,* 1974, *185,* 1124–1131.

Watson, J. B. *Psychology from the standpoint of a behaviorist.* New York: J. B. Lippincott, 1919.

Watson, J. B. *Behaviorism.* New York: Norton, 1925.

Wicklund, R. A., & Brehm, J. W. *Perspectives on cognitive dissonance.* Hillsdale, N.J.: Lawrence Erlbaum Associates, 1976.

Zajonc, R. B. Feeling and thinking: Preferences need no inferences. *American Psychologist,* 1980, *35,* 151–175.

Zanna, M. P., & Cooper, J. Dissonance and the pill: An attribution approach to studying the arousal properties of dissonance. *Journal of Personality and Social Psychology,* 1974, *29,* 703–709.

Name Index

Volume I and Volume II entries are listed following the designations I and II.

Subject Index

Volume I and Volume II entries are listed following the designations I and II.

Alfred Binet

Hermann von Helmholtz

Charles Darwin

Emil Kraepelin

Sigmund Freud

Karl Lashley